Food and Power
Proceedings of the Oxford Symposium on Food and Cookery 2019

Food and Power

Proceedings of the Oxford Symposium on Food and Cookery 2019

Edited by Mark McWilliams

Prospect Books
2020

First published in Great Britain in 2020 by Prospect Books, 26 Parke Road, London SW13 9NG.

The image on the title page is entitled *Muckamuck Strike Then and Now* (2018), a photographic mural by Dana Claxton in collaboration with Sean Griffin. Image courtesy of Morris and Helen Belkin Art Gallery.

ISBN 978-1-909-248-70-0

Design and typesetting in Gill Sans and Adobe Garamond by Catheryn Kilgarriff and Brendan King.

Printed and bound in Great Britain.

Contents

Foreword

The homepage of the American bakery Arnold proclaims its wholesome-sounding motto, 'From Seed to Slice'. Elsewhere the website tells the brand's heart-warming history: the company was founded 'back in 1940, when Dean and Betty Arnold opened their own bakery out of a tiny house in Stamford, CT', where 'the couple were able to give each brick-oven-baked loaf the attention it deserved'. There's only one hint, buried in the contact page, of how much things have changed: the bakery lists its address as Bimbo Bakeries USA. Along with its competitors Flowers Foods and Campbell Soup Company, Bimbo turns out to be one of the three mega-companies behind almost all the bread sold in American supermarkets: hundreds of bread varieties, dozens of bakeries, all owned by three corporations.

The wild variety of foods on offer in any modern supermarket is an illusion. The colourful packages filling the shelves camouflage the tight integration of the monoculture-based industrial food chain. Beyond the bakery aisle, except in a few sections on the periphery, almost all the products come from just ten international conglomerates. The situation may be even worse in the fields producing the corn and soy that fuel that system, with the seed and fertilizer of industrial agriculture controlled by barely a handful of corporations. While proponents of this system rightly cite its efficiency in feeding more and more people around the globe, study after study shows the impact of its ultra-processed food on those people's health through the unholy trinity of the western diet: obesity, diabetes, and heart disease. The system sickens the very bodies it feeds.

In such a world, a conference on the theme of food and power could be expected to be a depressing affair. Certainly, none of those gathered at this year's Oxford Food Symposium shied away from the facts. And yet, over three lovely July days at St Catherine's College, the focus almost imperceptibly shifted: slides hammering the dangers of and to industrial food yielded to excited discussions about the food movement resisting that system. The buzz in the dining room came not just from exclamations triggered by stunningly good meals, but also from symposiasts sharing ways to work for change. The women from the Hubb Community Kitchen cooked for us, ate with us, and most importantly reminded us how cooking and eating together can help people recover from tragedies as unspeakable as the Grenfell Fire. Roberta Wedge taught us that just editing a Wikipedia entry could, in a small way, rebalance the power of representation. Borough Market filled our communal tables with artisan foods produced by women and women-owned businesses. Fogo Island's Zita Cobb showed us the outsized influence a small island could have on a larger food system. And the presenters of the papers included in this volume embodied the way that studying food and power, over history and in our own time, is itself a formidable act.

Even in the collective euphoria of the concluding sessions, though, the symposiasts who came together in Oxford could hardly foresee the intense nostalgia they would later feel for that intimate gathering. The global pandemic that has devasted the restaurant world and revealed weaknesses in even the most advanced countries' food chains proved an almost existential threat to the Symposium as well. As this volume goes to press, however, preparations are furiously underway for the inaugural V-Symposium. Moving the Symposium online is a Herculean task, but the Trustees embraced this new opportunity to pursue our mission to change the conversation, expand the table, and improve the plate. What seemed a threat to our community instead revealed that it is larger and stronger and more compassionate and more committed than we realized, even when we were talking face to face.

This volume, like the thirty-seven that preceded it, is the concrete legacy of the Oxford Food Symposium. First in print and later online, its papers will reach an audience that is orders of magnitude larger than the crowd that can fit into the Bernard Sunley Lecture Theatre. Here I would like to thank everyone who helped me, particularly Elisabeth Luard, Ursula Heinzelmann, Cathy Kaufman, Peter Hertzmann, Gabi Shyne, Catheryn Kilgarriff, Brendan King, and, of course, the many symposiasts who, wherever they gather, are the Oxford Food Symposium.

I would like to conclude with good news, welcome good news in these uncertain times. First, this volume is made possible by a generous grant from Tokyo's RINRI Institute of Ethics, testifying to the Symposium's international community and its commitment to lifelong learning. Second, the winner of the 2020 Gourmand Award for the World's Best Series on Food and Drink Culture is this very *Proceedings of the Oxford Symposium on Food and Cookery*.

Mark McWilliams
Editor, Oxford Symposium on Food and Cookery

Foodnight

Len Fisher, Janet Clarkson, and Elisabeth Luard

A mock TV interview with a serious message, between interviewer "Emily Makeshift" (E) and a prospective UK Brexit Minister for Food Security (B).

E: Thank you for finding the time to be with us on *Foodnight*, Minister.

B: Always a pleasure to be interviewed by you, Emily. Love the skirt.

E: As I understand it, you've been offered the post of Brexit Minister for Food Security by both our prospective leaders. Briefly, can you tell us why they believe you're the right man for such a powerful new portfolio?

B: Well, I eat a lot of food, Emily. I also have a wide experience of the different types of food that they serve in the House of Commons dining room. And I'm a great fan of Brexit and how it will let us take control of the flow of food across our borders.

E: Minister, we're being warned that if it's a no-deal we'll be out of fresh food and pharmaceuticals within weeks, if not days.[1] Surely that's a problem for any government, whoever's the leader?

B: Well, we've got David Rutley to deal with that. He's the new Undersecretary of State for these short-term problems.[2] And as Boris Johnson said, 'there will be drinking water whatever happens … and there will be milk solids and glucose and whey for our Mars bars.'[3] So I don't see any real short-term problems, especially when we have a former supermarket executive to iron things out.

E: So – no short-term problems, then? Presumably there are plans in place for special powers to ensure food security? What sort of powers will you have?

B: Oh, very strong powers, Emily. I will be totally responsible for controlling the flow of food from all parts of the world.

E: So how will you make a deal with the ten multinationals – let's call them Big Food

– who control most of the world's food-supply?[4]

B: Well, Emily, we have very good relationships with those companies.

E: Even if their headquarters are outside the UK?[5]

B: Well, that helps with the tax arrangements.

E: You mean they don't pay tax?

B: Well, yes, they do pay tax. Just not here.

E: So we accept the status quo. Does that have anything to do with members of our own government who have close connections to the ten companies?[6]

B: Well, these connections are very valuable …

E: (interrupting) You mean they hand over huge amounts in political donations and spend a fortune on lobbying?[7]

B: … but we can only use the power of those connections if outsiders don't know about them.

E: You mean outsiders such as the voters?

B: Well, I was thinking more of outsiders like the countries of Europe. That's one reason for cutting ourselves off and taking back control.

E: Which won't be easy when the World Economic Forum says food security is a global problem that can only be solved through global cooperation. It's all in the Global Risks Report, surely that matters?[8]

B: Well, Emily, the world is full of reports.

E: You mean like the report that has just been suppressed by the Trump government that the vitamin content of rice is going down as the carbon dioxide concentration in the atmosphere is going up?[9]

B: Science, Emily, it's all just science.

E: And the Oxfam report based on solid scientific research that there is enough food to feed the world, only politics, war and corruption disrupt its distribution?[10]

B: Well it's a matter of taking a balanced view. Our Government's balanced view is that we are here to serve our constituents, particularly those who vote for us.

E: So it's a matter of keeping power?

B: Well, the power to do good, Emily.

E: Let's take a specific example. In 2016 your Government introduced the Soft Drinks Industry Levy, otherwise known as the Sugar Tax.[11] It came into effect last year, but already Boris Johnson is talking about removing it.[12]

B: Well. It's a tax on the poor, Emily.

E: But it's been introduced in many poor countries, and the World Health Organization says that the financial benefits to the poor from reducing obesity in countries like Mexico far outweigh the cost of the tax.[13]

B: Well, maybe educated British people are better at making their own decisions based on the evidence.

E: The manufacturers certainly seem to be. The evidence is that the tax is driving them to develop new drinks with much lower addictive sugar contents.[14] Let's move on. You've talked a lot about gaining power by taking back control, but how much power can we have if we cut ourselves off from the rest of the world?

B: Well, lots of power, Emily. Instead of being tied down by cooperative agreements, we can negotiate better deals for ourselves.

E: What if the other side uses the same tactics?

B: Well, yes, but we are really good negotiators. Just look at Brexit.

E: With the greatest possible respect, Minister, can I remind you of the Tragedy of the Commons?[15]

B: Well the House of Commons is always a tragedy.

E: I mean the problems that arise when everyone pursues their own self-interest at the expense of cooperation?

B: Oh, that Tragedy of the Commons? (Aside, to unseen secretary) Could you just

Google that for me? (Looks at phone) Well, I guess we can control that kind of thing as soon as we have the power.

E: That's not what Len Fisher says in his best-selling book on the subject.[16] He says you need really powerful incentives to maintain cooperation. Minister, let's move on to a different sort of power. There are claims that some foods take a huge amount more power and energy to produce than others. Also there are claims that the world agricultural system itself is a significant contributor to global warming, both directly through gas emissions and because much of the energy to produce the food that Westerners want is still coming from the burning of fossil fuels.[17] Do you have the power to deal with that?

B: Well, Emily, these are pretty big claims, and in any case we have David Rutley to deal with the global warming thing when he has time from his other duties.

E: But these claims are backed by pretty big evidence, including some that comes from the Future of Humanity Institute right here in Oxford, where we are doing this interview.[18]

B: Well, these are academics, Emily. My concern is with the real world.

14 E: But, Minister, doesn't the globally interconnected real world hold the actual power when it comes to controlling our food supplies? That's what the World Economic Forum believes, and it's certainly what some of your constituents think.[19] Some have even decided to try to become self-sufficient.

B: Well, yes, I have to admit that we are taking some precautions. We've even turned the gardens at the back of Number Ten over to growing vegetables.

E: That'll be a relief for the voters – the new PM will have enough potatoes. Seriously though, isn't it true that whatever we do, Britain will still be a net importer of foods, and the food supply is just part of a complex network that involves energy, water, land use, and labour?[20]

B: I'm glad you mentioned labour, Emily, because that's where our real advantage lies. Labour is much cheaper in third world countries, so we can buy our food more cheaply from them than producing our own.

E: Whatever the cost in slavery and child labour?

B: Well, the companies involved are upping their game there.

E: Do that you mean that changes in company policy are a direct result of public pressure after Oxfam blew the whistle?[21]

B: Well, not entirely. You have to consider the shareholders as well, you know. That's why Nestlé warned that the costs of weeding out slavery in the company would result in higher food prices and lower profits.[22]

E: Isn't it also true the Third World countries that provide most of the world's food are also those who going to be most affected by global warming?[23]

B: Well, maybe so, Emily, but that's not really our problem. We still hold the financial whip hand, so we still have the power.

E: You mean like the World Bank has the power to offer loans to Third World farmers so long as they produce food for the West but are unable to afford it for themselves?[24]

B: That's economics, Emily.

E: Like the economics that Monsanto uses to insist that Third World farmers use only their seeds, and can have the farmers jailed if they dare to exchange or use their own?[25] In fact, there was even a farmer in Tennessee who was jailed.[26]

B: That's market forces.

E: But if they are being controlled by market forces, surely we are too? Do we really have any power at all?

B: Well, Emily, we certainly have the power to control the flow of undesirable foreign foods across our borders.

E: Can you give me an example?

B: Well, not really, but ….

E: So really you have no power at all?

B: (looking at watch) Is that the time? I'm afraid I'll have to wind up this interview, Emily. I have to arrange a meeting with some food industry representatives.

E: Thanks very much for your time, Minister.

B: It's been a pleasure (then, off-camera, to the interviewer) Can you recommend a good local restaurant – Chinese or Italian for preference?

Notes

1   C. Morris, 'Brexit: What Would a 'No Deal' Mean for Food and Medicine?', *BBC News*, 3 August 2018 <https://www.bbc.com/news/uk-45047874> [accessed 15 December 2019].

2   Gov.UK 'David Rutley MP', *Gov.UK*, 2019 <https://www.gov.uk/government/people/david-rutley> [accessed 15 December 2019].

3   Greg Evans, 'Boris Johnson Said There 'Will Be Drinking Water after Brexit' and Everyone Made the Same Joke', *The Independent Indy 100*, 28 June 2019 <https://www.indy100.com/article/boris-johnson-brexit-drinking-water-tory-leadership-twitter-jokes-8979476> [accessed 15 December 2019].

4   Kate Taylor, 'These 10 Companies Control Everything You Buy', *Business Insider*, 4 April 2017 <https://www.businessinsider.com/10-companies-control-food-industry-2017-3/?r=AU&IR=T> [accessed 15 December 2019].

5   'The World's Biggest Food Companies in 2018', *Food Processing Technology*, 28 June 2018 <https://www.foodprocessing-technology.com/uncategorised/worlds-biggest-food-companies-2018/> [accessed 15 December 2019].

6   Martin Williams and Rajeev Syal, 'The Full List of Peers and MPs with Directorships or Controlling Interests in Companies Linked to Tax Havens', *The Guardian*, 20 September 2012 <https://www.theguardian.com/news/datablog/2012/sep/20/peers-mps-directors-companies-linked-tax-havens> [accessed 15 December 2019].

7   Gary Sacks, 'Big Food Lobbying: Tip of the Iceberg Exposed', *The Conversation*, 18 February 2014 <https://theconversation.com/big-food-lobbying-tip-of-the-iceberg-exposed-23232> [accessed 15 December 2019].

8   World Economic Forum, 'The Global Risks Report 2018', *World Economic Forum*, 17 January 2018 <https://www.weforum.org/reports/the-global-risks-report-2018> [accessed 15 December 2019].

9   Helena Bottemiller Evich, 'Agriculture Department Buries Studies Showing Dangers of Climate Change', *Politico*, 23 June 2019 <https://www.politico.com/story/2019/06/23/agriculture-department-climate-change-1376413> [accessed 15 December 2019].

10 Oxfam Canada, 'There Is Enough Food to Feed the World', *Oxfam*, 5 September 2017 <https://www.oxfam.ca/publication/there-is-enough-food-to-feed-the-world/> [accessed 15 December 2019]; Eric Holt-Giménez and others, 'We Already Grow Enough Food for 10 Billion People … and Still Can't End Hunger', *Journal of Sustainable Agriculture,* 36 (2012), 595-98.

11 HM Treasury, 'Soft Drinks Industry Levy Comes into Effect', *Gov.UK*, 5 April 2018 <https://www.gov.uk/government/news/soft-drinks-industry-levy-comes-into-effect> [accessed 15 December 2019].

12 Heather Stewart, 'No 10 Defends Sugar Levy after Johnson Vows to Review "Sin Taxes"', *The Guardian*, 3 July 2019 <https://www.theguardian.com/society/2019/jul/03/labour-urges-hancock-to-oppose-johnsons-sugar-tax-review-boris-johnson-tom-watson-matt-hancock> [accessed 15 December 2019].

13 World Health Organization, 'Taxes on Sugary Drink: Why Do It?', *World Health Organization*, 2017 <https://apps.who.int/iris/bitstream/handle/10665/260253/WHO-NMH-PND-16.5Rev.1-eng.pdf;jsessionid=1005B9D431D200E8AB46F1121DF43D3E?sequence=1> [accessed 15 December 2019].

14 Beth Newhart, 'Coca-Cola Cuts Back on Sugar with Bubbler Beverages', *Beverage Daily.com*, 23 May 2019 <https://www.beveragedaily.com/Article/2019/05/23/Coca-Cola-cuts-back-on-sugar-with-bubbler-beverages> [accessed 15 December 2019].

15 Garrett Hardin, 'The Tragedy of the Commons', *Science,* 162 (1968), 1243-48.

16 Len Fisher, *Rock, Paper, Scissors* (New York: Basic Books, 2011).

17 Andy Reisinger and Harry Clark, 'How Much Do Direct Livestock Emissions Actually Contribute to Global Warming?', *Global Change Biology*, 24 (2018), 1749-61.

18 Future of Humanity Institute, 'Research Areas', *Future of Humanity Institute*, 2019 <https://www.fhi.ox.ac.uk/research/research-areas/> [accessed 15 December 2019].

19 World Economic Forum.

20 Samuel White, 'UK Imports and Exports Will Suffer from Brexit Isolation', *Euractiv*, 15 June 2017 <https://www.euractiv.com/section/economy-jobs/news/uk-imports-and-exports-will-suffer-from-brexit-isolation/> [accessed 15 December 2019].

21 Oxfam, 'Oxfam GB Statement on Modern Slavery for the Year 2018/2019', *Oxfam*, September 2019 <https://oxfamilibrary.openrepository.com/bitstream/handle/10546/620873/ar-oxfam-modern-slavery-statement-2019-300919-en.pdf?sequence=1&isAllowed=y> [accessed 15 December 2019].

22 Matt Agorist, 'Nestlé Says Requirement to Report Use of Slave Labour Would Cost Consumers More Money', *The Free Thought Project*, 6 September 2019 <https://thefreethoughtproject.com/nestle-anti-slavery-bill-cost/> [accessed 15 December 2019].

23 'Study: Global Warming Hits Poorest Nations Hardest', *University of Melbourne and American Geophysical Union Press Release*, 2018 <https://eos.org/scientific-press/study-global-warming-hits-poorest-nations-hardest> [accessed 15 December 2019].

24 James Bovard, 'The World Bank vs. the World's Poor', Cato Institute Policy Analysis No. 92, *Cato*, 28 September 1987 <https://www.cato.org/sites/cato.org/files/pubs/pdf/pa092.pdf> [accessed 15 December 2019]; Eva Perroni '21st Century Famine: A Long Time in the Making', *Food Ethics*, 27 April 2017 <http://sustainablefoodtrust.org/articles/21st-century-famine-a-long-time-in-the-making/> [accessed 15 December 2019].

25 Clare O'Grady Walshe, *Globalisation and Seed Sovereignty in Sub-Saharan Africa* (London: Palgrave Macmillan, 2019), pp. 1-24.

26 Stephen Hill, 'The Survivability of Humanity Within the Current Economic Paradigm', in *The Kyoto Manifesto for Global Economics*, ed. by Stomu Yamash'ta, Tadashi Yagi, and Stephen Hill (London: Springer, 2018), pp. 13-34.

The Power of Enjoyment in the Face of Industrialized Food

Jane Grigson Trust Lecture

Joanna Blythman

I only had the privilege of meeting Jane Grigson once, but thanks to her constant presence in my kitchen in the form of her cookbooks, she feels like a dear old friend.

The world isn't short of good recipes, but what I love about Jane is that her books deliver so much more than that. Knowing I was giving this lecture, I picked up one of my favourites: her *Vegetable Book*. Revisiting it just brought home to me what a rich, rounded, wise, and inherently sensible way of thinking about food Jane had.

Jane located every ingredient available to us in a cultural context. That context was an understanding of history, seasons, traditions and artisan methods. Authenticity mattered to Jane, and she rooted her thoughts and recipes in specific geographies and landscapes. An ingredient for Jane was partly explained by the locality from which it came. An explanation of the ecology of a given region was one of the tools she gave us to truly comprehend the characteristics of native plant cultivars and breeds of animals.

Here's some typically educational advice from her on shallots: 'One thing to realize is that the flavour of shallots can vary from region to region and according to variety. There are three main types – the small greyish-brown skinned shallot, the kind the French call "*échalote rose*", then the pinkish-red ones, and the bronze-skinned, yellowish variety which keep well.'[1] Here you see her attention to detail, her focus on the distinctions within classes of ingredients.

Yet despite this respect for locality and local biodiversity, her tone was internationalist, never parochial. Jane drops in sentences that have a cosmopolitan sweep yet make universal links between apparently diverse food cultures. Here's an example: 'A Ghanaian friend told us that in Accra there is an [avocado] tree in every garden, like apple trees in some parts of England; everyone gets bored with the fruit during the season, as we get bored with endless Bramley windfalls in the autumn. In Kenya it's much the same.'[2]

Jane assumed she was speaking to an intelligent, enquiring reader, someone capable of understanding nuance. She talked up to her readers, not down. She took it for granted that understanding the background to ingredients would make us more capable at the stove. And her audience, her frame of reference, was the home cook. She assumed that home cooking, from the humblest daily food to a dish for a feast, was a worthwhile endeavour, an endeavour that lies at the very heart of a life well lived.

She also saw it as desirable, and perfectly possible, that people might be encouraged to grow some of their own food. This line from the entry on courgettes is typical: 'You can buy a couple of plants from a nurseryman and grow them in a backyard or tub. Until you have grown them yourself and picked them at 5-7 centimetres in length, you cannot imagine how delicious they can be.'[3] I keep coming across people who find courgettes dull. Perhaps if they had this experience Jane describes, they would feel differently.

Taste, of course, was the whole point of food to Jane, and she went to lengths to describe it. For instance on salsify she points out that it is sometimes called the 'vegetable oyster' but goes on to remark that it 'tastes of nothing but itself'. 'Others have compared it to the parsnip, but this won't do either,' she says: 'Parsnip has a softer texture than the clean waxy bite of salsify, and is much sweeter.'[4] For Jane, taste was crucial, the *sine qua non* of food.

Health? Her books have references to the medicinal and tonic properties of certain foods. She notes, for instance, that medieval doctors credited parsnips with keeping off adders and curing toothache. But Jane never felt any need to trouble her reader with calorie counts for her recipes, or computations of nutritional values for each of their components. I'd guess that Jane simply assumed that if we followed the eating patterns passed down to us through the generations, we wouldn't go too far wrong.

But the food world we inhabit now couldn't be more different from Jane's. Particular cultural contexts are being overridden by a universalist vision of eating that is said to be broadly applicable to all societies. This approach to food emerged after World War II, and ever since it has been advanced as a modern formula for good health.

In the UK, we are asked to eat according to a government prescription that is embodied by the 'Eatwell Plate', or the 'Eat Badly' plate, as a growing number of dissenters prefer to call it. This prescription tells us to base our meals on starchy foods, reduce saturated fat, red meat and sugar.[5]

You can see variations on this model all around the world. In the US, it appears as a pyramid. In the far north of Alaska, the Regional Board of Health and Social Services depicts healthy eating in the shape of an igloo. The traditional, local foodstuffs of the Inuit, such as fish and seal fat – the fat and protein got them through freezing winters – are now restricted to the very top of the igloo, and overshadowed in bulk terms by the very un-traditional refined carbohydrates.

You may remember that earlier this year, a self-appointed body called EAT-Lancet launched its global prescription for what it considers 'a universal healthy reference diet'. EAT-Lancet wants this to be the basis of an unprecedented 'great food transformation'.[6] So EAT-Lancet is fashionably on-message. It plays on the guilt and anxiety people feel about climate breakdown and uses its supposedly ethical stance to deflect any challenges.

But behind the green rhetoric, EAT-Lancet is advancing a highly debatable proposition. This proposition is that animal foods – meat, dairy, eggs, fish – foods that Jane used regularly, are somehow bad for us, or at least ought to be restricted. 'Plant' food, on the other hand, is promoted by EAT-Lancet as the saviour of human and planetary health.

19

EAT-Lancet makes me think of a very important figure in British nutrition, surgeon captain Thomas Latimer Cleave, whose 1966 book, the *Saccharine Disease*, first identified the negative health effects of consuming over-refined foods. He summed up my feelings on the current attack on animal foods, such as red meat, so pithily when he said: 'For a modern disease to be related to an old-fashioned food is one of the most ludicrous things I have ever heard in my life.'[7]

It's worth noting here that EAT-Lancet, despite the 'plant' tag, isn't actually a vegetable-rich diet. In fact, it tells us to get only 3% of our calories from vegetables, while recommending that half of our calories should come from wheat, grains, and soya. But it does drastically restrict animal foods. We're allowed an egg and a half each week, not more than a daily mouthful of red meat.

I think we can safely say that EAT-Lancet isn't a blueprint for eating that Jane would recognise. But these days, Jane's knowledge and philosophy of food would be roundly dismissed as not science-based and therefore irrelevant.

Nowadays, the whole discussion around what is appropriate for us to eat has been commandeered by so-called experts – academics, assorted health professionals – to whom we are told to defer because they know best. Let me give you a personal example. Recently, I was criticised by a dietician for writing an article in *BBC Good Food* that dared to question government diet advice on what constitutes a 'healthy oil'. I was merely a food writer, contributing to a women's cookery magazine, she pointed out. She, on the other hand had a four-year degree, had done work experience as part of her training, and followed science-based government guidelines to the letter. How dare I challenge her superior received knowledge?

But let me return to EAT-Lancet. Its 'animal foods are bad' script had an initially uncritical reception in mainstream media and its influence continues. Last month, for example, *BBC News* ran a feature aimed at school students. It contained this statement, citing the seemingly authoritative UN Intergovernmental Panel on Climate Change as its source: 'Buy less milk, meat, cheese and butter and more locally sourced seasonal food.'[8] Of course, in the UK, milk, meat, cheese and butter are our locally sourced food; and they never go out of season. Jane would have spotted this right away, but this logically inconsistent advice was a classic example of a phenomenon known as the Dunning-Kruger effect, that is, you don't understand enough about a subject to know that what you believe to be true doesn't stand up.

The world seemed entranced by EAT-Lancet until the Italians entered the fray. Thank heavens for Italians and their respect for good food! Gian Lorenzo Cornado, Italy's ambassador and permanent representative to the United Nations, attacked both the science and the sense of the EAT-Lancet vision: '"A standard diet for the whole planet" regardless of the age, sex, general state of health, and eating habits has no scientific justification at all' and 'would mean the destruction of millenary, healthy traditional diets which are a full part of the cultural heritage and social harmony in many nations.'[9] Jane, with her broad, holistic, educated understanding of food would have applauded his efforts. And he got results. The World Health Organization subsequently dropped its planned sponsorship of the EAT-Lancet diet.

It goes without saying that I share the Italian problem with any monolithic universal diet. But, I could support a very different sort of food message, one that I do believe is globally applicable. And here it is in three words: Avoid processed food. Or, if we come back to the topic of this lecture, I could say: Avoid industrialized food. Or, if that's too long, not clear enough, then here it is in one word: Cook.

Let me explain my thinking. I have an over-arching hunch that natural ingredients in their least processed forms are the best basis for our minds, bodies, and souls. And I was pleased to see that two major studies reported this year alone have provided robust scientific evidence to back up that sentiment, because they make the links between over-processed food and disease. But what exactly do I mean by industrialized, or that even trickier word, 'processed'? Jane used processed food all the time: cheese, olive oil, vanilla, capers, for example. We're not against these, are we?

Thankfully, an international alliance of researchers led by Professor Carlos Monteiro at the university of Sao Paulo has done us all a favour and given us what's known as the NOVA classification. Very usefully, it breaks down the weasel world 'processed' into four groups:

Group 1: Unprocessed or minimally processed foods (cold-pressed oils).
Group 2: Processed culinary ingredients (vinegar)
Group 3: Processed food (tinned tomatoes)
Group 4: Ultra-processed food and drink products (crisps would be a simple, old-fashioned example of an ultra-processed food)[10]

But let me give you a more up-to-date example of an ultra-processed food: The Impossible Burger, a plant-based rival to the classic beef burger. Its ingredient list is as follows: 'Water, soy protein concentrate, coconut oil, sunflower oil, natural flavors, potato protein, methylcellulose, yeast extract, cultured dextrose, modified food starch, genetically modified soy leghemoglobin, salt, soy protein isolate, and synthetic vitamins'.[11] I wonder if Jane might read this ingredients list, note the marketing assurances about its healthfulness, and still be left asking the question, 'What the hell is it?'

Now I'm grateful to the NOVA researchers for defining processed food in a way that allows a deeper, more sophisticated discussion of the increasingly industrialized food on our plates. They have made an impact. The term – 'ultra-processed' – is featuring more and more in debates about diet and health.

In the UK currently, just over 50% of the food we eat comes into the ultra-processed, industrialized category. We're being assured that hi-tech, cutting-edge, ultra-processed food of this type is going to replace real food as we know it. Pat Brown, the CEO of Impossible Foods, says he can replace meat from animals by 2035. 'Cows aren't getting any better at making meat. We are', he says, with breath-taking hubris.[12]

You might think such a scenario is implausible, but is it? Despite the body of science that links consumption of over-processed food to obesity and ill health, there are a number of powerful interests pushing it, and in power terms – power is the theme of the Symposium this year – they seem to outweigh those interests that defend relatively unprocessed, real food. So what's the driving motivation here?

Simply put, ultra-processing hands manufacturers a licence to print money. Take potatoes. There's only so much any retailer could charge for them in their natural form, even if they marketed them as exclusive heirloom varieties, hand polished in mineral water by virgins hand selected by M&S. But transform them into crisps, or microwaveable chips, and the sky's the limit. This is what food engineers refer to as 'adding value': they break down whole foods into standard components that they endlessly manipulate and tweak to produce a series of novel, lucrative configurations. Ultra-processing is a tried-and-tested formula for skinflint spending and profit generation.

'Value engineering' (keeping down ingredient costs) is the food manufacturer's overweening objective. They do it by replacing the costlier items – eggs, butter, meat, milk, for instance – with pre-processed industrial substitutes, artfully employed, using all the tricks in the food technologist's manual, to create a similar effect. Why use real eggs in your formulation for instance, when you can choose instead cleverly confected starches, which, along with synthetic egg flavouring and yellow colouring, will give your product an egg-like effect?

This strong financial incentive to reduce raw material costs is the reason why ultra-processed products as seemingly dissimilar as fish fingers, mayonnaise, chocolate mousse, frequently share so many common ingredients: added water, protein flours, industrially refined oils, gums, chemically altered starches, sugar, all tarted-up with synthetic additives and further confected with 'processing aids', such as enzymes, that do not even appear on the label.

It's worth noting that EAT-Lancet, through an alliance with a body known as Fresh – an acronym for Food Reform for Sustainability and Health – receives backing from powerful companies that have a clear vested interest in selling us ultra-processed food. Let me give you a flavour of the companies involved. There's Bayer, the company that owns Monsanto, a company that's fighting a snowstorm of lawsuits in the US raised by people who believe its weedkiller, RoundUp, also known as glyphosate, has given them cancer. There's PepsiCo, the sweet soft drinks company. There's Kellogg's, manufacturer of all those pseudo-healthy breakfast cereals. There's Nestlé, which aside from selling us tooth-rotting confectionery, ruthlessly promotes its formula milk to mothers who have no access to clean water. There's Symrise and Givaudan, two companies that manufacture synthetic flavourings. There's a posse of pesticide and chemical companies, grain refiners, and palm oil companies.

Now, the more industrialized our food has become, the more it is made by companies such as these, the less we understand it in the broad, holistic, intelligent way that Jane did. I don't know what you think, but my feeling is that many people are quite suspicious of these foods and what they might be doing to us, yet because they are so ubiquitous, we take heart in a safety-in-numbers trust. We think, well these foods are so available, and being eaten by so many of us that they must be safe.

A vast regulatory food safety apparatus has been put in place to convince us that these foods are safe. Food companies are obliged to operate a system of self-regulation known as HACCP – hazard analysis and critical control points – and their compliance is policed by the Food Standards Agency in the UK, and equivalent bodies in other countries.

To my mind, the very existence of this modern food safety establishment has helped to create an illusion, an illusion that food safety is best delivered by what the French sociologist Claude Fischler describes as an 'aseptic no-man's land' of promised biological purity, a purity best established in some distant place by faceless scientists in white coats.[13]

There was a classic example of this illusion of purity in May when environmental health officers stopped the local Women's Institute bringing in homemade cakes to cheer up residents of a hospice in Rutland, simply because they had been cooked in home kitchens. Yet although it can ban cakes that might cheer up a dying person and his or her family, this system is full of as many holes as a ciabatta loaf. So far this year in British hospitals five people have died because they were fed sandwiches contaminated by listeria. But you can bet your bottom dollar that these killer sandwiches had passed seamlessly through rafts of HACCP checks from factory to bedside. The suppliers involved, by the way, were back in production within a week or two.

Meanwhile, the power vested in this ineffective food safety establishment is used remorselessly against small producers. Some of you will know about the case of Errington Cheese, Scotland's oldest artisan cheesemaker. A child died from E-coli, that company's raw milk cheese was falsely blamed, and it was put out of production for three years. Exhausting its own funds, and with help from crowdfunding and the leading E-coli expert, Professor Hugh Pennington, the Erringtons were subsequently exonerated in a lengthy, expensive court battle that nearly bankrupted them. Now they are making wonderful cheese again and selling it to grateful customers. But the case has sent a chill through Scotland's cheesemakers. One cheesemaker has ceased production permanently, and others are pasteurizing their products. They fear public health authorities will effectively harass them if they don't.

The fact of the matter is that fear, not enjoyment, walks hand in hand with the industrialized, ultra-processed food system:

Fear of poisoning.
Fear of obesity.
Fear of whole groups of macronutrients, such as fat.

Fear, of course, is joined at the hip with another F: faddism. Lacking coordinates to navigate the industrial food system, we are encouraged to fixate on isolated nutritional micro-parts of whole foods that are identified as either saints or sinners, depending on which school of nutrition you adhere to. A host of dogmatic dietary tribes vies for our loyalty: low-fat, low carb, paleo, keto, vegan, flexitarian, red meat avoiders, gluten-free, intermittent fasting, and EAT-Lancet's 'plant-based'.

So how can we challenge these immensely powerful, and I would say hostile, forces that are encouraging us to eat a diet that is ever more divorced from ingredients in their whole, diverse, and most wonderful forms? How can we restore a normal, pleasurable, literate view of food that Jane would recognize, and put that at the heart of our lives?

As I said earlier, it seems to me that Jane simply assumed that enjoyment was the natural consequence of eating in a time-honoured, fairly traditional way. She saw that enjoyment began with an informed appreciation of the factors that create good food. She knew that for most of us, it was predicated on home cooking. And I see very many chinks of light these days that make me optimistic that we can reclaim her vision.

Let me slowly wind down this lecture by returning to the global south, to Brazil, where the NOVA classification originated, the country that currently has the sanest government eating guidelines in the world – guidelines that we would do well to adopt. Brazil doesn't patronize its citizens with simplistic, kindergarten visual images and deeply flawed nutrient profiling schemes. It doesn't blind them with red, amber, and green traffic lights, which give people the impression that diet Coke is healthier than mackerel. Instead it has seven clear principles that it asks its citizens to apply:

1) Make unprocessed foods the basis of your diet
2) Limit your consumption of processed foods
3) Avoid ultra-processed foods
4) Eat minimal oils [Referring to industrially refined cooking oil]
5) Eat in company
6) Shop where fresh foods are offered
7) Develop cooking skill

The first four are essentially nutritional recommendations, but the last three – eat in company, shop where fresh foods are on sale, develop cooking skill – are social. And I think that Jane would like this, for it brings us back again to the theme of this lecture, the 'power of enjoyment'. She would approve of these last three principles because they talk not just of what we eat but also of how we eat. They assume that eating well is a matter of culture, not merely nutrition.

Last year, about a week before Christmas, I was walking past a rather unremarkable café near where I live. I'd never paid much attention to it. But it had opened on its day off, Monday, its tables all nicely set with napkins and decorations, and was serving a complimentary proper Christmas meal to assorted homeless citizens. What an uplifting sight it was to see! A meal that offered dignity, safety, enjoyment, and companionship to people whose lives are often chaotic and frightening. And I'm sure it uplifted the mental health of the people who took the bother to host it. It reminded me, as Brazil's guidelines do, that it's always important to locate civilized, health-sustaining eating in conviviality round a table. However much we are encouraged to do so, it remains really important never to lose sight of the daily pleasure of sharing uncomplicated home-cooked food.

The prevailing industrial food complex wants to make passive consumers out of us, people who no longer have any intuition about the food they eat, people who trustingly go along with whatever big companies sell them.

But I do believe that an alternative vision of food, a vision that is predicated on enjoyment, on the hands-on participation of active citizens, is terribly seductive. I see it bubbling up at a grass roots level all around us. I see it expressed in the Real Bread movement. Bakeries that follow these principles are springing up everywhere. I see it on the allotment, and in the school playgrounds where little children tend vegetables in raised beds. I see it in the refilling shops that are springing up on shopping parades, where we rediscover the domestic economy our mothers and grandmothers took for granted by filling up our storage jars and old bags from gravity dispensers, instead of buying food over-packaged in plastic from the supermarket. I see it in organic box schemes that deliver to our homes, reconnecting our rural food producers with urban consumers. I see it in places like Liverpool, where the Can Cook initiative has pioneered a dignified alternative food proposition to meals on wheels. It gives me so much pleasure to see small independent food shops with progressive ideals actually doing better than they have for ages, even as the big chains disappear from our shopping parades. I see it in the seed savers movement where citizen groups are defending our planet's biodiversity against corporate patents. I see it in the ongoing strength and momentum powering not-for-profit workers' food co-ops, such as Locavore in Glasgow, Unicorn in Manchester, and Infinity in Brighton. I see it at work in places as unalike as Brixton, Bristol, and Totnes, where their eponymous pound is a local currency that helps people relocalize their food economies.

Currently, a self-seeded, resilient movement composed of enterprises of this kind is beginning to break through with an alternative to the monolithic industrialized food system. This movement demonstrates to me one extremely uplifting and empowering point: grass grows through concrete, eventually. For all that the post-World War II industrialized food system poses as normal, as a permanent, unchangeable status quo, it actually represents a brief, and problematic, episode in the history of how the world has fed itself since time began. So many people are hungry for the restatement of saner, more enjoyable, tried-and-tested eating patterns, and they are determined to make that happen. I like to think that if Jane was here with us today, she would recognize, respect, and cheer on their intention.

Notes

1   Jane Grigson, *Jane Grigson's Vegetable Book* (Lincoln, NE: Bison Books of the University Press of Nebraska, 2007 [1978]), p. 354.
2   Grigson, p. 61.
3   Grigson, p. 228.
4   Grigson, p. 443.
5   NHS, 'The Eatwell Guide', *NHS*, 28 January 2019 <https://www.nhs.uk/live-well/eat-well/the-eatwell-

25

guide/> [accessed 18 April 2020].

6   Walter Willett and others, 'Food in the Anthropocene: The EAT-Lancet Commission on Healthy Diets from Sustainable Food Systems', *The Lancet*, 393.10170 (16 January 2019) <doi.org/10.1016/S0140-6736(18)31788-4>.

7   T.L. Cleave and George Duncan Campbell, *Diabetes, Coronary Thrombosis, and the Saccharine Disease* (Bristol: Wright, 1966), p. 123.

8   'Climate Change: Answers to Your Most Asked Questions', *BBC News*, 24 May 2019 <https://www.bbc.com/news/science-environment-48213808> [accessed 18 April 2020].

9   Ingrid Torjesen, 'WHO Pulls Support from Initiative Promoting Global Move to Plant-Based Foods', *BMJ*, 365.l700 (2019) <doi.org/10.1136/bmj.l700>.

10 Carlos Augusto Monteiro and others, *Ultra-Processed Foods, Diet Quality, and Health using the NOVA Classification System* (Rome: Food and Agriculture Organization of the United Nations, 2019) <http://www.fao.org/3/ca5644en/ca5644en.pdf> [accessed 18 April 2020].

11 'What Are the Ingredients?', *Impossible Foods*, 2020 <https://faq.impossiblefoods.com/hc/en-us/articles/360018937494-What-are-the-ingredients-> [accessed 18 April 2020].

12 Pat Brown, 'Impact Report 2019: If Not Now, When?', *Impossible Foods*, 2019 <https://impossiblefoods.com/mission/2019impact/letterfromtheceo/> [accessed 18 April 2020].

13 See, e.g., Claude Fischler, '*OCNI: objets comestibles non identifiés*' in *Modernes et après: Les Immatériaux* (Paris: Autrement, 1985), pp. 80-86.

26

Serving Up A Slice of Africa: Reading Empire Adventure Stories as Textual Blancmanges of National Identity, Power, and Race

OFS Rising Scholar Award Winner

Siobhan Dooley

Of all the books produced since the most remote ages by human talents and industry those only that treat of cooking are, from a moral point of view, above suspicion. The intention of every other piece of prose may be discussed and even mistrusted; but the purpose of a cookery book is one and unmistakeable. Its object can conceivably be no other than to increase the happiness of mankind.

Joseph Conrad, 'Preface' to *A Handbook of Cookery for a Small House* (1923)

The relations of man with matter, with the world outside, and with history [were] in the colonial period simply relations with food.

Frantz Fanon, *The Wretched of the Earth* (1961)

White racism, imperialism and sexual domination prevail by courageous consumption. It is by eating the Other (in this case, death) that one asserts power and privilege.

bell hooks, *Black Looks: Race and Representation* (1992)

In the field of postcolonialism, Joseph Conrad is better known for the novella *Heart of Darkness* and its portrayal of Africans as 'black shadows of disease and starvation' than the preface he wrote for his wife Jessica's cookbook.[1] His assertion in it, however, that books about food and cooking are ideologically neutral is worth discussing and, as this paper intends to show, is disingenuous.[2] As Annette Cozzi points out in *The Discourses of Food in Nineteenth-Century British Fiction*, food 'is about more than physical nourishment or sensual pleasure, it is about power: power over life, and power over death, power over self and over the Other'.[3] This observation is borne out by Mrs Isabella Beeton's *The Book of Household Management*. She writes:

Creatures of the inferior races eat and drink; man only dines. [...] Dining is the privilege of civilization. The rank which a people occupy in the grand scale may be measured by their way of taking their meals, as well as by their way of treating their women. The nation which knows how to dine has learnt the leading lesson of progress. It implies both the will and the skill to reduce to order, and surround with idealisms and graces, the more material conditions of human existence; and wherever that will and that skill exist, life cannot be wholly ignoble.

This passage makes it clear that what 'a people' eat collectively determines the degree to which their nation has achieved 'civilization'. Mrs Beeton maintains one cannot call what the 'aboriginal Australian' or the 'native of Terra-del-Fuego' eats *dinner* (emphasis in original).[4] Her sentiments further thicken Cozzi's overarching argument that national identity is constructed, 'most often against a racialized Other', on the plates and pages of the British public.[5] I wish to expand on the work already done on the role of food and fiction in moulding a blancmange-like 'Britishness' by exploring how colonial-alimentary ideologies are constructed in the *Boy's Own Paper*, a periodical designed to educate and entertain children. These ideologies were subsequently swallowed and ingested by a Victorian public eager for narratives of the African continent that affirmed their racial superiority.

In its first year of publication, the periodical's readers were treated to many adventure stories set in Africa, various explorers' travel accounts as well as news reports of British heroics in the Anglo-Zulu war. Like India, Africa and its commodities were treated as comestible objects. However, where India, a country, was defined by exotic excess in the British imagination, the entire continent of Africa was more often portrayed as a barren wasteland, only flourishing where Europeans were brave enough to settle and cultivate the land.[6] Its inhabitants were either 'rabid' man-eaters or 'perish[ing] from famine'.[7] Still, the public remained voracious for details about Africa, as the paper's correspondence pages attest. There were multiple requests for a portrait of the Zulu king Cetshwayo kaMpande, as well as an appeal on how to pronounce his name.[8]

Their greed for knowledge about the British Empire in Africa appears to have been matched only by their sweet tooths, for readers did not only request information to know more and to master, but also recipes to make sugary childhood treats like ginger beer, strawberry ice-cream, and sherbet.[9] Such recipes are another expression of British imperialism, as Sidney Mintz argues in *Sweetness and Power: The Place of Sugar in Modern History*. Sugar and sweetness cannot be separated from the colonial enterprise, which enslaved millions of Africans in its quest to satisfy demand for a substance that Mintz connects to an all-consuming white desire for power.[10] The inclusion of such recipes constitutes covert assertions of British imperial power and privilege. More importantly, their positioning in amongst requests for information about Britain's colonies draws attention to the text's function of satisfying its consumers' desires, in which the representational force of food is simply another manifestation of knowledge. This collapse between food and knowledge to assert hegemony is explicitly expressed in an article found in the Christmas edition of the *Boy's Own Paper*. Entitled 'Odds and

Ends: Fireside Fun', it gives instructions – a recipe – on how to make an African using an orange, alongside those to craft a pig out of a lemon:

> Here is Sambo, an old friend of the Christmastide holidays, and very easily prepared withal! Select a suitable orange, and set to work as follows: – First cut away the peel where the eyebrows, eyeballs, nostrils, and teeth have to come. Then insert two currants for eyes, and fine raisins for the curly black hair. This done, 'Sambo' is quite ready to be introduced to the company.[11]

Representations of Africans, sometimes literally as is the case here, became something for young British children to cut their teeth on. This recipe for making an edible African is not dissimilar to the act of writing one into being. Reading and eating are similarly interchangeable.[12] The child's activity must, of course, begin with having read the text and then presumably ends with the consumption of the African/orange, rendering it a domestic re-enactment of Darwinism. In both instances, whether reading or eating, the British subject retains the position of apex consumer. This text offers a paradigm through which to read all imperial acts of consumption. The remainder of the paper will focus on two of the key ingredients frequently used to gelatinize racial hierarchy, namely the creatureliness, or animality, of the African Other and its alleged opposite, a civilized whiteness, which, in this case, is codified by an English Christmas.

The inherent creativity of any culinary act presupposes an agent who wills the words into a material existence. The imaginary white child that follows this recipe to make a 'Sambo' and a pig out of citrus fruits is therefore actively involved in the process of creation. This grants the child the status of god-like creator, whereas the African and the pig are portrayed as passive creatures. In this particular creation narrative, the African's status is called into question because he, like the pig, is a created thing. Is he human or animal, or something in-between? In *The Animal That Therefore I Am,* Jacques Derrida stresses that the notion of an animal is entirely a construct, designed to allow for the complete subjugation of whatever might be defined as 'animal for the benefit of man'.[13] The very constructedness of the animal as a category means that the boundary between the animal and human is always inherently unstable, allowing the definition of what is human and what is animal to be manipulated to ensure the hegemony of the group that identifies themselves as fully man.

This blurring between Africans and animals occurs frequently in the *Boy's Own Paper*.[14] In its first several volumes, there are multiple stories about monkeys and baboons either stealing food from Europeans or relying on them as a food source. The reader is clearly being encouraged to draw comparisons between these pilfering animals and the 'Hottentot waggon-driver[s]' in Mary Ann Carey-Hobson's 'The Feathered Policeman: A South African Story', where several groups of Africans are accused of stealing melons, mealies, and figs from Mr. Harrison, a South African farmer.[15] One group accepts a 'basketful of apples' from him, even after they have ruined the crop cultivated by Gubbins, 'the English gardener'. He declares 'them black rascals' are '[n]ot

29

content with stealing the very best, they cuts of all these as they couldn't want, just to try the weight of 'em, I suppose. Such a day as I've had there's three of four h'acres of they mealies as was just a getting fit to use destroyed!' Tom Harrison, a 'lad of sixteen or seventeen' and presumably the son of the gentleman farmer, challenges Gubbins's lower-class vitriol against 'black niggers', arguing that '[t]hey're not all bad' and that it's not 'because they're black that they cheat and steal, but because they don't know better'. The *Boy's Own Paper* reader is meant to admire his benevolent and progressive stance towards Africans, especially when he saves one of the thieves who runs into Romeo, the farm's resident ostrich, while trying to escape capture. Tom concludes that the 'poor fellow' had 'learnt a lesson', but in all likelihood, would require more tutelage to learn 'virtue is its own reward'.[16] Placed in Tom's mouth, the moral's self-congratulatory smugness draws a clear boundary between the civilizers and the uncivilized Other.

This hierarchy is only reinforced by Tom's repeated use of the phrase 'I think' to preface his thoughts, which is a dull echo of Descartes' *cogito, ergo sum*. Derrida identifies the 'I think, therefore I am' of 'Cartesian ontology' as one of the key philosophical ideas underpinning the belief that animals were inferior. Historically he argues, man was regarded as a 'rational animal' until Descartes' writings cause a 'moment of rupture with respect to the tradition', which re-defined man as a 'thing that thinks' and distanced an entirely rational human selfhood from an animality that could not reason or speak, but only 'imitate [...] without understanding or thinking'.[17] Tom's 'I think' affirms his superiority as a respectable white man who is not only able to learn, but also to teach the animalistic African Other. This is reinforced by the black character's last words: '"Ach mij Baas, if you *please*, mij Baas, oh take him away! Oh Heere! I shall die!"'.[18] Even when he is saved, he keeps repeating the same words, reinforcing his status in the text as the unthinking animal, who is compelled to recognize that without his master he would die.

Animalization of the African Other, however, does not solely occur as a result of parallels between these various texts, but within the story itself. For instance, it is unclear which 'overworked dumb creatures' Mr. Harrison is referring to at the beginning. Is 'the good-natured farmer' sorry for the 'waggoner' who was unable to loosen his oxen from the yolk at the dam, or for the oxen? Significantly, the word 'creature' is soon after applied to the African characters by Gubbins; he calls them 'ongrateful creatures' and hopes to catch them 'like eels in a basket'. In contrast, the named ostrich who strips the nameless thief of his clothing is anthropomorphized to become a 'policeman', or what Gubbins calls a 'peeler'. Gubbins makes a joke about the thief's clothes being 'a'most peeled off his back'.[19] The use of the word 'peel' here is striking; it is as if here were an orange. The peeling of his 'skin', the destruction of his clothing, symbolically strips this African Other of 'one of the "properties" of a man', leaving him naked like an animal.[20]

It appears Carey-Hobson's story about animalistic Africans appealed to the *Boy's Own Paper* editor as well as its readers, because another story of hers was published three years later. The first part features a baboon called Jacko who serves as a groomsman for a Dutch Boer. Charles, a British boy, watches as Jacko takes 'figs on the sly' from a pile of drying fruit. Interestingly, this is the same fruit the Africans in 'The Feathered Policeman' first steal. Another similarity is Charles offering Jacko an apple, echoing Harrison's gift of apples to the Africans. Charles also gives Jacko sugar, and judges him to be 'stupid' and incapable of 'know[ing] what's good' when he does not eat it straightaway. This then leads to a discussion between him and Jem Mastik, a young farmer, as to the differences between Africans and baboons; Jem starts by saying that:

> 'The Bushmen have a notion that the baboon could talk if they liked, but that, being afraid that the Boers would make slaves of them, they hold their tongues.'
> 'Queer creatures!'
> 'Which – the Bushman or the baboon?'
> 'Oh! both. They're much of a muchness, I think.'
> 'The poor little Bushmen haven't any tails, you know, though I'll acknowledge there's not much to choose between the two. I have two baboons at my farm, so you'll be able to study their propensities while you are there if you'd like.'²¹

Like Tom, the two boys conclude that thieving (and poor taste) is the result of a lack of intelligence combined with little or no education, and therefore neither the baboon or the Bushman should be judged too harshly. Regardless, when, Jan Bavian, one of Jem's baboons, threatens to attack Charles' mother, punishment calculated to correct his 'fierce savagery' follows swiftly.²² Intriguingly, it is in aping humanity that the baboon causes the most damage, arguably because he, an animal, attempts to 'imitate [… his betters] without understanding or thinking'.²³ He first attempts to 'mimic […] the mistress of the house' by petting the family cat. When this proves unsuccessful, Jan next plucks a chicken, but in a brutal twist on the housewifely duty, he does it while the animal is still alive and takes great joy in doing so. Carey-Hobson describes how the English boy is duly horrified, whereas the African bystanders find the spectacle amusing. The resemblance – the 'much of a muchness' between baboons and Africans discussed earlier by the boys – is supposedly proven by the latter's 'shrieks of laughter'. The Africans are chastised by Charles for laughing and the baboon is suitably '"peppered"' with gunshot, which teaches him to be 'amenable to the laws of his master'.²⁴ The parallels Carey-Hobson encourages her readers to draw between baboons and Africans give the reader the impression both are simply creatures to be tamed, taught, and civilized by enterprising young white adventurers.

Yet, in the colonial context, actual animals are usually hunted rather than protected by the would-be adventurer. Megan A. Norcia in her work on Victorian geography primers states '[t]he imperial food chain model was not strictly based on the relation of predator to prey'.²⁵ I would contend that the animalization of the African Other in *Boy's Own Paper* stories makes the predator-prey relationship an integral part of the colonial experience they depict, in which the strong survive, and the weak die. This is supported by Mervyn Nicholson's argument that the relationship between food and power causes the '[e]ater and eaten [to] modulate into hunter and quarry, the powerful and the powerless. Metaphorically, if you are weak, you are edible; if you are edible, you are weak'.[26] In the periodical, African bodies are often shown being threatened or eaten by wild animals. For instance, the story 'Crocodile Hunting in Africa' is accompanied by a drawing of a crocodile eating an African. This illustration is set against the narrator's portrayal of himself as a great white hunter who saves the natives from a 'deadly enemy'.[27] In Darwinian terms, the Englishman's triumphant survival is proof that the British occupy the top position of the imperial food chain.

Turning to the next ingredient, I believe it is not insignificant that the recipe for making an African out of an orange is found in the Christmas edition of the *Boy's Own Paper*.[28] Given that the festival, as we know it today, and its traditions were invented by the Victorians, 'Sambo' cannot be a very old friend after all.[29] He, and Africans in general, become, however, a vital ingredient in the construction of the 'Englishness' that the Victorian middle-class Christmas set out to promote, a season in which the nation's structural inequalities were temporarily elided, rich and poor, coming together to celebrate, and feast.[30] Tara Moore, in *Victorian Christmas in Print*, contends that the Christmas book genre:

> developed a Christmas symbolism that told an increasingly festive nation that Christmas stood for a particular myth of patriotic, traditional Englishness. The nature of the image in *Punch*'s discourse allowed the comic newspaper to construct the conflation of Englishness and Christmas. Illustrators mixed icons of Englishness like Britannia and John Bull with emblems of the season, especially Christmas food items [...].

According to Moore, it is the plum pudding that 'becomes synonymous with John Bull's Englishness', and was increasingly used in print to represent 'a British-dominated globe'.[31] By the twentieth-century, the ingredients list for a Christmas pudding had become a popular marketing tool to celebrate the reach of Britain's Empire. For instance, in the 1930 film *One Family*, a young boy is given the quest of collecting ingredients from across the British dominions to make a Christmas pudding fit for a king. In the film, South Africa is portrayed as a 'land of sun and fruit'.[32] The white farmer oversees the African workers, as they collect oranges and grapes. The young boy only brings back brandy, but oranges would also have been needed to make the candied citrus peel called for in Mrs Beeton's traditional Christmas (or plum) pudding recipe.[33] The consumption of African oranges, whether they are made into 'Sambos' or not, therefore remains a gastronomic expression of British superiority.

Another expression of Western hegemony is the ability to bring Christmas to the African continent. Or, to borrow the words to a well-known Christmas song, to let them know what Christmastime is, and from a British 'world of plenty', 'spread a smile of joy'.[34] In 1882, the *Boy's Own Paper* published 'The Middy's Plum Pudding, or a Christmas Dinner on Board a Slaver', a short story in which a group of British sailors aboard the *Foam* patrol the coast of West Africa in a bid to 'keep down the infamous slave trade'. It is almost Christmas, which prompts a discussion between Lieutenant Hill and Harold Browne, a midshipman, about food. The latter reports that there will be nothing special about Christmas dinner, and lays the blame on the last African '"empty belly" station' the ship stopped at, 'Jella Coffee'.[35] Ironically, the indigenous word for a village or hamlet ('cope/kofe/kope') is misspelt, becoming 'coffee', a colonial commodity.[36] This slippage exposes the contradiction within the stereotype Browne espouses: Africa is somehow empty, but simultaneously full of coffee and other cash crops to exploit. Still, he declares the station has nothing except 'a few' 'fowl[s]' that are 'old and tough'.[37] These are a poor substitute for the turkey Mrs Beeton envisions as an indispensable part of the Christmas celebrations of 'the middle classes of this empire'.[38] The lieutenant reassures the midshipman that 'there'll be the orthodox plum pudding to fall back on', as there is 'plenty of flour and raisins in the hold'. Subsequently, the men's ability to produce a 'tastefully decorated' table, 'groaning under the weight of enormous plum puddings, pasties and eatables of various descriptions' underscores their innate nobility as civilizers of the world.[39] This is the 'well-served table' of Mrs Beeton's imaginings, a 'striking index of human ingenuity and resource' that is made all the more remarkable given the conditions under which it has been made. They, indeed, possess 'the will and skill to reduce to order, and surround with idealisms and graces, the more material conditions of human existence', which set them apart from the empty bellies on the continent.[40]

In the length of time it takes the ship's puddings to be boiled, the British ship captures a slaver, rescuing 'two hundred of the wretched *creatures*' imprisoned aboard (emphasis added). Christmas celebrations ensue, and the freed African slaves are described as '[looking] on with wonder as the service proceeded, and although they did not quite comprehend what was going on, their faces beamed with pleasure when they heard the rising music'. Their reactions to the food are not given, and there is no suggestion they are included in the festive meal. In fact, they are not mentioned for the remainder of the story, having served their purpose. The plum-pudding, however, remains centre-stage. Its presence not only makes the men's Christmas dinner, but it saves Lieutenant Hill from being murdered by the slaver's captain, who is described as being a 'swarthy spaniard'. On the slaver, a table-cloth is thrown over what is left of the festive 'banquet'; 'the pudding at one end makes a capital head', and so it 'look[s] as if some fellow was asleep under the cloth'.[41] During the night, the slaver's captain escapes from the hold. In the dark, he thinks the pile of food is the lieutenant, and he attacks the pudding with an axe, only to find himself apprehended by the *Foam*'s crew. Food, once again, proves integral to the construction of this narrative of English superiority. It is the Christmas pudding that allows the sailors to triumph over the story's malevolent racialized Other, a Spaniard, and emerge as the true European saviours of the continent. Food asserts English supremacy in what Richard Dyer identifies as a 'hierarchy of whiteness', in which 'some whites are whiter than others'.[42] The *Boy's Own Paper* readers

33

are led to condemn the behaviour of the dark Spanish captain, who tries to enslave 'two hundred creatures' as well as murder a British officer while he is asleep.[43] At the same time, they are encouraged to admire and emulate the British characters, who, unlike their unsporting (and less white) competitors, are portrayed as honourable and benevolent empire-builders.

This essay has concentrated on one particular method for making and consuming white superiority in the nineteenth-century *Boy's Own* periodical, namely the animalization of the African Other and the contrasting image of an English Christmas. The role food plays in creating these imperial narratives, which were then consumed by British children, make it impossible to countenance Joseph Conrad's assertion that books about food and cooking are ideologically neutral. For Conrad, one's domestic arrangements and what one eats is apolitical. He insists the sole purpose of a cookery book, the product of 'human talents and industry', was 'to increase the happiness of mankind', but who qualifies as man in this statement? Who is excluded from Conrad's seemingly universal 'mankind'? What the essay has shown is how the *Boy's Own Paper* stories use food to animalize and exclude the African Other in order to increase the happiness of white men by affirming their superior 'human talents and industry'.[44] The representational force of food on both the pages and the plates of the British public therefore fuels the colonial enterprise and the overwhelming imperial desire to be the apex consumer. Food is, as Fanon points out, at the very centre of all relationships during the colonial period.[45] I have hinted here how the force of these colonial-alimentary ideologies are still felt in the present-day. For instance, the narrative that Africa is a continent that cannot feed itself, is enshrined in Band Aid's annual declaration that nothing ever grows in Africa. To quote bell hooks, such instances of 'white racism' and 'imperialism' only 'prevail by courageous consumption'.[46] They only exist because they are eaten. By analyzing the reading and eating habits of nineteenth-century consumers, we might gain an insight into twenty-first century consumption, with a view to starving the imperial and racist structures that feed off such representations of Africa.

34

Notes

1   Joseph Conrad, *Heart of Darkness and Other Tales* (London: Oxford University Press, 2008), p. 118.

2   Joseph Conrad, 'Preface' to *A Handbook of Cookery for a Small House* by Jessica Conrad (London: William Heinemann, 1923), p. v.

3   Annette Cozzi, *The Discourses of Food in Nineteenth-Century British Fiction* (New York: Palgrave Macmillan, 2010), p. 6.

4   Isabella Beeton, *The Book of Household Management* (Oxford: Benediction Classics, 2010), p. 923.

5   Cozzi, *Discourses of Food*, p. 5.

6   For an account of the food-related rhetoric that would shape India in the imperial British imagination, see Cozzi, '"Miss Sharp adores pork": Ingesting India from *The Missionary* to *The Moonstone*', *Discourses of Food*, pp. 105-26.

7   'Stanley's Adventures in Africa', *Boy's Own Paper*, 13 September 1879, p. 567; 'With the Zulus', *Boy's Own Paper*, 22 March 1879, p. 149.

8   'Correspondence', *Boy's Own Paper*, 20 December 1879, p. 192; 'Correspondence', *Boy's Own Paper*, 10 January 1880, p. 240.

9   The recipes mentioned can be found in the following *Boy's Own Paper* correspondence sections: 22 November 1879, p. 128; 1 May 1880, p. 528; 21 January 1882, p. 280.

10 Sidney Mintz, *Sweetness and Power: The Place of Sugar in Modern History* (London: Penguin Books, 1986), p. 71.

11 'Odds and Ends: Fireside Fun', *Boy's Own Paper*, 27 December 1879, pp. 206-07.

12 In *Discourses of Food*, Cozzi similarly points out that both eating and reading are acts of consumption (p. 4). Megan A. Norcia, in 'The Imperial Food Chain: Eating as an Interface of Power in Women Writers' Geography Primers', *Victorian Literature and Culture*, 33.1 (2005), also conflates reading and eating, suggesting school textbooks are the primary means by which the imperial apparatus is internalized, or rather ingested (p. 262).

13 Jacques Derrida, *The Animal That Therefore I Am*, ed. by Marie-Luise Mallet (New York: Fordham University Press, 2008), p. 25.

14 Though hardly only there: Jennifer Eberhardt argues that the black-ape association was also promulgated through nineteenth-century scientific essay ('The Scary Monster' in *Biased: The New Science of Race and Inequality* (London: William Heinemann, 2019), pp. 133-52).

15 In her obituary, Mary Ann Carey-Hobson is described as the 'well-known South African authoress'. She was, however, British-born, only moving to South Africa with her father, a surgeon, when she was twelve years old in 1845. A keen supporter of Britain's imperial enterprise, she briefly returned to England in 1862 to organize the South African court for the Great Exhibition. It was only after the death of her second husband that she returned to London. There she began her literary career, editing a magazine as well as writing novels and short stories about life as a settler in colonial South Africa. In addition to supporting the British Empire through her writing, she was a member of both the Imperial Institute and the Royal Colonial Institute. For the full obituary, see Anon., 'Death of Mrs Carey Hobson', *South Africa Magazine*, 21 January 1911 <www.1820settlers.com/genealogy/getperson.php?personID=I106389&tree=master> [accessed 29 October 2019].

16 Mary Ann Carey-Hobson, 'The Feathered Policeman: A South African Story', *Boy's Own Paper*, 19 July 1879, pp. 422-23.

17 Derrida, *The Animal That Therefore I Am*, pp. 74-77, 71, 52.

18 Carey-Hobson, 'The Feathered Policeman', pp. 423.

19 Carey-Hobson, 'The Feathered Policeman', pp. 422-24.

20 Carey-Hobson, 'The Feathered Policeman', pp. 423; Derrida, p. 5.

21 Carey-Hobson, 'Taming Baboons', *Boy's Own Paper*, 11 March 1882, p. 384.

22 Carey-Hobson, 'Taming Baboons: Part II', *Boy's Own Paper*, 18 March 1882, p. 401.

23 Derrida, p. 52.

24 Carey-Hobson, 'Taming Baboons: Part II', p. 401-02.

25 Megan A. Norcia, 'The Imperial Food Chain', p. 253.

26 Mervyn Nicholson, 'Food and Power: Homer, Carroll, Atwood and Others', *Mosaic*, 20.3 (1987), p. 39.

27 'Crocodile Hunting in Africa', *Boy's Own Paper*, 6 September 1879, pp. 540-41.

28 'Odds and Ends: Fireside Fun', *Boy's Own Paper*, p. 206.

29 John Storey, 'The Invention of the English Christmas', *Christmas, Ideology and Popular Culture* (Edinburgh: Edinburgh University Press, 2008), p. 18.

30 Storey, p. 30.

31 Tara Moore, *Victorian Christmas in Print* (New York: Palgrave Macmillan, 2009), p. 66.

32 Walter Creighton, *One Family*, BFI, 9 July 1930, www.bfi.org.uk/inview/title/6178 [accessed 20 May 2019]. For an in-depth analysis of the film, see Tom Rice 'One Family', *Colonial Film: Moving Images of the British Empire*, September 2008, www.colonialfilm.org.uk/node/40 [accessed 20 May 2019]. His observation that the film drew on 'existing EMB campaigns and adopted language used in other media' indicates the significance of the plum-pudding in showcasing Britain's imperial and national identity.

33 Beeton, pp. 689-90.
34 Band Aid, 'Do They Know It's Christmas?', *Do They Know It's Christmas-Single* ed., Phonogram, 1984, track 1.
35 'The Middy's Plum Pudding, or a Christmas Dinner on Board a Slaver', *Boy's Own Paper*, 25 December 1882, pp. 13-14.
36 Adam Jones and Peter Sebald, 'Appendix 10', *An African Family Archive: The Lawsons of Little Popo/Aneho (Togo) 1841-1938* (2005), p. 522.
37 'The Middy's Plum Pudding', p. 13.
38 Beeton, p. 523.
39 'The Middy's Plum Pudding', pp. 13-14.
40 Beeton, p. 923.
41 'The Middy's Plum Pudding', pp. 14-16.
42 Richard Dyer, 'The Matter of Whiteness', in *White: Twentieth Anniversary Edition* (New York: Routledge, 2017), p. 19; see the whole of Dyer's chapter (pp. 1-40) for further discussion on hierarchies of whiteness.
43 'The Middy's Plum Pudding', p. 14.
44 Conrad, 'Preface', p. v.
45 Frantz Fanon, *The Wretched of the Earth*, trans. by Constance Farrington (London: Penguin, 2001), p. 249.
46 bell hooks, *Black Looks: Race and Representation* (New York: Routledge, 2015), p. 36.

A Tale of Two Cities: Paris, London, and the Political Power of Food

Carolyn Steel

'The supply of food to a great city is among the most remarkable of social phenomena – full of instruction on all sides.'

– George Dodd[1]

How do you feed a city? It's a vital question, yet one that we rarely ask. Living in a modern city, it can be hard to grasp the importance of the relationship that underpins urban civilization – that which exists between city and country. Industrialization has obscured the vital connections without which our urban lives would swiftly grind to a halt: the complex supply chains that transport food from the land and sea where it is produced to our supermarkets, cafés, kitchens, and tables.[2] Food arrives as if by magic, and we rarely stop to wonder how it got there.

Before the age of steam, things were very different. In the pre-industrial world, the feeding of cities was an arduous, often overwhelming task that shaped almost every aspect of urban life and preoccupied every city administration. Above all else, what mattered to a city's fortunes was its geography. It is no accident that the world's first cities – the Sumerian city-states of Ur, Uruk, Kippur, and others that emerged some 5500 years ago in southern Mesopotamia – were built on a vast river delta, where the mighty Tigris and Euphrates merged to spill their mineral-rich waters just north of the Persian Gulf. The construction of elaborate banks and ditches to control the waters and channel them over the cities' palm groves, orchards, and fields effectively created the world's first countryside. Life in these early urban centres revolved around the annual harvest, a pivotal event that was both celebrated and overseen by the temple, which acted as the city's administrative, as well as spiritual, hub. Writing, money, and bookkeeping were among the skills and artefacts invented in Sumer in order to help with the new and unwieldy task of feeding a large, non-food-producing population; a problem with which every city since has had to grapple.

One lasting legacy of these prototypical cities was their division of land into two distinct territories – city and country – that have shaped urban civilization ever since. Although the urban and rural portions of early city-states were considered indivisible parts of an integrated whole, they nevertheless established a hierarchy between the leaders and led, and the feeders and fed, that would become more pronounced with time. In ancient Sumer, as in virtually every subsequent civilization, power resided with the temples, not with the farmers who toiled to fill their granaries.

Rome – Consumer City

'...the city appears a kind of common emporium of the world...'

– Aristides[3]

The city-state model pioneered in Sumer was sufficiently successful to dominate urban development for the next five or so millennia. When a city eventually bucked the trend, it did so in such spectacular fashion as to effectively rewrite the urban blueprint. That city was ancient Rome. With one million citizens at its zenith, Rome was the first urban centre to outgrow its local hinterland. The city was already relying on imported grain from Sicily and Sardinia from as early as the third century BCE, and subsequent conquests of Carthage and Egypt, in 146 and 30 BCE respectively, cemented this approach, securing access to farmland that expanded the capital's gastronomic as well as political horizons. For the best part of five centuries, the plains of North Africa (and especially those of the Nile Delta) served as the Imperial breadbasket, while other foods including olive oil, pork, wine, honey, and *liquamen* (a fermented fish sauce without which few Romans considered life to be worth living) were extracted from all across the Mediterranean, Black Sea, and North Atlantic coasts.

Rome's approach to feeding itself thus relied on what we would now call 'food miles': a strategy of conquest and trade enabled by slave labour and militarized mastery of the seas. Without sea transport (which has been estimated to be about fifty times cheaper than journeys overland), the city could never have grown to such a monstrous size.[4] Even so, feeding the capital was a constant headache for its leaders: during Augustus's reign, up to 320,000 citizens received a free 'grain dole', the *Annona*, which Cicero reckoned cost the state one-fifth of all its revenue.[5] Ruinous though it was, maintaining the dole was a smart move, according to Tacitus, who saw the political expediency of feeding the *plebs* and declared that Augustus had 'won over the people with bread'.[6] The Annona remained a thorn in the side of successive emperors, however, as a speech by Tiberius makes clear: 'This duty, senators, devolves upon the emperor; if it is neglected, the utter ruin of the state will follow.'[7]

As the world's first metropolis, Rome makes a revealing comparison with contemporary Western cities. With the bulk of the capital's food coming in from abroad, local farmers were free to concentrate on the highly lucrative practice of *pastio villatica* (villa farming), growing fruit and vegetables and producing such delicacies as milk-fed snails and nut-stuffed dormice for the luxury market, much as vertical farms and organic box schemes serve high-end urban markets today. While local farmers thrived, however, Rome's distant hinterlands suffered: by the third century, the soils of North Africa had become exhausted, and observers wrote despairingly of the white, caked earth, a sure sign of fatal salinization.

By effectively eating itself to death, Rome revealed the true extent of what I have called the 'urban paradox': the fact that, however powerful they may seem, cities have an inherent vulnerability, since they must depend on somewhere else – a territory we call 'countryside' – to feed them. Whatever their size, wealth, or influence, cities have always relied on a rural hinterland which, while ideally close at hand as in the case of early city-states, has since of necessity often been hundreds or even thousands of miles away, comprising territories many times larger than the cities themselves. In the pre-industrial world, this dependency made a city's geographical situation of critical importance, not just in determining its ability to eat, trade, and wage war (by no means mutually exclusive activities, then as now), but also to the ways in which it shaped the politics, economics, and culture of its host nation.

Paris – the 'New Rome'

> 'One would have trouble imagining that there are sources capable of meeting the needs of this vast pit.'
>
> – Dictionary of the Paris Grain Police, 1790[8]

Nowhere has the power of geography to shape national destinies been more evident than in the parallel fates of two rival European capitals, Paris and London. By 1750, Paris was one of the largest cities in Europe, with some 650,000 mouths to feed. Dubbed the 'New Rome' because of its size, the city's geographical situation differed from that of its ancient predecessor in one crucial respect: although also built on a river, it was 170 meandering miles up the Seine from the sea – too far to be navigable by ocean-going vessels. The result, as Stephen Kaplan details in his gripping account *Provisioning Paris*, was that the supply of grain to the city dominated and stifled the rural economy of northern France. A series of 'provisioning crowns' were declared around the capital, of which the first consisted of a zone twenty miles deep in which only grain for the city could be grown. With a good harvest, this 'first crown' could just about cope, but in a bad year (which could come as often as one in three) the capital asserted its right, by force if necessary, to acquire its grain from the 'second crown' of Picardy and Champagne; if that wasn't enough, the third or 'crisis' crown was invoked, consisting of most of France from its Atlantic to Mediterranean coasts.

Unsurprisingly, the capital's habit of putting 'a knife to the throat of the people', as one local put it, didn't go down too well in the countryside. When the harvest failed, country folk needed their grain just as much as city-dwellers did, but since they were less inclined to riot than their urban counterparts, they rarely got enough. Parisians were as dependent on the authorities to feed them as Roman citizens had been, and they were similarly bellicose. They were also fussy, insisting on eating so-called '*bis-blanc*' bread, a loaf so fine that, as one writer observed, 'the small artisan eats a more beautiful loaf than the best bourgeois of the provinces'.[9]

The Parisian authorities recognized, like those of Rome before them, that feeding the people was critical to their political survival. As the finance minister Jacques Necker put it in 1778, it was 'the most essential object that must occupy the administration'.[10] Without easy access to foreign grain, however, the authorities' options were limited. Rather than being able to expand their hinterland as the Romans had done, their only recourse was to extract as much from their existing one as possible. To this end, the city set up a 'grain police', an unwieldy hierarchy of thousands of officials, headed up by the 'baker of last resort', the King himself. The police oversaw every aspect of the grain trade, sending spies into the countryside to gather information on market conditions, likely yields, local gossip, and weather, reporting back at weekly meetings. Only licensed grain merchants were allowed to function within twenty miles of the city, and all transactions were supposed to take place in the open so that they could be monitored. The hoarding of grain was forbidden, and millers, bakers, and merchants were all prevented from engaging in one another's business.

So much for the theory. In practice, a great deal of trade went on illegally, via an extensive black market that included a network of illegal 'corn exchanges' held in taverns, farms, and even out on the open road. Institutions such as convents and hospitals that were licensed to hold stocks of grain for their own use acted as illegal granaries, allowing dealers to store their grain in exchange for a cut of the profits. Millers and bakers, meanwhile, battled to wrest control of the supply, with millers amassing vast wealth by dealing in grain, and then bakers milling their own flour, taking away the millers' business. Although the grain police were aware of these transgressions, they were powerless to stop them. As the officers themselves recognized, the black market – which effectively operated as an undercover free market – had an essential role to play in feeding the city, supplying about one third of all its food. The police were thus forced to turn a blind eye to the very practices they were supposed to prevent; their task was to control a trade that was inherently uncontrollable.

To make matters worse, the authorities tried to increase their grip on the food supply by concentrating it all in a single central market close to the Louvre, Les Halles. The market was split into various quarters selling different kinds of produce, each presided over by its own dynastic clan, who kept a mafia-like grip on their respective trade. Later dubbed *Le Ventre de Paris* (the Belly of Paris) by Emile Zola, the market was a city within the city, with its own population, customs, rules, taverns, and clocks. As Diderot noted, it also had its own political opinions: 'Listen to a blasphemy. La Bruyère and La Rochefoucauld are very ordinary and pedestrian books when one compares them to the wiles, the wit, the politics and the profound reasonings that are practised in a single market day at the Halle.'[11]

Bread, as most of us are aware from dimly-recalled history lessons, played a role in the French Revolution. Rather than seeing food shortages as a shared privation to be endured, Parisians saw them as a direct failure of the authorities to feed them. The crisis came in the 1780s, when a string of poor harvests (caused partly by the eruption of an Icelandic volcano) culminated with two disastrous years in 1788 and 1789. As the population became restive, it was the market porters, or *forts* (many of them ex-soldiers so named for their strength and fighting spirit) who spread rumours of food shortages

40

and blamed the King. As riots began to break out, the *forts* became natural leaders of the mob, turning the strength of their key role in the food system directly against those who had granted it. When the 'baker of last resort' tried to flee Paris and was apprehended, he was shown no mercy. Louis XVI had in fact stopped to change horses, but was portrayed as having broken his journey in order to eat a meal: the ultimate gesture of a monarch too greedy to save his own skin, let alone those of his people. With the possible exception of Rome, few cities provide as clear an example of why politicians loathe being responsible for feeding their people as Paris.

London – Feeding the Wen

Although never dubbed the New Rome, London deserved the title more than most. Already noted as a 'celebrated centre of commerce' by Tacitus just twenty years after its foundation in 43 CE, *Londinium* mimicked its mother city from the off, with a taste for foreign fare such as wine, olive oil, pine-nuts, raisins, pepper, ginger, and cinnamon – as well as the must-have *liquamen* – all shipped up from the Mediterranean to make life bearable for ex-pat Romans living in the frozen north.

Blessed with a tidal, navigable river, London had plenty of options when it came to feeding itself. The Thames not only gave the city easy access to imported foods, but it also provided the means by which produce from the fertile fields of south-east England could easily reach the city. The supply of grain to the capital already dominated the local economy by the thirteenth century, with market towns such as Ware, Henley-on-Thames, Faversham, Maidstone, and Rochester growing rich on the trade.[12] Yet despite the abundance of local supplies, London never lost its habit of importing food from abroad, and was already regularly supplementing its grain supplies from the Baltic by the tenth century.

Such abundance led London to develop a distinctly hands-off approach to feeding itself. Unlike their French counterparts, no English monarch took responsibility for feeding their citizens; on the contrary, royal interference in London trade was merely seen as a hindrance. Duties from the city's two main river ports of Billingsgate and Queenhithe went to City and Crown respectively, making the question of where ships docked a matter of great concern to the monarchy. The disadvantage caused by Queenhithe being upstream of London Bridge was something that successive monarchs attempted to overcome by issuing edicts, such as this from Edward IV in 1463, cited by John Stow:

> it was ordained, that all manner of vessels, ships, or boats, great or small, resorting to the city with victual, should be sold by retail, and that if there came but one vessel at a time, were it salt, wheat, rye, or other corn from beyond the seas, or other grains, garlic, onions, herrings, sprats, eels, whiting, place, cod, mackerel &c, then that one vessel should come to Queene Hithe, and there to make sale: but if two vessels came, the one should come to Queene Hithe, the other to Billingsgate: if three, two of them should come to Queene Hithe, the third to Billingsgate &c. always the more to Queene Hithe.[13]

41

As this litany suggests, regardless of where ships docked in London, there was no shortage of food flowing into the city, which perhaps explains why the English were so slow in exploring the possibilities of global trade. It was only when Christopher Columbus accidentally bumped into America while attempting to find a sea-passage to Asia in 1492 that the English finally woke up to what they were missing. Within three years of that momentous event, Henry VII had engaged two Venetian explorers – John Cabot and his son – to 'conquer, occupy and possess whatsoever such towns, castles, cities and islands' they could find on behalf of the Crown.[14] It marked the start of the age of trade and exploration (a.k.a. exploitation and piracy) that would turn England into a global superpower.

While Spanish explorers sought gold and silver and Dutch ones spices and silk, the trade that the English hit upon was sugar. When Admiral William Penn seized Jamaica on behalf of the Crown in 1655, he could hardly have imagined the wealth that would soon be pouring out of the new colony. Sugar was a food so irresistible to European palates that it would transform not just England's economic fortunes, but the very fabric of society. Demand for the stuff grew so rapidly during the seventeenth century that plantations were soon established all over the Caribbean, run like factories on African slave labour, the shameful 'false commodity' on which so much colonial wealth was based. To begin with, England exported half its sugar to the rest of Europe, but by 1750 home consumption had outstripped supply to such an extent that exports had virtually ceased. As the governor of the East India Company Sir Josiah Child pointed out, Britain didn't need to export its sugar; it could manage very nicely just trading with its own foreign colonies.

42 Thanks largely to trade in the new 'white gold', eighteenth-century London was a boomtown. One tenth of the British population lived in the capital, a quarter of them engaged in port trades, dealing with goods that flowed in from every part of the world. Walking through the busy dockyards, Samuel Johnson marvelled at the abundance to be found there:

> He that contemplates the extent of this wonderful city, finds it difficult to conceive, by what method plenty is maintained in our markets, and how the inhabitants are regularly supplied with the necessities of life; but when he examines the shops and warehouses, sees the immense stores of every kind of merchandise piled up for sale [...] he will be inclined to conclude that such quantities cannot easily be exhausted [...].[15]

London was getting rich, and as Daniel Defoe noted, the city was getting increasingly frivolous as it did so. 'It will hardly be believed in ages to come,' he wrote, 'that a pastry cook's shop, which twenty pounds would effectively furnish at one time with all needful things for sale, yet that fitting up one of these shops should cost upwards of £300, Anno Domini 1710: let the year be recorded!'. Disgusted though he may have been at such extravagance, Defoe was in no doubt as to its wider benefits to the nation, as he noted in his 1720 *Tour Through the Whole Island of Great Britain*:

It is not the kingdom which makes London rich, but London makes the rest of the kingdom rich. The country corresponds with London, but London corresponds with the world. The country supplies London with corn and cattle; and if there were not such a metropolis, what would become of the farmers? [...] The country send up their corn, their malt, their cattle, their fowls, their coals, their fish, all to London, and London sends back spice, sugar, wine, drugs, cotton, linen, tobacco, and all foreign necessaries to the country [...]. London consumes all, circulates all, exports all, and at last pays for all; and this is trade.[16]

The craving for sugar was turning Britain into the world's first consumer society. Alongside the bitter trio of coffee, tea, and cocoa, it created an intoxicating blurring of boundaries between luxury and need. As one of the first to witness the phenomenon, Defoe could see that the world about him was changing, yet it would take another fifty years before the events he described were acknowledged as a whole new economic order: the start of a hunger that could never be sated.

The Case for Free Trade

By the early eighteenth century, the contrasting fortunes of Paris and London were stark. With a population of 675,000, London had just surpassed Paris as Europe's largest city; yet while the French capital became increasingly crippled by the struggle to feed itself, Londoners were too busy making money to give the matter a second thought.

One man for whom the contrast did not go unnoticed was the Scottish moral philosopher and economist Adam Smith. While staying in Paris in 1766, Smith met the leading economists of their day François Quesnay and Jacques Turgot, the self-styled 'Physiocrats' (from Greek *phusis*, nature, + *kratia*, rule) then grappling with the vexed question of how to feed Paris, which they hoped to do by modernizing the medieval property laws and taxes that mired the rural economy. All three economists agreed that the ultimate source of a nation's wealth lay in the land: Quesnay even went so far as to say that farmers were the only productive members of society, since landowners merely distributed the wealth they created, while merchants and artisans produced nothing at all.

While disagreeing on the latter point, Smith was impressed by Quesnay's proposal to remove all internal barriers to trade, a principle that Turgot tried to implement while serving as controller-general of finances in 1774. History might have turned out very differently had Turgot's tenure not happened to coincide with a series of disastrous harvests that were blamed, not on nature's intransigence, but on the Physiocrats' meddling. Turgot was relieved of his duties, scuppering any chance of reforms that might have averted the food crisis that would eventually spark the French Revolution.

While events in Paris followed their tragic trajectory, a very different revolution was unfolding in Britain. As Daniel Defoe had already noted, the wealth flooding into London was not merely transforming the capital, but the countryside along with it. As marshes were drained and land enclosed in order to feed the city, a raft of new agricultural practices such as crop rotation, cattle breeding, and the growing of fodder crops imported from the Dutch were transforming British farming. The English countryside was a hive of entrepreneurial activity, as poulterers and warreners took out loans to expand their businesses, fruiterers planted orchards, and butchers became graziers and stockbreeders.

For Adam Smith, the contrast between such entrepreneurial buzz and the torpor of rural France was striking. The Physiocrats were right to want to deregulate urban-rural trade, he thought, but their insistence on farmers being the only source of wealth blinded them to a greater truth: that it was access to wider markets that multiplied that wealth. While the Physiocrats wanted to turn France into a protectionist agrarian economy, Smith saw Britain's potential to become something far greater: an industrial trading nation. In 1776, just two years after his Paris sojourn, Smith published what remains arguably the most influential economic tract ever written, *An Enquiry into the Nature and Causes of the Wealth of Nations*. In it, Smith laid out the principles of modern capitalism, arguing that, although land formed the basis of a nation's wealth, its generation depended on trade:

> The great commerce of every civilised society, is that carried on between the inhabitants of the town and those of the country [...]. The country supplies the town with the means of subsistence, and the materials of manufacture. The town repays this by sending back a part of the manufactured produce to the inhabitants of the country. The town, in which there neither is nor can be any reproduction of substances, may very properly be said to gain its whole wealth and subsistence from the country. We must not, however upon this account, imagine that the gain of the town is the loss of the country. The gains of both are mutual and reciprocal.

The relationship between city and country required no regulation, argued Smith, since the self-interest of many individuals in a free market would see to it that every available economic niche was filled. The 'hidden hand' of commerce would regulate itself, to the benefit of all. However, Smith acknowledged, the opening up of local markets to global trade could also have its casualties:

> The inhabitants of a city, it is true, must always ultimately derive their subsistence, and the whole materials and means of their industry, from the country. But those of a city, situated near either the sea-coast or the banks of a navigable river, are not necessarily confined to derive them from the country in their neighbourhood. They have a much wider range, and they may draw them from the most remote corners of the world [...]. A city might in this manner grow to great wealth and splendour, while not only the country in its neighbourhood, but all those to which it traded were in poverty and wretchedness.[17]

Although Smith didn't mention London by name, there can be little doubt as to what 'mighty city on a navigable river' he had in mind when he wrote these words. In contrast to Paris, London demonstrated what Smith called 'perfect competition': the forces of supply and demand in dynamic harmony. His economic model predicted great wealth alongside wretched poverty: a formulation that would prove remarkably prescient.

'Nobody Does It'

A century after *Wealth of Nations*, London's position as a global capital was secured. In the mid-nineteenth century, the social chronicler George Dodd published a fascinating and exhaustive account of the Victorian capital's food supply entitled *The Food of London*. Unlike modern food companies that shroud their operations in secrecy, the port and market authorities of Dodd's day seem to have been more than willing to share with him the minutiae of their trade, thanks to which we know how many tons of potatoes were sold at Covent Garden in 1853 (72,000), how many head of livestock arrived in London that same year (2.2 million) and how many ships docked each day at the city's ports: 121, of which 52 came from the colonies bringing, among other things, an annual 86 million pounds of tea from India and China. Despite his diligence in tracking down every cow and cabbage entering the city, however, Dodd admitted to being stumped when it came to explaining how this cornucopia of produce reached London:

> It is useless to ask by what central authority, or under what controlling system, is such a city as London supplied with its daily food. 'Nobody does it'. No-one for instance, took care that a sufficient quantity of food should reach London in 1855, for the supply of two millions and a half of human beings during fifty-two weeks. And yet such a supply *did* reach London.[18]

45

By George Dodd's day, the 'hidden hand' that fed London had barely changed for centuries. Cattle were still herded down St. John Street to the livestock market at Smithfield, geese still waddled in from Essex to be sold at Poultry, and tea clippers still sailed up the Thames. Yet things were on the verge of change. In 1835, the first railway line into London had been completed and, as Dodd recognized, the railways were set to revolutionize the way that cities were fed. 'It is scarcely possible', he wrote, 'to exaggerate the value of quick and easy transmission of food to so enormous a city as London; the variety of the commodities, and the prices at which they can be sold, are so intimately dependent thereon, that it becomes almost a matter of life and death to the inhabitants.'[19]

The most obvious transformative effect of the railways was to allow food to be transported rapidly in bulk over great distances, thus saving cities from the sort of fate that had engulfed Paris just fifty years earlier. Railways, in short, emancipated cities from geography, easing their ancient burden of feeding themselves and allowing them, for the first time, to be built any size, shape, and place. The urban age had arrived, and with it the transformation of the rural landscape on a scale never before seen.

As cities like London began to sprawl, a matching agricultural carpet was rolled out across swathes of previously inaccessible land such as the great plains of America's

Midwest. For the millions of bison and Native Americans who inhabited the prairies, the arrival of the railroads in 1830 spelt catastrophe. Within the space of just four years, the northern herd had been slaughtered, and their human companions scattered or removed to reservations, leaving the plains open for conversion to the largest area of grain production the world had yet seen.

All railroads led to Chicago, whose position at the base of Lake Michigan and near the top of the Mississippi watershed put it in pole position to profit from the new trade. With more grain pouring into the city than people could consume, Chicagoans came up with the novel idea of feeding the surplus to cows. By 1870, Chicago's Union Stockyards employed 75,000 people and processed three million head of cattle a year, raising the new problem of how to get so much fresh meat to lucrative East Coast markets in an edible state. Gustavus F. Swift, one of Chicago's biggest packers, cracked the problem by building a railway furnished with depots of lake ice, salted blocks of which were hung at both ends of each railway truck, so that chilled air flowed over the dressed beef and kept it fresh. Swift effectively invented what we now call the chill-chain: a refrigerated delivery network that formed the last piece of the food logistics puzzle. With aggressive marketing and cut-throat prices, he soon persuaded Bostonians and New Yorkers that factory beef slaughtered hundreds of miles away was a better bargain than fresh meat from their local butchers. Industrially produced cheap meat had arrived.

With their logistical mastery, efficiencies of scale, and ruthless business practices, Chicago's meatpackers were *de facto* founders of the modern food industry. By controlling the supply chain and using their economic heft to undercut rivals and drive them out of business, they pioneered the logic of control and consolidation that now dominates global food. By 1889, just four meatpackers controlled 90% of the Chicago beef trade; today just four (including JBS-Swift) control 85% of all US beef production.[20] The packers demonstrated what political leaders had always known but were afraid to admit: control of food is power.

Today, the corporate food genie is well out of the bottle, with global agri-food conglomerates such as Nestlé, PepsiCo, and Unilever making annual sales well above many national GDPs (Nestlé's sales in 2019 were worth $97 billion).[21] Today, our politicians have about as much control over our food as did the hapless Parisian grain police. When it comes to food, we're all free traders now; yet the fact that our leaders long ago ceded responsibility for feeding us is rarely acknowledged. On the contrary, the 'revolving door' between government and 'Big Ag' and the billions funnelled into the latter in the form of subsidies are kept as far as possible from the public gaze. Yet when leaders such as Brazilian President Jair Bolsonaro – who has strong links to the cattle industry – appoint their agribusiness buddies to government and give them a tacit green light to deforest the Amazon, the dangers of such cosy relationships are clear.[22] Today, it would be little exaggeration to say that the lack of political control over our food threatens our future and that of our planet.

Sitopia

Two millennia after Rome's demise, it's not hard to see parallels with our own perilous state. Rome exemplified what happens when city and country become fatally disconnected; however technically enabled we may be in comparison to our *liquamen*-guzzling ancestors, our essential dilemma remains the same. As Aristotle noted, we are 'political animals' – which is to say that we have an inherent duality: we belong in society, yet our ultimate home is in nature. This duality forms the core of the urban paradox: the more we gather together in cities in order to be social, the further we get from our sources of sustenance. All of which suggests that, after roughly two centuries of leaving the feeding of cities to the market – a.k.a. the agrifood industry – it's time we got political about food again.

Given the enormous importance of food to human society, it should perhaps come as no surprise to learn that it plays a key role in much utopian thought. Both Plato and Aristotle – good citizens of the Athenian *polis*, or city-state – argued that cities should remain small in order to be able to feed themselves. They argued for the principle of *oikonomia* (household management), an arrangement in which every citizen would feed their household from their own farm; a principle which, scaled up, would render the *polis* self-sufficient. The idea was echoed by Thomas More in his 1516 *Utopia*, in which he envisioned replacing the bloated Tudor capital of London with a network of semi-independent city-states. In 1902, Ebenezer Howard updated this notion in his *Garden Cities of To-Morrow*, which is essentially More's *Utopia* with railways. Recognizing our need for both society and nature, Howard dubbed his garden city a 'Town-Country Magnet', arguing that a network of dense communities of limited size surrounded by countryside could provide the benefits of city and country living, while negating the downsides of both. Crucially, all the urban and rural land in the garden city would be owned by its residents in the form of a public trust, so that when land values rose, it would be local citizens, not private landowners, who would benefit.

Contrary to its comfortable leafy image, therefore, the garden city was in fact a radical proposal for incremental land reform and an associated shift towards a more regional, participatory politics. All of which makes interesting reading in the current climate. As I have argued elsewhere, many of the social and ecological challenges we face – climate change, deforestation, mass extinction, pollution, water depletion, soil degradation, declining fish stocks, obesity, and diet-related disease – can be traced to the fact that we fail to recognize food's central role in shaping our lives and world.[23] Indeed, we might describe ourselves as living in a 'sitopia', or food-place (from the Greek *sitos*, food + *topos*, place); yet since we don't value the stuff from which it is made, our sitopia is a bad one. The question we might usefully ask is therefore this: what might the world look like if we were to value food again – and put it back at the centre of our politics?

That question is essentially what drives the Food Movement, a loose confederation of farmers, producers, cooks, writers, academics, campaigners, policy-makers, and organizations from all over the world, such as Slow Food and Via Campesina (the global peasants' movement), which argues for the recognition, protection, and production of food that is, as Slow Food founder Carlo Petrini put it, 'good, clean and fair'. A plethora of such initiatives as community gardens, food cooperatives, regenerative farming, Community Supported Agriculture, farmers markets, and organic box schemes have already shown how valuing food can transform lives, economies, cities, and landscapes for the better. What the Food Movement demonstrates is the enormous potential for bottom-up transformation through food; yet to build a truly good sitopia – a world in which every human and non-human would eat (and therefore live) well – would require government intervention at every level, from local to global.

Effects of Good Government

The most complete sitopian image ever made is arguably Ambrogio Lorenzetti's *The Allegory of the Effects of Good Government*, painted in 1338. Adorning one wall of Siena's great council chamber, the *Sala dei Nove*, it is a richly detailed evocation of daily life in the medieval city-state, showing a prosperous city and bustling countryside co-existing in perfect harmony. Then as now, the fields, vineyards, and olive groves that fed the city could be glimpsed directly outside the chamber's window. The fresco thus illustrates precisely what it says on the label: how the effects of good government are to foster a close partnership between city and country. Had Siena's councillors glanced up at the image during one of their meetings, its message would have been clear: look after your countryside, and it will look after you.

Like Plato and Aristotle before them, Siena's rulers clearly recognized that governments have a duty to mediate the relationship between city and country. This remains the responsibility of our leaders today, however much they might protest to the contrary. The Greek *polis* and medieval Italian city-state represent two brief periods in history when this principle was well understood. For most of history, however, the urban-rural relationship has been anything but balanced, with cities firmly holding the upper hand. Today, as we hurtle towards a predominantly urban future, that imbalance spells catastrophe.

As we face the dilemma of how to eat in future, is there anything we can learn from our past? One clear lesson is that feeding cities has never been easy – and that geography remains critical to it and to the shaping of the cultures that spring from it. Paris's struggle to feed itself relative to London, for example, created two contrasting attitudes that still resonate today (one hesitates to mention Brexit, yet it is arguably one outcome of that divide). As an early pioneer of free trade, London is also implicated in the growth of the global food system, just as Chicago – ideally placed by geography to exploit the Midwest – showed how it could be industrialized. Today, as urban appetites threaten even the world's furthest reaches, the time has clearly come to recalibrate our relationship with geography – or rather nature – through food.

If we are to flourish in the future, it seems clear that we must to put the *oikonomia* back into economics – and put food back at the heart of our political thinking. The beauty of *oikonomia* as a concept is that it shows how we can democratize food. Provided that we design and occupy cities and landscapes wisely, it suggests we can all produce food as well as consume it. Of course we needn't take this literally – even the most fervent of utopians recognized that cities need farmers to feed them – but the idea that food is something in which we all have at least some stake nevertheless matters. Unlike the Parisian mob or Roman *plebs*, we should have some sovereignty over what we eat, and not be mere passive consumers. As Carlo Petrini suggests, we should all become 'co-producers', actively engaged in various ways in the process of sustaining ourselves.

Food is too important to be left to the free market – or, indeed, to politicians. As the gastronomic *Tale of Two Cities* testifies, food doesn't lend itself well to top-down control; yet left to its own devices it tends to run rampant. If we are to rethink our future through food, therefore, our guiding principle must surely be one of balance: at every scale, we need to strengthen the bonds between city and country, producer and consumer, and, most importantly, between ourselves and nature.

Luckily, we don't have to invent the wheel in order to do this; indeed, the original urban blueprint – the city-state – remains an obvious model, keeping cities limited in size and surrounding them with a productive 'green belt'. Alternatively, as the regional geographer Patrick Geddes once proposed, we could preserve strips of countryside radiating out from urban centres, so that cities grow into star shapes. The physical form of urban and rural development isn't what really matters, but rather maintaining a strong connection between the two: as Geddes remarked, we must 'make the field gain on the street, not merely the street gain on the field'.[24] Somewhat surprisingly, the 1952 Japanese Agricultural Land Act achieved this in Tokyo, preserving an unlikely patchwork of organic farms in the core of the megacity that feed their local communities to this day. Modern efforts to reconcile city and country include Dutch architects MVRDV's Almere Oosterwald masterplan, which incorporates a mix of farms, factories, and housing in a deliberately fluid design, and British-based architects Viljoen and Bohn's concept of CPULs (Continuous Productive Urban Landscapes), which link underused urban spaces such as car parks and verges to create green corridors out into the countryside, echoing Geddes' star-shaped vision.

In the end, of course, it all comes down to people: if we want to change the world through food, we can. In 1973, some Brooklyn hippies decided that they didn't much like the way the US industrial food system was heading, and decided to set up their own alternative. Park Slope Food Coop was the result: now one of the oldest and biggest community food networks in the world, it has 17,000 members and a 45-year record of successful long-term contracts with local farmers in New York State. Coop members work a four-hour monthly shift in a shop that feels like an ordinary supermarket, yet is in fact full of high-quality food at near-cost prices from a network of trusted local producers. It may not quite be medieval Siena, but by putting the *oikonomia* back into economics, Park Slope has shown how we can all build a better sitopia.

By reconnecting us to one another and to nature, food can anchor us in our

49

increasingly complex and frenetic world. Sitopia can never be utopia – that, indeed, is its very point – yet by valuing food and putting it back at the heart of our politics, we can come close to the utopian dream of creating a fair, healthy, and resilient society. Food is, you might say, the most potent tool for transforming our lives and world that we never knew we had.

Notes

1   George Dodd, *The Food of London* (London: Longman Brown, Green and Longmans, 1856), p. 1.
2   For a detailed discussion of this phenomenon, see Carolyn Steel, *Hungry City: How Food Shapes Our Lives* (London: Chatto & Windus, 2008).
3   Neville Morley, *Metropolis and Hinterland* (Cambridge: Cambridge University Press, 1996), p. 13.
4   See Morley, pp. 63-65.
5   Geoffrey Rickman, *The Corn Supply of Ancient Rome* (Oxford: Clarendon Press, 1980), p. 170.
6   Tacitus, *Annals*, I. 5, qtd. in P. A. Brunt, 'The Roman Mob', in *Studies in Ancient Society*, ed. by M. I. Finley (London: Routledge and Kegan Paul, 1974), p. 102.
7   Rickman, p. 2.
8   N.T.L. Des Essarts, *Dictionnaire Universel de Police Paris 1786-90*, qtd. in Stephen Kaplan, *Provisioning Paris: Merchants and Millers in the Grain and Flour Trade During the Eighteenth Century* (Ithaca, NY: Cornell University Press, 1984), p. 24.
9   Kaplan, p. 44.
10 Kaplan, p. 24.
11 Denis Diderot, *Oeuvres Complètes* (Paris 1769, ed. Paris 1969), 8: 184, qtd. in Kaplan, p. 185.
12 See B.M.S. Campbell and others, *A Medieval Capital and its Grain Supply*, Historical Geography Research Series No. 30 (London: Historical Geography Research Group, 1993), p. 47.
13 John Stow, *Survey of London*, 1603, ed. by Charles Kingsforde (Oxford: Clarendon Press, 1908), II, p. 10.
14 Niall Ferguson, *Empire: How Britain Made the Modern World* (London: Allen Lane, 2003), p. 3.
15 Samuel Johnson, *On the Trades of London*, in *The Adventurer*, 1753, qtd. in Baron, I, p. 590.
16 Daniel Defoe, *The Review*, 8 Jan 1713, qtd. in Dorothy Davis, *A History of Shopping* (London: Routledge Kegan and Kegan Paul, 1966), p. 194.
17 Adam Smith, *An Inquiry into the Nature and Causes of the Wealth of Nations*, ed. by Edwin Cannan (London: Methuen, 1904; repr. Chicago: University of Chicago Press, 1976), pp. 401, 427.
18 Dodd, p. 2.
19 Dodd, p. 101.
20 Kimberly Kindy, 'This foreign meat company got U.S. tax money. Now it wants to conquer America.', *The Washington Post*, 7 November 2019 <https://www.washingtonpost.com/politics/this-foreign-meat-company-got-us-tax-money-now-it-wants-to-conquer-america/2019/11/04/854836ae-eae5-11e9-9306-47cb0324fd44_story.html> [accessed 15 March 2020].
21 'Nestlé Reports Full-Year Results for 2019', Nestlé, 13 February 2020 <https://www.nestle.com/media/pressreleases/allpressreleases/full-year-results-2019> [accessed 15 March 2020].
22 See for example Dom Phillips, 'Brazil Space Institute Director Sacked in Amazon Deforestation Row', *The Guardian*, 2 August 2019 <https://www.theguardian.com/world/2019/aug/02/brazil-space-institute- director-sacked-in-amazon-deforestation-row> [accessed 15 March 2020].
23 See Steel, *Sitopia: How Food Can Save the World* (London: Chatto & Windus, 2020).
24 Patrick Geddes, *Cities in Evolution* (London: Williams & Norgate, 1915, repr. London: Routledge, 1997), p. 96.

Forging the Future, Making Peace with the Past: The Case of *Ammachi* Canteens in Sri Lanka

Vidya Balachander

The concept of 'traditional food courts' has steadily gained in popularity in Sri Lanka since 2006. Run exclusively by women entrepreneurs, these open-air food courts – called *hela bojun hala* or traditional food stalls in Sinhalese – were set up by the central government's Ministry of Agriculture with a two-pronged mission in mind. They were aimed at reviving public interest in traditional Sri Lankan foods such as *appa* or hoppers, *kola kenda* or breakfast porridge, cutlets and other snacks, while also offering a source of livelihood to the women involved in cooking and overseeing the operations of these centres.

In 2016, under the direction of the district department of agriculture, a local government body, this idea was extended to the Tamil-dominated Northern Province of the country, which has been on the long road to socio-economic recovery since the country's twenty-six-year-long civil war ended in 2009.[1] Located in five cities in the North, these vegetarian canteens are called *Ammachi* or *Ammachi Unavagam* (grandmother's eateries in Tamil).[2]

While the *Ammachi* canteens are structurally similar to those in the rest of Sri Lanka, they serve a unique social function in the north. This paper examines the power of organized food vending to tilt – or at least impact – gender roles in a war-affected and deeply conservative part of Sri Lanka. It also explores the viability of *Ammachi* canteens as a potential avenue for the rehabilitation of war-affected women who have found employment therein.[3]

A Brief History

The first *hela bojun hala* was set up in the temple town of Kandy in Sri Lanka's Central Province. A part of the Women's Agriculture Extension Programme, the government term for vocational training programmes, the concept of *hela bojun hala* was introduced to offer entrepreneurship opportunities to underprivileged women, using food as the medium of business.[4] Offering freshly made Sri Lankan snacks such as *kos koththu* or baby jackfruit tossed with vegetables and *mung kiribath* or milk rice cooked with mung beans, at concessionary rates, the outlet soon became very popular in Kandy.

Encouraged by the runaway popularity of the first branch, in 2014 the Department of Agriculture allocated Rs 300 million (approximately $1.6 million) to construct six more outlets at the district level.[5] At the same time, other local, state, and non-governmental bodies, such as Provincial Departments of Agriculture, the Department of Agrarian Services, and the United Nations Development Programme, also contributed funds towards setting up outlets across the country.[6]

By early 2019, there were twenty operational canteens across Sri Lanka, as per statistics shared by the Ministry of Agriculture's National Food Programming Processing Unit. The press release also noted that as of mid-2019, six more branches had been sanctioned and were in varying stages of completion.

In the Northern Province, the canteens are called *Ammachis*, borrowing from the Tamil word for grandmother. The nomenclature is meant to evoke the nostalgic appeal of home cooking. In some cities of the North, such as Mullaitivu, the canteens have been supported and funded by non-governmental organizations such as the European Union-Sri Lanka Development Corporation and the United Nations Development Programme.

Gender Disparities and Economic Emancipation

In Northern Sri Lanka, the *Ammachi* canteens play an important role in redressing gender disparities caused by socio-cultural factors and the long years of civil strife.

For instance, Sudarshini is a forty-year-old mother of four schoolgoing children. The oldest of her children is seventeen, while the youngest is nine. In 2017, she completed a year-long training programme in cooking traditional Tamil food, organized by the Department of Agriculture, under the aegis of the Northern Provincial Council of Sri Lanka. Last year, she joined the *Ammachi Unavagam* located in Jaffna, the largest city and provincial capital of the formerly embattled Northern Province. Here, she works six-hour shifts making and selling Sri Lankan Tamil snacks such as *idli, kundu thosai* (savoury fermented pancakes made of a similar batter as dosas), *vadai, appam,* etc. Once a stay-at-home mom who ran small businesses to supplement the income of her husband, who is employed as a driver, Sudarshini is now the informal leader of the thirty-six women who are employed in this branch. Her motivation to enter the workforce was a fairly straightforward one. 'I wanted to earn and stand on my own feet,' she said.[7]

By itself, this may not be a particularly unusual assertion. However, when examined in the context of Northern Sri Lanka, where women's participation in the labour force is lower than in other parts of the country, this simple statement acquires a greater heft. In 2017, while the national average labour force participation was 36.6% for women, it ranged from 22.8 to 27% in the main districts of the Northern Province.[8] A range of socio-economic and cultural factors can be attributed to this disparity, including repeated displacement during the war, unfavourable socio-political conditions that dissuade women from working outside the home, and the deterioration of the local economy as a consequence of the conflict.[9]

Simultaneously, the end of the war also unveiled a harsh new reality – a stark rise in the number of female-headed households in the North. In 2015, the United

Nations Population Fund (UNFPA) estimated that there were 58,121 female-headed households in the Northern Province alone.[10] Although there are varying definitions of female-headed households, the term is broadly thought to refer to households where 'a female adult member is the one who is responsible for the care and organization of the household[...]'.[11]

While presenting an opportunity for economic emancipation, this change in gender norms has come at a commensurate cost. As Jeevasuthan Subramaniam notes in the context of Northern Sri Lanka:

> In many conflict regions, the customary roles of women in the family, the community, and the 'public' domain have completely changed. And the gendered roles of women and traditional family structures have encountered a remarkable transformation. This is an unintentional phenomenon. The collapse of family and community structures forces women to undertake new and unfamiliar roles. Women are compelled to bear a greater burden for their family members and of livelihood responsibilities.[12]

During the course of my interviews with ten employees of the Jaffna branch of *Ammachi Unavagam*, it became apparent that there were several reasons – excluding death and disability – that compelled several of these women to lead their households. These included sickness, inadequate household income, and economic inactivity on the part of their husbands. 'It makes no difference to me whether my husband is there or not there,' Sudarshini told me.[13] Implying that his financial contribution to the household was minimal, she added that it was with her earnings that she managed major expenses such as the children's school and tuition fees.

Despite its positioning, the *Ammachi* model is not exactly unconventional or non-conformist. It is fundamentally predicated upon what is considered a suitable occupation for women. But I argue that the social benefit offered by the *Ammachi* canteens is one of strength in numbers, and a sense of shared comradeship forged from common experience. In their interactions with me, many women mentioned that this job 'allowed them to be happy' and 'to forget their troubles back home', especially when they were in the company of their colleagues. Even though it is an unintentional consequence, I argue that the *Ammachi* canteens are an illustration of the powerful sense of community that is often fostered by cooking together. More poignantly, they serve as a means of allowing women to forget – or temporarily put aside – their difficult circumstances outside work. In this way, the *Ammachi* canteens are a successful example of the soft power of food as a currency of social change.

Entrepreneurship and Agency
Blurring the lines between open-air street vending and restaurants in the conventional sense, the *Ammachi* canteens marry the informality, immediacy, and easy accessibility of streetside dining with the social cachet afforded by eating in a relatively clean –

53

and therefore reliable – 'food court' setting. In cities like Kilinochchi – the de facto administrative capital of the Tamil Tigers, which was effectively decimated during the brutal end of the war – where the culture of eating out is still nascent and options are extremely limited, the *Ammachis* act as an affordable bridge.[14]

To give the canteens an air of professionalism – and to distinguish them from makeshift street stalls – they have a distinct and recognizable structure and ambience. In each of the locations in the north, the canteens have individual cooking stations arranged around a long counter or central island. Each woman, dressed in a white polo t-shirt, green skirt, and a green-rimmed cap, cooks specific dishes at her station and serves it to customers who pay her directly. By taking direct responsibility for their product and sales, the women become the 'face' of their own business. In a part of the country where the agency of women has been suppressed by complex socio-economic, cultural, and historical reasons, some of which have been discussed earlier in this paper, the *Ammachi* model has the potential to serve as a powerful counterpoint.

Besides their symbolic significance, the *Ammachi* canteens also offer tangible financial benefits to women entrepreneurs. The department of agriculture, occasionally with the aid of non-governmental organizations such as the United Nations Development Programme (UNDP), is responsible for providing the basic infrastructure, including constructing the physical space; procuring cooking facilities, kitchen utensils, and furniture; and also providing training in cooking, presentation, and business skills.[15] Once the women have been trained in cooking a menu of items that runs fairly standard across *Ammachis* – including crowd-pleasers such as *keerai vadai* (deep-fried spinach fritters), *puttu* (a steamed dish made of rice flour and grated coconut), *modakam* (sweet steamed dumplings), and *soosiyam* (deep-fried balls made of green mung and jaggery) – they become responsible for the running of their own business.

Since the *Ammachi* canteens function as cooperatives, each employee must pay for her own ingredients, and set aside a small sum every month for overhead costs such as utility bills and the salaries of the cleaning staff. Given that most food items are heavily subsidized and priced between ten and fifty rupees, the financial model may seem unviable. But the low price and strategic location of the canteens – on arterial roads and near intercity railway and bus terminals – attracts a large volume of customers. This translates to modest to robust sales. On an average, after accounting for miscellaneous expenses, each entrepreneur earns between Rs 500 to 1000 ($2.83-5.66) per day.[16]

In tangible terms, most of the women I interviewed were clear that this income makes a direct and crucial difference to the present and future prospects of their families. 'I would not be working here if it was not profitable. We can save up money and pay for our own needs,' said Kausalya, a thirty-year-old employee of the Jaffna branch.[17]

A New Beginning

One of the least discussed aspects of the *Ammachis* is that in cities that were at the epicentre of the war – such as Kilinochchi and Mullaitivu – the canteens employ a sizeable number of women who are widows of former Tamil Tigers fighters. Although they are reluctant to publicly share details, some of the women even served as former LTTE cadres.

In Kilinochchi, I spoke to Sunetra, a thirty-two-year-old ex-cadre with a frail, bird-like build and a wan smile.[18] In the final reaches of the war, during which an estimated 40,000 civilians were killed, Sunetra lost several members of her family. She also suffered grievous injuries, including bullets that are still lodged in her back. I argue that for women like Sunetra, who face ostracization within their communities and often find it difficult to reintegrate into civilian life, the anonymity of working alongside others in the business of food can serve as a tool to forge a more optimistic future.[19] As Thamotharampillai Sanaathanan, an art historian and professor at the University of Jaffna told me, 'The stories of these women [are] hidden behind their uniforms. Customers don't care about [their past].'[20]

Politics and the Future

The *Ammachi* canteens in northern Sri Lanka are a valuable case study in the potential of food vending to serve as a tool in challenging gender stereotypes, fostering a spirit of entrepreneurship, and potentially even as a vehicle of redressal and reconciliation.

However, their future is likely to be influenced by the socio-political climate of Sri Lanka. On 16 November 2019, the country held a crucial Presidential election, which is likely to shape the policies of the country in significant ways.[21] On 18 November, the country's former defence secretary, Gotabaya Rajapaksa, was sworn in as President. A hardline politician who is often credited with ending the war, Gotabaya Rajapaksa is also accused of serious war crimes and being involved with the disappearances of former rebel leaders, as well as aid workers and journalists who were seen as being political opponents.[22]

With many political analysts fearing that a return of Rajapaksa rule could deepen sectarian divisions between the Buddhist Sinhalese majority and minorities such as the Tamils, the future of progressive initiatives that benefit minorities, such as the *Ammachi* canteens, hangs in the balance.

55

Notes

1   Nyshka Chandran, 'Battle Scars: Sri Lanka's North Counts the Cost of a 26-Year War', *CNBC*, 27 April 2016 <https://www.cnbc.com/2016/04/27/sri-lanks-northern-province-poorer-undeveloped-after-26-year-civil-war-with-tamil-tigers.html> [accessed 15 June 2019].

2   Statistics provided by the National Food Production Programing Unit, Ministry of Agriculture, Sri Lanka [accessed 15 May 2019].

3   Meera Srinivasan, 'In Sri Lanka, Serving Hearty Meals and Fostering Sisterhood', *The Hindu*, 12 January 2019 <https://www.thehindu.com/news/international/in-sri-lanka-serving-hearty-meals-and-fostering-sisterhood/article25980310.ece> [accessed 15 June 2019].

4   Aisha Nazim, 'Hela Bojun: Empowering Rural Women Through Food And Agriculture', *Roar Media*, 8 November 2017 <https://roar.media/english/life/srilanka-life/hela-bojun-empowering-rural-women-through-food-and-agriculture/> [accessed 15 November 2019].

5   Ministry of Agriculture, Government of Sri Lanka <http://www.agrimin.gov.lk/web/index.php/component/content/category/12-project> [accessed 15 May 2019].

6   Statistics provided by the National Food Production Programing Unit, Ministry of Agriculture, Sri Lanka [accessed 15 May 2019].

7   Interview conducted by author, 24 May 2019.

8   Sri Lanka Labour Force Survey – Annual Report 2017, Department of Census and Statistics, 2017, <http://www.statistics.gov.lk/samplesurvey/LFS_Annual%20Report_2017.pdf> [accessed 15 May 2019].

9   Kethaki Kandanearachchi and Rapti Ratnayake, 'Post-War Barriers to Female Economic Empowerment', *International Centre for Ethnic Studies*, December 2017, p. 2 <http://ices.lk/wp-content/uploads/2017/12/Post-War-Realities-For-Circulation.pdf> [accessed 15 May 2019].

10   'Mapping of Economic Support Services to Female Headed Households in the Northern Province of Sri Lanka', *UNFPA*, 2015 <https://srilanka.unfpa.org/sites/default/files/pub-pdf/FemaleHeadedHouseholds.pdf> [accessed 15 May 2019].

11   Kandenarachchi and Ratnayake.

12   Jeevasuthan Subramaniam, 'War and Recovery: Psychosocial Challenges in Northern Sri Lanka', *International Centre for Ethnic Studies*, November 2017 <http://ices.lk/wp-content/uploads/2017/12/War-Recovery-Psychosocial-Chanlenges-For-Circulation.pdf> [accessed 15 May 2019].

13   Interview conducted by author, 24 May 2019.

14   Geeta Anand and Dharisha Bastians, 'Rebuilding Lives, and Homes, Shattered by Sri Lanka's Civil War', *The New York Times*, 17 May 2016 <https://www.nytimes.com/2016/05/18/world/asia/sri-lanka-civil-war-kilinochchi.html> [accessed 15 May 2019].

15   United Nations Development Programme, Sri Lanka.

16   This statistic is a broad estimate shared with me by some women employed at the Jaffna branch. The profit margins on drinks such as herbal teas and fresh fruit juices is lower. Since the Easter Sunday terror attacks in Sri Lanka on 21 April 2019, sales have dipped significantly.

17   Interview conducted by author, 18 October 2018

18   Interview conducted by author, 20 October 2018. Name has been changed.

19   Gethin Chamberlain, 'In Sri Lanka the War Is Over but Tamil Tiger Remnants Suffer Brutal Revenge', *The Guardian*, 21 May 2019 <https://www.theguardian.com/world/2009/may/21/sri-lanka-tamil-tigers-ltte-tamil-refugees-in-camp > [accessed 25 May 2019]; Kim Wall, Mansi Choksi, 'A Chance to Rewrite History: The Women Fighters of the Tamil Tigers', *Longreads,* 22 May 2018 <https://longreads.com/2018/05/22/a-chance-to-rewrite-history-the-women-fighters-of-the-tamil-tigers/> [accessed 15 May 2019].

20   Interview conducted by author, October 2018

21   Jayadev Uyangoda, 'A Week that Will Shake Sri Lanka's Future', *Groundviews*, 10 November 2019 < https://groundviews.org/2019/11/10/a-week-that-will-shake-sri-lankas-future/> [accessed 10 November 2019]

22   Brahma Chellaney, 'An Election that Could Threaten Sri Lankan Democracy', *LiveMint*, 20 October 2019 <https://www.livemint.com/opinion/online-views/an-election-that-could-threaten-sri-lankan-democracy-11571588144509.html> [accessed 20 October 2019].

Shooting them Softly: Photographing Lower-Class Eaters in Belle Époque Paris

Janet Beizer

As David Chang has poignantly shown in his Netflix series, *Ugly Delicious,* there are few more humiliating ways to exert everyday cultural hegemony than to mock the foods, diets, and alimentary practices of those perceived as cultural Others.[1] Photography and postcards, working together in their conjoined early twentieth-century golden age, provided prophetic evidence of Chang's observations about the xenophobic uses of food. One of the largest subcategories of the commerce in photographic postcards was the marketplace, and one of its prime targets, the lower-income people who flocked to the stands that sold leftovers and soup. Their photographers were bourgeois men – *flâneurs* with cameras – whose gender and class allowed free circulation all over Paris.[2] A salient dynamic pitting the bourgeoisie against the working class was reinforced by widely-circulating images of their food and eating practices.

Other People's Food

Soup sellers and vendors of leftovers (known as 'harlequins') in turn-of-the-century French urban marketplaces were often photographed together in a kind of diptych; they serviced a similar clientele and frequently sold their wares side by side.[3] Soup merchants used ingredients comparable to those of the harlequin merchant, albeit deteriorated one step further, and hence suited for soup. In narratives and images alike, soup becomes the degree zero of the leftovers trade, the lowest of the low. In soup-seller photos, assembled patrons tend to look far more threadbare and dishevelled than the average harlequin patrons; probably not coincidentally, photographers tend to shoot them in cold blood, exposing them in their infirmity, eccentricity, and indigence. Crutches, missing limbs, wrinkled clothes and faces, torn garments, sunken eyes, the look of misery, and crowds of people swarming: such is the stuff the camera consumes in soup-stand photos. As we follow photographers' socio-economic and gastronomic descent from harlequin to soup stands we plunge into more popular and populous scenes.

Postcard photographs of soup stalls share an unflinching visitation of working-class eating scenes. There is violence in exposing so many hovering spoons, opening mouths, avid downturned glances, teeth gnawing at scraps of bread. Intimate space is invaded as the private becomes spectacle. These scenes show hunger: brute animal need rather than civilized good taste (recalling Bourdieu's distinction between 'the taste of need and the taste of luxury').[4] Both food and human beings are reduced to their lowest common denominator as they converge in bodily function. The camera lens trained on ascending and descending spoons and devouring mouths reveals the nakedness of poverty and projects human corporeality and mortality onto it. We might paraphrase Villiers de l'Isle-Adam's play *Axël* here: 'Eat? The servants will do that for us.'[5] To photograph staunch bourgeois citizens standing outside swallowing soup or chomping bread would be unimaginable. If the modern viewer feels compelled to look away from some of these images it is to break a complicit triplication of our gaze with the eye of the photographer and the lens of the camera, which presume the availability of these Othered bodies, offered like pimped prostitutes or pinned moths or animals at the zoo.

Susan Sontag called the act of taking a picture 'predatory', explaining that 'to photograph people is [to see] them as they never see themselves, [to have] knowledge of them they can never have; it turns people into objects that can be symbolically possessed'.[6] Like most forms of predation, photography has a pecking order, tending first to devour its least defended, most visible, most abject objects. If it is true, as Roland Barthes reminds us, that photography's coming-of-age coincides with a new social phenomenon whereby 'the private is *consumed* as such, publicly', we must add that 'the irruption of the private' in public space is more than abstraction: it takes the conspicuous human shape of the denizens of the streets and its public feeding grounds.[7]

To think further about the assault on alimentary privacy, we might look at some better-explored exposures of peoples marginalized in France during the same period by race rather than class. The food choices, eating habits, and meal preparations of indigenous peoples imported from colonized spaces were deemed different enough from French bourgeois practices to warrant their being not only exhibited in fenced enclosures, but also being captured on film and affixed to cardstock.

Colonial Zoos

For at least as long as Malek Alloula's critique of Orientalizing postcards, *The Colonial Harem*, has been circulating, scholars have been critiquing the colonizer's gaze upon the colonized, the projection of imperialist phantasms upon subjugated people, and the use of constructed images and the discourses they support to justify so-called 'civilizing processes'.[8] That such challenges to, and deconstructions of, exoticizing projects have most often been addressed to 'exocolonialist' iconography and rhetoric (in the French context, picture postcards of West Africa, North Africa, Indochina, New Caledonia, the Antilles, and so-called French Polynesia and French Guyana) should not deter us from extending them to similar processes used in 'endocolonialism': collective phantasms projected on human groups within the hexagon subordinated on the basis of socio-economic rather than racial difference.

As Anne Maxwell contends in *Colonial Photography and Exhibitions*, live displays of ostensibly 'primitive' peoples at the Expositions Universelles and other fairs and well-circulated photographic images of colonized peoples were parallel representations of European hegemony.[9] Serving a variety of purposes ranging from promoting nationalism and imperialism to (not unrelated) advancing scientific theories about race, live or 'anthropological' exhibiting and photographing of colonized Others worked together to gird European expansion and tourism, both direct and vicarious.

In Paris, displays of primitive peoples were located alongside the animals as early as 1872 at the Jardin d'Acclimatation in the Bois de Boulogne. In the 1880s the Jardin, Maxwell notes, 'began to resemble a zoo: human specimens were placed behind fences and railings, and spectators began to throw them coins'.[10] Here a pattern began to set; in 1889 when ethnographic displays at the Exposition Universelle abounded, the 'native villages' were installed behind tall fences that caged in the 'natives'. The 1900 Exposition Universelle in Paris featured a Senegalese village fenced off from the crowds, the scene 'evoking a zoo', recounts Catherine Hodeir. A few decades later, Kanak and African 'native villages' at the Colonial Exposition of 1931 put their respective 'primitives' behind bars. The newspaper *Paris Soir* ran a photo representing 'an African "native" alongside zebras and monkeys from the Vincennes zoo', invoking the obvious social Darwinian trope. Crowds swarmed to gawk at the spectacle. There are traces of occasional disapproval, such as Sudanese militant Tiemoko Garan Kouyaté's denunciation of the Exhibition as a 'commercial and epicurean zoo of caged African lackeys'.[11]

The move to connect the exposition of exotic outsiders, or racial savages, to that of exotic insiders, or socio-economic primitives, is more glide than leap. There's a long history of assimilating the poor to the 'primitive', the 'savage', and the 'uncivilized' races. In 1842, well before the Belle Époque extension of what Michel-Rolph Trouillot calls 'the savage slot' from the indigenous to the indigent, Eugène Sue had appropriated James Fenimore Cooper's *Last of the Mohicans* to paint the 'dangerous classes' of Paris as 'the barbarians among us'.[12] Notions of race, not unproblematic today, were extremely fluid throughout the nineteenth century.[13] As Françoise Mélonio observes, old fears of the 'savage' peasant yielded quickly as the century progressed to 'fear [...] of the worker, savage or apache [...]. Rural populations and workers alike were freely assigned to 'another race' than the bourgeois city dwellers'.[14] The nineteenth-century poor, notes Judith Walkowitz, were constituted by the rhetoric of urban imperialism as 'a race apart'.[15]

Exhibitions of racial others and displays of socio-economic others, whether live or photographed, can be traced back to carnivals, fairs, circuses, and street shows that staged exceptional humans as oddities, based on perceived physical differences such as size, missing limbs, excessive hair, and gender crossing; ethnicity later joined such characteristics. But as Burton Benedict notes, 'behavioral "freaks" can be created from one's own culture, *especially if eating is involved*'.[16] What I'm suggesting is that postcards exhibiting the labouring classes slurping soup constituted anthropological displays or human zoos not unlike those of racially exotic postcards and live Colonial Expositions: such cards circulate traces of the feeding behaviours of Others publicly performing creaturely needs on behalf of those who could afford to do so in private.[17]

59

Feedings

The material factors of class and race loom everywhere around French turn-of-the-century postcard traces of eating Others. Food-related exposures of human displays at the zoos in Paris parks and the 'indigenous villages' of Expositions Universelles and Coloniales are models of spectacular and photographic violation. The corpus includes routinely exhibited imported colonial subjects along with exotic animals, at the zoos of the Jardin d'Acclimatation just west of Paris and the Jardin des Plantes in south central Paris. In both sets of photos, groups of visitors gather, rapt, to watch the feeding from behind a fence. While animal feeding shots often show the food being offered by the attendants (fish, for example, for the sea lions), in most postcard photos of mealtimes in human zoos and indigenous villages, we can no more make out the contents of the meal than we can discern those of soup bowls or harlequin plates in photos of the working class. The camera, along with the spectators' gaze, is trained on the *tableau vivant* of eating Others – again a practice bourgeois diners would not tolerate. Full-frontal exposure of eating and other material alimentary practices is reserved for the margins of French culture.[18]

The Erotic Gastronomic

In *La Cheffe, roman d'une cuisinière* (*The Cheffe*), the contemporary novelist Marie NDiaye remarks on 'the way certain guests behave toward the person cooking as they would with a lover or a mistress'.[19] Many postcard photos of indigenous food preparation and consumption frame cooking as an act of seduction, and ingestion as a gesture of titillation, presupposing and perhaps preordaining that their viewers will be those leering guests NDiaye describes. But if eating and cooking tend generally to be conflated with sex, for a nexus of reasons having to do with body boundaries and openings, desire, and pleasure, the history of such conflations is deeply marked by ideologies of race and class, as is the history of taboos differentially placed on their public exposure.

Consider, for example, a postcard photograph of a black male Saharan cook at the 1907 Exposition Coloniale. The photograph traps the man in a Thor or Vulcan-like posture. Bare-chested with upper body muscles rippling, he wields an enormous pestle poised mid-body at shoulder level, gripped in a taut fist in a suspended motion of pounding. Whatever pedagogical elements the cooking demonstration of a Saharan cook might purport to deliver are shadowed by an implicit racial message about indigenous male sexuality and the need for its containment.

While indigenous alimentary viewcards are often similarly bursting with sexual surcharge, they are typically gendered. Other cards tender the more common scenario of food work and foodstuff gendered in the feminine, and often in the nude. One such, from the Marseille Exposition Coloniale of 1922, shows two young Senegalese women, one undressed, surrounded by an array of pots, sieves, and bowls. The photo is ambiguously labelled *Cuisine sénégalaise*, equally translatable as 'The Senegalese Kitchen', 'Senegalese Cooking', or 'Senegalese Food', leaving open the question of what or who is available for consumption.

In almost every culinary image of the '*Villages indigènes*' that pretended to serve up lessons in ethnography and culture, the contents of the cauldron on the fire, the pots and the bowls, are indiscernible. Easily decipherable, however, are the facial expressions and body language of the people caught by the camera: suspicion and defiance in tensed arm and glance at the camera of people backed to an enclosing fence, apathy and despair in the eyes and the slumped posture of others. If anthropological education is the pretence of such exhibits of colonized Others in the early twentieth-century metropole, political messaging is the reality: foreign eaters and cooks are staged in a performance of Otherness that consistently subjugates France's backward overseas colonies to the technologically advanced, ultra-civilized hexagon.[20]

Inside Out

The many photos that impress postcards with scenes of indigenous peoples eating and cooking *en plein air* – on the grass, under trees, outside huts and tents, punctuated by clothes strung up to dry – offer bourgeois French viewers an inversion of their own everyday practices. Nineteenth-century Western ideology decreed that civilized orders live in increasingly interiorized space; take their meals, bare their skin, wash and dry their clothes out of sight.[21] Conversely, this logic imagined that primitive orders took all of nature as the theatre of their material life. Interior and exterior space were accordingly binarized and hierarchized, as were notions of subjectivity and objectivity, mind and body, culture and nature, individualism and collectivism.[22] What is kept inside in Western bourgeois culture – the body undressing, seducing, eating, laundering – is driven out in these images of non-Western Others: forced into the camera light, as if to fix the binary. The resistant shadows that determinedly offer and conceal in a striptease performance of invisibility flaunt a heart of darkness that must be maintained to make the show of routing out into the light function.

61

Similarly, pretences of authenticity upon which the indigenous villages are built coexist with occasionally voiced accusations that these scenes are theatrical montages rather than mimetic representations. An 1899 article in *L'Exposition Universelle de Paris* reports the dismay of various indigenous 'villagers' forced into role play, including a master jeweller from Senegal who testifies: 'We are very humiliated [...] to be exhibited this way, in huts like savages; these straw and mud huts do not give an idea of Senegal. In Senegal [...] we have large buildings, railroad stations, railroads; we light them with electricity. The Bureau of Hygiene does not tolerate the construction of this type of hovel.'[23] One revelation insinuates others; if the Senegalese mud huts are cliché constructions, might the Kanak cone tents and the Tuareg long tents be equally mythic renditions of colonial habitations? In much the same way, evidence that the Kanaks staunchly refused to perform in the nude suggests that images of topless African cooks might be more indicative of forced compliance with French Exposition directives than truthful representation of ordinary life at home.[24]

Certain peoples were particularly known for their reluctance to display their intimate lives to the public: the Kabyles were 'mysterious and determined to hide their [private] life', and the Okanda were 'careful to limit the exposure of their intimate life to visitors', journalists reported. That such reserve was noted indicates some awareness by the public of the theatrical nature of the ethnographic displays, an awareness further revealed by widely reported attempts, by journalists and the public alike, to gain access to the virtual wings of the Exposition as a space of higher truth. As Tran observes, this inner glimpse – what might endow the indigenous villages with the merit of authenticity – was often sought in alimentary practices, a 'direct pathway to the imaginary epicentre of the colonized peoples' culture'. The distinction between the theatrical staging of such practices and their ostensibly more realistic locus in the wings was understood to be temporal rather than spatial: so, for example, time of day was given as critical to viewing an authentic ethnographic experience of colonial eating. The public was advised by various articles to choose their hour wisely: 'Go visit them in the morning,' one journalist counsels, while another specified: 'In the morning, when visitors are scarcer, the Malays are occupied with their domestic life; they fastidiously clean their dwellings, do their wash, prepare or eat their meals – which is not the least curious part of the show.'[25]

This insistence on the need to seek out the hidden scene of the food show – what Tran articulates as 'the alimentary as the wings of the theater and the theater of the wings' – is perfectly congruent with the Western tradition which holds that 'the real show happens backstage', meaning, of course, in the most isolated, hidden, off-limits part of the theatre.[26] Of course, the distinction between backstage and frontstage spectacles does not hold. The 'wings' of indigenous cuisines at the Expositions, the behind-the-scenes show, shared performative elements with what was seen in the designated exhibit spaces, for many reasons, including that both were equally subject to French monitoring and regional and seasonal product availability.[27] Not the smallest paradox of the logic of Colonial Expositions is that they thrust their representations of the colonies into forced visibility, and then projected an aura of secret space behind them, recreating a Western model of specularity in which there is always yet another veil to remove. The quest for the infinitely regressive heart of ethnographic authenticity set curiosity in a dance with desire and scrutiny. If voyeurism was the dominant modus operandi for contemporary Exposition-goers who viewed imported 'natives' in *tableaux vivants*, in cooking and other craft demonstrations, and reviewed them in postcard photographs, it made future generations – who had only the photos – its heirs. For those of us today who look back at postcard traces of ethnographic displays, the line between research and prurience can feel a little thin.

Borderlines

And where are the soup eaters? How far must we turn from human zoos and indigenous villages to pick up the thread that leads back to society's fringes consuming its alimentary sludge? In the streets of Paris, leagues away from their birthplaces, the imported '*indigènes*' would temporarily have inhabited the same metropolitan territory as the urban poor, many of whom were more accurately indigenous to these spaces. The overseas people would have been interned on the outskirts of the city, while the

Parisian lower classes would predominantly have occupied inner city sites. But although the geographic quarters of the two sectors were not identically aligned, their semiotic spaces coincided. If 'indigenous' and 'indigent' are what the French call 'false friends' (*faux amis*), words that erroneously suggest a common source, they were nonetheless forced bedfellows in nineteenth-century French social thought.[28]

The organizers of the Exposition Universelle of 1867, the first international event to stage live human exhibits, considered but ultimately rejected a suggestion made by sociologist Frédéric Le Play, Commissioner of the Exposition, to incorporate the housing of French workers' families within the exposition so that visitors could observe their lifestyle first hand. Le Play was, however, able to implement an alternative: an exhibit of French workers demonstrating their trades.[29] Two decades later, at the 1889 Exposition Universelle, the social economy exhibit, which featured housing, hygiene, and public assistance for the French working class, was strategically situated across from the colonial area of the Exposition, implying that colonization was 'a natural extension of the social work accomplished within France', as Palermo has noted, and correlatively, that race was not the sole criteria for adjudicating civilized status.[30] In the carefully calculated architectural topography of the Expositions, the proximity of French working class displays to exhibits of colonized others would have graphically echoed the ideology so clearly adumbrated earlier in the century by Eugène Sue's epic fresco of the people of Paris as domestic barbarians and cannibals.[31]

Discussing pervasive fears of an invisible menacing Other throughout the fin de siècle in France and England, Kirsten Guest draws attention to the 'ongoing impulse to construct the poor as other', highlighting metaphors of savagery, primitivism, and cannibalism that analogized the peoples of the colonies and the domestic lower classes.[32] Disraeli's well-known evocation of class-rifted early Victorian England as a nation divided underscores the construction of the poor as a race apart: 'Two nations [...] who are as ignorant of each other's habits, thoughts, and feelings, as if they were dwellers in different zones or inhabitants of different planets; who are formed by a different breeding *and are fed by a different food.*'[33]

That Disraeli's portrayal of England's class schism relies on an alimentary synecdoche is not surprising: once more food traditions and eating habits crystallize group identity. Disraeli's alimentary rhetoric belongs to the same social discourse operative in training the camera on eating others to visualize racial difference, that is, to constitute race in the differential image of what goes into the body, and to construct difference in the racialized image of what is incorporated.[34] As Kyla Wazana Tompkins has argued in her work on alimentary discourses in nineteenth-century America, eating culture is 'a privileged site for the representation of, and fascination with, those bodies that carry the burdens of difference and materiality, that are understood as less social, less intellectual [...] less sentient: racially minoritized subjects, children, women [...,] animals [...which are] closely aligned with [...] the bottom of the food chain'.[35] In just this way, knowledge of indigenous and indigent Others was circulated on postcard photos through representations of their eating practices (at urban markets, Exposition villages, and zoos), as if the alimentary moment – 'the time of returning to the body and the heart of culture' – might offer not only a truly authentic glimpse of the Other, as Tran has contended, but also a revelation of the very core – the very most interior, which is to say, the intimate space – of alterity.[36]

On the horizon of that ideal alimentary moment held capable of revealing the bowels of the Other's culture, cannibalism lies immanent. It does not appear literally in photographic images of urban markets or colonial exhibits, precisely because it was a myth, but it is evoked there by the pointedly indiscernible contents of pots, kettles, and bowls, and it figures quite overtly in cartoons, caricatures, and narrative accounts of the period, where it is in fact a platitude.[37] In the discourse of eating Others, cannibalism looms inevitably, because it is the ultimate eating taboo, the boundary between nature and culture, the implicit pivot around which turned nineteenth-century ideologies of race and class.

While visions of cannibals hover most prevalently over images of Kanak mealtimes, given widespread contemporary legends of flesh eaters in New Caledonia, they are not absent from photos of the eating poor, who, along with other marginalized populations such as criminals and the insane, were charged with anthropophagy along with other varieties of barbarism. Guest refers to this group of alleged domestic cannibals constituted by the urban poor as 'borderline' because of its status of 'problematic' alterity: 'Unlike the colonial subject who is racially and culturally distinct from the colonizer, the "borderline" other shares significant physical attributes with the dominant population [...]. As a result, marginal groups can neither be dismissed as "irredeemable savages" nor comfortably assimilated to prevailing norms.'[38]

Projections of cannibalism onto the urban working class were part of the larger effort to codify difference and contain its threat, a threat that was increasingly posed by class difference in a way more materially powerful than that posed by colonial difference. Speaking of an evolving scepticism on the part of French commentators regarding Exposition representations of 'radical alimentary alterity' – including hot-coal ingestion, sword-swallowing, scorpion eating and the like, along with cannibalism – Tran astutely points out a corresponding migration of cannibal phantasms, from race- to class-based: 'With the humanist deconstruction of the cannibal myth comes a surging anxiety in the face of an Other who is closer, more worrying yet: the invasive, uneducated crowd swarming in Republican public space.'[39] This more menacing Other closing in on mainstream bourgeois France, this borderline crowd, immediately evokes that other borderline where nature and culture divide – and converge – the borderline where anthropology conventionally locates cannibalism.

Eating practices construct boundaries and determine borders within national, ethnographic, racial, and social groups, as well as between self and other. As Jean-Pierre Poulain summarizes, 'the alimentary act is the foundation of collective identity and hence, of alterity.'[40] Yet eating processes swallow boundaries, constantly dissolve the line between self and other, subject and object.[41] Within the dynamic system of eating, notions of borders and border lines turn into their opposites: passage, flux, indetermination, fusion, and borderlines, meaning not only the material edges that both divide and join, but the people who take that name, the classes and races who are marked off as unpalatable, indigestible, excluded, but are in the process symbolically reincorporated and internalized.

Notes

1   *Ugly Delicious*, prod. by David Chang and Peter Meehan, Season 1 (Netflix 2018).
2   See Naomi Schor, '*Cartes postales*: Representing Paris 1900', *Critical Inquiry*, 18.2 (Winter 1992), 188-244 (p. 216). Both statistical evidence and the camera angle support the trope of a viewing economy structured like the paradigmatic privileged male gaze dominating a feminized public exposed to the camera, in Laura Mulvey's classic formulation. See Schor, p. 216, and Abigail Solomon-Godeau, *Photography at the Dock* (Minneapolis: University of Minnesota Press, 1991), p. 263.
3   See Janet Beizer, 'The Emperor's Plate: Marketing Leftovers in Nineteenth-Century Paris', in *Food & Markets: Proceedings of the 2014 Oxford Symposium on Food and Cookery*, ed. by Mark McWilliams (London: Prospect Books, 2015), pp. 15-34.
4   Pierre Bourdieu, *Distinction: A Social Critique of the Judgement of Taste*, trans. by Richard Nice (Cambridge: Harvard University Press, 1984), p. 6.
5   Auguste Villiers de l'Isle-Adam, *Axël* (Paris: Editions du Vieux Colombier, 1960), p. 249. Translations are mine unless otherwise indicated.
6   Susan Sontag, *On Photography* (New York: Anchor Books, 1973), p. 14.
7   Roland Barthes, *La Chambre Claire: Note sur la photographie* (Paris: Gallimard, 1980), p. 153; my emphasis.
8   Malek Alloula, *The Colonial Harem*, trans. by Myrna Godzich and Wlad Godzich (Minneapolis: University of Minnesota Press, 1986 [1981]).
9   Anne Maxwell, *Colonial Photography and Exhibitions: Representations of the 'Native' and the Making of European Identities* (London: Leicester University Press, 1999), p. ix.
10 Maxwell, p. 17.
11 Catherine Hodeir, 'Decentering the Gaze at French Colonial Exhibitions', in *Images and Empires: Visuality in Colonial and Postcolonial Africa*, ed. by Paul S. Landau and Deborah D. Kaspin (Berkeley: University of California Press, 2002), pp. 233-52 (pp. 234, 237, 247).
12 Michel-Rolph Trouillot, 'Anthropology and the Savage Slot: The Poetics and Politics of Otherness', in *Global Transformations: Anthropology and the Modern World*, ed. by Michel-Rolph Trouillot (London: Palgrave, 2003), pp. 7-28; Eugène Sue, *Les Mystères de Paris* (Paris: Quarto-Gallimard, 2009), p 35.
13 Maxwell elaborates: 'the term 'race' was shifting and unstable. It was sometimes used as if it were synonymous with species, sometimes with culture and sometimes with nation, and sometimes to denote the ethnicity of sub-groups within national groupings [...]. This mobility of meaning can be attributed to competing ideas about the role played by skin colour and physical features, as against religion, education and other environmental factors, in determining the different levels of progress achieved by individuals and groups' (pp. 15-16).
14 Françoise Mélonio, '1815-1880: *Vers une culture démocratique*', in *Histoire Culturelle de la France*, ed. by Jean-Pierre Roux and Jean-François Sirinelli, vol. 3, *Lumières et liberté: Les dix-huitième et dix-neuvième siècles* (Paris: Seuil, 1998), p. 339.
15 Judith Walkowitz, 'Urban Spectatorship', in *The Nineteenth-Century Visual Culture Reader*, ed. by Vanessa R. Schwartz and Jeannene M Przybylski (New York: Routledge, 2004), p. 208.
16 Burton Benedict, 'Rituals of Representation: Ethnic Stereotypes and Colonized Peoples at World's Fairs', in *Fair Representations: World's Fairs and the Modern World*, ed. by Robert W. Rydell and Nancy E. Gwinn (Amsterdam: VU University Press, 1994), p. 29; my emphasis.
17 'Anthropological displays' was one of the euphemisms commonly used for live colonial exhibits of humans; I use it here for the postcard records of these as well. See Maxwell, p. 4.
18 I refer here to frank images of eating and food preparation rather than to undressed or otherwise

sexually marked eaters, though as will become clear the sexual innuendo is deliberate.

19 Marie NDiaye, *La Cheffe, roman d'une cuisinière* (Paris: Gallimard [Folio], 2016), p. 45.

20 The weight of figurative centrality and marginality should not make us forget that by 1889 France's colonial holdings covered an area ten times the size of the metropole. See Lynn Palermo, 'Identity under Construction: Representing the Colonies at the Paris *Exposition Universelle* of 1889', *The Color of Liberty: Histories of Race in France*, ed. by Sue Peabody and Tyler Stovall (Durham, N.C.: Duke University Press, 2003), p. 286.

21 For a historical analysis of the evolution of French architecture in conjunction with evolving mores, see Monique Eleb-Vidal and Anne Debarre-Blanchard, *Architectures de la vie privée: maisons et mentalités XVIIe-XIXe siècles* (Brussels: Editions Archives D'Architecture Moderne, 1989).

22 For detailed perspectives on the development of interiority, see the essays in *Interiors and Interiority*, ed. by Ewa Lajer-Burcharth and Beate Söntgen (Berlin/Boston: De Gruyter, 2016), especially the Introduction by Lajer-Burcharth and Söntgen (pp. 1-13) .

23 Palermo, p. 291.

24 Van Troi Tran, *Manger et boire aux Expositions universelles, 1889, 1890* (Rennes: Presses Universitaires de Rennes, 2012), pp. 233-34.

25 Tran, pp. 220-21, 224, 221-22.

26 Tran, p. 223. See Stefanie Diekmann (here quoting the tagline from the Canadian television series, *Slings & Arrows*), 'Scenes from the Dressing Room: Theatrical Interiors in Fiction Film', in *Interiors and Interiority*, ed. by Lacher-Burcharth and Söntgen, p. 93. Though Diekmann's focus is on cinema rearticulating theatrical traditions, cinematic renditions of backstage space are part of a larger cultural discourse: Emile Zola's 1880 *Nana* exemplifies novelistic uses of this tradition.

27 Tran, p. 228.

28 According to the OED, 'indigenous' comes from the Latin *indigenus*, to be born in, native, while 'indigent' derives from the Latin *indigere*, to lack or to want.

29 See Volker Barth, '*Des Hommes exotiques dans les expositions universelles et internationales* (1851-1937)' in *Exhibitions: L'Invention du sauvage*, ed. by Pascal Blanchard, Gilles Boëtsch, and Nanette Jacomijn Snoep (Paris: Actes Sud/Musée du Quai Branly, 2011), p. 181.

30 Palermo, p. 296

31 Sue, p. 6.

32 Kirsten Guest, 'Are You Being Served? Cannibalism, Class, and Victorian Melodrama' in *Eating Their Words: Cannibalism and the Boundaries of Cultural Identity*, ed. by Kirsten Guest (Albany: SUNY Press, 2001), pp. 109-10.

33 Benjamin Disraeli, *Sybil, or the Two Nations* (1845), qtd. by Guest, p. 110; my emphasis.

34 I include class difference under the banner of race, arguing that class is racialized in nineteenth-century Western European ideology.

35 Kyla Wazana Tompkins, *Racial Indigestion: Eating Bodies in the 19th Century* (New York: New York University Press, 2012), p. 8.

36 Tran, p. 223

37 To be clear: in the debate on whether cannibalism in fact exists, I do not place myself with those who contend it is a myth; I mean here that the purported cannibalism of the colonized exposed in nineteenth-century metropolitan France was a myth. See the essays in *Exhibitions*, ed. by Blanchard, Boëtsch, and Snoep for discussion of the cannibal myth at the human zoos.

38 Guest, pp. 109-11.

39 Tran, p. 238.

40 Jean-Pierre Poulain, '*La Nourriture de l'autre entre délices et dégoût; réflexions sur le relativisme de la sensibilité alimentaire*', *Revue Internationale de l'imaginaire*, 7: Cultures, nourriture (1997), 128.

41 Maggie Kilgour's *From Communion to Cannibalism: An Anatomy of Metaphors of Incorporation* (Princeton: Princeton University Press, 1990) is an excellent place from which to approach this paradox; see also Tompkins.

Gastrodiplomacy and the UK Diplomatic Network

Paul Brummell

The work of UK diplomatic missions overseas includes elements of both culinary diplomacy, the furtherance of diplomatic protocol through cuisine, and gastrodiplomacy, the use of cuisine to conduct cultural diplomacy. In the pursuit of the latter, the UK approach has focused on furnishing diplomatic missions with ideas and suggestions which can be adapted to the local context. This less directed approach to gastrodiplomacy than that adopted by some countries, for example the Thailand: Kitchen of the World campaign, reflects a UK Government concern not to weaken the attractiveness of British soft power through instrumentalization and recognizes the challenges of articulating a uniquely British cuisine. Diplomatic missions are alive too to the opportunities to celebrate citizen gastrodiplomacy activities arising outside governments. To a much greater degree than is typically discussed in the academic literature, both the culinary diplomacy and gastrodiplomacy work of UK missions focuses on showing an awareness and respect for local cuisines as well as promoting the British one, both in the furtherance of a positive bilateral relationship and in countering negative stories.

Soft power is defined by Joseph Nye as 'the ability to get what you want through attraction rather than coercion or payments' (2004: x). Nye identifies three sources of soft power: a country's culture, political ideals, and policies. Cuisine can be an important component of an attractive cultural offering, as witnessed by the food and drink-related listings as part of UNESCO's Intangible Cultural Heritage, including in 2010 both Mexican cuisine as a whole and the French gastronomic meal. Academics looking at the way gastronomic soft power is expressed have drawn a distinction between gastrodiplomacy, defined by Paul Rockower as 'how countries conduct cultural diplomacy through promotion of their cuisine' and culinary diplomacy, which is 'a means to further diplomatic protocol through cuisine' (2012: 235). Chapple-Sokol (2016) adds a third category of citizen culinary diplomacy, comprising activity which falls outside the remit of government. This paper looks at the promotion of the soft power of a nation's cuisine by diplomatic missions abroad from the perspective of a practitioner, drawing on my experience as a UK head of mission in Central Asia, the eastern Caribbean, and Romania between 2002 and 2018.

A first key observation is that, unlike the promotion of many other aspects of cultural soft power, the use of food and drink is not an optional activity for diplomatic missions. Senior visitors must eat. Meals provide an opportunity for discussions with influential host country figures in a setting which is more relaxed, more convivial to free conversation away from prepared briefing notes, than official meetings. The planning of meals is thus a central component of every visit programme. The choice of food and drink may face certain practical constraints: for example, a limited time slot, particularly for lunches, and the need to guard against offending religious sensitivities or common sources of food intolerance where hosts have incomplete information about their guests. But the choice of menu is also always influenced by the desire to create a positive tone for the discussions. This is an opportunity to showcase traditional British food and drink, but also to show respect for local cuisine. Thus the menu for the Foreign Secretary's visit to Romania in 2017 included *sarmale,* traditional Romanian stuffed vine leaves.

The balance between British and local dishes served during important visits is influenced by a range of factors. The experience and confidence of the Residence chef is one. Craig Harnden, Head Chef at the British Embassy in Washington DC, in an article sent out to posts as part of the Department for Environment, Food and Rural Affairs (DEFRA)/Foreign and Commonwealth Office (FCO) Food is GREAT Hospitality Toolkit 2017-18, offered a 'Best of British' dinner menu, starting with a scotch quail egg with celeriac and apple salad, followed by a herb-crusted loin of lamb with minted peas and fondant potato, with a dessert of 'Harvey's lemon tart', a Marco Pierre White recipe. Harnden notes, 'we have developed menus and canapes that reflect the classical dishes the UK is famous for with a modern twist and presentation. Our aim is to make sure all of our guests leave with a great impression of British food and drink, so even if we can't always use ingredients from the UK, everything has to taste delicious.' But many diplomatic missions are much smaller, with chefs less familiar with the UK, and for whom a senior visit is a rarer and potentially intimidating event for which the preferred option may be to fall back on the chef's tried and tested signature dish.

Other factors at play here include the preferences of the senior visitor themselves. It is not uncommon for visitors, especially if the country is unfamiliar to them, to encourage the diplomatic mission organizing their programme to show them something of local culture, including the cuisine. And while much less of a factor in today's globalized world than it would once have been, there is also the practical consideration of how well British cuisine resonates with the host population. Menus served during senior visits are designed to be appreciated by all those around the table, to aid positive discussions and a successful visit. In cultures with cuisines very different to those of the UK, serving dishes which are too unfamiliar to local palates may be avoided. One means of reconciling this challenge lies in serving dishes rooted in the cuisine of the host country, but which contain a nod or two to British dishes.

An example from Belgian diplomacy lies in a book called *Be Our Guest*, written by the spouses of two Belgian ambassadors, which includes a challenge set to seven Belgian chefs to create a menu for different Belgian Embassies overseas. Thus for Beijing, Gert de Mangeleer comes up with Dim Sum Stars, with a filling including Zeebrugge langoustine (Billen and van de Voorde-Heidbuchel 2018: 58).

The national day reception tends to be used more squarely by every diplomatic mission as a showcase of its cuisine. Typically the largest entertainment event of a post's year, the reception is targeted at a cross-section of influential local contacts, and may feature press attendance. While official lunches and dinners for senior visitors fall clearly into the category of culinary diplomacy, national day receptions incorporate an element of gastrodiplomacy too. For the UK, the National Day reception is the Queen's Birthday Party. In Romania its June timing at the height of summer favoured a garden party format, focused around drinks such as Pimms and British gins.

The DEFRA/FCO Food is GREAT Hospitality Toolkit offers posts ideas on how to promote British food and drink products at national days and other diplomatic receptions, as well as the crafting of opportunities to entertain local contacts around formats which highlight UK cuisine, such as afternoon teas. The British culinary calendar can also be a spur to events organized by posts, sometimes in conjunction with local British communities, charities, or other groups. One of the most widespread is the Burns Supper, combining cuisine with the poetry of Robert Burns. In some posts, particularly where there is no large resident Scottish expatriate community, the diplomatic mission itself may take on the organization of the event, as we did in Turkmenistan, while at others the Head of Mission may simply attend as a guest at an event organized, for example, by the local Caledonian Society. Sourcing the haggis is frequently the logistical challenge at the centre of the organization of Burns Suppers around the world.

Department for International Trade (DIT) teams support events to promote food and drink exports. In Romania, the food and drink sector was supported by the British Romanian Chamber of Commerce through an overseas delivery partnership with DIT: events hosted by the head of mission included a showcase of Speyside malt whiskies and another on behalf of Witley Neill gin.

The UK approach to gastrodiplomacy has, though, taken an essentially permissive structure, providing ideas and advice through the Food is GREAT Hospitality Toolkit, and leaving trade and investment teams to agree the format of food and drink promotional events with the companies concerned. Some other countries have taken a distinctly more directed approach. The Thailand: Kitchen of the World campaign, for example, incorporated the certification of Thai restaurants overseas on the basis of a set of criteria defined by the Commerce Ministry, including the use of raw materials and equipment from Thailand and the presence of a defined number of Thai dishes on the menu, drawn from a standard list. Peru also took a directed approach to its presentation of Cocina Peruana Para El Mundo, a campaign aimed

69

at securing a spot for Peruvian cuisine as part of the UNESCO Intangible Cultural Heritage of Humanity (Wilson 2013).

In part, this reflects a caution about instrumentalization. The United Kingdom has considerable soft power strengths, reflected in its top spot globally in the 2018 edition of *The Soft Power 30*, the annual ranking by Portland Communications and the USC Center on Public Diplomacy of the world's top soft powers, using a mix of objective data and international polling. An important part of this strength is around the independence of the cultural, sporting, broadcasting, and other institutions which make up so much of the UK's soft power. The BBC, for example, though in receipt of public funding, is a respected and trusted broadcaster globally precisely because its editorial independence from government is carefully maintained. It is difficult to envisage HM Government engaging in the business of assessing the quality of British restaurants overseas or providing recommended menus.

In part, the less directive UK approach also reflects the challenges of articulating a unitary British cuisine, as against a series of iconic elements (the cooked breakfast; Sunday roast). Yeatman argues that, in prioritizing variety, the connection between place and local dishes is weaker in England than in many parts of the world: 'to re-establish itself as a place to eat, rural England needs relabelling as *terroire*, populated by *terroire-istes*' (2007: 17). Great innovations in the manufacture of British foodstuffs in the Victorian era tended to be viewed by their creators as part of an Industrial Revolution in which Britain exported its know-how to the rest of the world, rather than local secrets to be guarded. A good example is provided by the 'father of Cheddar cheese', Joseph Harding, who readily shared his innovations with foreign cheesemakers, a largesse which was to lead to severe competition for West Country makers of cheddar from cheese produced in North America.

A Britain which developed into a colonial power, thriving through its free trade and openness, becoming a diverse multicultural country in the post-colonial era, finds its current culinary strength in developing and combining flavours and ingredients from around the world, a strength which means London alone has some sixty-nine Michelin starred restaurants. However, this all means that the articulation of an agreed list of British dishes in the manner of the Thailand: Kitchen of the World campaign would be decidedly problematic.

To a larger degree than is recognized in much of the literature, the public diplomacy gastronomic focus of UK diplomatic missions, as much as that of official dinners, also involves attention to local cuisines, as a means of showing respect and engagement. This has taken the form, for example, of social media work from the UK Embassy in Bulgaria showing the efforts of diplomatic staff to cook local delicacies.

Diplomatic missions have a central role to support the development of friendly bilateral relations between the UK and the host country. And some of the highest profile interventions have come when the host country feels that its cuisine has been slighted by a broadcaster or commentator in the UK. A good example here is

RendangGate. A Malaysia-born contestant on the cooking show *MasterChef*, Zaleha Kadir Olpin, was eliminated from the competition after judges Greg Wallace and John Torode had complained that the skin of her chicken rendang wasn't crispy enough. Malaysians took to social media to complain that chicken rendang is not supposed to be crispy (Coulter 2018). Faced with this barrage of local criticism of the UK, the then High Commissioner to Malaysia, Vicki Treadell, met up with Zaleha during a visit back to her home state of Pahang, and the two cooked a chicken rendang together, filmed on national television (Taylor 2018).

The UK Ambassador to Madrid, Simon Manley, having already appeared on the Spanish cookery programme *El Comidista* in a classic gastrodiplomacy effort of cooking up a Sunday roast lunch, came back onto the programme in 2017 following Spanish concerns that British chefs like Jamie Oliver were taking too many liberties with Spanish omelette, including adding ingredients like chorizo and coriander. Host Mikel Iturriaga cooked the Ambassador a tortilla in his kitchen, while the Ambassador prepared Jamie Oliver's recipe: 'one's a cake and one's a Spanish omelette' proclaimed a Spanish chef. The Ambassador wasted no opportunity to promote British food products on the programme, serving Iturriaga British beer and cheese and sporting a Union Jack apron (Jones 2017).

And posts are alive to the opportunities to celebrate positive citizen gastrodiplomacy efforts. One example here is the World's Original Marmalade Awards, a format developed at Dalemain Mansion near Penrith in Cumbria, which have been exported to Australia (UK and Australian marmalades compete in the 'Marmalashes') and now Japan. The awards enhance UK soft power through the product itself, the glorious eccentricity with which it is commemorated, and the emphasis on connecting people around the world.

In the same way that UK diplomatic missions around the world pay attention to local cuisines as well as our own in the furtherance of positive diplomatic relations, the Japanese expansion of the Marmalade Awards owes much to the interest shown by the Japanese Ambassador to London, an interest fuelled in turn by the gastrodiplomacy efforts of those Japanese citizens who have long been competing in the British festival. The Japanese ambassador has visited Dalemain, and encouraged the Japanese city of Yawatahama, at the centre of a citrus-producing area of southwest Japan, to take on the challenge of organizing the first edition of the Dalemain World Marmalade Awards and Festival in Japan in 2019.

The role of diplomatic missions is not to attempt to steer this citizen soft power, but rather to make connections and unblock obstacles where necessary, and above all to celebrate it.

The work of UK diplomatic missions overseas then includes elements of both culinary diplomacy and gastrodiplomacy. The academic literature has though mostly underestimated the extent to which the work of UK missions focuses on showing an awareness and respect for local cuisines as well as promoting the British one, both in the furtherance of a positive bilateral relationship and in countering negative stories.

References

Billen, Kathleen and Kristin van de Voorde-Heidbuchel. 2018. *Be Our Guest: The Ambassadors of Belgian Hospitality* (Tielt: Lannoo Publishers)

Chapple-Sokol, Sam. 2016. 'A New Structure for Culinary Diplomacy', *CulinaryDiplomacy.com*), 28 August

Coulter, Martin. 2018. 'MasterChef Judges Spark International Outrage After Telling Malaysian Woman her Native Dish "was not Crispy Enough"', *Evening Standard*, 3 April

DEFRA/FCO. 2018. *Hospitality Toolkit 2017-18*

Jones, Sam. 2017. 'Madre Mia! UK's Ambassador to Madrid Cooks "British" Tortilla on TV', *Guardian*, 27 July

Nye, Joseph. 2004. *Soft Power: The Means to Success in World Politics* (New York: Public Affairs)

Portland PR Limited. 2018. *The Soft Power 30: A Global Ranking of Soft Power*

Rockower, Paul. 2012. 'Recipes for Gastrodiplomacy', *Place Branding and Public Diplomacy*, 8.3 (August): 235-246

Taylor, Charlotte. 2018. 'A Crispy Crisis', *People and Places* (Foreign and Commonwealth Office Staff Magazine), August

Wilson, Rachel. 2013. 'Cocina Peruana Para El Mundo: Gastrodiplomacy, the Culinary Nation Brand and the Context of National Cuisine in Peru', *Exchange: The Journal of Public Diplomacy*, 2.1: 13-20

Yeatman, Marwood. 2007. *The Last Food of England* (London: Ebury Press)

Sushi, Sake, and Women

Voltaire Cang

Introduction

Japan is often portrayed in international media as a nation with acute gender inequality. The depiction is largely accurate, as Japan is frequently ranked on the lower end in most indices measuring gender equality worldwide, such as in political and economic participation, even as it ranks high in areas like educational attainment rates across genders.[1] In the culinary field, gender disparity in Japan stands on the same level as in many other nations, where men occupy most professional chef positions while women are often relegated to kitchens at home.

This paper investigates gender disparity in Japanese culinary culture by delving into the cultural histories of sushi and sake, Japan's most representative food and drink, respectively.[2] In particular, this study looks into the history of the production, with primary focus on the producers, of these emblems of Japanese cuisine in order to give context and provide some explanation on why women have been excluded from sushi and sake production and tradition, as well as shed some light on the existing gender disparity in Japanese society in general.

While history tomes on sushi and sake have been published inside and outside Japan within recent decades – significantly more for sushi than sake – very few studies have given attention to their producers, that is, the sushi chefs and sake brewers. With focus drawn more to the food (sushi) or drink (sake) rather than to the people behind them, the consequence has been the sidelining of gender issues in these culinary fields.

Several authors on women's history, though not in food studies, have considered the issue of women's exclusion in Japanese culinary culture, if cursorily. All are one in saying that the practice is primarily due to cultural beliefs regarding the polluting nature of women.[3] In sake brewing culture, for example, a proverb warns: 'Let a woman enter the brewery … and the sake will sour'.[4] While some of the studies conclude that these beliefs on female pollution became widespread in the late medieval era (fifteenth to sixteenth centuries) and resulted in the total exclusion of women from sake production by the early modern period (seventeenth century) – sushi as it is known today had yet to be invented – none of the works provide historical and cultural contexts behind the pervasiveness of such beliefs, especially in relation to traditional culinary practices in Japan. This paper attempts to rectify the situation to a certain extent, within the limited space allotted here.

Shokunin: Food and Drink Artisans

In the Japanese language, sushi chefs are called *sushi shokunin*, literally 'sushi artisans'; they are never referred to as cooks ('*ryōrinin*') or even chefs ('*shefu*'). *Shokunin* is defined in Japanese as a 'general term referring to skilled people in traditional art and handicraft industries, such as carpentry, plasterwork, gardening, tailoring, etc., who earn their living from producing things through their acquired skills', and is commonly used to denote artisans in the arts and crafts.[5] These include people in the culinary arts, although the term *shokunin* today is reserved mostly for artisanal producers of certain traditional foods, such as *soba shokunin* (buckwheat noodles), *unagi shokunin* (eel) or *wagashi shokunin* (traditional confectionery). The term, however, has recently been appropriated for chefs in professions considered artisanal by the public or the producers themselves, such as *pan shokunin* (bread) and *ramen shokunin*. The implication is that these artisanal producers are specialists in their fields and have undergone long and hard training like their counterparts in the arts and crafts. Sake brewers are also referred to as *shokunin*, although chief brewers are called by another name with gendered origins, as will be discussed later.

Shokunin is an ancient term that was originally used to describe any person engaged in any line of work (*shoku* 職=work/job; *nin* 人=job), although at least from around the fourteenth century, the word evolved to mainly describe people who worked in a specific craft, that is, craftspeople or artisans.[6] Since then, as now, the word *shokunin* has generally referred to workers involved in arts and crafts production, including certain culinary arts, whether they be growers, manufacturers, chefs, or brewers and whether involved in one, a few, or all stages of the production process.

Several in-depth studies have already been conducted on *shokunin* history, mostly in Japanese with a few notable works in the English language.[7] However, almost no academic work has focused on *shokunin* in the culinary arts, much less their history.[8] The omission is curious, as there is an abundance of textual information on culinary artisans even from pre-medieval (eighth to twelfth centuries) times, such as registers and gazettes. There is also a rich trove of visual data from traditional literature, particularly one category of illustrated scrolls featuring *shokunin* that have been published from at least the early twelfth century.

Illustrated scrolls were originally produced by and for the nobility and educated classes and thus typically depicted courtly life and aristocratic pursuits. However, several works in the corpus specifically feature artisans – who were commoners – as their main subjects. Due to their distinctive subject matter, these scrolls have since been categorized as a specific literary genre called *shokunin utaawase* ('artisan poetry contest'), the earliest examples of which are found from the Heian period (794-1185), at the height of courtly life in ancient Japan. Along with artisans such as metalworkers and potters, the scrolls invariably include depictions of culinary *shokunin*.

As the main producers and consumers of illustrated scrolls, the aristocracy were fascinated by the artisan class who played important roles in the capitalist economy;

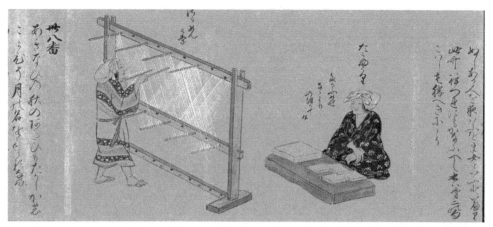

Figure 1. Pair 38, Tofu seller (r) and sōmen *noodle seller (l),* Shichijūichiban shokunin utaawase *scroll (replica) by Kano Seiseiin and Kano Shosenin, n.d. Tokyo National Museum.*

the fascination resulted in artisans being frequently portrayed in different forms of literature, especially in this category of illustrated scrolls.[9] The typical *shokunin utaawase* scroll usually contains drawings, often in colour, of artisans in their work attire, randomly arranged in pairs, and with accompanying descriptive texts. The *shokunin* are frequently shown going about their work, but at the same time pitted against another artisan in a poetry contest. (Hence the category name *utaawase* or 'poetry contest'.) To have *shokunin* declaim poetry is an inconceivable scenario that could only be the result of aristocratic fantasies: these depictions, even caricatures, of *shokunin* border on the perverse, but since they do show details of actual costumes, craft tools, and products of the era, they constitute a valuable reference on *shokunin* history.

The oldest extant scroll is the *Tōhokuin shokunin utaawase* dated from 1214 or earlier, but the most abundantly illustrated and comprehensive medieval-era work is the *Shichijūichiban shokunin utaawase*, published around 1500, which will be the focus here. Usually appearing in three volumes, the work depicts seventy-one numbered pairs of competing artisans (*Shichijūichiban* in the scroll's name means 'seventy-one pairs') representing 142 independent *shokunin* categories. Most of the artisans are at work, some of them holding tools, while reciting their poems. Among the 142 artisans, at least twenty-five represent *shokunin* working in food or drink craft traditions, such as artisans described as 'tofu seller' and '*sōmen* noodle seller' (Figure 1) – read from right to left – and 'salt seller' and '*kōji* (fermentation mold) seller' (Figure 2), including those who make dining utensils such as lacquer bowls and earthenware.[10] Ten of the twenty-five food and drink artisans are women. (Overall, there are thirty-four women among the 142 artisans in the *Shichijūichiban shokunin utaawase*, which several authors have indicated to be a testament to gender diversity in the workforce of the era.)[11]

75

Figure 2. Pair 39, Salt seller (r) and kōji *seller (l),* Shichijūichiban shokunin utaawase *scroll. Tokyo National Museum.*

One artisan stands out among the twenty-five: the 'sake brewer' – on the left – who is paired with the 'pot seller' (Figure 3). Not only is the brewer introduced early in the lineup, she is a woman who is explicitly identified as a producer, that is, a sake 'brewer' and not a 'seller', like all the other food and drink *shokunin*. That the sake brewer was a woman may be surprising in today's Japan, but it was the norm in medieval times when this scroll was produced, as it was also in the centuries before and later.

Shokunin continued to be featured as subjects in later illustrated works, including woodblock prints by famous artists such as Hokusai and Hiroshige, which frequently included artisans in food and drink occupations. While these works also merit detailed discussion, it is beyond the scope of this present paper; suffice it to say that by Hokusai's era (late eighteenth to mid-nineteenth century), there were no more illustrations of women sake brewers. As for sushi chefs, who began to be featured in art works only from around this period when sushi became common food, they were always male.

It was precisely in this period, Edo (1603 to 1868), when the exclusion of women in sushi and sake production was fully actualized. The following section will look at the historical process that led to this actualization. The discussion begins with sake brewing, as it has a much longer history in developing gender norms that critically influenced later sushi culinary culture.

Women in the Sake Craft

Japan's oldest written myth-history chronicles, *Nihonshoki* and *Kōjiki*, identify a female deity, Konohana no sakuya bime, as the originator of sake brewing, being the first to achieve the natural fermentation of rice by using enzymes in her mouth to activate the process. (She simply chewed the rice.)[12] This important historical role resulted in her enshrinement in several Shinto places of worship all over Japan, although one particular shrine, Tsumajinja in western Miyazaki Prefecture, has a commemorative stone marker

Figure 3. Pair 6, Pot seller (r) and sake brewer (l), Shichijūichiban shokunin utaawase *scroll. Tokyo National Museum.*

on its grounds declaring itself as the original site of sake brewing in Japan. The marker explains that it is the exact spot where Konohana no sakuya bime produced the first alcoholic drink from rice, *amazake* (a very low-, sometimes non-alcohol sweet drink made from fermented rice), which she had to make to cope for the lack of breast milk to feed her three infant children.[13]

Rice fermentation by chewing is an ancient method in Japan, and historical records mention that the process was often assigned to virginal girls; the practice has remained, quietly and in remote regions, into the present day. One author notes that this surviving 'prehistoric process [contains] no hint of pollution by women; instead young females were specified as the natural brewers'.[14] (After the girls assiduously chew the rice, they spit it into large bowls that are then sealed and made to sit for a few days. The chewed rice transforms into a viscous, alcoholic brew that is considered the prototype sake.)

This mode of sake production would change, however, around the Nara period (710-794) when the use of *kōji* as a fermentation starter was discovered; ever since, *kōji* and not enzymes in the mouth would be employed in all but the most rare and esoteric sake brewing traditions.[15] While young women chewers were no longer needed, sake brewing remained in women's hands, as attested in several records from Nara as well as succeeding periods. For example, *Harima no kuni fudoki* ('Harima Provincial Gazette', published c. 713) describes sake brewing in the region as an industry controlled by women who also brewed the sake themselves.[16] *Nihon ryōiki,* a collection of stories compiled from oral tradition that was written at the beginning of the ninth century or earlier, contains descriptions of female sake brewers and business owners. One popular anecdote in the collection is about a rich but corrupt noblewoman, Hiromushime, who owned much crop land and livestock, including slaves, and made huge profits from producing sake which she regularly diluted with water.[17] Her cheating ways – she was also a loan shark – saw her being reborn as a smelly and filthy half-human horned fox after her death, the result of the laws of karmic redistribution. Although Hiromushime's story warrants close reading and scrutiny, our main concern is the fact of her being the rice grower, sake brewer, and seller all together in the story, which was most likely the case for all sake brewers in that era and in the succeeding centuries, as evidenced in the *Shichijūichiban* scroll mentioned above, which had appeared some 500 years after this ancient story collection.

It was also around the Nara Period when codification was introduced and developed for the government and bureaucracy through the so-called *ritsuryō* (criminal and administrative codes) system. The government restructuring saw several craft industries, especially those that were considered important in the daily lives of bureaucrats and the aristocracy, fall under central (imperial court) administration. Sake brewing, along with metalwork, papermaking, and others, was among the earliest crafts to be so administered, leading to the establishment of the Sake-Making Office (*Zōshushi* or *Mikinotsukasa*) exclusively to oversee sake production for the court. Although the Office's head was male, the brewing staff consisted of both men and women assigned in several important roles in the production process.[18]

Outside the palace walls, however, sake brewing remained primarily the domain of women, mainly because it was made in households that were often headed by matriarchs. Called by the honorific *toji* ('lady' or 'madame'), these matriarchs were mostly older women who administered all household activities, which included sake production especially in the larger houses. In these households, *toji* supervised a staff of relatives and other villagers in all stages of sake brewing, from harvesting and cleaning the rice, to its steaming, mashing, fermenting, and storage.[19] The term *toji* has remained into the present, evolving into the word *tōji* (pronounced with a long *ō* and transcribed in different Kanji characters) but still referring to the master brewer in sake breweries, almost always male today, who supervises a staff of *shokunin* involved in different stages of sake production. *Tōji* are primarily responsible in handling the *kōji* for fermenting rice and determining the final taste of the sake.

Meanwhile, the establishment of the Sake-Making Office in the palace led to systematization of the sake brewing process and improvement of its quality standards. Sake production methods have remained unchanged since: when the historically important *Engishiki* book of laws and customs was published in the tenth century, one of its sections describing sake brewing procedures shows it to be similar to current methods, sans today's modern technology.[20]

The Office was able to achieve systematization and quality improvement in sake brewing through its frequent collaboration with the priestly class, who worked closely with the court in areas like research and personnel management. However, Buddhist temples would gradually gain more social, economic, and political clout – political leaders frequently used Buddhism to unify and rule – which allowed them to establish their own sake breweries. The aristocracy liked and consumed Buddhist-temple sake more often than those from the court breweries, and its popularity came to extend to the common populace.

The temples' growing wealth also enabled them to hire the best brewery workers, even luring experts from the palace, as they also regularly acquired information on the latest techniques for sake brewing that their monks brought back from travels abroad. Temple-made sake was so popular it became a category of its own, named *sōbōshu* (literally, 'priest and monk alcohol'), that was produced and widely sold until the Edo period, a remarkable span of more than 800 years engaged in the same business.[21] Indeed, Buddhist temples played very important roles in sake brewing history, especially as their systematic methods and techniques were copied by commercial sake brewing enterprises established later. As centres of Buddhism, the temples would also play a significant role in the shaping of gender practices in sake brewing tradition.

Buddhism and Sake

Although the few studies that discuss female exclusion in sake brewing point to cultural notions of female pollution as a major reason for the practice, none of these studies have specifically identified the notions as Buddhist in origin, much less linked these notions with the history of sake brewing in Buddhist temples. The oversight is odd, as Buddhist temples would have been the actual sites where these specific beliefs would have been formed and fomented.

That is not to say that Buddhism has always been prejudiced against women: religious studies scholar Haruko Okano has pointed out that during the religion's earliest years in Japan – in the Nara period – no discrimination was made between men and women, as evidenced in the custom of having monks and nuns work in similar roles or conduct rituals where they sit together while reciting sutras, among other practices.[22] In the succeeding Heian period, however, discriminatory practices against women in Mahayana Buddhism – the Buddhism tradition that entered Japan – came to be 'mixed with the indigenous Japanese idea of ritual purity and blood as a source of impurity', so that women were gradually seen as sources of defilement.[23] The exact source/s of these cultural views are not clear, and Okano stresses that the notions appear in neither the *Nihonshoki* nor the *Kōjiki*, the ancient chronicles mentioned above that relate the origins of the Japanese nation.

Moreover, from the fourteenth to fifteenth centuries (mid-medieval era), 'the introduction from China of the folk belief in the Ketsubon Sutra that all women who have given birth to a child will go to the hell of blood' promoted further discrimination against women.[24] According to the author, this belief was based on the notion that blood shed during childbirth polluted the earth, which in turn defiled the rivers, which eventually polluted monks if they drank tea made with water from these rivers. By the Edo period, menstrual bleeding would be subjected to the same notions, as Okano indicates.

The timeline of these shifts in thinking concerning female pollution runs parallel to the timetable of location shifts concerning the centres of sake production. That is, women were increasingly seen as defilers at the same time that Buddhist temples became dominant sake producers. One can easily draw the conclusion that the notion of female pollution and the resulting discrimination in sake brewing arose from Buddhism's – more precisely, Buddhist temple producers' – entry into the artisanal production and business of sake. These discriminatory beliefs would then be adopted by sake brewing enterprises that took over from Buddhist temples as the main sake producers, which happened mostly in the Edo period, which was also when the ideas of female pollution were found to be most widespread and pervasive. The same beliefs would in turn be adopted in sushi culinary culture, which itself was a product of Edo culture.

Sushi as Artisanal Food

Sushi has been described as an innovation from ancient culinary traditions in Southeast Asia; it was originally preserved food, made with gutted and cleaned fish placed over fermented rice and kept in storage.[25] However, the type of sushi that is most well-known today, that is, in the form of raw fish placed on top of hand-moulded rice (i.e. *nigiri*), is an invention from the Edo period. *Nigiri* is often described as *Edomae* ('Edo-style') sushi, for it was in Edo (later Tokyo), where these were invented. As *nigiri*, Edo-style sushi was a form of fast food that was easily eaten with bare hands. It was also cheap and popular among the working class who often ate on the go.[26]

Sushi gradually transformed from its fast food origins into haute cuisine and, as it consisted of expensive ingredients like rice and fresh fish, it came to be made exclusively by fully-trained and dedicated – that is, artisanal – chefs. It is not exactly known when the word *sushi shokunin* first came into use, although it could only have been coined from the Edo period after *nigiri* sushi made its appearance. The growing popularity of sushi, however, did coincide with the standardization of the *shokunin* system that also occurred in the same era, and this standardization of the artisanal profession would have created a suitable environment for the emergence of *sushi shokunin*. It was in Edo and during the Edo period when the *shokunin* training schemes in the different arts and crafts were standardized into the general system still existing today.[27]

The Edo period had been a relatively peaceful era lasting more than 250 years, during which time Edo's population ballooned and its infrastructure incessantly expanded and rebuilt. This required a constant influx of trained workers who could fill the various needs and niches in the booming economy. *Shokunin* training thus needed to be standardized: training programs began incorporating standard curricula which anyone who aspired to the profession had to undergo. (However, anyone could enter any *shokunin* profession as long as they underwent the required training for that particular *shokunin* craft.)

One study on Edo-era artisans described the typical training scheme for *shokunin* using the example of the carpenter, perhaps the most representative of all *shokunin*:

> The trainee would enter the master's household at around the age of ten. By the time he turned 14 or 15, he would first be given a saw and learn to cut wood. Next, he would be allowed to use the plane and learn to shave wood, followed by the chisel for making holes in the wood. Finally, he would be taught how

to sharpen his tools. Once he masters using the chisel, he is considered a full-fledged artisan. He then becomes independent when he turns 20.[28]

The age of ten may seem very young to begin one's training, but in the Edo period children at this age would already have had several years of education in *terakoya* (public schools affiliated with Buddhist temples) as well as having already learned to take care of themselves through their education at home. (Historians sometimes say that people in Edo had 'no childhoods'.) The trainee would live in the master's house throughout the standard ten-year training period, at first performing menial work, then learning the use of the trade's different tools and techniques in stages. He learns only by doing as he is told and faithfully imitating his master's work methods.

The use of 'he' in the paragraphs above is on purpose: almost all *shokunin* trainees, especially those who lived in their masters' households, were male. Girls were expected to stay at home, and, if they did work, it would mostly be in the entertainment and service industries, or in simple factory labour that was considered inferior to skilled and technical, as well as dangerous and difficult, 'men's' work.[29] The *shokunin* environment in Edo was tailored for men, even as the *shokunin* community and society in general was male-dominated, with many having left families in their provinces to seek their fortunes in the capital.

Most of the *shokunin* professions adopted the same training scheme as that described for carpenters above. That is, the trainee would live and work in the master's house for a period of ten years on average and be taught the different skills in stages during the period. This training scheme was also followed in most of the culinary *shokunin* professions and have largely remained until the present day. It has been retained in sushi chef training as well, as seen in the following description of sushi chef training recently outlined in one of Japan's largest online job-hunting sites for careers in the food industry:

Year 1: Washing/Cleaning duties, food delivery, hall duties
Years 2 to 3: Boiling rice, preparing shellfish and small fish, cooking eggs, preparing food for restaurant and kitchen staff
Years 4 to 6: Assisting in counter work, making maki and other rolls
Years 7 to 9: Making *nigiri*
Year 10: Becoming a full-fledged sushi chef[30]

This follows the same pattern as for traditional *shokunin*: menial work in the first few years, gradually learning the basic skills first, then on to acquiring major and career-defining techniques. Many in Japan consider *shokunin* training to be tough and, supposedly, not ideal for women.

Final Thoughts
It would be easy to conclude that the situation for sushi chefs would be different from that of sake brewers in the ways by which each profession came to exclude women. For sushi, the *shokunin* system standardized in the Edo period could be blamed; whereas for

sake brewing, the rise of Buddhist temples as centres of sake production (including their impure thoughts about women) would be the prime cause. But then that would be too easy and, as academics are wont to say, it is more complicated than it looks. And it is.

When asked about the gender disparity in their craft, some sake brewers will still allude to historical notions of female pollution. However, since this reasoning is flimsy and controversial at the least, even in Japan, many now say that work in the brewery is difficult and requires physical strength that most women simply do not have, which is an argument borrowed from *shokunin* tradition. According to brewers, the sake *shokunin*'s job is 'not only physically and mentally difficult, it is dangerous to the extent that you could die from it'.[31]

But sushi culinary culture also borrows notions developed in sake production. A few years ago, Yoshikazu Ono, the son of Jiro Ono, perhaps the world's most famous *sushi shokunin* – the latter of *Jiro Dreams of Sushi* documentary fame – was asked in a *Wall Street Journal* interview as to why women could not become sushi chefs. The younger Ono is also a sushi chef and works with his father (who turned 94 in 2019) in their tiny basement sushi shop (albeit Michelin three-starred) in Tokyo's Ginza district. Ono *fils* replied: 'because women menstruate. To be a professional means to have a steady taste in your food, but because of the menstrual cycle, women have an imbalance in their taste, and that's why women can't be sushi chefs'.[32]

Ono is employing the Buddhist trope on women's blood as applied in sake brewing, but with variations on the theme: he refers to blood as a reason for the unsuitability of women in his profession, though not because blood could pollute the food, but because it adversely affects women's taste buds. Yes, it is complicated.

Notes

1   World Economic Report, 'The Global Gender Gap Report 2018', 2018 <http://www3.weforum.org/docs/WEF_GGGR_2018.pdf> [accessed 30 March 2019]; United Nations Development Programme, 'Human Development Reports: Japan' <http://hdr.undp.org/en/countries/profiles/JPN> [accessed 30 March 2019].

2   In the Japanese language, *sake* means 'alcoholic drink' and refers to all kinds of alcohol. The common term in Japan for sake (i.e. 'rice wine') is *nihonshu* (literally, 'Japan alcohol'). This paper follows English language convention and uses the term sake to refer to 'rice wine'.

3   See Yasuko Tabata, 'Women's Work and Status in the Changing Medieval Economy' (trans. Hitomi Tonomura), in *Women and Class in Japanese History*, ed. by Hitomi Tonomura, Anne Walthall, and Haruko Wakita (Ann Arbor: Center for Japanese Studies, The University of Michigan; 1999), pp. 99-118; Haruko Wakita, *Women in Medieval Japan: Motherhood, Household Management and Sexuality* (Tokyo: University of Tokyo Press, 2006); Joyce Chapman Lebra, 'Women in an All-Male Industry: The Case of Sake Brewer Tatsu'uma Kiyo', in *Recreating Japanese Women, 1600-1945*, ed. by Gail Lee Bernstein (Berkeley: University of California Press, 1991), pp. 131-48.

4   Lebra, p. 131.

5   *Nihon kokugo daijiten* (*Great Japanese Language Dictionary*), 13 vols (Tokyo: Shogakukan, 2001) VII, 336.

6   Japanese historian Yoshihiko Amino dated the shift in the term's meaning to this period by pointing to records from Tōji temple in Kyoto, particularly the *Tōji shugyō nikki* of 1364, which specifically

described carpenters, metalworkers, stoneworkers, and those in other craft industries as *shokunin* ('*Chūsei shokunin wo megutte*' ('On Medieval-Era Artisans'), in *Kinsei fūzoku zufu* (*Illustrated Catalog of Modern Customs*), *Volume 12: Shokunin* (*Artisans*) (Tokyo: Shogakkan, 1983), 62-73).

7   For example, *The Artist as Professional in Japan*, ed. by Melinda Takeuchi (Stanford: Stanford University Press, 2004).

8   One noteworthy exception is Dorinne Kondo's anthropological study on an individual confectionery artisan: 'Multiple Selves: The Aesthetics and Politics of Artisanal Identities', in N. Rosenberger (ed.), *Japanese Sense of Self* (Cambridge: Cambridge University Press, 1994), pp. 40-66.

9   Yasutoshi Kita, *Takumi no kuni Nippon* (*Japan, Nation of Masters*) (Tokyo: PHP, 2008).

10 *Kōji* refers to the category of fermentation starters used in the production of liquor, vinegar, and seasonings like miso and soy sauce.

11 Tabata, 'Women's Work and Status'; Wakita, *Women in Medieval Japan*.

12 Lebra.

13 See Tsumajinja: <https://tsumajinja.webnode.jp>.

14 Lebra, p. 132.

15 Sake's only ingredients then, as now, were rice, *kōji,* and water.

16 Tabata.

17 Haruo Shirane, *Traditional Japanese Literature: An Anthology, Beginnings to 1600* (Columbia University Press, 2008).

18 Manabu Yunoki, *Sakazukuri no rekishi* (*History of Sake Brewing*) (Tokyo: Yuzankaku, 2005).

19 Akiko Yoshie, *Nihon kodai josei shiron* (*History of Women in Ancient Japan*) (Tokyo: Yoshikawa Kobunkan, 2007).

20 Yunoki.

21 Yunoki.

22 Haruko Okano, 'Women's Image and Place in Japanese Buddhism' (trans. Kumiko Fujimura-Fanselow and Yoko Tsuruta), in *Japanese Women: New Feminist Perspectives on the Past, Present, and Future*, ed. by Kumiko Fujimura-Fanselow and Atsuko Kameda (New York: The Feminist Press, 1995), pp. 15-28.

23 Okano, p. 19.

24 Okano, p. 21.

25 Naomichi Ishige, *Nihon no shokubunka shi: Kyūsekki jidai kara gendai made* (*History of Japanese Food Culture: From Paleolithic to Contemporary Times*) (Tokyo: Iwanami Shoten, 2015).

26 See Zenjiro Watanabe 'The Flavor of Edo Spans the Globe', *Food Culture,* 7 (2004), 9-14.

27 Kita.

28 Ikuo Nakano, '*Kinsei shokugyō kyōiku kunren no keifu* (Genealogy of Occupational Training in the Modern Era)', *Commercial Review of the Senshu University,* 7 (2009), 127-141.

29 Fuyuhiko Yokota, 'Imagining Working Women in Early Modern Japan' (trans. Mariko Asano Tamanoi) in *Women and Class in Japanese History*, ed. by Hitomi Tonomura, Anne Walthall, and Haruko Wakita (Ann Arbor: Center for Japanese Studies, The University of Michigan; 1999), pp. 157-60.

30 Kyūjin atto inshokuten dotto komu, '*Sushi shokunin no shugyō kikan* (Training Period of the Sushi Chef)', 10 April 2015 <https://job.inshokuten.com/foodistMagazine/detail/8> [accessed 15 February 2019] (author's translation).

31 Hiroshi Minato, '*Shuzō ga 'nyonin kinsei' ni natta riyū* (Reasons for Sake Breweries' Non-Admittance of Women)', 25 July 2018 <https://jp.sake-times.com/think/study/sake_g_no-woman-admitted> [accessed 15 February 2019] (author's translation).

32 Mary M. Lane, 'Why Can't Women be Sushi Masters?', *Wall Street Journal* (blog) <https://blogs.wsj.com/speakeasy/2011/02/17/michelin-chef-on-why-women-cant-be-sushi-masters/> [accessed 10 March 2019].

Food as Power in the Letters of Isabella d'Este

Allison Fisher

The historical study of food and feasting is inherently challenging because of the ephemeral nature of meals and the tendency of food to spoil. A scholar is nearly always unable to study the physical food itself, but must turn instead to secondary sources, including images, recipe books, ledgers, and letters for insight. Epistolary evidence particularly reveals a wealth of information about historical preparations and attitudes toward food. The letters of Isabella d'Este (1474-1539), one of the most influential female art patrons and political leaders of the Italian Renaissance, do just this. Her surviving correspondence frequently addresses how she used food, cooking, and comestible provisions to demonstrate her personal and political power in the dynamic years of the early sixteenth century in Italy.[1]

Born into the Este family, who had ruled Ferrara from 1240, Isabella later married Francesco II Gonzaga, the marquis of Mantua, and she acted as regent when he was abroad leading armies during the recurrent wars on the peninsula. Their son, Federico II, was subsequently granted the ducal title in 1530, and Isabella advised him on state matters until her death in 1539. As the daughter, wife, and mother of noble Italian leaders, Isabella was intimately familiar with the need to assert, maintain, and project power through a variety of means.[2] One notable approach was her letters. In fact, more than 16,000 letters by Isabella survive, forming a unique body of evidence that demonstrates how she used food as one mode to express her wealth and influence both domestically in Mantua and abroad in Italy and Europe.

With a focus on the recently published correspondence of Isabella by Deanna Shemek, this paper will explore the relationship between food and power in Isabella's letters through three themes: firstly, how Isabella used food gifts to cultivate and maintain relationships with other political leaders, including family members and close friends; secondly, how food laws and regulations promulgated by Isabella reinforced her elite position in society; and thirdly, how the preparation of food by cooks and its presentation at feasts attended by Isabella underscored her power and wealth. As this paper will demonstrate, Isabella's use of food as a tool to express authority is vital to her self-fashioning as a potent political figure in sixteenth-century Italy, and indeed it is an important intersection between history, food, and the status of women in the Renaissance.

A gift of food in the early modern world was viewed as an exchange of power, both for the giver and the recipient.[3] Particularly during the Renaissance, gifts of food were more than benevolent gestures as this was an era when the scarcity of food was a regular occurrence, especially among the lower classes. Poor harvests and unpredictable food supplies could lead to famine and starvation; much of the population lived in fear of food scarcity. To have enough surplus food that one could present it to another person demonstrated one's ability to afford extra or one's control of the production of foodstuffs. Thus, even a gift of simple fruits or fish could be a manifestation of power and wealth. Moreover, an element of trust came in to play with alimentary gifts. The recipient had to trust that the food gifted was safe to eat and not harmful or poisonous.[4] To accept a food gift was to display your trust in the giver as you might literally place your life on the line when consuming the gift.

In the letters of Isabella d'Este, food gifts are, in fact, the most frequent type of alimentary theme encountered.[5] From an early age, Isabella sent different foods with accompanying letters to describe her intentions to friends and family. As she grew older, the recipients of her comestible gifts expanded to include political leaders across Italy. This food diplomacy allowed Isabella to cultivate and maintain relationships with those both near and far geographically, including leaders such as the Holy Roman Emperor. In the Renaissance, it was a well-established convention in which both men and women participated as recipients and gift-givers alike.[6] As such, it is not surprising that Isabella gifted a wide variety of foods, such as cheese, wine, fish, and nuts, as one manifestation of her personal and political authority.

Typical for an elite woman of her time, Isabella most frequently sent food gifts to the closest members of her family, including her husband Francesco, her sister-in-law Elisabetta (the Duchess of Urbino), and her children. Her husband Francesco was a noted recipient of her magnanimity, receiving alimentary gifts from Isabella throughout their twenty-nine year marriage. For example, in a letter of 25 July 1495, Isabella detailed a list of the goods she was sending to Francesco, including 'four barrels of tart wine from Revere, two barrels of sweet wine to accompany melons, two small casks of white wine from Sacco, and one load of melons', along with sweets, preserved pears, and 'a basket of pears of different sorts'. At the time, he was away fighting the French armies, and Isabella was left to govern Mantua. In her letter, Isabella acknowledged that she knew Francesco had access to good wines, but she hoped he would be 'disposed to enjoy for love of me' the gift that she sent.[7] By sending her husband his favourite comestibles whilst he was defending their realm, Isabella was not only performing her appropriate wifely duties, but she was also highlighting the bounty of their local food production. This was the height of summer, and the rich agricultural lands surrounding Mantua must have recently yielded a crop of melons, and a successful harvest of wine the autumn previous.

In a subsequent letter, we see further evidence of how food gifts reflected status, and indeed, the volume of produce that the elite could access at the time. Isabella wrote to the Duchess of Urbino on 23 November 1499 to thank her for a gift of pomegranates, writing that 'I like the pomegranates from your orchard immensely [...]. When I tasted them, they seemed to me the best I had eaten in a long time, and this must be because they come from Your Ladyship, who could only send me something good, given our reciprocal love'.[8] Although Isabella's words follow the convention for formal correspondence at the turn of the sixteenth century, the two women did indeed share a close bond and sent each other food gifts on many occasions. In this instance, the Duchess had not only sent Isabella a gift of fruit, but it was a gift of 500 pomegranates, on account of Isabella's pregnancy. This would have been far too much fruit for one individual – or even several – to have enjoyed on their own. Thus, while Isabella may have enjoyed eating the fruit and appreciated the symbolic fertility as she herself was with child, the sheer volume of the gift underscores the wealth of the Duchess. During the Renaissance, the cultivation of fruit was strongly linked to the nobility. Fruit trees only yielded significant returns after many years of careful cultivation, and a subsistence farmer could never have afforded the effort and investment in fruit trees.[9] Moreover, according to Late Medieval and Renaissance thought, the natural order of the world held that because vegetables, particularly onions and beans, grew either underground or low to the ground, they should be eaten by the lowest levels of human society. Fruit, in contrast, which grew in trees, was prized for the tables of the elite. The more aerial the origin of the food, the more appropriate that it be consumed by the highest members of society.[10] It is telling, therefore, that fresh fruit was one of the most common gifts that Isabella both sent and received. Isabella's correspondence includes numerous varieties of fruit that ranged from figs to pears, citrons to peaches, depending on the season or what Isabella could access, either in the open market, by special order from producers, or from her own private orchards.

The food gifts – or lack thereof – sent by Isabella not only reveal her desire to maintain personal and political relationships, but they also demonstrate some of the complexities of politics on the Italian peninsula during the early sixteenth century. In January 1510, the Holy Roman Emperor sent a request to Isabella for grain. Isabella refused his request, explaining that 'it pains me to the depth of my heart to receive from Your Majesty an impossible request, which will not allow me to demonstrate my faithful service to you. To remove grain now from [Mantua] would be to take sustenance from our people, who at present are suffering from a grain famine'.[11] At the time, her husband was imprisoned in Venice after being captured on the battlefield the previous year. Mantua had been part of the League of Cambrai, which was formed to counter Venice; the alliance included France, the Holy Roman Emperor, the Pope, the King of Spain, and several Italian city-states, including Mantua. The Holy Roman Emperor suspected that Francesco Gonzaga might switch allegiance, and, along with the request for grain, he demanded Isabella's eldest son at his court as security. Indeed, in exchange for his liberation in July 1510, Francesco did side with Venice and accepted the command of the Venetian army.[12] Within three years, Mantua yet again switched sides to ally with the Venetians and the French against the Holy Roman Emperor and Spain.

Isabella's letter to the Holy Roman Emperor hints at the political complexity of the period, and indicates that she understood the frequency of changing allegiances. Mantua was a smaller state, and could not compete against the powerful Holy Roman Empire; therefore, it would be prudent to maintain at least a cordial relationship. At the same time, Mantua was surrounded by other states that often sided against the Holy Roman Emperor. Particularly during the absence of her husband, Isabella had to negotiate the shifting power of potential allies and enemies. Moreover, she revealed in the letter that her first priority was, in fact, her own subjects. As the wife of the ruler of Mantua, Isabella was morally responsible for feeding the citizens in her realm. In another letter of some ten days later, Isabella noted that the poor harvest was due to the 'many cavalcades and the continuous presence of armies' that ruined the crops of the territory around Mantua. A hungry citizenry could be dangerous and unstable for the rulers above them. Isabella had to feed the Mantuan populace first, lest her own position be compromised by domestic riots and violence. Four days later, however, Isabella did send the Holy Roman Empress a conciliatory package of fruit, game meat, cheese, and pheasants in order to keep the diplomatic channels open between Mantua and the Empire, and to urge the empress's assistance to liberate her husband Francesco.[13]

Isabella used food diplomacy to promote close relationships and alliances with both family members and other leaders. Indeed, she frequently sent her food gifts with the explanation that she was sending them 'for love of' the recipient, though her professed love could, of course, simply reference the formal, political allegiance that Isabella wished to strengthen. The acceptance of the comestible gift was 'a means of reinforcing bonds of trust and also reinforcing a vision of perfect political harmony' that a Renaissance woman like Isabella could literally cultivate in her garden and in her correspondence.[14]

A smaller group of Isabella's letters are those dedicated to the laws of food and agriculture. In addition to using food as gifts, Isabella used the laws and regulations surrounding food to reinforce her high status. By controlling the production and distribution of food, nobles like Isabella could hold sway over their subjects. In early modern Mantua, the economic classes competed for food and resource management, as a letter of 17 March 1496 reveals. Isabella wrote to the vicar of Goito to order the prosecution of anyone fishing in the Mincio River:

> Our farmers from the lake give us to understand that people are blatantly fishing in the Mincio for giltheads and other fish in violation of the law. We want you to reissue the commandment that no one, no matter who he may be, should dare catch those fish, on the penalty we have already specified several times in the past. And see that violators are diligently punished.[15]

During the Renaissance, freshwater fish were prized over saltwater varieties, and Mantua's lakes and rivers were famed for their fish, especially carp. More broadly, the fishing industry was crucial to the Renaissance diet, as several days of the week and many times throughout the year were fast days, which forbade red meat and dairy from the table of good Christians. Fish was an acceptable protein, and therefore played a large role in the diet, particularly for the higher classes. Interestingly, Isabella often sent carp and other fish varieties as food gifts to family members and allies, rather than game, fowl, or other highly-desired meats, building on both Mantua's reputation for fish and the popularity of fish during fast days. Control of the fishing rights in the region would supply the Gonzaga family and their court not only with fish to consume themselves on fast days, but they could also use in food diplomacy to highlight the alimentary abundance of the waters of Mantua. Furthermore, Isabella's letter indicates that illegal fishing in the Mincio River was an ongoing problem, as she had previously issued commandments against fishing there. Although the Gonzaga family ruled the region, they faced ongoing competition for the fish of the river from the lower social classes. Isabella's frequent issuing of edicts against fishing in the river were one attempt to assert the authority of the Gonzaga over an important food source.

Another issue faced by the elite in Renaissance Italy was contraband food. The market in contraband food distribution ranged from moving foodstuffs across borders without paying taxes, to trading foods that were monopolized by the nobles, including poultry and game.[16] In a letter of 28 September 1503, Isabella defended a Jewish man, David Hebreo, who was charged with 'having run contraband food' near Parma. Isabella wrote to Charles of Amboise, the viceroy of Milan for King Louis XII of France, that 'we cannot believe [the charges], since he is not a man capable of that activity but rather completely alien to it'. Isabella further requested that David 'may be freed from custody without harm, even if he has in some way disobeyed and transgressed the laws of the aforesaid city of Parma; for we will consider it a singular favour from Your Lordship, to whom we offer and commend ourself'.[17] By defending her subject and requesting his release, not only did Isabella act as the benevolent leader, but she also allied herself on a minor level to Charles of Amboise, and, by extension, the King of France. Isabella would have recognized her inferior status to the French monarch and his agents, and thus an allegiance – even if temporary – could have been partly motivated by a desire to keep her political options open at a time when the French army was occupying much of Italy.

In her later years, Isabella issued her own edicts surrounding food and its production. In 1529, for example, Isabella wrote to the commissioner of Castiglione Mantovano to order an edict against rice thieves. She wrote that 'we want you to publish an edict in our name, so that it comes to everyone's attention that whoever is found robbing our rice fields will be given three jerks on the strappado, with no exceptions'. Isabella further stated that 'those who come to steal our rice are for the most part Veronese' and she instructed the commissioner that 'if the Veronese arrogantly show up to do us harm, your men should block any obstructions [by them] to our managers' requisitions'.[18] Rice was a foodstuff that the Gonzaga had only recently begun to cultivate, perhaps as early as 1519; previously, rice was imported from Milan.[19] The development of a local rice industry would provide Mantua with further food autonomy from the larger, more powerful Duchy of Milan. Moreover, rice production was closely linked to the quality of Mantuan land and to water rights, as both were critical to cultivate rice.[20]

Isabella's letter demonstrates her desire to control the production of rice in her lands, and it also shows her interest in promoting new crops. Indeed, in a letter the following month, Isabella proclaimed the high yield of that year's rice crop to Alfonso Trotti, stating that 'she will be left with a good quantity of rice this year' and she was investigating if there were merchants who might buy some of the rice harvest from her.[21] Isabella's edict against the thieves must have been successful if she yielded such a successful harvest.

Similarly, Isabella's letters of 1530 reveal issues regarding a mill and water rights near the Bolognese border. Isabella wrote to the vice legate of Bologna regarding a mill from which the men of Castel Bolognese were trying to deviate water 'and they are diverting it out of its canal'.[22] Isabella lamented how much damage she could suffer from this water diversion if it impeded the grinding at her mill. The control of waterways was crucial to agricultural production at the time. A mill that was poorly served by a waterway would compromise the production of flour, as the mill would not have enough power to properly grind grain. Bread, made from flour, was one of the universal staples of the Renaissance diet. In the fifteenth century, for example, bread accounted for 40% of a family's total food bill and 60% of its caloric intake.[23] Every level of society consumed bread on a daily basis – the poor ate darker loaves that might be made with cheaper flours, like barley, rye, and millet, while the rich ate refined, white loaves made from the best wheats. Indeed, in his popular dietetic treatise, *De Honesta Voluptate et Valetudine* (c. 1465), the humanist Platina declared that 'nothing is more productive and pleasant or more nourishing than wheat'.[24] Isabella needed to have as much grain as possible grown and milled in her lands to feed her citizens, her court, and herself. Thus, when her complaints to the vice legate of Bologna went unheard, Isabella escalated the matter to the governor of Bologna, and insisted that he 'address this matter by whatever provision you understand is necessary'.[25] Isabella was willing to press the issue with whomever she needed in order to resolve the matter related to the most fundamental foodstuffs in her time.

A final important alimentary theme in Isabella's letters concerns the preparation and presentation of food at feasts and meals that Isabella attended. Feasts in the early modern era have provided fascinating insight into how elite diners expressed power through the food choices they made as hosts and guests.[26] Although the actual food and entertainments were ephemeral, descriptions of Renaissance banquets are a literary genre and preserved by works such as Bartolomeo Scappi's *Opera* (1570) and Cristoforo di Messisbugo's *Banchetti composizioni di vivande e apparecchio generale* (1549). Scappi and Messisbugo wrote about feasts from the perspective of cook and steward; in contrast, Isabella wrote about feasts in her letters from her viewpoint as a guest. As a member of the nobility, Isabella hosted and attended sumptuous banquets with other members of the highest echelons of Renaissance society. She would have dined on the most luxurious foods available, and this exclusivity of foods, preparations, and guests underscored her high status. In a letter to her husband of 23 March 1514, Isabella detailed the feasting during her visit to Salò, on the banks of Lake Garda:

> Under a loggia that borders on the lakeshore and over which is the salon of the house were tables loaded with baskets full of bread, Brasadella cake, apples, pears, grapes, boxes of candies, pine nut cakes, marzipan, *cera*, sugar, and plates of assorted fish in great quantity which these men presented to me with great long tributes and beautiful words, showing great fondness for Your Excellency.[27]

At Salò, Isabella could dine in a beautiful, relaxed locale on a wide variety of treats that were proffered at her welcome feast. Many contemporary descriptions of feasts focus on the entertainment, the setting, or the guests in attendance. For example, one feast hosted by Agostino Chigi, the richest man in Italy, which took place on 30 April 1518, was described as simply having 'plenty of food and luxurious fish [that was] provided for the reclining guests', which included cardinals and ambassadors.[28] It is revealing that Isabella listed the various foods served at the feast. Much as she had fine taste in antiquities, music, and fashion, she also had refined taste in foods, and wished to share the sumptuous details with her husband. The fruit offered was fitting for her noble status, while the cakes and candies were labour-intensive to prepare and usually contained the expensive ingredient of sugar. Thus, even the dainty marzipans and sweets served to Isabella at a lakeside meal reflect her social prestige and wealth.

Opulence at feasts could also be found in various forms of visual delights, such as one particular meal that was decorated with sugar sculptures which Isabella recounted to her secretary. In her letter to Benedetto Capilupi regarding a meal that she attended in 1514 in Naples, the birth town of her mother, Isabella wrote that the banquet lasted 'from noon until [one hour before sunset], and after countless and varied dishes, at the end each person was presented with certain different things made of sugar that were beautiful to see'.[29] Sugar sculptures were extremely elaborate and expensive objects, sometimes designed by leading artists; sugar could be gilded or coloured, and shaped into extravagant shapes like ancient gods or ships.[30] Their transient nature also added to the precious quality, as they could be eaten (in theory) or melted down to create a new, more lavish object at a future feast. To serve a meal with decorative sugar sculptures for guests flaunted not only the wealth of the host who served them, but also celebrated the diners, who enjoyed such delights.

To attend sumptuous feasts was a mark of power, but so too was the employ of a cook who could prepare such meals. Indeed, most elite households engaged numerous kitchen staff, including at least one head cook, and a steward to organize meals. Indeed, as Scappi outlined the hierarchy of a noble kitchen in his *Opera*, he noted that 'the Master Cook should have full authority – without, however, prejudicing the authority of the Master of the Household or of the Chief Steward – to engage and dismiss assistants, pastry workers, and scullions'.[31] Although most of the cooks who created the lavish banquets that Isabella and her equals attended remain unknown to us today, Isabella actually wrote about those who prepared her food in a pair of letters to her son, Ferrante, in February 1533. She wrote to her son to request that he send her favourite cook back to her. Previously, Isabella had sent Massimo the cook to serve her son whilst he was in Rome, but 'for some time now [she found herself] to be so lacking in appetite after the departure of Massimo, and [...] no cook has appeared who knows how to prepare anything that tastes good to me'. Isabella explained to her son that he 'does not need such delicacies, since he has the stomach of a young man and a soldier'.[32] In a letter of one week later, Isabella admitted that she could understand if Massimo the cook was reluctant to leave the great city of Rome to return to her service, but she noted that 'on account of this news, I suffer more than a little'.[33] Without the alimentary delights created by an accomplished cook, a ruler's appetite might suffer, and if he could not eat well, he could not rule well. By this period, however, Isabella was no longer in power, and thus she could send her prized cook to provide her adult son with a cook to help him eat and lead effectively.

The correspondence of Isabella d'Este provides unique glimpses into the complex relationship between food and power in the Renaissance, a time when what you ate and how you dined reflected your power and position in society. As her letters demonstrate, Isabella expressed her status through food in a variety of ways. Most prominently, she used food as diplomatic gifts with family, friends, and potential allies in order to solidify formal relations. While Isabella sent food gifts to her husband and other family members for personal reasons, she also sent food to leaders, such as the Holy Roman Emperor, for political reasons, including the maintenance of allegiances and to keep communication channels open. In addition, Isabella issued laws and edicts regarding food and food production to promote her interests and those of her subjects, including the cultivation of new crops like rice. Moreover, the luxurious feasts which Isabella had the privilege to attend highlighted her elevated position through the expensive ingredients and the labour-intensive methods used to prepare the meals that Isabella consumed. As her letters reveal, Isabella utilized food as a mode of self-fashioning; she asserted herself as a potent political leader, and above all as a woman of truly refined taste.

91

Notes

1 The food culture at the Gonzaga court has been explored broadly by Giancarlo Malacarne, *Sulla Mensa del Principe: alimentazione e banchetti alla Corte dei Gonzaga (Modena: Il Bulino edizioni d'arte*, 2000); however, his focus is not on the relationship between food and power in Isabella's letters.

2 On Isabella's use of cultural patronage, including literature, to promote herself, see Carolyn James, '"Machiavelli in Skirts": Isabella d'Este and Politics', in *Virtue, Liberty and Toleration: Political Ideas of European Women, 1400-1800*, ed. by Jacqueline Broad and Karen Green (Dordrecht: Springer, 2007), pp. 57-75.

3 Sarah Bercussen, 'Gift-Giving, Consumption and the Female Court in Sixteenth-Century Italy'

(unpublished doctoral thesis, Queen Mary College, London, 2009), p. 203.

4 Bercussen, p. 218.

5 Of the 830 letters published by Shemek, ninety-nine (over 10%) deal with alimentary themes.

6 Loek Luiten, 'Friends and Family, Fruit and Fish: The Gift in Quattrocento Farnese Cultural Politics', *Renaissance Studies*, 33.3 (May 2018), 342-57 (p. 357). In contrast, Bercussen maintains that in the late sixteenth century, it was primarily women who exchanged food gifts.

7 Letter from Isabella to Francesco II Gonzaga, 25 July 1495, in *Isabella d'Este: Selected Letters*, ed. and trans. by Deanna Shemek (Toronto: Iter Press; Tempe, Arizona: Arizona Center for Medieval and Renaissance Studies, 2017), pp. 76-77.

8 Letter from Isabella to Elisabetta Gonzaga, Duchess of Urbino, 23 November 1499, in Shemek, pp. 137-38.

9 Luiten, pp. 352-53.

10 Allen Grieco, 'The Social Politics of Pre-Linnaean Botanical Classification,' *I Tatti Studies in the Italian Renaissance*, 4 (1991), 131-49 (pp. 131-34).

11 Letter from Isabella to the Holy Roman Emperor (Maximilian I), 15 January 1510, in Shemek, pp. 314-315.

12 Shemek, p. 306.

13 Shemek, p. 314.

14 Bercussen, p. 219.

15 Letter from Isabella to the Vicar of Goito, 17 March 1496, in Shemek, p. 85.

16 Shemek, p. 226.

17 Letter from Isabella to Charles d'Amboise, 28 September 1503, in Shemek, pp. 226-27.

18 Letter from Isabella to the commissioner of Castiglione Mantovano, 30 August 1529, in Shemek, p. 527.

19 Rice had been cultivated in parts of northern Italy from at least 1475. See Diane Gherardo, 'Mediterranean Pathways: Exotic Flora, Fauna and Food in Renaissance Ferrara', *California Italian Studies*, 1.1 (2010), 1-11 (p. 1).

20 Shemek, p. 527.

21 Letter from Isabella to Alfonso Trotti, 20 September 1529, in Shemek, p. 527.

22 Letter from Isabella to the vice legate of Bologna, 25 October 1530, in Shemek, p. 541.

23 See Richard Goldthwaite, *The Buildings of Renaissance Florence: An Economic and Social History* (Baltimore: The Johns Hopkins University Press, 1980), pp. 346-47, qtd. in Ross King, *Leonardo and the Last Supper* (Toronto: Anchor Canada, 2012), p. 208.

24 Platina (Bartolomeo Sacchi), *On Right Pleasure and Good Health*, ed. and trans. Mary Ella Milham, Medieval and Renaissance Texts and Studies, 168 (Tempe, AZ: ACMRS Press, 1998), Book I, p. 16.

25 Letter from Isabella to the governor of Bologna, 30 December 1530, in Shemek, p. 545.

26 On the political nature of elite banquets during the Renaissance, see Ken Albala, *The Banquet: Dining in the Courts of Late Renaissance Europe* (Champaign, IL: University of Illinois Press, 2007), especially pp. 1-26.

27 Letter from Isabella to Francesco II Gonzaga, 23 March 1514, in Shemek, pp. 376-77.

28 Fabio Chigi, *Chigiae familiae commentarii* (1618), fols. 34r-v, qtd. in John Shearman, *Raphael in Early Modern Sources (1483-1602)*, 2 vols (New Haven: Yale University Press, 2003), vol. 1, pp. 335-37.

29 Letter from Isabella to Benedetto Capilupi, 8 December 1514, in Shemek, pp. 386-87.

30 For example, see June di Schino, 'The Triumph of Sugar Sculpture in Italy 1500–1700,' in *Look and Feel: Studies in Texture, Appearance and Incidental Characteristics of Food: Proceedings of the 1993 Oxford Symposium on Food and Cookery*, ed. by Harlan Walker (Totnes, U.K.: Prospect Books, 1994), pp. 203-06.

31 Bartolomeo Scappi and Terence Scully, *The Opera of Bartolomeo Scappi: L'arte Et Prudenza D'un Maestro Cuoco (The Art and Craft of a Master Cook)*, (Toronto: University of Toronto Press, 2008), Book I. 45, p. 131.

32 Letter from Isabella to Ferrante Gonzaga, 3 February 1533, in Shemek, p. 564.

33 Letter from Isabella to Ferrante Gonzaga, 11 February 1533, in Shemek, p. 564.

Food Production, Consumption, and Resistance by Japanese Americans Incarcerated by the United States Government During World War II

Paula I. Fujiwara

Introduction

Decades of anti-Japanese sentiment in the US, fuelled by racism and 'pro-American' business and political interests, reached a peak on 7 December 1941, after the bombing of Pearl Harbor in Hawaii by the Japanese government. In the ensuing months, mounting hysteria led President Franklin D. Roosevelt to issue Executive Order 9066 on 19 February 1942.[1] This paved the way for the eviction of approximately 122,000 people of Japanese ancestry – two thirds of whom were American citizens and one third of whom were children – from the west coast of the US and, ultimately, their incarceration in ten 'relocation camps' and other 'internment' and isolation facilities.[2] Authority was given to the Secretary of War and relevant agencies, primarily the newly created War Relocation Authority (WRA), to carry out the wholesale removal of these people to remote inland concentration camps away from the California coast (which was allegedly vulnerable to attack by Japanese military forces) and to furnish '[…] medical aid, hospitalization, food, clothing, transportation, use of land, shelter, and other supplies, equipment, utilities, facilities, and services'.[3]

The power dynamics of food production and consumption in the camps, informed by the resistance of the incarcerees, comprise three intertwined themes: most important, the relationship between the inmates and the WRA officials responsible for their care; second, the shifting power balance between *Issei* (first-generation immigrant) parents, and their *Nisei* (second-generation, US-born) children, caused by WRA's economic and political policies, as well as the physical layout of the camps; and third, the struggle between the American-born (mostly younger) citizen inmates given decision-making powers by WRA administrators, and the Japanese-born and/or educated cohort that did most of the low-rung kitchen work required to produce daily meals for the camp residents.

The Relationship Between the WRA Administrators and the Incarcerees

The dynamics of the relationship between WRA administrators and incarcerees were shaped in part by the physical layout of the concentration camps, particularly as it pertains to food production and consumption. The ten designated camps were scattered in isolated, inhospitable regions of the country.[4] Indeed, in most cases the camps became the predominant population centre of the surrounding area. They housed between 7318 (Granada) and 18,789 (Tule Lake) individuals in groupings called 'blocks' of approximately 12 to 14 military-style barracks, each measuring 120 x 20 feet and divided into four to six one-room units.[5] The barracks in each block accommodated approximately 250 to 300 people.[6] Families of up to three people were assigned 20 x 16-foot rooms, while the larger 20 x 25-foot units held up to seven individuals.[7] As the barracks had no plumbing, food preparation, bathing, laundry, and even toileting were done communally in specially outfitted rooms separate from the living quarters. All meals were taken in the block's mess hall, although incarcerees were not limited to eating in their own block, and some halls became favoured for the quality of their food.

A WRA Project Director ran each camp, supervising an all-Caucasian staff that was in turn in charge of the inmates. From the beginning of the incarceration, the WRA planned for community government, authorizing and encouraging ostensibly 'democratic', 'self-governing' community councils of elected representatives whose responsibilities were to provide guidance to the WRA director. Members were required to be US citizens, effectively making only the *Nisei* eligible, as the *Issei*, who had traditionally controlled decision-making, were barred from citizenship by US law.[8] Almost immediately, the council's ineffectiveness was exposed. The *Nisei* generally spoke little or no Japanese, and rumours proliferated that those favoured by the WRA were essentially '*inu*' (literally translated as 'dog' in Japanese, but used pejoratively for persons perceived to be informants and spies). The hitherto respected *Issei* elders, many of whom were parents of the *Nisei* councilmembers, were banned from participation, and the councils suffered from a lack of true authority, given that the WRA Director had ultimate veto power. In the end, the WRA administration was forced to use its parallel system of block managers (mainly *Issei* men nominated or elected by block residents), who were already in charge of block operations and were used to convey official information from the WRA Director's office and to enforce camp rules.[9]

The WRA also developed administrative guidelines for a Work Corps that encouraged all able-bodied adults to take on almost all the tasks needed to run the camps. While voluntary, a person who signed on agreed to 'certain definite obligations':

> *First* – He agrees to serve as a member of the Corps for the duration of the war, and for 14 days after the end of the war. *Second* – He swears or affirms that he will be loyal to the United States of America in thought, word and deed; that he will faithfully perform all tasks assigned him by the Authority; that he will accept in full payment for his service such cash and other allowances as may be provided by law or by regulations issued by the Authority [...]. Enlistment in the War Relocation Work Corps is accepted as a clear indication of the enlistee's patriotism and loyalty to the United States.[10]

The WRA also stressed the camps' self-sufficiency regarding food production. Inmates provided the day-to-day workforce to produce basic foods (planting and harvesting crops and caring for and butchering animals that provided meat). Pay ranged from $12 to $19 per month, deliberately kept below the pay scale for US soldiers, causing resentment over the inequity.[11] Although the incarcerees had a food allowance of 45 cents a day per person (versus 50 cents per day for an American soldier) and were subjected to the same rationing rules as the general public, the inmates were perceived by some as being coddled. In response, the WRA directors issued a decree that 'All centers were advised that at no time shall evacuees' food have higher specifications than or exceed in quantity what the civil population may obtain in the open market'. Each camp's director was 'also called upon (1) to see that all rationing regulations were strictly observed, (2) to submit their planned menus for each 30-day period to the Washington office for advance approval, and (3) to assume responsibility for accurately informing the public in the vicinity of the centers about WRA feeding policies and procedures'.[12] In spite of the Geneva Convention rules that required incarcerees to 'have the same rations as US soldiers in training', it was rationalized that daily food allowances could be less than the 45 cents per person because the inmate population included children and elderly, who did not consume as much food.[13]

Two key concepts of the Japanese psyche are resignation to life's vicissitudes, '*shikata ga nai*' ('it can't be helped') and '*gaman*' ('fortitude', 'tolerance', or 'perseverance'). However, despite this stereotype of 'passivity', inmates did resist their situation, often openly. Many of the inmates' complaints involved food – its quality, quantity, rationing rules, per-person expenditure, and diversion of food by WRA staff. Resistance took the form of petitions, work slowdowns, work and hunger strikes, and revolts.

Food Production in the Camps

The entrance of Japanese workers into the US agricultural economy that began in the late 1880s was driven by several factors: Japan's economic depression; the Chinese Exclusion Act of 1882, which prohibited the immigration of Chinese labourers to the US; and the need for a new workforce to cultivate and harvest labour-intensive crops. Though initially working as contract labourers, Japanese dominated the industry on the west coast by 1908. Immigrant leaders promoted their countrymen's transition from sojourners to permanent residents through their excellence at farming.[14] Japanese residents in California cultivated what was considered unproductive land and, despite controlling 'less than two percent of the state's total farmland before 1940, they produced a third or more of the state's truck crops, like fruits and vegetables'.[15]

From the earliest days of farming by the Japanese, envy surfaced in the white community, increasingly becoming a political issue, with multiple organizations attempting to curtail the perceived economic power of the Japanese.[16] Asians were deliberately barred from membership in the increasingly prominent American Federation of Labor.[17] The 1913 California Alien Land Law prohibited 'aliens ineligible for citizenship' from owning land and, later, even from leasing it.[18] The Japanese used various methods to circumvent these laws, such as forming corporations, using sympathetic white intermediaries, and obtaining deeds in the name of their American-born citizen children.[19]

Given the goal of the WRA to make the camps self-sufficient in food production, the wealth of experience of the incarcerated farmers was invaluable. One author posits that the site for what became the Tule Lake camp was chosen for 'the unique potential the area provided for agriculture on a huge scale. The other permanent centres were located in remote inhospitable areas where large scale agricultural operations were impossible' – the premise being that Tule Lake would provide food not only for its own inhabitants but also for the other camps. Some of the farm products were also sold on the open market (in direct contradiction to initial reassurances that this would not happen), yielding enormous profits for the WRA.[20]

Thus, the seasoned farmers who produced this bounty were relegated to becoming poorly paid government workers at $12/month; saw their highest-quality products, including chicken, eggs, and rationed pork, sold outside the camps; and were not allowed to share in the profits. Their manpower was so desperately needed that WRA authorities imposed fines of $20/month on able-bodied men refusing to work. At one point during the harvest, schools were closed so that students could be recruited.[21]

During the 1943 harvest season, grumblings continued regarding inadequate work clothing, equipment, food, and salaries. Tensions reached a peak when a truck carrying farmworkers to the field overturned, killing one man and injuring several others. Incarcerees organized to strike, confident of their negotiating position given the need for the timebound harvest to continue. They were soon outmanoeuvred by the WRA Director, who, to safeguard the crops, surreptitiously recruited incarcerees from other camps, paying them a dollar per hour instead of the eight cents that the Tule Lake camp workers received.[22] He also requisitioned food, including luxury items, for the offsite workers – an additional insult given the continual complaints about the inadequacy of mess hall meals. Outraged, the Tule Lake workers, led by a militant faction of incarcerees, attempted to negotiate with the WRA Director, who ignored their grievances, causing additional discontent among the general population. Early in November 1943, with thousands of dollars' worth of crops still awaiting harvest, the director declared martial law and called in the Army. Soldiers beat and arrested a group of men considered to be the main troublemakers, throwing them and eventually more than 200 other men into a stockade within the camp.[23]

In another example of the unequal power dynamics of camp life, incarcerees could be granted 'furloughs' outside the camps to harvest crops in danger of rotting in places such as Montana, Idaho, and Wyoming, which lacked local workers due to many opting to join the military. Even this was subject to the rules of the WRA including a requirement for the furloughed incarcerees to 'pay for the support of any dependents who may remain at Relocation Centers'.[24]

Food Preparation in the Camps

A dictionary definition of 'mess hall' is 'a large room where a particular group of people, especially members of the armed forces, eat meals together'.[25] It is no surprise that the term was used, given the War Department's responsibility for the planning of the camps.

Each block's mess hall was designed to serve approximately 300 people, although especially at the beginning of the incarceration, when camp construction had not been completed, this could mean handling 600 to 900 people in several shifts.[26] The sounding of a gong (or the banging together of pots and pans), called incarcerees to three cafeteria-style meals per day; people had to stand in long lines, in some instances without protection from the elements.

The quality of meals varied. Nationwide rationing was in effect, and although inmates were allocated a maximum of 45 cents per day, there were complaints that expenditures sometimes ran as low as 31 cents.[27] With the official WRA philosophy of self-sufficiency, costs went down as camps began to produce their own food supply; some sent their surplus to other camps, other government facilities, and the open market, although this last issue was not openly discussed.[28] In this context, incarcerees complained about inadequate amounts of food, especially for workers performing physical labour, but they also complained about a lack of variety and being given unfamiliar foods.[29]

Meals were prepared by people who were not necessarily trained cooks. The WRA released a monograph *The Relocation of Japanese Americans*, which can be accurately described as propaganda, to reassure the public that the inmates were being fed adequately, without special favours and within rationing restrictions.[30] In oral histories and written memoirs, inmates complained about the inadequacies of the diet; what one WRA official referred to as 'edible offal' was transposed by inmates as 'awful edibles'.[31] Some of their descriptions include:

> 'Often a meal consisted of rice, bread and macaroni, or beans, bread, and spaghetti. At one time we were served liver for several weeks, until we went on strike.'[32]

> 'I remember weenies. They were frozen, and when thawed out, part of it was green. I also remember smelt, mud shark, mutton and cow livers with big holes.'[33]

> '[W]einers [*sic*], dry fish, rice, macaroni, and pickled vegetables [...] Meatless days were regular at some centers – two or three times a week [...].'[34]

While such memories could be seen as misrepresentative, a US Army psychiatrist sent to Poston camp in Arizona as a government analyst confirmed their claims:

> Although the meals varied a good deal from one block to another they were in general very poor, lacking in variety, insufficient in quantity and not at all comparable to Army rations [...]. There was no adequate means of feeding infants and small children if the parents did not have the money to purchase their specialties and the situation was similar for invalids who required diets.[35]

In time, the incarcerees' tables were supplemented with produce from the camp farms and with food 'projects' under the Work Corps scheme implemented to develop products more acceptable to the Japanese palate, such as soy sauce, bean curd, and bean sprouts.[36]

Despite the privations experienced by the inmates, holiday dinners could be special. For Tule Lake's 1943 New Year's day celebration, the breakfast included the traditional dish to start the new year: *ohzoni*, a soup with chicken, vegetables, and a *mochi* (rice cake) 'dumpling'; the official WRA dinner was described using Japanese terms: 'Osakana – Pompana (*sic*) Fish; Onishime – Pork-Vegetables; Namasu – Daikon--Carrots; Kinton – Sweet Lima Beans; Kanten – Strawberry Gelatin; Mikan – Orange; Gohan – Blue Rose Rice'.[37] However, in Idaho's Minidoka camp, after the initial year's Thanksgiving celebration, where turkeys were provided by camp officials, interest and fervour among the inmates decreased in the following years as WRA promotion of the holiday dwindled, and the camp administrators focused on moving incarcerees to eastern states and making males subject to the military draft, despite their families remaining incarcerated.[38]

In the middle of the war, the US government, using a 'loyalty' questionnaire, forcibly removed inmates and their families deemed troublemakers to Tule Lake, which was rechristened as the only Segregation Center among the ten camps. A riot related to food production issues led to rioters being imprisoned (without being formally charged) in a stockade within the Center, where one prisoner kept a meticulous diary of every meal over the four months of his confinement. After initial meals that were an improvement over the usual mess hall fare, the quantity and quality of food declined as more people were locked up:

98

Thursday, November 25, 1943 – Thanksgiving in the stockade
Morning: 2 pieces of bread, coffee
Lunch: spaghetti, rice, tea
Dinner: rice, cabbage mixed with weenie, carrot
Today is Thanksgiving. Eating turkey is customary but was turkey on the menu? We hoped in vain.

Across the fence is the army mess hall (it's the same mess hall we ate in during our first three days of imprisonment in the stockade). We saw turkey after turkey being brought into the army mess hall. One soldier even held a turkey up for all of us in the stockade to see. What a cheap stunt pulled by a heartless person.

During lunch, we laughingly imagined the spaghetti as white meat and the weenies as dark meat.

The food they've been giving us recently is so sparse that it is barely enough to keep us from starving.[39]
Tuesday, November 30, 1943
Morning: hot cake, coffee
Lunch: rice, salt, tea

Dinner: rice, mackerel, tea

The amount of food is getting less, and the quality, getting poorer. This afternoon we ate a portion of rice too small to even feed a cat. Someone finally spoke up and said, 'We need to bring our complaints to the authorities and negotiate better treatment.'[40]

Eventually, in revolt against deteriorating conditions and inability to negotiate with the camp authorities, the 199 incarcerated men went on a hunger strike that lasted seven days.[41]

In addition to feeding the inmates, the mess halls served as community nerve centres and gathering spots for camp news, WRA information meetings, receptions, church services, film screenings, dances, exhibitions, and sales events. But they also were venues of resistance and contention, serving as places to plan protests against food shortages.[42] In the most significant example of their key role, during the winter and spring of 1943 they were used in all ten camps to hotly debate how to answer questions 27 and 28 on the infamous 'loyalty' questionnaire. *Nisei* men had to answer 'yes' or 'no' as to whether they were willing to serve in the US military (despite being imprisoned), and all adults were asked if they would pledge unqualified allegiance to the United States and renounce their loyalty to the Emperor of Japan. Poorly worded, the questionnaire raised resentment, resistance, and protest and ripped families apart when members voted in opposite ways.[43]

Erosion of Family Life

The initial wave of Japanese immigration (1885-1907) consisted mainly of labourers whose objective was to work abroad temporarily and return home after amassing capital. The second wave (1908-1924, when Japanese immigration was halted by the U.S government) was distinguished by the entry of women as 'picture brides', which led to families with American-born children who were automatically citizens thanks to the US birthright law.[44]

As a traditionally patriarchal society, the father dominated family life and was always accorded preferential treatment.[45] At the dinner table, he was served first, followed by the sons, then daughters, and finally the wife.[46] As the children became educated in American schools, learned English, and had the citizen-based right to purchase land and homes, they often became their parents' interlocutors with 'white society'.

Incarceration in the camps exacerbated and accelerated the change in family power dynamics. The cramped communal living conditions, minimal salary differences between parent and child, and the WRA-imposed rules stipulating that only US citizens could serve on community councils, undermined the authority and disciplinary power of the parents, particularly the fathers. Since all meals were prepared and served in communal mess halls, the women – the traditional preparers of food – gained a form of independence from this and other domestic tasks.[47] One important negative consequence was that the concept of the family meal disintegrated. Multiple written sources, oral histories, and interviews highlight the fact that children, especially teenagers, chose to eat with friends, despite an attempt to provide family tables in the mess halls.[48] Children and teenagers (as well as adults) sought out the halls serving the best meals, and they were able to eat multiple times as they roamed the various halls. Even the type of food offered could be a point of dissension. Although various camps eventually produced such Japanese staples as soy sauce, bean sprouts, miso paste, and tofu (as well as illegal sake), one early survey in Tule Lake reported that 65% of the inmates (assumed to be the younger *Nisei*) preferred American food over Japanese dishes.[49]

Tensions Among the Inmates

Disagreements around food-related issues also manifested among the inmates. The main power struggle was between the incarcerees who supported the Japanese American Citizens League (JACL) and those who favoured the traditional Japanese patterns of community leadership and consensus. The JACL was initially formed in 1929 as an umbrella group of already existing Japanese-American organizations, with membership restricted to US citizens. JACL members espoused a form of hyperpatriotism that accelerated during WWII, to the point of their informing on, and denouncing, fellow Japanese they felt were disloyal to the US They even favoured being allowed to volunteer for military service as a proof of loyalty of Japanese Americans. Within the camps, pro-JACL inmates were favoured by the WRA authorities, and they were the ones on the community councils, with a direct link to and relative influence on the WRA.[50]

Pro-JACL inmates excluded from membership and often labelled as dissidents the *Issei* and a group known as *Kibei* – Japanese born in the US, and thus American citizens, but raised in Japan for schooling. Most of the *Issei* and *Kibei* spoke English poorly and were often felt to be more aligned with Japan than with the US. In every camp, mess hall workers were mainly *Kibeis* and the elderly who could not get jobs elsewhere. In Manzanar, clashes between the pro- and anti-JACL factions were particularly intense throughout the summer of 1942. When pro-JACL leaders were defeated in an election by *Issei* and *Kibei*, camp officials intervened by strictly enforcing an earlier WRA ruling that only US citizens could hold elective office. They commissioned an all-*Nisei* group to draft charter rules, further inflaming the divide. In the fall of 1942, a *Kibei* cook's assistant, Harry Ueno, organized the 1500 mess workers (almost half of the entire Manzanar workforce of 4000) into a WRA-sanctioned (at least initially) Kitchen Workers' Union in hopes of collectively bringing the mess hall workers' concerns to the WRA administration. After noticing the lack of sugar (an item regulated by ration coupons during the war) in the mess halls while it was plentiful in the WRA staff dining areas, Ueno documented, through interviews and considerable independent investigation, that 'My figures were that up to September 30 more than 20,000 pounds were short. In October alone, the administration admitted a 6,100-pound shortage'.[51] Based on reports from internal camp police who witnessed sacks of sugar in the trunk of the widely disliked Assistant WRA Director when he drove out of the camp, Ueno accused him of stealing the sugar, as well as meat, and fruit and cookies meant for school children's snacks, to sell on the black market. The continued discontent around food, and the tensions caused by the WRA administration's favouring of the JACL group, led to the so-called 'Manzanar Riot', more properly described as a revolt.[52] The violence culminated in the death of two inmates, injuries (some of them severe) to nine others, and the arrest and removal of the alleged perpetrators without due process to isolated prison camps.[53]

Conclusion

Writ large, this shameful period of systematic government malfeasance took away people's livelihoods; stole businesses, land, homes, equipment, and other personal goods; decimated thriving communities; destroyed family solidarity; and stigmatized and shamed a people until they questioned their sense of self-worth. This paper shows how WRA policies shaped food production and consumption and describes the instances of inmates' resistance and its enduring memories. Both contribute to the Japanese-American communities' nationwide yearly recognition every 19 February of a 'Day of Remembrance' that marks the issuance of Executive Order 9066, and the battle in the current broader 'Never Again Is Now' movement against oppression of any kind, but particularly against the use of food as a weapon.

Notes

1   Executive Order 9066. 19 February 1942, in *Federal Register*, 7.38 (25 February 1942) <http://www.ourdocuments.gov/doc.php?flash=false&doc=74&page=transcript> [accessed 12 May 2019].

2   Brian Niiya, 'Common Myths of WWII Incarceration: "More Than Half Were Children"' *Densho*, 21 June 2016 <https://densho.org/common-myths-wwii-incarceration-half-children/June 21, 2016> [accessed 12 May 2019]; Roger Daniels. 'Words Do Matter: A Note on Inappropriate Terminology and the Incarceration of the Japanese Americans', in *Nikkei in the Pacific Northwest: Japanese Americans and Japanese Canadians in the Twentieth Century*, ed. by L. Fisnet and G. Nomura (Seattle: University of Washington Press, 2005): pp. 183-207; 'Sites of Incarceration', *Densho Encyclopedia*, 25 June 2012, 22:19 UTC, <https://encyclopedia.densho.org/Sites%20of%20incarceration/> [accessed 20 May 2019]. While several are mentioned in this paper, discussion concentrates on Manzanar, site of the 'Manzanar Riot', and Tule Lake, which was turned into a more restricted Segregation Center in the middle of the war.

3   Executive Order 9066.

4   Harlan D. Unrau, *The Evacuation and Relocation of Persons of Japanese Ancestry During World War II: A Historical Study of the Manzanar War Relocation Center,* Historic Resource Study/Special History Study, 2 vols. (Washington, DC: United States Department of the Interior, National Park Service, 1996), pp. 98-100.

5   Bonnie Clark, 'Amache (Granada)', *Densho Encyclopedia*, 25 June 2012, 22:19 UTC <https://encyclopedia.densho.org/Amache%20(Granada)/> [accessed 3 May 2019]; Barbara Takei, 'Tule Lake', *Densho Encyclopedia* 25 June 2012, 22:19 UTC <https://encyclopedia.densho.org/Tule%20Lake/> [accessed 3 May 2019].

6   Brian Niiya, 'Block', *Densho Encyclopedia*, 25 June 2012, 22:19 UTC <https://encyclopedia.densho.org/Block/> [accessed 12 May 2019].

7   Mei T. Nakano and Grace Shibata, *Japanese American Women: Three Generations, 1890-1990* (Berkeley, CA: Mina Press, 1990), pp. 142-45; Commission on Wartime Relocation and Internment of Civilians

(CWRIC), *Personal Justice Denied: Report of the Commission on Wartime Relocation and Internment of Civilians* (Seattle: University of Washington Press and Washington D.C.: Civil Liberties Public Education Fund, 1997), p. 158; for typical physical layout of the camps, see Unrau, pp.103-05.

8   Michi Weglyn, *Years of Infamy: The Untold Story of America's Concentration Camps* (Seattle: University of Washington Press, 1996), pp.119-21; Brian Niiya, 'Community Councils', *Densho Encyclopedia*, 25 June 2012, 22:19 UTC <https://encyclopedia.densho.org/Community%20councils/> [accessed 12 May 2019].

9   Niiya, 'Community Councils' (ultimately, the WRA in its final report conceded that community councils had been fraught with resistance and inconsistencies); Brian Niiya, 'Block Managers', *Densho Encyclopedia*, 25 June 2012, 22:19 UTC <https://encyclopedia.densho.org/Block%20managers/> [accessed 12 May 2019].

10 War Relocation Authority, *The War Relocation Work Corps, a Circular of Information for Enlistees and Their Families a Pamphlet Issued by the War Relocation Authority for Japanese-Americans Interned during World War II* (Washington D.C: War Relocation Authority, 1942), pp. 8-9 <https://digitalcollections. lib.washington.edu/digital/collection/pioneerlife/id/13694> [accessed 12 May 2019].

11 War Relocation Authority, *Relocation of Japanese Americans* (Washington D.C.: United States Government Printing Office, 1943), p. 8.

12 J. A. Krug and D. S. Myer, *WRA: A Story of Human Conservation* (Washington, D.C.: United States Government Printing Office, 1946), p. 102.

13 Russell Bearden, 'Life Inside Arkansas's Japanese-American Relocation Centers', *Arkansas Historical Quarterly*, 68 (Summer 1989), 169-96 (p. 186); Krug, p. 101.

14 Yuji Ichioka, *The Issei: The World of the First Generation Japanese Immigrants, 1885-1924* (New York: The Free Press, 1988), p. 80; Ichioka, pp. 3,5.

15 Heart Mountain WWII Japanese American Confinement Site, 'History – Before the War: Issei and Nisei Pursue the American Dream' <http://www.heartmountain.org/beforethewar> [accessed 12 May 2019].

16 Edwin E. Ferguson, 'The California Alien Land Law and the Fourteenth Amendment', *Calif. L. Rev.*, 35 (1947), 61-90 (pp. 69-70) <https://doi.org/10.15779/Z38221W>.

17 Ichioka, p. 91.

18 Ferguson, pp. 66-69, 70.

19 Cherstin Lyon, 'Alien Land Laws', *Densho Encyclopedia*, 25 June 2012, 22:19 UTC <https://encyclope-dia.densho.org/Alien%20land%20laws/> [accessed 5 May 2019].

20 Michael David Schmidli, '"Railcars Loaded With Crisp Fresh Vegetables": A Study of Agriculture at the Tule Lake Relocation Center 1942-1946' (unpublished master's thesis, Portland State University, 2008) <https://doi.org/10.15760/etd.2932> pp. 1-161 (p.1 of abstract, pp. 61,68).

21 Schmidli, pp. 119, 56-57, 62.

22 Schmidli, pp. 124, 126.

23 Takei, 'Tule Lake'.

24 'Harvest Season Calls for Laborers: Recruiting Procedures', *The Daily Tulean Dispatch*, 24 August 1942 <https://digitalcommons.wou.edu/tuldispatch/10> [accessed 12 May 2019]; Work Corps, p. 9.

25 *Webster's New World College Dictionary*, 4th ed. (Houghton Mifflin Harcourt, 2010) <https://<www. collinsdictionary.com/dictionary/english/mess-hall> [accessed 12 May 2019].

26 CWRIC, p. 160.

27 CWRIC, p. 163.

28 Unrau, p. 399; CWRIC, p. 168; Jane Dusselier, 'Does Food Make Place? Food Protests in Japanese American Concentration Camps', in *Food and Foodways*, 10 (2002), 137-165 (p. 155) <https://doi. org/10.1080/07409710213923>; Bearden, p. 177; Schmidli, p. 68.

29 Nakano, p. 144.

30 War Relocation Authority. Relocation of Japanese Americans, p. 7.

31 Nakano, p. 144.

32 Miné Okubo, *Citizen 13660* (Seattle: University of Washington Press, 2014), p. 143.

33 Noboru Shirai, *Tule Lake: An Issei Memoir* (Sacramento: Uteki Press, 2001), p. 216.

34 CWRIC, p. 163.

35 Alexander Leighton, *The Governing of Men* (Princeton: Princeton University Press, 1968), p. 116.

36 Unrau, p. 436

37 'Official WRA New Year Day Menu', *The Daily Tulean Dispatch*, 1 January 1943, p. 19 <https://digital-commons.wou.edu/tuldispatch/19> [accessed 12 May 2019].

38 Andrew Dunn, 'Barbed Wire Christmas: Holidays and Incarcerated Japanese Americans', *Activist History Review*, 2017 <https://activisthistory.com/2017/12/08/barbed-wire-christmas-holidays-and-incarcerated-japanese-americans/#_ftn4> [accessed 12 May 2019].

39 Tatsuo Ryusei Inouye, 'Chapter 3, More Prisoners', *Tule Lake Stockade Diary, November 13, 1943-February 14, 1944*, 1-12, pp. 5-6 <http://www.suyamaproject.org/?p=721> [accessed 12 May 2019].

40 Inouye, 'Chapter 4, Nothing to Eat', 1-10, p. 1.

41 Inouye, 'Chapter 11, Hunger Strike', 1-13, p. 7; 'Chapter 12, Debating Whether to End Hunger Strike', 1-6, p. 1; 'Chapter 13, End of the Hunger Strike', 1-8, p. 4.

42 Dusselier, p. 148.

43 Cherstin Lyon, 'Loyalty questionnaire', *Densho Encyclopedia*, 25 June 2012, 22:19 UTC <https://ency-clopedia.densho.org/Loyalty%20questionnaire/> [accessed 12 May 2019].

44 Ichioka, pp. 3-5.

45 Nakano, p. 34.

46 Harry H. L. Kitano, *Japanese-Americans: The Evolution of a Subculture*, second ed. (Englewood Cliffs, NJ: Prentice-Hall, 1976), pp. 70-71.

47 Nakano, pp. 62-63.

48 Unrau, p. 568.

49 'Tuleans Prefer American Food', *Daily Tulean Dispatch*, 31 July 1942, in *Tule Lake Directory and Camp News*, ed. by Harry Inukai (Hood River Oregon: Inukai Publishing, 1983), p. 182; Unrau, p. 399.

50 Cherstin Lyon, 'Japanese American Citizens League', *Densho Encyclopedia*, 25 June 2012, 22:19 UTC <https://encyclopedia.densho.org/Japanese%20American%20Citizens%20League/> [accessed 3 May 2019].

51 Kulberg Mitson, in *Resisters*, Part IV of Japanese American World War II Evacuation Oral History Project, ed. by Arthur A. Hansen (Munich: K. G. Saur, 1995): pp. 1-67 <http://www.oac.cdlib.org/view?docId=ft1f59n61r;NAAN=13030&doc.view=frames&chunk.id=d0e336&toc.depth=1&toc.id=&brand=oac4> [accessed 3 May 2019]; 'Sugar Situation Explained to Group', *Manzanar Free Press*, 2.53 (21 November 1942) <http://ddr.densho.orgddr-densho-125-11/> [accessed 11 May 2019]. In the article, the Acting Project Director, speaking to a special session of the Block Managers' Assembly, stated that the shortage was due to the receipt of 14,290 lbs of sugar, although it had requisitioned 20,392 lbs, and 'presumed that the shortages will be made up in November'.

52 Arthur A. Hansen, 'The Manzanar 'Riot': An Ethnic Perspective', in *Barbed Voices: Oral History, Resistance, and the World War II Japanese American Social Disaster* (Louisville, CO: University of Colorado Press, 2018), pp. 29-88 (p. 43).

53 Brian Niiya, 'Manzanar Riot/Uprising', *Densho Encyclopedia*, 25 June 2012, 22:19 UTC <https://ency-clopedia.densho.org/Manzanar%20riot/uprising/> [accessed 12 May 2019].

The Muckamuck: Restaurants, Labour, and the Power of Representation

L. Sasha Gora

'Sun dried chopped seaweed', 'Indian style smoked salmon', and 'Cold raspberry soup'. One side of the postcard-size menu shows baskets and wooden bowls decorated with carvings, shaped like animals and bursting with bread, fish, and greens.[1] Amongst a tableau of green vegetables and plants, baskets of white bread and clamshells, and different shades of wood, the yellow sticks out. The photograph's backside lists Muckamuck Restaurant's menu from circa 1975. 'Northwest Coast Native Indian Food' introduces the dishes that were once served at this Vancouver restaurant. In addition to 'Indian style smoked salmon', the menu lists a 'Wind and sun dried salmon appetizer' and fresh salmon that is 'barbecued over open alder fires'. Oolichans and trout are also on offer, as well an assortment of shellfish: oysters, clams, prawns, and crab. The 'Indian bannock bread' is 'baked fresh daily'.

As far as menus go, Muckamuck Restaurant's is rather sparse. Although the image depicts some plates, they are too small to glean any details beyond that a lemon is likely to accompany the fish. Instead, the photograph aims to visually signify 'Northwest Coast Native Indian Food'. That the dishes were photographed outside in a 'natural' setting and presented in carved vessels signify their 'Nativeness'. But how is the 'Watercress and spinach salad' dressed? Do the 'Pan fried oolichans' come with a side, or should one perhaps order the 'Sweet potato with roasted hazelnuts'? What is 'Indian tea'? This is a menu that needs a server. It is the server's task to announce the soup of the day and to explain what 'Indian tea' is.

Muckamuck Restaurant opened in Vancouver in 1971. It was one of the first, if not the first, Indigenous-themed restaurants in urban Canada. And it was popular: Andy Warhol ate there in 1976.[2] In addition to listing the dishes on offer, the menu indicates the Muckamuck is licensed, open seven days a week, and located on Davie Street. In fact, the history of Indigenous restaurants in Vancouver begins with this one address. 1724 Davie Street consecutively housed three different restaurants – first the Muckamuck Restaurant, from 1971 to 1981, then the Quilicum, which opened in 1985, and finally the Liliget Feast House, from 1995 to 2007. A condo building now stands at the same address, a rather typical Vancouver story.

Muckamuck Restaurant closed in 1981 due to a labour dispute. A 12 August 1978 newspaper photograph shows Debbie Mearns, the president of the Vancouver Indian Centre and a law student at the University of British Columbia (UBC), together with Christine Prince.[3] Behind them a man holds a sign: 'Doug deals from the bottom'. 'Doug' refers to Doug Christmas, one of the restaurant's owners. A woman to his left, Ethel Gardner, carries a sign with a photograph of Doug and the word 'Joker'. Another protester carries the sign, 'Walk the Muckamuck Walk. Sign a 1st Contract. SORWUC Local'. SORWUC stands for the Service, Office, and Retail Workers' Union of Canada, 'an independent, grassroots, socialist-feminist union', and one the Muckamuck employees joined. As one employee explained, 'racial issues emerged when employees realized that the owners were getting rich off Native culture'.[4] This labour dispute is the subject of writer, educator, and unionist Janet Mary Nicol's 1997 article '"Unions Aren't Native": The Muckamuck Restaurant Labour Dispute', as well as historian Julia Smith's 'An "Entirely Different" Kind of Union: The Service, Office, and Retail Workers' Union of Canada (SORWUC)'.[5] Unlike the Quilicum and the Liliget Feast House, Muckamuck was not Indigenous-owned, which is why I categorize it as 'Indigenous-themed'. Despite Muckamuck's policy of hiring Indigenous staff, the owners themselves were not Indigenous. As Nicol reveals, 'Three white American owners, Jane Erickson, Teresa Bjornson and Doug Christmas also had investments in art galleries and other restaurants in California and British Columbia'.[6] Early in the strike, however, Bjornson sold her shares.

An Edible Exhibition
So why did 'three white American owners' decide to open the Muckamuck, what was most likely Canada's only Indigenous-themed restaurant at the time? A July 1972 *Ottawa Journal* article states, 'Muck-a-Muck House started as an art gallery but soon turned into a work of culinary art'. Teresa Bjornson, a gallery employee, helped to transform the Ace Gallery's basement into a 'unique' restaurant. '"We just wanted to get some things together for an exhibit of Indian foods,"' she explained. But the gallery ran into issues with the Vancouver licensing department, and so '[f]rom there it was a short step to turning the basement into a restaurant'.[7] In the first couple of years it was called the Muck-a-Muck House (it is not clear when the article appeared and the hyphens and word 'house' disappeared from its name). In addition to Bjornson, another article mentions Jane Erickson as having co-started the restaurant and identifies both as former ballerinas.[8] Although Doug Christmas, who was actually born in Vancouver, owned the Ace Gallery, which backed the Muckamuck, his name does not appear in any of these articles. In any case, the gallery came first, then the idea for an exhibition of 'Indian foods', and, finally, its institutionalization as a restaurant.

The word 'muckamuck' comes from nineteenth century Chinook Jargon – also called Chinook Wawa – a pidgin language mixing Nuu-chah-nulth, Lower Chinook, Salishan, other Indigenous languages, English, and French. *The Canadian Encyclopedia* translates muckamuck as meaning a lot of food, but also compares it to the term 'highmuckymuck'.[9] The *Oxford English Dictionary* identifies muckamuck as a shortening of high muck-a-muck, which, ironically, means 'A person of great importance or self-importance'.[10] Today, the most common version of the word is 'muckety-muck'.[11] *The Canadian Enyclopedia* hypothesizes that highmuckymuck references 'someone who sits at head table'.[12] Just like the staged outdoor photograph of the Muckamuck dishes, the restaurant's name aims to signify its 'Nativeness'.

Before the restaurant could open, Bjornson and Erickson had to define the food they intended to serve: 'Indian food'. As the *Ottawa Journal* explains, '"Not many of the local Indian people keep up the traditional cooking," said Miss Bjornson. "We went through the whole province trying to get recipes typical of many tribes." Traditional cooking implements were also in short supply. "They don't make them any more [...] Things like boiling baskets are almost extinct".' Bjornson's account suggests that it was simply a choice to 'keep up' traditional cooking, which overlooks the history of regulations promoting assimilation and restricting the continuity of Indigenous foodways. Bjornson matter-of-factly announced: '"Many of the original Indian dishes just aren't done these days."'[13] In addition to playing culinary researchers on reserves, Bjornson and Erickson consulted an anthropologist and a botanist at the University of British Colombia and read 'a detailed old report of American Indian ethnology'.[14] If the Muckamuck owners were aware of the cultural responsibility of representing a cuisine, let alone someone else's, the articles suggest otherwise. The press largely viewed the restaurant's decision to hire Indigenous employees as a commitment to authenticity. This, however, omits the power dynamic of white owners – those writing the paycheques and drafting the menu – and Indigenous employees. But beyond lending the Muckamuck an air of 'authenticity', hiring Indigenous staff also provided economic benefits. The Muckamuck management hired employees through the Canada Manpower Training Program, 'offering to "train" First Nations people to work in the restaurant and, in return, received 75 per cent of the trainee's wages from the government'.[15]

In 1972 the restaurant did not have a menu; instead, it listed dishes on a blackboard and erased any that ran out. The Muckamuck demanded that its ingredients be local and used regional berries, such as salmonberries, salal, wild blueberries, black currants, and elderberries. What the restaurant was not able to gather or pick, it claimed to purchase from 'local Indians', including fish. But Bjornson identified sourcing ingredients as a challenge: '"Dried meat and dried fish were too difficult to come by"'. The restaurant was also restricted by which foods were legal. Bjornson explained, '"We know of a man who could supply us with all the mountain goat we could eat – but we're not allowed to serve it."'[16]

Government regulations affected not only what was allowed to be on a plate, but also the plate itself. '"Naturally we wanted wooden dishes and big serving bowls, in the traditional style. But the department of health said no way – wood is frowned upon because it can't be thoroughly cleaned,"' explained Bjornson. This leads this one reviewer to conclude: 'So Muck-a-Muck House is a little more like an ordinary restaurant and a little less traditional.'[17] Either the regulations changed – or were ignored – because in 1975 helpings were 'lavishly arrayed in large wooden bowls individually created by Indian woodcarvers of British Columbia'.[18] These wooden vessels are the ones the 1975 menu depicts. But by 1977, the hand carved wood bowls were off the table, although goat was now on it. Writing for *The Province*, restaurant critic and Muckamuck regular James Barber crowned the goat ribs 'the finest, gamiest tasting chops – the taste of smoke, rosemary, a wild night in the forest, it's dark and "we've only just got the fire going." Me Tarzan. You Jane'.[19] His praise is over the top, but also typical of the cultural stereotypes that snuck into restaurant reviews at the time.

Early press generally emphasized the restaurant's story, but in 1975 critic Sheila McCook prioritized its food. She ranked the soups – duck, salmon, and clam chowder – 'superb starting points for any meal' and described the first courses as 'hefty'. Labelling the restaurant's vegetable repertoire as 'familiar and exotic', she went on to list 'roasted hazelnuts, steamed fernshoots, dill carrots and cucumber, corn on the cob, boiled onions'. Minus the corn and the onions, these are similar options to Muckamuck's 1975 menu. Out of the bunch, fernshoots were presumably an example of the 'exotic' since they were less popular restaurant fare at the time. Another dish McCook considered exotic enough to have to spell out to her readers was made from soapberries. It appeared on the 1975 menu as 'Hot homemade applesauce with cream soapolallie (special Indian dessert known as Indian ice cream)'. McCook compared them in taste to huckleberries and described how they are 'whipped up with sugar into a tasty froth'. On their own, soapberries are bitter; the sugar tames their bitterness and transforms them into an acceptable dessert. McCook also mentions, 'There's juniper berry tea for those who like to polish off their meal with authenticity.'[20] This answers the question of what Indian tea is, but also reveals the value of authenticity for diners like McCook. In addition to what the 1975 postcard menu listed, other dishes came and went: the likes of pickled burdock root, juniper duck, herring eggs, and barbecued oysters.

Some ingredients, like 'grease', were pushed to the menu's margins. McCook explained: 'Grease is extracted from oolichan, a fish, and offered as a side dish for those preferring their soup authentic, if oily. It's optional, as is the sun-dried seaweed, to be sprinkled on food for a flavorful, salty effect'.[21] To make this seasoning optional is to compromise, to cater to cultural expectations. Thus, oolichan, a smelt-like fish also known as candlefish, raises the issue of taste: who can stomach what and how to navigate discrepancies between one diner's delicious and another's disgust. Another review spells out the restaurant's decision to offer grease on the side:

> Why not offer their customers a nice authentic soup flavored with the grease rendered from the oily little fish called the oolichan? No, their Indian cook warned them. They wouldn't like it. Oh yes, the two white women said, they would. So the cook made the soup with the oolichan grease and the women took a spoonful and they've never tried its sharp fishy flavor again.[22]

As most diners at the Muckamuck would have been unfamiliar with grease, to offer it on the side allowed the curious the chance to try it, without forcing them out of their culinary comfort zone.

McCook's review also points to the important role the servers played. In addition to taking orders and bringing food to the table, they acted as ambassadors of sorts. This is not true of all restaurants, but when a menu is sparse or a dish or cuisine unfamiliar to a customer it is the server's job to mediate. As McCook wrote, 'Almost everyone who comes to the Muck-a-Muck has questions to ask and the employees, all Indians, take the time to explain how each dish is cooked, what it tastes like, even how to eat it. They assist in making choices from the menu, encouraging the adventurous while steering more timid diners toward the European-like dishes.'[23] The servers not only explained the menu, but also educated diners about their 'exotic' Northwest Coast Native cuisine.

In the end, McCook recommended the Muckamuck. In addition to her own approval, she mentioned other positive reviews: 'The Muck-a-Muck is "one of the most interesting restaurants in Vancouver," according to Anne Hardy.'[24] Diners approved too, but beyond tourists and locals who are not likely to order grease even on the side, McCook stressed that 'Indian groups' have also given the Muckamuck their enthusiastic approval. Another article repeated this sentiment: 'And the restaurant is genuine enough that the Union of B.C. Indian Chiefs meeting in Vancouver recently held a dinner at the Muckamuck'.[25] That Indigenous diners also approved made it on to the reviewers' list of criteria by which they proclaimed the restaurant authentic.

A Restaurant Called Unique

With ten tables, 'similar to large picnic tables', the restaurant was mid-sized and, because it did not take reservations, diners frequently lined up.[26] Despite being located underneath an art gallery, the Muckamuck was bright. Fascinatingly, one review pointed out, at first glance many customers visually registered the restaurant as Japanese: 'This is because the cedar dining tables are at a low level over scooped-out wells where diners dangle their feet'.[27] This tellingly reveals that customers would have been familiar with Japanese restaurant décor, and less familiar with what a 'Native' restaurant might look like. So what did this 'Native' restaurant look like? Small stones covered the floor. The crunching sounds of people walking between tables gave the Muckamuck a soundtrack similar to a beach, layered over the actual musical soundtrack that alternated between 'Indian chants and country and western'.[28] Cans emptied of salmon and filled with sand served as ashtrays, contributing to the 'lost-in-the-forest picnicky' atmosphere.[29] Fir poles stood tall like totem poles.[30] 'Colourful ceremonial blankets' draped the walls. They were decorated with buttons arranged to resemble an eagle and a bear. The rest of the restaurant's colours were 'subdued' and 'natural'. Partially visible from the dining area, the kitchen provided further visual décor: cooks 'slowly turning their fish, meat and fowl over alderwood cinders'.[31]

From its food to its décor, the word 'unique' – and its relative 'unusual' – comes up repeatedly. In 1974, the *National Post* called it 'Delicious and highly unusual, even to the smoked salmon bellies and raspberry soup'.[32] Dave Brown called the Muckamuck 'an unusual place'. Despite being overwhelmed by the 'gargantuan' portions and having ordered too much – salad, clam chowder, barbecued salmon and the 'hot, spicy, and potent' 'Indian answer to Irish coffee' –Brown positively concluded his review: 'A different and thoroughly enjoyable evening'.[33]

News of the Muckamuck even travelled south of the border. Robert Trumbull, formerly the chief *New York Times* Canada correspondent, recommended it in a June 1977 article. 'Tops as a personal favourite', he wrote.[34] In the 1970s it certainly was not every day that a restaurant in Canada made American headlines, but Barber was not pleased. He blamed long lines on the fact that 'a couple of years ago *Time Magazine* discovered the Muckamuck and all those expense accounts from Toronto, Chicago and Los Angeles went and told all the other expense accounts'. Nonetheless, Barber exclaimed Muckamuck as 'the sort of restaurant we can all be proud of, without *Time Magazine*'s accolades'.[35]

The Line

In 1978, *The Minneapolis Star* published a profile of the Muckamuck; however, the restaurant was temporarily closed because of 'labour problems'. The article did not elaborate; instead, it focused on how the Muckamuck demonstrated Chinook food's popularity and shared three recipes: Muckamuck Watercress and Spinach Salad, Muckamuck's Baked Whole Wheat Bannock, and Muckamuck Clam Chowder (which surprisingly calls for canned clams).[36] On 11 May 1980, Catherine Watson's profile of the restaurant ran in the *Minneapolis Tribune*, which elaborated on the strike: 'Until two years ago, all food-curious tourists had to do was head for Vancouver's Muckamuck Restaurant.'[37] She summarized how the Indigenous employees went on strike after a quarrel over scheduling, wages, and the right to unionize. She further reported that Muckamuck closed the moment the strike began and its doors remained shut for seven months, and then reopened before Christmas. Watson did not advise against eating at the Muckamuck; instead, she informed American tourists of what they might encounter, leaving it to them to decide whether or not to cross the picket line.

Janet Mary Nicol was a 'regular on the Muckamuck picket line' together with Ethel Gardner, a Stó:lō member of the Skwah First Nation. Gardner got her job in the cold kitchen making drinks and salads through an employment agency. But, as she recounts, the working conditions were questionable: 'The cook was charged for getting the soup burnt and I was fined for leaving the bannock out overnight.' Despite the usual grievances associated with minimum wage restaurant work, Gardner added, 'We are also told that we must wear Native jewellery and if we not we are badgered about not being proud of our culture.' Gardner returned to the employment agency to say she wanted to quit, but a counsellor suggested she join a union instead. She and others joined the SORWUC, and on 21 February, 23 February, and 29 March, SORWUC 'launched charges of unfair labour practices on behalf' of Muckamuck's employees. Gardner was fired on 23 February. After the union's certification, Christina Prince fleshed out the racialized tensions at work: that 'management had told workers they "should be happy" to have a job because of their race'. Eighteen of twenty-one employees joined the union, the majority of which voted to strike, and the picket line formed on 1 June 1978.[38]

109

In addition to rallying for better working conditions, the picket line brought attention to larger issues related to Indigenous peoples and civil rights. The strike lasted a total of three years. Four-and-a-half months into the strike, Christmas and Erickson opened a new business on Davie Street where the Ace Gallery had been: Chilcotin Bar Seven. The Muckamuck was closed at this point, but above it this new restaurant sparked headlines like 'Cowboys lasso Muckamuck' and 'Muckamuck goes cowboy in bid to beat strike'.[39] In the former, Peter Comparelli penned a theatrical opening: 'The clump of cowboy boots has replaced the sound of moccasins on pebbles. It could be called Showdown on Davie, but it's not your typical late-night Western. In this case, the Indians are on strike'.[40] More than seventy picketers, he recounted, raised their voices at the opening, drawing further attention to the Muckamuck strike, as well as to the cultural insensitivity of opening a cowboy-themed restaurant in the midst of the strike initiated by Indigenous employees. The picketers were not amused. But like the average mechanical bull ride, Chilcotin Bar Seven did not last long.

The Muckamuck did, however, reopen in December 1978 with new employees. Co-signed by Florence Differ, a cook, the *Richmond Review* published a letter sharing the opinion of those working throughout the strike. 'To say that we were being exploited is so far from the truth. [… W]e are proud to be native and proud to be part of Muckamuck,' the four wrote. The editorial concluded with great emotion: 'If we destroy Muckamuck, we only destroy ourselves.'[41] This demonstrates the strike's complex layers. To some, it was confusing to see Indigenous employees both in the restaurant and on the picket line, making it unclear whom to support.

From a heated television debate, charges of violence (including raw eggs, a black eye, and a crowbar incident), and derogatory leaflets to missed hearings, late paycheques, and temporary picketing bans, Muckamuck's three-year strike has too many details to repeat. That both owners were living in California only made the strike a more complicated, transnational affair. The *Vancouver Sun* proclaimed it 'the longest-running strike in Vancouver' and *The Province* 'the ugliest strike in B.C. history'.[42] It is, however, worth noting the dedication that kept the strike going for three years. To summarize its end, the Muckamuck closed for good in 1981, and SORWUC shut down its picket line. A final legal ruling lingered for another two years. On 1 March 1983, the Labour Relations Board concluded that Muckamuck management had not bargained in good faith and owed the union $10,000.[43] However, because Christmas and Erickson no longer had assets in BC, SORWUC never received their compensation. In the end, SORWUC did not negotiate a contract with the Muckamuck, but the strike did bring great attention to working conditions at the restaurant, especially regarding cultural representation and power.

Yours for Indian Self-Determination

The month the strike began, the Union of BC Indian Chiefs Newsletter published a letter by Gardner asking for support. She concluded by contextualizing her experience at the Muckamuck in relation to the history of colonialism: "'We are part of the renewed struggle of Native people to gain the rights and respect denied us since Captain Cook landed here.'" Workers did express wanting more input in 'the menu planning of the cuisine', but Gardner's primary complaint was about its abuse of power. She claimed the issue was not that the owners were white but that they marketed the restaurant with the illusion that all staff, including the owners, was Indigenous.[44] Despite the illusion that the Muckamuck represented progress for Indigenous peoples in the commercial restaurant sector, it really only continued unequal power relations between those in charge and those providing labour.

In 1980, together with eight others, Gardner ended a letter published in *Kinesis* with what had become the picketers' sign-off: 'Yours for Indian Self Determination'.[45] In 2018 these same words swaddled the Morris and Helen Belkin Gallery, located on the UBC campus. The 1978 'Muckamuck strikers march, downtown Vancouver', image, taken by Sean Griffin, belongs to the *Pacific Tribune* Photograph Collection, the Communist Party of Canada's weekly newspaper. Lakota artist Dana Claxton revisited this photograph in the 2018 group show *Beginning with the Seventies: Collective Acts.*[46] Claxton used the archival image of the 1978 strike as a base for a large photomural that traversed one of the gallery's walls. Titled *Muckamuck Strike Then and Now* (2018), she digitally edited the image to include members of the ReMatriate Collective (Figures 1 & 2). Formed in 2015, the ReMatriate Collective is a play on the word repatriation. As the title suggests – *Muckamuck Strike Then and Now* – the work recovers

III

Figure 1. Dana Claxton in collaboration with Sean Griffin, Muckamuck Strike Then and Now, 2018, photographic mural. Image courtesy of Morris and Helen Belkin Art Gallery.

the strike's history in an effort to argue for its on-going relevance. In a similar spirit, Claxton's revisiting of the image credits both herself and Sean Griffin as the artists: a collaboration that crosses decades.

Beyond appearing in the photomural, the ReMatriate Collective also contributed a work connected to the SORWUC's 1978 strike against the Muckamuck. The collectives' 2018 red-on-red appliqué banner wrapped around the gallery's south side, spelling out the words in capital letters that double as its title: 'Yours for indigenous sovereignty'. These words framed the exhibition, and cast the gallery as a witness and an ally. To conclude, these words also summarized the Muckamuck picket line: a battle for

112

Figure 2. Dana Claxton in collaboration with Sean Griffin, Muckamuck Strike Then and Now, 2018, photographic mural. Installation view, Beginning with the Seventies: Collective Acts at the Morris and Helen Belkin Art Gallery, 2018. Photo: Rachel Topham Photography. Image courtesy of Morris and Helen Belkin Art Gallery.

self-representation and respect, for power. A battle for self-determination. This history of one particular restaurant in Vancouver in the 1970s attests to the power of restaurants to express a culture and the complexities this takes on in a settler colonial context, where said culture represents the minority Indigenous culture, but it is the majority settler culture that remains in charge.

Notes

1   'Muckamuck Restaurant: Northwest Coast Native Indian food', Pamphlet collection. AM1519-: 2011-045.1 Box: 632-A-02. City of Vancouver Archives, Vancouver, British Columbia, Canada.
2   Eve Johnson, 'The Impact He Made on Vancouver's Art Scene', *Vancouver Sun,* 19 April 1986, p. D3.
3   *Pacific Tribune* Photograph Collection, 'Muckamuck Strikers March, Downtown Vancouver', 12 August 1978, MSC160-396_03, Simon Fraser University Digitized Collections <https://digital.lib.sfu.ca/pt-1274/muckamuck-strikers-march-downtown-vancouver> [accessed 12 November 2018].
4   Janet Mary Nicol, '"Unions Aren't Native": The Muckamuck Restaurant Labour Dispute, Vancouver, BC (1978-1983)', *Labour/Le Travail,* 40 (1997), 235-51 (p. 237).
5   Julia Smith, 'An "Entirely Different" Kind of Union: The Service, Office, and Retail Workers' Union of Canada (SORWUC), 1972-1986', *Labour/Le Travail,* 73 (Spring 2014), p. 23-65.
6   Nicol, p. 236.
7   'Muck-a-Muck House Serves "just plain good food"', *Ottawa Journal,* 11 July 1972, p. 29.
8   'Muckamuck: Indian Fare Finds Favor in Vancouver', *Minneapolis Star,* 12 July 1978, p. 4C.
9   J.v. Powell and Sam Sullivan, 'Chinook Wawa,' *The Canadian Encyclopedia,* Historica Canada, 2017 <https://www.thecanadianencyclopedia.ca/en/article/chinook-jargon> [accessed 13 January 2019].
10   *Oxford English Dictionary,* 'Muckamuck' <https://en.oxforddictionaries.com/definition/muckamuck> [accessed 13 January 2019].
11   *Merriam Webster Dictionary,* 'Muckamuck' <https://www.merriam-webster.com/dictionary/muckety-muck> [accessed 9 May 2019].
12   Powell and Sullivan.
13   'Muck-a-Muck House Serves "just plain good food"'.
14   'Come to the Muckamuck: It Means Food. *Real Canadian* Food', *Ottawa Citizen,* 4 May 1974, p. 161.
15   Nicol, p. 237.
16   'Muck-a-Muck House Serves "just plain good food"'.
17   'Muck-a-Muck House Serves "just plain good food"'.
18   Sheila McCook, 'Eat Your Oolichan – And Enjoy It', *Daily Independent Journal,* 19 April 1975, p. M13.
19   James Barber, '$15 (Each) Will Buy Sumptuous Meals', *The Province,* 13 May 1977, p. 25.
20   McCook.
21   McCook.
22   'Come to the Muckamuck: It Means Food. *Real Canadian* Food'.
23   McCook.
24   McCook.
25   'Come to the Muckamuck: It Means Food. *Real Canadian* Food'.
26   Dave Brown, 'The Muckamuck: Gargantuan Meals Challenge the Biggest of Appetites', *The Ottawa Journal,* 3 June 1978, p. 28.
27   McCook.
28   Peter Comparelli, 'Indian Cooks, Waiters Battle Restaurant's White Managers', *Vancouver Sun,* 22 May 1978, p. B16.
29   Barber.
30   'Come to the Muckamuck: It Means Food. *Real Canadian* Food'.

31 McCook.

32 Thelma Dickenson, 'Vancouver's Spark: The Contrasts', *National Post*, 22 June 1974, p. 20.

33 Brown.

34 Robert Trumbull, 'What's Doing in Vancouver', *New York Times*, 5 June 1977, p. 7.

35 Barber.

36 'Muckamuck: Indian Fare Finds Favor in Vancouver'.

37 Catherine Watson, 'Muckamuck: Where the Food Is Intriguing', *Minneapolis Tribune*, 11 May 1980, p. 4E.

38 Nicol, pp. 236, 242.

39 'Muckamuck Goes Cowboy in Bid to Beat Strike', *The Province,* 11 October 1978, p. 44.

40 Peter Comparelli, 'Cowboys Lasso Muckamuck', *Vancouver Sun*, 11 October 1978, p. 1.

41 Florence Differ, Doris Olney, Matthew Jacob, and Doreen Harry, 'Letter to the Editor: No Exploitation Say Native Staff', *Richmond Review,* 10 November 1978, p. 5.

42 'Restaurant Management Now Willing to Bargain', *Vancouver Sun*, 26 April 1980, p. A12; Joey Thompson, 'Muckamuck Stew Is Back at the LRB', *The Province,* 14 May 1980, p. A4.

43 Nicol, p. 249.

44 Nicol, p. 239.

45 'Muckamuck: A Strike for Indian Self Determination', *Kinesis,* July 1980.

46 Morris and Belkin Art Gallery, 'Beginning with the Seventies: Collective Acts', 2018 <https://belkin.ubc.ca/exhibitions/beginning-with-the-seventies-collective-acts/> [accessed 9 May 2019].

Starving for Rights: Hunger Strikes as Weapons of Resistance inside Farms and Prisons in the United States

Melissa C. Gouge and Jennifer L. Hostetter

In 2018, farmworkers and incarcerated people in the United States used hunger strikes as forms of protest against injustice. While each group organized and participated in their own campaign, both had similar aims: to demand basic human rights and bring an end to oppressive, slave-like working conditions. As two of the most marginalized groups of workers in the US, (im)migrant farmworkers and prisoners typically earn only pennies an hour for their toil. They face gruelling working conditions or are forced to work against their will. With little recourse for complaint, few legal rights, and social invisibility, there is little they can use as leverage to fight inequality, apart from their own bodies.

In this sense, food – especially the voluntary abstention from it – can become a formidable weapon of resistance, given its function as both an essential means of subsistence and a powerful marker of identity. Hunger striking, or fasting for political and social change, is a common strategy employed by the disenfranchised with longstanding historical and religious roots. This act of starving oneself is a profound statement of self-defence that calls attention to one's plight, disrupts the existing power structure, and elicits the emotional involvement of others as a catalyst for change. The 2018 hunger strikes among migrant workers and incarcerated people similarly utilized food abstention in their common fight for improved living and working conditions. And though events such as these may not achieve their intended objectives overnight, their outcomes can be far-reaching nevertheless, as they raise awareness of oppression and recruit outside support.

In this paper we present two case studies from 2018 where hunger strikes were a critical form of protest. The first is the National Prison Strike, a campaign launched by imprisoned organizers following a brutal riot in a South Carolina correctional facility that left at least seven dead. Strikes were carried out in prisons across the country to raise awareness and to end inhumane living conditions, prison slave labour, death-by-incarceration legislation, and racial disparities within the criminal justice system. The second case is the Freedom Fast led by the Coalition of Immokalee Workers (CIW), where farmworkers and their allies fasted together in New York City outside the office of Wendy's restaurants' board chair. The demonstration was held to protest Wendy's ongoing refusal to participate in the CIW's Fair Food Program and to demand an end to sexual violence against women farmworkers in the fields.

Both cases highlight the continued significance of hunger strikes as what James C. Scott calls a 'weapon of the weak', whereby people with limited power use their bodies to resist injustice.[1] In settings like these, hunger strikes have proven to be enormously effective in (re)claiming human dignity and building solidarity among participants. This is significant for both populations, as the current socio-political landscape – rife with supercharged rhetoric and fear-mongering surrounding issues of race, crime, policing, and citizenship – has left them vulnerable to a host of injustices. While these attitudes are currently inflamed, history tells a familiar tale.

From the 1970s to the 1990s, a period marked by the rapid expansion of mass incarceration due to a series of strict sentencing policies accompanied by 'harsh rhetoric [...] against the poor, the foreign, and the criminal', we are reminded that underprivileged, immigrant people of colour have long been scapegoats for society's ills by those with institutional political power.[2] Both groups in our studies have limited access to resources and rights, are subjected to exploitation, and struggle with (in)visibility – often overlooked or forgotten by outsiders. Finally, and perhaps most interestingly, both incarcerated people and (im)migrant farmworkers make demands of those in power to recognize their dignity and invoke universal human rights in their struggles. For all of these reasons, these two hunger strikes from 2018 are particularly interesting to consider alongside one another.

We begin with a brief discussion of some of the origins of hunger strikes, to give context, meaning, and provide greater insight into their effectiveness. We then present our case studies, both of which are content analyses enriched by qualitative interview data, to illustrate how claimsmakers, whether in the field or behind bars, use their bodies to refuse food, increase the sympathy of outsiders, and, ultimately, initiate change. First we discuss the nationwide prison strikes, then we explore the five-day fast by farmworkers and their allies. Each case contains background and contextual material to provide a framework for understanding each group and their deprivation strategies more clearly. Common themes of rights, visibility, and solidarity are explored next. We close by addressing the overall successes each group achieved, for both the strikers and their campaigns.

Historical Background: From Fasting to Hunger Strikes

Abstaining from food to achieve some higher end – be it spiritual, social, or political – has been practiced throughout history. In ancient cultures, ceremonial fasting emerged out of necessity, mirroring the natural periods of feast and famine during the planting seasons.[3] These folk traditions extended into the spiritual realm, where fasting became (and remains) an important means of devotion among the world's major religions. Spiritual fasting also served a socio-political function, such as that performed by the fasting ladies of medieval Europe, who fasted to resist existing power structures in the family, the Church, or the larger community, and thereby elevated their otherwise lowly status.[4] Indeed, these medieval women could be viewed as early 'hunger strikers', who took fasting beyond church walls and used their bodies to gain power.

Beyond the church, there is a clear relationship between the hunger strikes carried out today and the early penal practices of India and Ireland. Both cultures encouraged citizens, especially the poor, to settle disputes and recover debt by fasting in protest on their offender's doorstep. The aim was to attract public attention, thus humiliating the offender. If the victim were to die, the offender would not only be fined, they also would be held in disrepute. The ancient Indian ritual, called *dharna* or *sitting dharna*, originated as a series of individual demonstrations, but over time became increasingly collective, whereby groups direct their grievances to the state.[5] *Dharna* also fuelled Mahatma Gandhi's famous hunger strikes.

In medieval Ireland, a nearly identical ritual was called *troscad*. For the poor in particular, *troscad* was a primary legal means of fighting for justice and establishing one's rights. While the custom is no longer enforced by law, *troscad* nevertheless remains a fixture of the Irish consciousness, and hunger striking continues to flourish.[6] The most well-known recent example is the Irish Republican Hunger Strikes of 1981, where ten strikers perished while demanding to be recognized as political prisoners.

The flurry of hunger strikes we have seen over the last century certainly take their cues from the past, demonstrating how food abstention remains a useful tool in the fight for justice. Notable examples are the strikes of incarcerated suffragettes in the UK and US in the early 1900s, demanding the right for women to vote, and the famous fasts of Cesar Chavez from California's United Farm Workers, in 1968, 1972, and 1988, in which he fought for union contracts and against the use of pesticides.

Case Studies: The National Prison Strike and the Freedom Fast

Life Inside: Conditions in US Prisons
The US has the highest rate of incarceration per capita in the world, with 698 people imprisoned per every 100,000 residents.[7] And though minorities represent only 30% of the general US population, they are disproportionately represented as 56% of those incarcerated.[8] Since the 1980s and 90s – when prison populations sky-rocketed due to the 'war on drugs' and increased sentencing legislation such as the three-strikes, mandatory minimums, and truth-in-sentencing laws – prisons have become virtual human warehouses where many will suffer death by incarceration, the majority of whom are poor people of colour.[9]

Behind bars, living conditions often are bleak. Incarcerated people are routinely subjected to myriad abuses, including overcrowded facilities, meagre and inedible food, contaminated water supplies, severe physical abuses, excessive solitary confinement, minimal access to fresh air and sunlight, and beyond. Prison labour is particularly exploitative, yet permitted by the 13th Amendment to the US Constitution. Wages are notoriously low, and working conditions are often forced and tyrannical. The average pay is $0.20 an hour, but in five states, prison workers receive no wages.[10] Moreover, many of these jobs are not voluntary; those who refuse to work, even if ill or injured, are frequently placed in solitary confinement.

These punishments are not merely circumstantial, but often are calculated and deliberate, and their impacts on prisoner health are extensive. Incarcerated people are stripped of nearly all of their rights, so by design, these places of confinement, and all activities within them, serve as additional punishments. Even everyday activities such as bathing and dressing do not escape humiliation. Prisoners are routinely strip-searched for contraband or forced to use the restroom openly. As such, privacy is virtually non-existent, and the level of debasement is profound.

Yet much of this brutality is hidden from public view. Prisons are built not only to house the condemned but to banish them from the community. While the people living behind bars have some basic legal protections (e.g. the right to adequate food, medical care, and freedom from cruel and unusual punishment), these rights are rarely enforced, given the lack of public awareness. Furthermore, prison administrators have broad legal freedom to apply disciplinary measures, citing the persistent threat of violence. Thus human rights abuses abound.

As institutions of violence, the threat of brutality is ever-present in prisons, provoked either by the incarcerated themselves or the vicious social control tactics employed by the guards. Social hierarchies exist much like those in the outside world, dividing across racial and socio-economic lines. These differences certainly can inflame tensions between prisoners, but more importantly, they highlight 'the ways in which incarcerated people are forced to create their own collective means for safety, survival, and camaraderie in a situation where hope is the scarcest commodity'.[11]

The 2018 National Prison Strike

In April 2018, a brutal fight broke out at Lee County Correctional Facility in South Carolina, where at least seven prisoners were killed and twenty seriously injured. State officials laid the blame squarely on prisoners, reporting that the conflict erupted between rival gangs.[12] However, incarcerated witnesses countered that guards provoked the fights by intentionally housing rival groups together, then waited hours before breaking up the conflict or providing medical aid.[13] This resulted in prisoners bleeding out during the melee, who might have otherwise survived with proper care.

As news of the massacre spread to other prisons, incarcerated activists were outraged by the lack of media attention and the flagrant abuse of power by guards. In response, a protest was organized to run from 21 August to 9 September, led by imprisoned organizers from Jailhouse Lawyers Speak, a group of incarcerated prisoners' rights activists. Inside organizers worked closely with allies on the outside, including the Incarcerated

Workers Organizing Committee (IWOC), a prisoner-led workers union. In contrast to previous strikes, the 2018 protests were planned over several weeks to allow more time for demonstrations and to combat suppression attempts by prison administrators.

Despite the challenges of spreading information inside high-security facilities, imprisoned organizers developed a complex network of communications, relying on contraband cell phones, social-media posts, prison newsletters, and outside support. Ahead of the strikes, prisoners in at least seventeen facilities signed on in solidarity, as did a number of outside groups. Organizers sought to bring their plight into the public conversation, to 'call a ceasefire' between rival groups on the inside, and to give agency to their own authority in the movement.[14] They created a list of ten demands to accompany the nationwide demonstrations, all of which were appeals to recognize prisoners' human rights. They included calls for humane living conditions, an end to slave labour, proper channels to redress grievances, an end to inhumane and racialized sentencing and gang enhancement laws, the possibility of rehabilitation and parole, access to education, and the reinstatement of voting rights.[15] While hunger strikes and commissary boycotts were the most common tactics, incarcerated protesters also used other nonviolent strategies, like work stoppages and sit-ins.

After the strike began, prison officials launched a series of retaliations. Numerous prisons went on lockdown, all communication was cut, and prisoners were confined to their cells. To minimize events, prison administrators issued statements denying any strike activity. Nevertheless, as word spread, more incarcerated people and outside allies became involved. Strikers' social-media posts went viral, and news coverage appeared across a broad spectrum of mainstream media outlets, both domestically and abroad. Prisons across the country came out in solidarity, and expanded to include at least one facility in Nova Scotia, Canada. Other international support came in from Palestine, Greece, Germany, and Mexico.

As we write this, the impacts are still being felt. Those incarcerated continue to suffer repercussions, such as lockdowns, suspension of mail services, restricted or banned family visitations, and solitary confinement of suspected organizers. Nevertheless, the protests had a profound impact. They attracted unprecedented media attention, brought prisoners' rights into the public discourse, and led to policy changes in some states.

Life Outside: Conditions on US Farms

With a history of abuses as extreme as in prisons, from slavery to the sharecropping system to the disastrous Bracero program from the 1960s and the failures of the contemporary H-2A guestworker program, farmworkers in the US are still struggling for fair wages and safe working conditions. New Deal legislation exempted agricultural workers from protections, and many of those exemptions still exist today.[16] Work that was once performed by slaves is now done by immigrants (and incarcerated people), the majority of whom have dubious authorization status. Precarious and dangerous working situations leave workers vulnerable to abuses with few avenues for recourse in the aftermath of mistreatment (e.g. wage theft and sexual violence). Since the 1990s, members of the CIW have cultivated more than tomatoes – they have grown a large network to support their efforts to fight the largest producers and buyers of produce in the country to demand their basic human rights to fair wages and dignity in the workplace.

Initially using a model similar to that of the United Farm Workers (UFW) in California, workers in Immokalee, Florida staged general and hunger strikes against farm owners, but long-term unemployment was unsustainable for already poor workers. Farm owners were hamstrung between retailers setting prices and farmworkers seeking fair pay. As a result, wages stagnated. Shifting gears, the CIW began to organize against buyers at the top of the supply chain – those who bore the greatest responsibility for their working conditions – rather than growers of tomatoes. Demanding increased pay and enforceable workplace safety standards established by the workers themselves – or 'worker-driven social responsibility', rejecting corporate social responsibility programs – seemed like a far-fetched idea until farmworkers cultivated a diverse network of allies. Together, they forced retailers like Taco Bell, Wal-Mart, Chipotle, and Trader Joe's grocery stores to work in partnership with the CIW.

2018 Freedom Fast

Fasting has been part of the CIW's repertoire since the early days of organizing. In March of 2012, they fasted for six days on the doorstep of Publix Supermarkets, one of the largest buyers of Immokalee-grown tomatoes with headquarters in Lakeland, Florida, near the small town. Like Publix, Wendy's has steadfastly refused to come to the table with farmworkers to discuss joining the Fair Food Program. In fact, responding to intense pressure from the CIW, Wendy's has outsourced the purchase of tomatoes to Mexico – where workers do not enjoy the benefits won by CIW successes. Working conditions in Mexico are so dire that they were featured in a Pulitzer-nominated series in the *Los Angeles Times*.[17]

Inspired in part by the lack of response from Wendy's President and CEO Todd Penegor and Chairman of the Board Nelson Peltz to a letter claiming 'the problem of sexual violence has been our daily bread for decades', written by the CIW's Women's Group, the CIW organized a fast to bring attention to the abysmal working conditions suffered by women who pick tomatoes in Mexico.[18] Astutely, they contrasted these conditions against the improvements enjoyed by women working in the same industry in the US after years of successes won by the CIW.[19] The reference to daily bread cleverly foreshadowed the fast to come during their annual March gathering. Organizers of the Freedom Fast also took advantage of media fury in reaction to the rise of the #metoo movement and the election of Donald Trump.

The Freedom Fast message directed at Wendy's focused particularly on ending violence against women in the fields – and recommended the CIW's Fair Food Program as the solution. Farmworkers from Florida and their allies from the Midwest,

California, Texas, Tennessee, and Massachusetts gathered to fast together in Manhattan outside of Trian Partners, the hedge fund offices of Nelson Peltz (who had not yet responded to the letter penned by the women's group). As the CIW has grown over the years, so has participation in their fasts. This year, about 100 farmworkers and their allies fasted together for five days, and about 2500 attended the march on the final day.[20] Farmworkers, their families, students, musicians, medical professionals, faith leaders, and unassuming bypassers were drawn into the activities.[21] There were also solidarity fasters, both individuals and faith groups, in other cities like San Francisco, CA; Stonybrook, NY; Marshall, MN, and Spokane, WA.[22]

During the five days, an air of solemnity and reverence alternated with joyous revelry as faith leaders offered homilies and prayers for the fasters in tandem with *son jarocho* music and festivity. Provocative displays of women silenced by tape-covered mouths and signs reading '*yo ayuno por un futuro mejor para mis hijos*' ('I fast for a better future for my children') and 'I stand with farmworker women' were prominent.[23] The power of the fast is particularly potent for those who produce our food but are unable to afford it – those often viewed as powerless by outsiders but whose power is unmistakable as they endure the suffering of hunger not only for themselves but for the suffering of all women. As Nely Rodriguez, a long-time CIW organizer and farmworker, said, 'if I am hurting [after fasting], it is nothing compared to the pain women feel when they experience different forms of sexual violence in the fields for simply thinking about how they will feed their kids.'[24]

Many fasts close with breaking bread together, and this fast was no different. The *121* farmworkers' children presented faith leaders with baskets of bread to be blessed and shared among fasters and non-fasters alike. The sharing of food together marked the end of the fast and the building of solidarity among fasters. Unmoved by their fast, Nelson Peltz allowed security guards to accept only a small fraction of the over 100,000 signed petitions from supporters at the end of the fast – and to date still refuses to meet with farmworkers.[25]

Discussion

As we introduced our cases and the reasons they are worthy of comparison, several topics emerged, one being the politically-charged milieu within which both groups exist. Rather than dedicate our entire discussion to the increased severity of racism and xenophobia that is readily visible in the US news, we are focusing on the other topics we referenced, including: access to resources, rights, and dignity; (in)visibility; and solidarity.

The Right to Have Rights

In the absence of material resources, the poor leverage the most accessible resource under their control – their bodies – to address inequities; in so doing, they position themselves as rights bearers even in the absence of state recognition.

Although farmworkers, especially the undocumented, have few rights, those who are imprisoned have a near total absence of rights. This distinction, combined with poor enforcement mechanisms for existing protections, is important when considering the effectiveness of hunger strikes inside 'total institutions'.[26] During the National Prison Strike, prison officials neither sanctioned the protests nor offered any protections to participants. Rather, every effort was made to tamp down protests, seeing that hunger strikes in the prison context are particularly disruptive. In addition, the debate remains in the wider public as to whether incarcerated people even have the right to strike, thus corrections facilities are given tremendous license in suppressing any form of prisoner resistance.

In contrast, the 2018 Freedom Fast was sanctioned by the state as permitted under New York law, thereby lending some protections and a sense of legitimacy to the Freedom Fast. Furthermore, the 'fasting on Nelson Peltz's doorstep' carried out by CIW farmworkers and allies was endorsed by the participation of leaders from many faith communities (e.g. T'ruah and Rev. Barber from the Poor People's Campaign).[27] The symbolic sanctuary these religious figures provided to vulnerable demonstrators is reminiscent of the safe harbour the Church offered to repressed women in medieval Europe.

Claims to human rights and dignity squarely oppose the dehumanization that occurs in US prisons and agricultural fields, so acts like these are means by which people can reclaim their bodies and sense of power over self to build communities capable of changing the social order. Jailhouse Lawyers Speak released a statement illustrating this point: 'We may be in cages, we may be treated like animals, we may be tagged as second class citizens upon release, but we are still humans.'[28] And during the Freedom Fast, Nely Rodriguez said in an interview, 'we are human beings and we are demanding justice'; later in the same interview she commented that 'their dignity as women is not respected'.[29]

Visibility

Visibility in the context of the National Prison Strike is different than that of the Freedom Fast. Though both groups have access to similar social-media platforms, the prison strike faced significant challenges in organizing, due to extreme levels of security and surveillance. Nevertheless, and at extraordinarily high risk to their very lives, inside organizers were able to coordinate a nationwide campaign. Freedom Fast organizers did not have such constraints in their organizing efforts.

The CIW fasts were not covered extensively in national news but they did occur in public spaces. Colourful signs and *son jarocho* Mexican folk music captivated bypassers. Participation by religious leaders and messages of support from celebrities and many others also provided a mainstream sense of legitimacy for strikers. In contrast, the prison strikes were distinctly less visible, hidden deep within institutional walls. Yet, they did receive widespread media attention, appearing in major news outlets, marking a clear break from previous strikes.

Solidarity

Long-term food abstention and basic human rights claims are not enough for hunger strikes to be successful. They must be visible to sympathetic outsiders and invoke public outrage in order to motivate change. For both groups, the 2018 events were designed to attract outside attention, arouse sympathy, foster group empowerment, and ultimately generate action. Visibility and solidarity are closely linked. Luke Nephew, a poet who attended the Freedom Fast, offered that 'this struggle is not just against corporations [... ,] it's about loving ourselves and loving each other and building connections'.[30] Similarly, Brooke Terpstra, an activist with the IWOC who helped coordinate the National Prison Strike, stated that 'solidarity isn't just a gesture, it's about sharing the burden'.[31]

What both groups clearly share is knowledge of how their collective suffering from hunger builds solidarity among themselves and with outsiders. In essence, it is an invitation to connection with the group's cause, as remarked upon by Rabbi Mira Rivera of T'ruah as he offered a prayer to start the second day of the Freedom Fast: 'we fast and pray in solidarity with our brothers and sisters, the Coalition of Immokalee Workers.'[32]

Conclusions: Evaluating Successes

While neither group has seen their demands fully satisfied and abuses remain, both farmworkers and prisoners made significant strides in their struggles for justice. In prisons, coordination by organizers of a strike of this magnitude without administrators shutting it down was remarkable. Equally astonishing was their ability to negotiate peace among themselves, bringing fellow prisoners together as a united front against a common enemy. Also, new platforms for social justice movements powered by cell phones and social-networking sites gave prisoners unprecedented access to the public, lending a powerful voice to the unheard. This public exposure was instrumental in bringing about policy changes, such as Florida Amendment 4, restoring voting rights to ex-felons. In fact, prisoners' rights have remained in the national conversation amid the 2020 Presidential election campaign.

As for the Freedom Fast, Wendy's did not join the Fair Food Program, yet the CIW's long-term strategy has won them a 'seat at the table' in other ways. Wendy's callous disregard for the lives of women farmworkers, as demonstrated in their knee-jerk media response accusing them of co-opting the Time's Up movement's message (later publicly countered by its founders), led to much broader press. Outlets like *People*, *Glamour*, and *The New York Times* ran stories critical of the fast-food chain.[33] The dozens of awards the group has received (e.g. the Roosevelt Freedom from Want and James Beard Leadership Awards) signify growing recognition for the CIW's work. Yet, the real successes have been won for the workers themselves – $26 million in payments under the Fair Food Program and the virtual elimination of violence and human trafficking in the US tomato industry.

While both of these cases illustrate how hunger strikes can fuel social justice movements, the work is far from done. US prison conditions continue to deteriorate. Farmworkers and prisoners are increasingly demonized. Their creative use of food deprivation challenges us not only to pay attention to their struggle but to respond to their emotional pleas to recruit us as accomplices in their calls for justice – as strikes have been similarly employed before. We also must take action. How might we learn from these groups and emulate them in our own spheres? If we wish to fulfil our ethical obligation to live justly and civilly with one another, must we not lift the iron curtain, peer in despite the ugliness, and fight to alleviate the suffering of the most vulnerable among us? After spending twenty-seven years imprisoned in South Africa, Nelson Mandela said in his autobiography *The Long Walk to Freedom*, 'no one truly understands a nation until one has been inside its jails […].'[34] The same must be said of its agricultural fields.

Notes

1 James C. Scott, *Weapons of the Weak: Everyday Forms of Peasant Resistance* (New Haven: Yale University Press, 1985), pp. 29-35.

2 Mary Bosworth, *Explaining U.S. Imprisonment* (London: Sage Publications, 2010), p.149.

3 Caroline Walker Bynum, *Holy Feast and Holy Fast: The Religious Significance of Food to Medieval Women* (Berkeley: University of California Press, 1987), p. 34.

4 Bynum, pp. 216-44.

5 Lisa Mitchell, 'The Visual Turn in Political Anthropology and the Mediation of Political Practice in Contemporary India', *South Asia: Journal of South Asian Studies*, 37 (2014), 515-40 (p. 527).

6 Peter B. Ellis, *The Druids* (Grand Rapids: Eerdmans Publishing, 1998), pp. 141-42.

7 Peter Wagner and Wendy Sawyer, 'Mass Incarceration: The Whole Pie 2019', *Prison Policy Initiative*, 19 March, 2019 <https://www.prisonpolicy.org/reports/pie2019.html> [accessed 26 October 2019].

8 Matt Vogel and Lauren C Porter, 'Toward a Demographic Understanding of Incarceration Disparities: Race, Ethnicity and Age Structure', *Journal of Quantitative Criminology*, 32 (2016), 515-30 (p. 515).

9 Bosworth, pp. 125-26.

10 Wendy Sawyer, 'How Much do Incarcerated People Earn in Each State?', *Prison Policy Initiative*, 10 April 2017 <https://www.prisonpolicy.org/blog/2017/04/10/wages/> [accessed 26 May 2019].

11 Jared Ware, 'Interview: South Carolina Prisoners Challenge Narrative around Violence at Lee Correctional Institution', *Shadowproof*, 3 May 2018 <https://shadowproof.com/2018/05/03/interview-south-carolina-prisoners-challenge-narrative-around-violence-lee-correctional-institution/> [accessed 30 May 2019].

12 Dwayne McElmore, Teddy Kulmala, and Emily Bohatch, '7 Inmates Killed in Mass Casualty Incident at SC Maximum Security Prison', *The State*, 16 April 2018 <https://www.thestate.com/news/local/crime/article208982719.html> [accessed 30 May 2019].

13 Heather Ann Thompson, 'How a South Carolina Prison Riot Really Went Down', *The New York Times*, 28 April 2018 <https://www.nytimes.com/2018/04/28/opinion/how-a-south-carolina-prison-riot-really-went-down.html> [accessed 30 May 2019].

14 Brooke Terpstra, 'End Prison Slavery: National Prison Strike 2018', *The Final Straw Radio*, 8 July 2018 <https://thefinalstrawradio.noblogs.org/post/2018/07/08/august21-prison-strike-2018/> [accessed 22 May 2019]

15 Jailhouse Lawyers Speak, 'National Prison Strike', *San Francisco Bay View*, 14 July 2018 <http://sfbayview.com/2018/07/national-prison-strike/> [accessed 25 May 2019].

16 Michael Holley, 'Disadvantaged by Design: How the Law Inhibits Agricultural Guest Workers from

Enforcing their Rights', *Hofstra Labor and Employment Law Journal*, 18 (2001), 573-621.

17   Richard Marosi, 'Product of Mexico', *LA Times*, 7 December 2014, 10 December 2014, 12 December 2014, 14 December 2014 <http://graphics.latimes.com/product-of-mexico-camps/> [accessed 7 March 2019].

18   CIW, 'Why we are Fasting…', *CIW: Coalition of Immokalee Workers*, 8 February 2018 <https://ciw-online.org/blog/2018/02/why-we-are-fasting-2/> [accessed 21 May 2019].

19   CIW, 'Letter to Mr. Todd A. Penegor', *CIW: Coalition of Immokalee Workers*, 5 October 2017 <http://ciw-online.org/wp-content/uploads/Oct17_CIW-letter-to-Penegor.pdf> [accessed 16 May 2019].

20   Lisa Held, 'Florida's Farmworkers Take Their Fight to Park Avenue', *Civil Eats*, 19 March 2018 <https://civileats.com/2018/03/19/floridas-farmworkers-take-their-fight-to-park-avenue/> [accessed 15 May 2019].

21   Rinku Sen, 'These Farmworkers Know How to End Sexual Harassment in the Fields. Will Wendy's Listen?', *The Nation*, 15 March 2018 <https://www.thenation.com/article/these-farmworkers-know-how-to-end-sexual-harassment-in-the-fields-will-wendys-listen/> [accessed 18 May 2019].

22   *Statements of Solidarity with the Freedom Fast* <http://www.boycott-wendys.org/solidarity> [accessed 18 May 2019].

23   Julie Taylor, 'The Power of Commitment: Reflections on the CIW's Freedom Fast 2018', National Farm Worker Ministry, 28 May 2018 <http://nfwm.org/news/reflections-on-ciws-freedom-fast-2018/> [accessed 21 May 2019].

24   Jake Ratner, 'CIW's Freedom Fast Day 4 – We Will Not Be Silent', *YouTube*, 16 April 2018 <https://www.youtube.com/watch?v=Mih6EcI74cY> [accessed on 14 May 2019].

25   Vera Lian Chang, 'Meet the Farmworkers Leading the #MeToo Fight for Workers Everywhere', *KQED*, 25 May 2018 <https://www.kqed.org/bayareabites/128564/meet-the-farmworkers-leading-the-metoo-fight-for-workers-everywhere> [accessed 17 May 2019].

26   Erving Goffman, *Asylums: Essays on the Social Situation of Mental Patients* (New York: Anchor Books, 1961), p. 4.

27   *Statements of Solidarity with the Freedom Fast.*

28   Jailhouse Lawyers Speak, 'One Year since Lee Prison Massacre that Sparked Nationwide Strike', *Liberation*, 15 April 2019 <https://www.liberationnews.org/jailhouse-lawyers-speak-one-year-since-lee-prison-massacre-that-sparked-nationwide-strike> [accessed 1 June 2019].

29   Ratner.

30   'Luke Nephew of Peace Poets joins @ciw during their #FreedomFast bc: this struggle is about loving each other. We are not alone when we are together' (@yoNYC1u – Young and Organized in New York City, 12 March 2018).

31   Terpstra.

32   Rabbi Mira Rivera, 'Morning Witness for the CIW and Allied Fasters', T'ruah, 2018 <https://www.truah.org/wp-content/uploads/2018/03/CIW-fasting-prayer-Rivera.pdf> [accessed 18 May 2019].

33   Noam Scheiber, 'Why Wendy's is Facing Campus Protests (It's About the Tomatoes)', *The New York Times*, 7 March 2019, p. B1.

34   Nelson Mandela, *The Long Walk to Freedom* (London: LittleBrown, and Co., 1994), p. 194.

Eating French, Being French: Gastronomy and National Identity in Contemporary France

Jennifer L. Holm

Food and eating have always been central to French national identity. Since the Middle Ages, chefs, authors, scholars, politicians, and laypeople have consistently aligned gastronomy either ideologically or symbolically with Frenchness. French food sociologist Jean-Pierre Poulain situates gastronomy as an integral, unifying component of the French patrimony and a 'social fact' that helps to understand France and her people.[1] French political scholar Vincent Martigny attributes the high value of gastronomy in crafting Frenchness to the fact that it brings people together literally and figuratively, promoting harmony and accord.[2] These views, while grounded in certain truths, seem increasingly idealistic. They are demonstrative of the French propensity to use food as a rallying force. However, as we see in contemporary France, food is not always cohesive. It can also be

a site of resistance or a tool of exclusion and discrimination. This dual function of food and eating, I argue, is key to its ability to craft and reinforce a specific national identity.

Looking at an ensemble of political measures and gastronomic discourses we see that the nation's gastronomy is increasingly a tool for national self-fashioning, defining French identity through themes of culinary tradition, heritage, and *terroir* that, in turn, allow for discrimination of immigrant foodways. Efforts to direct eating – through rules, regulations, and instruction – have historically been a means of control used to structure and form identity. Today, the use of food to sculpt a national self is occurring at multiple levels, from the local to the national. Central to this project is the successful inscription of the French gastronomic meal on UNESCO's List of Intangible Cultural Heritage (ICH). It is undeniable that France's bid to inscribe its gastronomic meal on UNESCO's ICH List was a protectionist effort to exert soft power and reify the nation's gastronomic importance on the international stage. However, I will show that a deeper reading of the nomination dossier and the surrounding gastronomic discourse reveals that this was also an effort to inform and define French identity through food. Couched in the rhetoric of inclusion, community, and togetherness, there is a parallel rhetoric of discrimination that gastronomic tradition enables and formalizes. The French gastronomic meal, now a cornerstone of gastronomic discourse and politics within the nation, communicates a certain idea of what it means to eat French and, thus, what it means to be French.

Over the past decade in France, there has been an uptick in the use of food as a tool of discrimination against the nation's Muslim population. This trend falls in line with a succession of government attempts to regulate Muslim bodies, practices, and beliefs and in marking members of the faith as other than the 'normal' French citizen.[3] Laurent Binet traces political gastronomic racism to the *soupes au cochon* (occurring between 2004 and 2006) of the Identitaires, an extreme far-right fringe group. These events were meant to feed non-Jewish and non-Muslim homeless populations. In the French high court and the European Court of Human Rights, the meals were deemed discriminatory and therefore illegal.[4] The next target of discrimination was halal food. At the end of 2009, the fast food chain Quick initiated a program to serve halal meat in some of its restaurants in areas with large Muslim populations. This decision was met with widespread criticism lasting into 2010. Many commentators in the press deemed it contrary to French republican values and discriminatory against France's majority non-Muslim population.[5] In 2012, Marine Le Pen of the Front National party pushed halal into the centre of the presidential campaign to stoke fear and try to win over voters while also bringing other candidates into the fray. She falsely claimed that all meat bought and sold in Paris was halal and that non-Muslim consumers had been duped.[6] In a related move the following year, what is now termed *kebabophobia* made its appearance. Locally elected officials began barring the establishment of kebab shops in town centres. The reasoning for this, according to Robert Ménard, the mayor of the southern town of Béziers, is that 'kebab shops are a threat to the historical image and the identity of the city'.[7] The implication is that eating kebabs is not French and has no place in France. Similar actions against kebabs have since occurred throughout France, leading food scholar Pierre Raffard to suggest that the kebab has become an emblem of a perceived 'islamization' of the nation.[8] More recently, in September 2017, Florian Philippot, then vice president of the Front National, was caught with political friends eating dinner at a couscous restaurant. The diners were deemed hypocrites, fostering anti-immigrant hatred while feasting on culinary pleasures immigrants brought to France. FN party members decried the meal as unpatriotic. In the wake of what is now termed #couscousgate, Philippot was forced to leave the FN.[9] While spectators may laugh at #couscousgate from afar, wielding political power and determining Frenchness through food is increasingly common in France.

In a nation built upon the ideals of universalism, solidarity, and secularism, religious-based food restrictions and some ethnic restaurants (namely those associated with immigrants of Muslim background) are seen as problematic. They are indicative of communitarianism, and, thus, in the French mindset, potentially threatening to the nation. Communitarianism has a distinct meaning in France that is tailored to mirror the importance of the nation as a singular, unified body. It is 'used primarily to define, symbolize and warn against perceived intent by minority groups to create distinct and separate communities and specific racial/ethnic political demands in violation of Republican norms'.[10] In France, it is illegal to ask questions about and collect data on ethnic and religious background; this is done to fight against communitarianism and as an attempt to foster unity and ward against discrimination. As such, political discourse and practice typically silence identifiers of diversity, a trope that arises in the language of the French gastronomic meal.

The rise of this gastronomic racism in France is a product, I contend, of two important events occurring within a span of six months at the end of 2010 and beginning of 2011. First is the inscription of the gastronomic meal on the UNESCO ICH List in November 2010. The meal sets up a sort of *régime*. In French, this word signals both a restrictive mode of eating and a political power. Likewise, the gastronomic meal dictates a specific way of eating and inscribes it into the identity of the nation, giving it the power to include and exclude people within the national community. Second is the enactment of the Muslim veil ban in April 2011. With the ban, the political far right won their cause *du jour* and would need a new symbol of the Muslim community toward which they could direct their angst and use to stoke fear. Nothing better, more tangible, or symbolic than food could fit the bill.

While it is perhaps tempting to focus on the discriminatory gastronomic rhetoric we witness in contemporary France, turning our attention elsewhere is more productive and informative in understanding how gastronomic actors including chefs, critics, food historians, and political officials are urgently engaged in efforts to simultaneously protect French gastronomy and fashion national identity in the process. Traditionally, the French state has remained largely silent in food matters beyond consumer health and safety, stepping in on occasion to protect traditional foods such as through the creation of the *Appellation d'origine contrôlée* system. Increasingly, though, intervention is becoming more common. The last three French Presidents – Nicolas Sarkozy, François Hollande, and Emmanuel Macron – each from a different political party, have made use of gastronomy as a political tool and have also worked to shore up the cultural element. We see, occurring in tandem to negative forms of gastronomic discrimination, a series of affirmative nation-wide events and policies aimed at concretizing gastronomy and its place at the heart of Frenchness. These processes are more subtle than the overt gastronomic racism making headlines: they speak to what is French through a rationalized and normative language rather than focus on difference. All of these events and policies stem from the gastronomic meal and its inscription on the ICH List. A close reading of the gastronomic meal nomination file reveals why and how it has become a touchstone for French national identity within and outside of French politics. It demonstrates the larger cultural implications of food in France during a time when the nation feels under threat and there are broad concerns about identity and belonging. As the file necessitates a continued gastronomic education for the people, it positions the meal and consequent gastronomic events squarely within the republican model of French citizenship – a model in which citizenship is conflated with adherence to French cultural values.[11]

The French gastronomic meal's inscription on the ICH List is anchored in French politics. President Sarkozy announced the effort to recognize a distinctly French way of eating at the 2008 Salon international de l'agriculture. By announcing the move to protect French gastronomy (and the human and economic systems that support it) in this venue, Sarkozy sought to gain the support of farmers by crafting an image as a protector, ready to safeguard France in the era of globalization.[12] In November 2010, French efforts paid off and the 'gastronomic meal of the French' was added to UNESCO's List of Intangible Cultural Heritage.

The gastronomic meal is 'a festive meal bringing people together to enjoy the art of good eating and drinking'.[13] It is defined through a series of practices that normalize eating *à la française*: a carefully orchestrated menu of dishes taken from a 'repertoire of recipes'; the selection and purchase of quality ingredients; the pairing of food and wine; a standard structure of courses beginning with the aperitif, moving on to successive courses including a starting course, a main dish of meat or fish and vegetables, a cheese course, dessert, and ending with liqueurs; setting the table according to 'classic French taste'; and specific actions including sharing food and gastronomic discourse.[14]

The language of the nomination file closely aligns the gastronomic meal with French identity. It is so essential to French identity, in fact, that it is a practice 'with which all French people are familiar'. To be French means to know of and partake in this ritual. Participation in the gastronomic meal 'constitutes an important reference point for identity' and gives rise to 'feelings of identity and belonging'. This is true not only among the French, but also among foreigners who 'see the gastronomic meal as a marker of French identity'. Sentiments of belonging, the file explains, arise from the meal's representation of national cultural values including 'attachment to the agricultural world', sharing of meals, manners, conversation, history, and 'happiness for all'.[15] These are the values to which all French people subscribe and about which they learn in school. They exemplify the French motto – *Liberté, Égalité, Fraternité* (Liberty, Equality, Fraternity) – that guides national ideology and arises from the Revolution, a central moment in the genesis of republican values.

The meal is deeply embedded in the long history of France. The nomination file explains how the 'collective experience' of the French nation 'has been built over several centuries'.[16] Partaking in the meal 'reminds the French of their history and thus gives them a feeling of continuity'. The file specifically relates the meal to the revolutionary period and the Enlightenment, key moments in the development of the rights of the citizen. Anchored in several centuries of history and linked to popular and aristocratic classes alike, the meal is seemingly an immutable part of the nation. The French, consequently, 'regard [the meal] as part of their heritage'. The file repeatedly uses possessive forms. Possession and history come together in the emphasis on the meal as part of a 'shared history' that is 'inherited' from the past.[17] Current practitioners are inserted into a continuum of eating linked to important moments in French history. As a result, French food and history become one. The file reminds us and the French that, as anthropologist Thomas M. Wilson states, 'a history of food is also a history of ourselves'.[18]

The knowledge that this practice occurs in every family and community throughout France creates the sense of imaginary communion around a national table across time and geography. The file heavily employs tropes identical to those necessary for constructing national identity such as a common history, heritage, culture, and landscape.[19] Here, the nation is an imagined community – one that exists in the minds of its members, all believing they practice similar, repeated actions binding them together. In his theory of imagined communities, historian Benedict Anderson argues nations exist precisely because their people 'will never know most of their fellow-members, meet them, or even hear of them, yet in the minds of each lives the image of their communion'.[20] While Anderson focuses his discussion largely on printed text as a source of this imagined group, his use of the word 'communion' seems particularly relevant to food studies. Communion is, after all, not only the sharing of thoughts and knowledge, but also of food and meals.

The framework of the gastronomic meal renders it a significant device in the structure and maintenance of a cohesive national body. The practices of the meal are defined as 'rites', giving them an initiating quality. Indeed, the gastronomic meal nomination file notes that the meal contributes to 'social integration', 'inclusion', 'intercultural dialogue', and 'social ties'. To practice the ensemble of rites is a means of inserting oneself or demonstrating membership in the community. Here, the community is national – the 'entire French people', which is 'large, diverse and unified'. The meal is such a powerful unifying force that it incorporates and homogenizes 'social and cultural mixes, regional plurality and contributions by immigrants'. The meal is assimilative and integrative; 'its values take in diversity and strengthen feelings of belonging for participants in the gastronomic meal'. The words 'homogenous' and 'homogeneity' appear throughout the file, for instance in noting that the meal is 'homogenous in the whole community'. Likewise, we read a repeated use of words like 'togetherness' and expressions such as 'bringing together'.[21] This discourse emphatically insists on the meal's role in crafting a nation united in its cultural sameness. Though its members may be diverse, they are all one because they subscribe to the homogenous practices like the gastronomic meal. Typical of the French view of citizenship, individual differences are subsumed by a feeling of national belonging and rendered obsolete.

The recurring emphasis on togetherness and belonging is reminiscent of the *vivre ensemble* discourse in French politics. While the idea of 'living together' may appear 'well-intentioned and like a message of inclusivity, it is often translated as a mechanism for disciplining those who "don't really understand" how to live in harmony with others. It has become a rather heavy and inflexible concept'.[22] The *vivre ensemble* ideology is restrictive, seeking to homogenize citizen behaviour within a set of specific values that define national identity. And, as the integration of immigrants is increasingly seen as a failure, and homogeneity less and less attainable, as is the case in contemporary France, national values and, thus, the national identity become increasingly grounded in cultural practices.[23] Cultural fields, in turn, become gradually more codified and defined against potential others.

The gastronomic meal file, despite its best and most inclusive intentions, falls victim to mainstream discussions about diversity in France and French gastronomy. Diversity in French gastronomy almost always refers to regional diversity and the rich variety of products that come from France thanks to its geography and climates, ignoring culinary contributions of immigrants.[24] Similarly, in the gastronomic meal discourse, diversity is largely French-specific. The meal 'combines folk and savant traditions, transcends local customs, generations, social class and opinions, and adapts to religious and philosophical beliefs'.[25] Certainly, the reference to religious and philosophical beliefs does open the notion of diversity, but it is hard to understand how a meal in which the careful selection and consumption of alcohol marks the beginning, middle, and end would easily adapt to Muslim family practices. Moreover, the insistence on the homogenous character of the meal and its embeddedness in a long-view of French history makes it difficult to see how the meal could ever adapt to truly diverse situations.

We might argue that the choice of dishes for the meal allows for inclusivity of non-French cuisines, but the file is contradictory on this issue. Twice the file notes that the meal is 'associated with a shared vision of eating well, rather than with specific dishes'. Consuming the same foods and wines is not a requirement. Consequently, the meal is 'open to the diversity of traditions, food and cuisines'. Nevertheless, the file also indicates that the food on the table should come from or reference 'a repertoire of codified recipes'. What are these recipes? What makes them codified? Would couscous, pho, or a barbecue make the list? Upon close reading, the file appears to link the repertoire of recipes to foods that would find their place in discussions of what is traditionally French as they have been 'long handed down from generation to generation'. The language of the dishes echoes the language of the meal itself as inherited history. Moreover, using local products from the market is of utmost importance because 'they have a high cultural value'.[26] Localizing ingredients, as Wilson contends, increases feelings of trust and quality, which are 'cornerstones of national culture and identity'.[27] The use of local foods further links the meal to notions of *terroir*, itself ingrained in beliefs about heritage, tradition, and Frenchness.[28] This language is at least, I contend, an effort to privilege traditional French cuisine within a framework that is suggested to be open.

The inscription of the gastronomic meal on the ICH List has spawned other initiatives to protect and promote French gastronomic identity. Though these initiatives are numerous, this analysis will discuss those of which education is the central component or purpose.[29] One month after the inscription of the gastronomic meal on the ICH List, the government initiated the National Food Program (*Programme national pour l'alimentation*). The program, which continues today, promotes innovation throughout the food system by awarding grants for projects in areas including social justice, education and transmission of culinary *savoir-faire*, and fostering the relationship between agricultural communities and the broader French population. Through coordinated actions across several government ministries, the program wishes to develop the 'consumer-citizen' and positions government food programs as facilitators of 'solidarity' within the nation.[30] The

Hollande administration went as far as to say that the goal of the program was to make French food culture 'one of the founding principles of citizenship'.[31]

The fall of 2011, one year following the gastronomic meal's success, saw the birth of the *Fête de la Gastronomie*, an annual three-day celebration of French food and agriculture. The event is meant to inform (*'sensibiliser'*) the French and tourists alike about all things culinary and to contribute to the nation's economic bottom line by promoting 'an essential element of French identity'.[32] A vast array of events, largely based on discovery and sharing of culinary *savoir-faire*, encourages appreciation and knowledge of the nation's culinary heritage and offerings.[33]

Both of these events, the creation of the National Food Program and the *Fête de la Gastronomie*, specifically refer to the gastronomic meal, as does nearly every gastronomic event and policy occurring in France since 2010, suggesting it is the *raison d'être* for all consequent political, food-based action. The continued transmission of the meal and of culinary knowledge is a condition for placement on the ICH List. The gastronomic meal nomination file goes further though, specifically explaining the necessity of educating the French public, noting that the French are unaware of the impact and importance of their own culture. The file also addresses threats to gastronomic culture in France and elsewhere by mentioning the perceived dilution of culture in the face of globalization, the increasing standardization of food production, and changes in French dining norms. Consequently, though without entering into specifics, the file proposes gastronomic education programs to be implemented in schools and communities. Noting that these efforts will aid in transmitting and safeguarding the meal, the file states that they will also contribute 'to the strengthening of social and family ties'.[34]

One specific promise of the nomination file is the creation of gastronomic sites dedicated to raising awareness about and transmitting both the meal and gastronomic heritage generally.[35] In June 2013, the French government consequently moved to create a network of four *Cités de la gastronomie*, or Gastronomic Cities, across France. Each *Cité* is dedicated to a different aspect of French gastronomic culture and has a mission of promoting culinary work, sharing culinary knowhow, developing professional education programs, encouraging research and innovation, and creating educational experiences accessible to the general public. Education is thus at the forefront of each site's existence. At present it is impossible to know the impact of these sites. At the time of writing this article, the *Cités* are in the final stages of development and not yet open to the public.[36]

What makes these repeated calls for education important in the larger national context and concerning the matter of who is and is not French is that education has long been central to the formation of French citizens. It is possible to view French schools as '"mills of citizenship" – and not just of citizenship but of Frenchness'.[37] With the creation of a national education system in the nineteenth century, Jules Ferry intended for schools to craft responsible and equal republican citizens so as to ensure the survival of the Republic by teaching a common language, universal values, and *laïcité* – the separation between state and religion.[38] Civic education aimed at cultivating national identity remains integral to the national educational curriculum at all levels even today.[39] Students learn about the fundamental rights of citizens, symbols of the Republic, key historic documents, monuments, and the history of the French language.[40] All of these elements construct and maintain the national identity by integrating regionally and ethnically diverse populations into a singular community. They also recall the values linked to the gastronomic meal.

Food is a concrete, lived experience that may provide the most efficacious medium through which to define, demonstrate, and diffuse a centralized concept of French identity. Food is easily accessible for students given its secure place in the everyday. Because it is a powerful, multi-layered symbol, food is an ideal medium for engaging more abstract themes through concrete examples. Indeed, for about the past thirty years, the French school system has been using food to promote national values and inculcate a dominant culinary definition of Frenchness through its school lunch program and the annual *Semaine du Goût*, or Taste Week.[41] Teaching French gastronomy means teaching national history, geography, taste, notions of quality, the values of community and citizenship, respect, table manners, and the art of conversation (in other words, the deployment of the French language). Gastronomy and nation are self-reinforcing. As Poulain claims, defining national identity and culinary identity are part of a circular process, one feeding off of the other, eventually becoming inseparable.[42]

For the nation to exist, the community not only needs to be singularly identified and constructed, it also needs to be regularly reified to prove itself convincing and permanent. This is particularly true during times of anxiety and tumult, words that aptly describe the French social climate over the past decade. Changes and threats to French culture, society, and values perceptibly touch everyone, and so everyone must reengage in their comprehension and daily practice of national identity, first and foremost around the table. When the French government enacts food policies and references the gastronomic meal, it is writing food into French citizenship in increasingly meaningful ways. By educating the public on how to eat French, actors across a variety of fields are promoting and enforcing what it means to be French. Defining model citizens is no longer about promoting traditional republican values, but about dictating what, when, where, and with whom the nation eats. Formalizing food education and French gastronomy itself affirms, codifies, and makes official what many have been arguing since nearly time immemorial – gastronomy is a key tool in constructing the nation and in defining what it means to be French.

133

Notes

1   All necessary translations are my own. Jean-Pierre Poulain, *Sociologies de l'alimentation: Les mangeurs et l'espace social alimentaire* (Paris: Presses Universitaires de France, 2002), p. 201.

2   Vincent Martigny, '*Le Goût des nôtres: gastronomie et sentiment national en France*', *Raisons politiques*, 37 (2010), 39-52 (p. 51).

3   Amélie Baras, 'France Citizenship in the Aftermath of 2015: Officializing a Two-Tier System?',

Citizenship Studies, 21 (2017), 918-36 (p. 918).

4 Laurent Binet, '"*Touche pas à mon pain au chocolat!*": The Theme of Food in Current French Political Discourses', *Modern and Contemporary France*, 24 (2016), 239-52 (p. 241).

5 Wynne Wright and Alexis Annes, 'Halal on the Menu? Contested Food Politics and French Identity in Fast-food', *Journal of Rural Studies*, 32 (2013), 388-99 (p. 389).

6 Edward Cody, 'In France, Halal Meat Drama Enters Election Campaign', *Washington Post*, 6 March 2012 <http//:https://www.washingtonpost.com/> [accessed 23 May 2019].

7 Elaine Sciolino, 'French Politics Served in a Pita', *New York Times*, 23 December 2014, p. D1.

8 Pierre Bafoil, '*De Béziers à Marseille, pourquoi des villes partent en croisade contre les kebabs?*', *Les Inrocks*, 5 July 2017 <http://www.lesinrocks.com> [accessed 16 September 2018]. See also Sciolino, p. D1.

9 Lauren Janes, '#CouscousGate?', *History News Network*, 8 October 2017 <https://historynewsnetwork.org/article/167070> [accessed 15 November 2017].

10 Dena Montague, 'Communitarianism, Discourse and Political Opportunity in Republican France', *French Cultural Studies*, 24 (2013), 219-30 (p. 220).

11 Christophe Bertossi, 'The Performativity of Colour Blindness: Race, Politics and Immigrant Integration in France, 1980-2012', *Patterns of Prejudice*, 46 (2012), 427-44 (p. 427-29); Dominique Schnapper, '*Peut-on encore être universaliste?*', in *L'Universel et la politique des identités,* ed. by Schmuel Trigano (Paris: Editions de l'Eclat, 2010), pp. 25-39.

12 Jean-Louis Tornatore, 'Anthropology's Payback: "The Gastronomic Meal of the French," The Ethnographic Elements of a Heritage Distinction', in *Heritage Regimes and the State*, ed. by Regina F. Bendix, Aditya Eggert, and Arnika Peselmann (Göttingen: Göttingen University Press, 2013), pp. 341-65 (pp. 349-53, 362).

13 For the purposes of this publication, I am using the English language version of the French gastronomic meal nomination file. There is also a French version. I have cross-referenced the language in each version to ensure consistency. UNESCO, 'Gastronomic Meal of the French, Nomination File No. 00437', UNESCO Intangible Cultural Heritage, 2010 <https://ich.unesco.org/en/rl/gastronomic-meal-of-the-french-00437> [accessed 1 June 2018] (p. 3).

14 UNESCO, pp. 4-5.

15 UNESCO, pp. 3-5.

16 UNESCO, p. 2. See also, the similar expression 'has flourished in France for centuries' on p. 3.

17 UNESCO, pp. 4-6.

18 Thomas M. Wilson, 'Food, Drink and Identity in Europe: Consumption and the Construction of Local, National and Cosmopolitan Culture', *European Studies,* 22 (2006), 11-29 (p. 20).

19 Anne-Marie Thiesse, 'The Formation of National Identities', in *The European Puzzle: The Political Structuring of Cultural Identities at a Time of Transition*, ed. by Marion Demoissier (Oxford: Berghahn, 2007), pp. 16-28.

20 Benedict Anderson, *Imagined Communities* (London: Verso, 2006), p. 6.

21 UNESCO, pp. 2-8.

22 Lori G. Beaman, 'Living Together v. Living Well Together: A Normative Examination of the SAS Case', *Social Inclusion*, 4 (2016), 3-13 (p. 9).

23 Bertossi, pp. 428, 438.

24 For examples of this argumentation, see Francis Chevrier, *Notre gastronomie est une culture* (Paris: Bourin Editeur, 2011), pp. 34-38; Alain Ducasse, *Manger est un acte citoyen* (Paris: Les liens qui libèrent, 2017), pp. 127; Martigny, p. 43.

25 UNESCO, p. 5.

26 UNESCO, pp. 3-6.

27 Wilson, p. 24.

28 Amy B. Trubek, *The Taste of Place: A Cultural Journey into Terroir* (Berkeley: University of California Press, 2009), pp. 18, 53.

29 Other political manoeuvres around food include the successful effort to inscribe the Champagne and

Burgundy wine regions on the list of UNESCO World Heritage sites, the desire to place both the baguette and the Parisian bistro on the ICH List, Goût de France, and President Emmanuel Macron's creation of the 2020 Paris Food Forum.

30 Ministère de l'Agriculture, de l'agroalimentaire et de la forêt, '*Le Nouveau programme national pour l'alimentation*,' November 2014, pp. 3-8.

31 Gouvernement.fr, *Une nouvelle politique de l'alimentation*, 15 May 2017 <https://www.gouvernement. fr/ action/une-nouvelle-politique-de-l-alimentation> [accessed 2 February 2019].

32 Ministère de l'Économie et des finances and Ministère de l'Agriculture et de l'alimentation, '*Fête de la gastronomie: Au cœur du produit*', *Dossier de presse* (2017), p. 5.

33 Ministère de l'Économie et des finances, '*Fêtez la gastronomie partout en France: Le Goût dans tous ses sens*', *Dossier de presse* (2018).

34 UNESCO, pp. 6-9.

35 UNESCO, p. 9.

36 Le Repas gastronomique des Français, *Le Réseau des Cités de la gastronomie* <https://repasgastronomi-queunesco.fr/les-cites-de-la-gastronomie/le-reseau/> [accessed 17 May 2019].

37 Christopher Caldwell, 'The Crescent and the Tricolor', *The Atlantic*, November 2010 <www.theatlantic. com> [accessed 28 April 2019].

38 Daniel Béland, 'Identity Politics and French Republicanism', *Society*, 40 (2003), 66-71 (p. 66); Gilbert D. Chaitin, 'Education and Political Identity: The Universalist Controversy', *Yale French Studies*, 113 (2008), 77-93 (p. 77).

39 Audrey Osler and Hugh Starkey, 'Citizenship Education and National Identities in France and England: Inclusive or Exclusive?', *Oxford Review of Education*, 27 (2001), 287-305 (pp. 295-96).

40 Ministère de l'Éducation nationale, *Bulletin officiel de l'éducation nationale, Numéro 30*, 26 July 2018 <www.education.gouv.fr> [accessed 26 March 2019].

41 Tina Moffat and Danielle Gendron, 'Cooking up the "Gastro-Citizen" Through School Meal Programs in France and Japan', *Food, Culture, and Society*, 22 (2019), 63-77; Ministère de l'Agriculture et de l'alimentation, '*La Semaine du goût*', *Dossier de presse* (2018), pp. 2-5.

42 Poulain, p. 23.

Marxist Analysis, in My Food Technology? Fuzzy Legibility, Flavour Connections, and the Recent Dialectical Emergence of Postmodernity in Cuisine

Arielle Johnson

1. What Is This All About?

This paper is concerned with the emergence of new food projects that combine practical/traditional and empirical forms of thinking in an unusual way. The term 'new food projects' is intentionally vague because some are based in restaurants, some around scholarly work, and some elsewhere. All do intentional knowledge-making, and involve both a focus on flavour and sites and individuals outside of the hegemony of academic institutions.

Two quintessential examples are the Washington State University Bread Lab and Restaurant Noma's various lab-building projects (the Nordic Food Lab, the Noma Fermentation Lab). Neither of these is wholly modernist in the sense of molecular gastronomy or embracing commodity-focused food systems, but neither takes a reactionary approach of looking backward to an earlier, and lost, type of food system.

In this paper I explore how a dialectical analysis of how these new projects relate to food, knowledge, and power makes them more understandable. By combining elements from traditional food systems and practical knowledge (valuing biodiversity, flavour, place, and culture, and reflecting comfort with fuzzy, chaotic, or approximate legibility rather than perfect engineering) with those from modernity (empiricism, adaptation and development of new technology, use of data and the literature review), they offer a synthesis to resolve the tension between traditionality (as a thesis) and modernity (as a synthesis), something that I will call 'postmodernity' in cuisine.

2. Métis, Modernity, and Dominance

On the topic of forms of knowledge, I'm going to start with something that cooks and chefs have a lot of: a traditional, practical form of knowledge that James Scott, in his seminal book *Seeing Like a State*, calls *métis*. To quote Scott:

> How frequently local knowledge, trial and error, or what we might more generously call the stochastic method has produced practical solutions without benefit of scientific method.

> *Métis*, with the premium it places on practical knowledge, experience, and stochastic reasoning, is of course not merely the now-superseded precursor of scientific knowledge. It is the mode of reasoning most appropriate to complex material and social tasks where the uncertainties are so daunting that we must trust our (experienced) intuition and feel our way.[1]

Much of what we might talk about here as traditional foodways – not just recipes or dishes, but also social and natural systems for producing food – are built upon *métis*.

By contrast, applied epistemic knowledge has invented things like the cadastral map, modern city planning, and the Green Revolution. This kind of knowledge-making is typically in the service of some kind of central authority, and it functions through simplification and legibility: by simplifying systems to optimize to a particular goal, like a forest which can yield as much timber as possible or more accurate farm taxes based on mapped size, epistemic knowledge and modernization flattens, and makes flattened versions of complex systems legible and orderly to a non-local.

As has been touched on most recently by Joanna Blythman during the first day of the 2019 Oxford Food Symposium, foodways based on tradition and locality are everywhere being encroached on by high modern processes of industrialization and standardization. This is not unique to food. In fact, Scott argues that it is in the nature of modernity, in its need to supplant the traditional, for it to hold practical and lived knowledge in contempt to help legitimize itself:

> a certain understanding of science, modernity, and development has so successfully structured the dominant discourse that all other kinds of knowledge are regarded as backward, static traditions, as old wives' tales and superstitions. High modernism has needed this 'other,' this dark twin, in order to rhetorically present itself as the antidote to backwardness.[2]

137

This tension would be resolvable – not necessarily for good or bad, but there would be a resolution of tension – if high-modern-style knowledge-making and the knowledge it makes could fully supplant traditional *métis*.

This doesn't happen, and hasn't happened, because through the process of flattening, simplification, and the drive for perfect legibility, high modern systems have created new problems.

3. Dialectical, Flavourful, and Fuzzy Wheat Breeding: The Bread Lab

Scott covers how these emergent issues have manifested in systems like forestry, agronomy, and urban planning. To look at a food-specific perspective from a scientist's own field, I turn to Dr Stephen Jones, a classically trained wheat breeder at Washington State University who has founded what he calls The Bread Lab. Jones, along with his frequent collaborator Bethany Econopouly, outlines the synthetic position of The Bread Lab in relation to conventional (modern) and heirloom (traditional) wheat varieties.

They note that '[c]onventional wheat breeding justifiably attempts to produce varieties that benefit the greatest number of farmers, producers, and consumers. Consistent targets aimed at large consumer bases are the easiest for public and private breeders to justify, receive funding for, and hit'. However, they explain:

> By breeding for uniformity, breeders have bred out diversity in the wheat gene pool with the end goal of also removing variation in milling and baking operations. The result is a loss of nutrition, flavour, and ultimately consumer choice of products and the businesses that make them [...]. Flour, bread, and wheat have lost their regional distinctiveness and today is most probably the clearest example of broad-scale uniformity in agricultural and food systems.[3]

What we would now call heirloom varieties of wheat, or before that, landraces, that were developed (using *métis*) to suit localities and produce quality bread have been supplanted by a smaller number of modern wheat varieties. While these hit specific targets for yield and for commercial sandwich bread qualities in ways that heirlooms never could, they bring with them a diminishment of wheat genetic diversity as well as an erasure of flavour and nutrition. In striving for a kind of perfect legibility (in this case, wheat that consistently performed to specific targets in an industrial bakery setting), high-modern, technical wheat breeding ignored and flattened other, sensable, but more difficult-to-measure qualities. By narrowing down the number of varieties, it also created a genetic bottleneck, making the shared wheat germplasm more susceptible to catastrophic, maladaptive disruptions.

138

One approach to ameliorate this lack of genetic diversity as well as flavour is to, simply put, return to the heirlooms. The idea of a return to preindustrial varieties of food, the slowing and turning back of time, has been attractive to a great many people and explicated in much more detail elsewhere. In the specific case of wheat, Jones points out some specific flaws in this method:

> Although some heirloom wheats are appealing to modern small-scale millers and craft bakers, to be sustainable and widely affordable, varieties need to work for farmers. So we find ourselves back at wheat's first path of life: yield, resistance to disease, efficient use of resources, and ease of harvest for a given locality. Heirloom varieties, when dislocated from place or time, have not kept up with changing climates or pests and disease.[4]

While returning and retaining has an important place (and, for many food categories, a deep cultural importance that cannot be dismissed), it in itself is insufficient to systemically resolve the tension between traditional and high-modern forms of knowledge embodied in wheat.

Fortunately, Jones offers a model:

Breeders must pull the two paths of wheat together so that the seed works for the farmer and the craft miller and the baker: high yields in the field and slow bread in the bakery, at a price that is more within a range of what more members of our communities can afford.

The mission of the Bread Lab is to combine science, art, curiosity, and innovation to explore ways of using regionally available grains to move the craft of whole grain bread baking and other grain usage forward. The farmer-breeder-chef collaborative approach seeks to leverage the agronomic skills and knowledge of the farmer, the culinary perspective of the chef and the logistical skills of the breeder to develop varieties with local adaptation and end-use potential.[5]

By giving up the high-modern goal of perfect legibility, and the high-modern scientist's need for intellectual supremacy, The Bread Lab creates a novel approach that defies norms of both *métis*-based and modern industrial knowledge-making. The targets for wheat are based on flavour and artisan baking performance; the process is guided by the experience-earned knowledge and intuition of skilled craftspeople. Scientific and high-tech methods are still very much used, but the legibility they are used to develop is deliberately fuzzier.

4. More Previously-Unthinkable Collaborations

Jones's Bread Lab is not alone in this type of model of work in food – in the last decade or so, a number of genre-defying science and science-adjacent projects in food have come into existence. Not only is the shape of their defiance similar to each other, but it is also different than forms of defiance or rebellion that came in the past.

Some of these projects emerge from academic sites. In this paradigm, they subvert both the expectations of the level of legibility and control of complexity that a scientific project should seek out, and avail themselves of what was previously anathema: input from the practical, *métis*-based knowledge of artisans and practitioners. Jones's Bread Lab breaks protocol by involving skilled artisan bakers in designing and carrying out the wheat evaluation process and turns the high-modern, industrial approach to crop science on its head. At Harvard, Drs Rachel Dutton and Ben Wolfe study cheese fermentation, not in the industrial context of optimized, controlled, single strains, but with microbial populations of artisan cheeses responsible for complex flavour formation.[6] Their collaborators are small producers and affineurs like Jasper Hill Farm in Vermont as well as experimental restaurants like Momofuku in New York.

A curiosity and openness to flavour, often not viewed as a subject worth studying in depth in its natural context, serves as an entry point for questioning other received assumptions about what is necessary for doing research. I have found this in my own work, and, separately, other scientists working on food have as well. By seeking out previously-unthinkable collaborations, and adopting a looser stance regarding the type of expertise that is worthy of taking seriously, these rebellious academic sites both find seriously novel research work to be done, and are helping define a new option for how to develop research on food in the first place.

5. Restaurants Making Labs, Cooks Making Knowledge

The role of restaurants, cooks, and food producers in this emergent paradigm is yet more intriguing. The projects I've already mentioned are obvious sites of knowledge generation – this is what academic institutions and academic credentials are supposed to be for. The other half of this new kind of knowledge-making takes place in restaurants, specifically with restaurants launching their own research labs.

Momofuku, founded by chef David Chang in New York, began a research program to better understand the functionality of fermentation and microbial *terroir*, apply it to locally available ingredients to serve in their restaurants, and disseminate this knowledge publicly. They collaborated with academics for some of this work, but the impetus and direction of engaging in explicitly knowledge-generating activity came from chefs without any formal scientific training or credentials, outside of a university or the food processing industry, in a self-built and self-run site.[7]

In my own personal experience, I've worked quite closely with several projects originating out of the Copenhagen-based restaurant Noma. Noma is organized around a creative constraint to work primarily, ideally only, with ingredients grown within the Nordic region, which rules out many common ingredients like lemons and olive oil and seriously brings seasonality, and the shortness of growing seasons, to the forefront.[8] Seeking out unconventional suppliers took the point of creation of Noma's cuisine out of the kitchen and brought it deep down the supply chain, situating it inextricably in a larger system and landscape of food production. The Nordic Food Lab and later the Noma Fermentation Lab were launched to develop a more systematic understanding of the roots of flavour in biodiverse ingredients and (like Momofuku) techniques of fermentation by instructing chefs to self-educate in microbiology, ethnobotany, entomology, and natural products chemistry and scientists to figure out how to construct experiments with flavour and kitchen performance as a target.[9]

Here, again, we have self-constructed sites explicitly for knowledge generation, outside the physical purview of academia, with traditional and practical knowledge and their holders on the same hierarchical level as those with formal credentials for generating knowledge. And again, flavour is an entry point and a goal, and, with this as a goal, larger forms of questioning and larger systems are engaged. Finally, the level of control and precision of the knowledge and tools resulting from this setup is much fuzzier and more open to chaos than that which typifies explicitly modern forms of doing research on food. By embracing a fuzzy legibility, these projects, whether they are intra muros or extra muros of academe, identify new ways of resolving tension between traditional and high-modern approaches to food by synthesizing aspects of both into something new.

6. Flavour as an Entry Point and Connector

Of course good flavour is a goal for chefs and their work; but when I talk about it as an entry point to genre-breaking work, I refer also to its physiological and ecological

Knowledge production & publication outside of academic hegemony	Academic labs working outside of norms of legibility and control	Interdisciplinary, Anti-hierarchical Connections
Noma, Copenhagen	The Bread Lab, Washington State University	MAD Symposium, Copenhagen
D.O.M., São Paulo	Oregon State University Multibarley project	Nordic Food Lab, Copenhagen
Momofuku, New York	Dutton Lab, Harvard / UC San Diego	Noma Fermentation Lab, Copenhagen
Central, Lima	Wolfe Lab, Tufts	Culinary Breeding Network, Oregon State University
Mikla, Istanbul	Dunn Lab Sourdough Project, North Carolina State University	Flavour Journal
Blue Hill at Stone Barns	Mazourek Lab, Cornell / Row 7 Seeds	International Journal of Food Science and Gastronomy
Indigenous Food Lab, North American Traditional Indigenous Food Systems, Minneapolis	Falise Lab, Cornell	London Gastronomy Seminars
Glenn Roberts, Anson Mills, South Carolina	Shepard Lab, Yale	
Neal's Yard Dairy, London	Mouritsen Lab, University of Copenhagen	
Basque Culinary Center, San Sebastian		
Mugaritz, San Sebastian		

Table 1: A list of 'postmodern' food projects, approaching empirical knowledge, métis, tradition, and flavour in similar ways

aspects. Flavour, in the sense of a sense that combines taste and smell that has been both philosophically and scientifically undervalued, as well as the ecologically-driven evolutionary adaptations that drive the creation of flavour molecules in nature also acts as a natural connector between disciplines.[10] Chefs that approach the flavour of their ingredients at all analytically or experimentally will eventually find that it is not sufficient to keep their mindset confined to what can happen in the kitchen, and that seeking flavour naturally takes them into microbiology, agronomy, ethnobotany, and beyond. Likewise, scientists who work on some part of this system that produces edible things – a wheat or a squash breeder, a cheese microbiologist – will eventually figure out that the parameters they can measure – environment, genetics, substrate – may be perceptually intangible, but translate into tastable flavour molecules. If they follow this line of inquiry, it will take them to the limits of what is considered important in the academy, and they will find that their understanding is enhanced, via this flavour inquiry, by seeking input beyond this boundary, from traditional knowledge or from practitioners and artisans (cooks, farmers, cheese makers, and others) who work with the same systems, but in practice, rather than *in vitro*. Flavour necessitates the alternative James Scott talks about to epistemic knowledge crushing and erasing *métis* and situated knowledge – a workable, harmonizing synthesis of both approaches.

7. Modernity and Modernism and Cuisine

Of course, this paper is hardly the first attempt to place contemporary food developments within a framework of cultural evolution. I would be remiss in talking about Modernity and Cuisine without mentioning its most famous coinage, Modernist Cuisine, which was defined by its greatest proponent and primary chronicler Nathan Myhrvold as fine cooking projects that 'transcend their primary utilitarian purpose and engage our minds in profoundly intellectual and emotional ways'. In *Gastronomica*, Myhrvold makes the case that the haute cuisine techniques and philosophy he writes about in *Modernist Cuisine* (2011), conceived of by chefs like Wylie Dufresne, Juan-Mari Arzak, Grant Achatz, and above all Ferrán Adria of El Bulli, make up a cultural development to create food that is 1) legitimately artistic, rather than craft and 2) legitimately in the artistic tradition of Modernism.[11]

Myhrvold particularly emphasizes that the haute cuisine of modernist chefs qualifies as art, as contrasted to craft, calling it 'one of the great intellectual questions for gastronomy in the twenty-first century'. The 'traditional ideas about food' hold that food is the product of craft, not art. The attributes that Myhrvold identifies as craft-like include a 'focus […] on the process of manufacture, or on the food itself, with less emphasis on the thoughts and emotions triggered by the food'. He concludes that '[f]ood is deeply constrained by rules and traditions', and while he does not elaborate on this point (except to later mention 'intellectually bankrupt rules of the past' and 'establishment rules' that exist to be overthrown), its inclusion with qualities that assume food to be craft, rather than art, suggest that these rules and traditions are to be read as negative constraints.[12]

Myhrvold and others use the term 'cuisine' to mean 'haute cuisine', but this is not the only meaning contained within that term. Sidney Mintz has discussed the use of 'cuisine' when one really is discussing 'haute cuisine', the food of 'sophisticated consumers' and 'cooks and diners free from the conventions of region or ritual'.[13] This

142

freedom from convention is similar to what Myhrvold identifies as a precursor to both food as art and cuisine as modernism, but in this case, the 'cooks and diners free from the conventions of region or ritual' are not in twenty-first-century Europe, but rather Sung-Dynasty China (960-1279 CE).

Contrast this to Mintz's more specific definition of cuisine: 'Cuisine [...] has to do with the ongoing foodways of a region, within which active discourse about food sustains both common understandings and reliable production of the foods in question.'[14] Haute cuisine requires sophisticated consumers, but the baseline for any kind of cuisine requires an ongoing discourse, and therefore familiarity, feelings, and thinking about food. Above all, cuisine is not just food: it is food, coming from a place, with associated production methods and a discourse around it.

If place and production are essential parts of cuisine (on top of cultural value and the kitchen), as Mintz argues, then cuisine is not only about food as a product of cooking and consumption, but also of landscape, environment, agronomy, and ecology. Place and region have a specific landscape, a specific environment, a specific ecology with species whose evolutionary history was impacted by their interactions with landscape and environment as well as each other, and specific choices about what plants and animals to cultivate as well as how to cultivate them.

In turn, the cultural role of food is not separable from the different disciplines that study and expedite its production – which means that any cuisine starts far away and a long time before any ingredients enter a kitchen. It also means that a cultural examination of cuisine, as well as the creation of food in a kitchen, can only be enhanced by engaging with these systems, and the disciplines that study them, that have an impact on food before it reaches the kitchen.

Going by this Mintz-influenced definition of cuisine – food situated in nature, a production system, and a culture – we have had, if not Modernist Cuisine, then pervasive 'Modern Cuisine' in the West for something like a century. In this case, I refer to 'modern' not as an avant-garde aesthetic project emerging out of late-nineteenth century artistic movements, but modern in the sense of containing modernity. Modernity, like modernism, is constituted as a break from tradition and traditionality, but instead of making art or architecture, it uses particular tools to configure a society and its economic and social systems.

8. Modernity in Cuisine: Dominance and Mythmaking

Some of the defining characteristics of modernity, besides a general discontinuity from traditional ways and systems, include a particular discontinuity and abstraction of time and space; the disembedding of social activities from specific, localized contexts; and the production of systematized and specialized knowledge.[15] These aspects of modernity are institutionalized in systems that consolidate power – namely, industrialism, capitalism, the surveillance state, and military power. Since food and cuisine (cuisine including the culture around food, as well as the place and systems that it comes from) pervade most of the functionings of society in one way or another, as well as a society's interactions with the natural world, all four of these institutions have a hand in the creation of Modern Cuisine. Capitalism and industrialism are particularly relevant, and an additional component to understanding the power dynamics that underlie how we perceive the role and future of food, modern, postmodern or otherwise, is the soft-power role of myth and narrative. As Roland Barthes puts it in *Mythologies*, 'In the account given of our contemporary circumstances, I resented seeing Nature and History confused at every turn, and I wanted to track down, in the decorative display of what-goes-without-saying, the ideological abuse which, in my view, is hidden there.'[16]

'What-goes-without-saying', the myth, the accepted narrative about the way things are – it is dressed up to appear natural and inevitable, but its accepted-ness and going-without-saying belie that it is not reality; it is what someone (or several someones) would like reality to be. Narratives both push and hide ideology simultaneously, and successfully getting others to accept an ideology is a potent method for subtly accumulating power. If something goes-without-saying, it also goes without questioning.

This particularly comes to bear on discussions about 'The Future of Food'. Will it be modern, or postmodern? I would argue that breathlessly covered projects like Soylent, meat substitutes, vertical farming, genetically personalized food-as-medicine, the engineered microbiome, robot kitchens, and CRISPR gene editing, all enabled by the big-data panopticon are both the dominant, goes-without-saying myth about what the future of food will be and uniformly late-modernist projects, contrasted to postmodern ones.[17]

All these projects rely on key modernist points of legibility and of control, control that comes with high start-up capital requirements, increasingly centralized oversight of and power over what a large group of people gets to eat, and how that food gets made. The mythmaking of future food takes ideas and hopes from earlier eras of modernity – the meal-in-a-pill, Winston Churchill's vision of growing chicken parts 'separately under a suitable medium' – and re-skins them with more updated tech, without evolving the underlying ideology or inevitable social system necessitated by its production needs.[18] The myth takes invented, but no longer new, ideas, and portrays them as eternal and inevitable and outside of history. The ideology that positivist future-of-food mythmaking hides in plain sight is about the inevitability of late capitalism and late modernity.

9. The Necessity of Synthesis and the Dialectic

If late-modern food projects go-without-saying as an inevitability and a logical endpoint of modern development, if there is no dialectical interplay between food ideas in history, then the new food projects I mentioned earlier do not make any sense at all. They don't use technology in the right way, and they don't use knowledge generation as centralizing power generation. They shouldn't exist, and yet they do; they've even developed similar philosophies and outlooks semi-independently of each other.

Within a context of synthesis, the pattern common to new food projects I mentioned earlier – flavour, blending epistemic and practical knowledge, an acceptance of imperfect control and fuzzy legibility – is subversive, and sticky, because it undermines the supremacy of high-modern, industrial ideas of power and value and the systems that support them. These projects borrow from both buckets, and in doing so, introduce this tension between modern food systems and traditional cuisines into a dialectic. As laid out by Hegel and Marx, the dialectic acts as a forward engine for the emergence of change in concepts and for real-life power dynamics, resolving unstable tensions not by tipping a hand in one of two directions, but by creating a third that synthesizes elements of both. In this case, we might identify the thesis in this dialectic as traditional systems of cuisine, its antithesis as industrial modernity, and these new projects – from rebellious academics and upstart cooks – as their synthesis, a new kind of postmodernity in cuisine.

Ideas that use modernity as a stepping stone to something else challenge this ideology in a dangerous way. A restaurant doing research, and using modernity as fuel for the dialectical engine of idea-synthesis, is not just an interesting curiosity, but also a revealer of deep power interests. An industrially produced meal-replacement is not just a meal replacement, a bread lab is not just a bread lab, and flavour that is both perceptually complex and systemically understood is not just a sensory phenomenon.

Where epistemic high modernity seeks perfect legibility, postmodern projects accept a fuzzy legibility, a result that falls within a range of predictability but tolerates a range of stochasticity and chaos – for example, a post-baking treatment, water and salt content, and controlled temperature and humidity range for incubation that can reliably take a restaurant's bread waste and transform it into a fermented miso-like product, which will vary in flavour and consistency but turn out something delicious ninety percent of the time. Or, a barley variety that contains a high degree of internal genetic variability, allowing it to adapt to different ecological conditions while still producing high-quality, if tolerably variable, beer malt.

Where modernity siloed the systems that produce food (where knowledge is generated by holders of specific technical qualifications and flows only outward) and the haute cuisine of elites (where the practically skilled producer engages in artistic activity that floats above the everyday and dirty work of considering and stewarding systems) into separate realms that do not converse without debasing themselves, postmodernity thrives on robust interchange between the two.

145

Notes

1   James C. Scott, *Seeing Like a State: How Certain Schemes to Improve the Human Condition Have Failed* (New Haven: Yale University Press, 1998), p. 325.
2   Scott, p. 331.
3   Stephen S. Jones and Bethany F. Econopouly, 'Breeding Away from All Purpose', *Agroecology and Sustainable Food Systems*, 42.6 (3 July 2018), 712-21 <doi.org/10.1080/21683565.2018.1426672> [accessed

5 May 2019].

4   Jones and Econopouly.

5   Jones and Econopouly.

6   Peter Andrey Smith, 'For Gastronomists, a Go-To Microbiologist', *The New York Times*, 17 September 2012 <https://www.nytimes.com/2012/09/19/dining/for-gastronomists-a-go-to-microbiologist.html> [accessed 5 May 2019].

7   Jane Kramer, 'The Umami Project', *The New Yorker*, 14 January 2013. <https://www.newyorker.com/magazine/2013/01/21/the-umami-project> [accessed 5 May 2019].

8   René Redzepi, *Noma: Time and Place in Nordic Cuisine* (London: Phaidon Press, 2010).

9   Ole G. Mouritsen and others, 'Seaweeds for Umami Flavour in the New Nordic Cuisine', *Flavour* 1.1 (21 March 2012), 4 <doi.org/10.1186/2044-7248-1-4>; René Redzepi, *A Work in Progress: Journal, Recipes and Snapshots* (London: Phaidon Press, 2013); Arielle J. Johnson, 'Artisanal Food Microbiology', *Nature Microbiology*, 1 (29 March 2016), 16039. It should be disclosed that I worked at Noma from 2014 to 2016 and collaborated on research prior to that in 2012 and 2013. In 2014 I was invited to take a job there, with my work including co-founding the Noma Fermentation Lab. While I cannot claim an unbiased perspective, I can claim one of particularly up-close observation, and, I hope, insight.

10 Dana M. Small, 'Flavour Is in the Brain', *Physiology & Behavior*, 107.4 (November 2012), 540-52; Gordon M. Shepherd, 'The Human Sense of Smell: Are We Better Than We Think?' *PLOS Biology*, 2.5 (11 May 2004), e146; S.A. Goff and Harry Klee, 'Plant Volatile Compounds: Sensory Cues for Health and Nutritional Value?', *Science*, 311.5762 (10 February 2006), 815-19 <doi.org/10.1126/science.1112614>.

11 Nathan Myhrvold, 'The Art in Gastronomy: A Modernist Perspective', *Gastronomica: The Journal of Critical Food Studies*, 11.1 (1 February 2011), 13-23 (p. 13).

12 Myhrvold, pp. 13, 20.

13 Here Mintz is quoting and critiquing Michael Freeman's conflation of 'cuisine' and 'haute cuisine' in 'Sung', in *Food in Chinese Culture*, ed. by K.-C. Chang (New Haven: Yale University Press, 1977), pp. 141-76 (p. 145), qtd. by Sidney Wilfred Mintz, *Tasting Food, Tasting Freedom: Excursions Into Eating, Culture, and the Past* (Boston: Beacon Press, 1996), p. 99.

14 Mintz, p. 104

15 Anthony Giddens, *The Consequences of Modernity* (Standford: Stanford University Press, 1990).

16 Roland Barthes, *Mythologies* (New York: Hill and Wang, 2012 [1957]), p. XI.

17 Joshua Spodek, 'Soylent Is Bringing You the Future of Food', *Inc.com*. 13 November 2018 <https://www.inc.com/joshua-spodek/soylent-future-of-food.html> [accessed 5 May 2019]; BBCClick, 'Lab-Grown Meat: The Future of Food?', *BBC News*, 7 July 2017 <https://www.bbc.com/news/av/technology-40496863/lab-grown-meat-the-future-of-food> [accessed 5 May 2019]; Chris Ip, 'Impossible Foods' Rising Empire of Almost-Meat" *engadget*, 19 May 2019 <https://www.engadget.com/2019/05/19/impossible-foods-burger-sausage-empire/> [accessed 5 May 2019]; Leila Abboud, 'Farm Labs That Grow Crops Indoors Race to Transform Future of Food', *Financial Times*, 21 February 2019 <https://www.ft.com/content/6a940bf6-35d4-11e9-bd3a-8b2a211d90d5> [accessed 5 May 2019]; Marion Nestle, 'NutraIngredients-USA on "Personalized Nutrition"', *Food Politics by Marion Nestle*, 29 November 2018 <https://www.foodpolitics.com/2018/11/nutraingredients-usa-on-personalized-nutrition/> [accessed 5 May 2019]; Megan Gibson, 'Meet The Robot Chef That Can Prepare You Dinner', *Time*, 14 April 2015 <https://time.com/3819525/robot-chef-moley-robotics/> [accessed 5 May 2019]; Stephen S. Hall, 'Crispr Can Speed Up Nature – and Change How We Grow Food', *WIRED*, 17 July 2018 <https://www.wired.com/story/crispr-tomato-mutant-future-of-food/> [accessed 5 May 2019]; Ashish Thusoo, 'How Big Data Is Revolutionizing the Food Industry', *WIRED*, 2018 <https://www.wired.com/insights/2014/02/big-data-revolutionizing-food-industry/> [accessed 5 May 2019].

18 Lizzie Widdicombe, 'The End of Food', *The New Yorker*, 5 May 2014 <https://www.newyorker.com/magazine/2014/05/12/the-end-of-food> [accessed 5 May 2019]; Benjamin Aldes Wurgaft, 'Where Is My Jetpack?' *Gastronomica*, 28 June 2012 <https://gastronomica.org/2012/06/28/where-my-jetpack/> [accessed 5 May 2019].

146

Counter Narratives: American and Canadian Feminist Restaurants from 1972 to Present

Alex D. Ketchum

Karen's Kitchen, 729 West Brompton, tel 525 7785. Wed nights only at 7 p.m. – it really is Karen's own kitchen so be sure to ring up first. Feminist.
— *Gaia's Guide* (1976)[1]

The women's and lesbian travel guidebook, *Gaia's Guide*, listed Karen's Kitchen in the restaurant section for the Chicago area in the 1976 through 1984 annual editions. This short entry speaks to the larger themes and central analytical questions of my paper. In these few, short phrases, the reader was told that Karen's Kitchen was 'feminist', that it existed in a non-traditional space of trade that blurred public and private spheres, that the business was run by a woman named Karen, and that customer practices would differ from those in a typical, mainstream restaurant. This entry in *Gaia's Guide* also raises a number of important questions. Why would Karen call her restaurant 'feminist'? What was a feminist restaurant? What kind of food was served? Other than through guidebooks, how did potential clients find out about the space? Was this space unique? The fact that Karen's Kitchen was listed in a travel guide demonstrates the need that women had for finding these sorts of spaces.

Why Call a Restaurant 'Feminist'?

Karen's decision to manage a food business out of her home demonstrates that some feminists during the 1970s and the 1980s used food as a way to support themselves financially, socially, and politically. The above entry likewise shows that, despite facing a political and economic system that was hostile to women's business ownership (particularly for women of colour and lesbians, and especially prior to the passage of the Equal Credit Opportunity Act in 1974 and the Canadian Human Rights Act of 1977), the owners of feminist restaurants and cafés crafted creative solutions to make the kinds of spaces they wanted. The owners founded these establishments even if it meant having to bend the laws, such as skirting health codes or manipulating tax statuses to their own advantage. The history of feminist restaurants and cafés in the United States and Canada in the 1970s and 1980s provides a history of feminist, food, and environmental movements, while also being relevant to today's debates around the need, or lack thereof, of single gender spaces, feminist consumption, and the relationship between feminist movements and other social justice movements, particularly food justice movements.

Definition

Feminist restaurants and cafés of the 1970s and 1980s in the United States and Canada acted as spaces that challenged the status quo around cooking and consumption through their creation of feminist food. These restaurants were 'feminist' due to their approach to workplace dynamics, supply sourcing, wage structures, and the ability to foster and support community. They could be 'breakfast joints' or specialize in meeting the needs of the lunch or dinner crowd. For the purposes of this research, in order to avoid policing who can call themselves feminist and to make the project the most manageable, I decided that a restaurant must be identified as feminist in its title, in flyers, in interviews, or in descriptions in restaurant reviews, magazines, or periodicals. Within these parameters, a central tenet of the restaurant owners' philosophy was a focus on the needs of women and feminists above all other goals. This paper further speaks to contemporary restaurant discussions around gender, feminism, and labour.

Feminist restaurant owners produced advertisements, business cards, and flyers for special events like concerts, poetry presentations, lectures, guest talks by feminists, and other forms of entertainment. In addition, restaurant owners wrote menus and cookbooks. In these documents, owners also identified their space as feminist, which could be important if the name was not explicit, such as Ms. Purdy's Social Club Coffeehouse and Restaurant of Winnipeg, Manitoba. Apart from self-definition, it can be difficult to categorize these businesses. Many, but not all of them, were either women-only spaces or had women-only hours at some point during their operation. Collectives ran many of the spaces, and radical lesbian separatist, socialist feminist, or ecofeminist ideologies influenced many of the owners. Most restaurants held events with feminist and lesbian poets, musicians, artists, and political speakers because creating a community space was important to many of the owners. However, the most important factor for this study was whether or not the restaurant was an intentionally feminist space.

The apex of American and Canadian feminist restaurants was from 1976-1985. Most feminist restaurants and cafés closed after only a few years of operation; however, this did not mean that they were failures. Feminist restaurants and cafés allowed for – and indeed fostered – cultural, economic, and social communities that played an important role in the women's movements. Despite acting as alternatives to hegemonic eatery culture, feminist restaurants, cafés, and coffeehouses were still liable to mainstream economic patterns and governmental regulations, which ultimately curtailed some of the owners' dreams.

The history of feminist restaurants and cafés in the United States and Canada is a history of business practices, political activism, and food politics. Feminist restaurants and cafés promoted women-owned and women-centred businesses and fostered non-capitalist and non-hierarchal business practices and models. Feminist restaurant history reveals the importance of physical space for socializing, activism, economics, and community building. These businesses were not isolated but, instead, were part of a larger economy and society that was not always amenable to their desires. The creation of women's spaces required innovative financial strategies. Balancing economic needs with feminist philosophies required compromises. This paper speaks to contemporary restaurant discussions around gender, feminism, and labour.

Utilizing business records, advertisements, feminist and lesbian periodicals, and original interviews, I examine the ways in which all feminist restaurants and cafés challenged the common contemporary view of cooking as antithetical to women's liberation and, instead, showed that the kitchen could, in fact, be a space for women's empowerment rather than an oppressive sphere. This project re-centres feminist entrepreneurialism and challenges narratives of post-war feminism. It focuses on how feminist restaurants challenged restaurant work structures.

This paper does not argue that feminist restaurants were the only type of establishment to challenge restaurant hierarchy. Other restaurants also tried to change the role of restaurant management. Moosewood Restaurant, in Ithaca, New York (1973-present), is one of the most famous restaurants that utilized collective management. However, it is not alone: a variety of restaurants, though still in the minority of the general restaurant population, have attempted non-hierarchical collective management. Many of the participating restaurants have had political reasons for doing so, whether they identified as anarchist, feminist, or were concerned with some idea of social justice. What made the feminist restaurants different was their emphasis on feminism. For them, it was important to create decidedly feminist spaces.

Work Structure

In the 1970s, feminists began to critique gender inequity in a variety of workplaces, including restaurants. Feminists believed that the relationships between restaurant managers and waitresses and between waitresses and customers systematically disempowered women.[2] However, most restaurants were managed in this hierarchical style, and most were owned and managed by men. According to the US Bureau of Labor Statistics (BLS), in the 1970s and 1980s far fewer women managed restaurants than in 2017 (ownership was not studied by BLS).[3] In 1972, only 32.4% of restaurant, cafeteria, and bar managers were women and 8.9% were Black men and women.[4] In 2017, 46.3% of food service managers (the category that has replaced 'restaurant, cafeteria, and bar managers,') were women, 9.5% were Black, 11.7% were Asian, and 16.9% were Latino or Hispanic.[5] The gender imbalance of who owns restaurants, who are the head chefs, and who gets the praise continues to present day. Traditionally, although women were cooks and waitresses, they have been noticeably absent from decision-making roles.

Most feminist restaurants and cafés in the 1970s and 1980s were begun by white, lesbian, English-speaking, radical or socialist feminists, who were working-class or middle-class and had some way to access capital outside of bank loans. Rather than cooking, the primary motivation was creating a woman-centred, feminist space where staff could live as 'out' lesbians and financially support themselves in an environment that reflected their values. The general trends among these restaurants were that most were built with sweat equity. Even for restaurants that lasted beyond the first-two-years period, when the majority of restaurants (feminist and not-feminist) fail, finances were always tight. The longer lasting restaurants were highly organized or at least adapted quickly to become so. They had a set idea of how the work would be structured and did not over-extend their programming. Importantly, these spaces had a plan to deal with emotional conflict, especially when operated by a collective. Having a liquor license provided greater economic stability, but alcohol was not always desired, as creating substance-free spaces was a factor that motivated some founders. Restaurants that employed accountants and professional legal counsel saved themselves from costly mistakes.

Feminist restaurants challenged the patriarchal capitalism of the typical business structure. For example, the owners of Bread and Roses feminist restaurant in Cambridge, Massachusetts, thought seriously about these ideas. Writing in 1976 about how the restaurant was different than others, interviewer Gale Goldberg remarked, 'The women at Bread and Roses and the physical space help create an easy, supportive atmosphere for women and their women friends. In urbanized America, other types of restaurants, including both inexpensive fast-food establishments and high-priced restaurants, are mostly owned and operated by men.'[6] In the 1974 Bread and Roses Business prospectus, the owners considered this difference and its implications:

> in contrast, the male tone of a restaurant business venture is aimed more directly at profit making, commercialism, and a hierarchical structure of organization. Traditionally, women have been noticeably absent from places at the decision-making level. The harried long hours on foot are more familiar to women. The often demeaning and thankless job of waiting on tables, servicing the patron, has fallen to women who receive low salaries and rely heavily on tips. There is little place for advancement in this arrangement. Rewards perhaps come in getting better hours – peak times – when the turnover is greater and the pace is quicker. Currently, the waitress must work harder for her gratuity [...]. The ideas of feminism encourage recirculation of profits into the women's community by supporting other women's energies.

These women were challenging the ideas of what it meant to run a restaurant in the process.

In the prospectus, Bread and Roses 'expanded the concept of restauranting from the feminist perspective' by building upon the typical three factors for customer satisfaction: '1. Good food that is well-prepared and attractively served, 2. Good service that is courteous, skillful, and prompt, and 3. An attractive environment'.[7] Feminist restaurant owners wanted to redefine who could own and operate restaurants and who could enjoy them.

While the solution of changing the system from within was popular amongst organizations such as the Women's Culinary Alliance, feminist restaurants sought to break away from the mainstream restaurant industry.[8] Feminist restaurants still had to function within the economic system but functioned in a periphery set apart. The owners' goal was not just to challenge the restaurant industry itself but capitalism and male-run spaces more generally. Feminist restaurants and cafés were founded out of desires to create different kinds of spaces. Within feminist restaurants themselves were important differences. Even within a single restaurant, employees and collectives could have different goals. As Marjorie Parsons reflected on the Common Womon [sic] Club of Northampton, Massachusetts, 'For some women this was a political project, for others this was a livelihood.'[9] Despite these differences, there were similarities between the spaces that set them apart.

Changing Work Relationships

Many feminists have talked about changing their workplace but few have done so [...]. By eliminating the hierarchy implicit in most businesses and by giving women employees the opportunity to be themselves, we think we have gone a long way toward making it possible for them to be feminists on the job.
– Colleen McKay, Los Angeles Women's Saloon and Parlor[10]

Feminist restaurants transformed the relationship between staff and customer. Changing the relationship between the customer's money and the establishment was also important. For instance, most feminist restaurants did not allow tipping. Bread and Roses had a jar on the counter, which was used to raise money for local feminist causes instead of tipping the staff.[11] Unlike other low wage restaurants in 1976, which encouraged their waitresses to smile, flirt, and ingratiate themselves with customers in hopes of getting larger tips, the *Lakeland Ledger* noted, the Los Angeles Women's Saloon and Parlor paid all its employees a high wage of $3 an hour.[12] In 1976, the minimum wage in California was $2 an hour for non-tipping jobs; jobs with tips have a lower minimum wage, and therefore the $3 an hour wages were far above the norm.[13] Poly Molina, who had worked as a waitress at other restaurants in Los Angeles before taking a job at the Women's Saloon remarked to the journalist, 'I don't feel like I'm an automaton here.' She continued, 'Other restaurants make you wear ridiculous costumes or walk with a silly grin on your face. Male managers permit and sometimes even encourage customers to insult or mistreat waitresses. Here no matter what job we do we are treated with respect.'[14] Similarly, the Common Womon Club of Northampton, Massachusetts also did not allow tipping. Eliminating tipping practices was an important factor in changing the relationship between staff and customers and thus was common in feminist restaurant business dynamics.

In another example of changing the work structure, feminist restaurants often requested each table to clear their own soiled dishes. In fact, there were no waitresses at Bread and Roses of Cambridge or Bloodroot of Bridgeport. When the food was ready, customers were called upon to serve themselves.[15] Clients picked up their own food from the counter and cleared their plates at the end. As Patricia Hynes of Bread and Roses explained to an interviewer, 'We don't feel comfortable with women waiting on other people.'[16] Although self-service was a concept that more traditional restaurants have employed with buffet tables, salad bars, and cafeterias to save money by requiring a smaller staff, these feminist restaurants used this technique for political reasons, to challenge the hierarchical and patriarchal standards of the regular service industry. According to the *Lakeland Ledger*, at the Los Angeles Women's Saloon and Parlor, most customers were sympathetic to the needs of the staff. If the waitresses were busy, the customers were encouraged to get their own silverware or help themselves to a second cup of coffee. One night a group of regular customers did all the cooking and cleaning so that the staff could have a night off.[17] For the most part, customers seemed unfazed by this arrangement.

Feminist restaurants also often had unique staffing procedures that differed from mainstream restaurants. In the case of the Los Angeles Women's Saloon and the Common Womon of Northampton, each woman working at the restaurant shared the management roles by taking turns planning the meals, doing the cooking, organizing the finances, washing the dishes, and doing the maintenance. By rotating positions and tasks, these feminist restaurants subverted traditional restaurant management hierarchy. At the Los Angeles Women's Saloon and Parlor, all of the fourteen employees participated in major decision making, although those who had expertise in areas of cooking and marketing oversaw the day-to-day functioning in those areas. For instance, the 'dirty work' was divided so nobody was stuck scrubbing the floor every day.[18] Collective structures tended to encourage people to share the work. The Common Womon Club began during a February 1976 meeting for women who wanted to get into business. All nine members worked in the kitchen, cooked, and cleaned. The collective also changed sizes – shrinking to seven. Interest in being involved in the collective actually impeded its efficiency. There was a limit to how many people could make a living wage. Different ideas about work and expectations led to problems.

Despite having a vision of challenging hierarchies, collective models were not the easiest to maintain. When asked if there were tensions within the collective, Berkeley's Brick Hut Café owner, Joan Antonnucio, replied, 'Hahaha. Always. It was a collective. With people.' Then more seriously she added, 'We usually tried for consensus, later a two-thirds quorum, then just majority rule.'[19] By creating a procedure to deal with conflicts, the Brick Hut Café was able to mitigate tensions. Personal conflicts and different expectations tore other restaurant collectives apart. Although Marjorie Parsons of the Common Womon Club emphasized repeatedly how committed the collective was to the project, she noted the downside to that level of emotional investment meant that 'also the anger and the resentment built up because some people did more work'. In order to compensate for this problem, the Common Womon Club held processing meetings in addition to their business meetings. Unlike the business meetings, which were used to work out scheduling, fundraising, event planning, discuss money matters, and draft tasks lists for jobs ranging from cleaning the bathrooms to writing the menu, process meetings offered the group important time to discuss emotions. Parsons remarked, 'There were times in the group when people didn't get along – had a really hard time with each other.' Over time tensions built within the collective; sometimes the conflict would be over former lovers and co-collective members fighting, and sometimes it would be over something as simple as a debate about whether or not to use butter or margarine.[20] Poor communication skills could result in businesses imploding over something as simple as how much butter to order.

Challenging mainstream restaurant hierarchy meant taking risks, and sometimes these risks led to failure. Collectives were dependent on members being able to trust that the other women would follow through on their tasks and commitments to the restaurant.[21] At the Common Womon Club, the constant infighting resulted in burnout. Marjorie Parsons recommend that future collectives 'get a good facilitator to come in once a month to come in and talk with the group'.[22] With a group therapy session once a month the anger could get released and people could move on. She also advised against overextending oneself. These businesses, especially in smaller towns, often served as the community centre, women's centre, or LGB centre. As a result, business owners were often trying to organize many events, and they became spread too thin. The Common Womon Club aimed to do care work for the entire women's community of Northampton, but the collective members forgot to care for themselves in the process. While Parsons's collective was unable to implement these techniques in time to save it, she wanted to share this advice with other women interested in beginning feminist businesses.

Lessons Learned

Feminist restaurants worked and looked differently from mainstream restaurants during the 1970s and 1980s. Bloodroot Feminist Vegetarian Restaurant began as a woman-centred space that reflected the owners' values. As Selma Miriam explained to the *Fairfield County Advocate*, 'We wanted to start a woman's center, but we needed a way to support it. So we decided on a restaurant and bookstore; mental food because feminist writings are so important to us.'[23] This creation of a women's centre in the Bridgeport area, a bookstore and a healthy place to eat, allowed them to 'make a living for themselves without selling out'. Selma Miriam found the values she wanted to reflect 'through much soul-searching, and with the support of her Bloodroot partners': she 'came to believe that her passions for orchid-growing and cooking were consistent with and spring from her relationship to Earth, and should be carried forward into her life as a radical lesbian feminist.'[24] Noel Furie of Bloodroot agreed, stating to *The*

Black Rock News that starting Bloodroot 'was a matter of doing something political … political in the sense of being able to have full control over our own lives and have our work in concert with our beliefs'. In the same article, Sam Stickwell commented that 'the joy of serving women from all walks of life is its own reward'.[25] Women from all over the world have visited Bloodroot, and the restaurant has many regular customers. Even forty years after its founding, some of the original customers continue to return to this place. Selma 'believed strongly in the fact that "you could make a community with food" and she and the collective certainly did'.[26] A similar theme follows from the reflection of other feminist restaurant owners. Feminist restaurants had an impact beyond that within just their businesses because they became a nexus for their communities. They were also part of a larger conversation about how to live and live out one's values within a capitalist society.

Feminist restaurants allowed women to live openly as feminists and challenge both the system and the restaurant as an institution. While reflecting on Mother Courage's first year, Dolores Alexander noted:

> Thank God the first year is over. The biggest lesson we learned is that nothing – nothing good – comes easy. But we are very satisfied with the choice we have made. We really see the best chances for personal fulfillment AND revolutionary change in women getting going their own enterprises and institutions. In the man's world, as far as women are concerned, the trend will be tokenism for years to come. And you can bet that not many feminists are going to be among these tokens. Of course, we still have to live in and deal with that world. You know, Mother Courage is a character in a Brecht play who endures and survives the Thirty Years' War by dealing with both sides. Obviously to survive we all have to compromise to some degree. The trick is to retain one's values with minimum compromise. That's what we are trying to do.[27]

Mother Courage's founders realized that they could not fulfil every aspiration, as they were solely two women constrained by the physical limitations of their bodies and time, in addition to economic and social systems. However, Dolores Alexander explained on a sign that she placed within the restaurant that she and Jill Ward had 'been working in the movement and we wanted to find a way to continue contributing to the movement and still make enough to support ourselves'.[28] She stated, 'neither of us wanted to compete in a man's world, a world created by men – which excludes us and yet which has taught us that it is because of our inadequacies that we don't make it.'[29] A feminist restaurant was a way to have feminist-oriented work connect with their daily lives.

Conclusion

While feminist restaurants and cafés embodied their feminist ideals uniquely, these businesses challenged the status quo of the food service industry's combination of cooking, capitalism, and consumption. These spaces had different aesthetics and work structures due to a mixture of needs, from lack of financial resources and from feminist values that sought to overturn the sexism experienced by women in mainstream restaurant culture. Feminist restaurants experimented with challenging restaurant hierarchies. Eliminating tipping, having customers serve themselves, and working in collective structures all changed the relationships between owners, staff, and clientele. The restaurants were political projects. The owners extended the meaning of restaurant management beyond orchestrating front and back of the house functions. While questions about how to manage a business within a capitalist society continued to be a matter debated by feminists, feminist restaurant owners sought to balance their values with practical needs. Feminist restaurants did more than serve food: the owners worked on serving the greater community, both of feminists and that of the neighbourhood.

While feminist restaurants and cafés challenged capitalism, they still had to be part of the economy. Balancing economics with philosophy meant compromises. These feminist restaurants and cafés were not isolated, but part of a larger economy and society that was not always amenable to their desires. The creation of women's space required innovative financial manoeuvrings.

Afterword

In March 2017, Bloodroot Feminist Vegetarian Restaurant of Bridgeport, Connecticut celebrated its fortieth anniversary. Three nights of dinners from the twenty-first to the twenty-third marked the actual anniversary. Bloodroot also hosted dinners by guest vegetarian chefs from around Connecticut, six different art exhibits, feminist guest speakers, a book fair, and four cooking classes over the course of six weeks. These anniversary events reflected the same commitment to community building that contributed to Bloodroot's initial success. Commenting on that success, founder Selma Miriam remarked, 'We just stuck with what we believe in,' adding, 'We have scraped and struggled, but we have always had devoted customers.'[30] In the year of its founding, Bloodroot was one among hundreds of feminist restaurants in North America. Now, forty-two years later, Bloodroot is the only remaining feminist restaurant founded during the 1970s in the United States and Canada.

Most contemporary restaurants that embody similar principles to feminist restaurants founded between the 1970s and 1980s do not label themselves in the same overt manner. It is far more common for restaurants to identify themselves as socially conscious spaces of social justice, or part of a food politics movement. Queer politics and postmodern theories of the body have shifted understandings of gender, and singular gender spaces of feminist political organizing, therefore, are less common. However, the human need of finding community spaces where one feels accepted and supported continues.

Feminist restaurants and cafés merit our attention because they provide a model for creating businesses that challenge workplace inequity. Studying these spaces combats

155

the erasure of feminist and lesbian feminist culture and underscores the contributions founders of feminist restaurants and cafés made to debates around food politics, community organizing, and labour rights, which continue today.

Notes

1   Sandy Horn, 'Karen's Kitchen', in *Gaia's Guide* (San Francisco: Women's Up Press, 1976), p. 52.

2   Historian Dorothy Sue Cobble has traced the evolution of waitresses' attitudes towards feminist proposals such as the Equal Rights Amendment and shown the way that waitresses have been engaged in activism over works right throughout the twentieth century ('"Practical Women": Waitress Unionists and the Controversies over Gender Roles in the Food Service Industry, 1900-1980', *Labor History*, 29.1 (1988), 5-31 <https://doi.org/10.1080/00236568800890011>.

3   Sections of this paragraph are included in my article on feminist business history. Alex Ketchum, 'Cooking the Books: Feminist Restaurant Owners' Relationships with Banks, Loans and Taxes,' *Journal of Business History* (2019), 1–27 <https://doi.org/10.1080/00076791.2019.1676233>.

4   According to economist Lisa Williamson at the U.S. Bureau of Labor, detailed occupational employment estimates were first made available in 1972. There were considerably fewer detailed occupations in the classification system used from 1972 to 1982 than those used for more recent data (only about 150 occupations versus 535 in the 2010 Census classification). Many of the detailed occupations were of a miscellaneous or 'all other' type (Alexandra Ketchum to Lisa Williamson, 'Data on Restaurant Employment by Sex/Gender', 26 February 2018; *Employed Persons by Detailed Occupation by Sex and Race* (U.S. Bureau of Labor Statistics, 1972-1982); *Employed Persons by Detailed Occupation by Sex and Race* (U.S. Bureau of Labor Statistics, 1983-2002)).

5   *Employed Persons by Detailed Occupation, Sex, Race, and Hispanic or Latino Ethnicity* (U.S. Bureau of Labor Statistics, 2017) <https://www.bls.gov/cps/cpsaat11.pdf> [accessed 15 May 2019].

6   Gale Goldberg, 'Feminism and Food: An Alternative to Restauranting' (unpublished thesis, Massachusetts Institute of Technology, 1976), H. Patricia Hynes Papers, Schlesinger Library, Radcliffe Institute, Harvard University, Box 1, Folder 3.

7   Patricia Hynes, 'Business Prospectus of Bread and Roses' (1974), H. Patricia Hynes Papers, Schlesinger Library, Radcliffe Institute, Harvard University, Box 1, Folder 3, 5-6.

8   After feminist restaurants had begun to change conversations around women, gender, feminism, and restaurants, organizations such as the Women's Culinary Alliance, founded in New York City in 1981, encouraged women to enter the restaurant industry. Rather than encourage women to create their own kind of businesses, this organization took a more liberal approach; their idea was to integrate more women in the already existing system and eventually become chefs, restaurant owners, or managers.

9   Marjorie Parsons, *Coffeehouse Meeting*, The Women's Coffeehouse Records, 1979, Northeastern University Archives and Special Collections, AV2316, M120.

10 Sharon Johnson, 'In Los Angeles Saloon Women Get the Red Carpet', *Lakeland Ledger* (Lakeland, Florida), 69: 244 (16 June 1976) <https://news.google.com/newspapers?id=d4ksAAAAIBAJ&sjid=2P0 DAAAAIBAJ&pg=7132%2C4566266> [accessed 15 May 2019].

11 Goldberg.

12 Johnson.

13 State of California, 'History of the Minimum Wage', *Department of Industrial Relations* <https://www.dir.ca.gov/iwc/minimumwagehistory.htm> [accessed 15 May 2019].

14 Johnson.

15 Goldberg.

16 Patricia Roth Schwartz, 'Bloodroot: Not by Food Alone', *Hartford Advocate* (Hartford, Connecticut, 23 November 1977), p. 27.

17 Johnson.

18 Johnson.
19 Alexandra Ketchum to Joan Antonnucio, 'Brick Hut', 9 June 2015.
20 Parsons.
21 Elizabeth Kent, 'A Journey Through "Lesbian Mecca": Northampton LGBTQ History Walking Tour', 2014.
22 Parsons.
23 'More Than Just a Restaurant', *Fairfield County Advocate*, 8 September 197-.
24 Emily Ferrar, 'Following Someone Else's Pattern Is Anathema: A Portrait of Selma Miriam', *Ways of Knowing,* 5 December 1998, p. 6.
25 'Five Feminists Run Bloodroot Gourmet Vegetarian Eatery', *The Black Rock News*, 28 June 1989.
26 Ferrar.
27 Dolores Alexander, 'Mother Courage Restaurant: Mother Courage' (Title of Periodical Cut Off), Smith College Archives, Dolores Alexander Papers (unprocessed), Box 21, Folder 180, 39.
28 Dolores Alexander and Jill Ward, 'Food', Smith College Archives, Dolores Alexander Papers (unprocessed), Box 21.
29 Alexander and Ward.
30 Joe Meyers, 'Famed Bridgeport Vegetarian Restaurant Approaches 40th Anniversary', *CTPost*, 20 November 2016 <https://www.ctpost.com/living/article/Famed-Bridgeport-vegetarian-restaurant-approaches-10624322.php.> [accessed 15 May 2019].

Weaponizing Food: Communism, the Democratic Transition, and the Transformation of Taste

Dorota Koczanowicz and Leszek Koczanowicz

In June 2014, public opinion in Poland was incensed by the revelation of illegal recordings of customers at Sowa i Przyjaciele, a fashionable Warsaw restaurant.[1] Bribed by a businessman, the staff had been taping politicians of the Civic Platform, the governing party at the time. Microphones placed under the tabletops by waiters registered controversial conversations between cabinet members and their allies. Ultimately, not only political statements but also culinary choices proved meaningful, troublesome, and, above all, costly.

Taste is perhaps the most intimate of all the senses, according to Carolyn Korsmeyer (1999), while Georg Simmel insists that it is the most selfish one (1997). However, neither the impact nor the explorations of taste concern only the private sphere, since taste also fulfils important social functions. The ingestion of certain foods is bound up with defined political and cultural allegiances and, as such, can be harnessed as a weapon in political struggles. Therefore, the Opposition expectedly seized the opportunity to use the tapes for its political purposes, citing the ministers' ill-suited comments that contravened their own professed policies, and decrying their profane language and contempt for the electorate. The culinary preferences of the cabinet members were censured as showcasing the social alienation of the governing political class. Their exorbitant bills, including pricey wines, were especially brandished, but what turned out to be the politicians' ultimately damning misstep was their partiality for baby octopuses. Explanations that baby octopuses were actually cheaper than pork did not help much: what mattered to the populists was that the 'elites' were worlds removed from the choices and tastes of 'normal' people. The 'baby-octopus eaters' were divested of power in 2015. To fully understand why baby octopuses proved such an efficacious weapon in political struggles, we must go back to Poland's communist past.

A baby octopus dish was successful as a weapon in political struggles for two reasons. The political opponents counted, rightly as it was to turn out, on Poles' dislike of foreign culinary traditions and on their distrust of the restaurant itself as an institution. This incident demonstrates that culinary preferences can usefully serve in political warfare, in our case, specifically in the populist combat against the elites (Koczanowicz 2016). Sketching a comprehensive historical background, we trace how transformations of culinary tastes were inscribed in the communist modernization and in the post-1989 democratic transition processes.

However, because the taping scandal is a classic example of populist rhetoric, let us make a short detour to the theory of populism before proceeding to our historical analysis. Defining populism has proved a challenging venture that has stirred considerable controversy in academia. In our argument, we follow Jan-Werner Müller, who observes that 'populism is a distinctly moral way to imagine the political world and necessarily involves a claim to exclusive moral representation' (2016: 181). One salient advantage of this approach is that populism can be studied not only as politically consequential, but also as culturally and aesthetically charged. The populist project crucially envisages comprehensive social change, and not merely political transformation. Populists claim for themselves the right to judge who are a true people and who are a depraved elite, and, although these categories are rather hazy, their differential assessments must rely on a set of criteria. It turns out that dietary preferences can effectively serve as one such evaluative yardstick. However, in the context of Poland and, probably, of other post-communist countries as well, the reliance on this particular benchmark breeds paradoxes which may be frustrating to populists. The point is that, while on the one hand they seek to radically repudiate the communist past, on the other they must largely adopt the communist perspective on a range of cultural issues, including food and eating. This paradox is fuelled by several factors.

Communism and Eating

Traditionally, Poles have eaten first and foremost at home. This practice resulted both from the organization of labour (under communism farmers accounted for 60% of the population) and from the special relevance attributed to home meals, which fulfilled important social functions, such as strengthening a family's communal bonding and consolidating its structure based on the traditional division of female and male roles. The seizure of power by communists was supposed to thoroughly remodel this structure, for the flagship goal of the communist revolution was to transform all spheres of social life. As a historian of post-war Poland insists, 'The Polish Workers' Party was not just another social institution searching for members and greater influence. It pretended to have responsibility for a wide range of social issues – such as housing, fuel, and food supply' (Kenney 1997: 38). The initial period of communist rule in Poland was marked by the collectivization of farming and the launching of what was referred to as the Battle for Trade, that is, a campaign of bringing entire trade, including the smallest local retail stores, under the state monopoly.

As the next step on their agenda, the communists planned to transplant the Russian models of mass catering to Poland, purportedly with a view to relieving the working people from daily cares involved in getting food provisions and tedious cooking chores. A developed network of state-subsidized mass caterers, such as factory canteens and cafeterias, milk bars and cheap restaurants, were expected to encourage Poles to eat out of home. Such policies carried a powerful symbolic load, since the politics of eating lay at the core of social transformations in a number of respects. Specifically, food and eating were meaningful as: 1) a means of total control, 2) a symbol of the social advancement of workers, 3) a factor in the system of the reproduction of labour force, 4) a way of national identification (inclusion and exclusion), and 5) a political token (the special role of meat).

Nevertheless, Poles did not take to eating out, despite efforts to tout the practice by the communist authorities. The state spared no effort to influence the quality of food served in restaurants by strictly controlling the composition of dishes, whose ingredients had to be listed in menus, together with their respective weights in grams. Menus also featured names and surnames of individuals who were responsible, for example, for coffee-brewing. All these exertions were of little avail. The main reasons behind the failure of this campaign, extensive though it was, were the low quality of catering services and the belief in the superior value of home-made meals cooked by a homemaker familiar with the family's individual needs.

Discontinuous Food Supplies

Food distribution was centrally controlled, and food trade was comprehensively monopolized by the state by introducing mandatory contracts for food producers, radically curtailing the private trade network, and implementing strict price control policies for food.[2] At the same time, the communist period was perennially plagued by the scarcity of basic food products, in particular meat, which resulted from the 'economics of shortage' (Kornai 1980). Kornai explains that as the communist economy was structurally beset by the shortage of several consumer goods, including food, the communist regime became increasingly embroiled in ideological contradictions. In interwar Poland, like all over the world in this period, the regular and plentiful consumption of meat was a nearly exclusive privilege of the upper classes. If the communist revolution was supposed to eliminate all inequalities, the working class should enjoy the prerogatives which had previously been reserved for the upper social strata. Consequently, one of the aspirations of communist governments was to make meat consumption common and ubiquitous. At the same time, however, the ineffectiveness of agriculture, as well as the fixed system of state-controlled prices, brought about permanent market shortages. The failures of agriculture were caused by the state's attempts to plan and control food production and distribution. Even though most farms in Poland were privately owned by farmers after 1956, which was an exception in the communist bloc, the state determined agricultural production through a system of mandatory deliveries and price control. While the state forced farmers to turn in obligatory supplies, illegal slaughter and trade soared. It was only towards the end of communist rule in Poland that farmers themselves were allowed to legally sell the food, including meat, which they produced.

Discontinuities in food supplies more or less directly triggered economic and even political transformations in communist Poland. Over the decades, huge strikes and demonstrations (1956, 1970, 1980) were related to food shortages and meat price increases. In the 1970s, the announcement of a rise in meat prices caused an uproar and, consequently, a wave of strikes, which were violently cracked down on, but which precipitated a radical change in the leadership of the communist party and the state. Nevertheless, the new government made the same mistake a few years later. The announcement of a considerable increase in the prices of low-quality yet very popular meat products saw another wave of strikes and demonstrations sweep across several cities of Poland. Although the government retracted the proclaimed price increase in the summer of 1976, the problems of discontinuous supplies remained unresolved. At the moment when the economic collapse was at its sharpest, shops appeared that sold meat without any limits, but at what came to be referred to as commercial (that is, free-market) prices. Such shops were called Meat Museums, as the average citizen could only come along and have a look at the meat they had on offer. At the same time, the shelves in regular butcher shops were entirely empty. Although food was rationed and the monthly meat quotas were quite modest, getting meat became a huge problem.

All this happened despite a variety of social-engineering devices to which the communist regime resorted in order to alleviate the effects of food scarcity. Because Polish Catholic society was known to observe fasts rather strictly, additional days without meat were put on the calendar. In the summer of 1951, meatless Mondays were introduced in retail trade, and Tuesdays and Thursdays in gastronomy. Reports critical of a meat-based diet started to proliferate in the press. It was vocally emphasized that meat consumption rates had far exceeded those from before the communist era, and that any further increase might jeopardize the nation's health.

At the same time, the belief was rife that the ruling class fed on the best foods in secret. Rumours circulated that discontinuous meat supplies were due to massive meat exports to the Soviet Union and China. This belief was elevated into a symbol of the colonial exploitation Poland was experiencing. As a matter of fact, the idea was not very far from truth at all.

Polish ham and sausages were export goods which the West highly appreciated as well. When the First Secretary of the Committee of the Polish United Workers' Party in Rzeszów visited Italy in 1963, he took five kilos of various cured meats with him as a gift for the Italian communists. Meanwhile Poland was going through another meat crisis, which made people line up in long queues in front of butcher shops. In the autumn of that year, meat factory employees were charged with corruption and fraudulence in meat trade and put on trial. The main defendant was convicted, sentenced to death, and executed.

While Polish food was exported in huge quantities, international agreements afforded Poles opportunities to taste foods which were produced in other communist countries. What the current Ministry-approved register of traditional Polish products lists as Szczecin paprikash perfectly exemplifies the international support Polish gastronomy received. Nearly all of the ingredients that went into the making of this canned food, whose recipe dates back to 1965, were imported: 'Initially, its main ingredient was the meat of various species of African fish, tomato pulp imported from Bulgaria, Hungary and Romania, prima, i.e., a variety of hot African peppers, vegetables and seasonings' (Ministry of Agriculture 2018). Starting in 1967, Chinese rice was also a mandatory ingredient of Szczecin paprikash.

Supplies of tropical fruit were rare, with tangerines from China, oranges first from Israel (until 1967) and then from Arab counties, and bananas from Central America being coveted and long-awaited delicacies. The top Party leadership, including the Political Bureau, was involved in decision-making about fruit imports, and the entire nation monitored the routes of the ships which carried the precious cargo. The changing locations of the ships were systematically reported by the press and on the radio. As the ships neared Poland, the tension grew, and their arrival at Polish ports was announced on TV in major news programs. When the longed-for goods finally made their way onto grocery shelves, the average citizen was entitled to purchase one kilogram (2.2 pounds) of lemons and two kilograms (4.4 pounds) of oranges. In the 1970s, Poland's contacts with the West improved, which resulted, among other things, in Poland purchasing licenses to produce Coca Cola and Pepsi Cola, the previously denounced imperialist beverages. Poland was divided into two zones: Coke was available in the central and northern parts of the country, whereas Pepsi could be enjoyed in the South and the West of Poland (Harbanowicz 2016: 98).

The Milk Bar

By the mid-1950s, the state had closed down nearly all privately-owned restaurants. The sector of private gastronomy was only revived in the late 1960s (Brzostek 2010: 306). In return, cheap mass catering was offered, and so-called milk bars began to mushroom. The milk bar was the epitome of communist gastronomy. Yet, the first milk bar in Poland was in fact opened in Warsaw as early as in 1896. Such canteens also throve in the interwar period. However, they had their heyday under the People's Republic of Poland. In the post-war era, Poland's first milk bar was established in Kracow in 1948, and it took barely one year before there were as many as eighty of them across Poland (Brzostek 2010: 268).

Milk bars were frequented by workers and students alike. Before 1989, the state heavily subsidized many ingredients going into the making of breakfasts and lunches in milk bars. The state-funded list did not include, however, such coveted goods as meat or cream. Milk bars offered a kind of unsophisticated, home-like cuisine of simple and filling dishes. Their menus always included a pretty wide selection of soups, such as red-beet soup, tomato soup, split-pea soup, and chicken broth, followed by several flour-based dishes, such as pancakes and various sorts of dumplings, as well as potato-based dishes, such as noodles of raw or boiled potatoes, *kopytka* (that is, the Polish variety of gnocchi), hash browns, and the like. The most popular meat dishes included various kinds of meatballs, *bigos* (a stew of sauerkraut and meat leftovers), and baked beans with sausage.[3]

Enclaves of foreign cuisine cropped up in big cities. Hungarian, Russian, and Bulgarian restaurants were opened, but the tastes and flavours from outside the socialist bloc were shunned more often than not. In the 1950s, the famed Shanghai was in operation in Warsaw. The two stories of the restaurant usually swarmed with customers, who were baited by a conspicuous, dragon-shaped neon sign and a Chinese cook who took care to secure original ingredients and spices from abroad:

> Soy sauce, Mun mushrooms, rice noodles and even century eggs flowed from China to Poland in a steady stream [...]. Although judging by its name, Shanghai could have been expected to serve spicy cuisine of South China, the restaurant rather specialized in mild-flavoured Beijing cuisine. It was renowned for veal and poultry, but did not have the Peking duck, a flagship dish of Beijing, on the menu. (Garlicki 2011)

Despite these enclaves, no cohesive and thorough project of radical social change was completely implemented in Poland, even though communism envisaged such a concept. Practices of social life proved particularly resistant to and defiant of communist pressures. Attempts to modernize both food and culinary tastes did not produce any radical change in the dietary habits of Poles. This failure resulted from the singularity of the communist modernization in Poland. Whereas profound economic and social changes were indeed effected, the cultural sphere was pervaded by the models derived from the traditional lifestyles of the gentry and the peasantry, which were taken over and cultivated by the new working class. The traditional patterns became petrified, as their relevance and validity were never examined in public debate, unlike in Western countries. With no interrogation of this kind, traditional rituals and gender divisions were systematically reproduced in everyday life (Koczanowicz 2008). For this reason, after 1989, Polish society openly re-embraced ideologies of old as if it had woken up from a long sleep. As a Polish philosopher vividly put it, ours was a 'revolution in slumber' (Leder 2014). These petrified traditions involved culinary culture as well. Eating at home still continued to be the most important norm, especially during religious feasts, as it additionally mobilized and united people in opposition to the new rituals imposed by communist ideology.

Skin-Deep Modernization: Post-1989 Transformations and the Resistance of Tradition

The tendencies described above were bolstered by the fact that Poles had hardly any access to non-traditional food products. Even if some exotic merchandise, such as squid, soy sauce, or prawn crackers, unexpectedly made their way from the allied socialist countries to grocery stores in Poland, Polish consumers ignored them entirely despite the paucity of any other produce, because they had no idea how to integrate them into their menus.

Consequently, when 1989 came, Poland stood at the threshold of the capitalist transition with its commonly accepted attachment to traditional food and eating habits entirely intact. Over the recent one hundred years, Poland's culinary tradition has twice been exposed to the crushing forces of socio-political transformation, which could have produced a radical change in taste: communism, which by default combated tradition and launched a far-ranging modernization, and the 'iron roller of capitalism', which also by default disregards tradition. After the fall of communism and the opening to the West, Poland was inundated with new commodities, and Poles enthusiastically fell for new forms of consumption. As canned pineapple became a favoured garnish for the traditional pork chop, Italian, Greek, and Chinese restaurants began to oust Polish ones from town centres. It did not take long before Poles turned into Europe's most fervent lovers of sushi.

Tourists visiting the most popular Polish cities today may have the impression that Poles prefer foreign cuisine to traditional Polish dishes. While it cannot by denied that Polish flavours hide in the thicket of Greek, Italian, and Indian restaurants, and in American fast food outlets, which burgeon in the centres of Polish towns, one should not rely on this to jump to conclusions about the contemporary Polish nutrition patterns.

Perhaps counterintuitively, it turns out that, for all these shifts, the fall of communism and the opening to the West have not significantly affect the culinary tastes of Poles. The processes of globalization have certainly multiplied and diversified food products on offer, but their easy availability does not immediately translate either into changes in consumption patterns or into the democratization of eating. As a matter of fact, it can serve as another tool of social stratification, as 'to be familiar with foreign products and versed in cooking them sometimes takes specialized knowledge and the wish to demonstrate it, which in broad lines requires considerable cultural capital' (Domański and others 2015: 21). In 2014, a large-scale sociological survey on the eating preferences of Poles showed that despite the globalization-related cultural and civilizational changes, Poland was still a bulwark of food conservatism: neither meal times nor favourite dishes had actually changed (Domański and others 2015). The majority of society still stick to three traditional meals – referred to as breakfast, dinner, and supper – consumed at pretty fixed times. Dinner, which is eaten between 2:00 and 3:00 p.m., continues to be considered the main meal. Another notable feature of Poland's culinary culture is a very strong attachment to traditional cuisine. Among soups, a distinct preference is given to chicken broth (particularly popular as the first course of Sunday dinners) and tomato soup, while the typical second course consists of pork chops or minced meat patties with a side dish of boiled potatoes. Entrenched eating habits go hand in hand with repeated declarations of partiality for familiar cuisine.

Nor have the kitchen roles changed: in most households cooking is still done by women (Koczanowicz 2018). Over 75% of dinners are cooked by women. Consequently:

> Cooking skill is invariably associated with the stereotypical representations of the 'good wife' and the 'good mother' – it is her major defining feature, as well as a tool of social control and assessment. At the same time, daily home cooking serves to reproduce family relationships: it involves activities performed as frequently and regularly as to become habitual and taken for granted. This reinforces intrafamily arrangements which are rarely, if ever, subject to reflection. Cooking is also strongly associated with love and care for others and, as such, is emotionally charged, which additionally perpetuates the existing gender-roles division. (Domański and others 2015: 206)

In spite of the ubiquity, diversity, and considerably improved quality of restaurants in Poland today, consumption styles of the Polish public have not changed significantly. For a majority of Poles, the restaurant is a venue where one goes rarely or not at all. Eating out is a relevant indicator of one's social position. Domański's research findings show that 87% of his respondents reported having dinners at home. Even if they had their meals at the workplace, they most frequently lunched on home-made sandwiches. Admittedly, over half of adult Poles visit restaurants, but for most of them such an outing is an extremely rare occasion. Eating out is a practice primarily undertaken by members of the middle class. This rarity results on the one hand from financial constraints, but on the other also from the belief that home-made food is best, a notion which was entrenched in the communist period. Symptomatically, 'most respondents state that what they would be most inclined to eat at a restaurant are the dishes to which they are accustomed' (Domański and others 2015: 203). The greatest openness to new, exotic, and sophisticated culinary experiences is displayed by business people, 'who tend to be somewhat ostentatious in their consumer eating habits, declare the greatest interest in purchasing luxury commodities among all socio-occupational group, and relatively seldom report worries over food expenses' (Domański and others 2015: 203).

The argument presented in this paper is located at the intersection of culture studies-oriented foods studies and political philosophy. As such, it fills a major gap in current scholarship since the existing studies in this complex field are largely marginal and anecdotal. We have shown several interrelations between politics and eating. Firstly, our research suggests that the specific modernization launched by the communist regime in Poland was also expressed in policies for producing, preparing, and distributing food. It turned out that, all its powerful influence notwithstanding, the totalitarian state failed to radically transform the eating habits of the Polish public. Similarly to other spheres of social life, the pressure of the regime and the resistance of society produced a grey zone of tacit compromise, which undercut, if not demolished, the strivings to fully command individuals' choices. This tacit compromise came at the price of petrification, with dietary changes halted and Poles preserving their eating habits, which had been passed down from generation to generation, basically unchanged through the end of the communist era.

165

Secondly, while the democratic transition has had a considerable influence on nutrition patterns, this impact has been limited to privileged social groups. The members of these groups are customers of refined restaurants which proliferate in big cities. They, rather than anybody else, also experiment with cooking exotic meals at home and form an enthusiastic audience of cooking shows and blogs. At the same time, the prevailing social eating habits continue to be thoroughly conservative and have moreover been erected into a sign of social identity and of an attachment to national values in the globalizing world.

These developments have led, thirdly, to an increase in the axiological and political relevance of food. What we eat is less an expression of individual preferences and more a manifestation of belonging to a particular socio-political group. Political theory shows that populism is founded on and fuelled by the us-them division, where 'we' are ordinary people and 'they' are an alienated political elite which is unable and unwilling to understand the concerns of common people. Eating habits serve as a vivid illustration for the populists to demonstrate that this division appears at a very basic level.

Shortly before the recent European election, Jarosław Kaczyński, the leader of the governing populist party, gave an interview which was designed to 'warm up' his image. He talked about his private life, his favourite cats, and first and foremost about what he ate. He obviously confessed that his diet consisted of traditional Polish dishes, such as dumplings, pork chops, and cabbage. He recalled being invited to a sophisticated restaurant in Paris, where he had been promised to be swept off his feet by extraordinary flavours. The visit had produced no effect of this kind, he put his voters at ease: 'It only confirmed what I'd known before: nothing compares to common Polish food!'

Acknowledgements
Research on this paper has been sponsored by Poland's National Scientific Centre (Grant 2018/29/B/HS2/00041).

Notes
1   Literally, Owl and Friends, with Sowa (Owl) being the proprietor's name.
2   Side by side with the legal distribution of goods and commodities, a half-legal trade network developed bypassing the state's role as an intermediary (Kochanowski 2015).
3   State-subsidized milk bars are still around in Poland. In 2014, the Ministry of Finance put up a new list of the funded ingredients that did not include any spices or herbs, not even pepper. The desired taste was expected to be achieved by salt only. The use of other products was to be penalized by funding cut-offs. This decision triggered a public discussion which was accompanied by a surge of protests from both cooks and clients, who collected signatures on petitions to the Ministry and organized pickets. This mobilization made the Ministry re-design the list and allow using ninety-four ingredients to cook state-subsidized dishes. This change added over twenty products to those in the previous regulation, including, among others, such spices as ginger, lovage, marjoram, coriander, and cinnamon. Meat is still not on the list.

166 References

Brzostek, Błażej. 2010. *PRL na widelcu* (Warszawa: Baobab)

Domański, Henryk and others. 2015. *Wzory jedzenia a struktura społeczna* (Warszawa: Scholar)

Garlicki, Andrzej. 2011. 'Przygody kulinarne w PRL', *Mówią wieki* <http://www.mowiawieki.pl/index.php?page=artykul&id=791> [accessed 25 May 2019]

Harbanowicz, Justyna. 2016. '*Internacjonalizm w kuchni PRL'u*', *Kultura-Historia-Globalizacja*, 20: 97-108

Kenney, Padraic. 1997. *Rebuilding Poland: Workers and Communists, 1945-1950* (Ithaca: Cornell University Press)

Kochanowski, Jerzy. 2015. *Tylnymi drzwiami. Czarny rynek w Polsce 1944-1989* (Warszawa: W.A.B.)

Koczanowicz, Dorota. 2018. *Pozycja smaku: Jedzenie w granicach sztuki* (Warszawa: IBL PAN)

Koczanowicz, Leszek. 2008. *Politics of Time: Dynamics of Identity in Post-communist Poland* (Oxford: Berghan Books)

Koczanowicz, Leszek. 2016. 'The Polish Case: Community and Democracy under the PiS', *New Left Review*, 102: 77-96

Kornai, János. 1980. *Economics of Shortage* (Amsterdam: Elsevier)

Korsmeyer, Carolyn. 1999. *Making Sense of Taste: Food and Philosophy* (Ithaca: Cornell University Press)

Leder, Andrzej. 2014. *Prześniona rewolucja. Ćwiczenia w logiki historycznej* (Warszawa: Wydawnictwo Krytyki Politycznej)

Ministry of Agriculture of the Republic of Poland. 2018. 'Regional and Traditional Products' <https://www.gov.pl/web/rolnictwo/paprykarz-szczecinski> [accessed 25 May 2019]

Müller, Jan-Werner. 2016. *What Is Populism?* (University Park: University of Pennsylvania Press)

Pop-Eleches, Grigore and Joshua A. Tucker. 2017. *Communism's Shadow: Historical Legacies and Contemporary Political Attitudes* (Princeton: Princeton University Press)

Simmel, Georg. 1997. 'Sociology of the Meal', in *Simmel on Culture: Selected Writings* (Thousand Oaks: Sage), pp. 130-35

Sugar and Show: Power, Conspicuous Display, and Sweet Banquets during Henri III's 1574 Visit to Venice

Michael Krondl

Introduction

In the summer of 1574, Henri of Valois, duke of Anjou and, at least for the moment, the elected King of Poland made a week-long stopover in Venice. Having fled (quite literally) his regal obligations in Poland, he was on his way back to France to take up his deceased brother's place as Henri III, king of France. For the maritime republic, it was a once in a lifetime opportunity to get into the monarch's good graces. Accordingly, they pulled out all the stops, organizing a non-stop extravaganza that began even before the twenty-two year-old royal set foot in the watery metropolis. Upon his arrival, the city presented him with religious processions and regattas, feasts and fireworks, theatrical performances and shopping trips, political tête-a-têtes with the doge and soirées with courtesans. It is as if the city of Venice – the canals, the squares, the palaces, and the churches – had transformed itself into a giant stage set for a performance for an audience of one.[1] Yet in reading over the chroniclers' accounts, what seems to have captivated the eyewitnesses most were the elaborate costumes worn by the Venetian hosts and the tables set with extraordinary quantities of sugar sculpture.[2] What left an impression was the sugar and the show.

As Sidney Mintz ably demonstrated, sugar is powerful as both an economic and symbolic force.[3] In the Renaissance, sugar was used to signal power through the display of what contemporaries dubbed *magnificenza* (magnificence), a system dependent on conspicuous consumption itself demonstrated by its quantity, quality, and cost. For Venice, given its history as sugar merchant and processor, sugar had enormous value as a signifier of wealth, power, and refinement: that is, it reified *magnificenza* as few other commodities could.

The Renaissance Feast

States have long used food to assert power, whether by providing 'bread and circuses' or manufacturing famines. But if governments have regularly used food to discipline their citizens, they have also employed food for its symbolic quality in pursuit of political ends. This was especially true in the pre-modern era when state banquets were staged for the express purpose of performing wealth and status. The feasts detailed, for example, by Cristoforo di Messisbugo in the mid-sixteenth century are more theatre than meal, a procession of symbol-burdened set pieces, some in the form of food, others in song and dance.[4]

Yet while the performance of conspicuous display was commonplace in pre-modern Europe, Italian spectacle shone brighter than its transalpine peers. During Henri's visit, foreign witnesses commented profusely on the dress and jewellery worn by the women as well as the men. The décor of the streets, palaces, and gondolas merited exhaustive description, as did performances of various kind. Interestingly, visitors barely mentioned the actual food served at the banquets with one notable exception: confectionary. The chroniclers documented no fewer than five occasions when the king was treated to a primarily sweet repast, in some cases relatively small in scale, in others staged as public displays.[5]

Signal and Subterfuge

Contemporaries were well aware of the utility of spending on public display. In his 1552 treatment of magnificence, Sienese philosopher Alessandro Piccolomini writes, 'only someone who makes great things while spending could be properly called "magnificent"', and goes on to explain as examples of these great acts the 'building of temples, porticoes and theatres' and the sponsoring of 'public festivals and comedies'.[6] The Venetian political theorist Paolo Peruta says much the same thing fifty years later: 'There are few occasions when one can demonstrate one's magnificence, but during those occasions, such as weddings, banquets and in building, it is appropriate to spend without worrying about the cost but rather the magnificence and greatness of the result.'[7]

To understand the social value of sugar in the Venetian context, sociologists Thorstein Veblen and Pierre Bourdieu provide additional insight, admittedly with serious provisos.[8] In the case of the American sociologist the idea of an aspirational middling class emulating the purchases and habits of their 'betters' can, with caution, be applied to the middling princes of Renaissance Italy. The form, and at least some of the content, of the Italian spectacles was meant to emulate the festivals of aristocratic Europe, especially the Burgundian court, seen by the Italians as a more genuine version of blood-based aristocracy than what they themselves could muster.[9] Certainly, it proved as useful affectation for a class of less than blue-blood rulers, like the Medici or Sforza, as for the Venetian Republic's oligarchs. Like Veblen's, Bourdieu's context is modern and bourgeois, but his idea that discernment or taste can be a tool to build and maintain social capital can, in part, inform a discussion of *magnificenza*.

More recently, Jonathan Nelson and Richard Zeckhauser, an art historian and an economist, have sought to apply economic concepts of game theory, signalling, and – perhaps even most useful in the Italian context – ideas of 'signposting' and 'stretching' to art patronage, an approach equally applicable to spending on other artistic endeavours.[10] Here, signalling is the idea that, since we are only partially privy to any individual's information, there are signals that can be read as a stand-in for that information. If we read those signals correctly, we can make a series of deductions about a person's status, performance, background, and so on: a Rolex watch acts as a proxy for wealth, a police escort as an indicator of power. Thus, in Venice, the pomp and display that greeted the French king can be read as a series of carefully curated signals. The concept of signposting refers to signals selectively chosen to include only information useful to the sender's cause, while stretching involves an actual manipulation of the truth. Thus, the signposting 'player' conveniently omits the fact that the Rolex was a hand-me-down and, when stretching, that the watch was, in fact, purchased for twenty-five dollars on Canal Street. Similarly, the Venetians' signals were often more show than substance. The show put on for Henri had elements of a Potemkin town, this one built of sugar and allegory.

While art historians focus on the most permanent forms of magnificence – that is painting, sculpture, and architecture – from a purely monetary sense, it could be argued that these were not the conspicuous displays most valued in the Renaissance. Enormous resources were spent on much more ephemeral displays and the props that went with them. While buildings were admittedly expensive, paintings were relatively affordable, vastly cheaper than any number of table appurtenances. When an inventory of Lorenzo de Medici (the Magnificent) was conducted in 1492, a panel by Fra Angelico was valued at 5 florins, yet a large, jewel-encrusted cup came in at 800 florins.[11] The outlay on less permanent table decoration could also be significant. In 1450, the Angevin Neapolitan court of King Alphonse paid an annual sum of 2000 ducats to the apothecary Bernat Figueres for sweets.[12] A single 1534 Venetian banquet consisting of sugar sculpture (*trionfi* in Italian, *spongade* in Venetian dialect) and other confectionary given in honour of Renée, the French-born duchess of Ferrara, cost 2000 lire.[13]

169

The performance-based display that characterized much of Renaissance signalling can be explained, in part, by the emulation of northern courts, which, due to their perambulatory nature, necessarily focused at least as much on processions, feasts, jousts, and other temporary interventions as on building sculpture-decorated palaces.[14] Perhaps equally, the structure and form of the signalling can be understood as a secular mirror of the theatrical nature of Counter-Reformation Catholicism with its emphasis on ceremony, procession, ornate fashion, and precious tableware.

Venice and Sugar

To understand the *magnificenza* deployed for Henri's benefit and the place of the sugar feasts in the week-long extravaganza, it is worth mentioning the geopolitics of the day and their impact on sugar's role in the republic's economy.

By 1574, Venice's star had begun to fade. As the centre of both the sugar and spice trade shifted from the Mediterranean to the Atlantic in the fifteenth century, the merchant republic increasingly found itself at the periphery of Europe's trading network. Even its watery backyard was now increasingly dominated by Dutch, English, and French merchantmen.[15] Politically it was losing ground to the Ottomans in the east and the Spanish Hapsburgs to the west. Thus, from a diplomatic standpoint, the Venetian government had every incentive to get into the French monarch's good graces. Venice had entered the sugar trade at least as early as the Crusades, importing both refined and raw sugar to the metropolis where it was further refined. At first the sugar had come from the Holy Land, then Cyprus, which became a de facto Venetian sugar colony until it was conquered by the Ottomans in 1571. After the loss of Cyprus, the most important source was Egypt which, despite the vagaries of relations with Istanbul after the Ottoman conquest in 1517, continued to provide the sweet commodity until the early seventeenth century, when Atlantic sugar made Eastern Mediterranean sources no longer economical.

Nonetheless, sugar remained expensive, and got dearer as increased demand outpaced a growing supply. Not only was it used as a ubiquitous seasoning in elite cuisine, it was also deployed for decorative purposes. In the 1500s, Italian chefs dusted it, typically alongside cinnamon, over any number of foods, often in elaborate patterns. Adding tragacanth gum to sugar paste made it as easy to sculpt as clay. Alternatively, it could be melted like gold or bronze and cast in much the same way. And like bronze, it was sometimes gilded in silver or gold to make the display even more magnificent.

In Venice, chroniclers mentioned sugary ornaments as early as 1341. By 1493, Beatrice d'Este, the wife of Ludovico Sforza, the duke of Milan, wrote of a *collazione* given in her honour 'composed of diverse things all made with gilded sugar, which numbered three hundred; with infinite plates of confectionary'.[16] In the sixteenth century, there are numerous reports of the city's *compagni della calza* hosting sugary feasts. (These associations were part college fraternities, part gentlemen's clubs, a way for the city's young elite to network.) Hosting banquets, festivals, and performances was the way to build social capital; sugar sculpture was a way of signalling standing. Marin Sanudo describes in his diary a *compagnia* event from 1523 where 'a triumphal carriage [in miniature?] decorated with a symbol of faith was presented to the duke of Urbino, a sugar eagle to the imperial legate and a biscione to the representatives of the duke of Milan, another gift to the Mantuan legate as well as to the other lords present'.[17] In 1530, Francesco II Sforza (Beatrice's son), the duke of Milan, was hosted by a different *compagnia* with a sweet feast at the Ducal palace.[18]

Henri's Visit

If these earlier displays were meant to show off Venetian power and wealth, they were nothing compared to the extravaganza prepared for Henri III. The Senate instructed that ships be decorated for the grand regatta that would greet the king; it ordered churches and monasteries to ring their bells; it enjoined the citizens, especially those owning palazzi lining the grand canal, to light torches to illuminate the young monarch's approach.[19]

The show wasn't merely for the king. The guest list was a reflection of the complex web of alliances and misalliances that ruled Italy. All of the peninsula's potentates either sent representatives or came themselves: the pope sent a cardinal, the duke of Florence a count, the duke of Mantua sent his man, as did the Duke of Urbino, and of Parma. Even Spain and Venice's arch-rival Genoa sent ambassadors. The dukes of Ferrara and Savoy both arrived in person with hundreds of retainers in tow.[20]

When the king finally arrived at the edge of the lagoon on the afternoon of 18 July, he was welcomed by senators, dressed to the nines, accompanied by a cannonade. From there the greeting party conducted the king in a gondola decorated with gold brocade to the city itself, escorted by a convoy of two thousand gondolas.[21]

Over the next week the Republic subjected the king to a non-stop series of performances and spectacles that mixed entertainment and politics in varying measure. Everywhere he turned there was the display of Venice's magnificence: swarms of gondolas, nightly fireworks, and glittering tableaux of sugar sculpture. Between the public spectacles the king apparently played the tourist: he saw a command performance of Venice's renowned *commedia dell'arte* troupe, the Gelosi; he visited the Merano glass works; and he went jewel shopping, supposedly incognito (spending money his mother had arranged to loan him from Italian bankers).

As in any state visit, there were numerous banquets, some sponsored by the government itself and others by the visiting potentates who jockeyed among themselves to capture the young Frenchman's attention. We know who threw which banquet where but we're mostly ignorant of the dishes served. Daniela Ambrosini thinks this is because the king himself didn't consume the food at the banquets; there are multiple mentions of his frugal eating. What meals he ate were prepared by his personal cook due to the fear of poisoning.[22] I do not find this explanation convincing. It assumes that the theatrical repasts described in other contemporary Italian settings were staged to give sustenance rather than as elaborate performances of wealth and power. It seems impossible to imagine that the menus presented at the Doge's palace were in any way meagre. Instead I would suggest that the chroniclers' attention turned to the most visible, extravagant elements of these meals, mainly those parts that demonstrated the most magnificence, and consequently left us with highly detailed descriptions of only the sugar feasts.

We know the least about the first of these *colazioni*, which took place on Wednesday, 21 July. Following mass at the Basilica of San Marco the king was conducted into the *sala del Maggior Consiglio* (the Doge's palace council hall), its windows all decorated with festoons of flowers and fruit. The magnificence on display was hardly subtle: the hall had been decorated for the occasion with paintings by Venice's most renowned artists, starting with Carpaccio and Bellini and ending with Titian, depicting 'glorious history from the time of Doge Ziani, the emperor Federico Barbarossa and Pope Alexander III'. On the side of the room with the doge's throne, an immense sideboard (*credenziera*) in the form of a three-sided pyramid reached almost to the ceiling. If the paintings conveyed the message of the city's power, the *credenziera* demonstrated the government's affluence: it was laden with vases, basins, bronzes, candelabras, plates,

171

bowls, and salt cellars, all in gold and silver, calculated to be worth 200,000 scudi, the price equivalent of a respectable navy.[23] The king had his own elevated table, while six tables were set up for the local and visiting grandees. We don't what they ate, but we do know that an adjacent room was also prepared for the king, this one featuring three tables boasting a display of confectionary (*confiture*).[24] Like the paintings, and the treasure tower of tchotchkes, the sugar work added to a cumulative expression of unlimited taste, power, and wealth.

The second sugar feast is the one that has caught most food historians' attention. This took place on Saturday, 24 July. After a morning of shopping incognito, the king was given an exhaustive tour of the Arsenale. To put this into context, the Arsenale was the city's military shipyard, where war galleys were built from scratch and armed for battle. Marin Sanudo, the prolific diarist, called it 'truly one of the finest things in the world'. In a 1509 declaration, the government pronounced it the 'heart of the state'.[25] During the king's tour, the guides gave special attention to the trophies captured at the battle of Lepanto less than three years earlier.[26] The pièce de résistance of the tour, however, was a demonstration of the workers vaunted efficiency: 'Then before his very eyes a "galea" was completely outfitted in a single hour; something that would not be credible had it not been attested by everyone present, and that was only possible due to the division of labour and the perfect order [in which it was executed]'.[27]

This performance of industrial efficiency was followed by another demonstration loaded with meaning, this one less obviously military but perhaps more to the tastes of the urbane monarch. An anonymous observer set down the details:

> [The king was] led to the chambers of the noble Council of Ten located in the same building as the Arsenale, where an abundant and regal *colazione* had been prepared, [the table] spread with confectionary, many kinds of candied fruit [...] even the tablecloth, napkins, plates, and knives and forks, and the bread were made of sugar, so well-crafted and so resembling their original forms that they seemed real and not simulated or counterfeit, to such a degree that the king, having sat down and picked up his napkin had it break into two and fall on the ground, he laughed that he had not realized [the ruse] earlier.[28]

Nolhac and Solerti point out how this meal was a 'curious contrast to the wood and steelworks' of the Arsenale tour. But was it? If the armament works were meant to signal Venetian naval heft, was not the sugar intended to convey the city's economic might? If the choreographed assembly of the *galea* demonstrated the city's military manpower, did not the extraordinary craftsmanship of the sugar table show off the city's superior commercial human resources? Moreover, the location was far from arbitrary: these were the very rooms where the council – in effect the city's ruling cabinet – made its policy and executive decisions. Yet if the signalling was all too clear, the truthfulness of the signals was rather more opaque. The Lepanto trophies conveniently camouflaged the fact that Venice was on the back foot in the Aegean, the quickly assembled *galea* disguised the Arsenale's labour shortage after the Turkish wars, and the sugar feast was perhaps the sweetest stretch of all. While Venice still retained significant refining capacity, and the craftsmanship of its artisans was unrivalled, it had lost its sugar island and now not only depended on Ottoman Egyptian sugar but was increasingly being sidelined as ever more sugar flooded Western Europe from Brazil. It wasn't all a lie, but it was more sleight of hand than the real thing.

The Arsenale *colazione* would prove as no more than a prelude to the sugar crescendo of the following day. This was to be the king's farewell banquet organized by a *compagnia della calza*, held once again at the *sala del Maggior Consiglio*, outfitted as it had been for the earlier banquet, yet the overall impression of *magnificenza* was even more conspicuous than it had been heretofore.

Although everyday display was rationed in many Italian cities including Venice through a variety of sumptuary laws, which, despite their lax observance, still dampened down quotidian display, these restrictions had been suspended for the purposes of Henri's visit. As a result, the women who attended the final event came dripping with pearls 'the size of hazelnuts'.[29] Yet as much as the French visitors were awed by the splendour and beauty of the female Venetians, they seemed even more taken by that day's sugary extravagance:

> Following a ball, and at about five o'clock in the afternoon, the ladies were conducted into the adjoining voting hall (*sala dello scrutinio*), adorned with yellow and turquoise garlands (*ciambellotti*) with golden fringes, where a sumptuous meal (*colazione*) of confectionary, pistachio and almond pastes, orzatas and other drinks had been prepared. Three tables were spread with the sugar figures that were then so much celebrated by their contemporaries, although Venice had the privilege of this art and had already given grandiose displays on other occasions. This time the sugar, skilfully formed by a famous spicer (*speziale*), Nicolò della Cavalliera (of the Pigna apothecary), was based on forms and models from Sansovino, resulting in a most extraordinary display.
>
> Before the high chair for the king, also set up in this room under a rich canopy, was a table with several of these figures, some almost one arm high [a *braccio*, equalling about two feet], between which stood a woman in a queen's dress sitting in the middle of two tigers, she wore one crown and held two others each in one hand, and the tigers had on their arms the arms of France and Poland. Then there were two lions, a Pallas [Athena], a figure of Justice, a Saint Mark and a David, all with allegorical meanings, and also two ships perfectly finished with masts, sails, ropes, and artillery, and then animals, fruit, and many other things, some covered with gold or silver leaf. On the other side of the hall above two long tables there were more than two hundred other figures also of sugar, representing popes, kings, doges and princes, the seven virtues, the liberal arts, the gods, the planets, and an infinity of inventions, all finely worked; each

173

of them carried a tag attached to a rod with an indication of what it represented, and some held bunches of flowers in their hands.

Meanwhile as the ladies squeezed together into formation, the King, the Doge and the princes and many gentlemen arrived, and proceeded to take those figures, so we knew which were the favourites, because some had several. Meanwhile Henri was not satisfied with admiring those little masterpieces as he had the day before the Arsenale, and he requested that he could take many home with him to France; indeed, we have certain news that he then chose thirty-nine other detailed and gilded figures from a certain Pietro Vicentino, to whom he gave twenty-five scudi. The plates of confectionary were dispensed by the *compagni della calza*, who saved twenty-eight containers to be sent the following day as a gift to the ambassadors and other foreign gentlemen.'[30]

If the week-long spectacle prepared for Henri's visit can be described as a fireworks show, this final ball was the grand finale, with so many rockets being set off that the intended audience of one may well have been blinded by the display. The message of taste, of wealth, of *magnificenza* was not merely unmistakable, it was overwhelming. To what degree it represented the real power position of the Adriatic Republic, ever more constricted in the Mediterranean and shut out of the trade routes across the Atlantic, is another matter entirely. It's a fair guess that the Venetian oligarchy hoped the young king wouldn't notice.

174

The Limits of Magnificence

Putting too much emphasis on the role of the sugar banquets in furthering the city's geopolitical goals would be overstating the case, but that is not to deny their important role in the performance staged to awe and impress the young French monarch. Certainly, the chroniclers were impressed by these as much as the processions, fireworks, and regattas. As was Henri, presumably, since he wanted to take them home as souvenirs.

Confectionary, but especially sugar sculpture, had a series of advantages in the 'game' played by the Venetians, not only when compared to more permanent forms of conspicuous display but even when compared to the extravagant banquets of that era. The quantity of confectionary signalled wealth and the craftsmanship showed sophistication, something that the Venetians could use as surrogates in the absence of actual nobility or lineage. Unlike the more permanent media used for bronze or marble sculptures, the sugar figures could be purpose-made to convey a message. In this sense, they had more in common with performance than more permanent forms of *magnificenza* such as architecture. They were by their very nature ephemeral – especially in Venice's July heat and humidity – yet they were nonetheless a desirable souvenir as the scrum at the end of the final Doge's banquet makes clear. All these features set the sugar feasts apart from more commonplace contemporary banquets, which were, admittedly, a literal manifestation of conspicuous consumption but could hardly be finely tuned to send a particular signal as was the case with the sugar sculpture. Just how effective all this sugar and show was in convincing Henri to take the Venetian side is unclear given the young king's mostly incompetent reign, but there's no doubt he could report to his Italian mother that there was no shortage of *magnificenza* in the Adriatic republic.

Notes

1 Estimates for the costs incurred run as high as 100,000 ducats. See Evelyn Korsch, 'Diplomatic Gifts on Henri III's Visit to Venice in 1574', *Studies in the Decorative Arts*, 16.1 (Fall-Winter 2007-2008), 83-113 (p. 87) <http://digitalcommons.uri.edu/cgi/viewcontent.cgi?article=1004&context=art_facpubs> [accessed 15 May 2019].

2 The most comprehensive collection of these is in Pierre de Nolhac and Angelo Solerti, *Il viaggio in Italia di Enrico III: re di Francia e le feste a Venezia, Ferrara, Mantova e Torino* (Turin: L. Roux ec., 1890).

3 Sidney W. Mintz, *Sweetness and Power: The Place of Sugar in Modern History* (New York: Viking, 1985).

4 Cristoforo di Messisbugo, *Banchetti Compositioni Di Vivande*, 1549.

5 In addition to the three state occasions discussed below, Nolhac and Solerti mention a private dinner on 21 July in the Doge's apartments of bread soaked in water ('as was his custom') followed by pistachio and almond marzipan (p. 134). Following his departure from Venice, he was also treated in Mantua on August 2 to a *colazione* of 'confectionery, waters [soft drinks] and other sugar works' (p. 184).

6 Qtd. in Jonathan K. Nelson and Richard Zeckhauser, *The Patron's Payoff: Conspicuous Commissions in Italian Renaissance Art* (Princeton: Princeton University Press, 2008), p. 69.

7 Paolo Paruta, *Della perfettione della vita politica* (Venice: Domenico Nicolini, 1599), p. 282.

8 See Thorstein Veblen, *The Theory of the Leisure Class* (New York: Macmillan, 1899); Pierre Bourdieu, *Distinction: A Social Critique of the Judgement of Taste*, trans. by Richard Nice (Cambridge, MA: Harvard University Press, 1987).

9 See Alison Cole, *Virtue and Magnificence: Art of the Italian Renaissance Courts* (New York: H.N. Abrams, 1995).

10 Jonathan K. Nelson and Richard J. Zeckhauser, *The Patron's Payoff* (Princeton, NJ: Princeton University Press, 2014).

11 Carol M Richardson, Kim Woods, and Michael W Franklin, *Renaissance Art Reconsidered: An Anthology of Primary Sources* (Oxford: Blackwell Publishing, in association with the Open University, 2008), pp. 295-297.

12 Mohamed Ouerfelli, *Le Sucre: Production, Commercialisation et Usages Dans La Méditerranée Médiévale* (Leiden; Boston: Brill, 2008), p. 638.

13 Pompeo Molmenti and Horatio Forbes Brown, *Venice: Its Individual Growth from the Earliest Beginnings to the Fall of the Republic* (Chicago: A.C. McClurg, 1906), p. 295.

14 For more on the itinerant nature of the northern Renaissance court, see Malcolm Vale, 'Courts, Art and Power', in *The Renaissance World*, ed. by John Jeffries Martin (New York: Routledge, 2007), pp. 287-306 (p. 288).

15 Domenico Sella, 'Crisis and Transformation in the Venetian Trade', in *Crisis and Change in the Venetian Economy in the Sixteenth and Seventeenth Centuries*, ed. by Brian Sebastian Pullan (London: Methuen & Co., 1968), pp. 88-105 (p. 91).

16 Molmenti and Brown, p. 122. At this time, the *colazione, collazione*, or *collatione* was a sort of light meal, though records indicate that, at least in some instances, these could be quite lavish and impressive.

17 Marino Sanudo, *I diarii di Marino Sanuto: (MCCCCXCVI-MDXXXIII) dall' autografo Marciano ital. cl. VII codd. CDXIX-CDLXXVII* (F. Visentini, 1893), p. 459. The *biscione* (a serpent devouring a man) was the heraldic symbol of the Visconti and later Sforza dukes of Milan.

18 June Di Schino, *Arte dolciaria barocca* (Rome: Gangemi, 2016), p. 29.

19 Nolhac and Solerti, p. 57.

20 Nolhac and Solerti, pp. 71, 113.

21 Nolhac and Solerti, p. 90.

22 Daniela Ambrosini, 'Les Honneurs Sucrés de Venise', in *Le boire et le manger au XVIe siècle: actes du XIe colloque du Puy-en-Velay*, ed. by Marie Viallon- Schoneveld (Saint-Etienne: Publ. de l'Univ. de Saint-Etienne, 2004), pp. 267-284 (p. 270).

23 The *scudo d'oro* was a gold coin roughly equivalent to a ducat. In 1580, a *galea* (light galley) cost about 6000 ducats; see Ruggiero Romano, 'Economic Aspects of the Construction of Warships in Venice in the Sixteenth Century', in *Crisis and Change in the Venetian Economy in the Sixteenth and Seventeenth Centuries*, ed. by Pullan, pp. 59-87 (p. 81).

24 Nolhac and Solerti, pp. 128-31.

25 Romano, p. 59.

26 It would not have been lost on the king that the alliance that defeated the Turkish navy included an awkward alliance of Venice, Genoa and Spain, but not France. Presumably he was also aware that the battle did no good, Venice had already lost its sugar island of Cyprus months before the battle.

27 Nolhac and Solerti, p. 143. The *galea*, the smallest of the city's war galleys, was the workhorse of the Venetian navy.

28 Qtd. in Ambrosini, p. 282.

29 Nolhac and Solerti, p. 148.

30 Nolhac and Solerti, pp. 148-149. Nolhac and Solerti suggest that this apothecary is likely the same Nicolò della Cavalliera alla Pigna who was elected 'prior' of the Collegio dei Spetieri medicinali in 1573 and 'consigliere' of the same guild in 1575.

Making *Yakiniku* Japanese: Erasing Korean Contributions from Japan's Food Culture

Christopher Laurent

Introduction

Almost a decade ago, a motley group of Japanese ultranationalists gathered in front of a Korean elementary school in Kyoto ostensibly to protest the school's use of the public park across the street. The school was an ideal target: it was affiliated with North Korea and did not have the means to fight back. For many students attending, the school was not so much a symbol of oppression and aggression toward Japan but a safe space to protect their identity, culture, and language in a society that sought to assimilate or exclude them. While the young Korean students remained inside for safety, the crowd began to stir and wave imperial flags, a symbol of Japanese colonial oppression. Some in the crowd began to chant, 'Go back home! You stink of *kimchi*!' – *kimchi* is often used as an insult to target Koreans that have lived in Japan for generations. At the same time, its consumption has slowly but surely permeated the Japanese diet. Today, *kimuchi* – the milder Japanese version of the side dish – is one of the most consumed pickles in Japan. While *kimchi* is used as an ethnic slur directed towards Koreans, *kimuchi* is celebrated as a uniquely Japanese innovation. How can food that delineates Korean ethnicity be the source of prejudice at the same time it is incorporated into Japanese dining habits?

Scholars have examined the processes of domesticating Korean foods to make them part of Japanese cuisine.[1] However, in an attempt to remain objective, these analyses have stayed neutral, silencing some of the greater injustices of this project: while Koreans living in Japan are relegated to subaltern status, their food is expropriated and celebrated as part of Japanese society. This paper seeks to clarify much of the confusion surrounding culinary appropriation by paying close attention to the structure of power that frames it. First, it will provide historical context to better understand the contemporary predicament of Koreans living in Japan. As many Koreans living in Japan reminded me, 'If you want to understand why we are here, you need to look at history'. Second, this paper will examine the food of Koreans living in Japan, a cuisine distinct from both that of South Korea and that of Japan. More specifically, it will focus on how *yakiniku*, a Korean grilled meat dish that clearly frames ethnicity, is being incorporated into contemporary Japanese dining habits. Third, it will broaden the discussion on culinary appropriation to assess what is at stake for marginalized communities. The theoretical implication is to reframe culinary appropriation as part of an integrated system that includes ethnic economy, minority marginalization, and systemic discrimination.

Koreans Living in Japan

An estimated 657,000 Koreans live in Japan, constituting one of the largest minorities in a nation otherwise perceived as homogeneous.[2] Many Koreans are second- and third-generation residents of Japan who speak better Japanese than Korean. Yet, they remain second-class citizens. The current predicament of this population is tied to Japan's colonial period (1910-1945) when large numbers of Koreans who migrated to Japan were often coerced into forced labour.[3] The use of the term 'coerced', even in the case of comfort women, is to this day a topic of contention between Korean and Japanese politicians.[4] Regardless, most historians will find it hard to argue that Japanese colonialism in Korea was not devised as a system of exploitation that pushed millions of Koreans to immigrate toward Japan. It is worth noting that Japanese colonialism was modelled on the success of European colonialism.[5] The Japanese colonial project was devised to reproduce strategies of subjugation, build colonial administration systems, and create a racial hierarchy within their empire. This hierarchy, with Japanese people at its apex, helped promulgate stereotypes that justified Korean subjugation. After the 1910 great Kanto earthquake, rumours of Koreans poisoning wells prompted the massacre of thousands of Korean civilians living in the Tokyo area.[6] These stereotypes – Koreans are unruly and prone to criminality – endure today in Japan's popular imagination.

178 After World War II, Japan was forced to surrender its colonies. Out of the two million Korean labourers, about 600,000 chose to remain after the war.[7] Although Koreans were located at the bottom of the social ladder in Japan, they chose to stay until the political and economic situation improved in Korea. Few ended up making it back home, and their descendants constitute the basis of the Korean population living in Japan. As former citizens of the Japanese Empire, Koreans living in Japan were stripped of their nationality and forced to choose between North Korean and South Korean citizenship. While some Koreans were given the opportunity to naturalize and take Japanese citizenship, most stayed second-class citizens in a country that treated them as undesirable foreigners. Why did most Korean residents choose not to adopt Japanese citizenship? First, the process is complex requiring vast financial resources. Second, it is perceived by some members of the community as a betrayal. Third, most Koreans living in Japan do not see why they should naturalize when they were citizens before Japan's surrender. As they were excluded from desirable occupations, Korean labourers were relegated to unwanted jobs like scrap collectors, gambling hall owners, and hole-in-the-wall restaurant workers. Unable to rent from the majority of Japanese landowners and unable to afford rent elsewhere, Koreans were relegated to living in ethnic ghettos and shantytowns where Japanese people would never live.

Today, Koreans remaining in Japan have inherited the ambiguous status of *Zainichi*, granting them long-term residence without giving them the same rights as Japanese nationals. They are living inside Japanese society as outsiders largely contained in the same neighbourhoods, the same occupations, and the same schools. In order to escape discrimination, many Koreans hide their identity 'passing' as Japanese. For example, the vast majority of Koreans today do not use their Korean names in public life, opting instead to use a Japanese pseudonym. As most *Zainichi* Koreans are born and raised in Japan, they are culturally, linguistically, and physically nearly impossible to differentiate from Japanese people. However, their citizenship prevents them from having the same civil rights, including equal access to employment and education opportunities. To make matters worse, most *Zainichi* Koreans were initially affiliated with North Korea, a regime hostile to Japan. Unlike South Korea, North Korea was proactive in protecting *Zainichi* Koreans' interest in Japan, building schools, providing business lending schemes, and encouraging civil rights activism. Although today the majority of Koreans in Japan have shifted their allegiance to South Korea, they remain perceived as infiltrators by Japanese far-right activists. Koreans that remain politically affiliated to the North suffer the most violent forms of exclusion.

This brief historical survey is essential to understand the current struggles of Koreans in Japan. Although Japanese colonialism is over, the legacy of this system endures within Japanese society. Koreans in Japan have resisted and achieved some victories. For example, they won important lawsuits enabling them to work in Japanese companies, repelled fingerprinting laws reserved otherwise for criminals in Japan, and managed to gain minimal reparations for their exploitation. Yet, by many measures, they still suffer much systemic discrimination, as they are far from gaining equal rights in Japanese society. In fact, with each hard-fought victory, like limited voting rights in local elections or access to pension plans, there has been considerable backlash. The far right has systematically portrayed *Zainichi* Koreans as playing the system, targeting Koreans residents in violent demonstrations and calling to expel them from the country or even exterminate them.[8] In the last few years, hate speech and online bullying against Koreans have drastically increased.[9] In this context, the food culture of Koreans has been a potent symbol of resistance and an economic resource. In *Zainichi* households, simple dishes like *kimchi* stew (*kimchi chigae*) endure the test of time as a reminder that after three generations in Japan they will not be completely assimilated. In *Zainichi* neighbourhoods, restaurants selling *Zainichi* specialties are hard to ignore as they are at the centre of the ethnic economy and social life of the community.

Korean Food Culture in Japan

It is important to remember that the vast majority of ingredients and food processing techniques that make up Japanese cuisine came from Asia via the Korean peninsula. The predecessors of emblematic foods like rice, miso, soy sauce, yuzu, sushi, and green tea all emerged outside of Japan. These foreign elements were transformed – some might claim refined – and adopted as uniquely Japanese. As the Japanese Empire began to expand in the early twentieth century, Japan began to swallow up the human, economic, and culinary resources of its growing empire. Dishes like ramen, today the most popular dish in Japan, were initially sold there by Chinese migrants.[10] A Taiwanese entrepreneur who immigrated to Japan during the colonial period developed instant ramen, a processing technique that played a crucial role in spreading this dish from Japan to the rest of the world.[11] Korean migrant labourers also played a significant role in cities with the closest links with the Korean peninsula. Today, cities like Osaka and Fukuoka have among the largest *Zainichi* Korean populations, and *Zainichi* Korean dishes have become an integral part of the local cuisines of those cities. More recently, South Korea's growing economic and cultural importance across East Asia has helped fuel considerable interest in South Korean popular cuisine. Although *Zainichi* Koreans have had some measure of success riding this wave of popularity, it is important to remember that their cuisine is significantly different from the contemporary cuisine of South Korea.

As explained earlier, a great number of Korean labourers migrated to Japan, voluntarily or against their will, in large part to support the war effort. This exploited workforce was relegated to dangerous and undesirable occupations like working in mines and factories. After the war, these labourers had two options: go back to a country ravaged by colonialism and civil war or stay in a country that had few opportunities for its citizens. To survive their exclusion from the labour market, a large number of Koreans that stayed in Japan turned to entrepreneurship. Restaurants, born out of large cities' ethnic enclaves, have shaped Japan's palate and foodscape. This phenomenon is not unique: throughout the world immigrant communities have turned to food entrepreneurship as a form of economic survival. Although restaurants can offer a means to generate income for immigrants, it is a risky endeavour requiring a lot of work with little initial return. *Zainichi* Korean entrepreneurs have had to be frugal to stay afloat. Restaurants are more often than not family businesses with family members working for little or no money. Savvy owners had to cut overhead costs wherever possible on ingredients and preparation time. Economic constraints can be limiting but they can also be the source of tremendous culinary creativity. Although few Japanese credit them for their entrepreneurial genius, Koreans in Japan have created a popular cuisine from the scraps leftover by Japanese consumers.

The resulting *Zainichi* cuisine blends Korean and Japanese influences; while created from the resources available to this disenfranchised community, the Japanese have often embraced the results, even when that means erasing their own violence. During and shortly after the war, Koreans were notorious for illegally brewing the unfiltered rice wine known as *makoli* in Korean and *doboroku* in Japanese. Although for many Koreans this strategy was a means to survival, illegal brewing was met with violent repression from the Japanese authorities.[12] The dismantlement of illegal Korean breweries periodically led to lethal confrontations between residents and the Japanese police. Although these events are all but expunged from Japanese historical consciousness, moonshine is experiencing a revival among the Japanese working classes.

The same pattern of erasing and embracing happens elsewhere in Japan. In Fukuoka, an ideal settling point for many Koreans due to proximity to the Korean peninsula, one of the city specialties, spicy cod row (*karashi mentaiko*), is now considered a Japanese dish. Similarly, Osaka has by far the largest population of *Zainichi* Koreans: while their influence on the local cuisine can hardly be ignored, the savoury scallion and seafood pancakes called *shijimi* that are such a common street food in the city are a likely precursor to Japanese *okonomiyaki*, a dish that is the pride and joy of Osaka residents. Members of the Korean community have also defended the idea that Japan's contemporary infatuation with meat is in great part due to the influence of Korean food culture. *Zainichi* dishes' popularity in Japan is seldom credited to the presence of the Korean postcolonial minority.

Meat-eating in Japan was popularized in great part through grilled meat restaurants called *yakiniku*. These restaurants serve small pieces of meat grilled by the customers at the table. Grilling your own meat at the table becomes a way to save labour in the kitchen while providing an entertaining activity for the guests. Scholars unanimously agree that these restaurants were started by *Zainichi* Koreans. As few Korean restaurateurs could afford more than leftover scraps, these restaurants first started out serving *horumon yaki* (grilled offal), which later morphed into *yakiniku* (grilled meat), a food adapted to Japanese tastes and Japanese sensitivities. Each restaurant developed its blend of dipping sauces that would, if the restaurant is famous enough, be an additional stream of revenue to stores. Originally, these restaurants were known as Chosen cuisine (the colonial name for the Korean peninsula) but to distance themselves from the negative connotation, entrepreneurs changed their name to *yakiniku*, which literarily means grilled meat in Japanese.[13] As with Koreans in Japan using their Japanese name, these restaurants also became known under a Japanese name to distance themselves from their Korean origins. This permutation operates under the same dynamics as the erasure of people: when something is bad, Japanese people use the Korean name, but when it is good they use the Japanese name.

Power and Appropriation

As fewer and fewer people associate *yakiniku* with *Zainichi* Koreans, the dish is more often than not considered Japanese. Today, this type of grilled meat is one of the most popular dishes among young people in Japan – who have little clue of its origin. Although Korean ethnic neighbourhoods still rely heavily on *yakiniku* restaurants to make a living, an increasing number of restaurants outside these enclaves are owned by Japanese. The remaining traces of Koreanness have been slowly erased from menus, and few restaurants classify themselves as foreign cuisine any longer. In fact, *yakiniku* restaurants are becoming increasingly popular outside of Japan as well. A rapid survey of the restaurants' websites reveals their classification as Japanese-style barbecue with no mention of their Korean origins.[14] The strategic deletion of Korean influence allows the restaurants to add value to its food thanks to a global hierarchy of cuisine where Japan reigns supreme. This tactic allows these restaurants to charge more than what they could for Korean barbecue. At the same time, as the popularity of *yakiniku* increases in Japan and abroad, so does anti-Korean sentiment in Japan. With the Japanization of *yakiniku* two different yet interrelated processes take place. Economically, *yakiniku* restaurants become monopolized by Japanese owners taking away an essential resource from a group with few recourses in Japan. Culturally, it erases the contribution and presence of *Zainichi* Koreans, thus validating the narrative that Koreans only take and have never contributed.

How does culture fit into global patterns of economic marginalization, erasure of disenfranchised communities, and social hierarchies? Contemporary fears of imminent immigrant invasion and misdeeds of ethnic minorities spread like wildfire across the media and political landscape. While nation-states – in particular the ones of East Asia – have historically strived to become linguistically, culturally, and ethnically homogeneous, they have in the process silenced the presence and the contributions of their minorities. Cultural production is one of the few resources excluded groups can exploit, which explains why these communities are sources of tremendous creativity. However, in order not to undo the myth of national homogeneity, the dominant group must expropriate these contributions to make them part of the nation. This process of plagiarism and erasure may often be presented as cultural borrowing, but it is not an accident: it follows similar patterns of dominance and power in societies that continue to internally exploit minority groups. *Tikka masala* in Great Britain, *couscous royal* in France, and *rijsttafel* in the Netherlands operate under similar patterns of appropriation. Although marginalized communities developed these dishes in a colonial context, they have become so familiar to those countries that some consider them native. This process of domestication would not be problematic if the communities that developed this food were not marginalized.

The United States has a long history of embracing the food cultures of ethnic minorities while excluding these same groups. Southern culinary heritage has been a longstanding area of contention, pitting against each other communities on both sides of the racial divide. For instance, white chefs and entrepreneurs like Paula Deen have long benefited from rebranding of cuisine created largely by African Americans as 'Southern', effectively monopolizing it both culturally and economically. Southern barbecue constitutes a prime example of this cultural dynamic. African American contributions to the craft are often minimized even though their historical primacy in its creation is well documented. As one measure of this minimization, the Barbecue Hall of Fame includes only three African American men out of twenty-four inductees.[15] This type of culinary appropriation follows a similar pattern: preventing minorities from making money from their cultural production and simultaneously erasing those contributions to that culture. The discussion over culinary appropriation, and more generally cultural appropriation, is one that is very much alive in the public but has garnered relatively less scholarly attention compared to other dimensions of systemic racism. There is an urgent need to understand culinary appropriation using the perspective of disenfranchised minorities. As we closely examine the dynamics that govern culinary appropriation, we must recognize that the marginalized have more at stake than the privileged.

Most criticisms of culinary appropriation argue that one cannot prevent culinary exchange from happening, that culinary poaching is simply homage to a cultural group that increases acceptance of marginalized minorities. However, few ask themselves how the dominant group is systematically benefiting from this transaction. At this point, it is worth stating the fact that not all culinary exchange is culinary appropriation. Power, more precisely the imbalance of power, between two groups is essential to

182

contextualize what constitutes culinary appropriation. When a group has the power to exploit, discriminate, belittle, and prevent upward mobility, taking the food culture of a marginalized group and making it the food of the dominant amounts to more than mere cultural borrowing. Culinary appropriation is, in fact, a system that transforms the foreign into the native, contributes to the economic marginalization of disenfranchised groups, and erases minority contributions from the so-called national culture. This system is embedded within a pre-existing framework of ethnic and racial oppression that operates in most nation-states. Food culture does not evade this framework as it is subject to similar dynamics of exclusion, discrimination, and racism. The forces that push people to the margins, that maintain racial hierarchies in place, and portray minorities as a burden on society need to be examined to understand the overarching framework that enables culinary appropriation. To ignore the forces that operate within this framework is to enable this project and to side with power.

Conclusion

This paper describes the position of Koreans living in Japan and considers the appropriation of their cuisine by the very group that persecutes them. Third and fourth-generation Koreans that are born and raised in Japan speak fluent Japanese, understand Japanese cultural norms, and are physically indistinguishable from their Japanese counterparts, yet they still do not hold the same rights. As a minority that came to Japan during the colonial occupation of Korea, they still suffer from prejudice and systemic discrimination in a society that seeks to erase them or exclude them. When one takes these elements into consideration, the Japanization of *yakiniku* and the Japanese takeover of the industry appear problematic. The appropriation of Korean cuisine in Japan exists within a system of oppression that predates the invention of the dish and continues historical trends. Patterns of subjugation that were devised during colonial times persist today in Japanese society; this subjugation erases the presence of Koreans and pushes them to the margins of society. *Zainichi* Koreans have been far from passive to this oppression, forging grass-roots resistance movements to better their status in society and making their presence heard to urge Japan to recognize their existence. However, this type of activism has focused on rectifying past and present discrimination rather than on their cultural erasure. As members of the Korean community are increasingly visible in the media, one can hope that Japan will have no choice other than to acknowledge their presence and contribution.

Patterns of cultural erasure and economic marginalization are not unique to Japan. In fact, they operate using similar mechanisms in postcolonial societies. As members of former colonial empires, our first instinct is to argue that culinary appropriation is benign borrowing, a homage or a way to provide visibility for the marginalized, but this view ignores the structure of power that exists in society. When the dominant group has the power to erase the culinary presence and contribution of a minority group, can we still consider it simply culinary diffusion? When members of the dominant group make a fortune with resources developed by a marginalized group, while the same

183

group struggles to make a living from these same resources, is it only flattery? When examining cases of culinary appropriation one must take into account the relative status of each group to grasp the larger implications of this one-way exchange. The power that one group or one person holds in relation to the other party becomes a reliable arbiter, or at least a good benchmark, to distinguish between what is culinary appropriation and what is not. Japanese hamburger restaurants are not appropriation, whereas white chefs building their reputation and fortunes on the cuisines of people of colour is. Members of the group profiting from culinary appropriation have attempted to undermine the concept, their voices amplified by the status they occupy in society. This is no accident: it is part of the overarching framework. One needs to pay close attention to the other voices, the ones with less power, take their grievances seriously and consider that they might be right, that culinary appropriation might, after all, be worth denouncing.

Notes

1   Katarzyna Cwiertka, 'Culinary Culture and the Making of a National Cuisine', in *A Companion to the Anthropology of Japan*, ed. by Jennifer Robertson (Oxford: Blackwell, 2007), pp. 415-28; Sonia Ryang, *Eating Korean in America: Gastronomic Ethnography of Authenticity* (Honolulu: University of Hawai'i Press, 2015).

2   This estimate does not include naturalized Koreans and children born of mixed marriages. See Yasunori Fukuoka, *Lives of Young Koreans in Japan* (Balwyn, North Victoria: Trans Pacific Press, 2000), p. 21.

3   Xavier Robillard-Martel and Christopher Laurent, 'From Colonization to Zaitokukai: The Legacy of Racial Oppression in the Lives of Koreans in Japan', *Asian Ethnicity*, 16 February 2019 <doi.org/10.108 0/14631369.2019.1575718>.

4   Haeng-Ja Chung, 'The Comfort Women: Sexual Violence and Postcolonial Memory in Korea and Japan by C. Sarah Soh', *American Anthropologist*, 112.2 (2010), 337-38; Hirofumi Hayashi, 'Disputes in Japan over the Japanese Military 'Comfort Women' System and Its Perception in History', *The Annals of the American Academy of Political and Social Science*, 617 (2008), 123-32.

5   William G. Beasley, *Japanese Imperialism, 1894-1945* (Oxford: Clarendon Press, 1987), p. 6.

6   Sonia Ryang, 'The Great Kanto Earthquake and the Massacre of Koreans in 1923: Notes on Japan's Modern National Sovereignty', *Anthropological Quarterly*, 76.4 (2003), 731-48.

7   Edward W. Wagner, *The Korean Minority in Japan, 1904-1950* (Honolulu: Institute of Pacific Relations, 1951).

8   Robillard-Martel and Laurent.

9   Tomomi Yamaguchi, 'Xenophobia in Action: Ultranationalism, Hate Speech, and the Internet in Japan', *Radical History Review*, 2013.117 (2013), 98-118.

10   Barak Kushner, *Slurp! A Social and Culinary History of Ramen – Japan's Favorite Noodle Soup* (Leiden: Global Oriental, 2012), pp. 13-14.

11   George Solt, *The Untold History of Ramen: How Political Crisis in Japan Spawned a Global Food Craze* (Berkeley: University of California Press, 2014), p. 91.

12   John Lie, *Zainichi (Koreans in Japan): Diasporic Nationalism and Postcolonial Identity* (Berkeley: University of California Press, 2008).

13   Miyatsuka Toshio, 'Yakiniku–Savory Dish with Simple Origins', *Japan Quarterly*, 46.4 (1999), 31.

14   'Montréal, Canada', *Gyu-Kaku Japanese BBQ* <https://www.gyu-kaku.com/montreal/> [accessed 4 June 2019]; 'Kintan at Oxford Circus', *Kintan.uk* <https://kintan.uk/oxfordcircus/> [accessed 4 June 2019].

15   'Barbecue Hall of Fame', *American Royal* <http://www.americanroyal.com/bbq/barbecue-hall-of-fame/> [accessed 4 June 2019]. As a response to increasing criticism, the organization nominated two African American chefs in late 2019.

The Community Cookbook as a Vehicle of Women's Empowerment in Nineteenth- and Early Twentieth-Century America

Don Lindgren

Introduction

For more than one hundred fifty years, groups of women have gathered around kitchen tables, in church basements, and in meeting halls to collect and organize recipes for a purpose more ambitious than their own use. They were doing the work of making cookbooks. To do this work, the women exercised all of the functions of commercial publishers: they solicited content; sought financial backing; edited, designed and illustrated; hired printers and binders; and finally marketed and distributed their product. They accomplished these tasks on a shoestring budget, with little or no exposure to, or guidance from, the traditional centres of publishing, and without the motivation of personal gain. The fruit of all this labour is a legacy of thousands of works, produced by amateurs (in the best sense of the word) in towns big and small across the United States, a distinctively American expression of fellowship, creativity, and purposefulness: the community cookbook.[1]

The Community Cookbook as a Genre

The community cookbook is generally considered to display three characteristics: the books were produced by members of a recognizable community, the recipes were understood to have been compiled from sources within that community, and the intention of the enterprise was to generate revenue for a charitable purpose or for the maintenance of the organization itself. Books fitting this definition have also been called charitable cookbooks, fundraising cookbooks, compiled cookbooks, local cookbooks, church cookbooks, and in more recent years (a little ambiguously), 'those spiral-bound books'.[2] As a genre, the community cookbook became an unexpected tool for the empowerment of American women at a time when there were many limitations on their participation in professional life.[3] Well into the beginning of the twentieth century, women negotiated social environments still imbued with a sentimentality about what might be called 'prestige without standing'. In the public sphere, women could be revered and disregarded at the same time. The empowerment of women began in the articulation of their concerns through domestic means. Paramount among these concerns were health, well-being, and prospects of their families in a changing world. But, whereas the origins of community cookbooks lay in these subjects, the physical means of production required avenues of access negotiated almost entirely by men. This was an age in America before women could, without intervention from men, own property or bank accounts, devise wills or other contracts, or exercise control over their own wages, to say nothing of political enfranchisement.[4] Despite variations in state and local ordinances, nowhere would women have been surprised to learn that legal practice required men to file papers of incorporation for the establishment of any civic organization. In principal, the entire enterprise from founding an association to publishing the community cookbook would have required supervision by men. But this story of limits is also a story of limits broken.

In this confining social, cultural, and legal environment, how were the community cookbooks produced, and what did the women achieve through these books? Some hurdles were overcome by dispensing with them altogether, a rare luxury afforded to many of the women's groups that existed outside of traditional publishing centres. Copyright registration, for example, followed a routine course at commercial publishing houses. However, copyright was not consistently filed for church and charitable cookbooks whose distribution was local, while books produced by social reform or relief communities, such as temperance unions or Women's Exchange societies, may well have sought counsel regarding property rights. The uneven application of copyright registration led to some unforeseen consequences, including the exclusion of many community cookbooks from the holdings of important institutional collections.[5] Compilers and editors of community cookbooks applied other somewhat vernacular standards to the rules of publishing. Title pages could be absent altogether, not just lacking copyright information. In some cases a titled wrapper might fill in for a title page.[6] Sadly, for the bibliographer, wrappers are often the first element to perish in the kitchen, leaving many books later unidentifiable.

Up-front publishing and printing costs were financed through a creative work-around. Advertisements were solicited from local businesses, including printers and binders. Barter for promotional consideration, coupled with advertisements for businesses within the community helped finance the costs of book production, leaving the proceeds from sales to be applied in full to the charitable or social cause.[7]

The cookbook's content, an expense for a traditionally published book, was compiled from within the community at no cost beyond labour, with recipes – frequently, but not necessarily – attributed to the contributing member of the community. In effect, women employed techniques that we today might call crowd-funding (pre-financing of production through advertising) and crowd-sourcing (gathering the recipes from community members) to get the cookbooks published.

In later years the communities, especially those in smaller towns, were faced with new production challenges, as local job printers and binders consolidated into larger operations in bigger towns and cities. Some community groups turned to a new breed of specialist book printers able to produce the smaller quantities often required (and often featuring the metal spiral or plastic comb binding).[8] Other groups applied creative do-it-yourself approaches to printing and binding, applying new printing technologies like mimeograph, ditto, and later Xerox copying, while new binding technologies like staples, ring binders, machine sewing and nuts and bolts, with inexpensive, easily available materials including wallpaper, construction paper, decorated oil cloth, and even linoleum.[9] Again, we see the women's groups able to confront a business challenge and 'make do' with adaptation, creativity, and a good deal of effort. But publishing community cookbooks and distributing useful and perhaps tasty recipes was not the only goal.

Some Goals of the Compilers

The aftermath of the American Civil War provided a backdrop of social need to which women's groups could respond by raising money through book sales. Needs included medical care, addressed through, for example, Maria Moss's *A Poetical Cook-Book* (Philadelphia, 1864), or the provision of clothing through the many cookbooks issued by independent chapters of the Dorcas Society.[10] Community cookbooks were quickly put to use raising funds for a much wider range of causes. With these funds, the women contributed significantly to the construction and outfitting of churches, hospitals, grange halls, libraries, and other civic buildings.

For example, Colorado's Monte Vista Library Association compiled and issued the *San Luis Valley Cook Book* (Monte Vista, c. 1909).[11] The Ladies' Literary Club of Monte Vista had established itself in August 1885 – a full year before incorporation of the town itself – specifically for the purpose of providing a public reading room and lending library. At first books were housed in the rear of a general store, but sufficient funds were raised, in part through sales of a cookbook, to erect a building in 1895. Fortuitously, the building, if small (sixteen feet deep and twenty-two feet wide), proved durable. Today it houses the archives of the Monte Vista Historical Society. A report filed a century later (May 1995) in application for the preservation of the library building added in its narrative: 'On Saturday evening of August 3, 1895 the ladies of the Monte Vista Library Association gave their annual reception at the new library building. The *San Luis Valley Graphic* reported that 'guests were invited to bring suitable books for the library and the request was liberally responded to. Refreshments were served, the proceeds of which are to go to the purchase of new books'. The president, Mrs H. H. Marsh, provided an historical review of the Association's patient work throughout the years to build up a fine library only to see it entirely destroyed by the Bonner block fire. Despite this and other calamities, the women persevered, and in 1916 applied to the Carnegie Foundation for funds to expand yet again. The result was a new building that opened in 1919 bearing the name Monte Vista Carnegie Library. Thus the efforts of the Ladies' Literary Club, in part through the sale of cookbooks, established the original informal library in a general store, built two successive library buildings, expanded one with the help of the Carnegie Foundation, and both still stand today as historical buildings in the town of Monte Vista.[12] Quite a

187

contribution to the built environment of this small Colorado mining town.

The proceeds from sales of community cookbooks were also put to use to support various social movements. Hattie Burr's *Woman's Suffrage Cook Book* of 1886 was one of the first of many community cookbooks to raise funds for suffrage, and contains contributions (more quotes than recipes) from figures in the movement including Harriet Beecher Stowe, Clara Barton, Lydia Child, Louisa May Alcott, and others.[13] In 1895, the *Green Mountain White Ribbon Cook Book* was offered by the Women's Christian Temperance Union of Vermont in their ongoing crusade against the perceived evils of alcohol. This small community cookbook contains recipes specifically thought to address the root causes of alcoholism; with better nutrition and more 'natural' foods would come less desire for drink.[14] In more recent years community cookbooks have been adapted to help build new movements and address new social needs, with books issued in support of many causes including nuclear disarmament, school lunches in South Africa, and AIDS/HIV research.[15]

How Effective Were these Cookbooks?

Groups of women were able to hurdle obstacles put in their way to compile, publish, and distribute cookbooks, and they used the sale of the books to raise funds for various causes. How effective could this homespun business really be? The answer is 'very effective'. One measure can be found in the records of money collected in support of church construction across the United States. Month after month, contributions from small congregations were sent to the Congregational Church Building Society, and then redistributed to new congregations or congregations with new building projects. The listings of donations, arranged by state and town, contain primarily the names of various local women's auxiliaries. The first nine months of 1898 show more than $120,000 collected.[16] This money was not exclusively from the women's groups, and the women had methods of raising funds beyond the sale of cookbooks, but for a single denomination in 1898, $120,000 was enough to build, in their entirety, about thirty-four churches.[17] So in addition to community cookbooks being composed of manageable parts, inexpensive to produce, genuinely helpful, and inclusively collaborative (members of the community with modest skills could still contribute), we see they can be used to raise useful and sometimes sizable sums of money.

The rapid geographic spread of community cookbooks is another indication of the extent to which they were recognized as effective fundraising tools. *Nantucket Receipts* is the earliest known community cookbook, appearing in Massachusetts in 1871 (on behalf of a public library in Dedham).[18] The same year another appeared in Michigan (for the Ladies' Fair of the Congregational Church, Grand Rapids); in 1872 in Connecticut ('for the benefit of Christ Church Fair', Hartford) and in Indiana (to aid the Congregational Church, Terre Haute); in 1873 in Ohio (for the First Presbyterian Church, Dayton); and in 1874 in Kansas ('for the benefit of the Home for the Friendless' in Leavenworth).[19] More than two hundred fifty community cookbooks with some charitable dimension had appeared before the end of the 1880s.[20] More than six times that number had been placed on offer by the century's close. The numerical surge also had geographical breadth. Between the end of the Civil War and the turn of the century, community cookbooks had been published in forty-three of the forty-five states and in the District of Columbia; examples from the territories constituting all of the present-day fifty states have been documented before 1910.

A further measure of the effectiveness of community cookbooks was their co-option by national food producers and publishers. *The Centennial Buckeye Cook Book*, a church cookbook issued in 1876 and compiled by women of the First Congregational Church of Marysville, Ohio, became the centrepiece of the small publishing empire of Estelle Hemans Woods Wilcox and her husband, Major Alfred Gould Wilcox.[21] The Wilcoxes recognized entrepreneurial opportunity and purchased the copyright of the Marysville cookbook – immediately, it would seem, as *Buckeye Cookery and Practical Housekeeping* appeared in 1877. Later issues were titled *Practical Housekeeping, The Dixie Cook-Book, The New Dixie Cook-Book, Buckeye Cooking*, and so on through at least 1909.[22] Content produced for charitable purposes in Marysville, Ohio was retitled, redistributed, and transformed into a purely commercial activity. With local production and a local audience, individual community cookbooks were largely a local affair. National food producers, especially those in aggressively competitive markets like baking powder (Rumford), flour (Swan's Down), and cocoa (Walter Baker) recognized that the books were trusted element in millions of American households and purchased advertising space in the books. The historical inclusion of local business advertising made these national advertisements an easy fit. Colour printing was introduced to the books by some of these advertisers, often a single page printed elsewhere and tipped into the books. Some companies sponsored an entire cookbook, simplifying work for the community organization, but also removing the local 'crowd-financed' advertising. Like local business advertisements, those from national products helped to raise the funds that paid for the book, which in turn raised the funds for charity. Other companies repackaged and published entire books that had first appeared as community cookbooks. C.I. Hood & Co. Apothecaries, makers of Hood's Sarsparilla, purchased the rights to *The High-Street Cook Book*, issued in 1885 by the Ladies of the High Street Church of Lowell, Massachusetts. The newly published work, now titled *Hood's High Street Cook Book*, was issued later the same year, crediting the Ladies on the title page, and featuring an image of two women instructing a chef on the pictorial wrapper.[23] For the food producer, the community cookbook served as a new vehicle to introduce their brand into kitchens across America and onto shelves where the books still, today, may sit.

Conclusion

While national food producers were eager to engage their audience through locally produced community cookbooks, it remains to be seen whether they understood why the cookbooks were such effective mechanisms for this engagement; but we can see why.

American women came together in groups, informal and formal, to get something done within the range of power available to them in their time and place. They creatively navigated the production and marketing of cookbooks, and they used the sale of the books to often significant financial effect. Beyond the books themselves, beyond raising funds for the physical churches, hospitals, and libraries that are the heart of American civic architecture, and beyond providing kindling for a range of American social and political movements, women's organizations in America used community cookbooks to build the very communities the books reflected. Each element of the process made connections and strengthened networks: compiled recipes are gathered from community members; local business advertisement supports the project while projecting the small-town businesses into the kitchens of families; local printing and binding (either professional or homemade) produces an object that in both process and material physically reflects the community. The funds raised enabled significant contributions to America's built landscape in cities, towns, and small villages, enabling the construction, repair, and outfitting of churches, hospitals, libraries, and grange halls. Other funds strengthened movements such as Temperance, Suffrage, and Social Justice: movements that changed the social face of the nation. Still others made more modest contributions, such as a 'no-spitting' ordinance in a Colorado silver mining town. But big or small, each charitable contribution was accompanied by a parallel contribution to the creation of the social bond of community. Through these dual achievements – solving a practical problem through organizing around the sale of community cookbooks, while building networks of social bonds within the community – these groups of women, these church ladies, grange members, temperance crusaders, and hospital auxiliaries, navigated restrictions, limits, and boundaries to empower themselves through community cookbooks.

Acknowledgement

This paper is largely based on an ongoing research project that consists of the collection and detailed bibliographic and historical exploration of early community cookbooks. See Mark Germer and Don Lindgren, *UnXld: American Cookbooks of Community & Place*, vol. 1 (Biddeford, ME: Rabelais Inc., 2019).

Notes

1   The phenomenon of community cookbooks was not uniquely American, as shown by an exemplary survey of a parallel tradition, see Sarah Black, 'Community Cookbooks, Women, and the "Building of the Civil Society" in Australia, 1900-38', in *Dining on Turtles: Food, Feasts, and Drinking in History*, ed. by Diane Kirkby and Tanja Luckens (Basingstoke: Palgrave Macmillan, 2007), pp. 154-70; Janet Theophano, *Eat My Words: Reading Women's Lives Through the Cookbooks They Wrote* (New York: Palgrave, 2002), pp. 11-48.

2   'First, such books must be spiral-bound, or they are not to be trusted' (Alton Brown, 'Foreword', in *The Southern Foodways Alliance Community Cookbook*, ed. by Sara Roahen and John T. Edge (Atlanta:

University of Georgia Press, 2010), p. [xi]). Some definitions in circulation, it should be noted, skew toward books of an age closer to the present day. But there is broad consensus (see Black, p. 155) on the other 'essential' traits in Brown's formulation: recipes contributed by members of an organization, a light editorial hand, and 'a strong sense of place'.

3   On the understanding that genres are resources constructed by communities to wield 'pragmatic power as social action', in the formulation proposed by Carolyn Miller, 'Rhetorical Community: The Cultural Basis of Genre', in *Genre and the New Rhetoric,* ed. by Aviva Freedman and Peter Medway (London: Taylor & Francis, 1994), pp. 67-78.

4   On the development of coverture laws during this period, see Joyce W. Warren, *Women, Money, and the Law: Nineteenth Century Fiction, Gender & the Courts* (Iowa City: University of Iowa Press, 2009), pp. 43-55.

5   Terra L. Gearhart-Sema, 'Women's Work, Women's Knowing: Intellectual Property and the Recognition of Women's Traditional Knowledge', *Yale Journal of Law & Feminism*, 21.2 (2009), 372-404 (see especially the section, 'Traditional Knowledge and Women's Work', pp. 380-84). For an overview of gender issues in copyright law, see Ann Bartow, 'Fair Use and the Fairer Sex: Gender, Feminism, and Copyright Law', *American University Journal of Gender, Social Policy & the Law*, 14.3 (2006), pp. 551-84.

6   For an example of a book published without title page, see [Soldiers Memorial Hospital Committee], *The Old South Cook Book* (Montgomery, Ala.: the Committee, 1920), see cover text.

7   For examples with advertisements throughout, see Ladies of the First Baptist Church, *Queen City Cook Book* (Sioux Falls, S.D.: the Ladies, 1891) and [A.W.H.N.], *Choice Receipts from Experienced Housewives* (Bridgeport: Standard Association Press, 1878)

8   *Cookbook Publishing Guide* [sales kit flier], (Kearney: Morris Press, 2015).

9   For an example with ring binders, see Ladies of the Covenant Presbyterian Church, *The Bisbee Cook Book* (Bisbee, AZ: c. 1905). A detailed inventory of the professional and vernacular printing and binding technologies employed in community cookbooks will be included in a forthcoming volume of *UnXld*.

10 Maria Moss's *A Poetical Cook-Book* (Philadelphia, 1864) is recognized as the first charitable or fundraising cookbook, though not strictly a community cookbook, as it was compiled by a single author; Dorcas Aid Society (Benton, IL), *Christian Church Cook Book* (Benton, 1922), serves as one example of many of its type.

11 Monte Vista Library Association, *San Luis Valley Cook Book* (Monte Vista, c. 1909).

12 *UNXLD*, vol. 1, p. 16.

13 Hattie A. Burr, *The Woman Suffrage Cook Book* (Boston: [n.p.], 1886).

14 Women's Christian Temperance Union of Vermont, *The Green Mountain White Ribbon Cook Book* (Jericho, VT: [1895]).

15 [Women Strike for Peace (Los Angeles Branch)], *Peace de Resistance: A Cook Book* (Los Angeles: [1965]); Mario Batali and Jim Dine, *The Lunch Box Fund Cook Book* (New York: 2015); Alice Waters and others, *Aid & Comfort Portfolio* (Berkeley, 1987).

16 [Congregational Church Building Society], *Church Building Quarterly*, 16.4 (New York, 1898), 269-80.

17 For estimates of the costs of building a church, see *American Carpenter and Builder*, 14.6 (Chicago, March 1913), pp. 52-54.

18 [New England Hospital for Women and Children], *Nantucket Receipts* (Boston, 1870).

19 [Ladies of the Congregational Church], *Grand Rapids Receipt Book* (Grand Rapids, 1871); *Choice Receipts* (Hartford, 1872); [Ladies of the Congregational Church], *The Terre Haute Receipt Book* (Terre Haute 1872); [Kansas Home for the Friendless], *The Kansas Home Cook-Book* (Leavenworth, 1874).

20 Numbers extracted from the corpus examined in Margaret Cook, *America's Charitable Cooks: A Bibliography* (Kent, OH: [the author], 1971).

21 [First Congregational Church of Marysville, Ohio], *The Centennial Buckeye Cook Book* (Marysville, 1876).

22 The succession is laid out in Katherine Bitting, *Gastronomic Bibliography* (San Francisco: A.W. Biting, 1939), pp. 495-96.

23 [Ladies of the High-Street Church], *High-Street Cook Book* (Lowell, 1885), the rights to which were purchased by C. I. Hood & Co. in order to promote Hood's Sarsaparilla; in later editions the title was changed to *Hood's Cook Book*.

The Power of Eating Together, or the Story of Why Banquets Were the Core of Marriage in the Past

Andrea Maraschi

Treasure-Givers and Solemn Weddings

First course: gilded suckling pigs, spitting fire from their mouths, and gilded fish (called '*porchette*'). Second course: gilded hares, gilded pikes. Third course: a large gilded calf and a gilded trout. Fourth course: gilded quails and partridges, along with gilded roasted trout.[1] The menu goes on and lists a total of eighteen courses, accompanied by rich gifts such as cloaks lined with ermine, silver belts, steeds with gilded head-stalls, coursers with gilded saddles, and crimson velvets. A quick peep into a lord's hall in the late Middle Ages reveals the feast given on 5 June 1368 by the ruler of Milan, Galeazzo II Visconti, for the marriage of his daughter, Violante, to Lionel, Duke of Clarence (Clare, Suffolk).[2] Twenty years had passed since one of the greatest catastrophes mankind ever experienced: survivors (like Galeazzo, Francesco Petrarca and Jean Froissart, also present at the wedding, maybe alongside Geoffrey Chaucer) and new generations (like Violante) wanted to shrug off fears and atrocities which must have been still fresh in their memory after the Black Death. Politics-wise, the marriage was a strategic union between the crown of England and one of the more powerful families of northern Italy: sumptuous celebrations were required. Yet, such a magnificent banquet, with courses meticulously described by the sources, was not there to be merely eaten: it was a symbol of status.

In fact, the story of marriage and of wedding banquets in Europe has a lot to do with status and power. Rulers needed to show their generosity, to share their wealth with their men, allies, retinues.[3] A ruler must be a *beaga bryttan*, 'giver of rings', or a *sinces bryttan*, 'treasure-giver'. These kennings are found in the Old English poem *Beowulf*, but point at a fundamental attribute of every medieval lord.[4] Three hundred years before Violante's wedding, the feast for the marriage of Matilda of Canossa's parents in 1037 was even more majestic. 'The banquet [for the wedding of Boniface and Beatrice] went on for three months', the countess's biographer Donizo writes. For the occasion, Boniface shod his horses with silver instead of iron, and ordered that the nails be incompletely hammered, so that the silver could be scattered around in the fields. In this way, 'the locals [i.e. his subjects] could see how great he was [...], and how immense his wealth was'. As for the food, Boniface spared no expense. Spices were considered a status symbol for nobles, a proper identity marker: unsurprisingly, they were provided in enormous quantities. Donizo tells that they 'were not crushed in mortars' – as one would expect – 'but ground at the watermills like spelt'.[5] The biographer does not dwell on other fundamental components of the marriage, such as Beatrice's rich dowry: the banquet is all he needs to describe in order to portray the count's power and prestige.

In 1549, thus almost two hundred years after the wedding of Violante and Lionel, Italian bishop and historian Paulus Jovius praised Galeazzo Visconti's extraordinary largesse: 'such abundance of treasure was spent, for he arranged a lavish wedding banquet, equestrian games, and gave great gifts to more than two hundred English counts.' The reason is immediately clear: Galeazzo wanted to 'surpass the magnificence of the most wealthy kings'.[6] And then the author lingers on the splendour of the banquet, on the courses, on the presents accompanying each of them. One should not conclude that Galeazzo had delusions of grandeur, though. This is what medieval wedding feasts were for: first and foremost, they were displays of power.

Now, it is to be noted that marriage did not consist of a mere banquet.[7] Many other elements had great importance, aside from the political aspects of the union: the dowry was one of them. Violante's precious dowry, for instance, consisted of the city of Alba; of towns such as Mondovì, Cuneo, and Cherasco; and of hundreds of thousands of florins. Among other things, these were just a part of the huge exchange of money and gifts that characterized her and other weddings of the medieval élite.

Modern readers would assume that the nuptial mass was a key moment as well: they would not be wrong. Violante and Lionel got married in the church of Santa Maria Maggiore in Milan – a much smaller predecessor of today's Cathedral dedicated to the Nativity of St. Mary – before many important secular and ecclesiastical guests. The ceremony was celebrated by the Bishop of Novara, and took place in accordance with protocol. The bride was accompanied by two kinsmen, her uncle Bernabò Visconti and Amedeo of Savoy, and the former held her finger, the one where the nuptial ring would be placed.[8] The union was celebrated with great solemnity ('*con grande pompa*'), for solemnity was a necessary condition when it came to weddings of the European élite.[9] However, the sources do not seem to linger more than necessary on the nuptial mass: there does not exist yet a norm which invalidates marriages that do not take place in accordance with said protocol. For that, one has to wait until the *Tametsi* decree of 1563, a ruling of the Council of Trent which changed matrimonial law.[10] The opening of the decree immediately exposes the essential controversy characterizing marriage up until that time:

> Although [*tametsi*] there should be no doubt that clandestine marriages made with the free consent of the contractants are valid [*rata*] and true marriages as long as the church has not rendered them invalid, so that those are justly to be condemned who deny that such marriages are true and valid and who falsely affirm that the marriages of minors contracted without the consent of their parents are invalid and that parents have the power to render them valid or invalid, nevertheless, the holy church of God for most just reasons has always detested and prohibited them.[11]

The word *tametsi* perfectly summarizes the whole picture. The church had been trying to oppose clandestine marriages since early Christian times, but had been forced to turn a blind eye on a practice which was a direct result of 'human disobedience'.[12] There could be different types of clandestine marriages: for instance, a) those arranged in secret; b) by force; c) incestuous unions; or, d) marriages between persons 'in a state of damnation' (that is, persons who abandoned their partners and started living with somebody else 'in perpetual adultery'). The *Tametsi* decree proposed a definitive solution: henceforth, marriages should be publicly announced by the local priest three times during Mass on three successive feast days. If no impediments had been found, the marriage was to be celebrated *in facie ecclesiae*, where the couple would express their mutual *consensus*, and the priest would recite the formula '*ego vos coniungo* [...]'.[13] From then on, the ceremony required the presence of the priest and at least two witnesses, for two reasons. First, the Church needed to extend its control over such an important institution.[14] Second, the celebration was to be made public in order to discourage unions characterized by 'hidden impediments'. The major difference between the past was that 'those who attempt to contract marriage otherwise [...] the holy synod renders entirely incapable of contracting thus, and it declares such contracts invalid and null'.[15]

Before 1563, however, the very role of the priest was optional, because the bride and the groom themselves were the ministers of marriage, and the priest's role only had a sacramental significance.[16] This contradiction is better explained in the following section.

194 Before 1563: The Debate around *Consensus*

The Church gained control over marriage only many centuries after Christianity became the official religion in the Roman empire – and only with great struggle. The institution of marriage predates Christianity, and for a long time it continued to be perceived as a mere contract which implied the 'exchange' of precious goods: wealth, properties, lands, power ... and women.[17] So, while the Church was trying to impose the performance of specific rituals that would have made a marriage solemn – such as the blessing of the couple by a priest, for instance – the core of Western marriage continued to consist of one main traditional practice, among others: the banquet.[18] And for many good reasons. Already in pre-Christian, traditional marriage, publicity was an important requirement, first and foremost from a social perspective: only in this way 'the community at large could witness the transition, recognize its validity, accept the new couple into the fold, and reaffirm the institution of marriage'.[19] This principle was endorsed by early Christians: 'report all of those who shall celebrate their marriage in secret', Pope Eutychian decreed in the late third century.[20] There were many sensible motives for requiring that a legitimate marriage be celebrated in public:

1) the families of the bride and the groom and all the members that were involved in the transaction could be acquainted with the nuptial agreement;
2) the community could be informed about the event, and (passively) confirm

that the union was not incestuous or the result of abduction;

3) a key moment in life – the formation of a new family – could be richly and merrily celebrated.

Marriage was legitimized by an implicit (under Roman law) or explicit (in medieval canon law) expression of mutual *consensus*. This fact also implies that marriage was quite the same among all tiers of society.[21] This is exactly the picture emerging from the famous *responsa* of Pope Nicholas I to Boris, the newly converted Khan of Bulgaria, in 866. Nicholas stated that if one could not afford to abide by formalities such as the giving of a ring as pledge (called *arrha*), the giving of a dowry, written agreements, and a church ceremony, then the *consensus* of the parties was considered enough.[22]

Marriage did not consist of a single act, as today, but was a process, consisting of two main steps: betrothal (*sponsalia*) and wedding. According to the Roman jurist Ulpian, the former only required the expression of consent (*nudus consensus*), whereas Germanic laws asked for a donation from the groom-to-be to the family of the girl.[23] In both cases, the expression of public consent was the field on which the game was played, as theological discussion was unable to settle the dispute over the role of *consensus* itself (whether a primary, undisputable position, or one of subordination to *copula carnalis*, that is, sexual intercourse).[24] Discussion also concerned who was supposed to express said consent, on the girl's side: the bride-to-be herself, or her male parents or guardian. What is sure is that, from late antiquity throughout the early Middle Ages, secular and spiritual authorities insisted that a legitimate marriage required public nuptials and a public manifestation of consent. Banquets had an extremely important social function from this perspective, for they could satisfy all of the aforementioned requirements at the same time. Curiously – though understandably – they were not mentioned by authorities and norms, except for some troublesome aspects (as will be shown later). Nonetheless, the sources are anything but reticent as for what concerns wedding banquets, for they represented traditional and fundamental social rituals.

195

The Banquet, an Unsung Protagonist, and a Point of No Return

Since late antiquity and throughout the Middle Ages, wedding banquets emerge as the unsung protagonists of marriage. Barbarian and Romano-Barbarian kings, from Attila to the Merovingian rulers, arranged sumptuous *convivia* to celebrate their weddings, for they needed to publicly celebrate such events alongside their clan. Weddings were often characterized by all sorts of excess, concerning eating and drinking *in primis*. According to the sixth-century Byzantine chronicler Jordanes (and to Priscus, his source), the feared King of the Huns died on the day of his marriage in 453 with the young and beautiful Ildico after indulging with wine: it is likely that Attila suffered from high blood pressure, and naively decided to lay on his back after the banquet.[25] Thus, when the usual rush of blood started flowing, it did not flow from the nose, but streamed down his throat and choked him to death. It may have been an unfortunate circumstance, but Paul the Deacon – commenting on the same fact – suggested that weddings were usually characterized by *profusa convivia* ('excessive banquets'), and thus excessive eating and drinking.[26]

By inviting their men to their wedding banquets, kings had the chance to display generosity and to share their wealth, a necessary condition for Germanic rulers in societies which were based on a thick network of social bonds. For instance, when the king of Austrasia Sigebert I (561-575) married Brunhilda, the daughter of the king of the Visigoths, Athangild, many *seniores* ('lords') of the kingdom were invited, and they merrily celebrated such an important political event with their ruler.[27] Similarly, King Sigebert II – Brunhilda's grandson – 'arranged a wedding banquet, and invited a considerable crowd of men [*principum*]' – that is, of the men whose consent and loyalty he needed in order to rule the kingdom.[28]

Wedding banquets were not taken into consideration by norms and theological debate concerning marriage. Yet, they were not unimportant in the collective consciousness of contemporaries. On the contrary, they seem to have been seen as actual rituals of passage: a point of no return for young women. The example of the Merovingian King Sigebert II's marriage is rather telling. The king had previously been betrothed to Fridiburga, the only daughter of a duke of Alemannia named Gunzo.[29] According to Wettinus (d. 824), the girl was gravely sick, so much so that she was believed to be possessed by a demon which tormented her. Gallus, an Irish monk who had reached the continent alongside Columban and a handful of other companions, was living as a hermit in the nearby forest: Gunzo sent for him, because such pious men were known to be able to work miracles like Christ and the biblical prophets.[30] Gallus was able to free her from the evil entity, and she secretly confessed to him that she would like to consecrate her virginity to God. Meanwhile, Sigebert commanded that a great wedding banquet be made ready, but Fridiburga begged him to let her not attend the *convivium*, due to her poor health. Sigebert accepted, and 'during the banquet many were surprised by the fact that the queen was not sitting by the king': as a matter of fact, Fridiburga never married the king.[31]

Was it because she did not join the wedding banquet? Not necessarily, but that was a public, crystal clear, passive statement. The same principle seems to be at work in the seventh-century Latin *Life of St. Brigid*, where the saint helps a girl flee an unwanted marriage that had been arranged by her father.[32] The girl wanted to take her vows to become a nun, and run away the night of the wedding, once the banquet had been made ready (*nocte nuptiarum praeparatis epulis*). Her father chased her to bring her back, but Brigid was able to change his mind by means of the sign of the cross: a miraculous act of persuasion. This story suggests that the girl made her decision known just in time – i.e. just before the banquet – and thus publicly and passively expressed her dissent by refusing to join the wedding table. Had she not done so, all of the invitees would have witnessed the celebration of the union, and would have legitimized it from a social perspective – by simply being present at the feast.

196

Too Lavish, to the Point of Being Dangerous

The example of Violante's wedding feast suggests that such events were the result of a rooted and shared 'culture of excess', so alien to an age of political correctness like the one we are living in today. In recent times of economic crisis, rulers seem to have preferred a different approach. On 29 April 2011, the English prince William and Kate Middleton opted for a 'green' and seemingly low-cost wedding: the menu consisted of organic and zero-km food, and the invitees were asked to replace wedding gifts with donations for charities, while the budget assigned to security was the highest in history. So, despite the fact that the feast respected traditional canons of splendour and magnificence, the message that was attached to it was one of spending review, economy, and respect for the environment. But this familiar 'culture of saving' and political correctness has been long preceded by an opposite taste for excess, and wedding banquets were among the main stages on which said system of values was displayed.

Opulence and excess played a specific role as a matter of honour for the families that were involved in the union. When, in 1487, Annibale Bentivoglio and Lucrezia d'Este – members of two of the more powerful Italian families of the time – got married in Bologna, there were served complex sugar sculptures, fully-feathered peacocks which looked alive (probably not so different than Maestro Martino's recipe), and many other gastronomically and aesthetically impressive dishes.[33] Furthermore, the courses were first displayed to the townspeople of Bologna, 'so as to show them the power of their Lord'.[34]

Actually, wedding feasts could be so lavish that proper sumptuary laws were issued in late medieval times, addressing the maximum number of courses that could be served and the maximum number of guests that could be invited. The Statute of 1288 of the same city – Bologna – established by law that no more than ten guests could be invited by each of the families of the bride and the groom, and that no more than three courses could be served.[35] Wedding banquets were seen as morally dangerous by late medieval and Renaissance public authorities, and certain birds in particular represented enemies *par excellence* of sobriety, for they embodied the idea of opulence that sumptuary laws were supposed to stifle. In 1343, the city of Siena followed Bologna's example as for what concerned the maximum number of courses that could be served (three: boiled meat, roast meat, and marzipans).[36] Two hundred years later, in 1556, the city of Forlì raised the limit to six (with the addition of a pie course). Among these, only one course could feature large game such as peacocks, while blancmange, candied fruit, and fish were banned. In 1559, the Statute of Parma similarly limited the consumption of peacocks – among other things – because excess was inflicting 'a universal wound to the soul and the body and the temporal goods' of the citizens.[37]

Unsurprisingly, the Christian Church was all the more preoccupied with wedding feasts. For centuries, ecclesiastic authorities repeated that priests should not attend wedding banquets because they were characterized by excess, lust, and laughter, and were thus occasions where gluttony and desire flourished.[38] In the third century, the Bishop of Carthage Cyprian held that wedding banquets were particularly dangerous for virgins, for they were 'contagious', but the nature of such a 'disease' is more clear in later council canons.[39] In the fourth century, the Council of Laodicea stated that good Christians (both laic and ecclesiastic) should avoid 'clapping their hands or dancing' when invited to weddings, and 'should dine or lunch soberly' – thus implying that these 'wrong' behaviours were habitual, and in 465 the Council of Vannes urged the clergy to avoid wedding banquets because erotic songs were usually played during such feasts.[40] Almost four hundred years later, in 851, a capitulary by the king of East Francia Louis II strongly recommended that priests and clerics leave the banqueting hall before the musicians were let in.[41] Warnings of this kind were anything but unusual in the early Middle Ages, which suggests two interesting conclusions: 1) the clergy did in fact attend weddings along with laypersons, and 2) banquets were the beating heart of marriage, where all the people who were involved (priests, families, spouses, relatives, friends) used to meet together and have fun.[42] To these points, it is safe to add a third one, which has been confirmed by the previous sections: wedding banquets were occasions where the 'culture of excess' (of all kinds) could freely let off steam.

The Middle Ages and Political Incorrectness

As stated by the Greek biographer Plutarch, we do not sit at the table to eat, but to eat together. It is a fundamental difference between the behaviour of humans and animals: for the former, the practice of eating gains a wide range of meanings, which goes far beyond the mere utilitarian purpose of ensuring survival. In this sense, wedding banquets represent an essential case study to understand the connection between food and power because they:

1) drew boundaries between people who were included in and excluded from the guest list;
2) were used to strengthen social bonds;
3) were actual rituals of passage which turned the betrothed into a married couple;
4) were considered dangerous for the soul by the Church;
5) were targeted by secular laws with the intention of moderating luxury.

The sources which meticulously recorded important marriages of their times – such as those of Lionel and Violante in 1368, and of Annibale and Lucrezia in 1487 – prove extremely interested in preserving the memory of the banquets rather than of anything else. The reason was that sumptuous banquets were actual forms of legitimation of the union and of the lord's power. In fact, such records seem even too concerned about the menu, considering that they were meant to be historical accounts: evidently, the courses and the act of 'eating them together' played a fundamental role in the collective consciousness of contemporaries.

The Middle Ages were a time characterized by a developed taste for what we would consider political incorrectness: medieval society zealously fabricated boundaries and marginalities and was proud of displaying excess.[43] Distances were to be highlighted, and status was to be underscored, in the belief that such differences had been predetermined by God's will. Undoubtedly, wedding banquets were one of the fundamental fields on which the games of power, of marking identities, and of reinforcing social bonds were played.

Games for treasure-givers.

Notes

1   Bernardino Corio, *Storia di Milano*, ed. by A. Butti and L. Ferrario, 3 vols (Milan: F. Colombo, 1855-1857), II, pp. 226-27.
2   Lionel was the second eldest son of King Edward III. A brilliant analysis of the event is in Albert Stanburrough Cook, 'The Last Months of Chaucer's Earliest Patron', *Transactions of the Connecticut Academy of Arts and Sciences*, 21 (December 1916), 1-144.
3   Katherine O'Brien O'Keeffe, 'Values and Ethics in Heroic Literature', in *The Cambridge Companion to Old English Literature*, ed. by M. Godden and M. Lapidge (Cambridge: Cambridge University Press, 2013), pp. 101-19; Lars Hermanson, 'Holy Unbreakable Bonds: Oaths and Friendship in Nordic and Western European Societies c. 900-1200', in *Friendship and Social Networks in Scandinavia, c. 1000-1800*, ed. by J. Viar Sigursson and T. Smaberg (Turhout: Brepols, 2013), pp. 15-42.
4   *Beowulf. A Dual-Language Edition*, ed. by H. D. Chickering, Jr. (New York: Anchor Books, 2006), pp. 50, 68, 134, 160.
5   Donizone, *Vita di Matilde di Canossa*, ed. by P. Golinelli (Milan: Jaca Book, 1984), p. 84 (translation mine).
6   Paulus Jovius, *Vitae Duodecim Vicecomitum Mediolani Principum*, in Johann G. Graevius, *Thesaurus antiquitatum et historiarum Italiae*, 45 vols (Leiden: P. Vander Aa, 1704-1725), III, cols. 241-331 (col. 313).
7   Andrea Maraschi, *Un banchetto per sposarsi. Matrimonio e rituali alimentari nell'Occidente altomedievale* (Spoleto: CISAM, 2014), pp. 61-74.
8   *Annales Mediolanenses ab Anno MCCXXX usque ad Annum MCCCCII, ab Anonymo Auctore literis consignati*, ed. by Ludovico Antonio Muratori, RIS XVI (Milan: Typographia Societatis Palatinae, 1730), cols. 635-840 (col. 739).
9   Corio, p. 226.
10 Philip L. Reynolds, *How Marriage Became One of the Sacraments* (Cambridge: Cambridge University Press, 2016), pp. 977-79.
11 *Decrees of the Ecumenical Councils*, trans. by N. P. Tanner, 2 vols (London: Sheed & Ward, 1990), pp. 755-56.
12 Philip L. Reynolds, *Marriage in the Western Church: The Christianization of Marriage During the Patristic and Early Medieval Periods* (Leiden: Brill, 1994), p. xix; Jean Gaudemet, *Le mariage en Occident. Le moeurs et le droit* (Paris: Cerf, 1987), pp. 290-95; *Decrees of the Ecumenical Councils*, pp. 755-56.
13 *Decrees of the Ecumenical Councils*, pp. 755-756.
14 Irven M. Resnick, 'Marriage in Medieval Culture: Consent Theory and the Case of Joseph and Mary', *Church History*, 69.2 (2000), 350-71.
15 *Decrees of the Ecumenical Councils*, pp. 755-756.
16 Reynolds, *How Marriage Became One of the Sacraments*, p. 916; Maraschi, *Un banchetto per sposarsi*, pp. 1-16.
17 Reynolds, *How Marriage Became One of the Sacraments*, p. 160; Christopher N. L. Brooke, *The Medieval Idea of Marriage* (Oxford: Oxford University Press, 2002), pp. 39-60.
18 Maraschi, *Un banchetto per sposarsi*, pp. 151-53.
19 Reynolds, *How Marriage Became One of the Sacraments*, p. 162. See also Maraschi, *Un banchetto per*

sposarsi, pp. 43-58.

20 Pope Eutychian, *Exhortatio ad presbyteros, Patrologia Latina* V, ed. by J.-P. Migne (Paris: Sirou, 1844), col. 167.

21 Philip L. Reynolds, 'Marrying and Its Documentation in Pre-Modern Europe: Consent, Celebration, and Property', in *To Have and To Hold. Marrying and Its Documentation in Western Christendom, 400-1600*, ed. by Id. and John Witte, Jr. (Cambridge: Cambridge University Press, 2007), pp. 1-42 (pp. 1-15, 13).

22 Pope Nicholas I, *Epistolae*, MGH *Epistolae 6, Epistolae Karolini aevi* IV, ed. E. Perels (Berlin: Weidmann, 1925), pp. 257-690 (p. 570).

23 *Digesta Iustiniani*, ed. by T. Mommsen, 2 vols (Berlin: Weidmann, 1870), 23.1.4; Reynolds, *Marriage in the Western Church*, p. 76.

24 Resnick, pp. 352-53; Reynolds, *Marriage in the Western Church*, pp. 22-24; Georges Duby, *Medieval Marriage: Two Models from Twelfth-Century France*, trans. by E. Foster (Baltimore, MD: Johns Hopkins University Press, 1978).

25 Jordanes, *Storia dei Goti*, ed. by E. Bartolini (Milano: TEA, 1991), p. 118.

26 Paul the Deacon, *Historia Romana*, MGH SSRG 49, ed. by H. Droysen (Berlin: Weidmann 1879), p. 115.

27 Gregory of Tours, *Libri Historiarum X*, MGH SSRM 1, 1, ed. by B. Krusch and W. Levison (Hannover: Hahn, 1951), IV, 27, p. 160.

28 Wettinus, *Vita Galli*, MGH SSRM 4, ed. by B. Krusch (Hannover: Hahn, 1902), pp. 256-80 (p. 268).

29 Wettinus, pp. 267-68.

30 Andrea Maraschi, 'I miracoli alimentari di San Colombano: l'originalità, la tradizione e la simbologia', *Studi Medievali* LII (2011), 517-76 (p. 520).

31 Wettinus, p. 268 (translation mine).

32 *Vita prima S. Brigidae Auctore Anonymo*, AA SS, Feb. I, Dies I (Antwerp: I. Meursium, 1658), p. 134.

33 Maestro Martino of Como, *The Art of Cooking. The First Modern Cookery Book*, ed. by L. Ballerini, trans. by J. Parzen (Berkeley: University of California Press, 2005), p. 54; Andrea Maraschi, 'Parlare attraverso il cibo. Banchetti e artifici gastronomici per le nozze Bentivoglio-D'Este (Bologna, 1487)', *Proposte e Ricerche*, 74 (2015), 179-86.

34 Cherubino Ghirardacci, *Della Historia di Bologna, Parte terza*, ed. by A. Sorbelli (Città di Castello: Lapi, 1912), p. 238 (translation mine).

35 Maria Giuseppina Muzzarelli, ed., *Legislazione Suntuaria nei secoli XIII-XVI. Emilia Romagna*, Pubblicazioni degli Archivi di Stato, Fonti XLI (Bologna: Clueb, 2002), pp. 50-51.

36 Maria Giuseppina Muzzarelli and Antonella Campanini, eds., *Disciplinare il lusso. La legislazione suntuaria in Italia e in Europa tra Medioevo ed Età Moderna* (Rome: Carocci, 2003), p. 67.

37 Maria Giuseppina Muzzarelli, ed., *Legislazione Suntuaria nei secoli XIII-XVI*, pp. 331, 463 (translation mine).

38 Andrea Maraschi, 'When Banquets Were Dangerous for the Soul. Church Opposition to Wedding Feasts in Medieval Times', *Proceedings of the 2018 Dublin Gastronomy Symposium* (2018) <https://arrow.dit.ie/cgi/viewcontent.cgi?article=1114&context=dgs> [accessed 15 May 2019].

39 Cyprian, *Liber de habitu virginum*, PL 4, ed. by J.-P. Migne (Paris: Sirou, 1844), col. 460.

40 *Sacrorum Conciliorum nova et amplissima collectio*, ed. by J. D. Mansi (Florence: A. Zatta, 1692-1769), II, col. 582 B, c. 53; VII, col. 954 C, c. 11.

41 *Hludowici II Capitularia*, MGH LL 1, *Capitularia regum Francorum*, ed. by G. H. Pertz (Hannover: Hahn, 1835), pp. 415, n. 23.

42 Maraschi, 'When Banquets Were Dangerous for the Soul', pp. 4-5.

43 Jacques Le Goff, *Il meraviglioso e il quotidiano nell'Occidente medievale*, trans. by M. Sampaolo (Rome: Laterza, 1983), pp. 18-28.

Not in One Place: Parenteral Nutrition and Time-Space Compression

Jacob A. Matthews

While Cyrano de Bergerac's seventeenth-century novel *L'Autre Monde ou les États et Empires de la Lune* is perhaps better known as an early example of science fiction literature, the work also treats its reader to a particular view of the human gut. The biblical patriarch Elijah describes to an intrepid interstellar voyager how the human gastrointestinal tract is far from a simple organ, but instead a living snake, a punishment given to both humans and Satan alike following their eviction from the Garden of Eden. The sounds that our bellies make, Cyrano writes, are our resident serpent's cries for food, harkening back to the first temptation that led Adam and Eve to the forbidden fruit.[1] There is something in this way of imagining the gut that still rings true: as the burgeoning pharmaceutical, supplement, and probiotic foods industries are so quick to remind us, the gut can often be a source of significant discomfort and anxiety. Eating, for all the sensory and social pleasures it may offer, only precedes food's journey through the body. It might seem we eat not only for ourselves, but also for this serpentine other whose tastes can differ from what we conceive of as our proper appetites. The corridors of delicate flesh that course through us, which move without – and sometimes against – our conscious direction, defy conceptions of the body and self as a unified whole. As our digestive systems grumble and groan, they communicate with us in a language not quite our own, at odds with the raw intimacy of ingestion and digestion.

For those suffering from severe illness or the side effects of aggressive medical interventions, the digestive system can come to represent more than a simple inconvenience: the serpent can and does rebel outright, ceasing to function and refusing in whole or in part to transfer nutrients back to its host. Unsurprisingly, the lack of a working gut meant almost certain death in Cyrano's Europe during the seventeenth century. It was only in the mid-twentieth century that medical science could claim the same circumvention of the digestive system as it could for the heart and kidneys. This would take the form of intravenous feeding, or parenteral nutrition (PN), eventually giving rise to the idea of an 'artificial gut'.[2] I will only outline a short history of PN's development here, as this has already been well documented in medical and historical literatures. Rather, instead of reconstructing a genealogy of the artificial gut as such, I am more interested in interrogating early conceptual frameworks applied to feeding-by-vein within these literatures. The idea of an artificial gut and the possibility of intravenous feeding can, I argue, inform the way in which we engage with our contemporary, global alimentary landscape, problematizing our understanding of what it means to eat, ingest, and digest.

In this paper, after a brief examination of intravenous feeding's origins and rhetorical presentation in the late-1960s, I place my reading of these materials in conversation with more recent work in geography and political theory. By considering intravenous feeding within a broader critical framework, I interrogate the idea of alimentary prosthesis as not only a medical technology, but also as a sociocultural and economic phenomenon, thus highlighting the extent to which ingestion and digestion have become, in both a figurative and literal sense, increasingly exteriorized via the effects of globalization. I will employ David Harvey's notion of time-space compression as articulated in his 1989 paper 'Time-Space Compression and the Postmodern Condition' in order to analyze historical and discursive links between PN's development and emerging global trade in perishable foods.[3] I claim that the dream of the artificial gut meaningfully foreshadows the contemporary role of food supply and distribution networks. I then open my analysis to Soylent, a relatively new brand of meal-replacement product, in order to demonstrate how this food experience also points to departures from normative understandings of bodily and digestive autonomy.

Intravenous Feeding and the Artificial Gut

202

Histories of intravenous feeding tend to begin in 1628 with William Harvey's *On the Motion of the Heart and Blood in Animals*, credited as one of the first descriptions of the circulatory system.[4] Vassilyadi, Pateliadou, and Panteliadis, however, further trace this legacy into antiquity and medieval Europe: they identify Herophilus and Erasistratus 'as the first to distinguish between veins and arteries [and to map] the course of veins in the human body' in the third century BCE, and they date the first documented explorations in parenteral nutrition to the twelfth century CE with Ibn Zuhr's experiments in supplying a nutritive solution to a patient through a needle. These authors do admit that William Harvey's work was integral to later advances in parenteral nutrition in that it permitted the earliest documented successful experiments in intravenous feeding by Sir Christopher Wren in 1658, who administered 'wine, ale, and opiates into a dog'.[5] Advances throughout the nineteenth century would eventually lead to experimental short-term use of PN as early as 1869 and successful employment of the technique on humans in 1909, though these infusions were subcutaneous as opposed to intravenous. One of the primary hurdles in developing long-term and lower risk intravenous feeding techniques was in creating nutritive solutions suitable for intravenous administration that were also sufficiently dense in calories: fat emulsions proved problematic early on, as did solutions which relied primarily on glucose.[6] Delicate, iterative refinements of intravenous feeding methods relied not only on developments in clinical practice, but also on technical advances in the manufacture of lipid emulsions, a process that would continue throughout the twentieth century.

Long-term intravenous feeding only became feasible in the late 1960s, and it was in 1967 that medical doctors Douglas W. Wilmore, Stanley J. Dudrick, and Jonathan E. Rhoads were the first to feed human beings exclusively by vein for an extended period of time through total PN (TPN). In one noteworthy case, Wilmore and Dudrick treated a severely malnourished infant suffering from 'near total atresia [malformation] of the small bowel'. They intravenously administered an experimental nutritive solution following techniques developed during earlier trials on beagles in the 1940s at the University of Pennsylvania, a method first invented by Harry Vars and later modified for human beings by Dudrick and Rhoads. This patient went on to survive over a month of entirely intravenous nutrition; the doctors reported that the treatment resulted in an otherwise straightforward and successful recovery.[7] Dudrick later reflected on this period of his early career, satisfied that '[total PN] has been credited for having been instrumental in saving countless lives, and has clearly demonstrated the relevance of adequate nutrition to the achievement of optimal clinical results in surgical patients of all ages'.[8]

Only a year after this initial clinical success, Rhoads associated the new possibilities offered by advances in PN with the notion of an 'artificial gastrointestinal tract' or artificial gut. In his 1968 address to the American Society for Surgery of the Alimentary Tract, Rhoads presented his vision of parenteral nutrition's potential to develop a kind of globally distributed alimentary prosthesis:

> The human gastrointestinal tract is a vast chemical laboratory limited to processes which can occur at about 37°C in aqueous solution […]. It has been the objective of those who have developed artificial feeding to find methods of reducing foodstuffs to the forms in which they circulate in the blood stream and then to produce these substances with a high degree of purity and sterility so that they may be injected directly into the body. *Thus the artificial alimentary tract is not in one place.* An industrial organization may be making glucose in one state while another industrial organization is making hydrolyzed protein in another, and a third can be making fat emulsion in a foreign country. If one turns to pure amino acids, many producers may be involved in their production, separation, purification, and recombination in the desired concentration.[9]

As Rhoads observes here, the sterile nutritional solution used in PN must already contain the nutrients that would otherwise be extracted through the process of digestion. The artificial gut is thus a network of industrial production, laboratory synthesis, and sterile assembly. Importantly, its intravenous formula is merely an element in a series of necessary stages, not an input distinct from a mechanical intravenous apparatus. This process of 'reducing foodstuffs' to their chemical components, Rhoads suggests, represents a kind of spatiotemporally distributed digestion. Importantly, this solution is not food: industrial and clinical processes function to strip 'foodstuffs' simultaneously of the nutritionally non-essential and of their individuated identities. From food – understood implicitly as heterogeneous containers of nutrients – exogenous laboratories mimic the endogenous laboratory of the gut. PN thus involves a vertiginous redistribution of the gastrointestinal tract's processes, the artificial gut becoming a delicate dance across space and time, digestion and nutrition occurring decidedly 'not in one place.'

Alimentation and Time-Space Compression

Though Rhoads opens his address by comparing the artificial intestinal tract to the dialysis machine and artificial heart, it is clear that the former differs from either of the latter prostheses: it lacks, by Rhoads's description, a kind of spatiotemporal containment. Despite their genuine complexity, one could explain dialysis or an artificial heart in simple, mechanical language: the former is like a pump for blood, the latter like a filter. One cannot, however, do the same so easily for the artificial intestinal tract, something that is less device than technique and distributed network. Its mechanical components are only a part of its overall function and design, and it not only replaces the process of digestion, but also supplies its own nutrients to the body. From this perspective, it seems even to surpass the role of the biological gut: the artificial intestinal tract not only would process heterogeneous inputs in an interrelated sequence of mechanical and chemical stages, but also replace the exogenous steps involved in procuring these nutrients. In this way, it is less superficially mimetic than a prosthetic kidney, heart, or limb, as it does not immediately appear to perform the same actions as the parts of the body that it replaces. The everyday mysteries of our bodily interiors are projected onto this anonymous intravenous substance, one determined as much by factory, supply chain, and communication network as by solution, tube, or intravenous catheter. The artificial gut is not an object or a device, but closer to, in Rhoads's words, 'a veritable history of biochemistry' brought to fruition.[10] It envelopes a globe and converging histories in flux, peopled by humans and machines and transport infrastructure.

In a similar spirit to his emphasis on the fundamental equivalence between the intestines and a laboratory, Rhoads concludes his address with a description of the body in terms of its 'economy', comparing a patient's nutritional needs to a family's income and expenses:

> The economy of the body may be likened to that of a family. The rate of consumption may rise due to illness or accident but there is a seemingly irreducible minimum that the wife must spend each week. If the breadwinner earns less than must be spent, the family is in the red and headed toward bankruptcy and starvation. If he earns more than this, they are in the black, potentially on their way to real affluency. The practice of providing by vein a part, often a substantial part, of the nutritional requirements of a patient with an alimentary handicap is old and well established throughout the civilized world [.... I]t is now possible to

204

cross far into the black on the nutritional balance sheet. The difference as judged clinically is often as sharp a contrast as the contrast of bankruptcy and affluence.[11]

This comparison presents a similar image to a gut that would exist not in one place. Here, Rhoads's casts his vision of the prototypical family back into the body, composed of the breadwinner husband, homemaking wife, and dependent children, a family which is itself at risk of physical starvation as a result of the father's illness or accident. It is as if the family's fiscal and nutritional 'balance sheets' collapse into one, each reflecting back onto each other. Taken together with Rhoads's spatially and temporally dispersed vision of alimentary prosthetics, nutritional, familial, and global economies blur together; sterile laboratories replace the fleshy biology of the gut; the human being, from the confines of the clinic, leaves its body, partially scattered in space and time.

It is difficult to read this way of comprehending digestion (prosthetic or otherwise) without also considering global food distribution networks. While Rhoads hardly considers his nutrient solution 'food' as such, quotidian alimentary experiences evolved throughout the mid- to late-twentieth century due in part to the very same economic and social developments that enabled PN's widespread adoption. Food and PN, of course, do not occupy entirely separate worlds, even if their associated discourses have rarely overlapped. Though Rhoads expresses a sense of wonder when he speaks of the world in which he lives, one so interconnected that it could produce the artificial gut and each vital component of the 'nutritional balance sheet' is assembled and distributed with just-in-time finesse, he does not extend such an understanding here to his broader alimentary universe.

In 'Time-Space Compression and the Postmodern Condition', David Harvey reflects at length on the scale of worldwide social and economic transformation between 1970 and 1989. Though his analysis does not centre on food, he employs the image of the supermarket to illustrate his understanding of time-space compression, a palpable consequence of a world increasingly governed by the logic of flexible accumulation. He observes here just how global the experience of food in the United States and Great Britain became in less than twenty years:

> Innumerable local food systems have been reorganised through their incorporation into global commodity exchange. French cheeses, for example, virtually unavailable except in a few gourmet stores in large cities in 1970, are now widely sold across the United States [.... The] food market [...] now looks very different from what it was twenty years ago. Kenyan haricot beans, Californian celery and avocados, North African potatoes, Canadian apples and Chilean grapes all sit side by side in a British supermarket.[12]

There is certainly some room to quibble with Harvey's broad-strokes approach to food history. What he describes as evidence of remarkable change to 'local food systems' are effectively limited to international trade in perishables, which was not unprecedented in the mid-1900s. As geographer Susanne Freidberg chronicles in *Fresh: A Perishable History* (2010), the cold storage and transatlantic sale of eggs, for example, had been well-established in the United States even at the turn of the twentieth century, while egg-production rates, 'still jagged in the mid-1930s, had essentially flattened out by the mid-1970s'. Freidberg's account of international vegetable shipping mostly agrees with Harvey's assessment, however, as she notes that the use of Boeing 747s for transporting perishables, as well as the introduction of airport refrigeration throughout the 1970s and 1980s, allowed for fresh produce to move worldwide with previously unknown ease and speed.[13]

But Harvey's general argument in 'Time-Space Compression' rests on his observation of a rapidly accelerating rate of change in – as opposed to absolute levels of – international trade in regional foods, and he highlights the unique challenges that these developments pose for coherent engagement with broader cultural and economic phenomena. His analysis explores the ways that global networks – not only of food and tangible consumer goods, but also media, services, and labour – significantly impact a subject's lived experience of time and space:

> The whole world's cuisine is now assembled *in one place* in almost exactly the same way that the world's geographical complexity is nightly reduced to a series of images on a static television screen. [...] *The interweaving of simulacra in daily life brings together different worlds (of commodities) in the same space and time.* But it does so in such a way as to conceal almost perfectly any trace of origin, of the labour processes that produced them, or of the social relations implicated in their production.[14]

There is an intriguing symmetry between the supermarket 'in one place' and the 'not in one place' of the artificial intestinal tract. The food market, for Harvey, is indicative of the broader compression of earth's spatiotemporal geographies via the almost instantaneous delivery of the image, which all but destroys the perception of physical distance. Likewise, for Rhoads, the manufacturing processes behind parenteral nutrition similarly compress global heterogeneity into sterile formula, bending his sense of possibility around the limits of body, location, and object.

Soylent: Eating Without Food

We are reminded here of a similar, more recent reckoning with the body's abdominal serpent, less than fifty years after Wilmore and Dudrick's clinical breakthrough with total PN. In 2013, engineer and writer Rob Rhinehart published 'How I Stopped Eating Food' on his since-deleted blog, in which he claims to have not 'eaten a bite of food in 30 days, and [that] it's changed [his] life'. Contrary to what his title might imply, Rhinehart had not spent the prior month fasting, nor had he received any kind of supervised medical intervention. Instead, he had solely subsisted on an off-white, milkshake-like product of his own design, a beverage he named 'Soylent' in an apparent nod to the 1973 film *Soylent Green*. Unlike its fictional namesake, Rhinehart's Soylent was free of human remains and supposedly contained 'every substance the body needs to survive, plus a few extras shown to be beneficial'. He describes his experience with Soylent as a kind of liberation from the perceived ugliness and economic constraints of food, born out of his '[resentment of] the time, money, and effort the purchase, preparation, consumption and clean-up of food was consuming'. Moreover, he attributes all manner of health and aesthetic benefits to a Soylent-only diet: decreased Body Mass Index, clearer skin, faster reading comprehension, even an increased capacity to enjoy music.[15] Instead of circumventing the gut's machinery and demands, Soylent is designed in its image, a supposedly perfect fit for the human body, all without the seemingly-extraneous matter that makes up food.

But only the definitional vagaries around the word 'food' in Rhinehart's original blog post – he considers it at once the 'fossil fuel of human energy' and also restricted to things like 'meat, fruits, vegetables and breads' – allow his title's claim of not 'eating food' to parse. A tall glass of thick, protein-rich liquid certainly sounds like food, just as much as drinking it sounds quite a bit like eating. Only if so restricted to the heterogeneous field of plants, animal flesh, and culinary staples can food-*qua*-food remain distinct from his creation. He envisions Soylent as the cure for a kind of external malady particular to this narrowly-defined food, a response a perceived infringement of subjective freedoms and self-fulfilment. What is more, Rhinehart considers a movement away from human reliance on food – analogous to a movement from fossil fuels to renewable energy sources – as part of a greater duty to progress, understood both in its technological and political sense. Food-as-we-know-it is then decidedly anti-modern. *207* These objects, Rhinehart argues, are themselves to blame for so many of the apparent ills that plague our world, such as obesity, hunger, even the infidelity of human appetites: '[Soylent is] like finding a partner you really care about. When all your needs are met, you don't have a desire to stray.' He goes so far as to suggest that broad adoption of his uniform, 'quantified diet' could liberate women from 'the stereotype of the housewife in the kitchen': 'How wasteful society has been with its women! The endless hours spent cooking and cleaning the kitchen could be replaced with socializing, study, or creative endeavors.' Reinforcing his idiosyncratic understanding of food's power over the human being, he concludes that 'The food is eating us'.[16]

Rhinehart went on to transform Soylent into the main product offering of a fully-fledged corporation over the next several years, though he resigned from his post as CEO in 2017.[17] Today, Soylent is available at Walmart, among other brick-and-mortar retailers, and ships anywhere in the United States from their webstore, which advocates purchasing the drink on a subscription basis.[18] The product is a not uncommon sight in the supermarkets, pharmacies, and bodegas of major US cities, where it tends to share the same shelves as energy drinks, kombuchas, and other protein-rich beverages like Muscle Milk. Online, an unaffiliated Reddit community of over thirty-four thousand members continues to document users' experiences with Soylent and similar products; some users continue to tinker with homemade blends adapted from Rhinehart's original open-source recipes.[19] Something in his message and the product's promise appears to resonate with a segment of the American public, with those who either consciously share in his pessimistic view of food or simply desire a convenient, low-hassle meal in a disposable plastic bottle.

We can note several parallels here between Rhinehart's understanding of alimentation and Rhoads's artificial intestinal tract. While they both have markedly different motivations, each understands food in terms of its heterogeneity, in terms of its status as object. They necessarily contrast this understanding of food with how they define their respective liquid solutions. Both emphasize their inventions' capacities for the total replacement of food via homogeneous substance, both of which are defined as distinct from food due either to their route of administration or lack of a familiar taste and appearance. More intriguingly, though, is the way in which Rhoads and Rhinehart each comprehend alimentation in terms of its effects on their worlds at large. While Rhoads explicitly understands the artificial intestinal tract as a global enterprise that has the capacity to open the barriers of the body in order to maintain it, Rhinehart has a more ambiguous sense of his relationship to this global space. Rhinehart erroneously locates the consequences of broader economic and historical forces within edible things themselves, a tendency that echoes Harvey's claim that our contemporary relationship to food obscures the labour that produces them and 'the social relations implicated in their production'.[20] It is as if Soylent appears as a condensation of alimentary time-space compression, like a supermarket in a bottle, where geography and labour are doubly effaced. Unlike Rhoads, who is conscious of the relationship between production networks, objects, and the body, Rhinehart has little consideration for the broader system of relations that produce and move objects outside of his own kitchen.

I do not mean to overstate the material similarities between parenteral nutrition and Soylent but, instead, to suggest that each occupies a place on an historical and ideological throughline that continues to influence our contemporary understanding of eating. It is here, I argue, that Rhoads's way of conceptualizing the artificial alimentary tract can help us to begin to make sense of contemporary questions around food and eating, such as those posed by something like Soylent. This framework, if imperfect, is useful for three reasons. First, Rhoads defines alimentation not only in terms of the consumption or manufacture of identifiable edible objects, but rather in terms of a complex system of human and non-human relations. We can contrast this with Rob Rhinehart's goals with a product like Soylent, which endeavours to locate the solution to contemporary food-related problems in the manufacture of novel foodstuffs, all the while obfuscating the incredibly complicated production, transportation, and agriculture networks involved in their fabrication. Soylent is, in this sense, made of people, or at least their labour, as well as animal, plant, microbial and machine activity.

Rhoads's approach also represents a departure from what Jane Bennett identifies as the 'conquest model of consumption', which 'disregards the effectivity of not only animal bodies, but also the "bodies" of vegetables, minerals, pharmaceutical, bacterial or viral agents [and] presents nonhuman matter as merely the environment for or the means to human action'. In her case for the recognition of the political agency of matter, Bennett understands the ingested as an 'actant', as opposed to strictly inanimate stuff: 'Edible material is an agent inside and alongside intention-forming, morality-(dis)obeying, language-using, reflexivity-wielding, culturemaking human beings. Food is an active inducer-producer of salient, public effects, rather than a passive resource at the disposal of consumers'. We can view bodies, organs, and the ingested, then, as a woven material and societal mesh that forms, in Bennett's terms, larger 'economic-cultural prostheses'.[21] This kind of nuanced approach to objectal agency differs, however, from what is at play in Rhinehart's understanding of food's power as a labour-intensive commodity. Instead, what Bennett suggests here is an ethical and political model for eating that mirrors the way in which Rhoads's artificial gut smears the barriers of the human, non-human, and edible.

Lastly, the socio-economic forces behind parenteral nutrition's development that Rhoads mentions with respect to the artificial alimentary tract are largely the same as those that so drastically changed our relationship to food: communication and transport infrastructure, advances in industrial technologies and nutritional science, and so on, have drastically reshaped and continue to shape food systems. Just as Rhoads's artificial alimentary tract exists 'not in one place' as the product of spatiotemporally dispersed manufacturing and assembly processes, it is as if our fleshy guts have also been scattered around the world. When we consider our biological ingestion-digestion paradigm as inseparable from our inconstant spatiotemporal geography, we arrive at the inverse of Harvey's supermarket: globally-produced foods brought together 'in one place' produce a reterritorialization of the biological gut. Foods are not only grown and slaughtered far from where we live and work, but they are also reduced, synthesized, recombined, studied, and advertised throughout our networked globe at a dizzying scale and with incredible speed. While this state of affairs can disorient us and cause us to yearn for a more secure sense of location and individual identity, it should also push us towards a much more fundamental reconsideration of the human body's relationship to alimentary space and the powers that occupy it, that course through it, and that connect it back to us.

209

Notes

1   Cyrano de Bergerac, *L'Autre Monde ou les États et Empires de la Lune* (Paris: Éditions de Boucher, 2002), p. 22.

2   Ryan T. Hurt and Ezra Steiger, 'Early History of Home Parenteral Nutrition: From Hospital to Home', *Nutrition in Clinical Practice*, 33 (2018), 598-613 (p. 603) <dx.doi.org/10.1002/ncp.10180>.

3   David Harvey, 'Time-Space Compression and the Postmodern Condition', in *The Condition of Postmodernity* (Cambridge: Basil Blackwell, 1992), pp. 284-307.

4   Hurt and Steiger, p. 599; Jonathan E. Rhoads, 'Presidential Address: Approaches to an Artificial Gastrointestinal Tract', *The American Journal of Surgery*, 117 (1969), 3-10 (p. 4) <dx.doi.org/10.1016/0002-9610(69)90278-5>; Stanley J. Dudrick, 'History of Parenteral Nutrition', *Journal of the American College of Nutrition*, 28 (2009), 243-51 (pp. 243-44) <dx.doi.org/10.1080/07315724.2

009.10719778>; Stanley J. Dudrick and Jonathan E. Rhoads, 'Total Intravenous Feeding', *Scientific American,* 226 (1972), 73-81 (p. 75).

5   Frank Vassilyadi, Alkistis-Kira Panteliadou, and Christos Panteliadis, 'Hallmarks in the History of Enteral and Parenteral Nutrition: From Antiquity to the 20th Century', *Nutrition in Clinical Practice,* 28 (2013), 209-17 (pp. 211-14) <dx.doi.org/10.1177/0884533612468602>; Jonathan E. Rhoads and Stanley J. Dudrick, 'Weight Gain, Growth, and Development Induced in Man by the Intravenous Administration of Pure Chemicals', *Proceedings of the American Philosophical Society,* 117 (1973), 152-61 (p. 152), <www.jstor.org/stable/986540>.

6   Vassilyadi, Panteliadou, and Panteliadis, pp. 212-214; Rhoads, pp. 4-6; Dudrick, 246-47.

7   Douglas W. Wilmore and Stanley J. Dudrick, 'Growth and Development of an Infant Receiving All Nutrients Exclusively by Vein', *JAMA,* 203 (1968), 860-64 <dx.doi.org/10.1001/jama.1968.03140100042009>; Hurt and Steiger, pp. 601-02; Janet H. Weinberg, 'Nutrition through a Needle: Closing Pandora's Box,' *Science News,* 106 (1974), 90-91 (p. 90) <https://www.jstor.org/stable/3959211>.

8   Dudrick, p. 250.

9   Rhoads, pp. 3-4, (emphasis added).

10   Rhoads, pp. 4-9.

11   Rhoads, p. 9.

12   Harvey, pp. 299-300.

13   Susanne Freidberg, *Fresh: A Perishable History* (Cambridge: Harvard University Press, 2010), pp. 93, 117, 193-96.

14   Harvey, p. 300 (emphasis added).

15   Rob Rhinehart, 'How I Stopped Eating Food', *Mostly Harmless,* 13 February 2013 <http://web.archive.org/web/20170316060410/http://robrhinehart.com/?p=298> [accessed 29 May 2019].

16   Rhinehart.

17   Rob Rhinehart and Bryan Crowley, 'Soylent's Next Chapter', *Soylent Blog,* 2017 <https://soylent.com/blogs/news/soylent-s-next-chapter-1 > [accessed 29 May 2019].

18   'Frequently Asked Questions', *Soylent Help Center* < https://soylent.com/pages/faq> [accessed 30 May 2019].

19   'r/soylent', <https://www.reddit.com/r/soylent/> [accessed 30 May 2019].

20   Harvey, p. 300.

21   Jane Bennett, 'Edible Matter', *New Left Review,* 45 (2007), 133-45 (pp. 133-38).

Encounters of Food and Power in the Australian Colonial Contact Zone

Frieda Moran

For Joseph Banks, botanist onboard the *Endeavour* in 1770, the freshness and flavour of the Coral Sea turtles was remarkable: 'Our Turtles are certainly far preferable to any I have eat in England'. This taste was so delicious, it triggered hostilities between the *Endeavour* crew and peoples of the Guugu Yimithirr nation of Northern Queensland. This was a foundational conflict; Captain James Cook and his crew were challenged over the taking of turtles, a critical food resource for the local people.[1] From the start, food was central in the Australian colonial contact zone.[2] Food and food knowledge were exchanged, refused, or disputed as power dynamics were established.

Stranded awaiting ship repairs, Banks recorded the slow development of trust between newcomers and locals through food exchanges. Attempting to gain the goodwill of a group of men, 'Cloth, Nails, Paper, etc.' were offered without success until 'at last a small fish was by accident thrown to them on which they expressd the greatest joy imaginable'.[3] Evidentially, the fish was the critical factor. The following day the gift was reciprocated, thus establishing trust and an equilibrium of power.[4] On the twelfth, Guugu Yimithirr men asserted, through food, that they held power, dictating the circumstances of meeting on their land. Given fish, 'They receivd it with indifference, signd to our people to cook it for them [...] they eat part and gave the rest to my Bitch'.[5] While the groups became 'very good friends', discord followed.

Having observed the British collecting several turtles at a time over the several weeks of their stay, the Guugu Yimithirr men made no objection. When the *Endeavour* had eight or nine turtles on deck, however, this changed. The British were visited by local men bearing spears: 'They soon let us know their errand which was by some means or other to get one of our Turtle [...] by signs askd for One and on being refusd shewd great marks of Resentment; one who had askd me on my refusal stamping with his foot pushd me from him with a countenance full of disdain.' A turtle was seized from the British, then taken back; the Guugu Yimithirr men 'repeated the expiriment 2 or 3 times'. Onshore, the conflict continued. In Cook's account (more dramatic than Banks's version), one man 'made a large circuit round about us and set fire to the grass [...] the whole place was in flames'.[6] Cook fired a musket, wounding one of the Guugu Yimithirr. Later, an older man made peace with the British, and quiet prevailed until the *Endeavour* departed over a week later.

This confrontation over who controlled food resources reflected the different ontologies of the two groups. While the British regarded the animals as theirs because they caught them, the Guugu Yimithirr men asserted their rights to turtles taken from their sea-country. While accepting the newcomer's initial taking of a few turtles, a threshold was exceeded that violated their political economy. The Guugu Yimithirr did not demand all of the British catch, but only the share of the resource they believed theirs. Bearing firearms, the balance of power appeared to be tilted in favour of the British. Banks, however, realized how precarious this control was, and how vulnerable their situation was in this tense contact moment: 'We had great reason to thank our good Fortune that this accident happned so late in our stay'. Crew members stumbled upon goods they had given to the Guugu Yimithirr, and Banks appeared to comprehend the value of the food resource denied to them: 'they seemd to set no value upon any thing we had except our turtle'. Both groups appreciated the turtles as a resource for sustenance. Yet the turtles were not critical to survival of either group in this moment, with Cook offering the locals bread, 'which they rejected with scorn as I believe they would anything else excepting turtle'.[7] Here tastes collided, sparking conflict over who had the right to control access to this food.

Australia is large continent. Pre-colonization, it is estimated that over 200 Aboriginal language groups and 650 dialects existed, constituting many different cultures; there was no such thing as a 'pan-Aboriginal' culture.[8] Experiences of the colonial contact zone were many, given cultural and geographic variances. Early British explorers of the seventeenth century were preceded by other European explorers and by seasonal trading outposts from Asia. Well before British arrival, Makassans, from southern Sulawesi, visited the Northern Coast of Australia for several hundred years, collecting a food and medicinal resource, trepang. Exchanges and relationships with the local people were established, some of whom travelled with the visitors to their homelands.[9] Tangible living evidence of the Makassans' visits include tamarind trees. Too often Australian Indigenous cultures are conceived of as isolated and unchanging, but the Makassan tamarind trees speak of earlier exchanges of food and culture.

From the outset, food was an instrument of colonial power. European food sources, such as cattle and sheep, damaged the land, critically fracturing the foodways of Aboriginal people; rations were used to control and 'civilize'; and accounts of Indigenous food practices were used as evidence supporting racial hierarchies of the time, which in turn were used to justify colonization. The very legal basis of British colonization of Australia rested on perceptions of the production of food. The assertion of *terra nullius,* or land belonging to no one, was used as justification for British settlement, practiced for a long time before being formally described as legal doctrine.[10] The central tenet of *terra nullius* was concerned with the production of food and Lockean ideas of property rights gained through tilling the land and through British narrow definitions of agriculture.[11] Because Indigenous Australians did not cultivate the land in a manner understood by the British, they thus were perceived to lack a property system, and it was asserted they were inhabitants rather than proprietors.[12] The Australian people were predominantly portrayed as primitive hunter-gathers by the imperialists, an idea which had to be constantly remade through discursive practices in order to justify British colonization. There were, of course, historical critiques of *terra nullius*, and current scholarship has increasingly shown that Aboriginal Australian people were connected to their land in complex ways, practicing many forms of 'agriculture', such as 'fire-stick farming'.[13] One way *terra nullius* was claimed from 'primordial' peoples was through discourse around the foodways of Indigenous Australians.

In Michel Foucault's formulation, power is not simply repressive, but productive. We must study 'the mechanisms of power', which are particularly instructive in the contact zone. He viewed power and knowledge as deeply connected: since power was informed by 'discursive forms of knowledge', he was interested in how 'discourse creates relations of power/knowledge', from which human thought and action become possible. Foucault showed that power/knowledge never simply flows in one direction: there is always a counterforce, a constant circulation of power.[14] Applying Foucault's ideas helps reveal uncertainties amid the workings of power and discourse.

Food and eating can produce and express power in a multitude of ways. I am interested in 'food as a mediator of power relations' and how relationships and responses to food can be read as indicative of power dynamics.[15] Food has the capacity to bond people and communities, but it also has the capacity to divide. Notions of what is considered 'edible' or 'food' are largely culturally constructed: the very definition of what constituted food was challenged in the contact zone.[16] Central to constructions of identity, food can signify aspirations and communality, or be used as evidence of 'otherness'. Food and eating can perform social difference, but also subvert or reject assertions of power. Control over access to food dictates lives. From the individual and group to the institutional and imperial, food and power intersect and generate certain relationships between peoples at all levels. It is possible to examine power dynamics from many perspectives, but I think food expresses subtleties in telling ways. Food discourse has been central to the construction of ideas of Aboriginal people into the twenty-first century, with implications still felt today. Historical depictions of Australian Aboriginal people as 'rudest savages' in racial hierarchies must be deconstructed. Derogatory assertions concerning food habits often sit alongside moments of respect and admiration in primary sources, emphasizing how inherited knowledge and discourse clouded imperialists' perspectives and informed power structures for centuries to come.

In examining power dynamics in the Australian colonial contact zone, I have consciously looked for encounters that involve food, deliberately sought moments that exemplify expressions of power. The writings of those implicated in British Imperial projects, as Ann Laura Stoler reminds us, not only reflected or legitimized European power, but were themselves the 'site of its production'.[17] Although contact zones are generally understood as spatial, bodies were also important sites of contact.[18] Food, too, is then a contact zone: a meeting place, binding people in relationships to place and to one another.[19] Without ignoring the atrocities of the colonial contact zone, I seek to avoid simplistic dichotomies of oppressed and oppressor, presenting more nuanced understandings of decentred power, agency, and collaboration. Both peoples were not monolithic or even necessarily united groups, but were comprised of individuals with varying ambitions and desires.[20]

Food and power intersected in colonial contact zones throughout the globe and imperial history. As scholars such as Rebecca Earle, Trudy Eden, and Cecilia Leong-Salobir have variously shown, studying food in contexts from the Americas to Southeast Asia reveals some of the more paradoxical elements of colonialism.[21] While there is a growing body of work on Indigenous Australian foodways and agriculture, and some on the collision of food cultures in the contact zone, Zane Ma Rhea has argued that 'food has been an under examined and barely theorized central factor in explaining the impact of colonization into the contemporary era [.... F]or original inhabitants, the food security crisis forced on them by colonization has not been overcome'.[22]

In the first two decades of colonization, both British and Aboriginal peoples experienced hunger and starvation, although for different reasons. What was abundance for one culture was scarcity for another. The British found Australian conditions difficult as they struggled to establish agriculture in unfamiliar conditions where inherited knowledge was inappropriate; inadequately prepared or supplied by imported goods, they often found food sources wanting. The British were motivated to experiment with local foods, leading at times to disputes, but also sometimes cooperation, with local peoples. Competition for food resources was an increasing issue, with more bodies relying on the land and sea. European hunting dogs and technologies, such as guns and seines (nets), interrupted existing environmental balances. The introduction of hooved animals compacted the soil, harming important tubers, grains, and fruit; fences altered movements of peoples and animals; and sedentary populations polluted waterways.[23]

Aboriginal groups turned to newly available food sources present on their country: the cows, sheep, and other animals and vegetable crops of the colonizers. The British regarded these actions as theft, and conflict became increasingly common. The changes to the country were so profound, historian Robert Kenny has argued, that the familiar Aboriginal country was 'replaced'.[24] Beyond, and because of, hunger and conflict, Aboriginal people were left susceptible to disease, with high numbers dying from imported smallpox, sexually transmitted diseases, and other viruses. Violence and power were negotiated not only in the moment of contact, but in discourse as well.

Food expressed and shaped relationships of power in the Australian contact zone. In 1791, a Burramattagal guide to an exploration party from the First Fleet asserted his

214

taste preferences and power as a critical procurer of food. Refusing to retrieve shot duck, Boladeree argued he:

> had the trouble of fetching it ashore, only for the white men to eat it. This reproof was, I fear, too justly founded; [...] little had fallen to their share except the offals, and now and then a half-picked bone. True, indeed, all the crows and hawks which had been shot were given to them; but they plainly told us that the taste of ducks was more agreeable to their palates.[25]

As with the turtle incident, food was again the source of dispute, revealing complex power at play. Boladeree was treated worse than a servant, given the animal-like work of 'fetching' the dead ducks, which he was not deemed worthy of eating. He was given only foods which were disregarded, if not considered inedible. What was considered food, and who it was appropriate for, was an expression of power: hawks, crows, bones, and offal were not good enough for British, but thought suitable for Aboriginal people who received 'all' of the flesh-eating birds. By disputing this distribution, Boladeree negotiated power and argued his equality, as the holder of food and country knowledge.

Without Indigenous knowledge of food, and assistance in procuring it, many European explorers and colonists would have starved. A group of British and South Asian sailors were twice shipwrecked in the late 1790s, first on Bass Strait islands, then on the shores of eastern Victoria, attempting to make their way to the Sydney settlement. Having run out of their remaining rice supplies, the sailors were largely reliant on the generosity of local Aboriginal people. Supercargo William Clarke recorded that 'a party of natives [...] gave us plenty of fishes. It seems they had met the Moor whose friendship we experienced yesterday, and were by him informed of our distress, so that we were indebted to that kind-hearted fellow for his guidance and this day's protection'. In this example, the gift of nourishment undoubtedly shaped the European perceptions of Indigenous people – those individuals and groups who gave food were 'friends' and given very human characteristics; those who did not were variously described as 'treacherous', 'hideous', and 'disgusting', with their hair 'serv[ing] them in lieu of a towel to wipe their hands as often as they are daubed with blubber or shark oil, which is their principal article of food'.[26] This description of what and how foods were consumed illustrates how food practices were used to articulate racial superiority and otherness. The sailors had little power in the hands of those people whose lands they crossed, but Clarke retrospectively claimed power discursively, representing the 'inhospitable' aboriginal people as 'savages'.

Eating habits and food were central to the British idea that Australian Aboriginal peoples represented some of the lowest forms of a human racial hierarchy; they were used as evidence for the 'inferiority' of a group of people. The power of a culturally-dictated disgust response could rob peoples of their humanity, rendering them animal-like. Across the continent, the charge of eating raw, half-cooked, or scorched meat followed Indigenous peoples. Eating raw food was equated with savagery: from fish 'thrown' into the fire, and when 'a little warmed they take it off [...] then peal off with their teeth the surface', to 'they are very fond of the entrails which they eat half raw'.[27] The trope of raw-flesh-eating-savages was not confined to this time or place, but, as scholars have shown, one that has been present in many geographical locations through time, serving various purposes.[28]

Food preference signalled otherness as well. Bungaree, a man from the Kuring-gai cultural-linguistic group north of Sydney, acted as a mediator on explorer Matthew Flinders' circumnavigation of Australia from 1802 to 1803.[29] Having caught three skates and a mullet, Bungaree sacrificed the 'most delicate' fish to Flinders, leaving himself hungry rather than eat taboo skate. In discussing the food preferences of others, Flinders revealed his own food prejudices, and detailed complex relations of power: 'The natives of Port Jackson have a prejudice against all fish of the ray kind, as well as against sharks; and whilst they devour with eager avidity the blubber of a whale or porpoise, a piece of skate would excite disgust.' Flinders implied his own repulsion for whale and porpoise fat, the taste for which naturalizes his casual designation of Bungaree as a 'savage' for the intended European reader. Despite much ridiculing of Bungaree 'for this unaccountable whim', he held fast to his belief.[30]

Yet it was not only Bungaree, but also another sailor, presumably European, 'who preferred hunger to ray-eating!' Flinders attributes the sailor's avoidance as stemming from time spent with Aboriginal people:

216

> It might be supposed he had an eye to the mullet; but this was not the case. He had been seven or eight years with me, mostly in New South Wales, had learned many of the native habits, and even imbibed this ridiculous notion respecting rays and sharks; though he could not allege, as Bongaree did, that 'they might be very good for white men, but would kill him'.[31]

Food knowledge and culture were negotiated and exchanged in the contact zone. Lastly, Flinders insisted on sharing the mullet with Bungaree and the sailor, showing a paradoxical mixture of respect and prejudice for the men and their food preferences. This example speaks of the power and tenacity of food beliefs, as well as how exchange is, in some small way, a melding of cultures.

Food, eating, and taste were also central when, in the five years from 1829, Government-backed 'conciliator' George Augustus Robinson was charged with negotiating for Tasmanian Aborigines to come under government protection after the violence of the Black War. A devout Christian, his objective was the 'Amelioration of Aborigines of Van Diemen's Land' through civilization and Christianity. 'Amelioration' entailed maintaining a sedentary population, building huts for habitation, and imposing agriculture, namely potato fields; it also meant 'to prevail to them to cook their food after the manner of Europeans, to catch fish to eat with potatoes, [...] to eat at one table'.[32] For Robinson, British conceptions of 'civilization' dictated not only what was eaten, but also how food was grown, prepared, and consumed.

Food rations were to be extremely limited, with the intention of making the community agriculturally productive. Rationing was a tool of the colonial agenda through Australian history, from private settlers and missionaries to government policy.[33] Discussing twentieth-century central Australia, Tim Rowse observed that rationing occurred for numerous reasons 'with a variety of expectations about the mentality and behaviour of recipients'.[34] Here, rationing was intended to encourage a 'European', and thus civilized, way of life. Further, rations were constructed to fit with European gender norms: as 'rewards', Robinson requested rations of tea and sugar for women and tobacco for men.[35] As Damian Mosley argued, Indigenous peoples were instructed which foods were 'correct', and shown that their very 'humanness connected to their palates'.[36] But at various times the people of Tasmania can be seen to have rejected, accepted, subverted, and/or selectively responded to Robinson's offerings.

With numerous Indigenous peoples from across Tasmania and a few other Europeans, Robinson travelled on foot around the island, encouraging Aborigines to come under his, and thus the British Government's, 'protection'. Bread, which Robinson offered to each group he encountered, illustrates the complex role food played in the colonial mission, and moreover illustrates the varied power dynamics of each moment. Sharing bread, for Europeans at least, was highly symbolic. Bread here was an offering, a gesture of goodwill, but also inextricably bound with Robinson's mission to civilize. By getting Aborigines to consume bread, he was getting them to imbue civilization and Christianity. Moreover, it was a performance of Robinson's ability, if they were to accept his 'protection', to provide for their needs and comfort. For the 'Conciliator', the local peoples' unfamiliarity, distrust, or distaste for bread was evidence of their lack of civilization:

217

> I gave them bread, when they put it to their noses, smelling and looking at it. It appeared to them an object of great curiosity. TIME.ME.DENE.NE told them to PAR.TIG.GER.RER, to eat it, that NUM PARTIGGERRER. With some persuasion they ate a little of it, and before I left could [eat] it as well as the natives I had with me.[37]

In a statement that at once admired the food knowledge of the people he had contact with and acknowledged their agency, Robinson recorded: 'Their resources are indeed prolific when hunger craves and there is a variety of unknown herbs or roots or plants to which they fly when hunger compels […] They hold our luxuries in the utmost antipathy and contempt'. In choosing which foods were consumed, individuals negotiated power balances in these moments, in the form of the maintenance of foodways, taste preferences, and both resistance and adoption of European foods and tastes. Robinson repeatedly recorded foods being discerningly chosen or rejected. A group of the remote southwest 'were highly pleased with the variety of objects', but became more selective with what was ingested. 'They would not eat bread, but would eat biscuit; They would not eat oysters', he noted, and they often had to be convinced to consume: 'Gave them

Biscuit: some of them would smell it and give it back again, others at the entreating of the two females [who travelled with Robinson] would eat it'.[38]

At a time when many of the people he was in contact with were dying of influenza-like symptoms, presumably viruses brought by Europeans, Robinson connected the local diet with illness, noting the people's 'pernicious obstinacy in rejecting proper nourishment'. Despite admiring resourcefulness, Robinson himself feared eating Aboriginal foods. Imported supplies ran out, 'and so I resolved to partake of their diet provided my stomach could bear the same'. Another time, Robinson ate muttonfish (abalone), which he elsewhere described as having 'a strong rancid taste', to gain trust of a hesitant family.[39] We are reminded of the power and belief in established foodways.

Depictions of Australian Aboriginals as savages were rationalized by what they considered food, how their food was produced and prepared, and how much food they ate. Another example that speaks of Foucault's ideas on the production of power through discourse comes again from Tasmania. The island provides a useful case study, with a relatively contained body of ethnographic and historical literature discussing Tasmanian Indigenous peoples, and an even more limited collection of primary sources. Within these works, we can trace the origins of discourse threads. In nineteenth-century literature, Tasmanian Aborigines were commonly described as eating 'greedily' and 'voraciously'; they were: 'like all savages, gross feeders'.[40]

In one anecdote published in a Hobart newspaper in 1846, a 'native woman' on Flinders Island gorged herself on sooty petrel eggs, 'besides a double allowance of bread'.[41] Later discussed by the Tasmanian Royal Society in 1847, this episode became exaggerated: 'a woman would eat from fifty to sixty eggs, larger than a duck's [...]. Ogilby stated it to be no uncommon circumstance for an individual, at a single meal, to eat 12lbs. of meat, and wash it down with a gallon of train oil'. Another member of the Society argued that Ogilby 'surely meant his remarks to apply to the aborigines of some other country, as those in Tasmania never had the opportunity of obtaining *train oil*'.[42] It is not apparent which of these remarks are made in jest, although they are clearly absurd. In the original, the author wrote the claims could be 'scarcely credited', yet from here, this episode entered the histography, was included in prominent texts published in the 1870s, 1880s, and 1890s, usually without questions of accuracy, and placed alongside other accounts of gluttony. At a Royal Society lecture, J.B. Walker stated of the egg tale 'whether this story is true or not, I do not venture an opinion. But it is well known that the Australian native, like other savages [...] has a boaconstrictor-like power of gorging himself far beyond the extreme capacity of a European'.[43] Although not included in these texts as 'fact', the story was not discounted, thus perpetuating stereotypes of Tasmanian Aborigines as animal-like and less than human.

What constituted food differed between groups in the Australian colonial contact zone, and these differences were critical to how individuals perceived one another, not only in the instance of encounter, but also through discourse, informing and reinforcing power and racial hierarchies into the future. But food also allowed individuals to maintain personal agency and make connections across cultures. Reading further into primary accounts reveals many moments of respect and admiration, emphasizing how inherited knowledge and discourse clouded imperialists' perspectives and informed power structures for centuries to come. For Australia today, as a settler-colonial society with huge power disparities, the examination of ideas of food and power in the colonial contact zone is critical.

Notes

1   The Guugu Yimithirr are a cultural-linguistic group from Hopevale in North Queensland (John B. Haviland, 'Guugu Yimithirr Cardinal Directions', *Ethos*, 26.1 (1998), 25-47); Joseph Banks, '15 July 1770', *The Endeavour Journal of Sir Joseph Banks* <http://gutenberg.net.au/ebooks05/0501141h.html> [accessed 27 April 2019].

2   Mary Louise Pratt, *Imperial Eyes: Travel Writing and Transculturation* (London: Routledge, 1992), p. 4.

3   Banks, '10 July 1770', *The Endeavour Journal of Sir Joseph Banks*.

4   Banks, '11 July 1770', *The Endeavour Journal of Sir Joseph Banks*.

5   Banks, '12 July 1770', *The Endeavour Journal of Sir Joseph Banks*.

6   James Cook, '19 July 1770', *Cook's Endeavour Journal* <http://southseas.nla.gov.au/journals/cook/contents.html> [accessed 6 March 2019].

7   Cook, '19 July 1770'.

8   Anna Haebich, 'The Battlefields of Aboriginal History', in *Australia's History: Themes and Debates*, ed. by Martyn Lyons and Penny Russell (Sydney: University of New South Wales Press 2005), pp. 1-21 (p. 3).

9   Denise Russell, 'Aboriginal-Makassan Interactions in the Eighteenth and Nineteenth Centuries in Northern Australia and Contemporary Sea Rights Claims', *Australian Aboriginal Studies*, 2004.1 (January 2004), 3-17 (p. 3).

10 Stuart Banner, *Possessing the Pacific: Land, Settlers, and Indigenous People from Australia to Alaska* (Cambridge, MA: Harvard University Press, 2007), pp. 11-12, 30-32; Virginia Marshall, *Overturning Aqua Nullius: Securing Aboriginal Water Rights* (Canberra: Aboriginal Studies Press, 2017).

11 John Locke (1690), *Second Treatise of Government* <http://www.gutenberg.org/files/7370/7370-h/7370-h.htm> [accessed 30 May 2019].

12 Banner, p. 39; Bruce Pascoe, *Dark Emu Black Seeds: Agriculture or Accident?* (Broome: Magabala Books, 2014).

13 For example, see Rhys Jones, 'Fire-Stick Farming', *Australian Natural History*, 16.7 (1969), 224-28; Bill Gammage, *The Biggest Estate on Earth: How Aborigines Made Australia* (Allen & Unwin Sydney, 2011).

14 Michel Foucault (1976), *The History of Sexuality. Vol. 1: The Will to Knowledge*, trans. by Robert Hurley (London: Penguin, 1998), pp. 92-93, 97, 95.

15 Nancy Shoemaker, 'Food and the Intimate Environment,' *Environmental History*, 14 (2009), 341-42.

16 Damian M. Mosley, 'Breaking Bread: The Roles of Taste in Colonialism', *Food, Culture & Society*, 7.2 (2004), 49-62.

17 Ann Laura Stoler, *Carnal Knowledge and Imperial Power: Race and the Intimate in Colonial Rule* (Berkeley: University of California Press, 2002), p.13.

18 Penelope Edmonds, *Urbanizing Frontiers: Indigenous Peoples and Settlers in 19th-Century Pacific Rim Cities* (Vancouver: University of British Colombia Press, 2010), p. 16.

19 Mary Douglas, *Purity and Danger: An Analysis of Concepts of Pollution and Taboo* (London: Routledge & Keagan Paul, 1979).

20 Zane Ma Rhea, *Frontiers of Taste: Food Sovereignty, Sustainability, and Indigenous-Settler Relations in Australia* (Singapore: Springer, 2017), p. 104.

21 Rebecca Earle, *The Body of the Conquistador: Food, Race and the Colonial Experience in Spanish America,*

1492-1700 (Cambridge: Cambridge University Press, 2012); Trudy Eden, 'Food, Assimilation, and the Malleability of the Human Body in Early Virginia', in *A Centre of Wonders: The Body in Early America*, ed. by Janet Moore Lindman and Michele Lise Tarter (Ithaca: Cornell University, 2001), pp. 29-42; Cecilia Leong-Salobir, *Food Culture in Colonial Asia: A Taste of Empire* (London: Routledge, 2011).

22 Ma Rhea, p. 94; Charlotte Craw, 'Gustatory Redemption?', *International Journal of Critical Indigenous Studies*, 5.2 (2012), 13-24; Greg Blyton, 'Hungry Times: Food as a Source of Conflict between Aboriginal People and British Colonists in New South Wales 1804-1846', *AlterNative: An International Journal of Indigenous Peoples*, 11.3 (2015), 299-310; Shannon Woodcock, 'Biting the Hand That Feeds: Australian Cuisine and Aboriginal Sovereignty in the Great Sandy Strait', *Feminist Review*, 114.1 (2016), 33-47.

23 Ma Rhea, p. 95.

24 Robert Kenny, *The Lamb Enters the Dreaming: Nathanael Pepper & the Ruptured World* (Melbourne: Scribe Publications, 2010), pp.168-79.

25 Watkin Tench, *A Complete Account of the Settlement at Port Jackson* <http://www.gutenberg.org/files/3534/3534-h/3534-h.htm> [accessed 5 May 2019]; Matthew Fishburn, 'The Field of Golgotha: Collecting Human Skulls for Sir Joseph Banks', *Meanjin*, 76.1 (2017), 104-16 (p. 104).

26 'Narrative of the Shipwreck of Captain Hamilton and the Crew of the Sydney Cove', *Historical Records of New South Wales*, ed. by F.M. Bladen <http://gutenberg.net.au/ebooks13/1300541h.html#ch-02> [accessed 29 January 2019].

27 Claude Levi-Strauss, *The Raw and the Cooked* (New York: Harper & Row 1969), p. 164; Tench, *A Complete Account of the Settlement; Friendly Mission; the Tasmanian Journals and Papers of George Augustus Robinson, 1829-1834*, ed. by N.J.B Plomley (Hobart: Tasmanian Historical Research Association 1966), p. 9.

28 Brent D. Shaw, '"Eaters of Flesh, Drinkers of Milk": The Ancient Mediterranean Ideology of the Pastoral Nomad', *Ancient Society*, 13 (1982), 5-31; Keir Waddington, '"We Don't Want Any German Sausages Here!" Food, Fear, and the German Nation in Victorian and Edwardian Britain', *Journal of British Studies*, 52.04 (2013), 1017-42; Zona Spray Starks, 'Arctic Foodways and Contemporary Cuisine', *Gastronomica*, 7.1 (2007), 41-49.

29 F.D. McCarthy, 'Bungaree (?–1830)' <http://adb.anu.edu.au/biography/bungaree-1848> [accessed 29 May 2019].

30 Matthew Flinders, '25 February 1802', *Voyage to Terra Australis* <https://ebooks.adelaide.edu.au/f/flinders/matthew/voyage-to-terra-australis/complete.html> [accessed 27 April 2019].

31 Flinders, '25 February 1802'.

32 Plomley, p. 56.

33 *Conciliation on Colonial Frontiers: Conflict, Performance, and Commemoration in Australia and the Pacific Rim*, ed. by Kate Darian-Smith and Penelope Edmonds (London: Routledge, 2015), p. 5.

34 Tim Rowse, *White Flour, White Power: From Rations to Citizenship in Central Australia* (Cambridge: Cambridge University Press, 1998), p. 3.

35 Plomley, p. 57.

36 Mosley, pp. 49-62.

37 Plomley, p. 153.

38 Plomley, pp. 66-7, 131, 153.

39 Plomley, pp. 119; 79, 155-6.

40 J. Milligan, 'The Aborigines of Tasmania', *Empire*, 28 September 1855, p. 3; James Bonwick, *Daily Life and Origin of the Tasmanians* (London: Low, Son, & Marston, 1870), p. 17; H.L. Roth, *The Aborigines of Tasmania* (Hobart: Fullers, 1968), p. 86.

41 R.H. Davies, 'On the Aborigines of Van Diemen's Land', *Courier*, 7 March 1846, p. 4.

42 'Minutes of the Tasmanian Society,' *Tasmanian Journal of Natural Sciences*, 3.3 (1847), 238.

43 J.B. Walker, *Early Tasmania* (Hobart: Government Printer, 1973), p. 243.

220

Meat and Power in Communist Romania

Simona Moti

Recent scholarship on socialist Eastern Europe frequently intersects with questions of food and eating practices.[1] This essay maps the role of one particular food item, meat, in the articulation of power relations in communist Romania during the 1980s. Meat, especially pork and the products derived from it, is a traditional staple food that plays a constitutive role in social and family life in Romania, where it has powerful cultural and symbolic connotations. Historically, the consumption of meat symbolized wealth and strength. During the 1980s, however, meat was invested with a different social significance – in the words of Arjun Appadurai, it entered a different 'social life' – becoming involved in the deep play of politics and inseparable from power, as the state experimented with feeding and starving the entire population as a means of enacting governance.[2]

In several Dictionaries of Communism, which compile lexical inventories that characterized social, economic, cultural, and political life under communism, 'meat' is one of the entries that stand emblematic for this period because they provoke associations in the most condensed or symbolic manner.[3] Meat played an important role in the collective imaginary of the 1980s, and its entanglement with power is vividly remembered by ordinary people. Among the hardships that marked people's lives – the repressive political apparatus, the limitation or deprivation of freedom, censorship and surveillance, the abject poverty, as well as the feelings generated by living under these circumstances (fear, anxiety, rage, revolt, humiliation, and the constant concern with survival) – food in general and meat in particular constitutes an accurate metonymy of the life experience under communism. Needs and desires, power relations between the state and society, as well as between individuals, often revolved around food. The unavailability of basic food items and the survival strategies that entailed form the recurring themes and resilient memories about this decade.

Deprivation as an Instrument of Domination and Control

Romanian communism is often regarded as one of the most densely regulated and repressive regimes in Eastern Europe. Nicolae Ceaușescu ruled Romania from 1967 until he was toppled in 1989. In 1981, asserting the need to be independent from the USSR and the West, Ceaușescu decided to pay off the country's foreign debt.

Consequently, during the 1980s, at a time when other countries in the Eastern Bloc liberalized their economies, Ceaușescu's regime launched a foreign and home policy that implemented extreme austerity measures causing an unparalleled economic crisis. Industrial and agricultural products were exported, leading to extraordinary levels of hunger and hardship for the population. Food was rationed, and energy supplies were often cut off. No other Eastern Bloc regime inflicted such deprivation that denied the basic living needs of its people.

Basic foodstuffs, including bread and meat, were rationed. Meat was even scarcer than other commodities and disappeared almost completely from state-regulated stores. Ceaușescu justified these measures in the name of good health, promoting his program of 'scientific nourishment', which reduced daily caloric intake.[4] The regime's food policy was patented by Dr Iulian Mincu (nicknamed Dr Mengele), who justified the regulation of meat under the guise of promoting a 'rational' healthy vegetarian diet. In reality, the underlying agenda of this forced vegetarianism was aimed at transforming the population into 'a herd of domestic harmless ruminants'.[5] The concern for food became a central and often all-consuming preoccupation, and meat in particular became a real obsession.

The intersection of food and power occurs at different levels: the macro level of government control over food production and distribution seeps down into the micro level of biopolitics and impacts the lived experience of individuals and their social interaction. In communist Romania, state strategies of inflecting the food system and rationing certain foods extended upon the everyday life of the individual, taking hold of households, minds, and bodies. The rigid control of consumption was used by the state as a programmatic repressive measure. Food shortages became an instrument of controlling, disciplining, and passivizing the population, channelling potentially subversive popular energies into the struggle for survival.[6] The gruelling effort needed to obtain the daily food left little time and energy for involvement in civic administration or protest.

The 'Meat Folklore' of Communism

The state's attempt to regulate consumption left indelible marks on people's lives: Romania was the most malnourished country in the Eastern Bloc. In turn, this resulted in specific practices related to coping with the limited supply, social differences, and power relations that were often measured in terms of access to and distribution of food in the context of a generalized social disintegration. Practices around meat – namely the production, procurement, mediation, and distribution of meat through complex social networks along with various modes of consumption – became instruments for negotiating power, as did some of the discourses produced around meat, namely the ambivalent representation of meat and slaughterhouses in the collective imaginary and in fiction. Together these practices and discourses engendered by the harsh socio-political environment were constitutive parts of 'meat folklore'.

Queuing for Meat and the Experience of Shopping as 'Hunting'

When meat was available on occasion in state-owned stores – usually pig's hooves, nicknamed 'adidas', or a bag of chicken bones (heads, necks, wings, and claws) – it was only at the cost of endless shopping queues. The queue, this ubiquitous attribute of the communist economies, reached dramatic proportions in Romania during the 1980s. According to the Romanian researcher Codruța Alina Pohrib, the queuing experience was 'a commonplace of representations of communism, the totem of humiliation, poverty or, at best, forcible solidarity'.[7]

The queue for the most basic foodstuff became a daily experience, providing stark visible evidence of the economic and ideological bankruptcy of the system. Queuing was prevalent, a 'normal way of life' accepted with resignation by an increasingly desperate, starving population. Queues could appear anywhere, anytime, at irregular hours, prompting people to carry a shopping bag at all times. Food availability in stores was kept purposefully unpredictable as a totalitarian instrument for extending control over the individual; the regulation of such mundane activities as shopping increasingly connected state power to individual bodies.

On a symbolic level, the queue represented the alienation of individuals, their transformation into 'human insects' and the annihilation of individuality through repressive regimentation.[8] In the 1980s, queues became more numerous and surveillance got stricter. The queue became one of the territories surveiled by the secret police, overhearing conversations and monitoring public dissatisfaction and dissent.[9]

Queues for meat were especially large, disorderly, and aggressive. The meat supply was usually barely enough for 10-20% of the population in the queue, so only the lucky ones in the front or the strong ones who could fight their way into a better position were rewarded. Consequently, people queuing for meat would often rediscover their primitive hunting instincts, while the struggle for meat acquired the apocalyptic dimensions of what Romanian author Paul Cernat called a real 'meat epic'. Writing retrospectively about the lines he used to stand in as a teenager, Cernat testifies to the dehumanization of his fellow citizens: 'The people were ugly, stinking, deformed, brutish, frustrated, scornful, monstrously envious, and some of them would have gladly collaborated with the secret police in order to get some extra meat […] I have never seen uglier, more degraded people than in those queues'.[10]

The Black Market of Meat and the Complicity of the Whole Nation

The extreme austerity measures of the 1980s facilitated the emergence of complex social networks of connections and exchange in which people sought to produce and distribute goods outside of the strict confines of state-sanctioned consumption. This accelerated second economy sustained widespread illegal circulation and consumption in the Eastern Bloc.

Although Romania under Ceaușescu was known for its harsh political repression, the regime, like others in the region, tolerated the second economy on some level because it provided the necessary corrective for the scarcity induced by extreme austerity measures. But the rampant black market that resulted became deeply embedded in the Romanian economy, producing intricate webs of complicit officials and ordinary citizens.[11]

Practically everyone, at all levels of the social hierarchy, was complicit, since everyone, including state actors, participated in some form of illicit economic activity. It might appear as if the black market challenged the regime's control of the economy, but the authorities themselves encouraged corruption and were involved in it. The local administrators and the secret police were willing accomplices as they became enmeshed in these illegal webs of exchange and consumption. The collusion of state actors and the prevalence of such practices made the black (or grey) market a commonplace experience. Power relations and influence networks were carefully perfected over the years.[12]

In practical terms this meant that procuring meat required a direct or indirect connection to a 'supplier': somebody in the countryside who raised animals illegally or a well-connected acquaintance who worked in a store or restaurant where they had access to meat which they stole and redistributed or bartered for other goods. This parallel economy transformed meat products – one of the most coveted foodstuffs – from mere objects of consumption into much more, namely tokens of social standing and leverage in power relations: 'The mere access to certain products, including food, could become a marker of the owner's or the trafficker's power, who could use them, sell them, offer them as gifts. Sometimes it was tantamount to social success'.[13] This effectively altered the perception and social standing of certain jobs that provided access to meat: those who worked in stores, restaurants, or food processing plants suddenly found themselves in privileged positions. In other words, access to meat restructured social hierarchies.

As Jonathan Bach notes with reference to East Germany, 'the socialist system worked to constantly deprive and stimulate consumer desire in an ongoing cycle.'[14] The scarcity-induced obsession with meat in the late 1980s elevated the role of slaughterhouses in the collective imaginary. As a constitutive part of the 'meat folklore', slaughterhouses are vividly remembered by people reminiscing about this decade and feature as a recurring motif in memoirs and fictional works. Workers in slaughterhouses were allotted a monthly meat ration, some of which they resold to common people forced to buy meat on the black market at a much higher price. These workers usually sold the meat they received officially, but many stole and smuggled more products out of the gates and ran their own meat trade operations: 'Some stole one kilogram, others trucks full of meat – the bosses and managers'.[15] In the collective imaginary, slaughterhouses thus acquired utopian dimensions of almost unlimited access to meat. The correlative representation of slaughterhouses in fiction is often that of dystopian spaces linked to the degradation of the individual and the disintegration of the social fabric under totalitarian rule.

The Illicit Domestic Processing of Meat

As belts were tightened out of necessity, people were forced to find creative means in order to make ends meet and get food on the table: 'Making do became an art form as women concocted meals out of an odd array of seasonings and inferior meat trimmings'.[16] A new skill set that women acquired was meat processing in the domestic sphere, since the pigs or calves that were bought on the black market needed to be butchered at home. Most families have memories of clandestine pig slaughtering in the bathroom and subsequent processing on the kitchen table, as well as of the smell of blood lingering for days after. Butchering was usually gender-specific, performed by women who became knowledgeable about the anatomy of the animals and acquired a butcher's mastery of separating meat from bones to provide their families with food.

The meat history in communist Romania created the context for people to acquire such skills through the forced proximity to animal carcasses and the sensory experience of handling raw meat. This was quite different from the current experience of buying packaged meat in the supermarket – sanitized, plastic-wrapped, chopped into pieces, and ready to use – which facilitates the dissociation of meat-eating from the animal it comes from. Today, raw meat, especially offal, is considered abject and evokes disgust. During the 1980s, when the consumerist buffer between meat-eaters and the origin of meat products was often eliminated, meat was 'ambivalent to the bone', evoking simultaneously 'the value of life and the abjectness of the carcass lying on the kitchen table' – a perfect metonymy for the sacrifices and (Faustian) compromises made in the cause of meat.[17]

The Ambivalent Representation of Meat and Slaughterhouses in Fiction

In fictional works about this period, meat and slaughterhouses are frequently represented as ambivalent symbols linked to the degradation of the individual and the erosion of society under totalitarian rule. For example, the work of Herta Müller – the German-Romanian author and 2009 Nobel Prize laureate for literature who left Romania in 1987 as a political dissident and immigrated to Germany – frequently depicts Romania under the repressive dictatorship of Ceauşescu.

Her best-known novel, published in German in 1994 and translated into English as *The Land of Green Plums*, illustrates how power held sway at all levels of society through the lasting effects of terror, and portrays a society that is materially impoverished, desperate, and alienated.[18] Extreme culinary metaphors, including raw meat, play a central role in depicting the crimes of an inhuman regime that mutilated and destroyed individuals. Bleak scenes in the novel describe slaughterhouse workers and their families fighting against starvation by consuming raw offal and drinking fresh blood, becoming addicted to them like vampires. While these brutish acts save the people from starvation, poverty and greed dehumanize them, reflecting how the experience of totalitarianism poisons the physical, mental, and moral well-being of individuals, as well as depicting the perverse blend of coercion and complicity that characterized Romanian communism in the 1980s.

The original German title of the book, *Herztier* (literally 'heart-beast') is a complex metaphor that congeals the themes of meat (inner organ, offal), bodily experience, greed, fear, power, alienation, and dehumanization under totalitarianism, but also the struggle for survival, vitality, and life force under extreme circumstances.

Notes

1   *Communism Unwrapped. Consumption in Cold War Eastern Europe*, ed. by Paulina Bren and Mary Neuburger (Oxford: Oxford University Press, 2012).

2   Arjun Appadurai, *The Social Life of Things: Commodities in Cultural Perspective* (Cambridge: Cambridge University Press, 1986).

3   Maria Todorova, 'Introduction: Similar Trajectories, Different Memories', in *Remembering Communism: Private and Public Recollections of Lived Experience in Southeast Europe*, ed. by Maria Todorova, Augusta Dimou, and Stefan Troebst (Budapest: Central European University Press, 2014), pp. 1-25 (p. 14); Smaranda Vultur, 'Daily Life and Constraints in Communist Romania in the Late 1980s: From the Semiotics of Food to the Semiotics of Power', in *Remembering Communism*, ed. by Todorova, Dimou, and Troebst, pp. 175-200 (p. 190).

4   Jill Massino, 'From Black Caviar to Blackouts. Gender, Consumption, and Lifestyle in Ceauşescu's Romania', in *Communism Unwrapped*, ed. by Bren and Neuburger, pp. 226-49 (p. 238).

5   Vultur, p. 181.

6   Paul Cernat, '*Cozi şi oameni de rând în anii '80* ', in *Viaţa cotidiană în comunism*, ed. by Adrian Neculau (Iaşi: Polirom, 2004), pp. 191-200 (p. 193).

7   Codruţa Alina Pohrib, 'The Romanian Latchkey Generation Writes Back: Memory Genres of Post-Communism on Facebook', *Memory Studies*, 12.2 (2019), 164-83 (p. 174).

8   Adrian Neculau, '*Manipularea contextului şi controlul reprezentărilor sociale*', in *Viaţa cotidiană în comunism*, ed. by Neculau, pp. 35-46 (p. 43).

9   Vultur, pp. 180, 193.

10 Cernat, pp. 193, 192.

11 Narcis Tulbure, 'The Socialist Clearinghouse: Alcohol, Reputation, and Gender in Romania's Second Economy', in *Communism Unwrapped*, ed. by Bren and Neuburger, pp. 255-276 (p. 256).

12 Vultur, p. 194.

13 Vultur, p. 194.

14 Jonathan Bach, 'The Taste Remains: Consumption, (N)ostalgia, and the Production of East Germany', *Public Culture*, 14/3 (2002), 545-556 (p. 550).

15 Vultur, p. 198.

16 Massino, p. 243.

17 Inga Iwasiow, 'Meat', *Journal of Postcolonial Writing*, 48.2 (2012), 209-18 (p. 217).

18 Herta Müller, *The Land of Green Plums* (London: Picador, 2010).

Going Hungry in the Magdalene Laundries, 1922-1996

Giulia Nicolini and Alice Mulhearn-Williams

Introduction

'I was so skinny. Because I ... you know ... work, work, work and not a bite to eat.'[1]

'You were told what time to get up in the morning, you were told what to put on, you were told what to eat, you were told what to do.'[2]

Food Studies literature has long been focused on 'food that tastes good'; however, as an object of study, Jon Holtzman argues that 'bad food' may be more 'telling' and negative memories of food more powerful.[3] With this in mind, our paper will explore the experience of hunger as an expression of power and powerlessness within the Irish Magdalene laundries – institutions run by the Catholic Church in which 'wayward' women were forced to work for free, often in dire living conditions.

As a locus of punishment, discipline, identity, and, in some cases, resistance, hunger held a complex position in the daily life of the Magdalene women. Using oral histories of survivors, this paper asks what it means to 'be hungry' in the context of punitive institutions. It will use hunger as a lens through which to explore the relationship between food and power, while also picking apart the complex meanings of hunger in the specific context of the laundries. In so doing, it locates the 'lived body' as part of a wider interplay of power relations, and seeks to contribute to an embodied understanding of food and power.

The Magdalene laundries present a unique institution in which to explore the relationship between food and power. Mandated by the state, run by the Church, and legitimized by a national moral discourse, the laundries' existence in post-independence Ireland was framed by institutional power. Yet within their walls, power often worked in more indirect ways: a discourse of ascetic hunger met with punitive food deprivation, and monotonous food regimes were coupled with emotional starvation. In focusing on the period after 1922, our paper situates the meanings of hunger in the laundries within the broader socio-cultural landscape of post-independence Ireland, at a time when Irish identity was being actively shaped on and through the bodies of women. Moreover, while the Magdalene laundries have received increased scholarly and popular attention in recent years, there has been little to no consideration of how food shaped the everyday experience of women confined in these institutions.

Our research is based on oral testimonies collected as part of the *Magdalene Institutions: Recording an Oral and Archival History* project, funded by the Irish Research Council. Led by the Justice for Magdalene Research group, the project aimed to contribute to a better understanding of the Magdalene laundry system in Ireland by collecting and archiving testimonies from survivors and key informants. Angela Maye-Banbury has observed that oral histories foreground 'the ontology of personal experiences', thereby giving voice to 'people whose experiences have become marginalised from history'.[4] The interviews offer an unprecedented insight into everyday life within these institutions, particularly given the refusal of religious congregations to release written records of the Magdalene laundries post-1900. As a version of history that 'speaks from within the shadows', these testimonies therefore allow for an analysis of the laundries' food regimes as experienced by the survivors themselves.[5]

Historical Background to the Magdalene Laundries

Originating in the thirteenth century, Magdalene institutions were conceived as places where 'women who lived sinful lives', typically (but not exclusively) prostitutes, could go to repent and be reformed before re-entering society.[6] The repentant women came to be known as 'Magdalenes' in the image of Mary Magdalene, who was branded as a reformed prostitute by Pope Gregory the Great (A.D. 540-604).[7]

Magdalene convents multiplied rapidly from the mid-eighteenth century onwards, across Europe as well as in North America and Australia, and were aimed at alleviating prostitution and related socio-economic problems.[8] The rise in Magdalene institutions coincided with changes in social attitudes towards women and sexuality, widening the definition of 'fallen' or 'wayward' women. In post-independence Ireland, this came to include single and unmarried mothers, lower-working class women, and women living in poverty, but also girls who were deemed 'sexually precocious' and whose 'moral well-being' was seen to be at risk.[9]

As the moral discourse of post-independence Ireland shifted, so too did the role of the laundries. Following the creation of the Irish Free State in 1922, the Church enjoyed a resurgence in power and a 'moral monopoly' over Irish society, its influence extending beyond religious life into education, health, and social welfare.[10] Four religious orders of nuns took over the operation of the Magdalene institutions. As independent charitable foundations which received no state funding, they relied on private donations and their own economic enterprise, which in Ireland took the form of commercial laundries.[11] The Magdalene laundries thus became part of a system of 'custodial institutions', including mother and baby homes and industrial schools, which James Smith has referred to as Ireland's 'architecture of containment', a definition that extends beyond institutions to include legislation as well as public and official discourse surrounding sexual immorality.[12]

Feminist historians have highlighted how Catholic morality was 'intimately bound up with Irish identity' in ways which became particularly oppressive for women in the period following independence.[13] The Magdalene laundries sat within a 'disciplinary regime that was [...] highly gendered, focusing almost exclusively on the regulation and self-regulation of women', and whose ostensible aim was to 'produce "decent" women'.[14] The result was a network of punitive institutions located on the periphery of the Irish state. Cloaked in shame and shuttered from the outside world, the Magdalene laundries in post-independence Ireland held a unique sociocultural position that would play an integral role in their survivors' experience of hunger.

What Is Hunger?

Being hungry is as central to the human condition as being satiated. Yet few of us consciously track the ebbs and flows of hunger – not in the same way that we revel in the multi-sensory experience of tasting, eating, and cooking. For historians of food too, hunger is framed by a wider focus on politics and poverty. The result is that it is rarely afforded the same phenomenological analysis as eating, when in reality the experience – or at least the threat of it – profoundly shapes the way we feed ourselves and others. As Carole Counihan writes, control of alimentation is powerful precisely because 'it satisfies the most basic, compelling, continuous and agonising human need: hunger'.[15]

So what does it mean to be hungry? In a purely physiological sense, hunger is triggered when electrical signals point to the emptiness of the stomach – sensations that are reinforced by metabolic signals like blood glucose and the secretion of the hormone ghrelin. Throughout this process, sensory and cognitive processes prime the body for the next meal with anticipated reward and pleasure.[16]

Hunger is, however, more complicated than all that. Just as the act of eating 'encompasses physiological, psychological, hedonistic, and broadly cultural aspects of the self', hunger is more than a dichotomy between longing and satiety, physiology and psychology.[17] On a discursive level, it is shaped by complex cultural notions of morality, pleasure, and aesthetics, all of which channel into our embodied experience of hunger, influencing, supplementing, and oftentimes contradicting our own subjectivities.

Historian James Vernon has argued that the experience of hunger has a cultural history that goes beyond its seemingly physiological form: 'how [hunger] has hurt has always been culturally and historically specific'.[18] In a similar vein, in their study of gastric bypass patients, Line Hillersdal, Bodil Christensen, and Lotte Holm draw on Judith Farquhar's notion of 'the political phenomenology of eating' to propose a double focus on 'lived experience' and the 'political, cultural and historical contingency of embodiment' in the study of hunger. They argue that radical changes in how patients perceive hunger and fullness after surgery '[produce] new sensory experiences' which cause a 'displacement from the patients' sense of self'; however, they suggest that this displacement is naturalized within the setting of the hospital through the 'interrelation between politics and eating'.[19]

This paper will follow that argument in considering how the interplay between politics and eating within the particular institutional setting of the laundries shaped the lived experiences of hunger among Magdalene women. In discussing the relationship between food and power within carceral institutions, literature concerning food regimes within prisons is also relevant. Significantly however, where the nature of the laundries diverged from prisons – for example, in their concealment from the public eye – our case study provides new avenues for exploring the meanings of hunger in relation to power.

Beginning with an exploration of memories of food deprivation, we will then widen the lens to consider how a lack of flavour and variety of foods aggravated feelings of hunger, deepening the experience of powerlessness and abjectivity. Finally, we assess how food deprivation was also a source of empowerment within the laundries through hunger strikes.

Hunger as Food Deprivation

Institutional food is notoriously bad. Tasteless, meagre, monotonous, and often prepared without care, it is one of the defining features of Erving Goffman's 'total institution', which seeks to control every aspect of an individual's life – right down to what they taste.[20] The food served in the Magdalene laundries does not break step. Among the prevalent comments on food was the lack of it. For one survivor, Martha, dinner times felt similar to a Dickensian orphanage: 'You'd get a small plate with your dinner on it, it could be chips and eggs and beans it could be, but you'd count the chips like...you'd count what you'd get I tell you there wasn't a lot there, you dare ask for more, it was like Oliver [Twist].'[21]

Without the power to control their own portions, hunger became a permanent condition for many of the women, amplified by a strict regimen of manual labour:

'God we were starving! You couldn't ... y ... you know, after working so hard, you couldn't get enough to eat, do you know what I mean?'[22]

'The memory of it! I don't ... can't remember having a ... a full meal. I can't...'[23]

Here food deprivation is interpreted by the women as an extension of the physical and emotional mortification experienced on their arrival to the laundries. The practice of hair cutting, the forced removal of names, and the refusal of privacy were common practices intended to ensure the systematic erasure of individual personhood. For Martha, memories of collapsing in the laundry from hunger soon after her arrival are mnemonics for other mortification practices, including having her name changed, being labelled 'the devil's child' by the nuns, wearing 'rags' as a uniform, and being forced to eat foods she disliked. If satiety is to be understood as a metaphor for physical and emotional fulfilment, we can see this constant condition of hunger as contributing to the women's sense of 'abjectivity', which Nora Kenworthy has described in relation to undocumented migrants as a feeling of 'discomfort in one's own physical body' that arises out of not knowing when an experience will end.[24]

Food deprivation was not only experienced as a form of punishment, but also wielded as a disciplinary tool. One survivor, Maureen Sullivan, remembers a woman who had to stand outside the dining room while the others ate because of 'something she's done'.[25] In another account by Catherine Whelan, hunger is framed as penance for a sin: 'You had to get up out of your seat, go into the middle of the room and kneel down in front of her and apologise for causing the nun … what shall we say … discom … she didn't say … disobedience. And for your penance, "you're … you're going to do without your supper today," usually on Sunday'.[26]

Just as the women hungered for an uncertain release from the laundries, they too hungered for meals that would satiate their hunger. For some of the survivors, this chronic sense of unease – or abjectivity – worked to strip away their 'manners', turning mealtimes into purely pragmatic occasions: 'So, they would be in those three or four plates right in the centre of this big long table. And I'd learned to have … to grab them when they came, otherwise you'd go hungry. And so I'd learned if you went in with manners you came out without! It doesn't matter, it was survival really.'[27]

The rupture between discourse and experience of hunger is particularly noteworthy here. Following Foucault's argument that the 'disciplinary apparatus' of punitive institutions is aimed at reforming an individual, historians might be tempted to view these examples of food deprivation as a means of moral reform based upon the ascetic rules of monastic institutions.[28] Yet in reality, hunger was experienced as part of a complex mortification process. Hunger did not reform women through a Foucauldian notion of 'self-regulation'. Instead, it was experienced as part of a punitive regime that stripped the women of their agency, fulfilment and sense of self.

Conversely, accounts of women being forced to eat despite the food making them sick highlight the tensions which characterized the experience of both hunger and satiety in the laundries, as well as the experience of hunger as powerlessness: 'You had to swallow it because you know if you didn't eat it, number one you'd … you'd go hungry, number two you didn't like it and it made you feel sick, but your body … it's strange how your body becomes accustomed to it.'[29]

The words of Margaret Burke here highlight the way in which the experience of hunger, as well as the food itself, caused women's bodies to become subjects, and the women to become disembodied from their experience of hunger. Disgust towards inadequate, unappetizing food therefore added to the sense of unease and abjectivity which characterized the experience of hunger in the laundries.

Bad Food as a Form of Starvation

Hunger may relate to the absence of food, but the material reality of food also shapes the experience of hunger. A number of former Magdalene women describe the food in the laundries as 'disgusting', 'slop', or 'horrible', others as 'bland' or at best 'edible'. The monotony of the meals, as well as their lack of flavour ('pure water'), unpleasant mouthfeel ('full of fat lumps and gristle'), and unappetizing odor ('the smell of the cabbage used to make me ill') contributed to both the experience of eating as a punishment and the sense of hunger as a permanent state of longing.

As already noted, the Magdalene laundries held much in common with prisons. Food practices are central to carceral life, and are in many ways symbolic of the prison experience.

The repetitive and monotonous nature of work and life in the laundries was reflected not only in the structure of mealtimes, but also in the substance and quality of the food itself.

Aside from bread and butter or dripping, few women recall specific meals in the laundries. Rather, impressed in their minds tends to be a more embodied and sensorial memory of the kinds of foods they ate: steamed or boiled vegetables; watery stews; fatty, gristly meat; porridge and other 'rice pudding type food'.[30] Rebecca Godderis, who has written about the prison food stories of Canadian male inmates, similarly found that cooking methods were a salient part of individual narratives about carceral food. The inability to decide whether food was baked or fried, for example, 'reflected their inability to make beneficial consumptive choices' and, as a result, prevented them from exerting full control over their own health.[31] Within punitive institutions, food functions as a technology for controlling the self; what women ate, or were made to eat, contributed as much to the process of subjectification as much as how much they ate or didn't eat.

It is worth noting that throughout the nineteenth and early twentieth centuries, conservative tastes and styles of cooking predominated in Ireland. The first national nutrition survey in 1948 found that 'bread and spread' was the most common meal among Irish households for breakfast, tea, and supper, and that overall eating patterns were characterized by monotony.[32] To some extent then, diets within the laundries would have reflected those of the Irish population at the time. However, while eating habits began to change in post-war Ireland, as a result of greater economic prosperity and the influence of food media, former Magdalene women report eating the same kinds of foods as late as the 1970s. In addition, some interviewees point to inadequate food safety standards, such as Lucy's recollection of baking with cockroach-infested flour. More significantly however, the experience of hunger is highly contextual; the content of meals alone does not define the experience of hunger and satiety. Rather, the lack of control not only over what, but also when, how much, and under what conditions one eats, all contribute to the situated meanings and experiences of hunger.

Writing about inadequate immigration detention centre food, Megan Carney notes that the absence of both pleasure and satiety in detainees' experiences of food, itself a form of 'corporeal suffering', was compounded by other forms of violence.[33] In the Magdalene laundries, abuse was sometimes explicitly tied to food; for example, Philomena tells of women who were made to sit at a table in the middle of the dining room, eat their meals off it, and kiss the floor, in order to apologise for trespasses such as laughing or speaking during mealtimes.[34] The denial of pleasure through food represented a kind of symbolic violence; coupled with physical forms of abuse, this moulded the experience of hunger as a permanent state of physiological and emotional longing: 'you can dream of nice food but that's only a dream'.[35]

Hunger as Resistance

If food deprivation is an assertion of power in carceral institutions, the hunger strike is perhaps the ultimate method of resistance. Due to the centrality of food to the modern prison experience, food refusal by detainees 'directly challenges the normal disciplinary workings of prisons' and has the potential to subvert the power relations which shape such institutions. The hunger strike is a highly communicative act, particularly within the carceral setting, insofar as it allows the individual to 'reassert bodily control in an environment deliberately designed to curtail individual choice and decision-making'.[36] Within the Magdalene laundries, food refusal provided an avenue for women to regain control over the meaning and experience of hunger, empowering them and ultimately enabling some of them to leave the laundries.

Four of the women interviewed by JFM discuss going on hunger strike while in the laundries. Nora Lynch and Kathleen R both spent time in the Good Shepherds' Sundays Well laundry in Cork during the late 1950s and early 1960s. Both women describe 'sitting on the stairs' on multiple occasions, as a form of protest: 'I didn't want to spend the rest of my life there, so I rebelled again, I went up the stairs, sat on the stairs, I wouldn't do no work, I wouldn't eat nor nothing'.[37] Philomena similarly describes going on hunger strike for over a week at the Good Shepherd laundry in Limerick in the late 1950s: 'I remember, there was three of us out together in the cloister. And there was three auxiliaries, we were all on hunger strike to go.'[38]

The refusal to eat was clearly bound up with the refusal to work, and its meaning was also tied to particular locations in the laundries. Hunger striking was referred to by some women, including Philomena and Mary, as the 'ran' or 'going on the ran': 'When we'd want to get going we used call it the 'ran', we'd go out but we wouldn't do no work. I often starved myself to get out'.[39] Nora Lynch and Kathleen R were eventually released from the laundries due to their continued hunger strikes and refusal to work; Philomena also believes that her hunger striking was one of the reasons for her being moved from one laundry to another (she spent time in five different laundries).

All four women discuss going on hunger strike as a form of rebellion and as a means of explicitly demanding their release from the laundries. Indeed, Nora Lynch describes learning about hunger strikes as a way of getting out, from women who had tried doing it themselves, albeit unsuccessfully: '[I] said to Martha, "how can you get out of here if all the doors are locked? How can you actually get out?" She says, "well some people go on hunger strike".'[40]

Karin Andriolo has observed that words 'do not grip unless one gives them hands to do so, unless one embodies them'.[41] Within the Magdalene laundries, hunger strikes were a form of embodied protest born out of a sense of injustice at indefinite, unexplained containment, and the denial of their demands for release. Kathleen R explicitly refers to hunger striking as a form of 'complaint', which she deemed the only way to communicate with the nuns: 'Verbally I didn't complain, there was no point in complaining… You couldn't complain, because there was no one to complain to because they won't listen to you.'[42]

As Amanda Machin argues, the hunger strike 'draws attention, although its meaning is not fixed or predetermined'.[43] Prisoners' hunger strikes have often been viewed as political acts intended to attract attention from the media and communicate with the

233

public through carceral walls. However, the deliberate concealment of the Magdalene laundries from society suggests that their protests were directed inwards, at the immediate and tangible abuses of the nuns, rather than at the broader political, social, and discursive structures that perpetuated the system of which the laundries were a part. While a comprehensive analysis of hunger striking in the laundries is outside the scope of this paper, these limited insights nonetheless provide a counterpoint to the relationship between hunger and power explored in the previous two sections.

Conclusion

This paper has used oral accounts of hunger in the Magdalene laundries as a case study through which to explore both the meaning of hunger and the relationship between food and power in carceral institutions. Carney's study of women held in detention centres shows that hunger feeds a sense of abjectivity and non-belonging in liminal spaces; for survivors of the Magdalene laundries too, it led to feelings of powerlessness. Yet hunger held complex and sometimes contradictory meanings in these institutions.

Bernadette's account of her time in the laundry in 1966 encapsulates these complexities. For Bernadette, hunger was not linked to food rationing. Instead she felt a longing for variety, flavour and agency over her own meals. As a way of asserting her 'individuality', she remembers requesting her own pepper mill from the woman in charge of the shopping: 'She bought me my black pepper, and it was brilliant because it came in a little mill, so I had ... my ... my black pepper every day.'[44] When faced with 'no end to [her] incarceration', this pepper mill gave Bernadette the autonomy to season her food, in turn giving her back a measure of control over her sense of self and her daily life within the laundry. Bernadette's experience of hunger is therefore multilayered, shaped by her 'middle class' hotelier background, her hatred of the strict food regimen, and her anxiety over when she would be released.

What Bernadette's and other survivors' accounts demonstrate is that hunger is not merely a longing for physical nourishment. Rather, it is a spiritual-physical experience mediated through culture, discourse, and personal history. For many of the survivors of the Magdalene laundries, this meant experiencing – and remembering – hunger within a milieux of abuse, neglect, and rejection. The result is an interpretation that is not tied simply to food deprivation, but multilayered memories of longing, un-fulfilment, and abjectivity.

In the Magdalene laundries, much like in prisons, the nuns, as authority figures, used food as a disciplinary tool and a technology for controlling the self at both a physical and spiritual level; this contributed to the women's sense of subjectification and alienation from their own bodies. However, as we have noted, the laundries were situated within a unique 'architecture of containment' which sought to control sexual immorality and socially deviant women more broadly. The position of the Magdalene laundries on the peripheries of the state imbued physical hunger with feelings of longing, unease, and powerlessness. However, this liminal position also complicated power relations, turning hunger strikes into a more introverted, local form of resistance than those experienced in carceral institutions.

We have suggested that the Irish Magdalene laundries present an interesting and in many ways unique setting through which to investigate the 'interrelation of politics and eating', insofar as they shed light on the relationship between discourse and experience in carceral institutions. On one hand, religious instruction was a crucial part of the supposed aim to reform such women, and, as some oral accounts show, the deprivation of food was often tied to moral discourse surrounding repentance. On the other hand, we have suggested that the discourse of reform and self-regulation which upheld these institutions diverged from the lived experiences of survivors, who recall memories of violence, abuse, and mortification.

The experience of hunger was therefore highly contingent on the nature of the laundries, themselves a product of the socio-political and religious landscape of post-independence Ireland. Hidden from the outside world and held indefinitely, the women hungered for the privileges of a life that they were owed but not permitted. Meals prepared with care, the agency to provide food for themselves and others, the homely security of a kitchen table – these comforts represented a life beyond the confines of the laundry walls. Deprived of the opportunity to look towards a 'release date' nor repent for a crime committed, the Magdalene survivors were left to hunger not just for bodily sustenance, but for emotional fulfilment.

Notes

1   Katharine O'Donnell, Sinead Pembroke, and Claire McGettrick, 'Oral History of Pippa Flanagan', *Magdalene Institutions: Recording an Oral and Archival History* (Ballsbridge: Government of Ireland Collaborative Research Project, Irish Research Council, 2013), p. 39. For brevity, only the name of the interviewee will be given in subsequent citations. All names of interviewees are pseudonyms.

2   Bernadette, *Magdalene Institutions*, p. 21

3   Jon Holtzman, 'Remembering Bad Cooks', *The Senses and Society*, 5 (2010), 235-43 (p. 237).

4   Angela Maye-Banbury, 'The Famished Soul: Resonance and Relevance of the Irish Famine to Irish Men's Accounts of Hunger following Immigration to England during the 1950s and 1960s', *Irish Studies Review*, 27 (2019), 195.

5   Jose Medina, 'Towards a Foucaultian Epistemology of Resistance; Counter-Memory, Epistemic Friction and Guerilla Pluralism', *Foucault Studies*, 12 (2011), 9-35 (p. 15).

6   Brian Titley, 'Heil Mary: Magdalen Asylums and Moral Regulation in Ireland', *History of Education Review*, 35.2 (2006), 1-15 (p. 1).

7   Rebecca Lea McCarthy, *Origins of the Magdalene Laundries: An Analytical History* (Jefferson: McFarland & Co, 2010), p. 1-2.

8   McCarthy, p. 10.

9   Leanne McCormick, *Regulating Sexuality: Women in Twentieth-Century Northern Ireland* (Manchester: Manchester University Press, 2009), pp. 37-38.

10   Tom Inglis, *Moral Monopoly: The Rise and Fall of the Catholic Church in Modern Ireland* (Dublin: University College Dublin: 1998), pp. 245-47.

11   Titley, p. 4.

12   Titley, p. 2; James Smith, *Ireland's Magdalen Laundries and the Nation's Architecture of Containment*

(Indiana: University of Notre Dame Press, 2007), p. 2.

13 Maryann Gialanella Valiulis, 'Power, Gender, and Identity in the Irish Free State', *Women's History Review*, 20 (2011), 569-78 (p. 575); Smith, p. 3.

14 Una Crowley and Rob Kitchin, 'Producing "decent girls": Governmentality and the Moral Geographies of Sexual Conduct in Ireland (1922-1937)', *Gender, Place and Culture*, 15 (2008), 355-72 (p. 367).

15 Carole Counihan, *The Anthropology of Food and Body: Gender, Meaning, and Power* (New York: Routledge, 1999), p. 4.

16 Gareth J. Sanger, Per M. Hellström, and Erik Näslund, 'The Hungry Stomach: Physiology, Disease, and Drug Development Opportunities', *Front Pharmacol*, 1 (2010), 145.

17 Andrea Borghini, 'Hunger', in *Encyclopedia of Food and Agricultural Ethics*, ed. by P.B. Thompson and D.M. Kaplan (New York: Springer, 2016), p. 4.

18 James Vernon, *Hunger: A Modern History* (London: Belknap Press, 2007), p. 8.

19 Line Hillersdal, Bodil J. Christensen, and Lotte Holm, 'Changing Tastes: Learning Hunger and Fullness after Gastric Bypass Surgery', *Sociology of Health & Illness*, 39 (2017), 474-87 (pp. 476, 485, 476).

20 Erving Goffman, *Asylums: Essays on the Social Situation of Mental Patients and Other Inmates* (London: Routledge, 2017).

21 Martha, *Magdalene Institutions*, p. 29.

22 Kathleen, *Magdalene Institutions*, p.34.

23 Bernadette Murphy, *Magdalene Institutions*, p.45.

24 Nora Kenworthy, 'Asylum's Asylum: Undocumented Immigrants, Belonging, and the Space of Exception at a State Psychiatric Center', *Human Organization*, 71.2 (2012): 123-34 (p. 127).

25 Maureen, *Magdalene Institutions*, p. 49.

26 Catherine Whelan, *Magdalene Institutions*, p.14.

27 Margaret Burke, *Magdalene Institutions*, p.14.

28 Michel Foucault, *Discipline and Punish: The Birth of the Prison* (New York: Knopf Doubleday Publishing Group, 2012).

29 Margaret Burke, *Magdalene Institutions*, p. 26.

30 Bernadette, *Magdalene Institutions*, p. 41.

31 Rebecca Godderis, 'Dining in: The Symbolic Power of Food in Prison', *Howard Journal of Criminal Justice*, 45 (2006), 255-67 (p. 258).

32 Department of Health (DOH), 'National Nutrition Survey: Parts I-VII: Complete Reports on Dietary and Clinical Surveys', *Lenus: The Irish Health Repository*, 1948 <https://www.lenus. ie/bitstream/handle/10147/252421/NationalNutritionSurveyParts1_7_1948DOH_Part1. pdf?sequence=1&isAllowed=y> [accessed 28 May 2019].

33 Megan A. Carney, 'Border Meals: Detention Center Feeding Practices, Migrant Subjectivity, and Questions on Trauma', *Gastronomica*, 13.4 (2013), 32-46 (p. 34).

34 Philomena, *Magdalene Institutions*, p. 11.

35 Margaret Burke, *Magdalene Institutions*, pp. 26-27.

36 Ian Miller, *A History of Force Feeding Hunger Strikes, Prisons and Medical Ethics, 1909–1974* (Palgrave MacMillan, 2016), p. 11.

37 Kathleen R, *Magdalene Institutions*, p. 2.

38 Philomena, *Magdalene Institutions*, p. 31

39 Philomena, *Magdalene Institutions*, p. 19.

40 Nora Lynch, *Magdalene Institutions*, p. 46.

41 Karin Andriolo, 'The Twice-Killed: Imagining Protest Suicide', *American Anthropologist*, 108 (2006), 100-13, (p. 102).

42 Kathleen R, *Magdalene Institutions*, p. 82.

43 Amanda Machin, 'Hunger Power: The embodied protest of the political hunger strike', *Interface*, 8 (2016), 157-80 (p. 170).

44 Bernadette, *Magdalene Institutions*, p. 28.

Cooking in Calais: Resistance to the Food Desert in Northern France

Féilim Ó Cuireáin

Introduction

Exiles have been living in makeshift camps along the coast of Northern France for over twenty years.[1] In this time, the French government has alternated between tolerating the exiles' spaces and expelling them from their camps. Small grassroots organizations and international NGOs have been working in the region for all of this period, providing aid and solidarity against the state's repressive treatment. Last winter I worked for Refugee Community Kitchen (RCK), cooking and serving food for exiles living in the Jungles of Calais and conducting interviews with other volunteers. RCK is a British grassroots NGO comprised primarily of volunteers from the UK. My interviews and research explored how exiles' lack of access to food could be interpreted within the concept of a 'food desert' and how this condition could be resisted by the exiles. This resistance was aided by the NGOs' attempts to translate the ideals of food justice and food sovereignty into forms of practice for their distributions. This work contrasted that undertaken by the state, whose own food distribution practice may actually promote the development of food deserts.

These interviews highlighted how grassroots humanitarian aid focused on food justice in Calais through concern for the exiles' nutrition, dignity, and right to pursue autonomy within their food systems. In contrast, 'state food' was distributed in ways that failed in respect to food justice or food sovereignty.

Performing the Food Desert

This essay explores three major sets of concepts in the discussion of food provision for exiles. The first set comes from 'bio power', a term used to describe methods to control the bodies of subjects and internalize the rules of the state, and 'bare life', a term coined by the Italian philosopher Giorgio Agamben to describe the abandonment of those subjected to it by the state, those stripped of their identity as citizens and left to a life bared down to survival.[2] While the effects of bare life can be focused on in many forms, here food provision is most relevant, which is considered using the second concept: the food desert. Exiles have resisted the food desert imposed by the state; their methods are considered through the third set of concepts from food justice and food sovereignty.

Bio power draws on Michel Foucault's concept of power: those subjected to it internalize the rules of the state imposed by the threat of force. Bio power has been applied previously by scholars to the use of hunger as a tool of control, such as Tamara Nair's calling hunger a 'state-created construct' used to control Myanmar's Rohingya population.[3] Foucault's use of bio power was extended by Agamben through his concept of 'bare life', which he often discussed in relation to the conditions of the exile and the camp.[4] The exiles' marginalization is described as a state of exception, which enforces bio power through secluding its subjects entirely from society. For the state, the benefit is the economical use of resources – for example, heavily monitoring the camps persuades exiles to remain there, avoiding the city centre.[5]

Since Agamben, later authors have used bare life to discuss the lives of exiles in camps – especially Calais. Michel Agier has referenced it often in his writing, rephrasing the term as that used in the title for his *Managing the Undesireables* (2011) and further expanding on it in his history of the Calais camps in *The Jungle* (2019): both books describe the method of unconscious population control used by the state.[6] This essay suggests that the construction of bare life is part of the rationale that leads to the development of a food desert: halting services through policing aid providers and replacing them with state services may appear as alternatives, but effectively perform another act of control. This creates conditions similar to spaces seen before considered as food deserts.

Today there is no single, consistent definition of what a food desert is. In general it refers to a physical location where obstacles hinder access to healthy foods. Most definitions focus on the physical boundaries around those living within the food desert. Rather than these physical boundaries, this study defines food deserts based on the social boundaries seen in Calais. The Jungle is not a neighbourhood in the traditional sense; instead the food desert in this analysis is an artificial construction, one which forms around the exiles due to their exclusion rather than being limited to one place.[7]

Drawing on characteristics identified by the USDA, I've chosen conditions relevant for Calais:

> 1) Lack of transport to and distance from healthy food stores. The biggest Jungle in Calais today is in an industrial estate due its proximity to the motorway and ferry terminal: with few bus links, it is at least a quarter of an hour walk to the town centre.
>
> 2) General levels of income and quality of facilities/services which will be examined in the next section.

Food deserts are often considered a result of poor management: with regards to urban planning, difficulty accessing healthy food is seen as occurring 'organically'. For example, when urban decay leads to the flight of supermarkets from marginalized communities, those business decisions curtail access to healthy groceries and create reliance on fast food and corner stores stocked with processed staples: generally the result is much poorer diets. While conventional food deserts occur as an unintended effect of bad administration, in places like Calais food deserts are a consequence of policies deliberately designed to isolate communities. The state's management of aid, their own and that of other charities, is used to subtly enforce the behaviour of those living in the Jungle.

This process is halted when humanitarian food aid creates a space for the pursuit of 'food sovereignty'. Food sovereignty is defined by the Declaration of Nyéléni as 'the right of peoples to healthy and culturally appropriate food produced through ecologically sound and sustainable methods, and their right to define their own food and agriculture systems'.[8] In this sense, the pursuit of food sovereignty in the Calais camps can be understood as a form of resistance to the isolation which is manifested as a food desert.

While food sovereignty is most often linked to agricultural issues and land ownership, discussions about food deserts tend to rely primarily on the concept of food justice in urban environments. Although food justice may better fit the situation in Calais, I still plan to examine the benefits of considering the values of food sovereignty to the daily actions of the organizations with which I worked. Most volunteers interviewed justified their efforts through the values of either food justice or food sovereignty; although no interviewee ever explicitly used the terminology of either.

Arguably food justice is one topic in the larger discussion of food sovereignty, seen as accessing nutrition and closely tied to social justice concerns. In the framework of this essay, though, food justice is seen as a more local solution. Food justice tends to work 'around' issues instead of solving them, such as through volunteers bringing healthy food into locations where inhabitants cannot prepare food for themselves.[9] Food sovereignty seeks instead to address the structural cause of inequality, taking a more long-term approach to problems within food systems – the goal is to address why access and facilities are lacking, and hoping these volunteers will eventually not be needed at all. While grassroots volunteers may now only promote the immediate goals of food justice, this essay still asserts that pursuing food sovereignty is more beneficial in the long term.

The next section offers a brief examination of the state organization providing food in Calais; it considers how the state's policies effectively create and weaponize a food desert. The following section then contrasts the methods used by grassroots activists to resist this creation.

La Vie Active

The state enforces its politics and tactics on the bodies of the people waiting on the border in a myriad of ways. When outright enforcement is not the most effective tactic, whether for cost, manpower, publicity, or other reasons, it has shifted to more subtle means to exclude this population. These methods included creating 'hostile environments' where the landscape itself is used to push exiles from Northern France.[10] Instead of attempting outright expulsion of exiles from Calais, state policies of constant, daily harassment exhausts those living on the border until they decide

239

themselves to leave: the state's use of bio power shows in the exiles' internalization of the state's desires. This harassment is often blatant: disrupting sleep by destroying tents and evicting exiles from the Jungles to prevent the formation of new camps. But the harassment can be more sophisticated as well, such as the creation of a food desert by the disruption and replacement of aid services.

The Calais government was forced to start distributing food last year, when, in an impromptu remark during a visit to Calais, President Macron declared that the state would now be the primary provider of food for the exiles. This claim caught the Calais government by surprise, and the service was contracted out to La Vie Active (LVA) who started their distribution in March 2018.

For full disclosure, I never managed to interview anyone connected to LVA directly during my time in Calais. I sent emails with no reply and was turned away when I approached them in person. However, their reluctance to speak to me was notably different to every other charity working in the city. La Vie Active is a charity working in Calais and across the country, but it faces criticism from other humanitarian organizations based in Northern France. Although an independent charity, LVA is so closely aligned with the state that the phrase 'state food' was used during interviews with volunteers and mentioned by exiles themselves. LVA has been working with the exile population in Calais since the time of the big Jungle around 2015: they ran the Jules Ferry Centre, a daytime drop-in centre for exiles to get meals, and faced criticism for their management of services even then.[11] The shanty town that developed around the centre became the most infamous Jungle, 'Camp de La Lande'.

The state taking responsibility and caring for displaced people was considered by many a move in the right direction. When LVA began to distribute food after Macron's statement last year, other aid organizations halted their own food distribution, giving LVA a chance to provide for the exiles. However, the charities soon discovered that state food distribution was being boycotted by the exiles, who reasoned that they could not take food from hands that also beat them.[12] During meal distribution, the main LVA centre was surrounded by police, the same forces who conducted evictions and stole tents the nights before.

There was also disappointment with LVA's decision to concentrate services on the city's peripheries. Since the demolition of Camp de La Lande, smaller Jungles had arisen around the city, and LVA chose three of those sites. However, Auberge de Migrants had closed a distribution site in the city centre, assuming that state food could take over this responsibility. LVA's plan meant exiles in the centre had less access to services, forcing them to remain out of sight in the cities' outskirts to receive food.[13]

Many of my interviewees, including the exiles themselves, dismissed the food which LVA provided. Its food project was described as purely a 'money making business for them' to fund other projects nationwide. LVA's food is produced by a kitchen in Calais that is also hired to provide hospital and school dinners, but many interviewees feared their menu methods of preparation lost any nutrients within the meals, that it had 'no energy in it'. There was also lack of cultural considerations: One volunteer mentioned seeing pork served to Muslim communities.

These problems, combined with the physical location of the camps and the social exclusion of the exiles, arguably create conditions in these spaces that resemble a food desert. The points of distribution used by the state for food aid are only accessible to exiles in campsites on the edges of the cities' wasteland and industrial estates.[14] While these locations may be convenient, they simultaneously limit the exiles' mobility; creating a reliance on these services keeps exiles excluded from the city centre.

This exclusion is seen as an effect of bare life, reducing the exiles' existence to pursuits that merely maintain their own survival – stripped of dignity and autonomy – in conditions resembling a food desert. The state services seem driven more by the minimum they are required to provide than by concern for the exiles themselves. These services become a method of bio power, an effort to dominate and influence behaviour. In the Jungle, they deter exiles from leaving their campsites.

Often, such exclusion is couched in the pretence of concern and the language of humanitarian goals. When LVA administered sites in Camp de La Lande, the eviction and demolition of the old Jungle was justified as necessary to ensure the health and safety of the exiles living there. The French interior minister called the action 'a humanitarian stage of intervention'.[15] State aid and administration is not only passively detrimental due to ineffectiveness, but also actively used to control displaced populations.[16]

As a result, exiles are paradoxically framed both as victims and security threat, something to be protected and also protected against. This dynamic was seen repeatedly when policies appeared to simultaneously work for and against those living in the camps such as in 2016 when 'the state built a camp with shipping containers by day, while the police tear-gassed men, women, and children by night'.[17] These tactics create conditions of a 'state of exception' and the food desert by using the same tools and language that should halt their creation.

This control over food provision was directed against not only the exiles but also other humanitarian providers in the city. There were repeated health inspector visits to kitchens feeding the exiles such as RCK's. Regular fines and tickets were given to delivery vehicles, and food distributions in the field were shut down as 'illegal operations'. On the surface these appear as benign administrative acts, but their continual use as a measure of harassment suggested more malicious intentions.

'The same government employed both the police forces that smashed people's heads, stole their shoes, and sprayed their bedding with chemicals and the authorities that confronted charities by asking, "have you washed their salad? Is it washed well enough?"' As one aid worker noted, 'You're kind of like, you know, if you really cared about the welfare of these people. *Really* cared. You wouldn't be helping your agents to be doing what they're doing'.[18] An interview with a founder of RCK highlighted the charity's need for constant vigilance against the prefecture's interference and threat to shut their operations. During one health inspection, the inspector mentioned he had been called by the mayor to conduct that visit; the mayor had never personally requested a business be inspected before.

While the state uses its own services to perpetuate the conditions that exclude this population, the exiles themselves still can resist that coercion, often with the help of grassroots organizations such as RCK.

Resistance and Humanitarian Aid Organizations

After seeing how state food was received, other humanitarian organizations quickly restarted their own operations to feed the exiles in spite of the presence of LVA in Calais – this in turn enables the exiles to strengthen their own resistance to the government's influence. Antje Ellerman discusses how acts of sovereignty may be created even in the face of the state's complete bio power; she quotes James Scott's use of the phrase 'weapons of the weak' in describing exile's behaviour.[19] For Scott, these 'weapons' are 'everyday forms of resistance' focused on short term goals, rather than systematic change.[20] These acts of resistance may not appear explicitly as acts of defiance, merely those of survival. However, in the face of the state's imposing of bare life through an individual's removal, survival itself becomes an act of resistance.

This resistance may come from the exiles themselves or that enabled through the aid of humanitarian organizations. Some exiles have been able to maintain a boycott of state food distribution since its inception over a year ago. Members of the Eritrean community in Calais still refuse state food, LVA eventually decided to halt distribution near to their campsite all together. This boycott may not have been possible were it not for the humanitarian organizations that are also providing food aid.[21]

These grassroots organizations manage to – consciously or unconsciously – draw on food justice and/or food sovereignty to inform the framework of decisions about their methods used when serving food. At present, these values lead to commitments to serve healthy, culturally appropriate food and to support the dignity and autonomy of how people may eat. By contrast, LVA's policies seem to be missing any discussion, implicit or explicit, of food justice or sovereignty in their framework. By allowing these values to inform decisions that affect the lives of the exiles, these aid groups provide alternatives to state food that halt the creation of the food desert.

Calais has various organizations working in order to feed the exiles, each taking a different time and place to spread aid out as effectively as possible. During my time I was most familiar with RCK, although I also managed to work with and interview people with the French charities Utopia 56 and Salam. Utopia and RCK were closely linked, operating from the same warehouse under the umbrella of the organizations Help Refugees and L'Auberge de Migrants. Salam has been working in Calais and Dunkirk since the crisis began over twenty years ago. There are also other groups working in the town such as Secours Catholique (SC) and Care4Calais. Each of these groups had differing stances on aspects of food justice, from nutritional needs to culturally appropriate foods.

The food cooked by RCK generally consisted of a serving of curry or stew, rice or pasta, and salad. During our distribution people were able to take as much as they wanted of what was on offer. The ideal was that the food would go from pot to mouth within an hour, which was achieved most days. The stews were usually a mixture of vegetables and soaked beans. Dried beans were preferred over tinned, first as a cost measure but also due to the belief that the nutrition possible with soaked beans was far better than that with tinned. Vegan food was preferred for cost as well. The money spent to feed a thousand people a day on fresh vegetables was a fraction of what it would be serving chicken or beef instead. The primary goal with their food was to enable people to have access to as many calories as possible in one meal, especially when they are dealing with stresses such as exposure to the elements.

RCK also hoped to run their charity in as sustainable a manner as possible, citing the renewability of a primarily plant-based diet over that of one based on animal products. Whilst this was not as primary a concern as compared to exiles' welfare, it still showed a commitment to other aspects of food sovereignty wherever they could. However, halal meat was bought for special occasions such as the end of Ramadan, reflecting respect for the cultural needs of the people who were being served. Most groups operated on the same or similar guidelines, building relations with the exiles in the hope of delivering food and services to them with dignity and respect.

Previous to this period, there were also other kitchens based in the old Jungle in 2015, including Ashram Kitchen, Belgian Kitchen, and Kitchen in Calais – all of which have left the city, either pursuing other projects or ceasing operations. One of the founders of Kitchen in Calais helped explain the difference between food provision then and in the current situation. I hoped to understand to what extent food justice and autonomy may have been possible in the old Jungle at the time. In terms of the creation of bare life for exiles, it appears that the Jungle as it was then actually allowed greater autonomy and space for food sovereignty than is possible today. During that time of the Jungle, several kitchens operated their services to provide more stable distribution. The exiles had space to set up their own cooking facilities and choose their own food, some were even able to set up shops and restaurants catering to their own communities.[22] Interestingly this contrasts with most descriptions of refugee camps written about currently as states of exception which leave exiles at the full mercy of the state. Even in times and places such as that seen with Camp de La Lande, whilst looking desperate, they may still have provided a chance for exiles to create their own sovereignty at times. At least in comparison to what is seen today.

Conclusion

This paper has examined whether the mechanisms and tactics of exclusion enforced on the exiles by the state in Calais can be interpreted as the creation of a food desert. This concept is considered as only one small aspect of a much larger system, seen as an extension of the creation of bare life.

The food desert has been used to describe the effect that a geographical location may have on people living within it, generally in a built-up area. This work was inspired by research conducted primarily in America to study these effects and to see how the work of food justice organizations can counteract them. Aid organizations in Calais probably align closer with the concerns of food justice over that of sovereignty, similar to projects such as the Food Justice Truck, a mobile farmers market delivering fresh fruit and vegetables to locations which might struggle to access them otherwise.[23] Food justice does address immediate situations by tackling lack of access to healthy food. However, the more far-reaching goals seen in the values of food sovereignty should ultimately be pursued to address the systematic blocking of independent food systems, including the inability of exiles to leave the Jungles in search of their final destination, the lack of care from the French state, and the harassment of heavy policing that keeps people from settling long enough to prepare their own food.

Although the concept of the food desert originally applied to built-up areas, this research shows its application may be used in other, more temporary spaces also. The spaces inhabited by the exiles – forests, scrubland, wasteland – are places where there was never any intention to build services. Discussions about food deserts tend to be, essentially, about revitalizing areas deprived of resources instead of areas that never had resources to begin with. These discussions miss how the concept of the food desert may be usefully applied to more transient populations, but that is beginning to change. While the majority of food desert research involves residents with fixed abodes, Chery Smith, Jamie Butterfass, and Rickelle Richards studied the navigation of a food desert from the perspective of a homeless population in Minnesota.[24] This paper has attempted to apply this same concept to the nomadic populations of the exiles in Calais – their situation that may be considered a 'mobile desert'.

LVA is seen as enabling this food desert by deploying its services without considering the values of food justice or sovereignty as a replacement of other grassroots organisations. However, other food aid organizations at work within Calais recognize that LVA's service is a step in the right direction in terms of state responsibility for aid. Interviewees I met described good relations with the staff of LVA, even if they were not satisfied with their methods. They are all there for the same reasons. Not everyone I met was critical of their distribution; representatives of Care4Calais spoke positively of their service, mentioning their serving of fresh fruit and decent portions but this was the only interview I had which supported La Vie Active's work.

During their time working in the old Jungle, LVA supported other organizations with financial aid, such as funding for Kitchen in Calais to build their site within the Jungle. Before LVA came in, they had planned to leave due to a lack of funds. Kitchen in Calais, a kitchen run by a Malaysian couple, cooked culturally appropriate food for other Muslims such as themselves, receiving a lot of respect from the exiles during their time in the Jungle. I was surprised to hear in an interview with the organiser of their kitchen that LVA were the ones who helped them to build their own unit within the site of Camp de La Lande. Depending on its circumstances, in the past LVA has also shown support for other groups working with principles of food justice. Administering aid designed to enable food justice is a process which must be regularly revisited to ensure its principles are being met.

The provision of services provided by the state should, ideally, be served with considerations for enabling food justice immediately and pursuing food sovereignty eventually by tackling the systematic reasons for unequal access to food. Such an approach would keep state aid from becoming another tool of domination wielded by the state to create bare life for the exiles living in Calais. Until then, various groups currently in operation in Calais are doing their best to fill the gaps not properly addressed by LVA.

Notes

1 ' Exiles' is my preferred term to refer to displaced people living in the Jungles around Calais while avoiding arguments about whether they are properly refugees or migrants. This choice follows the French term Exilé used by French academics, such as Michel Agier, to discuss the same situation. This essay will use 'exile' unless in reference to someone else's phrasing or names of aid organizations (Michel Agier, *Managing the Undesireables: Refugee Camps and Humanitarian Government* (Cambridge: Cambridge University Press, 2011)).

2 Giorgio Agamben, *Homo Sacer: Sovereign Power and Bare Life* (Stanford: Stanford University Press, 1995).

3 Tamara Nair, 'The Rohingyas of Myanmar and the Bipolitics of Hunger', *Journal of Agriculture, Food Systems and Community Development*, 5.4 (2016), 143-47 (p.143).

4 Adam Ramadam, 'Spatialising the Refugee Camp', *Transactions of the Institutes of British Geographers*, 38 (2013), 65-77.

5 Michel Foucault, *The History of Sexuality* (New York: Pantheon Books, 1976).

6 Michel Agier and others, *The Jungle: Calais's Camps and Migrants* (Cambridge: Polity Press 2019).

7 USDA, 'Definition: Food Access', *USDA Economic Research Service*, 2019 <https://www.ers.usda.gov/data-products/food-access-research-atlas/documentation/#definitions> [accessed 30 May 2019].

8 WDF, 'Declaration of Nyéléni', *World Democratic Forum*, 30 January 2007 <http://world-governance.org/en/declaration-of-nyeleni> [accessed 30 May 2019].

9 Jessica Clendenning, Wolfram Dressler, and Carol Richards, 'Food Justice or Food Sovereignty? Understanding the Rise of Urban Food Movements in the USA', *Agriculture and Human Values*, 33.1 (July 2015), 165-77.

10 Mallet and Hicks, *Lande: The Calais 'Jungle' and Beyond* (Bristol: Bristol University Press, 2019). (p. 37).

11 Calais Migrant Solidarity, *Jules Ferry Centre: Another Step towards Segregation/Le centre Jules Ferry: Un autre pas vers la segregation*, 29 January 2015 <https://calaismigrantsolidarity.wordpress.com/2015/01/29/jules-ferry-centre-another-steps-towards-segregation-le-centre-jules-ferry-un-autre-pas-vers-la-segrega-tion/> [accessed 30 May 2019].

12 Tom Steadman, 'Refugees in Calais Boycott State Food Distribution', *Help Refugees*, 20 March 2018 <https://helprefugees.org/news/calais-state-food-distribution/> [accessed on 30 May 2019].

13 Charlotte Boitiaux, 'French Government Starts Distributing 700 Meals a Day in Calais', *Info Migrants*, 8 March 2018 <https://www.infomigrants.net/en/post/7942/french-government-starts-distributing-700-meals-a-day-in-calais> [accessed 30 May 2019].

14 Refugee Info Bus, 'Calais Update – French Government to Begin Food Distribution for Refugees', *The Warehouse*, 5 March 2018 <https://medium.com/thedigitalwarehouse/calais-update-french-govern-

ment-to-begin-food-distribution-for-refugees-f73fd4742c08> [accessed 30 May 2019].

15 Debarati Sanyal, 'Calais 'Jungle': Refugees, Biopolitics and the Arts of Resistance', *Representations*, 139 (Summer 2017), 1-33, (p. 2).

16 Sarah Mallet and Dan Hicks, *Lande: The Calais 'Jungle' and Beyond* (Bristol: Bristol University Press, 2019).

17 Sanyal, p. 2.

18 S. R. Jones, personal interview with the author, Calais, 19 February 2019.

19 Antje Ellerman, 'Undocumented Migrants and Resistance in the State of Exception', (unpublished paper prepared for European Union Studies Association, 2009), p. 4 <http://aei.pitt.edu/33054/1/ellermann._antje.pdf> [accessed 30 May 2019].

20 James C. Scott, 'Everyday Forms of Resistance', *Copenhagen Papers in East and Southeast Asian Studies*, 4 (1989,) 33-62.

21 Steadman.

22 Maria Hagan, 'Disassembling the Camp: The Politics of Policing Exiles in Calais, France' (University of Amsterdam, Unpublished Masters Thesis, 2018) .

23 Fiona H. McKay and others, 'Food-Based Social Enterprises and Asylum Seekers: The Food Justice Truck', *Nutrients*, 10.6 (June 2018) <doi.org/10.3390/nu10060756>.

24 Chery Smith, Jamie Butterfass, and Rickelle Richards, 'Environment Influences Food Access and Resulting Shopping and Dietary Behaviours among Homeless Minnesotans in Food Deserts', *Agriculture and Human Values*, 27.2 (2010), 141-61.

Everything but the Kitchen Syndicate: How Parisian *Cuisinières* Cleaned Up Their Reputation by Tapping into Social Stereotypes

Samantha Presnal

Hot off the presses, straight from the kitchen: French cuisine was dying. In February 1884 this pre-emptive obituary made the front page of Paris's top daily press, *Figaro*. This was certainly not the first time the death knell had tolled for French cuisine, but in this instance there was a culprit. In his piece 'Women Cooks in Paris', columnist Adrien Marx accused *cuisinières*, or hired female cooks, of compromising the integrity of French cuisine with 'academies of false stews, institutes of pseudo-salmis, pernicious dens where horrible mixtures of bones and skins are combined in an atrocious sauce [...] which allows the novice and idle cook to conceal her ignorance or laziness'.[1] Marx's commentary prompted a flurry of responses from *cuisinières* who defended their 'offensive' sauces by pointing the finger at their hands-off employers. As one *cuisinière* 'of good sense' wrote, cooks had been corrupted by mondaine mistresses who quibbled over the cost of a carrot, disdained the stove, and never dared enter the kitchen themselves. She had faith that French cuisine could be resuscitated if 'mistresses went to the market, lent advice and guidance to their cooks, and inspired the love of cooking through their presence and kindness'.[2]

Within the next decade, her aspirations came to fruition. Throughout the 1890s, as affluent ladies enrolled in Paris's new culinary schools, they started to see the situation of the *cuisinière* as a social cause and began to advocate for formal training, fair placement practices, and social services for their kitchen staff. While our *Figaro cuisinière* seemed to have presaged these patronesses' philanthropic initiatives, her rebuttal was also a sign that *cuisinières* were ready to fight for themselves. Although many bourgeois women believed that the home cooking movement depended on their benevolence, not all *cuisinières* were charity cases. Some of them acted as their own advocates who persuaded powerful people to invest time and money in their cause. Through the case study of the little-known cité d'Antin cooking school and its mutual aid society, 'La Cuisinière', this paper explains how marginalized working-class women found personal and professional enfranchisement by using prejudice and politics to their advantage.[3] Through the close reading of written records left by and about the organization and its *cuisinières*, it argues that by conforming to certain expectations, La Cuisinière was able to defy others and reach new levels of professional legitimacy and personal distinction.

The very existence of the mutual aid society La Cuisinière upsets our prevailing image of domestic cooks as repressed laborers who lived and toiled in solitude.[4] Founded at the Ecole de Cuisine cité d'Antin in March 1897, La Cuisinière was singular among mutual aid societies in its composition and purpose. It was the first society to professionalize cooking as a trade for women through formal training; a recipe and news digest, *L'école de cuisine*; a suite of benefits; and regular reunions and social events. Prejudices about 'the weaker sex' and women's inferior wages had left women officially or effectively out of professional mutual aid societies for much of the nineteenth century.[5] And while there were a number of cooperative associations for male chefs in Paris, the vast majority refused entry to female cooks.[6] La Cuisinière was part of a small minority of exclusively female mutual aid societies, and one of the few whose mission was not aimed at protecting women as mothers but skilled workers.[7]

To pursue its progressive agenda, female cooks of La Cuisinière secured – and leveraged – partnerships with chefs, philanthropic ladies, and food and hospitality professionals. From the very beginning, these women capitalized on the celebrity status of their school's founder, chef August Colombié. Having served as chef to Prussian heirs, French princes, and Spanish aristocrats, Colombié found a following among high-paying clientele, helping him build his brand as a high-end chef.[8] When he arrived in Paris in 1878, he was stunned by the disrespect toward chefs and the dearth of professional associations. In 1881 he set about establishing the first federation, the Circle of Cooks, which evolved into the Academy of Cooks in 1883. A vocal proponent for chefs and *cuisinières* alike, the charismatic Colombié also found popularity among amateur female cooks who participated in his pop-up demos, referred to his recipes in women's magazines, and purchased his cooking guides.[9] His notoriety brought publicity and money to the cité d'Antin cooking school, but it also helped to bring La Cuisinière's cause to the attention of the administration.

The organization had submitted its official statutes to the Bureau of Public Assistance for formal sanctioning in early March 1897. After two months without word from the administration, on 4 May 1897 chef Colombié addressed his own letter to the bureau requesting that it review La Cuisinière's petition with 'a bit of rapidity'.[10] Just two days after Colombié sent his letter, the bureau ordered the prefect to conduct its investigation 'as promptly as possible, and at the latest 14 May'.[11] The report, which was delivered on 17 May, credited chef Colombié with founding the society and for having served as the 'chef of a royal European court'.[12] The minister found this information 'satisfactory in all respects', and issued formal approval on 19 May – just two weeks after chef Colombié had prodded the bureau, but two months after La Cuisinière first sent its application. With contacts in European high society and Paris's elite circles, chef Colombié's credibility seemed to help speed up La Cuisinière's approval.

One of the organization's first objectives was to raise the status of the *cuisinière* trade by 'developing the taste and need for theoretical and practical study'.[13] With their annual dues of twenty-four francs, La Cuisinière's members received free admission to all courses and conferences held at the organization's headquarters at the cité d'Antin.[14] These *cuisinières* benefitted from the cooking school's robust programming, featuring subjects like 'menu composition and orthography, history of the culinary arts, and food science'.[15] If a mistress employed a member of La Cuisinière, she could rest assured that her new employee's virtuosity in the kitchen would be matched by her *savoir-vivre*. Since dinner parties communicated many things about hosts, from the family's wealth to a woman's taste, selecting a *cuisinière* was a high stakes business.[16]

To appeal to a particularly upper-class clientele, who could afford to pay better wages, culinary practicum at the cité d'Antin was geared toward expensive, rather elaborate dishes in French cuisine.[17] At the cité d'Antin, members of La Cuisinière learned how to make *sauce à l'asperge* 'unctuous, thick, tender green and of rare delicateness', how to meticulously reduce a *sauce au madère* so that it was 'beautiful to the eye and fine to the palate', and how to gently incorporate whipping cream in a *sauce mousseline* to ensure that its taste was 'absolutely fine and delicate' with a 'creamy body'.[18] According to Colombié, this ability to embellish familiar dishes would earn cuisinières 'the approval of your guests, especially the male gourmands – no matter what is said about them and what they say – especially them'.[19] Although he conceded that male connoisseurs were often sceptical about female *cuisinières*, Colombié assured his students that prejudices would dissipate with proper plating and technique.

While delicious sauces like these exemplified France's tradition of decadent dishes, most medical authorities and laymen believed such sauces were taxing on the stomach. At the cité d'Antin, however, *cuisinières* learned to adapt classic cuisine to modern health concerns. Every issue of its journal, *L'école de cuisine,* featured a different treatise on diet, explaining how to alter regiments and dishes to alleviate certain symptoms or recurring dietary issues like indigestion or diarrhea. One issue of *L'école de cuisine* even called for replacing the orthodox roux made up of flour and butter with one comprised of cream and butter, a combination that upended culinary doctrine, but would be less upsetting on the stomach of diners with diabetes.[20] By staying current with developments in nutrition and curating menus to meet dietary needs, La Cuisinière's corps of female cooks augured a new era of healthful home cooking that could regenerate the body while preserving French traditions.

Equipped with an understanding of food chemistry and human anatomy and nutrition, *cuisinières* – long faulted for assaulting diners' digestive systems – became their first line of defence. In one of his lectures, chef Colombié expounded on the 'capital importance' of distinguishing between *sauce au beurre* and *sauce hollandaise*.[21] What he called the 'regrettable error' of confusing the flour-based sauce for the egg-thickened look-alike would be even more egregious if served to a gluten-intolerant guest. At the cite d'Antin medical specialists and pharmacologists delivered guest lectures about nutritional principles and how to manipulate recipes to improve diners' overall health. In one speech on pharmaceutical cooking to a crowd of mistresses and cooks, Docteur Foucard alluded to one of the many advantages of having a cook with an advanced understanding of food's chemical composition: 'Have you eaten asparagus? You are not unaware, then, that their eliminations are so recognizable that they conjure a poignant memory of the vegetable, emitting its tenderness in a persistent, bothersome odour. You will certainly be grateful for the hand that knows to add a pinch of potassium permanganate to soften the penetrating stenches.'[22] In his urine euphemism, the doctor alluded to the everyday benefits to be had by hiring a *cuisinière* trained at the cité d'Antin: not only would she allay dietary discomforts, she could help avoid awkward social situations.

La Cuisinière also addressed anxieties about personal hygiene, actively inviting mistresses to attend its semi-regular conferences on hygiene at the cité d'Antin.[23] By the late nineteenth century, germ theory had seeped into popular consciousness through the appeals of social hygienists, giving age-old concerns about cooks as contaminants scientific grounding.[24] Rather than denying or deflecting such stereotypes, experts at the cité d'Antin actually played up the risk posed by servants in order to accentuate their own *cuisinière*'s exceptional sanitary knowledge and impeccable hygiene. Lecturers also urged mistresses to make kitchen safety and sanitation a top priority by describing how, through their deleterious effects on *cuisinières*, hazardous kitchens ultimately compromised the health of all an apartment's inhabitants.[25]

While speakers attempted to persuade mistresses to be proactive, they conceded that *cuisinières* needed to take the first step to disinfect themselves. Beyond predictable topics like hand-washing, speakers lectured on teeth-brushing, ear-cleaning, feet-scrubbing, hair-combing, and feminine hygiene.[26] Such self-care rituals promised to purify the image of the female cook. According to Docteur Villechauvoix, cooks were exposed to toxic waters, decomposing garbage, and 'smells that emanate from the pots and pans [which] spread throughout the kitchen, seep into the walls, and give them an odour characteristic to the kitchen and to the female cook'.[27] As he presented it, the cook herself oozed the effluvia of the kitchen, and this tainted her reputation. By attending these conferences, *cuisinières* signalled their willingness to clean up their bad behaviour or bad rap, but also their expectation that the mistress would do her part to ensure a more salubrious workspace. With their polished cooking and purified cuisine, students at the cité d'Antin set themselves up to shine and set themselves apart from other *cuisinières* and *chefs*.

As the female cooks of La Cuisinière strove to protect their employers' health with their hygienic cooking, they also fought to secure a livelihood for French girls from the lower classes. During the fin-de-siècle, cooking, like many other service industries, saw an influx of immigrant labour willing to work for less.[28] And as in other sectors, where organizations used the threat of foreign invasion to bolster collective action, members of La Cuisinière played to nativist sympathies to garner support for their cause. Administrative positions were reserved for French citizens. And while only three months of residency in the Seine commune was required for entry into the organization,

250

only women nominated by two current members could be considered for admission, effectively limiting membership to women with strong roots in the local community.[29] According to chef Colombié, such exclusions would combat 'the strong competition from skillful cooks coming from Switzerland, Germany, England, the US etc. etc.'[30] La Cuisinière's journal frequently reprinted pieces from other presses on the progress of home cooking schools in other western nations and the lag in France. Editors used these reports to pitch La Cuisinière's mission as a matter of national importance. In 1899 one wrote, 'In this review we have frequently discussed professional culinary training for young girls in the countries which surround us, training that allows them to secure the best posts in our country, to the detriment of our own proletariat girls.'[31] The use of 'we' in reference to La Cuisinière's journal recalled the sororal spirit of the organization, while the repetition of the first-person plural pronouns – 'the countries which surround *us*', 'in *our* country' – conjured protectionism, reminding Frenchwomen of their collective duty to cultivate homegrown home cooks over outsiders. And in concluding its appeal with a first-person possessive – '*our* own proletariat girls' – La Cuisinière positioned its mission as a democratic and humanitarian one.

The associations of male chefs that preceded them had also framed theirs as a fight for national pride. But these men had legitimated their *métier* through gender tropes depreciating female culinary compatriots.[32] In contrast, La Cuisinière borrowed from its kitchen brethren in their efforts to professionalize. In the vein of culinary expos in vogue at this time, La Cuisinière organized annual exhibitions for members to showcase their specialties. Free and open to the public, these events were prime opportunities for the organization to promote the skills of its members and solicit support. Subscribers to La Cuisinière's journal found numerous columns devoted to exhibition coverage: advertisements in the weeks preceding, an announcement of award recipients, a recap of proceedings, and recipes for winning dishes. In its third year La Cuisinière branched out of the halls of cité d'Antin to reach a much broader audience at the 1900 Universal Exhibition in Paris. But unlike chefs, whose imposing *pièces montées* appeared to be more edifice than edible, La Cuisinière did not aim to dazzle. In a piece condemning chefs for their food monstrosities at the Culinary Expo, one *Figaro* correspondent expressed his optimism for La Cuisinière's showing the following day: 'It won't be artful, but it will at least be good, appetizing food.'[33] But in an occupation long shrouded in silence, La Cuisinière welcomed all publicity – even when it was condescending – and tried to turn it in its favour. In this instance chef Colombié responded to the *Figaro*'s low expectations with his own opinion piece in the pages of La Cuisinière's journal: 'Not only did I find that my students made beautiful and interesting dishes, but all of it was appetizing and ready to be eaten – can you imagine! And the eight hundred visitors, who honoured our exhibition with their presence, they praised my students' work much more highly than I would permit myself.'[34] The journalist's critique provided perfect pretext for chef Colombié to plug La Cuisinière's accomplishments and do it impartially, positioning himself as a mere a messenger relaying rave reviews from the audience. In deferring to the female visitors, Colombié referred to their high turnout and high status, casually conferring cachet to La Cuisinière's showcase.

Colombié used his star power to attract a posh crowd at La Cuisinière's dinner parties. Like many associations at the time, La Cuisinière held an annual banquet to foster solidarity among members and court prospective donors, including restaurant moguls, celebrity chefs, government dignitaries, and charitable mistresses. Guests experienced a 'true shock' in entering the banquet at the magnificent restaurant Marguery, a favourite of business tycoons on Paris's Boulevard Bonne Nouvelle.[35] The *Almanach des gourmands* described the building as 'sumptuous' in 'its richness of ornamentation, the infinite numbers of salons and private rooms, marvelous sculptures and mosaics, and the profusion and variety of decoration'.[36] The menus for the banquet were as elaborate as the restaurant's interior. For example, on the occasion of La Cuisinière's third anniversary, guests dined on bisque, sole in white wine, beef in béchamel, duck *à la* presse, a tower of seafood, ice cream, waffles, assorted desserts, fruits, fine wines, and, to top it off, champagne – all served by a discrete and stealthy male waitstaff.[37] The menu was not as ornate or over-the-top as what was served at government galas or chefs' expos, but reflected the repertoire *cuisinières* had perfected at the cité d'Antin and the polish and sophistication employers could expect.

An evening of fine dining and dancing priced at seven francs per head, the banquet helped raise funds and raze negative stereotypes of female cooks. Attendees at the annual banquet for La Cuisinière were surprised to find female cooks looking 'charming and young' with 'excellent dress and modest urbanity'.[38] These *cuisinières* assimilated seamlessly with the hundred other guests from high society and haute cuisine, with whom they dined, danced, and sang into the wee hours of the morning, when the 'idyllic ball' ended 'to the great regret of this group, at fifteen past six in the morning'.[39] Seeing female cooks mingling with donors and social influencers, 'one would have never imagined that this picturesque, elegant, and proper group was made up of young women, having worked all day in kitchens'.[40] Banquets allowed female cooks to slip out of their aprons and step out of the shadows, distancing themselves from the grime of the kitchen. Like the legions of chefs seeking to professionalize, the female cooks of La Cuisinière emerged from behind the stoves to align themselves with the grandeur of gastronomy. But at these banquets *cuisinières* carried themselves less like great chefs and more like *dames,* foregoing displays of masculine professionalism and utilizing their feminine charms to attract supporters.

Members used exhibitions and banquets to prove their sophistication, as artists of the plate and as feminine fashion plates. As crucial as these events were in piquing the public's curiosity, they may have been even more important for their role in fostering confidence in women employed in what had been seen as a seedy occupation. In doing so members of La Cuisinière rebranded themselves as desirable additions to the household. Indeed, during the proceedings of the first meeting, the president of La Cuisinière identified the 'true goal' of the organization as educating female cooks about 'their duty and responsibilities vis-à-vis their mistress'. La Cuisinière calmed fears about the cook as an outsider encroaching on and corrupting the family, matching mistresses with graduates of the cité d'Antin and vouching for their credentials and character. The society thus added transparency and reassurance to what had been a shady business of placement services.[41]

The organization's impact on the lives of its members and contemporary mentalities is more difficult to assess. The number of domestic servant syndicates did in fact grow from 1900 to 1910, increasing threefold from five to sixteen, with nine headquartered in Paris.[42] Within its first three years, La Cuisinière had placed more than one hundred graduates from the cité d'Antin and its membership had more than doubled.[43] Its patronage had also expanded, the guest list to its annual banquet multiplying five-fold from its first to second year, from fourteen to seventy, and more than tripling again in its third with 220 attendees.[44] As the number of members and donors grew, so too did the circulation of its journal. In 1900 the editor's mailbox was filled with letters from followers in the French provinces wondering where to find La Cuisinière at the Universal Exposition.[45] By 1904 it was receiving requests from subscribers in Spain, Italy, and as far away as Argentina.[46] However, the number of participating members remained modest, and on 6 June 1908, after only an hour of deliberation, La Cuisinière voted overwhelmingly to close the society.[47]

While La Cuisinière's existence was short-lived, it did seem to induce incremental shifts in the chauvinistic attitudes displayed toward female cooks. The disbanding of La Cuisinière coincided with the ascendance of the Mères Lyonnaises, women who created demand for consuming *bonne cuisine bourgeoise* outside the home and spurred culinary tourism in the post-war period.[48] Famous food critics like Curnonsky praised the Mères Lyonnaises and other restaurant matriarchs around France as the guardians of authentic, unadulterated French cuisine.[49] Although it was only after WWI that culinary regionalism really took off in France, at the turn-of-the-century there were already indications that the tide was changing. In 1906 chef Colombié published his final cooking manual, *La Pâtisserie bourgeoise*, which featured a 'never-before-seen' recipe authored by his co-instructor at the cité d'Antin, chef Pierre Chatelain. The chef had dedicated his dish to one Madame Caroline Peters, who in his preface he praised as the 'very devoted President of La Cuisinière'.[50] Calling his cakes 'Petites Carolines', chef Chatelain bucked the convention of naming dishes after illustrious diplomats or masters in favour of a more democratic nomenclature. His gesture signalled that Adrien Marx's earlier estimation had been invalidated, that *cuisinières* were no longer seen as sabotaging French cuisine, but as the only people capable of saving it.

253

Notes

1   Adrien Marx, 'Les Cuisinières à Paris', *Le Figaro*, 25 February 1884, p. 1.
2   Françoise, 'Réponse d'une cuisinière', *Le Figaro*, 29 February 1884, p. 1.

3   Société La Cuisinière, Sécurité sociale, *Sous-direction des accidents du travail, régimes spéciaux et de la mutualité, Bureau mutualité, Seine* 19760252/7, Paris, Archives Nationales (AN).

4   The extant scholarship on *cuisinières* does not consider them as an occupational category, but rather as isolated, repressed individuals without formal affiliations. Theresa McBride states that 'the servant gained no sense of class solidarity and the great majority remained politically inactive' (*The Domestic Revolution: The Modernisation of Household Service in England and France, 1820-1920* (New York: Holmes & Meier, 1976), p. 9). Amy Trubek found 'no evidence that women were members of professional associations' (*Haute Cuisine: How the French Invented the Culinary Profession* (Philadelphia: University of Pennsylvania Press, 2000), p. 123). According to Pierre Guiral and Guy Thuillier, a handful of mutual aid societies for domestic servants did exist at the turn of the century, but these were not specific to a particular occupation ('*Interventionnisme*', in *La Vie quotidienne des domestiques en France au XIXe siècle* (Hachette Education (programme ReLIRE), 1978), pp. 224-35.

5   Michel Dreyfus, *Les Femmes et la mutualité française de la Révolution à nos jours* (Paris: Editions Pascal, 2006), pp. 20-21.

6   I have identified only one exception to this in my research. In 1893 Edith Clarke, the director of the National Cookery School of London, was admitted to the Académie de Cuisine.

7   Dreyfus, *Les Femmes et la mutualité française*, pp.39-45.

8   Auguste Colombié, *Dossier de l'Officier d'Académie, Ministère de l'Instruction Publique*, F/17/40194, AN.

9   F. Barthélemy, '*Nos Célébrités culinaires: Auguste Colombié*', La Cuisine française et étrangère, 25 July 1893.

10 Correspondence of Auguste Colombié to the Ministère de l'Intérieure (Institutions de Prévoyance), 4 May 1897, 19760252/7, AN.

11 Correspondence of the Ministère de l'Intérieure to the Préfecture de Police, 6 May 1897, 19760252/7, AN.

12 Correspondence of the Préfecture de Police to the Ministère de l'Intérieure, 17 May 1897, 19760252/7, AN.

13 Statutes, Chap. 1. Art. Premier, Société 'La Cuisinière', 19760252/7, AN.

14 Statutes, Chap. 5. Art. 23, 1897, Société 'La Cuisinière', 19760252/7, AN.

15 Statutes, Chap. 9. Art. 38, 24, 1897, Société 'La Cuisinière', 19760252/7, AN.

16 Rachel Rich, *Bourgeois Consumption: Food, Space and Identity in London and Paris, 1850-1910* (Manchester: Manchester University Press, 2011), p. 101.

17 Barthélemy noted that multi-step sauces are one of the features that distinguish *cuisine bourgeoise* from *cuisine ménagère* ('*Cours complet de cuisine pratique*', La Cuisinière cordon bleu, 1899).

18 '*La Crème Irmanette*', L'école de cuisine, 10 June 1903; '*La Sauce au madère*', L'école de cuisine, 25 June 1903; '*Sauce mousseline pour poisson*', L'école de cuisine, 25 February 1904.

19 Auguste Colombié, '*Cours de cuisine: Timbale aux pommes douces*', L'école de cuisine, 10 November 1900.

20 '*Traité diététique ou spicilège alimentaire medical: sauces pour diabétiques*', L'école de cuisine, 25 January 1898.

21 Auguste Colombié, '*Ecole de Cuisine au gaz, cours de cuisine, turbotin, sauce au beurre, la sauce au beurre*', L'école de cuisine, 25 September 1899.

22 '*Au Jour le jour: la cuisine pharmaceutique*', L'école de cuisine, 21 April 1899.

23 The first conference on the subject of *hygiène alimentaire* was held on 29 April 1898; see Michelle Boucheix, '*Annonce*', L'école de cuisine, 25 April, 1898. In 1899 M. P. Foucard led a special three-part conference series on the subject of *cuisine pharmaceutique*; see '*Cuisine pharmaceutique*', L'école de cuisine, 10 December 1899 and '*Annonce*', L'école de cuisine, 10 December 1901.

24 Séverine Parayre, *Hygiène à l'Ecole: Une Alliance de la santé et de l'éducation, XVIIème – XIXème siècles* (Saint-Étienne, France: Publications de l'Univerité de Saint-Étienne, 2011).

25 '*Les Cuisinières et l'hygiène*', L'école de cuisine, 10 May 1898.

26 '*Conférence faite à la mairie du IXème arrondissement le 29 avril 1898 par M. le Dr. Villechauvoix*', L'école de cuisine, 10 August 1900.

27 '*Les Cuisinières et l'hygiène*', L'école de cuisine, 10 May 1898.

28 Bernard Moss, *The Origins of the French Labor Movement 1830-1914* (Berkeley: University of California Press, 1976), pp. 13-14.

29 Statutes, Chap. 3. Art. 5, 12 ; Statutes, Chap. 2, Art. 3, 11, 19760252/7, AN.

30 'Le mouvement social, une école professionnelle ménagère', L'école de cuisine, 10 August 1899.

31 'L'enseignement de nos jeunes filles et le Conseil municipal de Paris', L'école de cuisine, 10 January 1899.

32 Trubek.

33 F. H., 'L'Exposition culinaire', Le Figaro, 17 March 1900.

34 Auguste Colombié, 'Echo', L'école de cuisine, 10 April 1900.

35 'Société des secours mutuels', L'école de cuisine, 25 March 1899.

36 F. G. Dumas, 'Restaurants d'aujourd'hui', Almanach des gourmands (Paris: Librairie Nilsson, 1904), 159.

37 'Société de secours mutuels', L'école de cuisine, 25 March 1899.

38 'Société de secours-mutuels', L'école de cuisine, 25 March 1899.

39 Auguste Colombié, 'Le Troisième Banquet de la société de secours mutuels "La Cuisinière"', L'école de cuisine, 10 April 1900.

40 'Société de secours-mutuels,' L'école de cuisine, 25 March 1899.

41 Anne Martin-Fugier, La Place des bonnes: la domesticité féminine à Paris en 1900 (Paris: Grasset, 1979).

42 Guiral and Thuillier, p. 237.

43 In its first year, La Cuisinière counted thirty-five members. While I have not been able to locate precise figures for subsequent years, in 1901 eighty membres participantes attended the annual banquet. We can thus be certain that at least this many were adherents of La Cuisinière. See 'La Société la Cuisinière', L'école de cuisine, 10 April 1901.

44 'Banquet de la Société Secours-Mutuel La Cuisinière', L'école de cuisine, 10 April 1899; 'La Société la Cuisinière,' L'école de cuisine, 10 April 1901.

45 'Boîte aux lettres: A plusieurs abonnées de province', L'école de cuisine, 10 May 1900.

46 'Boîte aux lettres: M. V. de C…,San Sebastian,' L'école de cuisine, 10 April 1904; 'Boîte aux lettres: Mme. A, Italie', L'école de cuisine, 25 April 1904; 'Boîte aux lettres: S. R. y V., Buenos Ayres', L'école de cuisine, 10 May 1903.

47 Correspondence of Madame Peter, Présidente de La Société secours mutuels 'La Cuisinière' to the Ministère de l'Intérieure (Travail et de la Prévoyance), 25 July 1908, 19760252/7, AN.

48 Maguelonne Toussaint-Samat, Histoire de la cuisine bourgeoise du Moyen Age à nos jours (Paris: Albin Michel, 2001).

49 Alain Drouard, 'Cuisiniers et cuisinières de maison bourgeoise (France, XIXème-XXème siècle)', Food and History, 15.1-2 (2017), 255-72; Curnonsky and Marcel Rouff, La France gastronomique: guides des merveilles culinaires et des bonnes auberges françaises Paris, 1921-1928.

50 Pierre Chatelain, 'Petites Carolines', in La Pâtisserie bourgeoise: biscuits, brioches, madeleines, crèmes, tartes et tartelettes…, by Auguste Colombié (Meulan: A Rety, 1906), p. 215.

Sustainable Gastronomy: Power and Energy Use in Food

Christian Reynolds

Power. **Noun**. Energy that is produced by mechanical, electrical, or other means and used to operate a device.
Power. **Verb**. Supply (a device) with mechanical or electrical energy.
Sustainable. **Adjective**. 1. Able to be maintained at a certain rate or level. 2. Conserving an ecological balance by avoiding depletion of natural resources.

– Lexipro.com

Globally, food production accounts for 70% of water use, 90% of land use, and 30% of greenhouse gas emissions (Brodt, Chernow, and Feenstra 2007; Clune, Crossin, and Verghese 2017; FAO 2012; Hendrickson 1994; Poore and Nemecek 2018; Steinhart and Steinhart, 1974; Whiffen and Bobroff 1993; Woods and others 2010). On the current trajectory, food production will need to increase by 60-100% in the next thirty-five years, posing questions for the sustainability and viability of such a future food system. Concurrently, present food consumption patterns cause large environmental and societal issues, including health problems. The UK obesity epidemic costs £6 billion a year and is linked to diet and lifestyle choices.

Many (myself included) have suggested that we should aspire to move the population towards a healthy sustainable diet (Aleksandrowicz and others 2016; Green and others 2015; Macdiarmid and others 2012; Perignon and others 2017; Reynolds and others 2014, 2019; van Dooren and others 2015).

Most recently a ground-breaking report has been jointly published by the EAT forum and the *Lancet* (Willett and others 2019). This EAT-Lancet report has proposed a global, healthy, sustainable diet, which would provide for not only human health but also a healthy planet. The main recommendations are to increase consumption of healthy foods (such as vegetables, fruits, whole grains, legumes, and nuts), and to decrease consumption of unhealthy foods (such as red meat, sugar, and refined grains).

However, a critique of the EAT-Lancet diet is that it lacks consideration of local and traditional diets, foodways, or systems of production, and the report has limited suggestions for how the suggested global, healthy, sustainable diet could actually be implemented (Edman and others 2019; Jonas 2019; Torjesen 2019).

In addition, there are also only two mentions of 'cooking' within the EAT-Lancet report. First, cookery is mentioned in relation to the sustainability and healthiness of using different oils. Second, there is discussion of the role chefs can have in championing a healthy, sustainable diet, through designing new menus, being a voice in national public campaigns, and leading peer education (Chefs Manifesto 2017; Culinary Institute of America and Harvard T.H. Chan School of Public Health, 2013; Nordic Co-operation 2004; Relais et Chateau and UNESCO 2014; Sustainable Restaurants Association 2018).

This absence of understanding that there might be cultural barriers towards global dietary change – and that cooking is an important aspect of the domestic food system – may be due to the EAT-Lancet report being written primarily by nutrition, agriculture, and sustainability researchers who are removed from the gastronomy or food studies communities. However, as cooking, food culture, and food history are intrinsically linked to the diets and foods people eat, this lack of discussion in relation to a global diet is problematic. To this end, there needs to be an engagement between gastronomy and the current heathy, sustainable diets interdisciplinary research.

In this paper, I introduce the current multidisciplinary, heathy, sustainable diets research knowledge to the gastronomy community by discussing how power (energy) is used and embodied in food and cookery, and how modifying cookery methods and ingredients can result in reduced environmental impacts. I then use document analysis (as per Higgs 2016; Lamey and Sharpless 2018), to examine how 'sustainable' and 'low carbon' cookbooks communicate, employ, construct, and manipulate the discourse around sustainability and food – and see if they consider the impacts of ingredients and cooking in their recipe and method selection.

257

Power, Energy, Cookery, and Climate Change

Cooking can require large amounts of power or energy use. Although household energy use associated with cooking has more than halved since the 1970s (Cooper and Palmer 2011), home cooking still accounts for 10% of yearly UK household energy use and 20% of peak UK load (DECC 2014; Owen 2012; Palmer and others 2014). In the UK energy is generated from environmentally damaging sources (such as coal and gas) and is linked to greenhouse gas emissions. In 2017 only 18% of the UK's power was from low carbon sources, including nuclear power (BEIS 2018). This means that cooking has a direct negative climate change impact.

The impact of cooking changes with the food cooked and the method of cooking used. Many estimates have the proportion of greenhouse gas emissions from cookery linked to up to 30% to 50% of total greenhouse gas emissions for some foods (Berlin and Sund 2010; Calderón and others 2018; Carlsson-Kanyama and Boström-Carlsson 2001; Carlsson-Kanyama and Faist 2000; Davis and Sonesson 2008; Davis and others 2010; Defra 2008a, 2008b; Foster and others 2006; Mattsson, Nybrant, and Ohlsson 2005; May and others 2013; Muñoz, Milà i Canals, and Fernández-Alba 2010; Reynolds 2017a, 2017b; Rivera and Azapagic 2016; Schmidt Rivera, Espinoza Orias, and Azapagic 2014; Williams, Audsley, and Murray 2006).

Foods with production systems that are linked to producing large amounts of greenhouse gas emissions (such as beef with an average of 28kg of CO_2-eq per kg of bone free meat (Clune, Crossin, and Verghese 2017)), will have a lower proportional impact related to cookery (Reynolds 2017a). However, foods with production systems linked to producing low amounts of greenhouse gas emissions (such as legumes with 0.66 CO_2-eq per kg of edible bean) will have a much higher proportional cookery impact.

The choice of cookery method (and the time spent cooking) is important to the exact amount of energy used and the resulting climatic impact. Ovens are one of the most energy inefficient methods, using 2-2.5 kWh of energy (Newborough and Augood 1999; Whiffen and Bobroff 1993; Wood and Newborough 2003), meaning the act of roasting a casserole for an hour would be 0.56kg of CO_2-eq – the equivalent of driving 1.4 miles (GOV.UK 2018). Likewise, stovetop cookery has a modest energy consumption of 0.7-0.9 kWh, meaning that the greenhouse gas emissions related to the energy used in boiling of pasta for ten minutes (0.042kg of CO_2-eq) is nearly equal to the greenhouse gas emissions produced in the production of the pasta (~0.051 kg of CO_2-eq).

Low energy cooking methods include slow cooking (in an electric slow cooker), microwaves, and – most recently – sous vide cookery. The sous vide (French for 'under vacuum') method has become an increasingly popular form of cooking that provides cooks with exacting control over the 'doneness' and texture of foods (Baldwin 2012). The hospitality industry has used sous vide cookery since the 1970s, with the method having wider industry adoption by the mid-2000s. Since the early 2010s sous vide machines have been available to the global domestic market. The sous vide cooking method involves the placing the raw food in a vacuumed plastic pouch/bag and submerging this in a heated water bath until the internal core temperature reaches the desired temperature for the desired time duration. Reynolds (2017a) found that using sous vide methods with roast beef could reduce cookery related energy use by 18%, and using the sous vide cooking method in combination with organic ingredients and a reduced portion size of beef could further reduce the energy footprint of the production and cooking of roast beef by 53%.

Is There Such a Thing as a Sustainable Cookbook?

Cookbooks are important sources of knowledge that can be used to understand – within the limits of prescriptive instead of descriptive sources – cooking and eating behaviours of the past and present. Cookbooks can reflect (and create) the development of anxieties, trends, and events within society (Albala 2012; Bower 1997; Higgs 2016; Hörander 1981; Mitchell 2001; Theophano 2003). The cookbook is still a relevant medium for information transfer: 21%-54% of UK respondents use cookbooks as their main source for recipes (YouGov 2019). Previous research indicates that cookbooks are both a trusted place to learn to cook and a source of information and recipes later in life (Caraher, Lange, and Dixon 2000). This relevance makes cookbooks' communication of sustainability concepts important as a way to shift cooking and food choices towards sustainable options.

A rapid review was conducted, searching Google books, Booko.com, and Amazon.com using combinations of search terms (sustainable, cookery, cook book, food, low carbon, foot print, planet, diet). Books 'suggested' by search engines (categories as 'Frequently bought together' and 'Customers who viewed this item also viewed') were also added to the sample.

All books in scope were read and then surveyed to determine the number of recipes, the understanding and discussion of the term 'sustainable', the discussion of cooking (or only food selection) as a way to impact sustainability, the restrictions on sources of protein (i.e. vegan, vegetarian, or omnivorous), and the geographic/cuisine types listed. Books which used the term 'sustainable' in a dietary context (i.e. diets that can be kept long term), rather than in an environmental context, were excluded from the review as being outside of scope.

As shown in the table of Appendix 1, twenty-three books were found. Three books did not have any recipes (Gershon 2007; Ghazi and Lewis 2007; Lappe 2010), but were self-described as books that address changes individuals could make towards sustainability and diet. One book was described as manual on preservation methods rather than as a cookbook (Astyk 2009). Five books were published as part of the Rome Sustainable Food Project (Behr 2016; Boswell 2014, 2013; Talbott and Misenti 2010; Talbott 2012).

The oldest of the surveyed books (*Diet for a Small Planet*) was published in 1971 (F.M.   *259* Lappe 1992), this was accompanied by a 'follow up' book (*Recipes for A Small Planet*), from the same publisher, by a different author in 1973 (Ewald 1983), which provided recipes. However, later editions of *Diet for a Small Planet* have included recipes.

Diet for a Small Planet proposes the shifting of diet towards environmental vegetarianism due to concerns that animal-based diets were wasteful and a contributor to global food scarcity. Although there is mention of animal-based diets being high in environmental impact, carbon and greenhouse gasses related to foods are not discussed at all. The diet proposed is focused on combining multiple ('complimentary') sources of plant based protein so that their combined amino acid pattern better matches that required for human health. Recipes provided in *Recipes for A Small Planet* and later editions of *Diet for a Small Planet* are similar to those found in other 'classic' US/UK vegetarian cookbooks of the era (Katzen 1974; Canter 1985), and though legumes and nuts form the majority of the recipes, the geography of cuisine styles represented is large, including middle eastern, Indian, Brazilian, Mexican, Greek, Italian, and 'oriental'. There is no discussion of the environmental impacts of cooking; the books focus on shifting readers from animal-based diets towards environmental vegetarianism.

After the publication of these two books in the 1970s, there is a lapse of over thirty years, with *The Sustainable Kitchen: Passionate Cooking Inspired by Farms, Forests and Oceans* (Stein, Dern, and Hinds 2004), published the year before the Kyoto protocol on climate change was made legally binding. This book provided multiple omnivorous recipes (containing beef), understood 'sustainable cuisine' to be 'local' and small scale (supporting Community Supported Agriculture), and asked the cooks to understand ingredients (and their complex production processes and histories). It also highlighted that sustainable food needed to be more than more than just low environmental impact, but also needed to sustain heritage and community economies. It did not mention the environmental impacts of cookery method and energy use.

The next books published were *The Low-Carbon Diet* (Ghazi and Lewis 2007) and *Low Carbon Diet: A 30 Day Program to Lose 5000 Pounds* (Gershon 2007) published the same year as the fourth Assessment Report of the International Panel of Climate Change (IPCC 2007). However, neither of these books contain recipes but instead provide advice on how to lower carbon footprints (including changing cooking methods).

From 2008 onwards greater numbers of 'sustainable' and 'low carbon' recipes were published. The majority were omnivorous recipes (containing beef or lamb), with only two vegetarian and no vegan recipe books. In addition, none of the books list the actual amount of carbon embodied in their recipes but instead ask the readers to change behaviours and embrace concepts such as using leftovers, shopping organic, buying local, practicing mindful eating, and eating seasonally. The cuisine types offered are either distinct (i.e. Indian or Italian) or pitched as multi-cultural, modern American, or modern British. Some of latest published (2017 and later) cookbooks feature text, images, and recipes similar to those found in contemporary 'wellness' cookbooks of the same time period.

260

The discussion of the environmental impacts of different cooking method is only discussed in three of the books. However, even in cookbooks that alert the reader to the impact of different methods, the publication of recipes featuring energy inefficient cooking methods (such as baking and roasting) is common. Likewise, the use of beef and lamb in the majority of omnivorous 'sustainable' cookbooks seems misaligned with the large environmental impacts of these foods – even if some of the cookbooks alert the reader to these impacts.

In all books, the selection of food, dietary choice, and (to some extent) cooking was discussed and framed as an act of rebellion and protest, a decision that individuals could make to change themselves, society, and the planet. However, this review shows that many of the books may not have the best advice or evidence integrated into their recipes (such as eating beef and lamb and using high-impact cooking methods). Part of this problem must be due to the difficulty for food writers to source open and accessible information of food and cooking's environmental impacts – which is often trapped behind paywalls and hidden in technical manuals.

In this respect, it could be understood that just as the EAT-Lancet report was lacking in the perspectives from the gastronomy community, the cookbooks reviewed are lacking the scientific evidence with which to ground their recipes and advice. If we are to encourage the world to adopt a sustainable gastronomy and create a sustainable food system, both parties must begin to share their collective expertise for equal benefit.

Appendix 1

A table listing the twenty-three 'sustainable' cookbooks found in the Rapid Review. (Please note that full analysis of these texts is intended in another publication.)

Author and publication year (of edition studied)	Title	Discussion of cooking method impacts	Vegan, Vegetarian, Omnivorous
F.M. Lappe 1992 (originally 1971)	*Diet for a Small Planet*	No	Vegetarian
Ewald 1983 (originally 1973)	*Recipes For A Small Planet*	No	Vegetarian
Ghazi and Lewis 2007	*The Low-Carbon Diet*	No	NA
Cool 2008	*Simply Organic: A Cookbook for Sustainable, Seasonal, and Local Ingredients*	No	Omnivore (contains beef)
Astyk 2009	*Independence Days: A Guide to Sustainable Food Storage & Preservation*	Yes	Omnivore
Bhattacharya 2014	*Spices & Seasons: Simple, Sustainable Indian Flavors*	No	Omnivore (contains lamb)
A. Lappe 2010	*Diet For A Hot Planet: The Climate Crisis At The End Of Your Fork And What You Can Do About It*	No	NA
Koch and Hough 2012	*The Clean Plates Cookbook: Sustainable, Delicious, and Healthier Eating for Every Body*	Yes	Omnivore (contains beef)
Henry 2010	*Plenty – Good Uncomplicated Food for the Sustainable Kitchen*	No	Omnivore (contains beef)
Gershon 2007	*Low Carbon Diet: A 30 Day Program to Lose 5000 Pounds*	No	NA
Dudley 2017	*Land & Sea: Secrets to Simple, Sustainable, Sensational Food*	No	Omnivore (contains chicken and fish, no beef/lamb)
Stein, Dern, and Hinds 2004	*The Sustainable Kitchen: Passionate Cooking Inspired by Farms, Forests and Oceans*	No	Omnivore (contains beef)
Newgent 2009	*The Big Green Cookbook: Hundreds of Planet-pleasing Recipes and Tips for a Luscious, Low-carbon Lifestyle*	Yes	Omnivore (contains beef)
Woodvine 2011	*Didsbury Dinners: The Low-Carbon Community Cookbook*	No	Vegetarian. Local. Low carbon
Duncan and others 2011	*The Sustainable Table*	Yes	Omnivore (contains beef)

Talbott 2012	*Zuppe: Soups from the Kitchen of the American Academy in Rome (Rome Sustainable Food Project)*	No	Omnivore (contains beef)
Boswell 2013	*Pasta: Recipes from the Kitchen of the American Academy in Rome (Rome Sustainable Food Project)*	No	Omnivore (contains beef)
Boswell 2014	*Verdure: Vegetable Recipes from the Kitchen of the American Academy in Rome (Rome Sustainable Food Project)*	No	Omnivore (contains beef)
Talbott and Misenti 2010	*Biscotti: Recipes From The Kitchen Of The American Academy In Rome (Rome Sustainable Food Project)*	No	Omnivore
Behr 2016	*Carne: Meat Recipes from the Kitchen of the American Academy in Rome (Rome Sustainable Food Project)*	No	Omnivore (contains beef)
Van Huis, Van Gurp, and Dicke 2016	*The Insect Cookbook: Food for a Sustainable Planet*	No	Omnivore
Wells 2012	*The Small Planet Vegetarian Cookbook: Planet-Friendly Global Mezze*	No	Vegetarian
Australian Women's Weekly Staff 2016	*The Sustainable Cookbook*	No	Omnivore (contains beef)

References

Albala, K. 2012. 'Cookbooks as Historical Documents', in *The Oxford Handbook of Food History*, ed. by J.M. Pilcher (Oxford: Oxford University Press, Oxford)

Aleksandrowicz, L., and others. 2016. 'The Impacts of Dietary Change on Greenhouse Gas Emissions, Land Use, Water Use, and Health: A Systematic Review', *PLoS One* 11.e0165797 <doi.org/10.1371/journal.pone.0165797>

Astyk, S. 2009. *Independence Days: A Guide to Sustainable Food Storage & Preservation* (Gabriola Island, BC: New Society Publishers)

Australian Women's Weekly Staff. 2016. *The Sustainable Cookbook* (Sydney: Bauer Media Books)

Baldwin, D.E. 2012. 'Sous Vide Cooking: A Review', *International Journal of Gastronomy and Food Science*, 1, 15-30 <doi.org/10.1016/j.ijgfs.2011.11.002>

Behr, C. 2016. *Carne: Meat Recipes from the Kitchen of the American Academy in Rome* (Rome Sustainable Food Project) (New York: The Little Bookroom)

BEIS, 2018. *UK Energy in Brief 2018* (London: UK Department of Business, Energy, & Industrial Strategy)

Berlin, J., and V. Sund. 2010. *Environmental Life Cycle Assessment (LCA) of Ready Meals*, SIK Report No. 804 2010 <http://www.sik.se/archive/pdf-filer-katalog/SR804.pdf> [accessed 26 May 2019].

Bhattacharya, R. 2014. *Spices & Seasons: Simple, Sustainable Indian Flavors* (New York: Hippocrene Books)

Boswell, C. 2013. *Pasta: Recipes from the Kitchen of the American Academy in Rome (Rome Sustainable Food Project)* (New York: Little Bookroom)

Boswell, C. 2014. *Verdure: Vegetable Recipes from the Kitchen of the American Academy in Rome (Rome Sustainable Food Project)* (New York: Little Bookroom)

Bower, A. 1997. *Recipes For Reading: Community Cookbooks, Stories, Histories* (Amherst, MA: University Of Massachusetts Press)

Brodt, S., E. Chernoh, and G. Feenstra. 2007. 'Assessment of Energy Use and Greenhouse Gas Emissions in the Food System: A Literature Review', *Agricultural Sustainability Institute, University of California, Davis* <https://asi.ucdavis.edu/sites/g/files/dgvnsk5751/files/inline-files/litreview-assessmentofenergy-use.pdf> [accessed 26 May 2019]

Calderón, L.A., and others. 2018. 'Environmental Impact of a Traditional Cooked Dish at Four Different Manufacturing Scales: From Ready Meal Industry and Catering Company to Traditional Restaurant and Homemade', *International Journal of Life Cycle Assessment*, 23, 811-23 <doi.org/10.1007/s11367-017-1326-7>

Canter, D.S. 1985. *The Cranks Recipe Book* (London: Grafton)

Caraher, M., T. Lange, and P. Dixon. 2000. 'The Influence of TV and Celebrity Chefs on Public Attitudes and Behavior among the English Public', *Journal for the Study of Food and Society*, 4, 27-46 <doi.org/10.2752/152897900786690805>

Carlsson-Kanyama, A., and K. Boström-Carlsson. 2001. *Energy Use for Cooking and Other Stages in the Life Cycle of Food – A Study of Wheat, Spaghetti, Pasta, Baley, Rice, Potatoes, Couscous and Mashed Potatoes* (Stockholm: Stockholms universitet)

Carlsson-Kanyama, A., and M. Faist. 2000. *Energy Use in the Food Sector: A Data Survey* (Stockholm: Swiss Federal Institute of Technology, Stockholm University)

Chefs Manifesto. 2017. *Food Is Life: The Global Goals* (Stockholm: Chefs Manifesto Network)

Clune, S., E. Crossin, and K. Verghese. 2017. 'Systematic Review of Greenhouse Gas Emissions for Different Fresh Food Categories', *Journal of Cleaner Production*, 140.2, 766-83. <doi.org/10.1016/j.jclepro.2016.04.082>

Cool, J.Z. 2008. *Simply Organic: A Cookbook for Sustainable, Seasonal, and Local Ingredients* (San Francisco: Chronicle Books)

Cooper, I., and J. Palmer. 2011. *Great Britain's Housing Energy Fact File* (London: UK Department of Energy and Climate Change)

Culinary Institute of America and Harvard T.H. Chan School of Public Health. 2013. 'Menus of Change', *The Culinary Institute of America* <http://www.menusofchange.org/> [accessed 26 May 2019]

Davis, J., and U. Sonesson. 2008. 'Life Cycle Assessment of Integrated Food Chains – A Swedish Case Study of Two Chicken Meals', *International Journal of Life Cycle Assessment*, 13, 574-84 <doi.org/10.1007/s11367-008-0031-y>

Davis, J., and others. 2010. 'Environmental Impact of Four Meals with Different Protein Sources: Case Studies in Spain and Sweden', *Food Research International*, 43.7, 1874-84 <doi.org/10.1016/j.foodres.2009.08.017>

DECC. 2014. Powering the Nation 2: Electricity Use in Homes and How to Reduce It (London: DECC and DEFRA)

Defra. 2008a. FO0409 *Understanding the GHG Impacts of Food Preparation and Consumption in the Home. Phase 2* (London: Defra) <http://sciencesearch.defra.gov.uk/Document.aspx?Document=FO0409_8192_FRP.pdf> [accessed 26 March 2020]

Defra. 2008b. FO0406 *Understanding the GHG Impacts of Food Preparation and Consumption in the Home* (London: Defra) <http://sciencesearch.defra.gov.uk/Document.aspx?Document=FO0406_7256_ABS.doc> [accessed 26 March 2020]

Dudley, A. 2017. *Land & Sea: Secrets to Simple, Sustainable, Sensational Food* (London: Orion)

Duncan, C. H., and others. 2011. *The Sustainable Table* (Port Melbourne: Yaubula)

Edman, S., and others. 2019. '*En global diet skulle leda till katastrof*', *Dagens Nyheter* <https://www.dn.se/debatt/repliker/en-global-diet-skulle-leda-till-katastrof/> [accessed 26 May 2019]

Ewald, E.B. 1983. *Recipes for a Small Planet* (New York: Ballantine Books)

FAO. 2012. *Energy-Smart Food at FAO: An Overview* (Rome: FAO)

Foster, C., and others. 2006. *Environmental Impacts of Food Production and Consumption: Final Report to the Department for Environment Food and Rural Affairs* (London, Manchester Business School, Defra)

Gershon, D. 2007. *Low Carbon Diet: A 30 Day Program to Lose 5000 Pounds* (White River Junction, VT: Chelsea Green Publishing)

Ghazi, P., and R. Lewis. 2007. *The Low-Carbon Diet* (London: Short)

GOV.UK. 2018. 'Greenhouse Gas Reporting: Conversion Factors 2018', *GOV.UK* <https://www.gov.uk/government/publications/greenhouse-gas-reporting-conversion-factors-2018> [6 February 2019]

Green, R., and others. 2015. 'The Potential to Reduce Greenhouse Gas Emissions in the UK through Healthy and Realistic Dietary Change', *Climate Change*, 129, 253-65 <doi.org/10.1007/s10584-015-1329-y>

Hendrickson, J. 1994. 'Energy Use in the U.S. Food System: a Summary of Existing Research and Analysis', *Center for Integrated Agricultural Systems, University of Wisconsin, Madison* <https://www.cias.wisc.edu/wp-content/uploads/2008/07/energyuse.pdf> [accessed 26 May 2019]

Henry, D. 2010. *Plenty – Good Uncomplicated Food for the Sustainable Kitchen* (London: Mitchell Beazley)

Higgs, A. 2016. 'Margarine for Butter: Budget Cooking in America', *Graduate Journal of Food Studies*, 2.2 <https://gradfoodstudies.org/2016/07/01/margarine-for-butter-budget-cooking-in-america/> [accessed 26 May 2019]

Hörander, E. 1981. 'The Recipe Book as a Cultural and Socio-Historical Document: On the Value of Manuscript Recipe Books as Sources', in *Food in Perspective: Proceedings of the Third International Conference on Ethnological Food Research*, ed. by A. Fenton and T.M. Owen (Edinburgh: John Donald Publishers), pp. 119-144

IPCC. 2007. Climate Change 2007: *Mitigation. Contribution of Working Group III to the Fourth Assessment Report of the Intergovernmental Panel on Climate Change* (Cambridge: Cambridge University Press)

Jonas, T. 2019. 'Then They Buy You – the Eat-Lancet Commission Report on Healthy Diets', *Australian Food Sovereignty Alliance* <https://afsa.org.au/blog/2019/02/11/then-they-buy-you-the-eat-lancet-commission-report-on-healthy-diets/> [accessed 26 May 2019]

Katzen, M. 1974. *The Moosewood Cookbook* (Berkeley, CA: Ten Speed Press)

Koch, J., and J.S. Hough. 2012. *The Clean Plates Cookbook: Sustainable, Delicious, and Healthier Eating for Every Body* (Philadelphia: Running Press Book Publishers)

Lamey, A., and I. Sharpless. 2018. 'Making the Animals on the Plate Visible: Anglophone Celebrity Chef Cookbooks Ranked by Sentient Animal Deaths', *Food Ethics*, 2, 1-21. <doi.org/10.1007/s41055-018-0024-x>

Lappe, A. 2010. *Diet For A Hot Planet: The Climate Crisis At The End Of Your Fork And What You Can Do About It* (New York: Bloomsbury)

Lappe, F.M. 1992. *Diet For A Small Planet* (New York: Ballantine Books)

Macdiarmid, J.I., and others. 2012. 'Sustainable Diets for the Future: Can We Contribute to Reducing Greenhouse Gas Emissions by Eating a Healthy Diet?', *American Journal of Clinical Nutrition*, 96, 632-39 <doi.org/10.3945/ajcn.112.038729>

Mattsson, B., T. Nybrant, and T. Ohlsson. 2005. 'Industrial Processing versus Home Cooking : An Environmental Comparison between Three Ways to Prepare a Meal', *AMBIO: A Journal of the Human Environment,* 34.4-5, 414-21.

May, D., and others. 2013. *Energy Dependency and Food Chain Security* (London: Defra), pp. 1-41.

Mitchell, J. 2001. 'Cookbooks as a Social and Historical Document: A Scottish Case Study', *Food Service Technology*, 1, 13-23 <doi.org/10.1046/j.1471-5740.2001.00002.x>

Muñoz, I. L. Milà i Canals, and A.R. Fernández-Alba, 2010. 'Life Cycle Assessment of the Average Spanish diet Including Human Excretion', *International Journal of Life Cycle Assessment*, 15.8, 794-805 <doi.org/10.1007/s11367-010-0188-z>

Newborough, M., and P. Augood. 1999. 'Demand-Side Management Opportunities for the UK Domestic Sector', *IEE Proceedings: Generation, Transmission, and Distribution*, 146, 282-93 <doi.org/10.1049/ip-gtd:19990318>

Newgent, J. 2009. *The Big Green Cookbook: Hundreds Of Planet-pleasing Recipes And Tips For A Luscious,*

Low-carbon Lifestyle (Hoboken, NJ: Houghton Mifflin Harcourt)

Nordic Co-operation. 2004. 'The New Nordic Food Manifesto', *Nordic Co-operation* <https://www.norden.org/en/information/new-nordic-food-manifesto> [accessed 26 May 2019]

Owen, P. 2012. *Powering the Nation-Household Electricity-Using Habits Revealed* (London: Defra)

Palmer, J., and others. 2014. *Further Analysis of the Household Electricity Survey: Energy Use at Home: Models, Labels and Unusual Appliances* (London: DECC and Defra)

Perignon, M., and others. 2017. 'Improving Diet Sustainability through Evolution of Food Choices: Review of Epidemiological Studies on the Environmental Impact of Diets', *Nutrition Review*, 75.1, 2-17 <doi.org/10.1093/nutrit/nuw043>

Poore, J., and T. Nemecek. 2018. 'Reducing Food's Environmental Impacts through Producers and Consumers', *Science,* 360.6392, 987-92 <doi.org/10.1126/science.aaq0216>

Relais et Château. 2014. *Le Manifeste: un monde meilleur, par la table et l'hospitalité* (Paris: Relais et Châeau)

Reynolds, C.J. 2017a. 'Energy Embodied in Household Cookery: The Missing Part of a Sustainable Food System? Part 2: A Life Cycle Assessment of Roast Beef and Yorkshire Pudding', *Energy Procedia*, 123, 228-34 <doi.org/10.1016/j.egypro.2017.07.248>

Reynolds, C.J. 2017b. 'Energy Embodied in Household Cookery: The Missing Part of a Sustainable Food System? Part 1: A Method to Survey and Calculate Representative Recipes', *Energy Procedia*, 123, 220-27 <doi.org/10.1016/j.egypro.2017.07.245>

Reynolds, C.J., and others. 2014. 'Are the Dietary Guidelines for Meat, Fat, Fruit and Vegetable Consumption Appropriate for Environmental Sustainability? A Review of the Literature', *Nutrients*, 6, 2251-65 <doi.org/10.3390/nu6062251>

Reynolds, C.J., and others. 2019. 'Healthy and Sustainable Diets that Meet Greenhouse Gas Emission Reduction Targets and Are Affordable for Different Income Groups in the UK', *Public Health Nutrition*, 22, 1503-17 <doi.org/10.1017/S1368980018003774>

Rivera, X.C.S., and A. Azapagic. 2016. 'Life Cycle Costs and Environmental Impacts of Production and Consumption of Ready and Home-Made Meals', *Journal of Cleaner Production*, 112, 214-28 <doi.org/10.1016/j.jclepro.2015.07.111>

Schmidt Rivera, X.C., N. Espinoza Orias, and A. Azapagic. 2014. 'Life Cycle Environmental Impacts of Convenience Food: Comparison of Ready and Home-Made Meals', *Journal of Cleaner Production*, 73, 294-309 <doi.org/10.1016/j.jclepro.2014.01.008>

Stein, S., J.H. Dern, and M. Hinds. 2004. *The Sustainable Kitchen: Passionate Cooking Inspired By Farms, Forests And Oceans* (Gabriola Island, BC: New Society Publishers)

Steinhart, J.S., and C.E. Steinhart. 1974. 'Energy Use in the U.S. Food System', *Science*, 184.4134, 307-16 <doi.org/10.1126/science.184.4134.307>

Sustainable Restaurants Association. 2018. 'One Planet Plate', *Sustainable Restaurants Association* <https://oneplanetplate.org> [accessed 26 May 2019]

Talbott, M. 2012. *Zuppe: Soups from the Kitchen of the American Academy in Rome (Rome Sustainable Food Project)* (New York: Little Bookroom)

Talbott, M., and M. Misenti. 2010. *Biscotti: Recipes from the Kitchen of the American Academy in Rome (Rome Sustainable Food Project)* (New York: Little Bookroom)

Theophano, J. 2003. *Eat My Words: Reading Women's Lives Through the Cookbooks They Wrote* (New York: Palgrave Macmillan)

Torjesen, I. 2019. 'WHO Pulls Support from Initiative Promoting Global Move to Plant Based Foods', *BMJ*, 365, l1700 <doi.org/10.1136/bmj.l1700>

Van Huis, A., H. Van Gurp, and M. Dicke. 2016. *The Insect Cookbook: Food for a Sustainable Planet* (New York: Columbia University Press)

van Dooren, C., and others, 2015. 'Combining Low Price, Low Climate Impact and High Nutritional Value in One Shopping Basket through Diet Optimization by Linear Programming', *Sustainability*, 7, 12837-55 <doi.org/10.3390/su70912837>

Wells, T. 2012. *The Small Planet Vegetarian Cookbook* (Northampton: New Internationalist)

Whiffen, H.J., and L.B. Bobroff. 1993. *Managing the Energy Cost of Food*, Report EES-99 (Florida Cooperative Extension Service, Institute of Food and Agricultural Sciences, University of Florida)

Willett, W., and others. 2019. 'Food in the Anthropocene: The EAT-Lancet Commission on Healthy Diets from Sustainable Food Systems', *Lancet*, 393, 447-92 <doi.org/10.1016/S0140-6736(18)31788-4>

Williams, A.G., E. Audsley, and D.L. Sandars. 2006. *Determining the Environmental Burdens and Resource Use in the Production of Agricultural and Horticultural Commodities. Main Report,* Defra Research Project IS0205 (London: Defra)

Wood, G., and M. Newborough. 2003. 'Dynamic Energy-Consumption Indicators for Domestic Appliances: Environment, Behaviour and Design', *Energy and Buildings*, 35, 821-41 <doi.org/10.1016/S0378-7788(02)00241-4>

Woods, J., and others. 2010. 'Energy and the Food System', *Philosophical Transactions of the Royal Society B: Biological Sciences,* 365, 2991-3006. <doi.org/10.1098/rstb.2010.0172>

Woodvine, A. (Ed.). 2011. *Didsbury Dinners: The Low-Carbon Community Cookbook* (New York: Harmony Publishing)

YouGov. 2019. 'Is the Future of Food Flexitarian?', *YouGov* <https://yougov.co.uk/topics/resources/articles-reports/2019/03/18/future-food-flexitarian> [accessed 26 May 2019]

266

Mom vs. the FDA: How One Woman Got the U.S. Food and Drug Administration to Correct Their Evaluation of the Mid-Atlantic Golden Tilefish

Charity Robey

When it comes to wild seafood, the men and women whose lives and livelihoods depend on it are a source of information that government agencies ignore at their peril, for no stakeholder has more at risk in a fishery than the fisher. The commercial fishermen and women of Montauk, New York have a history of pushing back against what they see as ill-informed government regulations going back to the middle of the twentieth century.

In 2003, a group of concerned fishers led by Laurie Nolan conducted a successful campaign to have mid-Atlantic golden tilefish (Figure 1) removed from a list of fish containing high mercury levels. This fish had been added to that list erroneously in 1976 when tilefish from the Gulf of Mexico in the vicinity of oil drilling (which can produce a mercury by-product) had been tested for mercury and found to have high levels. Laurie Nolan's role as David to the FDA's Goliath resulted in what is today a successful and sustainable fishery.

Laurie Nolan, a self-described mom, put new test data together with her understanding of the biology, behaviour, and habitat of the tilefish to convince the FDA to stop listing mid-Atlantic tilefish as having high mercury levels.

Figure 1. Mid-Atlantic golden tilefish (Charity Robey).

Figure 2. The Seacapture steams into Montauk Harbor with Laurie Nolan standing on the jetty to welcome them home (Charity Robey).

Fishing in a Nor'easter

In mid-October of 2018, a vicious Nor'easter was blowing off of Montauk, and Laurie Nolan's 32-year-old son John was in the middle of it. Captaining the 82-foot *Seacapture* together with a crew of three, he made the decision to stay at sea, far enough from shore to ride out the storm safely. This decision added another two days to a trip that had already gone longer than planned. The stakes were high, not only for the lives of the crew members, but also for the livelihood of his family. He had 10,000 kilos of tilefish in the hold.

John Nolan III's cousin and former crewmate Robert Aaronson stood on the Montauk jetty with Laurie Nolan in a stiff cold wind to take in the *Seacapture*'s safe return, passing from the Atlantic Ocean past the boulders and sand of the jetty and into Montauk Harbor (Figure 2). Once the *Seacapture* had passed, they joined the rest of the family at the dock, along with his father, John Nolan II, John III's sister Molly, and his sister Jean's baby, Bodie. Nolan III pointed proudly to the hold, packed full of cleaned, iced fish, and said, 'Oh yeah'.

'We had a little bit of weather,' Nolan III said. 'But we fished every day. We have a good boat for it. We were getting beaten up pretty good, good-sized waves one day. Stuck it out and caught some fish.'[1]

Biology and History of the Mid-Atlantic Golden Tilefish

One of the earliest known records of the presence of the golden tilefish in the North Atlantic was a sighting in the waters south of Nantucket in 1879 by a certain Captain Kirby out of Gloucester. He described it as colourful and highly edible (Figure 3).

Given the scientific name *Lopholatilus Chamealeonticeps* by Goode and Bean, the fish's common name, 'tilefish', is possibly based on the 'tilus' in the scientific name. Three populations of tilefish are known to live in North American ocean waters: those of the mid-Atlantic, South Atlantic, and Gulf of Mexico. The mid-Atlantic tilefish are found far offshore on the edge of the continental shelf and slope from Nova Scotia, Canada to Suriname (Figure 4). The majority of the fishery is concentrated between Nantucket Island, Massachusetts, south to Cape May, New Jersey, and particularly concentrated between the undersea canyons, Hudson and Veatch.[2]

A large and long-lived creature, the tilefish lives in deep water and does not migrate. It reaches reproductive age between two and four, and its life span can extend to over forty years. Atlantic tilefish live at depths of 76 to 365 meters.

Extremely cold weather in the winter of 1882 caused the near extinction of golden tilefish in the North Atlantic, and great numbers of fish floated dead in the Gulf Stream. It is estimated that 10 million to 100 million tilefish died in the cold weather event of 1882. It was not until 1897 that tilefish were seen again in the North Atlantic, and the population gradually came back, building to the point that tilefish were an important

Figure 3. Atlantic tilefish is a colourful and beautiful creature (Charity Robey).

food fish by the middle of the twentieth century.[3] Today, 1.5 million pounds of tilefish are landed in Montauk every year.[4]

A Boat and a Line

When John Nolan started tilefishing in 1978 on *The Rainbowchaser*, a 17-metre fiberglass Bruno & Stillman hull, the fleet was fishing for tilefish with 67-metre sections of line with leaders and J-hooks tied in every three meters.

In the early 1980s, tilefishing out of Montauk was in decline, so John Nolan decided to try bottom fishing in Florida. With Laurie as crew they fished out of Key West, Florida, where fishers were catching tilefish on a longline, using baited hooks that snapped on and off the mainline. This was an extremely labour-intensive way to catch fish, but it got results. John and Laurie returned to Montauk and began to fish side by side with fisherman who were still using the old gear.[5] The new gear outperformed the traditional methods, resulting in much less bycatch and fish that were in much better shape since they were not being beaten up in a net.

In the 1980s the Nolans added a second boat, the *Restless*, and now had two crews on two

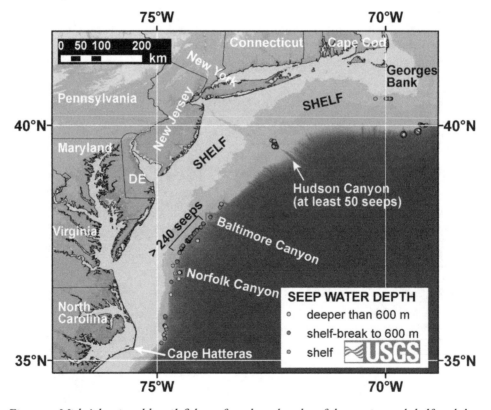

Figure 4. Mid-Atlantic golden tilefish are found on the edge of the continental shelf and slope (courtesy United States Geological Survey).

25-metre boats. When one crew came in, they'd unload, put on fresh provisions and a fresh crew, and send the boat right back out the same night, completing 33 trips a year for up to 330 days. This was the time before quotas, when tilefish were so abundant that the National Oceanic and Atmospheric Administration (NOAA) placed no controls on who could fish for them or limits on how many they could take. In 1999, tilefish were declared over-fished, a management plan went into place in 2001, and the fleet began to consolidate.[6]

When tilefish began to be managed, the Nolans moved from two 25-metre boats to one, the bigger *Seacapture*. 'Once the quotas were in place, we did not need two boats to catch the amount of fish we are allowed to catch,' said Laurie Nolan.

In 2009, an amendment to the tilefish FMP (Fishery Management Plan) implemented an ITQ (Individual Transferable Quota) system. At the start of the fishing year, each vessel was allocated the number of pounds to catch, based on the vessel's past landings.

In the United States, the Magnuson-Stevens Fishery Act of 1976 established a structure of management and regulation for U.S. fisheries between 5 and 321 kilometres off the coast that now controls almost every aspect of commercial and recreational fishing in offshore waters. Eight regional fishery management councils were created with representatives of commercial and recreational fishers, as well as state environmental and conservation representatives. These councils are charged with implementing conservation measures such as permitting and quotas, but they also function as advocates for fishers with the Department of Health and Human Services and the U.S. Food and Drug Administration.

Part of the management plan for tilefish that has been in place since 2000 is annual assessment of the tilefish population using a CPUE (Catch Per Unit Effort), which measures how long it takes fishers to catch their quota. The faster they do so, the greater the population. Other fish species' population are assessed using trawler surveys – boats that fish in the same place and time year-to-year and then assess the population by looking at the change in numbers. Laurie Nolan prefers the CPUE system because it relies on the experience of fishers. 'I think it's a simple and accurate way to assess the health of the tilefish stock, by comparing how quickly the fleet catches the quota,' she said. 'They (fishers) are doing it as a business. They are the best at finding the fish.'

Today, there are more than thirty species of fish that have recovered to the point that they can be fished again, thanks to management of the fisheries. The regulations keep the biomass stock at a certain level and allow permit-holding fishers to harvest the excess.

A 'Mom' vs the FDA

A few years after the mid-Atlantic Fishery Council began managing tilefish, the Nolans, this time with Laurie in the lead, began to effect another important change in the industry. Since the 1970s, the FDA had put all varieties of tilefish in the same category as shark, swordfish, tuna, and king mackerel – fish that contain elevated mercury levels and should not be consumed by pregnant women or small children.[7]

That classification was based on six samples that the FDA found had high levels of mercury in 1976; all came from Gulf of Mexico tilefish, taken in an area where oil drilling – and the dangerous levels of mercury that come with it – were a problem. Tilefish are long-living bottom-dwellers that feed on other bottom-dwelling animals; in this respect they share important characteristics with fish that tend to accumulate high levels of mercury in their flesh.

What Laurie Nolan knew from her years fishing for tilefish in the mid-Atlantic and South Atlantic convinced her that what was true for Gulf of Mexico tilefish in 1976 did not necessarily apply to mid-Atlantic golden tilefish in 2003:

> Tilefish don't migrate up and down the coast. The FDA threw up this blanket warning for nursing mothers, and young children for tilefish. They should have sampled each area if they wanted to warn the public correctly. Worse, the warnings come out again every six months or so, even though they may be working off of very old data. It's ridiculous that they were using data from the 70s and from the Gulf of Mexico, without letting the public know that. They think they are doing their job, but it's not very thorough.[8]

She decided to have tilefish caught by her family tested for mercury. After identifying a lab, Cebam Analytical, an FDA-approved lab, to do the testing, she followed the protocols to the letter: 'We sent twenty samples of twenty different fish sizes; the whole fish was filleted and skinned, then ground up with a sample taken from that. I had to use glass jars with stainless steel lids, keep the fish refrigerated and send the samples overnight in a box with dry ice.'

Her expenses came to $2500 for jars, processing, mailing, and the fee to Cebam Analytical. 'If you can get your species a clean bill of health for $2500 that's worth it,' she insisted. The response from Cebam Analytical, dated January 31, 2003, had several

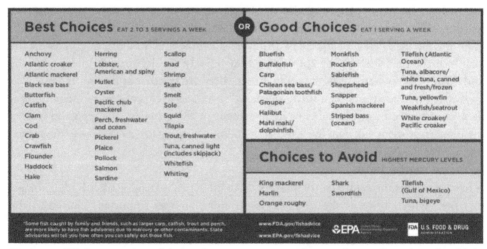

Figure 5. FDA categorizes fish in three groups according to how often they should be consumed. Tilefish is classified under 'Good Choices' (courtesy of the FDA).

pages of data that confirmed what Laurie Nolan had suspected. The independent study by Cebam Analytical, an EPA-certified laboratory, showed mercury concentrations in the tilefish tissue samples at levels between 0.0330% and 0.2668%, well within acceptable levels (Figure 5).

At the time, Laurie was on the Mid-Atlantic Fishery Management Council and brought the results of the tests to their attention. The council got behind her, writing letters to the FDA to push them to reclassify the fish and forcing the FDA to add a line item to the descriptions of tilefish on their websites.[9]

The FDA revised its recommendation on mid-Atlantic golden tilefish in 2004, but the fight is not over. Although they line-itemed mid-Atlantic golden tilefish in their recommendations, many other sites that gather data from them do not distinguish between Gulf and mid-Atlantic tilefish.[10] As Laurie explains, 'If you just google tilefish, you are still going to come up with a mercury warning. Call it mid-Atlantic golden tilefish, and maybe someday people will see.'

Back in 2003 when Laurie Nolan prepared samples from twenty tilefish for testing, she had many pounds of fresh fish left at the end of the day, so she made dinner for her family: 'We had a lot of ground tilefish that day.' She sautéed onions and garlic in olive oil, added them to the ground up meat with some shredded parmesan and diced red peppers. She shaped it into patties, rolled them in panko, and grilled them.

Leadership and Transparency

Sean Barrett is the founder of Dock to Dish, the first community supported fishery in the United States and the only one operating out of Montauk. Until about ten years ago, Montauk was about farming and fishing, but it has recently become better known for its nightlife, although it is still the largest fishing port in New York state. 'You would think, surrounded by water, we would have local fish,' Barrett said, but in the United States, 90% of the seafood consumed is imported, and in New York state at least 95% of seafood is imported.[11]

Dock to Dish sells fresh, sustainable local fish to subscribers, who are generally restaurants and individuals. Their subscribers agree to take a certain amount of sustainably harvested, fresh fish (often including tilefish) without knowing what kind of fish in advance – the true catch of the day. 'We are adamant about having traceability,' said Barrett. 'A QR card goes out with all the Nolan's tilefish. You aim it at your phone and it tells you about the Nolans.'[12]

The Nolans have worked with the same distributor for thirty years, Paul Farnham, who is himself a former tile fisherman and long-time owner/operator of the Montauk Fish Dock. *Seacapture* unloads at the Fish Dock, and Farnham takes it from there, distributing the fish to Gosmans, where it is filleted and sold to local restaurants as well as to Dock to Dish for delivery to their subscribers and corporate clients. Most of it goes to Lockwood (the company that also owns Citarella) at Hunts Point, a large wholesale market in the Bronx where restaurants and seafood shops from all over the Northeast go to buy fish.[13]

Tilefish have a firm texture and pinkish white, dense flesh similar in flavour to lobster (because of their habit of eating crustaceans). A group of Japanese business people approached the Nolans about buying tilefish directly and came to the boat for a tasting, Laurie Nolan was impressed with their gill-to-fin approach to eating the fish: 'They were cooking them up in the galley, sucking the bones and licking the skin. If you fry a tilefish whole, you can devour every last inch of that fish. If you leave the skin and scales on it's a richer flavour, like eating the dark meat of the chicken.'

Dock to Dish played an important role in elevating tilefish in the culinary world. Barrett said, 'Tilefish checked all the boxes. Local, sustainable, line caught and you knew your fishermen.' Chef Dan Barber is a champion of tilefish, which is supplied to Blue Hill at Stone Barns in Tarrytown by Dock to Dish. Dock to Dish also supplies Nolan tilefish to the Google corporate cafeteria in New York, which feeds 5000 employees in the Chelsea office.

Barrett considers himself a comrade in arms with Laurie Nolan: 'We fought for tilefish at the DEC (the state level). Only two years ago a local Long Island councilwoman wanted to publish mercury warnings, without the line item about golden Atlantic tilefish. We are fighting for the same things; Laurie on the Federal level and me on the state level with the DEC.'

Laurie Nolan's leadership has encouraged fishers of the Southern Atlantic tilefish industry to conduct similar testing at their own expense, to determine if those fish contain high levels of mercury, and if not, to push the FDA to reclassify them. As Laurie puts it, 'The FDA can be made to listen to the people who fish,' Laurie said. 'It's great to inform the public, but make it accurate information.'[14]

Conclusion

Wild-caught fish can be a sustainable source of healthy food, but they are under increasing pressure from climate change, pollution and other human activity, and fishers are the most vital stakeholders in this future.

The FDA has developed a system of regional fish councils that includes the voices and experience of fishers. Its work toward re-establishing fish populations, such as sea scallops, bay scallops and tilefish, is an indication of how things can go when the experience of fishers is considered. With increased pressure on wild ocean life, troubling questions about farmed seafood, and a dearth of useable information for consumers about both what kinds of seafood are good to eat and how human activity affects wild fish, the voices and experience of fishermen are ever more vital to understanding the past and future of seafood.

Notes

1 John Nolan III, Captain of the *Seacapture*, personal interview with the author, Montauk, NY, 30 October 2018.

2 K.O. Emery, *Atlantic Continental Shelf and Slope of the United States: Geologic Background*, Geological

Survey Professional Paper 529-A, US Department of the Interior (Washington, DC: US Government Printing Office, 1966) <https://pubs.usgs.gov/pp/0529a/report.pdf> [accessed 29, May 2019].

3   Robert Marsh and others, 'The 1882 Tilefish Kill – a Cold Event in Shelf Waters off the North-Eastern United States?', *Fisheries Oceanography*, 8.1 (1999), 39-49.

4   National Oceanic and Atmospheric Administration, 'Annual Commercial Landing Statistics', *NOAA Fisheries*, US Department of Commerce <https://www.fisheries.noaa.gov/national/commercial-fishing/commercial-landings/annual> [accessed 30 October 2019].

5   Laurie Nolan, co-owner of *Seacapture,* personal interview with the author, Montauk, NY, 22 October 2018, 26 October 2018, 2 April 2019, and 26 April 2019.

6   Letter from Paul Farnham to Daniel T. Furlong, 1 September 1999, in Mid-Atlantic Fishery Management Council, *Tilefish Fishery Management Plan*, Appendices – vol. 2 <https://books.google.com/books?id=Pi83AQAAMAAJ&lpg=PT243&ots=S5lUjtfRq2&dq=Paul%20Farnham%20Fish%20Dock&pg=PT243#v=onepage&q=Paul%20Farnham%20Fish%20Dock&f=false> [accessed 29 May 2019].

7   US Food and Drug Administration, 'Advice about Eating Fish: For Women Who Are or Might Become Pregnant, Breastfeeding Mothers, and Young Children', *FDA.gov*, 2019 <https://www.fda.gov/food/consumers/advice-about-eating-fish > [accessed 29 May, 2019]

8   Laurie Nolan.

9   Laurie Nolan.

10 US Environmental Protection Agency, 'EPA-FDA Fish Advice: Technical Information', EPA.gov < https://www.epa.gov/fish-tech/epa-fda-fish-advice-technical-information> [accessed on 30 May 2019].

11 Sean Barrett, Dock to Dish, personal interview with the author, Montauk, NY, 26 April 2019.

12 Sean Barrett.

13 Paul Farnham, owner of Montauk Fish Dock, personal interview with the author, Montauk, NY, 2 April 2019 and 26 April 2019.

14 Laurie Nolan.

Perceptions of Food and Italy's Colonization of Libya, 1911-1912

Or Rosenboim

What role did food imagery play in the Italian liberal imperial project in the twentieth century? This question provides the setting for this research project, which seeks to link food studies, intellectual history, and the history of imperialism and empire. Through the historical case study of Italy's liberal empire, this essay reflects on perceptions of agricultural utopia, plenty, and food abundance as motivations for modern colonization. Such images of food reflect Italy's quest for power in the Mediterranean, understood in terms of food abundance and agricultural fertility.

In 1911, Italy's liberal government embarked on a military campaign to conquer the Ottoman provinces of Tripoli and Cyrenaica, which were later named Libya. The war did not result in effective colonization, and guerrilla battles continued until 1923. Despite Italy's limited military and industrial power, the colonization of this North African territory had been one of Italy's political objectives since the late nineteenth century. The acquisition of a fertile colony would, Italians hoped, raise their international prestige and economic resources. The imperial project was also motivated by the aim to provide an outlet to the hungry farmers of southern Italy, who were emigrating in large numbers to the Americas. Thus, the colonization of Libya was publicly discussed in terms of food, fertility, and abundance.

Italian academics, journalists, and intellectuals depicted Libya as a food heaven in a utopian vision based on agricultural plenty. This vision contrasted with the image of Southern Italy as a space of hunger and scarcity, which were deemed the main cause of the significant waves of emigration from Italy abroad. Emigration was seen as a national shame, draining Italy's demographic and economic resources. Empire was thus envisioned as a necessary solution to ensure food security, by directing the flood of emigrants to plentiful colonies. The traditional trope of the New World as the promised land of opportunity was therefore substituted by a new image of North Africa as a land of fertile soil and food plenty.

The paper looks at writings by Italian intellectuals and journalists to trace the emergence and development of this utopian vision of Libya. The term 'utopia' was coined in 1516 by Thomas More, indicating a non-place, or a non-existent good place. As Quentin Skinner has suggested, More's utopian vision was not meant for realization: it was an ideal rather than a plan for action.[1] For More, utopia served to criticize his own society. Yet the term has since been extended to imagined alternative existences, good places, and ideal societies. Utopian thinking raises a fundamental issue: the relationship between experience and imagination. Utopias are constructed by extending the limits of the possible beyond the existing present, but this act of imagining typically does not lose touch with reality. Rather, utopias often serve as implicit or explicit criticism of existing reality. Utopia is therefore an effective means to project contemporary and contingent political concerns onto an imagined temporality and spatiality.

Italian authors in the early twentieth century can be inserted into an earlier tradition of 'booster literature', to use the term coined by historian James Belich.[2] This literary form sought to depict colonies as ideal destinations for emigration, 'exaggerating and sometimes fabricating the realities in order to justify imperial and colonial projects'.[3] While, as Belich suggests, in the British case the phenomenon of emigration within the imperial sphere was spontaneous and free from government control, Italian governments considered the creation of a colonial empire as a potential solution to the ongoing problem of emigration to other destinations in Europe and the Americas. Belich outlines an ideology of 'settlerism', both formal and informal, which was manifested in 'booster literature': books, pamphlets, newspapers, and journal articles surged after 1815. The 'Garden of Eden', paradise, and biblical lands were frequently invoked in the British booster literature, reflecting nineteenth century religious sensibilities. Inevitably, the distance between the literary descriptions and the actual places was significant, leading to sceptical and satirical contemporary reception. As we shall see, hyperbolic and exaggerated descriptions were not in short supply in the Italian booster literature; yet this form of literature was capable of generating a strong sense of nationalism and a significant degree of popular support for the colonial enterprise to convince the government of its feasibility and desirability.

277

In the context of the Italian colonial war for the conquest of Tripoli and Cyrenaica in 1911-1912, the use of utopian thinking was widespread as a means of rounding support and legitimacy for the war.[4] Utopian thinking had a dual function in this context: highlighting the desirable attributes of the potential African colony and underlining the social, economic, and political shortcomings of Italy. In this sense, Libya served as a non-place, a utopian space capable of containing the ideal – and idealized – imagined projections of a better future. Lack of systematic knowledge of the North African territory did not hinder the development and elaboration of utopian vision; on the contrary, liberated from the burden of empirical proof, Italian writers adopted a lenient relationship with the truth when imagining the Libyan utopia.

One of the main aspects of the Libyan utopia was food. In the press, the colony was described as a particularly promising and fertile land, often in contrast to reports from Libya and scholarly studies of the local geology and agriculture, which undermined the potential of the colony to deliver on the promise of food plenty. Nonetheless, this idea remained a powerful rhetoric in the context of Italy's liberal empire, as well as in the later fascist phase of imperialism.

How did ideas about food shape international visions in the twentieth century and reveal the importance of perceptions of food to political decision-making and imperial expansion? Food provided a strong motivation for colonization in ancient times, when empires were based on agricultural resources. Yet the interplay of food and empire in modern times remains less explored by scholars today. I investigate the modern aspects of the links between food and power in the international sphere by showing the ways in which ideas about food generated impulses of expansion and colonization. Rather than focusing on the actual existence of agricultural resources and food, the Italian protagonists of this study sought to create and shape perceptions of food plenty for use as motivation for empire.

The interplay of ideas and materiality forms a key aspect of their writings, providing a meaningful contribution to the contemporary study of food history and intellectual history. These two scholarly fields contain great potential for dialogue, which has not been so far realized. I draw on the interpretative methods of intellectual history, in particular on the contextualist approach advanced by Skinner, to locate ideas about food in their historical context and understand them as parts of a wider debate about food, empire, and power in the early twentieth century. Through the Italian case study, this research will examine how ideas about food shaped international visions of empire and world order before the First World War.

Utopias of Food in Tripoli and Cyrenaica

The construction of utopian visions of Tripoli and Cyrenaica was not, strictly speaking, based on a factual analysis of empirical reality. Emotions such as hope, enthusiasm, pride, and desire played a significant part in the formation of the utopian visions, both before and after the beginning of the war. Nonetheless, many of the proponents of such visions were writers who travelled to the provinces and could boast direct and personal knowledge of these regions. As we shall see, a visit to Tripolitania and Cyrenaica was no guarantee of a truthful rendition of the economic, cultural, and political life of the region, as the writers projected on the reality they saw an idealized vision that served their own purposes as advocates of empire. The result was complex and at times contradictory utopias, based on a mixture of romanticized agricultural fertility and a racialized vision of modern technology.

Enrico Corradini (1865-1931), a leading Italian novelist and journalist, was an admirer of Gabriele D'Annunzio, who developed a right-wing nationalist vision of Italy's future as an imperial power.[5] In 1910 he was among the founders of the Italian Nationalist Association, which provided enthusiastic support for the colonization of Libya.[6] The association soon became an influential lobby in favour of Italian imperialism, with Corradini serving as its most vociferous member. In his articles for the periodical *L'idea nazionale* and his best-selling books, Corradini sought to convince his readers that the colonization of Tripoli and Cyrenaica was a worthy project. His nationalist campaign was effective in reaching not only the wider public but also the ears of policy-makers and politicians, who felt inclined to take his demands into consideration.

One of the key points in Corradini's pro-imperial propaganda is the construction of a dual vision of a food utopia in Libya, which the Italian colonizer had the right – and the duty – to exploit. The duality of his vision consisted in emphasizing the fertility of the land while highlighting the local population's incapacity to properly develop it. Alongside the descriptions of plentiful abundance of food in orchards and desert oasis villages, Corradini dramatically invoked hungry local children, who apparently called to him in Italian: 'for the Holy Lord, *we haven't eaten*, viva Italy, viva the King, viva the Statute, give me a penny!'[7] Italy had, therefore, a duty to conquer the fertile lands to maximize their food-production potential using modern means. It was a civilizing mission based on an agricultural utopia of food that could only be created using modern knowledge, tools, and skills to which Italy had access.

A visit to Tripoli before the Italo-Turkish war generated, for Corradini, an ambivalent impression of 'beauty and misery'. He saw tall palms between the desert and the oasis, and underneath them 'olive trees laden with olives, a fig marking the border of the oasis reaching deep into the desert with its roots'. Yet when he reached the city, he saw 'a human herd with their mouths all green for all the grass devoured'.[8] The image of the bestiality of the locals, who eat indigestible grass for lack of better food, is neatly contrasted with the image of fig and olive trees, ancient symbols of plenty. The message is clear: the land promises abundant food, but only to those capable of cultivating and nurturing it.

At the market place, Corradini was impressed by the 'minute information of the fertility of the Tripoli soil' provided by his guides, members of the Dante Alighieri society, a world-spanning association founded in 1889 to promote Italian culture and initially also national interests. He was told that 'vegetables could be collected twice a year, in January-February as well as June-July, that the watermelons attained an extraordinary size, and that citrus fruit was exported even to Sicily'. Corradini was impressed not only by the abundance of food, but also by its 'extraordinary', almost miraculous qualities: the size was indicative of unusual fertility, which rendered Tripoli particularly desirable from the point of view of agriculture and food-production. Other local residents, the Jewish Nahum family, showed him local 'vineyards with beautiful grapes, palms, figs, quince, great rose gardens, jasmine, oleanders, mulberry, olives, corn'.[9]

The pleasant and appealing landscape that Corradini described, and encouraged the Italians to conquer, encapsulated a pre-modern, uncontaminated perception of food. Nutrition was based on the provision of the land: fresh fruit and vegetables represent the key ingredients of the Mediterranean diet that would relieve the hungry, both Italians and locals. No reference was ever made to cooked food. While Corradini's travel account is doubtlessly marked by a touch of 'orientalism', to follow Edward Said's term, he was also astute in highlighting the similarities between Italy and Libya.[10] By listing the available crops of Tripoli and Cyrenaica, he tacitly suggested their resemblance to familiar crops in Italy, thus creating a unified mental space that includes both the north and the south shore of the Mediterranean. The idealized vision of food and plenty serves, therefore, not only to ignite the pro-imperialist Italian imagination, but also to bridge over the sea and create a united mental-political – and culinary – space in the region.

On the road between the desert oases, Corradini saw caravans loaded with bags of flour, protected by armed guards, as well as 'flourishing pastures'. So great was his enthusiasm for local gardens he had seen that he chose to cite directly from his travel notepad, to retain the vivacity and stupor of the first gaze:

> the gardens are in the middle of the desert. There is a greenhouse of plants. Green, magnificent mulberry. Vine with stupendous bunches [of grapes]. No disease. One should see how the desert arena would become, when cultivated! Olives, apples. Under the plants the soil transfigures into compact land, grassy, excellent [...] tomatoes. It is a reddish soil, very fine, without any rocks. What great olive trees, unpruned, wild, loaded with olives! [...] But what desert! We are in the promised land. There is no disease in the vineyard: the leaf is pure, clean, without bubbles, never dry, very green.

The image emerging from Corradini's account is a neat opposition between the natural abundance of food in Tripoli and the human incapacity to make use of it. What it lacked, for him, was modern intervention in the form of 'civil institution': the locals live of the land 'which they don't know how to cultivate'. Hunger was not to be blamed on lack of natural resources or rainfall, but on 'agricultural unskilfulness' of a 'primitive people cut off the human consortium'. Tripoli embodied, for him, a space of discontinuity within the sphere of civilization: while Tunisia and Egypt could be considered civilized, Tripoli was 'a country alone in the world, like a wild territory, yet undiscovered'. Civilization meant, for Corradini, participating in an international society of knowledge, skill, and technology which embodied his sense of modernity. Those who remained outside of this sphere of modern civilization were doomed to live 'with the failing means of subsistence provided by solitude'.[11] It was, he argued, Italy's duty to become masters of the territory and reconnect the fertile yet underdeveloped land to the 'human consortium' of civilization.

Corradini's argument can be read as another link in the chain of Saint-Simonian visions of development through technology and knowledge, aiming to insert the 'natives' into the family of civilization and progress, as part of a world-spanning human society.[12] Expertise serves for progress, industrialization, profitable agriculture. Thus, the utopian descriptions of the Libyan deserts were not merely idealized versions of the panorama Corradini encountered in his actual visits there, but they embody also the proposal of an intentional imperial intervention. The utopia could not be realized without Italian effective rule over the territory. Thus, the interplay of imagination and reality plays a central role in Corradini's writings. The civilizing mission of the Italians in Libya was to introduce progress, based on modern agricultural expertise, and support the natural resources in the creation of food plenty. Nature in itself was not enough: technological knowledge was needed to ensure the realization of a food utopia in North

Africa and relieve the region – as well as the Italian emigrants – of hunger.

The Italian journalist and author Arnaldo Fraccaroli (1882-1956) was a popular figure in early twentieth century Italy, famed for his travel writing and theatrical pieces. His book *In Cirenaica con i soldati* (1913) recounts his first-hand experience in Benghazi and Derna during the Italo-Turkish war. Fraccaroli described his impression of Derna, a 'garden city' that seems the realization of a dream: 'a marvellous nest'. Again, he highlighted the tension between the land's natural fertility and the lack of attention given by the local inhabitants: 'the trees are weighted down by the countless apricots, old olive trees are distorted by the displeasure of not being cultivated with care [...] and the land is not angry of the mistreatment, with no criterion, and gives its fruits equally, generous and inexhaustible.' He argued that the soldiers themselves had already demonstrated how Italy could contribute to enhancing the land's fertility: near the military camps, soldiers cultivated gardens to provide 'all the vegetable one wants'. These were 'real experimental vegetable gardens that show how on the apparently arid mountain soil, and not only on the very fertile plane, it is possible to obtain excellent results with little effort'.[13]

Fraccaroli highlighted a theme that was present in Corradini's writings as well: the potential aspect of the utopian vision of food plenty in Libya. The description of Tripoli and Cyrenaica as ideal spaces of nutrition was conditional, since it depended on the capacity of the Italians to employ their modern know-how and technological skills to master the local agriculture. This potential, which could be fully realized by the Italians, was evidently left unexplored by the existing residents of the region, who were too uncivilized, unskilled, or unwilling to make the land yield fruit. This argument sought to respond to the evident tension in Fraccaroli and Corradini's descriptions of the region in terms of both plenty and hunger, both glory and misery. To overcome these inconsistencies, they resorted to a civilizational scale which exalted the difference between the colonizers and the colonized. Even meagre results, such as the cultivation of a vegetable garden by soldiers, were considered successful demonstrations of the civilizational gap between the Italians and the Arabs.

Giuseppe Bevione, a leading journalist at *La Stampa* and the newspaper's correspondent in Libya in 1911, also visited the gardens of the Nahum family at the outskirts of Tripoli. He found there 'figs, almonds, olives, oranges, lemons, full of leaves and over burdened by vegetative power. In the internal courts there was trifoglio, grain and barley, broad beans and tomatoes growing [*verdeggiano*] with happy energy'. It was 'a generous spectacle of natural happiness and earthly opulence'. Nearby, he noted:

> the date palm is the father tree of the floridity of North Africa. It is the indicator of the presence of water in shallow and the essential living condition of the most fragile vegetation. Its copious shade allows grain to grow and flourish. The oasis of Tripoli, they say, possesses over two million palms. I don't know if this huge number is correct. Sure, you need to turn your eyes to the sea to avoid limiting your gaze by countless vertical stems, that open wide in the transparent air the

281

fans of their leaves. This is the surest sign of fertility in the Tripoli plain.[14]

These images of a desert utopia, based on fertility of land and wealth of crops, became the foundation of Bevione's political argument in favour of the conquest of the North African colony. Importantly, such images were contrasted with the descriptions of desolation and hunger in Italy, most significantly in Sicily. The southern island emerged in Bevione's articles as a land of strife and deprivation, which he targeted as the main cause for its political unrest. Bevione is not unique or particularly original in suggesting that poverty and unemployment do not only undermine food security but also cause political tensions and even rebellion. The conquest of a fertile African colony, geographically close and agriculturally similar and better than Southern Italy, would relieve social and political tensions in Europe. In this sense, the utopian depiction of Tripoli and Cyrenaica was part and parcel of the author's pro-colonial argument, and a fundamental aspect of his political thought.

Resistance: Utopia or Dystopia?

The images of Tripoli and Cyrenaica as a food heaven were contested by contemporary writers. One of the main voices of opposition, who sought to portray an alternative, dystopian vision of the Libyan territories, was Gaetano Salvemini, a socialist journalist and writer for the newspaper *La Voce*, directed by Giuseppe Prezzolini (who shared his dissent from the colonial project). Salvemini (1873-1957), became known later on as a leading anti-fascist intellectual, who spent the war time in exile in the United States. Yet in the earlier days of his writing career, he dedicated his efforts to countering what we might now call a 'fake news' campaign on the part of the pro-colonial political commentators in Italy. One of the key aspects of his dystopian imaginary of Libya was centred on the effective assessment of the land's fertility and its capacity to generate agricultural plenty for the native population and the Italian colonizers.

In one of his emblematic contributions, Salvemini ironically commented about the veracity of the arguments advanced by Bevione on the fertility of the North African soil.[15] He started by assessing the reliability of the travelling journalist's account of the territory, and argued that a short visit to a limited part of the land cannot constitute a reliable source to assess its agricultural potential. A more significant question is that of the availability of water: Salvemini showed that Bevione relied on a partial limited interpretation of a study conducted in the region by the Italian geologist Paolo Vinassa de Regny in 1902. Whether intentional or not, Bevione's account provided a hyperbolic interpretation of Vinassa de Regny's findings, without any substantial supportive evidence.

Moreover, Salvemini criticized Bevione's argument in favour of the Italian agricultural genius, capable of generating wealth from a challenging agricultural industry. Thanks to Italian knowledge and investment, the argument goes, Italians would be able to render the lands of Libya even more fertile than they were, left destitute by the local Arabs. Salvemini highlighted the contradiction within this argument and the notion that the colony should support a deprived southern Italy: if the Italians were so good at cultivating crops in difficult conditions, why not start with investing in Sicilian agriculture? Such a critique resonates in an article from a British newspaper, published in the early stages of the war, asking why Italy should conquer Africa when 'it has Africa at home'?[16] Salvemini's anti-imperial critique thus fed into European prejudices about Italy and its limited potential for empire, due to its own 'backwardness' not only in politics but also in economics, culture, and social structure.

During the Italian war against the Ottoman army and the local Arabs for the conquest of the territories of Tripoli and Cyrenaica, Salvemini was even more direct in his accusations of falsehood and misrepresentation against fellow journalists. In 1912, he wrote an article for the left-wing newspaper *L'Unità* titled 'How to fabricate a "promised land"'.[17] This time he directed his arrows at the journalist Giuseppe Piazza, who published in the newspaper *La Tribuna* an euphoric rendition of Tripoli and Cyrenaica, based on the travels of an Italian consul in the region a decade earlier. The textual comparison helped Salvemini sustain the argument that Piazza suppressed negative aspects of the consul's report, while adding fantasy details about the abundance of palm trees, figs, and grain, orange trees and olives, 'spontaneously growing' in the oasis. By stamping his report with the mark of an 'eyewitness', pretending to base it on his own impressions of the territory, Piazza created a persuasive yet false account of the local agricultural abundance.[18]

Salvemini's polemics were not the only source of opposition to the arguments about a food utopia in the Libyan region. The Italian government was concerned with the contrasting views of utopia and dystopia and sought to back their decisions with scientific scholarship. Concrete knowledge, based on empirical and quantitative field study, was considered to be a foundational aspect of the government's debates in favour or against colonization. Such information could be, potentially, provided by a study conducted for the Jewish Territorial Organization, a London-based organization led by the Jewish political thinker Israel Zangwill.[19]

The JTO sought to find a territory, potentially within the realm of the British Empire or in its proximity, that could become a new homeland for the Jewish people, as an alternative to Palestine, which was considered both materially and politically undesirable for lack of resources and local conflicts. Among other locations, notably Uganda in East Africa, the JTO also sent an expedition of British scientists with geological expertise to Cyrenaica, to explore the territorial potential for a Jewish settlement. The report, written by Prof J. W. Gregory, was published in 1909, causing great alarm among Italian diplomats and politicians.[20] Interestingly, they were less concerned with the damning conclusions that Gregory and his colleagues drew from their visit, in relation to the fertility of the land, its suitability for agricultural crops, and the presence of natural resources. Rather, they were worried of the competition posed by the Jewish lobby for the Cyrenaica province to the Italian colonial project.[21] Indeed, the considerations offered by the scholars were not taken seriously in weighting the desirability of the colonial project from a material point of view, and the document was read by Italian politicians with a sense of relief, rather than concern.

Conclusion

In 2014, to celebrate the republication in English of Filippo Tommaso Marinetti's *Futurist Cookbook* and the closure of an exhibition on futurism, the Guggenheim museum in New York City organized a 'futurist dinner' based on recipes from the 1932 culinary compendium.[22] The curator, Vivien Greene, explained that Marinetti 'threw ingredients together to shock people out of monotony, to shock them out of cooking bourgeois food'. In her *New Yorker* review of the evening, Sophie Brickman described the last course as an example:

> Case in point: the last dish of the evening, Libyan Airplane. Marinetti's formula calls for candied chestnuts to be steeped in eau de cologne and milk, then served on a purée of bananas, apples, dates, and peas 'shaped into the form of a slender aeroplane.' [Chef] Lo Monte's take was benevolent: she nixed the cologne and included two cannoli as 'wings' on top of a small Martini glass filled with the chunky green purée. Alas, even her interpretation couldn't lift this poor dish out of sludgedom. 'it's chalky,' said one diner. 'You know, I really prefer desserts that are sweet,' said another. 'This just isn't for me.' Everyone ate their cannoli wings and quietly let their purée fuselages be.[23]

While the museum's rendering of Marinetti's culinary musing may have departed from the original intentions, the recipe envisioned by the futurist encapsulates the transition in visions of food and plenty from the earlier colonization of Tripoli under Giolitti's Liberal government to later fascist colonialism. Earlier writers emphasized an evocative – if at times predictable – utopian vision of food plenty, founded on almost biblical notions of agricultural abundance, fertility, and nutritious Mediterranean nature. Yet later culinary interpretations of Libya were motivated by a radicalized, extreme notion of food long departed from any promise of subsistence, nutrition, or even pleasure: an exotic combination of ingredients – very few of them local, most distinctly the dates – made up a dish imbued with political message and little relation to existing culinary practices. In clear contrast to Bevione, Piazza, and Corradini, Marinetti's recipe hails technology (Libyan airplane) over nature, and celebrates unusual and unappealing concoctions as a food of the future. From a site of natural relief of hunger, Libya became a symbol of a radical modernity.

This essay engaged with conceptions of food in the context of the Italo-Turkish War of 1911-1912 for the conquest of the Ottoman provinces of Tripolitania and Cyrenaica. Leading authors and journalists resorted to utopian imaginaries of Tripoli as a city of plenty, and Cyrenaica as a land of agricultural fertility. Alongside the natural abundance, the authors highlighted the contrast between the lazy and incompetent local population, unable to exploit natural resources, and the skilled Italian farmers and soldiers. The result was a persuasive political argument that played a role in leading Italy to a war that would last over two decades. Alternative accounts, which portrayed Libya as a dystopian desert, remained marginal and politically ineffective. The essay therefore sheds light on the interplay of ideas and materiality as a key aspect of the history of Italian imperialism and provides a meaningful contribution to the fields of food history and intellectual history.

Notes

1   Quentin Skinner, 'Sir Thomas More's Utopia and the Language of Renaissance Humanism', in *The Languages of Political Theory in Early-Modern Europe*, ed. by Anthony Pagden (Cambridge: Cambridge University Press, 1986). pp. 123-58.

2   James Belich, *Replenishing the Earth: The Settler Revolution and the Rise of the Angloworld* (Oxford: Oxford University Press, 2009) p. 154.

3   Andrekos Varnava, 'El Dorados, Utopias and Dystopias in Imperialism and Colonial Settlement', in *Imperial Expectations and Realities: El Dorados, Utopias and Dystopias,* ed. by Andrekos Varnava (Manchester: Manchester University Press, 2015), p. 14.

4   Giuseppe Finaldi, 'Dreaming in the Desert: Libya as Italy's Promised Land, 1911-70', in *Imperial Expectations and Realities*, pp. 191-209.

5   Antonio Schiavulli (ed.), *La guerra libica: Il dibatito dei letterati italiani sull'impresa di Libia (1911-1912)* (Ravenna: Giorgio Pozzi, 2009).

6   Gabriele Proglio, *Libia 1911-1912, Immaginari coloniali e italianità* (Milan: Quaderni di storia, 2016).

7   Enrico Corradini, *L'Ora di Tripoli* (Milan, Treves, 1911), p. 67 (emphasis mine).

8   Corradini, p. 67.

9   Corradini, pp. 66-68.

10 Edward Said, *Orientalism* (New York: Pantheon, 1978).

11 Corradini, pp. 67ff.

12 Walter M. Simon, 'History for Utopia: Saint-Simon and the Idea of Progress', *Journal of the History of Ideas,* 17 (1956), pp. 311–331.

13 Arnaldo Fraccaroli, *In Cirenaica con i soldati* (Milan: Treves, 1913), pp.105 ff (my translation).

14 Giuseppe Bevione, *Come siamo andati a Tripoli* (Turin: Fratelli Bocca, 1912), p. 13.

15 Gaetano Salvemini, *La coltura Italiana e Tripoli, republished in "Come siamo andati in Libia" e altri scritti dal 1900 al 1915* (Milan: Feltrinelli, 1963), pp. 102 ff.

16 Qtd. in William Clarence Askew, *Europe and Italy's Acquisition of Libya 1911-1912* (Durham, NC: Duke University press, 1942), p. 70.

17 Gaetano Salvemini, 'Come si fabbrica una "terra promessa"', *L'Unità*, 26 (8 June 1912), 103.

18 Giuseppe Piazza, *La nostra terra promessa : lettere dalla Tripolitania marzo maggio 1911* (Rome: Bernardo Lux, 1911).

19 See for example Gur Alroey. *Zionism without Zion: The Jewish Territorial Organization and Its Conflict with the Zionist Organization* (Detroit, MI: Wayne State University Press, 2016).

20 J. W. Gregory, *Report on the Work of the Commission Sent Out by the Jewish Territorial Organization under the Auspices of the Governor-General of Tripoli to Examine the Territory Proposed for the Purpose of a Jewish Settlement in Cyrenaica* (London: ITO, 1909).

21 The Italian Ambassador in London, Imperiali, to the Minister of Foreign Affairs, Di San Giuliano, 27 September 1912, in *Documenti diplomatici italiani*, series 4, vol. VII-VIII, n. 1019 <www.farnesina.ipzs. it> [accessed on 21 March 2020].

22 Filippo Tommaso Marinetti, *The Futurist Cookbook* (London: Penguin, [1932] 2014).

23 Sophie Brickman, 'The Food of the Future', *The New Yorker,* 1 September 2014.

'To Make the Whole World Homelike': Gender and Power in the Food Revolution

Laura Shapiro

> Nigella is a celebrity, no question about that, but is she a chef? Of course not. Which is fine. Her show is about eating well, not so much about cooking. [...] Let's face it: Nigella probably cooks better than your mother. And she's a lot better looking, and cooler. Nigella wouldn't mind if you smoked weed in your bedroom before dinner, would she?
>
> — Anthony Bourdain, *The Nasty Bits*[1]

I've spent a fair amount of time poking and prodding at this excerpt from *The Nasty Bits,* trying to figure out what on earth Bourdain wanted to say. *The Nasty Bits* is a collection of his journalism – articles turned out for numerous publications after the whopping success of his first book, *Kitchen Confidential,* in 2000, and the TV programs that followed. This particular passage appears in an essay about celebrity chefs, and I was struck by how uneasy Bourdain seems here, beneath the verbal swagger that was his trademark. It's as if he's casting around for reasons to keep Nigella Lawson off the team. She's cool enough, he admits; she's certainly famous enough, her recipes are hugely popular, but is she tough? Is she scary? Or is she just another mom, minus the orthopedic shoes?

Later in this essay, Bourdain meets up with Donovan Cooke, who was then the chef at Ondine, in Melbourne. Unlike the amorphous description of Lawson, these passages are confident. Bourdain loves to sing in this key:

> When I dropped in on him unannounced, he was standing behind a busy stove. [...] He is absolutely obsessed with flavour – and sauce-making in particular. [...] 'You reduce the fucking jus, right? And you don't bloody skim it. You emulsify the fucking fat right in – at the last second. If the sauce breaks? What do you mean if the sauce breaks? If the sauce breaks – you're a fucking cunt.'

Bourdain wraps up this portrait with a hearty slap on the back: 'That's a celebrity chef I want to see on TV.'[2]

Aha! Now the passage about Nigella Lawson starts to make sense. Everything Bourdain is trying to tell us is tucked deep inside the word 'cooking', a term he refuses to associate seriously with Lawson even when she's standing right in front of him working with fresh ingredients and deploying all the usual knives and mixing bowls. 'Her show is about eating well, not so much about cooking.' In other words, it doesn't count as cooking if it's uncomplicated. Or if it takes place at home instead of a restaurant. Or if the voice-over isn't laced with profanity. Or if the person at the stove is calm, pleasant, and female.

More than half a century after a good home cook in California managed to launch a food revolution, I can't help marvelling at the efficiency with which a bunch of guys brandishing TV contracts moved in and ran away with it. We could see it happening practically in real time: money and maleness, the original power couple, conducting yet another takeover. One minute ordinary Americans were reaching for the organic broccoli that had just shown up in the supermarket, and the next minute all eyes were on Emeril Lagasse shouting 'Bam!' at his ingredients, and Gordon Ramsey flinging himself into temper tantrums. Fortunately this testosterone invasion was confined to popular culture, so the civic and political activism associated with the revolution – supporting small farms and farmers markets, rallying communities around hunger and nutrition issues, organizing and lobbying against Big Food – is thriving to this day. But I wonder how much more, and more affordable, organic broccoli we'd be putting in our shopping baskets, how much more frequently we'd cook at home rather than summon our meals from a delivery app, if the original impetus behind the food revolution hadn't been elbowed out of the way when the celebrity chefs came marching in.

I'm going to suggest a specific date for the birth of the food revolution: 24 January 1968. And a specific place: the *San Francisco Express-Times*, page 9, bottom right-hand corner. That's where a beautifully illustrated little recipe appeared under the heading 'Alice's restaurant'. It was a very simple recipe indeed, for a dish called 'Pepper Toast'.

1. take two slices of good bread; whole wheat or rye is best:
2. spread thickly with butter:
3. liberally grind coarse fresh-ground or cracked black pepper over each slice:
4. broil until golden brown. eat hot.[3]

The *San Francisco Express-Times* was an alternative paper crammed with the rambunctious politics of the 1960s. Sharing the page with Pepper Toast was a photograph of David Harris, the anti-war activist, speaking at a demonstration in Oakland just before he set fire to his draft notice. There was also a short piece written by the beat poet Lawrence Ferlinghetti, who had just spent a week at a rehab centre where officials told him he had too many books and took away his copy of Stokely Carmichael's *Black Power*. Now and then the *Express-Times* published a comfortable, semi-stoned cookery column by a writer identified as 'grandma schulman': for example, 'Slice eggplant like ¼ inch, tomatoes a little fatter. Dip in beaten eggs, then crumbs, and fry in enough butter or margarine to keep from sticking. [...] Fry as hot as you can without burning. [...] The eggplant is RICH, the tomatoes out of sight. [...] Don't light up until you've at least begun the cooking or you know damn well you'll opt for peanut butter and crackers.'[4]

'Alice's restaurant' was different. In the course of the year, dozens more recipes in the same format as Pepper Toast showed up – framed lino-cuts bordered with illustrations of herbs or carrots or apricots, the instructions in lush calligraphy. Reading the *San Francisco Express-Times* online (and you should: it's funny and a little painful and will flood you with nostalgia even if you weren't born yet), it's startling to encounter such radiant culinary imagery. The pictures look as though an unseen hand had dropped them onto the page and left them there, islands of serenity in a sea of clamouring newsprint. Chocolate mousse, carrot bread, potatoes with dill, crepes filled with yogurt – the food was simple, the ingredients classic. As a perspective on home cooking in what was still very much the canned-soup casserole era, these easy yet refined recipes were a revelation. You didn't have to smoke a joint to find the food a pleasure.

Alice, of course, was Alice Waters, and the artist was her then-boyfriend, the printmaker David Goines. They had broken up by the time she and a few friends borrowed enough money to open a restaurant; nonetheless, he designed the first menu and has created anniversary posters for the restaurant ever since. None of the founders was looking to change culinary history when Chez Panisse opened in 1971 – all they wanted was a personable French restaurant where they could indulge their love of good food and share it with everyone else in Berkeley. Since they were wholly inexperienced, they expected a few rough patches and got plenty of them, but Chez Panisse became a sensation anyway. Today it's a landmark on the world's restaurant map, credited with inspiring a new, ingredient-based standard of excellence for postwar professional cooking in the U.S. and elsewhere. 'Fresh and local' became the mantra for a restaurant philosophy that now touches even coffeeshop menus, whether or not the food itself lives up to the ideal.

From the outset, men and women alike have been involved in Chez Panisse and crucial to its success. But restaurants don't start revolutions; people do, and this where we turn to Alice Waters, who's most likely wearing something vaguely vintage and carrying a few radishes. 'When I cook, I usually stand at my kitchen table,' she wrote in her first book, *The Chez Panisse Menu Cookbook*:

> I may pull a bunch of thyme from my pocket and lay it on the table; then I wander about the kitchen gathering up all the wonderfully fresh ingredients I can find. [...] While this method may appear chaotic to others, I do think best while holding a tomato or a leg of lamb. Sometimes I wander through the garden looking for something appealing, absorbing the bouquet of the earth.[5]

This may be over-the-top lyrical, but it's also intensely political. She was telling homemakers to bypass the food industry – a multi-gazillion dollar enterprise dedicated to gaining full control over what we eat – and go straight to the fresh ingredients. It was a message about power.

If we think of Alice as a figure in culinary history, we see her standing alongside Elizabeth David, M.F.K. Fisher, and Julia Child. But she emerged from the history of

288

women's activism as well. To me she is a figure in that remarkable lineage of women who seized hold of their beliefs and pursued them headlong across the late nineteenth and early twentieth centuries. Abolition, suffrage, public health, workers' rights – every issue was a feminist issue, and believers fought on many battlefields at once. Looking back at that eager, determined army, the sort of women who used to be called, with irritation, 'strong-minded', one in particular stands out as Alice's sister in revolution. I'm thinking of Frances E. Willard (1839-1897), the most famous crusader of her time and a leader so widely revered that, when she died, flags were lowered to half-mast and some 30,000 people filed by her casket in Chicago. Alice herself would be appalled even to be named in the same paragraph as Willard, much less depicted at her side, for Willard was the long-time president of the Woman's Christian Temperance Union and fought hard against wine, beer, and liquor all her life. But she was also the feminist visionary who made the WCTU the biggest and most influential women's organization in the world. Her cause was Prohibition; her larger goal was to start building a political system based on the humane social values traditionally associated with women. Alice has pursued a very different cause – and the same goal.

Willard was sixteen when she cut out this verse from a magazine:

A pledge we make no wine to take,
Nor brandy red that turns the head,
Nor fiery rum that ruins home,
Nor brewers' beer, for that we fear ,
And cider, too, will never do. [...]
So here we pledge perpetual hate
To all that can intoxicate.[6]

She had everyone in her family sign it – she called it 'the first bit of temperance work I ever did'. There was nothing unusual about taking a stance against alcohol in those years: many people did, even if they had no objection to a little social or medicinal wine, even a glass of beer now and then. The real enemy was drunkenness: in an era when married women's legal rights were few and inconsistent, an abusive husband or one who drank up his earnings could leave a family in ruins. Many of the early feminists had started out as temperance activists, only to be propelled into the suffrage movement when they saw how desperately women needed the power of the ballot box. Willard had the opposite trajectory: she never forgot the day she had to stay home and watch in angry frustration as her father and brother went off to vote. Nor did she ever get over the misery of having to leave childhood behind and start dressing like a lady. 'Mine was a nature hard to tame, and I cried long and loud when I found I could never again race and range about with freedom,' she wrote in a memoir.[7] Although she came close to marrying, she decided against it. Instead she threw herself into women's causes, with the WCTU her prime vehicle. Campaigning around the world, she made innumerable public speeches, forged prominent alliances with socialists and foreigners, and published copiously, all the while shying away from cooking and housework. Yet even as she broke one rule after another for female propriety, she managed to project an image of perfect womanliness. On the speaking platform she wore dark, modest gowns, and always took a tone more comfortable and intimate than oratorical – a style of self-presentation so magnetic that Susan B. Anthony described it as an 'occult force'.[8]

Willard's rhetoric drew on familiar themes of God, alcohol, and suffering children, but she gave them a new political spin. 'Dear Christian women who have crusaded in the rum-shops, I urge that you begin crusading in halls of legislation, in primary meetings and the offices of excise commissioners,' she pleaded in 1876. A decade later she had raised the stakes considerably and was promoting a policy she called 'Do Everything'. In speech after speech she exhorted women to apply the latest knowledge of sanitation and ventilation to their homes, set up public laundries and community kitchens, quit wearing corsets, petition for workplace health and safety regulations, and lobby for equal pay, equal access to education, a six-day work week, and an end to the double standard in 'personal purity and morality'.[9] Many women activists described their work as 'municipal housekeeping'; Willard expanded the metaphor into a wide-open demand for female power across the public sphere. Her proclamation on the subject became legendary: 'If I were to ask the mission of the ideal woman, I would reply: IT IS TO MAKE THE WHOLE WORLD HOMELIKE.'[10]

Frances Willard was not a gastronome, but if it had ever struck her as a possibility that maybe a few radishes would help her reach an audience, she'd have walked onstage and talked about radishes. Alice talks about them because she believes in them. She, too, has a liking for domesticity as a metaphor. As far as she's concerned, the kitchen – the place where we turn our minds to food, where we cook, eat, share, and teach – is the place where we start to change the world.

Organized feminism was still new when Alice arrived in Berkeley in 1964, but it was a time when political activism and a free-wheeling counterculture seemed to be making all things possible, or at least a lot more fun than they'd been in the 1950s. She liked what she was hearing from Mario Savio, who drew huge crowds to campus rallies of the Free Speech Movement. 'I absorbed his idealism and his conviction that people are more than cogs in the machine,' she once wrote, and she never forgot his image of a desiccated America: '"the utopia of sterilized, automated contentment"'.[11]

That winter Alice took her first trip to France, where the food bedazzled her palate and changed the course of her life. Earlier American gastronomes had had the same experience, M.F.K. Fisher in the 1930s and Julia Child in the 1940s. But Alice's conversion took place in quite a different context: she was a creature of Berkeley and the 1960s. If a woman fell in love with food, she didn't have to confine her passion to writing, or going to cooking school. She could open a restaurant, even if she knew absolutely nothing about opening restaurants. And she could infuse her restaurant with her own ideology – teamwork, not hierarchy; women cooking, not just waitressing; an enterprise dedicated to serving delicious food even if nobody made much money from it.

This moral and political backdrop was what allowed 'fresh and local' to emerge and ultimately reign over Chez Panisse. Most American restaurateurs were guided by cost and consistency when it came to ingredients; Alice, still obsessed by her French awakening, wanted flavour above all. At first the cooks just tried to find decent ingredients in Berkeley and San Francisco markets; gradually the notion of working with small farms begin to surface. Jeremiah Tower, the flamboyant chef who took over the kitchen in 1973, later claimed credit for introducing the practice. But Tower left after three years, and it was Alice who nurtured the idea until it became an entire philosophy of shopping, cooking, eating, and life.

Only in Northern California could such a philosophy have spread so quickly across the restaurant world. No other region in America had the right climate, and by that I mean the cultural climate as well as the weather. *Nouvelle cuisine*, the most talked-about restaurant trend of the moment, was inspiring ambitious chefs in New York and elsewhere to showcase fresh ingredients in all their simple splendour, but it was the Bay Area that was able to make this idea wholly American. Once Chez Panisse zeroed in on local farms, other restaurants caught on, and soon there was a thriving network of hands-on producers marketing their lettuces, chickens, goat cheese, and much else directly to chefs. These relationships were personal, at least in the early years: the grower herself dropped off the green beans and tomatoes at the back door. The ethos was small-scale, not industrial; the sensibility favoured generosity, not simply competitiveness. The values at work here were stereotypically female, especially in the context of food. I'd call them feminist values, though maybe that's wishful thinking on my part. At any rate, these were the values that helped make the Bay Area one of the world's great culinary regions.

Meanwhile, a posse of writers and environmental activists around the country was also focused on food, staging a more overtly political attack against industrial farming and the increasingly tasteless, chemical-laden meats and produce it was delivering. The time was right for Americans to start developing a new relationship with food. Farmers markets began to show up in many cities, and people who hadn't seen such appealing fruits and vegetables since childhood, or perhaps ever, were quickly addicted. 'Fresh and local' sped around the country, reaching people who had never heard of Chez Panisse and inspiring masses of journalism, countless recipes, and a pile of cookbooks as well as innumerable restaurants. A genuine revolution was at hand, a public speak-out against the processed techno-food beckoning from every street and supermarket.

Revolutions are crowd-sourced, by definition; but they always acquire a symbolic leader, and Alice was the obvious choice. She was there first, and she was relentless. 'She has stayed on message for forty years,' wrote the chef Joyce Goldstein in her comprehensive *Inside the California Food Revolution*.[12] The book was published six years ago; Alice is still on message. Every time she speaks or writes, she's addressing home cooks and telling them about farms, about cherishing good ingredients, about cooking from scratch, and about feeding their families. Over the years, thanks to her and many,

many others, this message became a kind of national anthem for food-lovers. It still rings out – though nowadays maybe a little absent-mindedly. Public attention has shifted elsewhere.

*

Sometime in the 1980s, I started to notice that well-off people in New York, where I live, had become obsessed with restaurants. It turned out other cities were experiencing the same thing, a Reagan-era tulip mania focused on getting into one or another wildly hyped, often insanely expensive new place. I couldn't figure it out: was this a food fad, an entertainment fad, a conspicuous-consumption fad, or just a culinary Beanie Baby that would disappear after a season or two? I asked the long-time food writer Barbara Kafka, who had been tracking high-end restaurants for many years, what was going on. Why were people suddenly so intoxicated with quail eggs and 'beggars' purses' filled with caviar? 'There used to be something called "'a dollar bill on a plate,"' she explained. 'It never really went away, and now it's back.'

That seemed to jibe nicely with what I was seeing. And as the mania raced on, it became clear that this was no Beanie Baby: it was a real turning point in mainstream American culture. Thanks to more widespread affluence and an increased popular sophistication about food, restaurants had changed their role in American life. People were talking about them, reading about them, debating the merits of this one over that one. Spending a lot of money to eat out, once viewed as an extravagance, had become acceptable, then desirable, and finally essential for those who aspired to what *Gourmet* called 'good living'. For the first time in our history, it was restaurants – not home cooking – that drove the public conversation about food.

The original food revolution didn't go away, but the centre of gravity was shifting from a women's world to men's. There's a dictionary definition of 'power' that's apt here: it comes from the science of optics, where it expresses a degree of magnification. Unlike home cooks, who tend to be female and invisible, professional cooks tend to be male and very visible indeed – magnified, aggrandized, publicized, and known as chefs. Of course, only a tiny percentage of Americans would ever be able to eat in the sort of restaurants where the chefs had names known to the public. But millions of people became fascinated with chefs when they started turning up in magazines, on cookbook covers, and finally on television. These newcomers on the culinary stage became famous by virtue of publicity. Of course they knew their way around a stove, but that wasn't really the job. The job was to be male, complete with plumage.

In 1990, the famously rude and raffish British chef Marco Pierre White published *White Heat*, a celebration of himself in recipes and, especially, photographs. Back then Anthony Bourdain was just another anonymous cook in a New York restaurant, and when somebody brought a copy of the book into the kitchen, he joined the rest of the crew to get a look. The recipes didn't interest him; the pictures did. There was the notorious White – 'long scraggly hair, dark rings under the eyes, haunted, smoking a cigarette,' Bourdain recalled years later, and he credited those pictures with changing his life. '"That's us!"' he thought. '"That's what a chef looks like."'[13]

Well, no. Judy Rodgers didn't look like that. Anne Rosenzweig didn't look like that. Nora Pouillon didn't look like that. But female chefs were the exceptions in a profession that had long thrilled to its own misogyny. What was important about Bourdain's epiphany was that it supplied him with the image that made him a star. Really tough, really smoked a lot, looked really sullen for no apparent reason, and always seemed to have a motorcycle waiting just out of camera range. This lurid version of masculinity would have been wholly out of place in a gingham-curtain home kitchen, which is surely why more chefs picked up the look with enthusiasm when they made it to television. Rebels, outlaws, and wildmen swarmed across the screen, while other male experts became gonzo intellectuals, avidly explaining the science of cooking as if home ec had suddenly awakened from its long nap and was ready to party.

Women, too, hosted some of the new food programs with great success, but mostly by teaching in traditional daytime formats. There were cross-overs – a few women became culinary rogues or adventurers, a few men did the friendly teaching – but on the whole, the stereotypes ruling food TV would have been familiar in the 1950s. Or the 1850s. This remarkable fealty to traditional sex roles has relaxed in recent years, maybe because feminism is back in favour at the moment or maybe just because of the prodigious amount of hot air it was taking to keep the clichés of maleness fully inflated, season after season. Men know science! Men fight! Men go to faraway places! Men love to eat messy food!

293

Bourdain eventually developed his own version of food travel, one that took up political and social questions as he investigated culinary realms, and he was in the midst of filming a new series when he committed suicide last year at the age of 61. An immense outpouring of sorrow swept the internet, including a number of tributes from people who had known him in person. Invariably they described a pleasant, decent guy, thoughtful and respectful, with good manners and good work habits. In other words, the persona he displayed in print and onscreen – cynical, raunchy, born to be subversive, so potty-mouthed he had to be bleeped into silence on network television – was pretty much a front. The baddest guy in the food revolution was a closet mensch.

*

These days it's de rigueur in the food world to dismiss Alice Waters as elitist. After all, we never see her slurping noodles in a Thai street stall, muttering, 'Shit, that's delicious', while the locals stand around respectfully like figures in a global-issues diorama. What's more, she's unabashed about insisting on 'fresh and local' at any cost, whether you're rich or poor. She can't imagine a better use for your household income, and if you really have very little to spend, why not plant a garden and simply grow your own asparagus and sugarsnaps? She does have a way of making herself an easy target. But she's spent nearly five decades working to counter the food industry, while her peers with more camera-ready politics are scrambling to endorse soft drinks, potato chips, bouillon cubes, and whatever else they can rationalize. Unlike many famous restaurateurs, moreover, she's never opened Chez Panisse II in Las Vegas or CP Quick in an airport. Instead she created a foundation called the Edible Schoolyard, which helps children develop an honest relationship with food by growing, cooking, eating, and studying it. The Edible Schoolyard started in a Berkeley middle school; today it encompasses more than five thousand programs across the nation and around the world.

Not long ago the widely-admired chef José Andrés, famous for his dozens of restaurants as well as his non-profit World Central Kitchen, which travels to communities hit by disaster, sat on a stage with Alice and reminisced about the first time he ate at Chez Panisse. What astonished him, he said, was dessert: a single clementine, unpeeled, on a plate with some dates. This was pure Alice: the end-of-meal equivalent of a few radishes. He still remembers the flavours in that extraordinary, unembellished fruit; he still remembers the moment he had to stop and wonder, for the first time, what 'cooking' meant. 'She made people like me think,' he told the audience. 'That's her real power.'[14]

Notes

1 Anthony Bourdain, *The Nasty Bits* (New York: Bloomsbury, 2006), pp. 71-72.

2 Bourdain, *The Nasty Bits*, pp. 73-74.

3 'Alice's Restaurant', *San Francisco Express-Times*, 24 January 1968, p. 9.

4 grandma schulman, 'Grow Your Own', *San Francisco Express-Times*, 21 January 1968, p. 110.

5 Alice Waters, *Chez Panisse Menu Cookbook* (New York: Random House, 1982), p. 6.

6 Qtd. in Frances E. Willard, *Glimpses of Fifty Years* (Chicago: Woman's Temperance Publication Association, 1889), p. 331.

7 Willard, *Glimpses of Fifty Years*, pp. 331, 69.

8 *Let Something Good Be Said: Speeches and Writings of Frances E. Willard*, ed. by Carolyn DeSwarte Gifford and Amy R. Slagell (Urbana: University of Illinois Press, 2007), p. 27.

9 Willard, *Let Something Good Be Said*, pp. 23, xxvi, 128.

10 Frances E. Willard, *How to Win* (New York: Funk & Wagnalls, 1888), p. 54.

11 Alice Waters, *Forty Years of Chez Panisse* (New York: Clarkson Potter, 2011), p. 15.

12 Joyce Goldstein, *Inside the California Food Revolution* (Berkeley: University of California Press, 2013), p. 42.

13 'A Conversation with Anthony Bourdain', in Anthony Bourdain, *Kitchen Confidential*, updated ed. (New York: Harper Perennial, 2007), p. 11.

14 'Food for Thought: A Conversation with José Andrés and Alice Waters', *The Washington Post*, 27 October 2017 <https://www.washingtonpost.com/podcasts/post-live/food-for-thought-a-conversation-with-jos-andrs-and-alice-waters/?utm_term=.ce73c401c8d2> [accessed 28 May 2019]

True Bread, *Pizza Napoletana*, and Wedding Cakes: The Changing Ways Legal Power Has Shaped Bakers' Lives

Richard Warren Shepro

The power of the law has historically been less than kind to bakers. However, as the role of bread and bakers has changed – nutritionally and spiritually bread is no longer vital to much of society – the law has become a tool bakers can use. Revolutionary France abolished slavery and emancipated the Jews, but retained laws that prohibited bakers from leaving their profession without permission.[1] Moreover, it was not enough just to remain a baker: the law also imposed a legal obligation to keep the bakery well stocked with good bread.[2] French bakers were not even allowed free choice in selecting their vacation days until 2015.[3] At the beginning of the twentieth century in the United States, legislators attempted to protect bakers from overwork, but the United States Supreme Court overturned the law designed to do so. In dramatic contrast, in the twenty-first century, artisan pizza makers in Naples were able to harness legal power for their own benefit in defining, marketing, and protecting their product, and in 2018 the United States Supreme Court affirmed the right of a specialty cake maker to refuse to design and bake a special cake to celebrate the marriage of two men.

The nature and force of regulation have varied greatly depending on the country, the historical period, and – especially – the economic and symbolic role of the bakers' products at that time in their particular milieu. This paper is intended to provide a cross-cultural comparison of four salient episodes in the history of the legal regulation of baking and bread in three countries and over more than three centuries.

Food regulations are generally sought by governments in order to protect the consuming public, as in most meat inspection laws, or to protect an industry that has significant importance to the economy the government represents, such as with the *Reinheitsgebot*, a Bavarian law adopted in 1516 to limit the ingredients of beer to water, barley and hops. The most draconian food regulations arise when public health appears to be truly threatened, as in the 'mad cow' scare of the 1990s.[4] When sought by industry groups, legal rules are generally thought to be aimed at giving existing practitioners an advantage over new entrants, reducing competition by creating barriers to entry. Medieval guilds are the classic example, although some recent scholarship suggests their actions were often not so purely protectionist as popularly believed.[5]

In looking at these four episodes it is helpful to consider why each government was motivated to intervene in the lives of bakers. Was the government attempting to help bakers? Or to protect a public whose well-being might depend on the use of governmental power? Did the bakers themselves feel a need for protection? Or did regulation reflect some broader philosophical goal?

It is not easy to draw valid conclusions across countries and centuries, but these four episodes appear to suggest that, as bread and baking have moved from being categorically essential to being less vital to society, legal regulation has changed from a harsh regime inflicted on bakers to a tool bakers respect and appreciate for marketing and for protection of their sense of self-expression.

Bread and Baking in Pre-Revolutionary France

There is no way to overstate the importance of bread in pre-Revolutionary France and the influence of bread quality, bread availability, and bread pricing on the French Revolution. Workers and most others lived mainly on bread, often consuming two to three pounds a day.[6] The percentage of caloric intake that bread represented is difficult to assess, but there is no doubt that France was deeply dependent on bread. What the historian Steven Kaplan has called the 'tyrannie des céréales' dominated the economy. Bakers generally worked essentially non-stop from 8:00 p.m. to 7:00 a.m. under arduous working conditions, but they produced deeply aromatic loaves that both fed the people physically and had a profound symbolic significance for the entire country.

The government, largely through the police, enforced maximum prices and regulated quality of ingredients, of leavening, and of baking. Bad bread was a matter for the police. The government and its theorists asserted that their extraordinary regulatory regime protected bakers from what they termed 'the rage of the populace', who indeed rioted, at times so ferociously that the wave of riots in April and May 1775 became known as the *Guerre des Farines* (Flour War). The expressed goal of regulation was two-fold: to maintain traditional quality and to keep prices fair. The deeper goal, expressed by the most prominent *commissaire* of police, Nicolas Delamare (who in old age became a great scholar and theorist of police work and regulation), was social tranquillity, for which true bread – *le bon pain* ('the good bread') – was the *sine qua non*.[7] In furtherance of social tranquillity, anyone who entered this sacred profession had a legal obligation to keep his bakery well stocked, with good bread, sold at a legal price. Of course, social tranquillity was not ensured for long. In 1789, during the Revolution, baker Denis François was hanged in an act of vigilante justice for hiding loaves for wealthy customers who would pay more than the official price during a bread shortage. Contemporary engravings of this grisly event circulated widely.

Although strong regulation was a constant, the philosophical, economic, and scientific underpinnings of the regime were debated hotly, in the style of the Enlightenment, and rules changed frequently. Prominent economists and mathematicians analyzed pricing with a plethora of statistical data, gathered in ways that were impressive for the time but with sampling methods unlikely to lead to a successful planned economy. Other arguments were simply based on theories, with some arguing that price-setting by the police was a way to maintain quality because it would prevent bakers from competing on price, only on quality, and that therefore consumers would then choose to buy the best bread – while still others argued that setting maximum prices actually degraded quality because prices would be set too low to prevent riots and then bakers could not afford the best ingredients and best fermentation and baking practices. Bread was viewed as so important that the market-based idea that price controls can themselves lead to shortages did not seem to be considered.

The nature of 'quality' did not seem to be viewed as evanescent. Rules as to what quality actually consisted of were influenced by experimental scientists, who often argued the superiority of their scientific methods over bakers' lore and experience handed down from father to son.[8] Prominent in the debates was Antoine-Augustin Parmentier, the chemist-agronomist known today largely for having persuaded the Paris Faculty of Medicine to declare potatoes edible in 1772. Parmentier argued strenuously that bread leavened with separately-produced brewers' yeast (a relatively novel but increasingly popular product) was unhealthy, whereas true or good bread made by a 'perfect baker' using natural yeast (*pain au levain*: sourdough) was healthy.[9] Bread made using commercially produced yeast was viewed by its detractors as impure or even poisonous, and, at the very least, disagreeable. However, it could be produced quickly and, unlike 'true bread', did not require bakers to go through the laborious process of nursing and feeding their starters, continuously taking care of a developing dough – and so did not require a thirteen-hour work day.

Delamare, Parmentier, and others responsible for or influential in regulating bread were not afraid to regulate the process by which bread was made. It is reasonable to ask, to what extent should laws interfere with how bread is made. Unhealthy bread is one thing. When you move from keeping out poisonous bread to regulating process in a quest to ensure quality and flavour, you enter an area that is less popular in the modern world. To what extent should the focus be on the bread? Or, alternatively, should the focus be on the well-being of workers? This question was brought to the United States Supreme Court in 1905, but by then, at least in the legislatures, the concern had shifted from the quality of the bread to the welfare of the bakers.

The U.S. Supreme Court's 1905 decision in *Lochner* v. *New York*[10]

In 1895, the state of New York, concerned about workers' well-being, passed a Bakeshop Act declaring that no employee of a bakery could be 'required or permitted to work' more than ten hours a day and sixty hours a week. Joseph Lochner, who owned Lochner's Home Bakery, was fined twice for violating the law. The second time he challenged the law, claiming that it violated his rights under the Fourteenth amendment to the U.S. Constitution, which expressly prohibits states from 'depriv[ing] any person of life, liberty, or property, without due process of law'. Mr. Lochner argued that his right to contract freely was 'liberty, or property' and was being taken away.

After the bakeshop law had been upheld successively by a trial court and two lower appellate courts, the United States Supreme Court accepted the case.[11] The U.S. Supreme Court has an immense role in the United States, and its decisions are often of great historical significance. The Court heard oral argument, considered the case, and then struck down the law by a contentious bare majority vote of the nine men who then served on the Court, five justices to four. The Court held that the state had no right to impose such a law because it interfered with the 'right and liberty of the individual' baker and bakery owner to enter into a contract under the terms they wanted'.[12]

The *Lochner* case was so influential in promoting the idea of freedom of contract that the following period in legal history is known as the *Lochner* Era, a period during which social welfare legislation was routinely overturned. Legal scholars still debate the legal principles, but any special role of either bread or bakers is generally forgotten. For a decision that could so influence the lives of bakers, and in stark contrast to the discussions in pre-Revolutionary (and post-Revolutionary) France, the Supreme Court arguments were not about bread, but about pure social theory: the laissez-faire ideal of free rights to contract versus paternalistic protection of workers.

The idea that it might take ten hours to produce 'true bread' or 'good bread' was never mentioned. In fact, bread quality was only mentioned in a single sentence in the majority opinion that asserted, without any discussion, 'Clean and wholesome bread does not depend upon whether the baker works but ten hours per day or only sixty hours a week.' The time it takes to make good bread and the quality of bread, so carefully considered in eighteenth-century France, had in a matter-of-fact way become an issue of no possible concern to the Supreme Court of the United States. As to the safety of bakers themselves, the Court simply stated that 'there can be no fair doubt that the trade of a baker [...] is not an unhealthy one'.

The concept that certain vocations needed special protection was ridiculed as a slippery slope that could lead to unnecessary protections for 'clerks, messengers' and even 'lawyers' or 'bank clerks'. The Court took note that '[t]here is no contention that bakers as a class are not equal in intelligence and capacity to men in other trades' or unable 'to assert their rights and care for themselves without the protecting arm of the State'. These notions reflected the waning days of a prevailing economic and social theory favouring minimal government intervention and the social Darwinism espoused by the English philosopher Herbert Spencer. Today, the *Lochner* decision is generally viewed as one of a handful of clear mistakes made by the Supreme Court, although a few conservative and libertarian scholars have begun to embrace it.[13]

Justice Oliver Wendell Holmes, Jr., wrote perhaps the most famous dissenting opinion in U.S. legal history, including these words that are today cited by every scholar who argues for judicial restraint and deference to legislatures:

> This case is decided upon an economic theory which a large part of the country does not entertain. If it were a question whether I agreed with that theory, I

should desire to study it further and long before making up my mind. But I do not conceive that to be my duty, because I strongly believe that my agreement or disagreement has nothing to do with the right of a majority to embody their opinions in law [...]. The Fourteenth Amendment does not enact Mr. Herbert Spencer's Social Statics.

Mr. Justice Holmes never mentioned 'bread' or 'bakers'. The quality of bread did not appear to be important to any of the justices.

Pizza Napoletana

Although there is significant controversy over the history and cultural meaning of pizza, it is certain that, from the late nineteenth century and increasingly as pizza has spread throughout Italy and the world, the pizza makers of Naples have sought to differentiate their gastronomic and artistic pizza endeavours from those of the increasing numbers of pizza makers outside Naples. One thoughtful commentator described the situation this way: 'Pizza is like a manufactured object from an archaeological age of which we have lost all other trace. It is that archaeological quality that enables pizza to shake off its geographical origin and gives it a place within the landscape of the big city, in locales that offer easily prepared poor foods [...].'[14]

The Neapolitan pizza makers began in earnest in 1984 to obtain legal protections to differentiate their pizza with the formation in Naples of the *Associazione Verace Pizza Napoletana* (VPN), a private organization of (then) twenty pizza makers that within a few years began to work toward creating a trademark or Italian legal designation of origin (*Denominazione di origine controllata* or DOC) that could give prestige to their product and possibly restrict the use of certain names by competitors.[15] The initial step was to obtain a trademark for the term '*Pizza Napoletana*' and set a highly detailed set of standards that had to be met for others to use their trademark. Borrowing from the artistic history of Naples, they adopted the character Pulcinella from the commedia dell'arte as their symbol, depicting him using a *palo* to place pizza in a wood-burning oven.

Their initial work inspired some degree of ridicule by competing pizza makers around the world who thought, probably incorrectly, that the group had been formed to try to trademark the term 'pizza'. This criticism accelerated once they began joint actions with Italy's flamboyant and nationalist then-Minister of Agriculture Giovanni Alemanno (later mayor of Rome). They actually had a different role. The DOC rules related to what has come to be known as 'indications of geographical origin', which are based on a complex interrelationship of various treaties and rules of supra-national organizations that can give significant protection to the name of a product. The European Union began to give EU-wide designations to food products in the 1990s.[16] In 2004, the group, with Alemanno's assistance, embarked on an effort to expand the reach of the Italian regulation to the entire EU. They abandoned Pulcinella in favour of a stylized drawing of a pizza Margherita and filed their extensive declaration with the European Union for a newer certification known as STG or TSG (Traditional Specialty Guaranteed). The EU TSG designation is designed to provide protections for traditional food products of 'specific character'. Under EU rules this kind of protection requires that specific production methods or raw materials have proved 'traditional' for 'a period that allows transmission between generations [...] at least 30 years'. However, this is a weaker form of protection than the EU's 'protected designations of origin', which protects products such as Champagne or Parmigiano Reggiano by requiring that the product be produced in a specific geographical location.

Italy's application was initially opposed by Germany and Poland but after some modification of the proposed rules was granted in February 2010 as Commission Regulation (EU) No 97/2010 of 4 February 2010 'entering a name in the register of traditional specialities guaranteed: Pizza Napoletana (TSG)'.[17]

These definitional rules, based on the VPN rules ('*disciplinare*'), run the length of a novella and contain extraordinary precision and detail. A few of the requirements give the flavour of the instructions:

- The central part is 0,4 cm thick, with a tolerance of ± 10 %, and the rim is 1-2 cm thick.
- Using an oil dispenser with a spout and a spiraling motion, distribute over the surface area, from the centre outwards, 4 to 5 g of extra virgin olive oil, with a tolerance of + 20 %.
- The baking time must not exceed 60 to 90 seconds.[18]
- The 'Pizza Napoletana' should preferably be consumed immediately, as soon as it comes out of the oven, in the same location as it was produced. However, if it is not consumed at the place of its production, it cannot be frozen or deep frozen or vacuum packed for later sale.[19]

Commercial brewer's yeast, though anathema to Parmentier, is required.

The Naples pizzerias thus voluntarily subjected themselves to regulation under rules that they themselves set forth, but that are so specific they are unlikely to be followed precisely and allow for no innovation at all. Were these restrictions worth the marketing advantage they received? This question might never be answered because, in practice, a degree of innovation continues. Some of the best makers of pizza around Naples no longer follow the rules because they (like Parmentier) feel it is important to use natural yeast for fuller, deeper flavour and for reasons of artistry.

This relatively weak type of legal designation gives only limited protection to the product (and only applies within the EU). The stronger designation of origin protection, DOC, which would include a geographic requirement, was proposed in the 1990s but seems to have been abandoned.[20] The DOC designation would have required the pizza to be made in Naples, giving the term *Pizza Napoletana* no special protection elsewhere, except as a set of rules that pizza makers elsewhere could assert that they followed if they felt that would give them a marketing advantage. It would not be helpful to obtain a geographical designation of authenticity for a product that under its own rules of authentic preparation cannot be preserved or transported elsewhere. Champagne and Parmigiano Reggiano do not face this issue. And a DOC designation would not particularly attract gastrotourists to Naples because people would already assume the pizza in Naples to be Neapolitan pizza.

The TSG rules and VPN rules both specify procedures for the two official types of *Pizza Napoletana* – pizza Margherita and pizza Marinara – but they do not receive protection of those names from use by others, and competitors whether in compliance with the rules or not can also use these pizza terms freely so long as they do not affix the letters STG or TSG to the term. Enforcement of the use of the designation is also a problem.

The TSG rules, as part of EU law, are not easy to amend, while the VPN rules can easily be amended by the *Associazione,* and in fact the two sets of rules have already diverged. Moreover, some of the celebrated pizza makers in and around Naples who are ignoring some of the EU rules have also chosen not to join the VPN, again pursuing their own artistic path. In short, the EU approval of the designation may be a mixed blessing. However, EU Regulation 97/2010 does serve as perhaps the longest and most complete and precise recipe ever written.[21]

The TSG status for *Pizza Napoletana* does not seem contentious any more, at this point, and in that sense the Neapolitans behind the rulings may be satisfied. They certainly received a lot of publicity as the designations were moving through the Italian legal system and eventually the EU. Even less contentious, because it does not in any way restrict competition, was the separate recognition Naples received in 2017 when the 'Art of the Neapolitan "Pizzaiuolo"' was added to UNESCO's Representative List of the Intangible Cultural Heritage of Humanity at the behest of a different organization, the Association of Neapolitan Pizzaiuoli.[22] (Others who have successfully applied for and been added to UNESCO's list include France for 'the gastronomic meal of France' (2010) and Jamaica, for reggae (2018)). This, the quasi-legal power of a United Nations agency, may in the end prove more valuable than TSG or VPN status because it grants a certain prestige without imposing significant restrictions.

The Same-Sex Wedding Cake

By contrast, the U.S. Supreme Court case *Masterpiece Cakeshop, Ltd.* v. *Colorado Civil Rights Commission* arouses extreme feelings.[23] This is the case about whether Jack Phillips, a master baker, could be sanctioned for refusing to create a custom-designed cake for a same-sex wedding that he disapproved of on religious grounds. The case was heard by a very different Supreme Court from that of 1905: no longer consisting of nine white Protestant males, the court included three women, three Jews, six Catholics, and one black man.

In contrast to the *Lochner* case's limited discussion of bread and baking, in *Masterpiece Cakeshop* the oral argument before the court on 5 December 2017, and the seven-to-two decision, two concurring opinions, and one dissent handed down on

4 June 2018, dealt in detail with the process of sketching, designing, sculpting, baking, and hand decorating of custom-made wedding cakes. Phillips argued that the Colorado Civil Rights Commission violated his right to free exercise of religion. In a confusing opinion, the Court held for Phillips, declaring that the Commission did not act properly in sanctioning him and thus set the Commission's order aside. The decision is equivocal and gives almost no basis for determining how the Court might come out in a different but similar case. However, the case leaves no doubt that a majority of the Court viewed the cake baker as an artist worthy of some degree of legal protection for his artistry.

At oral argument the justices focused with unusual concern on the symbolic importance of wedding cakes and to what extent a food – a cake – can be considered art or speech entitled to Constitutional protection. Justice Sonia Sotomayor was of the opinion that a cake is just food and said, somewhat scornfully, 'The primary purpose of a food of any kind is to be eaten.' By contrast, Justice Clarence Thomas, in his concurring opinion, cited books about desserts and weddings and noted that wedding cakes are often described as 'inedible' – a point Jack Phillips would not have agreed with – in order to make Phillips's point that a wedding cake is deeply symbolic and conveys messages that an artisan should not be forced to deliver.

Courts, especially supreme courts, usually try to decide cases narrowly, in part to avoid inadvertently deciding cases where facts are similar but significantly different. However, despite this effort to decide cases narrowly, the public – especially with controversial cases – often imbues the decisions with a broader significance than they have. With the *Masterpiece Cakeshop*, a common, but mistaken, belief, is that the Court ruled that a baker can refuse to serve gay couples. In fact, the Court's decision was exceedingly narrow, and the opinion of the Court took pains to explain that how a future similar case might be decided is very much in doubt.

The Colorado Civil Rights Commission had held that the baker's refusal to craft a custom cake for the couple violated the state's Anti-Discrimination Act. The court, trying to balance Phillip's right to free exercise of religion against the State's right 'to protect the rights and dignity of gay persons', noted that gay marriage was not allowed in Colorado at the time. Presumably, this fact alone would distinguish subsequent similar cases, now that gay marriage is protected across the United States by the Supreme Court decision in the case of *Obergefell* v. *Hodges*, which was decided in 2015 – after Phillips was prosecuted but before the Supreme Court took up his case.[24] As to the question of whether 'a beautiful wedding cake' might be 'protected speech', no group of five or more justices (out of nine) held similar enough views for any consensus to be formed – another reason it is impossible to know how the Court would handle a future case. In the end, it appears that the coalition of justices who made up the majority decided the case based largely on the Colorado Civil Rights Commission's hostile attitude toward Phillips: they found the Commission's behaviour demeaning in the way it dismissed what the Court concluded were Phillips's 'sincere religious beliefs and convictions'.

The Court did not decide whether forcing a baker or an artist to express a view

302

he did not agree with would constitute a kind of involuntary servitude – a return to eighteenth-century French baking laws when bakers needed permission to leave the profession. Many people were surprised that this arguably anti-gay decision of the Court was written by Justice Anthony Kennedy, who in 2015 had written the *Obergefell* decision, the very opinion that had legalized gay marriage in the United States. Cognizant of the fine lines he had drawn in the *Obergefell* case to garner the votes of a bare majority of the justices, in *Masterpiece Cakeshop* Justice Kennedy noted some unusual specific facts of the case and therefore the uncertainty of predicting 'the outcome of some future controversy involving facts similar to these'. More recently, the Court has sent some similar cases back to lower courts for further consideration, and it is likely that at least one of those reconsidered cases will come back in the future to the Supreme Court.

It is interesting to note that in his dissent in *Obergefell*, Chief Justice John Roberts mentioned the 1905 *Lochner* decision sixteen times, agreeing with Justice Holmes's belief that a court should not use a popular philosophical idea to impose a view that a legislature has not yet adopted.

Conclusion

This paper does not argue that there is no longer a balance between a government's interest in protecting the public and bakers' interest in protecting their own interests. In the case of bakers, there has not simply been a switch from protection of the public to protection of bakers' privilege. There has always been an ebb and flow of laws, and elements of both sorts of regulation combine. As early as the reign of Louis XIII, the royal household gave extraordinary legal protection and privileges to twelve master bakers who served the king in his travels, and the harsh regulatory regime and grim lives of most bakers in the eighteenth century does not mean bakers were never favoured or protected.[25] There are also, to be sure, significant regulatory burdens put on bakers today, who must comply with local health and safety laws affecting their product and their employees, with ingredient requirements, labelling requirements, and surprise inspections by health inspectors. Contemporary regulation still seeks to protect the public from adulterated or harmful bread and at the same time to protect workers.

However, the four historical episodes do illustrate a dramatic trend. In most households, the economic significance of bread has fallen far: from a critical staple to an accompaniment, however cherished it may be. No one needs bread to survive. Bread does still have immense cultural significance to many people, even as it is viewed as a poison by some in the anti-carbohydrate and paleo-diet movements. Governments have eased up on bakers. At the same time, bakers are finding special protections for themselves in the law. The emphasis on making quality a legal matter, so important in eighteenth-century France, is essentially gone, often replaced by an emphasis on the well-being, ambition, and freedom of expression of the baker.

The simplest test of the changes since eighteenth-century France might be to rush to the police to show them a loaf of bread that does not meet one's standards. Where substandard loaves are concerned, the contemporary view of police duty would not be the same as that of *Commissaire* Delamare.

Notes

1   For example, see Frances Malino, *The Sephardic Jews of Bordeaux: Assimilation and Emancipation in Revolutionary and Napoleonic France* (Tuscaloosa: University of Alabama Press, 2003).
2   Steven L. Kaplan, *The Bakers of Paris and the Bread Question 1700-1775* (Durham: Duke University Press, 1996), pp. 464, 692 n. 8.
3   The restrictions contained in the '*loi du 16-24 août 1790*' and subsequent revisions were finally abrogated by the simplification law 2014-1545, 20 December 2014.
4   See Richard Shepro, 'Outlaw Offal: The Curious Cases of Tête de Veau and Foie Gras', in *Offal: Rejected and Reclaimed Food*, ed. by Mark McWilliams (London: Prospect Books, 2017), pp. 346-58.
5   Gary Richardson, 'A Tale of Two Theories: Monopolies and Craft Guilds in Medieval England and Modern Imagination', *Journal of the History of Economic Thought* (June 2001), pp. 217-42.
6   On the subject of the difficulty of separating lore, tradition, and myth from historical fact as to what people ate in eighteenth-century France, see Philippe Meyzie, *La Table du Sud-Ouest et l'émergence des cuisines regionals (1700-1850)* (Rennes: Presse Universitaires de Rennes, 2007).
7   Steven L. Kaplan, *La France et son pain* (Paris: Albin Michel 2010), p. 146. Delamare's *Traité de la Police*, published in four volumes between 1705 and 1738, compiled and commented on the laws of Paris.
8   Bakers (*boulangers*) were exclusively male, while *boulangères* (bakers' wives) generally worked selling bread in the shop. A recent female graduate of a top baking school in Paris told me that she prefers to be called using the masculine name, *boulanger*, because she actually bakes and does not work in a shop.
9   He argued this view relentlessly, including in Antoine-Augustin Parmentier, *Le Parfait Boulanger, ou Traité complet sur la fabrication et le commerce du pain* (Paris: Imprimerie Royale 1778). See commentary in *Dictionnaire Universel du Pain*, ed. by Jean-Philippe de Tonnac (Paris: Éditions Robert Laffont, 2010), pp. 606-18.
10   198 U.S. 45 (1905). The *Lochner* case eventually was effectively overruled by several cases in the 1930s, notably *West Coast Hotel Co.* v. *Parrish*, 300 U.S. 379 (1937) (upholding minimum wage laws).
11   The U.S. Supreme Court is a court of limited jurisdiction that generally may determine whether or not to accept a case decided in a lower court. It has nine justices who may group together to join the written opinions of other justices, but in most cases only a majority vote or opinion may determine the resolution of a case.
12   References to the decision of 'the Court' or 'how the Court held' refer to the actual, binding decision and opinion of the majority of justices. The dissenting opinions are only opinions of those justices who write or join the particular dissenting opinion, and do not have precedential value, although they sometimes become highly influential at a later time.
13   See Paula Fujiwara's paper in this collection for the effects of an even more reviled U.S. Supreme Court decision, *Korematsu* v. *United States*, 323 U.S. 214 (1944). For those seeking arguments in favour of the decision, see, for example, David E. Bernstein, *Rehabilitating Lochner: Defending Individual Rights Against Progressive Reform* (Chicago: University of Chicago Press, 2011) and Richard A. Epstein, 'The "Necessary History" of Property and Liberty', *Chapman Law Review* (2003).
14   Franco LaCecla, *Pasta and Pizza*, trans. by Lydia G. Cochrane (Chicago: Prickly Paradigm Press, 2007), p. 80.
15   The person who actually produces the pizza in front of a wood-burning oven is known as a *pizzaiolo* but the association was formed by the owners of pizza establishments (some of whom may be or have been *pizzaioli*).
16   See, generally, Vadim Mantrov, *EU Law on Indication of Geographical Origin* (Heidelberg: Springer 2014). The general, current EU law is Regulation (EU) No 1151/2012 covering 'quality schemes' for

agricultural products and foodstuffs.

17 Official Journal of the European Union, 'Commission Regulation (EU) No. 97/2010, entering a name in the register of traditional specialities guaranteed [Pizza Napoletana (TSG)]' (4 February 2010) <https://eur-lex.europa.eu/eli/reg/2010/97/oj> [accessed 4 March 2020].

18 It is unclear why a do-not-exceed time is given as a range instead of simply a maximum.

19 The word 'preferably' was not contained in the original regulations of the *Associzione VPN,* which required immediate consumption on the premises, without exception.

20 The relevant terms at the EU level are 'Protected Designation of Origin' (PDO) and 'Protected Geographical Indication' (PGI).

21 For those who might happen to have a wood-burning oven at home, these extensive rules can be a real inspiration.

22 This group uses the older spelling.

23 584 U.S. ___ (2018).

24 576 U.S. ___ (2015).

25 de Tonnac, p. 460.

I'll Tell You How to Cook to Tell You Who I Am: The Culinary Identity Constructions of the Eaton Sisters

Koby Song-Nichols

In 1914, Sara Bosse and Onoto Watanna published the *Chinese-Japanese Cook Book* in Chicago. This book served as many North Americans' first introduction to cooking Asian cuisine; however, there was something contemporary readers did not know as they were perusing and attempting each recipe. The authors guiding them were not an American woman and her Japanese interlocutor but rather sisters, born as Sara and Winnifred Eaton to a British father and a Chinese mother. This plausible case of culinary identity fraud becomes even more complex when one considers their elder sister Edith, who adopted a conspicuously Chinese pseudonym Sui Sin Far (Narcissus flower in Cantonese). Together these sisters left a large collection of texts that detailed their experiences as Eurasian women, at times seemingly undermining or bolstering part, or all, of their ethnic background. The history of these Eurasian sisters, and their assumed names and identities, reveals the complexities of racialized and non-racialized experience under American and Canadian Chinese Exclusion acts that extended from the late nineteenth century into the mid-twentieth century. The Eurasian background of these sisters not only further complicates the production of this cookbook, which arguably represents one of the first 'Asian American' voices on Chinese and Japanese cuisine in North America, but also provides a unique historical moment to understand how agents used the combination of food and writing to articulate their own identities. This paper analyzes these three sisters' discursive approaches to food to advance our understanding of how racialized and gendered beings articulate their own identity with, and against, broader cultural constructions and expectations.

Three Sisters, Three Paths

The history of the Eaton family begins in China with Lotus Blossom (1847-1922), who also went by Grace, meeting Edward Eaton (1838-1915). Grace was born in China and worked with a Chinese circus group before London missionaries took her to be raised in England. In later life Grace returned to Shanghai to train for local mission work; here she met Edward who was in the region for business. They quickly married and in 1864, they had their first son, Edward Charles. The Eatons moved to England, where Edith was born in 1865, and then to America where Sara was born in New York in 1868. After transiting between America and England following business failures, the Eatons eventually settled in Montreal, Canada in the 1870s, where Winnifred was born in 1875. The Eaton family would eventually have sixteen children in total. In Montreal, a city where at the time it was exceedingly rare to see a Chinese person, the Eaton siblings experienced some of their first encounters with racism. Often referred to as '*les pauvres enfants...Chinoise, Chinoise*' (the poor Chinese children) by neighbours, the Eaton siblings knew from early on to feel ashamed of their mixed-race heritage.[1] In both Canada and United States, the late nineteenth to mid-twentieth centuries marked an intense period of anti-Chinese and anti-Asian sentiment, most prominently seen in the Chinese and Asian exclusionary laws enforced in each country.

The three sisters centred here, Edith, Sara, and Winnifred, each chose different life paths, and, to the delight of the historian, they all chose to document their thoughts as writers and journalists. From their writings, we can trace each sister's experience with racism and better understand how they negotiated their identity against these experiences. This paper follows these three sisters not only because of their distinctive choices to present more Chinese, Anglo-American, or Japanese identities but also because they each wrote about food to articulate these identities.

Since the rediscovery of Edith and Winnifred's writings in the 1970s, scholars and biographers have meticulously pieced together the Eaton family's history, accruing an extensive historiography and collection of literary analysis, particularly on Edith and Winnifred. In this historiography, scholars often champion Edith as the mother figure to Asian American literature following a period of Asian American activism that was developing in the 1970s. Scholars valorized Edith's efforts to speak for Chinese Canadian and American communities during a time of great anti-Chinese sentiment, and either ignored or demonized Winnifred's more Orientalized depiction of Japonica.[2] Since this initial wave of Asian American scholarly attention, the Eaton sisters experienced an academic renaissance in the late 1990s and early 2000s when scholars sought to challenge ahistorical assessments of the sisters' writings that placed twentieth-century understandings of race and ethnic authenticity onto these late nineteenth-century writings.[3] During this second period, Winnifred's writing gained attention, and efforts to collapse the binary view of the sisters in which Winnifred stood as a negative foil to her more 'politically engaged sister' Edith emerged. Dominika Ferens's work exemplifies this, pointing out that this 'good sister-bad sister' paradigm overlooks 'Winnifred's subtle antiracist interventions and the muted orientalism of Edith's work'.[4] Contemporary scholars including Rosmarin Heidenriech and Megan Chapman continue to work on collecting these sisters' work and theorizing their complex identity constructions. This paper builds on this historiography by examining the food texts that have been overlooked by previous scholars and by bringing Sara's work into the conversations surrounding the identity constructions of these sisters.

Chinese Food Is Clean and Healthy

Throughout her life, Edith used her writing to combat negative stereotypes of Chinese people in Canada and the United States. As the eldest daughter, Edith had the closest relationship to their mother and remained in Montreal until she was nearly thirty-two years old to help take care of her siblings.[5] Although faced with family pressures, Edith still managed to establish a successful career as a writer and a journalist. She began as a stenographer for the *Montreal Daily Star*, eventually publishing anonymously (as per publishing practices at the time) articles about the Chinese of Montreal in the newspaper in the late 1880s. Many of her pieces were published under the name Sui Sin Far; however, as Chapman has noted, Edith also adopted other viewpoints outside of her Chinese diasporic mainstay.[6] Edith's decision to adopt a primarily Chinese diasporic voice in her writings is connected to the many bouts with racism during her childhood in England and Montreal. In these experiences, she found solidarity in her experience with the Chinese men she encountered in her childhood, inspiring her to write and reflect on her heritage throughout her life.[7]

In her thirties, Edith left Montreal and travelled to the Caribbean and across the continental United States, documenting Chinese American and Chinatown experiences as she went. Some of her most notable works include *Mrs. Spring Fragrance* (1912), a collection of writing that captures a more sympathetic view of Chinatown communities, and 'Leaves from the Mental Portfolio of an Eurasian' (1909). Edith achieved only modest success during her lifetime, most of which came from the Chinese communities she connected with. Her writings about Chinese food and food culture further reveals her commitment to changing the anti-Chinese public opinion of her time. These writings also demonstrate a nuanced engagement with Chinese food that advocated for the Chinese community through asking for recognition of similarity rather than a respect or acceptance of difference.

Edith's defence of Chinese food and food habits began in her early writings published in the *Montreal Daily Star*, where on 25 November 1895, Edith published a piece titled 'Chinese Food'.[8] Published anonymously, Edith began by informing her readers that she had 'been through a Chinese kitchen in the city and eaten of many Chinese dishes, all of which [...] were very good and nutritious,' establishing her authority on the topic not through her ethnic background but through having visited these kitchens, as well as a tone of respectful but curious engagement with Chinese food and people. She went on to identify rice as 'a very wholesome grain', and declare that Chinese people cook 'cleanly and beautifully'. Here she glorified Chinese food as wholesome, clean, and nutritious, seemingly attempting to undo all the negative stereotypes of Chinese food as dirty and lesser than that followed Chinese food and bodies during this period of anti-Chinese sentiment. Her comment on rice, in particular, seems to have predicted the anti-Chinese attacks via food that would come later. Such attacks are most notably seen in the efforts of American labour union leader, Samuel Gompers, who wrote an anti-Chinese document titled 'Meat vs. Rice' in 1902, painting Chinese as harmful to American labour practices specifically because of their ability to sustain themselves on rice rather than meat like their Caucasian counterparts. As opposed to looking at Chinatown, Chinese restaurants, and Chinese food with disdain, Edith encouraged a more admiring appreciation of Chinese food. In the same format that anti-Chinese agents sought to stigmatize Chinese North Americans through their food, Edith worked to elevate Chinese cooking and by extension improve the status of Chinese people in Montreal. For example, in this article she describes how everything in a Chinese meal is cut into small pieces so that they can be handled by chopsticks, stating that 'the Chinaman comes to the table to eat – not to work – his carving is done in the kitchen'.

Later in her career Edith wrote a collection of pieces for the *Los Angeles Express* in the voice of a Chinese American man named Wing Sing who was traveling across North America. In Wing Sing's travels to New York City, published on 9 June and 14 June 1904, Edith gave us insight into New York City's Chinese restaurant scene and its significance to the city's inhabitants. In the article published on 9 June, Wing Sing finds himself in the city dining at a restaurant known as the 'Chinese Delmonico' with a gentleman named Ju Chu who is reported to be the president of the Reform Party of China in New York. At this restaurant, Wing takes the time to note that 'American people think chop suey [is] the best Chinese dish, but [that] the Chinese, they know plenty better'.[9] In this account, Edith first established Chinese restaurants as a site for important meetings through the company Wing Sing eats with. Secondly, she meets her most likely non-Chinese readers by placing the meeting at one of the most well-known Chinese restaurants in the city and then uses the aside about chop suey to invite her readers to recognize that there is more to Chinese cuisine than chop suey. In the second account, Wing Sing talks about a sense of solidarity between Chinese Japanese and Jews in the city; her narrator is surprised to note that Jewish people in the city like Chinese food and frequent Chinese restaurants, stating that it seemed 'strange' since the Chinese put pork in their dishes.[10] Through this account, Edith demonstrates the intercultural interactions occurring in Chinese restaurants between different ethnic minorities; in this sense she works to paint a fuller picture of the roles Chinese restaurants and food played within the city.

In these accounts, Edith reported on the more quotidian experience of Chinese food, using her knowledge of and experience with Chinese North American communities to invite her non-Chinese readers to recognize the humanity of her Chinese subjects. Her pieces on Chinese food and restaurants work within her larger corpus of writing that sought to speak out against anti-Chinese sentiment through this process of humanization. Emma Teng describes Edith's rhetorical strategy as demonstrating that those 'who have been treated as "different" [are], in fact, very much "like" the readers themselves.'[11] Edith used food and Chinese restaurants in her writing to achieve her larger goal of fighting against anti-Chinese racism, a process that perhaps relied on her position as a mixed-raced individual. Her ability to convey this humanity involved the

309

key recognition of the connection between her own racialized experience with other Chinese individuals and the ability to deconstruct and explain that experience to those of non-Chinese heritage and appeal to their understandings of humanity.

An Idea for a Cookbook

Sara's life is harder to trace in comparison to her better known and documented sisters: she published less prolifically, and her perceived implicit decision to claim a 'white' or 'Anglo-Canadian/American' identity removed her from the focus of Asian American and ethnic scholarship. However, by closely reading the biographical information assembled on Edith and Winnifred, slivers of Sara's life come through. While Sara was born in New York in 1868 during one of Edward and Grace's briefs stays in the city, she spent most of her childhood in Montreal. As she grew up, she followed in her father's footsteps and became a painter. She eventually married German artist Karl Bosse and is said to have lived a 'happy, bohemian, childless life in New York' with him.[12] In New York she published two articles in *Harper's Bazaar* (1913) and briefly operated as their Asian food correspondent. Her entry into writing may have had something to do with the fact that she lived with Winnifred for a time in New York, growing close and collaborating on writing projects, most notably the *Chinese-Japanese Cook Book*.[13] When read closely, Sara's food articles and work on the cookbook offer insight into the form of negotiation she may have gone through in claiming her heritage.

310

Sara's two articles in *Harper's Bazaar* concerning Chinese cuisine on the surface present as a Caucasian upper class engagement with an Orientalized understanding of Chinese culture and cuisine. The first article came out in January 1913 titled 'Cooking and Serving a Chinese Dinner in America'.[14] It detailed how readers can cook Chinese dishes at home through the information provided in the article and encouraged them to explore Chinese establishments in larger cities in America. One of the more interesting parts of this piece is her explanation as to why it may be difficult for diners to have tried to cook Chinese at home in the past. She first explains how Chinese cooks have fooled diners by leaving out 'a vital ingredient' when sharing recipes. She then provides recipes for a full Chinese meal at the end of the article as well as further tips on how not to be duped by 'Mr. Chinaman' into buying 'gaudy articles ("American-Chinese")' to recreate a Chinese dinner. This combination constructs an image of Chinese men in Chinatown seemingly actively working to thwart a home production of Chinese cuisine, which speaks to a possible societal distrust of Chinese people. However, this approach also implies that Sara is some form of insider to be aware of this deception and/or knowledgeable enough to provide assumedly full and authentic recipes of Chinese dishes; she did not provide an explanation as to how she procured those recipes or this cultural knowledge. By the follow-up article that came out in March of the same year, Sara may have realized that she did not provide an origin to her knowledge and thus credits her recipes to 'Vo Ling', an apparently 'worthy descendent of a long line of Chinese cooks' and himself the 'head cook to Gow Gai, the highest mandarin of Shanghai'.[15]

In these articles, Sara covers many aspects of entertaining guests with a Chinese meal from decorations and ambiance (including a suggestion of having a 'Chinese "boy" wait on the table if possible' or asking one's maid to 'wear her hair Chinese fashion' and instruct her to 'walk noiselessly'[16]) to assuring that all the necessary ingredients can be found in local Chinatowns. She also clearly used these articles as a starting point for the cookbook she wrote with Winnifred, with several sentences and sentiments transferring at times verbatim into the cookbook, including the attribution of all the Chinese recipes to Vo Ling. Vo Ling's ownership over the recipes becomes exceedingly doubtful in reading the cookbook, especially as many of the recipe names are written in a Romanized Cantonese (a dialect not native to Shanghai) and also due to the fact that there is a large section dedicated to chop suey, a dish that scholars have convincingly linked to being primarily developed in America and rarely found in China. This further provides evidence that Sara and Winnifred obtained this culinary knowledge by other means, the most obvious being through their family connections.

Altogether Sara offers a bohemian upper class engagement with Chinese cuisine, a move that would not be surprising considering the New York circles she operated in. However, one key aspect of Sara's writing, which perhaps reveals a more complex story, is how she echoes the sensitivities towards Chinese people promoted by her elder sister Edith. In her writing, Sara emphasizes that readers should go to Chinese restaurants to develop a taste for Chinese food and stresses the cleanliness of Chinese cuisine, stating that cleanliness was 'the first and the most important rule for Chinese cuisine'.[17] The cookbook also emphasizes the importance of rice to Chinese and Japanese culinary culture, elevates 'Oriental peoples' as 'past masters' of rice preparation, and notes that 'mushy, wet, overcooked rice is unknown to the Chinese and Japanese'.[18] Her and Winnifred's emphasis here on the culinary expertise of Chinese chefs reflects an admiring tone that is similar their sister Edith's view of Chinese food and people.

Sara's writing did not simply echo the Orientalized depictions of her euro-American counterparts but upon closer reading offered a more sensitive portrayal of Chineseness that was more palatable to white upper class individuals. Acknowledging Sara's background and paying closer attention to her writing suggests that this exercise with Chinese cuisine could have been an attempt to unite her bohemian New York lifestyle with the Chinese knowledge and experiences that operated behind her experience as a Eurasian. It demonstrates how one's cultural tools are formed by surrounding cultural agents and societal influences and how those tools offer different forms of access and expression of one's heritage.

Chinese-Japanese Cook Book
Winnifred followed in her sister Edith's footsteps, deciding to become a writer at an early age; however, unlike Edith, Winnifred was not limited by familial obligation and left home at the age of seventeen to go to Jamaica. She then moved to New York in 1901 having already published one novel and dozens of stories under her pseudonym,

Onoto Watanna. As Onoto, she claimed that she was descended from English nobility on one side and Japanese nobility on the other, an act of 'passing' as Japanese that she took seriously and performed consistently throughout her career.[19] Once in New York she soon published her novel *A Japanese Nightingale*, which sold approximately 200,000 copies, was turned into a Broadway play and a silent movie, and cemented Winnifred's fame.[20] In New York, Winnifred emerged as a literary celebrity. Winnifred's success both commercially and in constructing her own Japanese identity persona offers an opportunity to further examine how she used food not only to continue to articulate her identity but also to invite the reader to participate in her identity construction.

Analyzing the cookbook requires revisiting how and why Winnifred created and propagated her Japanese identity to the public. Winnifred's biographer – and granddaughter – Diana Birchall, cites several reasons and methods pertaining to Winnifred's identity. At the same time anti-Chinese sentiment was on the rise in the late nineteenth century in the United States and Canada, the perceived prestige of Japan was increasing as it was becoming known as a 'powerful modern nation' especially due to the Japanese success in Russo-Japanese and Sino-Japanese wars. There was also a craze for 'Japonica' following Commodore Matthew Perry's 'opening' of Japan in the 1850s, Japanese exhibits at the Philadelphia Centennial Exhibition of 1876, and the installation of the popular Japanese pavilion at the World Exposition in Chicago, which would have created a market for Winnifred's Japan-inspired works.[21] Ferens offers three explanations as to how Winnifred was able to convince her readers of her Japanese identity and cultivate an audience to create a lucrative and successful writing career. First, nineteenth century scientific theories had conflated race and culture, creating a popular understanding that there was an 'essential Japaneseness' that Onoto could claim through her reported Japanese half. Second, although there were events like world fairs and exhibitions that presented Japanese artefacts, few readers had any sense of Japanese literary conventions, allowing Winnifred to construct her own literary voice and authority over her claimed Japanese identity. Lastly, Winnifred's narratives 'resonated well' with other widely accepted ethnographic narratives of the time.[22] Birchall also points to Winnifred's access to multiple libraries and perhaps also to recollections of her father who had gone on business trips to Japan earlier in his life. Winnifred's ability to pass led to great financial and social success, demonstrating a strong plasticity of identity she had access to in response to broader societal conversations and understandings of race.

With this cookbook, Sara and Winnifred entered a new engagement with their readers, inviting their readers to participate in their identity creations. Although Winnifred did publish several nonfiction articles on Japanese subjects early on in her career, including factual pieces titled 'Every-Day Life in Japan', 'The Marvelous Miniature Trees of Japan', and 'The Life of a Japanese Girl', a cookbook presented a different form of nonfiction that implied a more active engagement with her Japanese identity.[23] Yong Chen conceptualizes cookbooks as 'social texts' that reflect 'the collective wisdom' of communities more than 'the individual ingenuity of the author' as well as reflecting contemporaneous 'social conditions and trends'; Yong Chen also noted that the cookbook offered Chinese Americans a 'high-profile platform' and authority to large educated non-Chinese audiences and shape the reception of Chineseness by mainstream American society.[24] With this in mind, the *Chinese-Japanese Cook Book* becomes the perfect medium to assess Sara and Winnifred's negotiation between community and societal understandings of Asianness and the construction of their own authority.

Winnifred's careful and methodical construction of her Japanese identity continues in the cookbook. As Birchall has noted, Sara's name appears before Onoto's, implying that the Chinese recipes were provided by Sara and the Japanese by Onoto.[25] Following on this construction of authority, unlike the Chinese recipes which, as mentioned above, were attributed as a gift from a family of Chinese chefs, there is no explicit explanation as to where the Japanese recipes came from, suggesting that they all came from Onoto and implicitly equating her perceived authority over Japanese cuisine to that of the Chinese chef family cited by Sara. The cookbook format allows Winnifred to extend Onoto's cultural authority towards Japanese culinary knowledge. Similar to the Chinese recipes, the Japanese section presents an array of dish types from soups and fish to omelettes, relishes, and dessert. Although these categories would have been familiar to her readers, through the reasons discussed above, historical conditions prevented these readers from questioning whether Japanese cuisine structured their dishes under the same categories.

The general balance of the cookbook perhaps belies Winnifred's limited mastery over Japanese cuisine; the Chinese section of the cookbook is significantly larger than the Japanese section, and a guide on how to cook is omitted in the Japanese section while present in the Chinese one. The voice used in the recipes also at times strays from the voice of a Japanese native towards an individual who rather researched Japanese culture. This is particularly evident in the cookbook's recipe for 'Katamochi', which compares the Katamochi to the Jewish 'Matzoth cracker' and states that this similarity 'has caused students often to point to it as another interesting evidence that the Japanese people are of Semitic origin – perhaps the "lost tribe"!'.[26] If we continue the assumption that the Japanese recipes came from Onoto, this recipe could hint at the studious origins of Winnifred's Japanese identity. It would be unlikely that contemporary readers would have noticed this shift, particularly due to the co-authorship of the book, thus as a whole this effort helped Winnifred further expand her authority over Japanese culture by capitalizing on contemporary interest of Asian cuisine and demonstrating a form of expertise over another realm of Japonica.

Conclusion – Sui Sin Fu Candy

Hidden within the *Chinese-Japanese Cook Book* on a list of groceries is a peculiar ingredient: 'Sui Sin Fu candy'. While I have not been able to locate to what exactly this ingredient refers, its close resemblance to their elder sister's moniker led me back to Edith's writings, searching for any mentions of candy. What I found was a piece published by Sui Sin Far called 'The Candy That Is Not Sweet'.[27] The short story recounts the actions of a young Chinese boy who steals his mother's money to purchase candy; however, due to guilt the candy did not taste sweet. This tale about not being able to enjoy one's bounty if achieved by dubious means resonates with Winnifred's success that has been troubled particularly by today's notions of cultural appropriation. While I cannot prove that Sara or Winnifred read this piece or whether it contributed to 'Sui Sin Fu' candy appearing in their cookbook, I do know that the timing of their cookbook came during a difficult moment for the Eaton family. A year before the cookbook came out, Edith passed away. Considering this, I am tempted to read the *Chinese-Japanese Cook Book* as Sara and Winnifred's way of paying homage to Edith and their Chinese ancestry, and as such the inclusion of 'Sui Sin Fu' candy becomes a recognition of Winnifred's change of heart in claiming a Japanese identity.

The conditions surrounding this cookbook offer us the opportunity to reflect on the relationships between these sisters and locate each of their identity explorations within broader society. Although Edith may have disagreed with Winnifred's choice to identify as Japanese, Amy Ling argues that Edith did not blame her sister for adopting a Japanese identity but rather criticized broader society for pressuring her sister, and other Chinese Eurasians, to identify that way. Ling also goes on to point out that Winnifred's writing shifted away from Japonica following Edith's death; the cookbook was one of the last pieces on Japan that she published.[28]

Through writing, these three sisters found ways to construct their own identities, whether it was through working to dispel racist stereotypes, promoting a bohemian Chinese luncheon, or expanding their constructed cultural expertise. Each sister creatively used food and writing to negotiate their own status in a society defined by racial binaries. Food became a realm for conversation and authority to be claimed and explored. By understanding how these sisters articulated their identity, we can continue to think about how the preparation and consumption of food and food knowledge interacts with constructions of identity and authority, especially for those who do not fit in, and/or challenge, hegemonic social categories. While much more could be said, we can be sure of at least one thing: these sisters took control over their Eurasian experience and identity, telling everyone how to cook in order to let everyone know who they were.

Acknowledgements

I need to thank everyone who helped me develop this piece, particularly Christopher, my family (especially Kallyn), Yang, Jeffrey Pilcher, the University of Toronto Asian Canadian Studies Research Network, the Oxford Food Symposiasts (2019) and all who let me talk about these sisters incessantly (especially Valeria and Kathy). This paper benefited immensely from their support, perspectives and edits, and I am very grateful. Any and all errors are my own.

Notes

1   Emma Teng, *Eurasian: Mixed Identities in the United States, China, and Hong Kong, 1842-1943* (Berkeley: University of California Press, 2013), p. 55; Diana Birchall, *Onoto Watanna: The Story of Winnifred Eaton, The Asian American Experience* (Urbana: University of Illinois Press, 2001), p. 4; Sui Sin Far and Mary Chapman, *Becoming Sui Sin Far: Early Fiction, Journalism, and Travel Writing* by Edith Maude Eaton (Montreal: McGill-Queen's University Press, 2016), p. xvi; Rosmarin Elfriede Heidenreich, *Literary Impostors: Canadian Autofiction of the Early Twentieth Century* (Montreal: McGill-Queen's University Press, 2018), p. 203; Annette White-Parks, *Sui Sin Far/Edith Maude Eaton: A Literary Biography, Asian American Experience* (Urbana: University of Illinois Press, 1995), p. 10.

2   *Aiiieeeee! An Anthology of Asian-American Writers*, ed. by Frank Chin (Washington: Howard University Press, 1974).

3   Amy Ling, *Between Worlds: Women Writers of Chinese Ancestry, Athene Series* (New York: Pergamon Press, 1990); White-Parks; Birchall.

4   Dominika Ferens, *Edith and Winnifred Eaton: Chinatown Missions and Japanese Romances, The Asian American Experience* (Urbana: University of Illinois Press, 2002), p. 2.

5   Xiao-huang Yin, *Chinese American Literature Since the 1850s, The Asian American Experience* (Urbana: University of Illinois Press, 2000), p. 89; White-Parks, p. 26.

6   Mary Chapman, 'Finding Edith Eaton', *Legacy: A Journal of American Women Writers*, 29.2 (2012), 263 (pp. 264-65) <doi.org/10.5250/legacy.29.2.0263>.

7   White-Parks, p. 18.

8   Sui Sin Far and Chapman, pp. 73-74.

9   Sui Sin Far and Chapman, pp. 223-25.

10 Sui Sin Far and Chapman, pp. 225-26.

11 Teng, p. 178.

12 White-Parks, p. 31; James Doyle, *The Fin de Siècle Spirit: Walter Blackburn Harte and the American/ Canadian Literary Milieu of the 1890s* (Toronto: ECW Press, 1995), p. 27; Ling, p. 27; Birchall, p. 25.

13 Birchall, pp. 23, 108.

14 Sara Bossé, 'Cooking and Serving a Chinese Dinner in America', *Harper's Bazaar*, January 1913, pp. 27, 29, 31.

15 Sara Bossé, 'Giving a Chinese Luncheon Party', *Harper's Bazaar*, March 1913, pp. 135, 146.

16 Bossé, 'Giving a Chinese Luncheon Party'.

17 Sara Bosse and Onoto Watanna, *Chinese-Japanese Cook Book, Hotel Monthly Handbook Series* (Chicago: Rand McNally, 1914), p. 9.

18 Bosse and Watanna, p. 2.

19 Ferens, p. 119.

20 Birchall, pp. xv, 74-77.

21 Birchall, pp. 55-56; Jean Lee Cole, *The Literary Voices of Winnifred Eaton: Redefining Ethnicity and Authenticity* (New Brunswick, NJ: Rutgers University Press, 2002), p. 25.

22 Ferens, pp. 120-21.

23 Birchall, p. 56.

24 Yong Chen, 'Recreating the Chinese American Home through Cookbook Writing', *Social Research; New York*, 81.2 (2014), 489-501.

25 Birchall, p. 107.

26 Bosse and Watanna, p. 104.

27 Edith Maud Eaton, *Mrs. Spring Fragrance* (Chicago, A.C. McClurg & Co., 1912), pp. 303-08 <http:// archive.org/details/cu31924075243513> [accessed 12 October 2019].

28 Ling, pp. 31-32.

Lebanese Sea Power: Food and the Phoenicians

David C. Sutton

Of the four great powers which shaped Ancient Mediterranean civilization and culture – Egyptian, Lebanese, Greek, and Italian – the extended power and influence of the Lebanese have been the least acknowledged and evaluated. Recognition of the importance of the Lebanese traditions (Phoenician and Carthaginian) in the Ancient World has been hampered by the loss of many of their archives – the most extensive in all antiquity, according to Josephus, but written on perishable papyrus – and by destructive military defeats at the hands of the Assyrians, the Babylonians and the Romans.[1]

This essay suggests that the story of the sea power (the thalassocracy) of the Phoenicians is essentially a story of food and food supply: first, a story of the fishing fleets of the Lebanese coast (where the very meaning of the word 'Sidon' is 'Fishery') from which evolved the legendary boatbuilding and navigational skills of the Phoenicians, and then a story of the food shortages in the fertile but overpopulated Lebanese lowlands that forced the Phoenicians to take to the high seas.

Phoenicians or Lebanese?

The Phoenicians never called themselves Phoenicians. They called themselves people of Ga-na-ne (Canaan) or La-ba-na-an (Lebanon).[2] The use of the term 'Canaanite' in the Hebrew Bible to designate all the peoples who were in the Near East before the Hebrews has caused ambiguity; hence the preference for 'Lebanese'. The Ancient Lebanese also identified strongly with their coastal cities: Ugarit, Byblos, Aradus, Beirut, Sidon, Tyre, Acre. The use of the term 'Sidonian' in both Homer and the Old Testament to describe the whole Lebanese people is, logically, an argument against those who have suggested that there was no single Phoenician culture.[3] (Famously, the much-maligned Queen Jezebel of Israel, daughter of the King of Tyre, is described in the Bible as Sidonian.) Using the word 'Lebanese' to describe the Phoenicians was until recently considered tendentious, and even political, but DNA research in the past fifteen years has established beyond doubt the continuity from the Phoenicians to present-day inhabitants of Lebanon, notably in the Maronite Christian community, but including Lebanese people of all religions. DNA-based projects have also produced very close matching between the Lebanese and peoples in their former colonies of Malta and Ibiza.[4]

Fishermen Who Wanted to Catch Whales

Naturally the early inhabitants of the Lebanese coastal plain looked to the sea for food. Some traditions even credit them with the invention of the fishing net. The National Museum in Beirut displays copper fishhooks from Byblos dated as early as 4000 BCE. The eastern Mediterranean was abundant in fish, and soon the Lebanese had fish to sell as well as fish to eat. Nehemiah is angry about men from Tyre living in Jerusalem who sold fish there on the sabbath (13:16). Nehemiah's indignation must have concerned salted fish, given the distance from Jerusalem to the sea. The Lebanese coastal cities enjoyed fresh Mediterranean fish from the earliest times.

There were some foods from the sea, though, which the first fishermen could not take. Texts from ancient Ugarit, about 4000 years ago, talk, rather wistfully, about the sea-monsters they could not catch, including *anharu* (the sperm whale) and *tunnanu* (the ancient Ugaritic word which survives in many European languages as tuna).[5] By the time of the Assyrian dominance, however, between about 1100 BCE and 850 BCE, the Lebanese had mastered hunting for cetaceans. Tiglatpilasar I (who reigned 1112-1074 BCE) reports killing a dolphin, on a hunt organized by his Lebanese hosts, 'in ships of Aradus', and tributes paid to Assurnasipal II (who reigned 883-859 BCE) by the Phoenician kings collectively similarly included *nakhiru* (probably salted dolphin-meat).[6]

Lebanese Foods other than Fish

From the earliest times, the Lebanese coastal strip was rich in the archetypal vegetable foods of the Mediterranean: cereals and fruit (notably lemons, oranges, figs, and pomegranates), olives and grapes (and hence oil and wine). Egyptian chronicles around 1500 BCE speak of Lebanese wine flowing like water, of the richness of the vegetable gardens near Byblos and the proliferation of cereals – notably barley, spelt, and wheat.[7] The cereals were baked as bread and biscuits, but especially eaten in porridges and pottages (as with the story of Esau in the Old Testament). It was a particular characteristic of Lebanon, then as now, that cereals were mixed with an abundance of lentils, peas, chickpeas, and broad beans (in what we now know to be a protein-rich combination), as well as onions, garlic, and leeks. Eggs came from hens and geese, but also from the (now extinct) Syrian ostrich. The cereals led to the availability of beer as well as wine, and also to various forms of flatbreads (the wine, then as now, came principally from the Bekaa Valley). Limited amounts of meat came from geese, wild birds, sheep, and some cows. Fish were much more significant. And two iconic foodstuffs, emphasized in the Old Testament account of Canaan, were milk and honey ('leben' in Arabic means fermented milk, which was seen as the colour of the snows on Mount Lebanon). For the most typical flavouring, archaeological digs in Lebanon have drawn attention to the supreme importance of cumin.

The frequent use of rice in modern Lebanese cookery (for instance in the staple of rice, cumin, and lentils) raises the question of the availability of rice to the Phoenicians. It was previously often discounted, but more recent research, using Assyrian, Akkadian, and Elamite sources for early rice production in the Near East – up to 3200 years ago – now makes it seem more likely.[8]

Food and Trade

Despite this abundance of attractive foods, however, it became clear very early that Ancient Lebanon could not produce enough food to feed the growing populations of its thriving coastal cities. The Phoenicians are sometimes described as 'natural' sailors, but it was food shortages in their rich and fertile land which made sea travel and trade essential.

Let us consider the well-known transfer of vital foods from Jerusalem to Tyre in the time of kings Shlomo [Solomon] and Hiram: 'Shlomo gave Hiram 100,000 bushels of wheat as food for his household and a thousand gallons of oil from pressed olives – this is what Shlomo gave Hiram each year' (1 Kings 5:11).

Different interpretations have been offered for these annual shipments, including king-to-king gifts, annual tithe from vassal to overlord, and a form of payment for expertise and for supplies of cedar. Whichever interpretation is preferred, it is clear that already, around 960 BCE, the coastal cities of Lebanon had great need of additional food.

The Mediterranean Sea has always been, and remains to this day, a transit zone across which peoples from under-resourced and under-nourished areas travel in search of food and a more viable lifestyle. What is unusual about Ancient Lebanon is the combination it presents of a rich and varied range of food products together with permanent problems of food shortages deriving not from poverty but from overpopulation.

318

Sources ancient and modern describe the Ancient Lebanese people as 'hemmed in' or 'squeezed' between the mountain ranges (of Lebanon and Anti-Lebanon) and the sea. Furthermore, beyond the mountains were the hostile military powers of Assyria and Babylon. The Mediterranean Sea was all too welcoming by comparison, and the need to trade was compelling, with voyages first southwards towards Egypt, then northwards into the Aegean, and later over the greater distances westwards.

Their first export comprised the emblematic cedars of Lebanon, which had to be brought down from the heights of the Lebanese mountains, floated, and bounced down mountain streams. Whole cedar trunks were being exported from Byblos to Egypt over 4500 years ago, and other early markets for cedar timber were found in Crete and Iraq. Initial exports to Egypt included numerous other products from the mountains of Lebanon, ranging from cedar-resin perfume to live wild bears. Carved wooden bowls from Byblos found in Egypt have been dated to the Third Dynasty (around 2592-2544 BCE).[9] And it is said that Lebanese cedar resin could still be clearly smelt in Ancient Egyptian tombs when they were opened thousands of years later.

The remarkable sailing skills required to transport huge cedar trunks, up to thirty metres long, from Lebanon to Egypt (with a combination of ships and towed barges) were already in evidence by around 2700 BCE.

Sea trading generally requires durables rather than perishables. Salted and dried foods, wine, and olive oil will travel well, but the Lebanese sailors, from the earliest times, also understood the importance of small high-value items, notably jewellery, spices and perfumes, carved marble, silks and linens, worked ivory, amber and ebony, and decorative glass. Their purple dye, their dyed products, intricate glassware, gems, amulets, torques, ornate jewels, and their precision design (for example of weighing scales) were among the exported products that are mentioned in sources from all around the Ancient World.

The cargo of a Lebanese boat, shipwrecked off the Turkish coast near Uluburun, carbon-dated to around 1305 BCE and discovered in 1982, gives wonderful confirmation of this early sea trade.[10] These were some of the durable objects found on board, mostly of high value:

- Lebanese-style jars[11]
- Ingots of copper and tin
- Ingots of blue glass
- Ivory from hippopotamus teeth
- Ostrich eggs
- Swords and other weapons
- Jewellery, gold, silver, and soapstone

And the foods identified on board represent an ageless Lebanese larder:

- Figs
- Pomegranates
- Olives
- Grapes
- Almonds
- Pine nuts
- Cumin
- Sumac
- Coriander
- Wine
- Olive oil

It is worth recalling that the Lebanese pursuit of tin, which took them to Atlantic Spain and then on to Cornwall, was a key factor in the transition to the Bronze Age in the Near East and Europe.

The presence of amphorae in the Uluburun shipwreck, indicating trade in wine and olive oil, is replicated in other Phoenician shipwrecks around the Mediterranean, notably one in Xlendi Bay, Gozo, which is still being explored, and two off Sinai which were discovered in 1997 when the US Navy was assisting the Israeli Navy in searching for a lost submarine. The amphorae on the various seabeds indicate an extensive oil and wine trade which was controlled from Lebanon even when the pottery is more local in origin (the amphorae found in Xlendi Bay were Maltese-made).

It seems clear that in the early period of Lebanese Mediterranean trade (approximately 2800 to 1100 BCE) there emerged a mixture of state-organized trade and private enterprise. The state-organized trade is sometimes described as typical of 'palace culture'. Some of the private entrepreneurs are even known by name, notably Sipit Ba'al, who traded between Tyre and Ugarit a little over 3200 years ago. Another prosperous Ugarit trader whose name recurs in the sources was called Yabninu. The texts from Ugarit between 1400 and 1200 BCE describe the emergence of a wealthy class of merchants, who owned their own land and property and who had a trading relationship with various palace cultures.[12]

Finally, one vile aspect of trade at this time must not be ignored: namely, the Mediterranean slave trade. This assessment is from a Greek perspective: 'In these early days the Greeks were no traders. The articles of luxury which we meet in abundance in the homes of the wealthy came from the East, in Phoenician ships, which also brought slaves. Eumaeus, the faithful swineherd of Odysseus, was one of them.'[13]

Salt and Trade

Salt trading was closely associated with successful fishing communities. Historic coastal centres which wanted to sell their fish inland needed access to salt. Salt was produced, as it still is (despite twenty-first century commercial struggles), on the Lebanese coast.[14] It was also produced extensively in several of the early Lebanese colonies, including Ibiza, Malta, Kition in Cyprus, Leptis Magna in Libya (later famous as a Roman city, but founded by the Phoenicians), Tangier, Pantellaria (still celebrated for its capers and caperberries in sea salt), western Sicily, and southern Sardinia. The historic salt pans in western Sicily, between Marsala and Trapani, can still be visited today, while the salt plants around Cagliari in southern Sardinia (the Lebanese settlement known as Caralis) remain of great significance.

The historic importance of salt in Lebanese culture can be traced back to at least the time of the apogee of Ugarit (around 1400 BCE), when salt is regularly mentioned in the royal texts.[15] Thereafter access to salt supplies was a driving force in Phoenician expansion throughout the Mediterranean area.[16] Lebanese sellers of salt fish became known throughout the Mediterranean region and (as we have seen) inland at least as far as Jerusalem. As well as being a national food staple, with the help of the salt trade, fish became another source of Lebanese wealth. The representation of fish and dolphins on Phoenician and Carthaginian coinage is particularly striking and significant.

The Dye Dealers and Their Wealth

The Phoenicians were identified from the earliest times with the purple dye which they were able to obtain from a mollusc known as murex. This is a marvellously successful development from their early fishing expeditions. The colour, widely coveted around the palaces of the ancient world, is known as 'royal purple' or 'Tyrian purple'. It was one of the most lucrative and distinctive items of Lebanese trade.

The murex was important to the wealth of Ancient Lebanon, and was sought by the Lebanese seafarers not only in the eastern Mediterranean but also (as with the salt trade) around several of their colonies. For example, the Lebanese colony of Kerkouane, on the tip of Cap Bon in Tunisia (a breathtaking archaeological visit, to this day) was known as a centre of the trade in murex and purple dye. The murex dyes, in fact, permitted silks, linens, and yarns to acquire a range of colours from floral pink to deepest purple. Cloth which came to be known as *dibapha* was double-dyed purple, and the most prized of all.

Tyre at its apogee was seen by its neighbours as wondrously wealthy and so powerful as to determine the fate of the region's kings, as two quotations from the Bible illustrate:

> Tyre has built herself a stronghold, she has heaped up silver like dust, and gold like the dirt of the streets. (Zachariah 9:3)

> Tyre, the bestower of crowns, whose merchants were princes, whose traders were the honoured of the earth. (Isaiah 23:8)

'Bestower of crowns' is a resounding phrase, and underlines that power can come from trade as well as from war.

The Navigators

The sailors who sailed westwards from Lebanon have been described as the world's greatest navigators, and the first to navigate by the Pole Star. They traded first with Cyprus, Egypt, and Greece, as we have seen, but soon began to travel much greater distances, and to found distant colonies, out into the Western Mediterranean and beyond.

Among the celebrated cities founded by colonizers from Lebanon are Thebes in Greece and Cadiz and Malaga in southern Spain, but they also created trading settlements in Malta, Sicily, Sardinia, and Morocco. Cadiz was one of the earliest Phoenician settlements, with a traditional foundation date around 1102 BCE. Pliny gives the founding date of Útica in Tunisia as 1101 BCE.

Herodotus (who had himself been on a visit to Tyre to study the temples attributed to Hercules, but actually built for the Phoenician god Melqart) graphically describes the journey commissioned by the Pharaoh Necho II that saw Phoenician sailors travel down from the Red Sea along the east coast of the African continent, around the Cape of Good Hope and back to their Moroccan settlements and through the Straits of Gibraltar back into the Mediterranean Sea.[17] This would have been around the year 600 BCE. The story told by Herodotus has always been seen as plausible, both because of his personal knowledge of Tyre and because of his sceptical reference to the accounts by the Lebanese sailors of the sun appearing to be to the north of them once they had crossed the Equator.

No other country in the Ancient World had such intrepid, skilled, and successful sailors and navigators. 'Phoenician' became a by-word for travel to the extreme limits of the known world.

The Spread of the 'Phoenician Alphabet'

The alphabet is sometimes described as the greatest of all Lebanese inventions. It was a consonantal set of letters which fitted the requirements of the Phoenician and other Semitic languages. It was rapidly adopted and modified by neighbouring cultures and was an essential component in the creation of early works of literature including the Old Testament in Hebrew and the works of Homer in Greek.

The first four letters of the Phoenician alphabet, which can be pronounced and written as *alep, bet, giml* and *dalet*, clearly show the characteristics which were inherited by later alphabets. In addition to the Greek alphabet, it is generally accepted that the Latin, Cyrillic, Anatolian, and Coptic alphabets all ultimately derive from the Phoenician.

Herodotus attributes the invention of this alphabet to the Phoenician king Kadmos, the founder of Thebes in Greece. This, however, is probably best regarded as the first story in a long literary tradition associated with the Phoenician alphabet. In fact, the most rapid development and spread of the alphabet is more probably derived from the mundane requirements of the extensive Lebanese trade networks.

Cities, Locations, Lifestyles

As we noted above, the Ancient Lebanese people identified primarily with the coastal cities where they lived – Ugarit, Byblos, Aradus, Beirut, Sidon, Tyre, or Acre. There is nothing in this identification to negate a sense of shared (Lebanese or 'Phoenician') identity, culture or lifestyle.[18] (The Greeks a few centuries later similarly identified with Athens, Sparta, Corinth, or Thebes more than 'Greece'.)

322

The greatest of the Lebanese coastal cities at the period of 'Phoenician ascendancy', and indeed the recognized mother-city, was Tyre. The supremacy of Tyre began around 1000 BCE, following the destruction of the earlier great city of Ugarit around 1200 BCE by the invading 'Peoples of the Sea', and then a period of Sidonian supremacy for about 150 years from 1150 BCE.[19]

The earliest Lebanese settlements overseas tended to be given the name Qart-hadasht (new city, or Carthage). The first such Carthage was established in Cyprus, possibly as early as 1500 BCE, and probably in the location which later became known as Kition (now Larnaca). The most famous, Carthage, on the Tunisian coast, has a traditional foundation date of 814 BCE.

The major Lebanese settlements around the Mediterranean region – for example at the Tunisian Carthage, Motya, Cadiz, and Malaga – were often modelled on the city of Tyre. Tyre was recognized as the patrimonial home in Lebanon by such cities, and they continued to pay substantial tithes to Tyre, even after its subjugation by the Babylonians. (Carthage continued to send 10% of its public treasure annually to Tyre, even though it had grown into far the greater city of the two.)[20] The urban planning model provided by Tyre was very distinctive. It led to a preference for offshore islands, or promontories which were almost islands, often facing out westwards (Tyre, Cadiz, Motya) and with sophisticated and secure harbour facilities.

Amongst the other settlements, the Lebanese origin of the Greek city of Thebes has been less easily accepted, although it forms an important theme of the play by Euripides entitled *Phoenician Women*, which emphasizes the links between Tyre and Thebes. Herodotus dated the Lebanese foundation of Thebes to a time before the Trojan War, perhaps during the thirteenth century BCE, but this is so far unconfirmed by archaeology.

Motya, in western Sicily, and Cadiz, on the Atlantic coast of Spain, are fascinating towns in which to study Ancient Lebanese culture and social life. The geographical similarity of the Cadiz peninsula to the one in Tyre has been widely noticed, and, naturally, being on the far side of the Pillars of Hercules opened up the Atlantic Ocean to the Lebanese voyagers for their trading visits to coastal locations from Cornwall to west and south Africa. The Pillars of Hercules have many other names, including *Madik Jabal Tariq*/Straits of Gibraltar, but probably the most evocative is *Bab al Maghrib*, the Gateway to the West. The Greek god Hercules is recognized to be derived from the Lebanese god Melqart, tutelary god of Tyre, and the name-form Herakles-Melqart is used in some specialist archaeological texts. Some scholarly works also refer to the Pillars of Hercules as the Pillars of Melqart.

The Ancient Lebanese especially valued their Atlantic colonies, which, besides Cadiz, included several in Morocco and, further to the north, Figueira da Foz in Portugal, where the municipal museum now holds some interesting Phoenician pieces. They provided starting points for the most spectacular of all the Ancient Lebanese voyages (to South Africa and Cornwall, maybe also to the Azores and Brazil). Strabo, improbably, claimed that sailors from Tyre had founded 300 colonies on the Atlantic coast of Africa.

The Lebanese colonies clearly maintained contact with each other. One interesting fishing story, collected by the writer known as 'Pseudo-Aristotle', tells how fishermen from Cadiz sailed four days south to the waters around the Canary Islands, where they found great quantities of very large tuna, which they salted, stored in jars, and then took to Carthage.

Phoenician civilization was urban and coastal. It was collective and regulated and based on long-distance trading by sea. The Phoenician version of a 'colonial empire' was an interconnected network of coastal towns and cities. Especially in the western Mediterranean, the strategic locations of the Lebanese colonies, notably in western Sicily and southern Sardinia, Pantellaria, Ibiza, Gibraltar and Malaga, and the Tunisian coastline, effectively gave them complete control of sea travel through all the key straits. For a period, the western Mediterranean was a Lebanese lake:

> International trade, then, was in Phoenician hands, and in certain parts of the Mediterranean it continued to be a Phoenician preserve until the end of the third century B.C.: for Carthage was a Phoenician colony [...] and the Carthaginians managed to keep Greek traders out of the triangle formed by the western end of Sicily, the Straits of Gibraltar, and the eastern end of the Pyrenees.[21]

Following the Routes of the Phoenicians Today

As a result of their established trade routes, their extensive network of colonies, and their 'symbolic conquering of the farthest limits of the world', the Ancient Lebanese exported aspects of their way of life and their culture all around the Mediterranean Sea and beyond – their urban design, architecture, and style of harbours; their religion and their gods; their language and their alphabet; their notions of justice and especially elected magistrates and 'a just monarchy'; their admiration for beautiful luxury goods and imposing sarcophagi; their use of wine in ceremonials and celebrations; and their culinary traditions.[22]

It is rewarding, reorienting, and informative to explore the Mediterranean as a Phoenician sea. The Lebanese influence on the cultures of Tunisia and Libya, Malta and Pantellaria, Sicily and Sardinia, Ibiza and Malaga, enriches the historical understanding of all those places. In cultural terms, including food culture, the Lebanese adventurers and traders brought oriental norms to Spain and the west. Spanish archaeologists use the phrase *el periodo orientalizante* to describe the steady infiltration into Spanish culture of norms and foodways from the eastern Mediterranean, from about 1000 BCE onwards.[23]

Following the Foods of the Phoenicians Today

The fish diet of the Lebanese coastal cities spread to the Lebanese colonies throughout the Mediterranean area and out to the Lebanese cities on the Atlantic coasts of Spain, Portugal, and Morocco. These 'western Phoenicians', including the Carthaginians, ate molluscs, prawns, and other seafood, whose shells are often found in archaeological digs; they are also known to have eaten sea bream, red mullet, mackerel, sturgeon, eels, sole, and perhaps above all tuna – a fish which appears frequently in ancient Lebanese iconography. The discovery of Lebanese coins with images of tuna in or near their colony-settlements at Cadiz, Almuñécar (Sexi in the Phoenician language), Abdera, and Soluntum (Sicily) is a powerful form of physical evidence for the economic importance of the ancient Lebanese fish trade.[24]

Among the favourite recipes associated with these fishing traditions, my own choice would be *sabbidije bi houbro* (cuttlefish with ink) from the favourite cookbook of my Lebanese mother-in-law.[25] This simple recipe has an authentic and traditional nature. It requires a large quantity (over a kilo) of cuttlefish and a lot of olive oil, in which the cuttlefish is simmered with onions and leeks for forty minutes. The ink (slightly thinned with water) is then added for a further ten minutes, before the dish is left to stand and served cold. It is a truly Mediterranean delight.

The archetypal flavouring in Lebanese culinary traditions is that of cumin. Shown by both palaeobotany and archaeological excavation to be native to the Levant, cumin was characteristic of the lands of the Levantine great powers, including the Assyrians, the Babylonians, the Persians, and the Phoenicians. The use of cumin around the Mediterranean was especially typical of the lands where the Ancient Lebanese established colonies. The Maltese island of Comino was named after cumin, and cumin plants still grow there. The dish of cooked spinach with chickpeas and cumin (*espinacas con garbanzos*), which is considered traditional in southwestern Spain, is a typical blend of Lebanese flavours.

Cumin traditions and other Lebanese food traditions spread into the parts of the Mediterranean region where Lebanese colonies had developed and in which for several centuries Lebanese seapower, Lebanese culture, and the Lebanese language were predominant.

Originally pushed out to sea from a fertile seaboard with a rich food culture but not enough food, the Lebanese colonizers left their permanent mark not through a continuous empire but through a well-connected network of strategically-located seaports.

The Phoenicians as a global power, as traders and as exporters of knowledge and traditions (and food culture too), have been seriously neglected by western historians, for reasons including ignorance, hellenocentrism, racism, and anti-Semitism, as Martin Bernal has emphasized:

> It is striking, in this context, that the latest edition of the *Cambridge Ancient History*, Volume 3, Part I – *The Middle East and the Aegean World, Tenth to Eight Centuries BC* – has chapters on Assyria, Babylonia, Urartu, the Neo-Hittite states of Syria and Anatolia, Israel and Judah, Cyprus and Egypt – but none on Phoenicia, which was the dominant power in the Mediterranean of the time.[26]

There is a Lebanese proverb which says 'If you have understood something about Lebanon, that means it has been badly explained to you', a witty and eloquent paradox. Nonetheless, I hope that this essay has provided a new way of looking at food and the Phoenicians, and in particular has developed the idea of food supply as essential to the growth of Ancient Lebanese sea power. [27]

325

Notes

1   Jack Goody, *The Theft of History* (Cambridge: Cambridge University Press, 2006), p. 65.
2   Maria Eugenia Aubet, *Tiro y las colonias fenicias de occidente*, 3rd edn (Barcelona: Bellaterra Arqueología, 2009), p. 29.
3   See, for example, Josephine Crawley Quinn, *In Search of the Phoenicians* (Princeton: Princeton University Press, 2018).
4   José Miguel L. Romero, 'Un studio revela el ADN libanés de los fenicios de Ibiza', *El Diario de Ibiza*, 25 September 2017.
5   Janny de Moor, 'In the Beginning was Fish: Fish in the Ancient Near East', in *Fish: Food from the Waters: Proceedings of the Oxford Symposium on Food and Cookery 1997*, ed. by Harlan Walker (Totnes: Prospect Books, 1998), p. 87.
6   Antonella Spanò Giammellaro, 'Les Phéniciens et les Carthaginois', in *Histoire de l'alimentation*, ed. by Jean-Louis Flandrin and Massimo Montanari (Paris: Fayard, 1996), pp. 91-92; Sabatino Moscati, *The World of the Phoenicians* (London: Weidenfeld and Nicolson, 1968), p. 10.
7   Giammellaro, p. 86, and for the rest of this paragraph pp. 85-92. The sources contain hints that the Egyptians, who had mostly barley wine and palm wine, were envious of Lebanese grape wine.
8   Sureshkumar Muthukumaran, 'Between Archaeology and Text: The Origins of Rice Consumption and

Cultivation in the Middle East and the Mediterranean', *Papers from the Institute of Archaeology*, 24.1 (2014) <doi.org/10.5334/pia.465>.

9   Josette Elayi, *Histoire de la Phénicie*, rev. edn (Paris: Perrin, 2018), pp. 62-71, 82, 88.

10 Cemal Pulak, 'The Uluburun Shipwreck: An Overview', *International Journal of Nautical Archaeology*, 27.3 (1998), 188-224.

11 For Ancient Lebanese pottery, see C. Leonard Woolley, *Guide to the Archaeological Museum of the American University of Beirut* (Beirut: American University of Beirut, 1921), pp. 13-15.

12 Marisa Ruiz-Gálvez Priego, *Con el Fenicio en los talones: los inicios del Edad del Hierro en la cuenca del Mediterráneo* (Barcelona: Bellaterra Arqueología, 2013), pp. 17, 27-34.

13 H. D. F. Kitto, *The Greeks,* rev. edn (Harmondsworth: Penguin, 1957), p. 41.

14 Ibrahim Chalhoub, 'In Lebanon, Salt Producers Fear Craft is Drying Up', *Phys.org*, 18 August 2017 <https://phys.org/news/2017-08-lebanon-salt-craft.html> [accessed 1 May 2019].

15 Giammellaro, p. 92.

16 On Phoenician salt-trading, see papers published online in the splendidly entitled symposium *Fish and Ships* (Rome, 2012), e.g. Antonio Manuel Saez Romero, 'Fish Processing and Salted-Fish Trade in the Punic West: New Archaeological Data and Historical Evolution', *Fish & Ships: Production and Commerce of salsamenta during Antiquity, Bibliothèque d'Archéologie Méditerranéenne et Africaine 17*, ed. by Emmanuel Botte and Victoria Leitch (Aix-en-Provence: Centre Camille Jullian, 2014) pp. 159-74 <https://hal.archives-ouvertes.fr/hal-01471805/document> [accessed 1 May 2019].

17 Herodotus, *The Histories*, trans. by Aubrey de Sélincourt, rev. by A. R. Burn (Harmondsworth: Penguin, 1972), pp. 147, 283.

18 This section is clearly in disagreement with the arguments of Josephine Crawley Quinn, *In Search of the Phoenicians*.

19 Carlos G. Wagner, *Historia del Cercano Oriente* (Salamanca: Ediciones Universidad Salamanca, 1999), pp. 228-29.

20 Aubet, p. 173.

21 Kitto, p. 42.

22 Wagner, p. 230.

23 See for example *Arqueología & Historia*, 12 (April-May 2017), pp. 10, 12, 20-25, 49, etc. This special issue entitled *Tarteso* demonstrates how modern research increasingly indicates peaceful co-existence and cultural intermingling of Tartessians and Phoenicians in south-western Spain.

24 Giammellaro, p. 97.

25 Georges N. Rayes, *L'art culinaire libanais* ([Beirut?]: [Imprimerie Nasrallah?], [1957]), pp. 70-71.

26 Martin Bernal, *Black Athena: The Afroasiatic Roots of Classical* Civilization (London: Free Association Books, 1987), vol. I, p. 433.

27 This essay was researched in various former Lebanese colonies in Spain, Sicily, Tunisia, Malta, and Cyprus, and in the tumultuous city of Beirut, with special thanks to all at the Phoenicia Hotel Floriana-Valletta and at the Phoenicia Hotel Beirut.

Cannibalism and Power: Resituating the Narratives of Post-Soviet Foodways Through Vladimir Sorokin's *Feast*

Svetlana Tcareva

In studies of Soviet and Russian culture, the engagement with food has been limited at best, especially if one looks at the intersection of foodways and literary production. Many scholars seem to believe that Russian and Soviet literature has rarely engaged with food.[1] Even Vladimir Sorokin himself, the writer whose short story will be at the centre of this paper, has stated that in Russian literature there have been no representations of satisfaction coming from food.[2] Sorokin is a controversial contemporary writer in whose works graphic violence, scatology, and nonsensical absurd scenes are abundant. He is also the only major Russian writer to engage consistently with the theme of food in his literary works. In his collection of short stories, *Feast* (*Pir*), the consumption and philosophy of food is the major theme. In one short story from *Feast* in particular, 'Nastia', Sorokin's critique of state power and his close attention to the body's digestive processes and food come together in graphic scenes of cannibalism.

I argue that in 'Nastia' Sorokin portrays nostalgia for Russia's past as being tantamount to nostalgia for times when cannibalism was common. Sorokin creates a surreal nightmare in which an aristocratic dinner turns out to be a cannibalistic feast, and by doing so offers a critique of Soviet and Russian state abuses of power. I follow Elspeth Probyn in her statement that 'food and its relation to the body is fundamentally about power'.[3] Cannibalism, then, is a trope in which power over someone's body and food consumption are linked most explicitly. The fact that Sorokin wrote 'Nastia' in 2000, less than ten years after the collapse of the Soviet Union, sets the important historical context for the story's analysis: amid the ruins of the former empire, a new national identity had to be created, and Sorokin issues a dark warning against trying to replicate the nation's past, as the past was a time, figuratively, of cannibalism.

We can start by briefly reviewing the plot of the story. The story begins when a teenage Russian girl, Nastia, wakes up on the morning of her sixteenth birthday, anticipating something with excitement and trepidation. What she knows, and the reader does not yet know, is that on this day she is going to be put into the oven, baked, and consumed by members of her family. This breaking of humanity's most sacred taboo, that of not eating human flesh, is set within a pseudo-nineteenth century landscape. This background is reflected in the narrator's language and the way that the characters' dialogue imitates the realist novels of nineteenth-century Russia. The characters even occasionally speak French, as was customary among the Russian aristocracy of the time. The setting of the story is also unmistakably the nineteenth century: it takes place at a manor; there is a cherry orchard and a church; the house has a samovar; and there is even a linden alley, a typical feature of an aristocratic estate in Russia.

After Nastia is baked, she is served whole, and guests gather around her body at the table. They discuss the flavours of different parts of her body while engaging in some philosophical banter about Nietzsche. A brief quotation can convey a sense of how it reads, and the following is one of the less graphic passages:

> Nastia was served to the table at seven o'clock. She was cheered with an excitement of dizzy intoxication.
>
> Golden brown, she was lying on an oval dish, holding her legs with darkened nails. She was surrounded by white rose buds, her breasts, knees, and shoulders were covered by slices of lemon, and river lilies gleamed white on her forehead, nipples and pubis. 'Here comes my daughter' – Sablin got up with a glass in his hand. 'I highly recommend, gentlemen!' Everyone applauded.[4]

It is important to note that the whole body is displayed, and no attempt is made to conceal the appearance of the food being offered, or its human source. Moreover, a whole conversation at the table revolves around different parts of the body. This makes it a scene of gourmet cannibalism, and these elements of upper-class banquet etiquette and the elaborate food decoration make the act of cannibalism even more shocking.

At the end of the story, we are presented with a surprising twist: all the guests at the dinner create a kind of hologram of Nastia by putting nails into a wall and projecting light from the window so that her face appears projected over her skeleton. Thus they materialize what they understand to be the Nietzschean idea of transcending the limits of one's physical body and becoming a higher being. This ending explains why Nastia was waiting for her birthday with such anticipation, since the birthday ritual gave her an opportunity to transcend herself. And, of course, this is why she is named Nastia: a shortened form of Anastasiia, a Greek name which means 'one who has been resurrected'. This is one common way of interpreting this story: critics have emphasized the Nietzschean aspect of the story and the dangers of the Russian intelligentsia playing with different -isms. For example, Keith Livers has argued that the story demonstrates 'the central precept of Nietzschean transcendence as transmitted through a distorted and distorting Russian lens that is being uncritically consumed'.[5]

Another possible reading is to see the story as expressing a fear of being consumed by monsters, such as cannibals or zombies, associated with a fear of losing one's personal identity. This fear is highly relevant for this particular historic period, as the new Russian identity, as well as the new Russian culinary identity, was just being created amidst the ruins of the old Soviet identity.[6] The question of national identity is important here, since food and national identity are very closely linked. However, such a reading still does not fully explain Sorokin's meticulous attention to this scene of gourmet cannibalism, nor does it allow us to fully unpack the story's political critique.

This paper offers an alternative reading of this story, one which takes its food-related imagery and cannibalistic corporeality fully into account. I argue that we should consider carefully the physical and fleshy nature of the cannibalistic trope Sorokin uses. Sorokin has often, and quite rightly, been seen as a writer who is merely indulging in postmodernism as a kind of game. He himself once said that words are just 'marked-up scraps of paper'.[7] But my own inclination is to follow Mark Lipovetsky, a scholar who has emphasized the physiological effect that Sorokin's texts produce in readers' bodies, and who proposes a useful term to talk about this process: 'carnilization'.[8] By choosing to depict an image of cannibalism, and by discussing the physical properties of the baked body in such excruciating detail, Sorokin acknowledges that his metaphor has a physical function: it has an ability to disgust readers on a deep and visceral level. When readers confront this scene, they are almost certain to have some physiological reaction: it is impossible to read it calmly and analytically.[9] This story and the many scenes of cannibalistic consumption it describes disgust and horrify, and it can serve as a good illustration of Julia Kristeva's statement that food consumption has a uniquely intense ability to evoke abjection in one's body.[10]

To show the physical reality of cannibalism, and to avoid treating it solely as a metaphor, I propose to situate the story in the context of Russian food history, and, more specifically, the cultural history of bread. A focus on bread makes it possible to fully unpack and analyze one episode in the story that has been overlooked by previous scholarship, specifically, the mention of 'French bread' (*frantsuzskaia bulka*) at the cannibals' dinner.

Bread is mentioned casually in the story when the father appeals to his guests at the dinner table to acknowledge the high quality of the meal that is being served. The guests, who have been debating the best methods of harvesting wheat, are reminded of the physical nature of the product they are consuming at this very moment. The father says: "'What do you mean that I am serving my guests some bread? Are you saying that this" – he grabbed Arina's dish with the unfinished pelvis area – "is this French bread, you are saying?'"[11] The guests laugh hysterically, interpreting the father's words as a joke.

This scene with the discussion of bread might seem to be only a passing moment in the text, but bread is a highly symbolic substance in Russia. The fact that the guests have just been discussing harvesting wheat brings out several important contexts. Firstly, bread has a long history of being equated with flesh on a symbolic level. In this, Sorokin joins a long tradition that includes the Christian symbolism of the Eucharist as well as Russian folk beliefs. In the Christian service of communion, churchgoers eat bread and drink wine, which they believe to be the body and blood of Jesus Christ.[12] Also, in Russia, traditionally, a premature baby was treated in a quite specific way: the baby was covered with dough and placed momentarily in a traditional Russian oven – which was warm, but of course not fully heated – to finish 'being baked', a symbolic practice known as re-baking [*perepekanie*]. In a similar practice, newborns were covered with sugar and honey, thus furthering the image of the human body as a meal.[13] In these ways, human flesh and the most basic dietary staple of the Russian peasant, bread, were joined on a symbolic level: both bread and flesh, in a certain ritual manner, could be eaten.

Secondly, in the context of Russian history, bread has always been closely linked with power.[14] The promise of the 1917 Bolshevik revolution was 'Peace, Land, and Bread', and wheat is even a part of the Soviet coat of arms.[15] In these early years of the Soviet Union – just as in many other places, of course – wealth was equated with an abundance of food, and the achievements of the new Soviet state were portrayed metaphorically in quite a few sculptures and paintings as an overabundance of wheat and/or bread. As Evgeny Dobrenko notes, while pleasure is subjective, abundance is objective, and thus food abundance becomes a trope meant to show the success of the Soviet Union.[16] Consider, for example, Ilya Mashkov's painting *Soviet Bread* (1936), that presents a hyperbolic vision of plenitude of bread, a plenitude that overpopulates the canvas and prevents the viewer from even being able to see the perspective or identify the background.[17]

Yet, the upheavals of the revolution and the Civil War led to mass starvation in some places; for example, the death toll of the Volga famine of 1921 and 1922 was immense, and there were rumours of restaurants serving human meat.[18] Famines, both in pre- and post-revolutionary Russia, often led to cases of survival cannibalism. In fact, one of the famines, that of 1891-92, happened around the time in which 'Nastia' seems to be set, and this famine is estimated to have caused 500,000 deaths from starvation.[19] Famines, then, were a regular feature of Russian history. It is interesting to note that the Russian tsar Alexander III prohibited the use of the word 'famine'; instead, the word 'bad harvest' (*nedorod*), was to be used. This word covered and masked the realities of the situation in the country, just as the beautiful language of nineteenth-century Russian novels masked certain realties. Human flesh and bread were linked: when there was not enough bread, the last resort for starving peasants became, in some cases, human flesh, to which they would resort after having exhausted all other options, including eating tree bark and even clay. Of course, in Sorokin's 'Nastia', human flesh is ironically treated as a rare delicacy to be enjoyed by the refined upper classes, and not a last resort for starving peasants.

Why French bread, specifically, and not just bread, and why did the guests laugh hysterically when the father mentioned it?[20] There is a phrase that is used often on the Russian-language internet and in popular culture: 'crunching on French bread' (*khrust frantsuzskoi bulki*). This expression is used when someone is expressing nostalgia for pre-revolutionary Russia, presenting Tsarist Russia as a lost utopia, with balls, poetry readings, and the aristocratic manners of men in suits. This expression became popular in 1998, when a song by the band Bely Orel was released that mentioned crunching on French bread and other stereotypical images from Tsarist Russia. The lyrics contained the following:

Balls, beautiful ladies, butlers, cadets,
And Schubert waltzes, and the crunch of French bread,

Love, champagne, sunsets, back alleys,
How delightful are evenings in Russia.[21]

By characterizing nostalgia for Tsarist Russia as nostalgia for 'crunching on French bread', this nostalgia is comically devalued.

So what then can this context tell us about the story 'Nastia'? When her father states that the guests are not 'crunching on French bread', he suggests that they are not living this idyllic aristocratic life of balls and Schubert waltzes, but have actually regressed to cannibalism. The fact that the Russian aristocracy, the ones who live in manors, have servants, and discuss philosophy, are the ones who engage in acts of gustatory cannibalism makes this taboo scene even more appalling. We are accustomed to seeing cannibalism in contemporary films and literature used to 'other' groups of people who belong to lower social classes. A good example of this is the cult horror movie *The Texas Chainsaw Massacre* (1974), which has been analyzed by the literary critic Jennifer Brown as a contribution to 'the idea of redneck foreign Others which has spawned a plethora of hillbilly cannibal movies in which inbred, gap-toothed, po' white folk feast on chirpy, middle-class camping families or adventurous, smug college students'.[22] And in nineteenth-century European literature, cannibalism was used to portray other countries as barbaric and thus justify colonial expansion. The cannibal in European literature of this period was often located on a faraway island and was a member of a different race or ethnicity.

What is shocking about 'Nastia' is the fact that its cannibalism is not being performed by faraway tribes or low-class rednecks; it is instead the Russian aristocracy who are eating their own kind within a setting like that of a nineteenth-century novel (which many readers would consider to be sacred). Since the story is written in the years immediately after the collapse of the Soviet empire, the image of the ruling class consuming its own kind suggests that the Soviet empire, too, collapsed because of its unlimited appetite that led to devouring its own. And, finally, Sorokin suggests to his readers that the cannibals are us, or at any rate those who want to bring back monarchist Russia to replace the legacy of the Soviet state.

In 'Nastia', Sorokin presents his own version of Russian gastrohistory, one where one sometimes ate actual, not symbolic, flesh. With the crunching of French bread against the backdrop of a nineteenth-century manor, Sorokin exposes the dynamics of corporeal exploitation in pre-revolutionary Russia and Soviet Russia; his story evokes memories of the famine and starvation that led to survival cannibalism and exposes the legacies of corporeal exploitation in a conservative patriarchal society. He then sees post-Soviet nostalgia for pre-Soviet times, as well as any search for a new Russian identity in Russia's past, as essentially in truth a nostalgia for cannibalism. The collapse of the Soviet Union increased food insecurity and inequality in food access, yet this socio-economic situation has been a feature of many, if not all, periods of Russian history. For Sorokin, it does not matter whether one is nostalgic for Tsarist Russia or

Soviet Russia, because all of Russia's past is marked by violence and abuses of power. In fact, in his novel *Day of Oprichnik* (2006) Sorokin envisions a dark dystopia in which post-Soviet Russia turns into a kind of medieval society, reminiscent of the terror under the sixteenth-century Russian tsar Ivan the Terrible. Not a single period of Russian history is to Sorokin worth replicating.

By using the trope of cannibalism as a means of political critique and satire, Sorokin joins a long tradition, seen most iconically, perhaps, in Jonathan Swift's 1729 essay, 'A Modest Proposal'. However, when Swift attacks economic disparities in Ireland by issuing a satirical proposal to sell the children of the poor to the rich for food, it is clear that his cannibalistic imagery is being used in a wholly metaphorical way. In the case of Sorokin, what is different is how the detailed description of gourmet cannibalism evokes feelings of disgust and abjection in readers' bodies. Sorokin does not just use cannibalism as a metaphor, but takes it to another level by making the non-symbolic nature of cannibalism in Russia apparent. He engages in the 'carnilization' of language and the insertion of the bodily into the text. It is impossible to read 'Nastia' calmly and analytically, and that is why Sorokin's political critique can affect his readers.

Sorokin is not the only one during this period to use the trope of cannibalism in Russian culture as a part of a political message during this period. In 1988, two years before Sorokin published 'Nastia', two Moscow-based artists created a performance in which a cake shaped as Vladimir Lenin's body was baked and eaten.[23] The performance was meant to symbolize the end of Soviet rule. Yet, this act of symbolic cannibalism of the communist leader carries different connotations than the cannibalism in 'Nastia'. In the artistic performance, the consumption of the cake is an act of power, one which shows how the old regime's remains can be consumed and digested after its loss of power by those who belong to the new regime. It is interesting to note here that in *Totem and Taboo* (1913), Sigmund Freud used the image of cannibalism to talk about how sons internalize and perpetuate the power of their fathers. If we look at the Lenin cake performance through the lens of Freud's psychoanalysis, we can say that by eating Lenin the citizens of the state wanted to achieve full control over the communist past and take its power, but they instead internalized the power of the communist past over themselves. Cannibalism in 'Nastia' carries the opposite message; it does not signify power but rather the utmost degradation of the ruling class.

The trope of cannibalism in Sorokin's 'Nastia' exposes a few important things about the relationship between the culture of food in Russia and abuses of state power. Firstly, Sorokin shows that in a Russian context, cannibalism cannot be just a metaphor, as it has had a real historical presence in Russian lives. Secondly, the new political identity, as well as the new gastroidentity, of Russia cannot and should not be based on the Russian past, since Russia's past is based on inequality, exploitation, and abuses of power. Finally, looking at Sorokin's 'Nastia' as a case study can demonstrate that the complex relationship between food consumption, hierarchy, and power can find its expression in a literary context.

Notes

1   There have been, of course, a few scholars who have analyzed food in Russian literature and culture from a variety of disciplines. I should note here Ronald LeBlanc's scholarship, especially his monograph, *Slavic Sins of the Flesh: Food, Sex, and Carnal Appetite in Nineteenth-Century Russian Fiction* (Durham, NH: University of New Hampshire Press, 2009). From the field of anthropology, see the scholarship of Melissa Caldwell, especially her edited volume *Food & Everyday Life in the Postsocialist World*, ed. by Melissa L. Caldwell, Elizabeth C. Dunn, and Marion Nestle (Bloomington: Indiana University Press, 2009). From history, see Alison K. Smith, *Recipes for Russia: Food and Nationhood Under the Tsars* (DeKalb: Northern Illinois University Press, 2011). For a well-written, non-academic, semi-biographical history of Russian foodways, see Anya Von Bremzen's *Mastering the Art of Soviet Cooking: A Memoir of Love and Longing* (New York: Crown Publishers, 2013). Darra Goldstein has been working on popularizing Russian cuisine and has published several cookbooks. I should also mention the most recent monograph on food and gender in late socialism, *Seasoned Socialism: Gender and Food in the Late Soviet Everyday Life*, ed. by Anastasia Lakhtikova, Angela Brintlinger, and Irina Glushchenko (Bloomington: Indiana University Press, 2019).

2   Sorokin said this in an interview following the publication of his collection of short stories, *Feast* (*Pir*). This book, unfortunately, has not yet been translated into English. See Vladimir Sorokin and Igor Smirnov, '*Dialog o ede*' <http://www.guelman.ru/slava/texts/eda.htm> [accessed 29 May 2019]. Sorokin continues his engagement with the theme of food in one of his most recent novels, *Manaraga* (2017). This novel is set in a dystopian society, and the story centres around a practice called book'n'grill; that is, preparing food by burning the manuscript of canonical books that no one reads anymore. The consumption of food is thus equated with the consumption of culture.

3   Elspeth Probyn, *Carnal Appetites: Foodsexidentities* (New York: Routledge, 2000), p.7.

4   Vladimir Sorokin, *Pir* (Moscow: Ad Marginem, 2001), pp. 27-28. The original text is: '*Nastiu podali k stolu k semi chasam. Ee vstretili s vostorgom legkogo op'ianeniia. Zolotisto-korichnevaiia, ona lezhala na oval'nom bliude, derzha sebia za nogi s pochernevshimi nogtiami. Butony belykh roz okruzhali ee, dol'ki limona pokryvali grud', koleni i plechi, na lbu, soskakh I lobke nevinno beleli rechnye lilii.*'

5   Keith Livers, 'From Fecal Briquettes to Candy Kremlins: The Edible Ideal in Sorokin's Prose', *Gastronomica: The Journal of Critical Food Studies*, 17.4 (2017), 26-35 (p. 29).

6   Nostalgia for Soviet times is often expressed in contemporary Russia by maintaining that during the Soviet Union there was no food adulteration and that, because of the strict enforcement of government standards, all of the food was high quality. In advertising, quite a few food products choose to claim that they follow Soviet recipes and adhere to the Soviet standards of production known as GOST. For a case study of using 'Soviet' in advertisements for sausages in Lithuania, see Neringa Klumbytė, 'The Soviet Sausage Renaissance', *American Anthropologist*, 112.1 (2010), 22-37.

7   '*Eto prosto bukvy na bumage…*', *Vladimir Sorokin: Posle literatury*, ed. by E. Dobrenko, I. Kalinin, and M. Lipovetsky (Moscow: Novoe literaturnoe obozrenie, 2018), p. 8.

8   See Mark Lipovetsky, '*Sorokin-trop: carnalizatsiia*', *NLO*, 120 (2013), 225-242.

9   Elena Petrovaskaia proposes a similar interpretation of the function of the trope of cannibalism in 'Nastia'. She argues that the meticulous visualization of cannibalism in the story provokes a visceral reaction in readers that lays bare subconscious taboos of the culture and prevents a purely rational engagement with the text. See Elena Petrovskaia, '*Uzhin kannibalov, ili o statuse vizual'nogo v literature Vladimira Sorokina*', in '*Eto prosto bukvy na bumage…*' *Vladimir Sorokin: Posle literatury*, ed. by Dobrenko, Kalinin, and Lipovetsky, pp. 435-51.

10   Kristeva proposes the term 'abjection' in *Powers of Horror: An Essay on Abjection* (trans. by Leon. S. Roudiez (New York: Columbia University Press, 1982)). For Kristeva, abjection is that which threatens meaning and the symbolic order, and in order for society and the self to function properly what is abject must be excluded. Food loathing, Kristeva states, is the 'most elementary and most archaic form of abjection', since food crosses the boundaries of the body and may threaten its wholeness (p. 2).

11   '*Eto kakim zhe, pozvol'te vas sprosit', khlebom ya kormliu muzhchin?! A? Vot etim, chto li? – On skhvatil*

tarelku Ariny s nedoedennym lobkom. – Eto chto po-vashemu – bulka frantsuzkaia? (Sorokin, *Pir*, p. 39).

12 Sorokin explores the cannibalistic undertones of the Eucharist in an earlier short story 'A Month in Dachau' (*Mesyats v Dakhau*) (1990).

13 G. I. Kabakova and Francis Conte, eds. *Telo v Russkoi kulture: Sbornik statei* (Moscow: Novoe literaturnoe obozrenie, 2005), p. 9.

14 Bread plays a very important part in today's political imagination in Russia as well. Prices on certain brands of bread are kept low by government mandate, and this low-priced bread is called social bread (*sotsialyi khleb*). Also, the importance of bread in Russian culture has been acknowledged by creating the bread museum in Saint Petersburg, which was established in 1988 at the site of a former bread factory and features a range of exhibitions.

15 I should note here that rye, not wheat, is the main crop in Russia. Rye bread was a staple of everyday food consumption, and bread made from wheat was baked only on holidays.

16 See Evgeny Dobrenko, '*Gastronomicheskii kommunizm: vkusnoe vs. zdorovoe*', *Neprikosnovennyi zapas*, 2.64 (2009), 155-73.

17 For more examples of using wheat imagery in Soviet art, see Diana Kurkovsky, 'Monumentalizing Wheat: Soviet Dreams of Abundance', *Gastronomica*, 7.1 (2007), 15-17.

18 For more on this famine and the US's famine relief support, see Bertrand M. Patenaude, *The Big Show in Bololand: The American Relief Expedition to Soviet Russia in the Famine of 1921* (Stanford, CA: Stanford University Press, 2002), especially chapter 14, 'Tales of Cannibalism'.

19 To learn more, see Richard G. Robbins, *Famine in Russia, 1891-1892: The Imperial Government Responds to a Crisis* (New York: Columbia University Press, 1975).

20 I should note that this French bread is not a baguette, but rather a kind of loaf.

21 See the lyrics in Russian here: '*Tekst pesni Bely Orel – Kak upoitel'ny v Rossii vechera*' <http://textlyrics.ru/belyy-orel/kak-upoitelny-v-rossii-vechera-text-pesni-klip-9dca20ca93.html> [accessed 29 May 2019].

22 Jennifer Brown, *Cannibalism in Literature and Film* (London, UK: Palgrave Macmillan, 2013), p. 12.

23 For a CNN news article on the event, see 'Let Them Eat Lenin!', *CNN*, 31 March 1998 <http://www.cnn.com/WORLD/9803/31/fringe/let.them.eat.lenin/index.html> [accessed 29 May 2019].

The Shared Power of Hunger Artists and Viennese Actionists

Carolyn Tillie

Introduction

In late seventeenth-century Europe and America, a bizarre and disquieting phenomenon appeared and grew in popularity: the Hunger Artist. These performers, who would deliberately starve themselves over extended periods of time, were a precursor to modern-era Performance Artists arising from the Futurist, Dadaist, and Russian Constructivist art movements. Although the Hunger Artist may appear to be the antithesis to the ferocious, transgressive Viennese Actionist artists Günter Brus, Otto Muehl, Rudolf Schwarzkogler, and Hermann Nitsch, both sets of performers are connected by themes of religious mythology or spirituality, fascination and disgust as depicted in human suffering, food (or lack thereof), and the power inherent in both participation and observance.

Hunger Artists

For the purposes of this investigation, while the Hunger Artist is defined as one who indulges in fasting and self-starvation, I have further categorized them as: Fasting Woman, Living Skeleton, and Endurance Artist. While much has been written about fasting and hunger – with the reasons and rationale behind such acts – the point of the three ascribed is that, in their abstinence of food, all relied on an audience for their validation. They were literally starving for attention.

From the eighth to the twenty-first centuries women, more than men, have subjected themselves to inedia (fasting) for various reasons. The earliest adherents ascribed their disciplined fasting as a religious devotion and a way to purge themselves of sin. These medieval ascetics 'suffering' from *anorexia mirabilis*, the miraculous loss of appetite, claimed special healing powers through their touch or saliva. Unlike the sufferers of the modern *anorexia nervosa*, a disorder associated with body image distortion, these religious penitents revelled in their starvation, seemed to thrive on the attention and notoriety, but were ultimately conflicted between desire and the struggle for autonomy.

During the Victorian era, sensational cases of women refusing food exploded in the popular press in the United Kingdom and the United States. Whereas the medieval abstainers ascribed religious motivations for their fasts, the Victorian Fasting Women abstained either due to supposed supernatural phenomena or owing to a physical ailment, be it fictional or legitimate. The male counterparts to the Fasting Women were twofold: Endurance Artists and Living Skeletons. Endurance Artists would deliberately refrain from food, whereas many Living Skeletons had healthy appetites, but were simply naturally thin. Living Skeletons were human oddities, most often seen under the auspices of sideshow organizers who would display their abnormally lean bodies for entertainment purposes. Fasting Women and Endurance Artists were usually self-represented in the display of their emaciated bodies to paying audiences. In all cases, by rejecting bodily needs and 'transcending the body's mortality by portraying the spectacle of spirit' (Gooldin 2003: 20), the Fasting Women, Living Skeletons, and Endurance Artists all proved their ability to overcome difficulties and suffering related to desires and corporeal existence.

Historic Examples

Female inedia has a venerable history in Europe, primarily manifested in religious contexts. Of the 810 canonized Roman Catholic saints, more than 260 are women. Of that number, upwards of 170 or more of these sainted, blessed, or venerable women have displayed clear signs of anorexia (Bell 1985). From the age of seven, Catherine of Siena (1347-1380), the youngest of a large family, began having religious visions and devoted herself to God. At the age of sixteen, with the death of a beloved sister in childbirth, she began a three-year abstention from both speech and food, with the exception of Holy Communion. This was only one of many periods of fasting throughout her life, accompanying political fissures within the church and her own attempts at church reform. Through her extensive writings and travel, Catherine gained many followers until her last prolonged fast, which she commenced shortly after the election of Urban VI and the subsequent Great Western Schism. She died at the age of thirty-three in 1380, claiming she could neither eat nor drink; her attempts to wield power and reform the church through acts of austerity having ultimately failed.

A later example of a Starving Aesthete is Therese Neumann (1898-1962) (Figure 1). Beginning in 1923 until her death, Neumann claims to have consumed nothing but the Holy Eucharist and, like many Fasting Women, was subjected to a 'watch' to ensure the veracity of her claims. Neumann was also subjected to medical tests which suggest her inedia was fraudulent. The question of legitimacy and deception becomes a recurring theme with the Starving Woman, although less so for her counterparts, the Living Skeleton or Endurance Artist.

Figure 1. Therese Neumann

Figure 2. Anne Moore

Anne Moore's (1761-1813) (Figure 2) prolonged fasts were not immediately evident as a scam. Conditioned to a long religious history of Fasting Women, the public was prepared to accept her apparent inedia as *anorexia mirabilis* in the manner of Catherine of Siena. Born in Derbyshire, Moore married a farm worker who abandoned her. In her thirties and with several children in tow, she travelled to Tutbury where her health began to decline. She started working as a washerwoman and attendant for a man afflicted with scrofulous ulcers. His stench was so offensive that no one would assist her. He died on 30 October 1806 and by 4 November, she was no longer able to work at all, losing 'all desire of food, as well as her ability to take it' (Henderson 1810: 18). She ate nominal amounts over the next few months but, with claims of vomiting, stomach ailments, and related digestive disorders, by June 1807 supposedly gave up food entirely. At first only local doctors attended Moore, but as stories of her fast grew, many sceptics came to see for themselves.

In September 1808, physician Alexander Henderson arrived in Tutbury to be one of the many who watched Moore for signs of food consumption. For more than two weeks, working in four-hour shifts, almost a hundred people offered up testimonials that Moore was not eating. Initially, she had been receiving a small stipend from the local parish, but with her fame extending beyond Britain to America – and a wax likeness of her created for the Columbian Museum in Boston – 'the number of people who go to see her is astonishing' (Henderson 1810: 24), leaving monetary gifts amounting to upwards of 400 to 500 shillings (Ruffles 1992: 10). In 1813, after six years of supposed abstinence, her subterfuge finally fell apart with the discovery of soiled bedclothes. It is speculated that some of the witnesses of the watch, as well as her children, had collaborated to supply her with nominal supplements through the pretence of kissing, or in the guise of damp rags, which Moore had requested to cool herself.

The practice of presenting oneself as hunger artist was rampant during the Victorian era when Sarah Jacob (1857-1869), the 'Welsh Fasting Girl', gained notoriety. It was claimed that she stopped eating at the age of ten. Her publicity garnered her numerous gifts and donations from those who believed she was miraculous. Placed in a hospital to be monitored under strict supervision, after two weeks it was clear she was suffering severe starvation. Despite pleas from a local vicar and nurses at the hospital to feed her in the face of imminent death, her parents refused, stating only they had frequently seen her like this before and were confident she would endure. The girl died of starvation a few days later and it was found that she had actually been consuming small amounts of food secretly, which was not possible once placed under medical scrutiny. Her parents, Hanna and Evan Jacob, were convicted of manslaughter and sentenced to hard labour.

Living Skeletons are usually men – although there are a few cases of women thus afflicted – who are born with deficiencies that preclude them from being able to gain weight, such as the infant malady marasmus, a severe deficiency of all nutrients. One of the earliest documented cases of a Living Skeleton is Claude-Ambroise Seurat (1797-1833) of Troyes, France (Figure 3). Born healthy except for *pectus excavatum* (a depressed chest cavity), by his fourteenth year his body was almost entirely skeletal, eventually growing to a height of 1.70 metres (5'7") but weighing only 35.4 kilograms (78 pounds) (Cruikshank 1825). Fascinating to both the layperson and the medical professional, Seurat peddled his only asset: his body. The medical establishment was appalled at those who profited from Seurat's misfortune, calling it 'one of the most impudent and disgusting attempts to make a profit

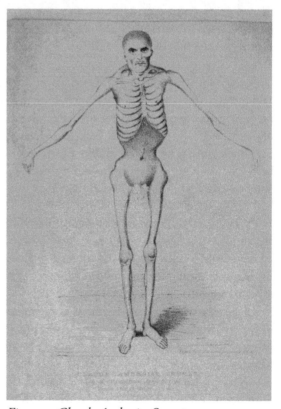

Figure 3. Claude-Ambroise Seurat

from the public appetite for novelty, by an indecent exposure of human suffering and degradation' (Altick 1978: 262). Besides the six shows a day where Seurat was forced to crawl around stage, he was also subjected to having his 'extremities squeezed by hundreds' (Cruikshank 1825: 4).

Afflicted with a physical condition that rendered him emaciated, Seurat's condition provided him little choice in profession and required him to capitalize on the opportunity of his misfortune. The Endurance Artists of the era made an explicit choice of their vocation. Giovanni Succi (1850-1918) of Italy – the likely model for the unnamed protagonist in Franz Kafka's short story, *Ein Hungerkünstler* (*The Hunger Artist*, 1922) – purposefully pursued a fasting profession. He conducted more than thirty public fasts over twenty-five years, five of them in 1888 alone. Succi claimed to have been provided a magical elixir during an adventurous trip to Africa, which allowed him the ability to abstain from nourishment for extended periods of time. Having subjected himself to psychologists and physiologists, a scientific commission was assigned the task of monitoring Seurat's fasts and restricting visitors as a method of controlling the experiment. By the turn of the century, the public's interest in professional fasters was waning, but in 1907, Succi endeavoured one last, remarkable fast in conjunction with the inauguration of the first cinema in Bologna. Enclosed in a glass cage in the waiting room, thousands of onlookers came to see him over the course of thirty days when he completely abstained from any food.

Ninety-six years later the public would see the ghostly echo of Succi's glass cage. David Blaine (1973-) advertises himself as a magician and endurance artist and has made his name by performing stunts on the edge of human capability. In 2003, Blaine withstood forty-four days in a clear plexiglass box measuring 1m x 2m x 2m (3' x 7' x 7') hoisted thirty feet above the banks of the Thames River without any food or nutritional supplements, although he was allotted 4.5 litres of water a day. Considered his most controversial stunt, *Above the Below* utilized technology by providing a webcam that allowed anyone to participate in the voyeuristic spectacle. Blaine was subjected to all manner of humiliations, from being pelted with eggs to all-night drumming and even the taunting of barbecues grilling meat, wafting appetizing aromas in his direction. The public reaction varied from anger to boredom to strong support. The proliferation of over 1600 articles in the British press attest to the public interest in this stunt.

Historic Overview

In 'Fasting Women, Living Skeletons and Hunger Artists: Spectacles of Body and Miracles at the Turn of a Century', Sigal Gooldin states, 'the act of fasting expresses one dimension of the act while the other is the spectacle itself'. It did not matter that Anne Moore was ultimately found to be a fraud. Moore and other Fasting Women such as Theresa Neumann and Sarah Jacob *appeared* to be fasting: 'They were visible, they were "gazed at" by an audience, they were admired, they were suspected, and they were, above all, present in the social world' (Gooldin 2003: 32). Those who witnessed Moore and the others added to the power of the presentation, whether real or not. In

Kafka's short story, the artist terminates his relationship with his impresario and joins a sideshow, where he is placed near a menagerie of animals. His performance evolves around achievement – one that was acquired through the labour of pain, suffering and self-inflicted hunger. Slowly wasting away, the throngs show more interest in the livelier animal attractions nearby. Kafka's *Hungerkünstler* eventually dies because no one was present to acknowledge his feat. The artist could not exist without the audience.

Viennese Action Movement

The Viennese Actionists were four performance artists – Günter Brus, Otto Muehl, Hermann Nitsch, and Rudolf Schwarzkogler – who collaborated during the 1960s on more than 150 *aktions* intended to 'shock, amuse, fascinate, and nauseate audiences in Austria, Germany and beyond' (Green 1999: 7). Trained as painters, they celebrated the grotesque and the violent, using techniques of butchery and self-mutilation, coupled with acts of gastronomy. As early adopters of Abstract Expressionism, taking their art off the canvas and into performance, they formed a non-canonical brotherhood by pushing the envelope of acceptance within the group's self-ascribed *aktions*. In interviews, many of these artists have cited Sigmund Freud's philosophies of liberating the consciousness from oppression through psychoanalysis, Wilhelm Reich's theories of sexual liberation and revolution, body psychotherapy, and Frederic Nietzsche's concept of the 'superman'. Witnessing the atrocities of WWII and its aftermath, their work was, in part, a manifestation of the subconscious associations related to the war and an attempt at abnegation of mainstream normality. Their art directly confronted the savagery of the war and made mockery of the entrenched political and religious conservatism that clung to Viennese life despite the cataclysms of Fascism and the *Anschluss*. Having come of age in hellish surroundings and immersed in the angst of being at ground-zero of the new Cold War, their reaction to the carnage was manifestations of revulsion in an artistic setting.

Artistically, the Aktionists had as their Austrian patron saint the first Viennese transgressionist, Egon Schiele, whose work is known for its raw intensity, frank sexuality, twisted body shapes, and naked self-portraits. At the beginning of the century, the Cubists deconstructed what the eye sees, and, by the 1920s, the German Expressionists expanded upon the Cubists' endeavours by emphasizing their feelings in simplified shapes and stark, gestural brushstrokes, replicating reality in bright, contrasting colours. Nitsch expressed a simpatico with the splatter paintings of Jackson Pollock and the figurative brutality of Willem de Kooning: 'I understood immediately that these painters were searching for the same thing I was through my theatre; nothing else but sensory-stimulating processes were being directly intuited and shown' (Morgan 2018).

Seemingly offensive acts were perpetrated upon their bodies along with organic materials such as blood, milk, urine, eggs, breadcrumbs, and entrails, manifesting both destruction and violence with emancipatory motives. At times, the artists themselves were the subject of public scandal – occasionally fined, jailed, or driven into exile. The mainstream art community all but ignored them and their work, or dismissed them out of hand. The artists, following a belief that they needed to come to terms with the suppression of collective societal memories of the atrocities of war, challenged and rebelled in a way that had not been seen before. Though ridiculed in their own time, the Viennese Actionism movement is now cited as one of the most important in post-war Europe, and, linked with Fluxus, Gutai, and Happenings movements, became a driving force for the onset of postmodern performance art.

Historic Examples

In 1957 Hermann Nitsch, a trained musician and dramatist as well as a visual artist, began theorizing his *Orgien Mysterien Theater* (Orgies Mysteries Theatre), an action piece involving music of his own composition, a small army of devotees, acts of butchery and evisceration using farm animals, and a live crucifixion. Nitsch's intent for the latter was not an austere crucifixion *à la* Diego Velázquez or Matthias Grünewald, but a living, blindfolded, naked man or woman strapped (not nailed) to a cross, splattered with and fed crimson blood (Figure 4). Wanting his creative endeavours to be experienced with all five senses, Nitsch first coined this style of performance painting as an *aktion*, invoking Dionysian and Apollonian mythologies as ascribed by Nietzsche's *Kunsttriebe* (artistic impulses).

341

With acolytes in white robes doing his bidding, Nitsch became the high priest of his own mysteries. Orchestrating the cathartic, gnostic ritual wherein his male and female Maenads acted out *sparagmos* – ripping asunder the sacrificial beast – his work was instilled with mystic intent as he drove to rediscover spiritual purpose through participation in the frenzied action. As Nitsch put it, 'I take upon myself all that appears negative, unsavoury, perverse, and obscene, the lust and the resulting sacrificial hysteria, in order to spare YOU the defilement and shame entailed by the descent into the extreme' (Morgan 2018) (Figure 5).

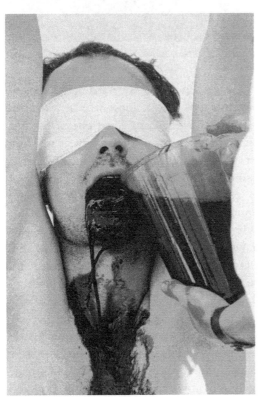

Figure 4. Aktion 2 Cibulka-Frey

There are many misconceptions about the work of the Viennese Action artists, and much contradictory information has been attributed to their work and to the artists personally. The established dogma is that they are fascists, anarchists, and Satanists. They have been described as everything from 'godless blasphemers to saints and shamans' (Green 1999: 11). While Nitsch is still actively continuing his blood-themed artwork, Günter Brus has turned away from his nihilistic performances and settled on a post-performative career of drawing and painting. One of Brus's most famous works, *Action Number Six: Vienna Walk* (1965), had the artist walking through the centre of Vienna dressed as a 'living painting'. His body painted entirely white, a roughhewn black dividing line was painted up Brus's back, over the

Figure 5. Aktion 2009 NF Foto Roland Rudolph

top of his head, through his face, and down his suit, extending down his right leg to his shoe (Figure 6). Friends and collaborators of Brus took pictures of him as he wandered the town and interacted with police in what can now be considered one of the first documentations of performance art – taking the event out of the gallery or museum and into the street, with unsuspecting passers-by unwittingly made part of the spectacle.

Brus's renown as an artist centred around proving Austria's fascist essence, most notably in the piece *Kunst und Revolution* (Art and Revolution, 1968). Taking over a student gathering at the University of Vienna, Brus and Otto Muehl with two fellow compatriots, Peter Weibel and Oswald Wiener, staged one of the most aggressively taboo-bending *aktions*. After breaking into the lecture hall, the four stripped down and, standing on chairs atop a large lectern, proceeded to smother each other in excrement, urinate into glasses and consume each other's urine, whip each other, masturbate and vomit, all while singing Austria's national anthem. For this heinous act all four men were arrested and sentenced to six months in prison.

Otto Muehl passed away in 2013, but not without a lifetime of controversy after establishing (and later apologizing for) an authoritarian commune from which he was arrested and jailed as a sex offender. Muehl, the most psychologically and artistic transgressive of the four, used the human body as a canvas and scene of action: 'a person is not treated in the material action as a person but as a body. the body, things, are not

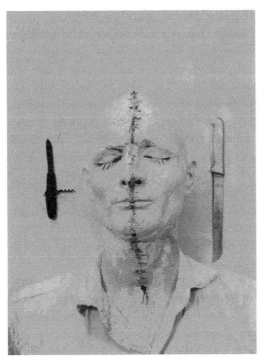

Figure 6. Gunther Brus

viewed as objects for our purposes, but have all purpose radically removed from them. the body is not seen as a human being' [*sic*] (Green 1999: 87). Muehl worked within classic themes like the still life or classical mythology in art for his subjugation. *Material Action 9: Still Life, Action With One Female, One Male and One Ox Head* (1965) had Muehl creating his own version of a living still life where his models would push their heads up through a table set with a cow's head and other edibles such as pickles, eggs, and bread. As part of the action, however, the artist would start interacting with the heads; feeding them, brushing their teeth, covering them with jam or milk. In effect, the *memento mori* of a Flemish still life is made real with the mortal act of destruction upon those involved in the debacle.

343

Rudolph Schwartzkogler's untimely death at the age of twenty-nine was caused by a fatal fall from his fourth-story apartment window. Whether or not this was suicide or an accident has never been determined, but legend had it that Schwartzkogler's death was due to self-inflicted mutilation of his own penis. This rumour came about due to an action which was entirely staged and mythologized. Robert Hughes, journalist for *Time* magazine originated this falsehood in an article:

> Those interested in the fate of the avant garde should reflect on a Viennese artist named Rudolf Schwarzkogler. His achievement (and limited though it may be, it cannot be taken away from him; he died, a martyr to his art, in 1969, at the age of 29) was to become the Vincent van Gogh of body art. As every movie-goer knows, van Gogh cut off his ear and presented it to a whore. Schwarzkogler seems to have deduced that what really counts is not the application of paint, but the removal of surplus flesh. So he proceeded, inch by inch, to amputate his own penis, while a photographer recorded the act as an art event. In 1972, the resulting prints were reverently exhibited in that biennial motor show of Western art, *Documenta V* at Kassel. Successive acts of self-amputation finally did Schwarzkogler in. (1972)

In fact, the artwork in question, *3rd Action* (1965) is part of a series of images in black-

and-white of a model named Heinz Cibulka. The photographer was Michael Epp. It was Schwarzkogler who orchestrated the scenes, wrapping Cibulka in white bandages and placing a fish where a seemingly butchered penis would lie. What appeared to be blood from the evisceration was actually ink. Schwarzkogler created these themes of mutilation, gore, and pain to manifest an understanding of societal flaws in his audience. Unlike the other Actionists, Schwarzkogler performed his works in private and had them photographed to let his intentions be narrated by his audience. We see juxtaposed images of pain and healing, not knowing if what we are viewing is real or imagined. The power lies in the fear that the mind supposed to be truth in what is being presented.

Similarities

As documented in Kafka's short story, *Ein Hungerkünstler,* themes of death, isolation, and corruption directly relate to the subsequent work of the Viennese Actionist artists. Hunger Artists protested political regimes and their motivation was to display control in uncontrollable circumstances. The Hunger Artist's refusal to eat was a practice in control and a protest against corruption, although it ultimately ended in isolation and death. Brus, Muehl, Nitsch, and Schwarzkogler endeavoured to protest fascist factions in Austria and flaws in society. Their performance art was often used to convey the death, isolation, and corruption that stemmed from the repressed totalitarianism of 1960s Austria.

Although Hunger Artists and Viennese Actionists were different in nature and time span, several similarities emerge. First, food was used to protest. For Hunger Artists, abstention from food was a form of protest and spectacle. Hunger Artists used their own human bodies to shock their audience to invoke pity and encourage financial assistance. For Viennese Actionists, the foodstuffs were part of the protest. Both utilized their own bodies for manipulation and attraction to become the spectacle and become empowered with the witnesses of their acts.

Another important theme is that of the spectacle. For both the Hunger Artists and the Viennese Actionists, the strength and power of their existence was in direct relation to their visibility and appearance. Otto Muehl said, 'i was a great artist because i did everything i could to make the artist unacceptable to society. and i totally succeeded, not only with society, but also myself' [sic] (Green 1999: 122). Their need to resort to extreme measures, either by starving themselves or subjecting their bodies to drastic actions, had the same motivation. They were both performance artists, desirous of attention, regardless of the cost: 'Taboo-breaking artworks often present a spectacle of excess, a passing beyond limits, one in which the spectator is not invited to participate, but instead must observe, apart, alienated, even repelled' (Julius 2003: 191).

The Viennese Actionists were nihilistic, taboo, frightening performance artists, but the same could be said of the Hunger Artists who deliberately starved themselves. Where the Hunger Artist would refrain from consumption, blurring the line between installation and performance art, the Action artists used their bodies to wreak wilful transgressions upon their very selves. Both groups manifested self-destruction and violence, motivated by the political strains of their place and time, as well as a desire to confront conventionality and the nature of art itself. Shocking and transforming their eager audiences, these early performance artists redefined the nature of art itself. The Actionists pushed the transgressive energy of early Viennese modernism to its logical extreme; moving from those bits of ourselves that we hide from the public gaze to actively performing human self-destruction. Ultimately, there is a demand in these horrors that we face up to what they expose, rather than accept the claims that we have become too desensitized to react.

References

Albala, Ken. 2014. 'Fasting', in *Springer Encyclopedia of Food and Agriculture Ethics*, ed. by Paul B. Thompson and David M. Kaplan (New York: Springer), pp. 916-22

Altick, Richard D. 1978. *The Shows of London* (Cambridge, MA: The Belknap Press of Harvard University Press)

Bell, Rudolph M. 1985. *Holy Anorexia* (Chicago: University of Chicago Press)

Bogdan, Robert. 1988. *Freak Show: Presenting Human Oddities for Amusement and Profit* (Chicago: University of Chicago Press)

Brumburg Jacobs, Joan. 1989. *Fasting Girl: The History of Anorexia Nervosa* (New York: Plume)

Cruikshank, Robert. 1825. *Memoir of Claude Seurat, the Living Skeleton* (Ludgate Hill: John Fairburn)

Ellmann, Maud. 1993. *The Hunger Artists: Starving, Writing, and Imprisonment* (Cambridge, MA: Harvard University Press)

Goldberg, RoseLee. 1979. *Performance: Live Art, 1909 to the Present* (New York: Harry N. Abrams)

Gooldin, Sigal. 2003. 'Fasting Women, Living Skeletons and Hunger Artists: Spectacles of Body and Miracles at the Turn of a Century', *Body & Society*, 9.2 (June): 27-53

Green, Malcolm (ed.). 1999. *Writings of the Vienna Actionists* (London: Atlas Press)

Henderson, Alexander. 1810. *An Account of the Extraordinary Abstinence of Ann Moor [sic], of Tutbury, Staffordshire, Who Has, For More Than Two Years, Lived Entirely Without Food* (Philadelphia: Joseph Sharpless)

—— 1813. *An Examination of the Imposture of Ann Moore Called the Fasting Woman of Tutbury: Illustrated by remarks on other cases of real and pretended abstinence* (London: J. Moyes)

Hughes, Robert. 1972. 'The Decline and Fall of the Avant-Garde', *Time*, 17 December, p. 111

Julius, Anthony. 2003. *Transgressions: The Offences of Art* (Chicago: University of Chicago Press)

Kloecker, Hubert. 2014. *Rite of Passage: The Early Years of Vienna Actionism 1960-1966* (New York: Snoeck)

Morgan, Robert C., 2018. *Writer and Artist, in conversation with Hermann Nitsch, Artist*, 16 April <https://www.youtube.com/watch?v=YYz1C5KM0jU&t=797s> [accessed 25 May 2019 accessed 25 May 2019]

Ruffles, Tom. 1992. 'Ann Moore: The Fasting Woman of Tutbury', *The Skeptic*, 6.6 (December): 9-11

Russell, Sharman Apt. 2005. *Hunger: An Unnatural History* (New York: Basic Books)

Sakoilsky, Paul. 2010. 'Breaking Out of the Reality Asylum: Hermann Nitsch and the Orgies Mysteries Theatre', *Galerie Zimmermann Kratochwill Catalogue*, August, pp. 32-33

Simanowtiz, Stefan. 2010. 'The Body Politic: The Enduring Power of the Hunger Strike', *Contemporary Review*, 292.1698 (Autumn): 324-31

Stiles, Kristine. 2016. *Concerning Consequences: Studies in Art, Destruction, and Trauma* (Chicago: University of Chicago Press)

Ursprung, Philip. 2009. 'More than the Art World Can Tolerate: Otto Muehl's Manopsychotic Ballet', *Tate Etc*, 15 (Spring) <https://www.tate.org.uk/tate-etc/issue-15-spring-2009/more-art-world-can-tolerate> [accessed 25 May 2019]

Vergine, Lea. 2000. *Body Art and Performance: The Body as Language* (Switzerland: Skira)

Wee, Lionel. 2007. 'The Hunger Strike as a Communicative Act: Intention without Responsibility', *Journal of Linguistic Anthropology*, 17.1 (June): 61-76

White, Murray. 1996. 'Schwartzkogler's Ear', *New Yorker*, 3 November: 36

Empire of Wheat: Bread, Power, and Colonialism in the French Empire (1890-1940)

Nicholas Tošaj

Introduction

In his 1931 book *L'Indochine française pour tous*, French author Louis Cros cited the average bread consumption of a French man at 200 kilograms per year.[1] Bread occupied a crucial place within French foodways, a position which placed the national government in a deep quandary; demographic growth and fluctuating agricultural production meant that at the dawn of the twentieth century France was no longer capable of producing enough wheat to supply its people with the bread they believed was their right.[2] This sense of entitlement complicated matters in the colonies where colonists continued to consume bread, yet were dependent on imperial rivals such as the British Commonwealth to deliver the wheat with which to bake it.

Though troubled by the fact that the wheat he was consuming in Indochina was not French, Cros sought to reassure his readers. He articulated that the wheat was Canadian, descending from seeds originally cast in Quebec centuries ago by French settlers.[3] In reality the wheat which Cros consumed was most likely Canadian Marquis wheat, a cross between Ukrainian and Himalayan varietals and a product of British imperial agricultural engineering.[4] Cros's urge to qualify Canadian wheat in the colonies as a food with a French legacy demonstrates the power embodied in concepts of *terroir* and gastronationalism. Consuming French bread abroad played a significant role in performing 'Frenchness' in the colonies, a performance which was shaped in varying degrees by the sourcing of wheat and labourers throughout the empire.

The provisioning of the empire with bread led to manifestations of both hard and soft power. Imperial trade currents were engaged to deliver wheat to the colonies at great expense. In order to meet these expenses, the French resorted to the selling of colonial goods, including staple foods such as rice. In Cambodia, discrimination against independent indigenous bakers in the form of preferential contracts and selective hygiene inspections unfairly benefited European bakers. In Morocco, agricultural policies were restructured to produce European-style wheats rather than traditional Moroccan hard wheats. While my dissertation seeks to address these topics more deeply, this paper is limited to surveying manifestations of power through wheat and rice in Cambodia and Morocco: the former, to which wheat was exported, and the latter, which was intended to be made into a breadbasket for the French Empire.

Bread as a Symbol of 'Frenchness'

Ideas of French culinary exceptionalism have long been tied to bread, baking, and French culture. The obvious springboard from which to understand the value attributed to French bread is the work of Steven Kaplan. Kaplan's *Good Bread Is Back*, alongside his other works, provides useful insight into the status of bread, its production, and consumption in France.[5] The centrality of bread to French culture and its democratization has also been discussed by Rachel Laudan in her *Cuisine & Empire*.[6] By following French bread to Cambodia and Morocco we not only expand the scope of seminal works in food studies, we also gain insight into how the identity of French bread shifted in an exoticized context. French bread became a symbol of colonial power – one which, unlike other symbols of colonialism, was directly consumed.

French nationals in Indochina eagerly grasped at overpriced supplies of canned food from the mainland in order to reassert their 'Frenchness' as opposed to eating significantly fresher and healthier local foods.[7] This tendency, substantiated by a combined nostalgia for French cuisine and a chronic fear of 'going native' is particularly relevant in the context of bread. Among some members of the French public, bread consumption was perceived as a relevant yardstick against which to measure the civilization of a people. *Le Boulanger-pâtissier*, a French professional journal for bakers, made this clear when it published a tract in 1938 by Professor L. Neuberger of Geneva who claimed that wheat bread was a strong marker of cultural superiority and social progress. Neuberger backed this claim by stating that the Japanese, the most westernized (and thus in his belief most developed) civilization in Asia ate more wheat bread than other Asian peoples.[8] Opinions such as those of Neuberger bolstered European claims to superiority at the height of the imperial era, embedding these notions of racial and national dominance into even seemingly mundane aspects of daily life.

The French affinity for wheat bread was steeped in centuries of tradition and dedication. Bread's availability as well as its embodiment as the quintessential French food in a world increasingly shaped by crystalizing national identities made the French staple particularly susceptible to perceived threats of hybridization, be it in the form of foreign grains, a fear of non-European bakers, or a distaste for the breads of other peoples. Fear of colonial cross-pollination permeated the attitudes of the colonists. The French 'civilizing mission', an equivalent to Kipling's *White Man's Burden*, armed French colonists with moral justification for their colonization efforts. However, to maintain their sense of superiority the French necessarily had to uphold their own cultural markers when abroad.[9]

Rice, Bread, and Power in French Cambodia

Phnom Penh, the administrative capital of French colonial Cambodia, stood as it does today at the intersection of the Tonlé Sap, Mekong, and Bassac rivers. A thriving trade hub with a long history as the Khmer capital, Phnom Penh became the heart of the French Protectorate when it was formed in 1863. Of the 1.5 million people that lived in Cambodia in 1867, 300 were French.[10] By 1933, Cambodia boasted a population of 2,450,000 people, 80,000 of whom lived in Phnom Penh; 1500 of these were European, constituting the bulk of Cambodia's French population.[11] This relatively small proportion of the population reflected Cambodia's peripheral nature within the 'Jewel in the Crown' that was French Indochina. Cambodia's relatively light density of French settlement was in part due to its nature as principally an agricultural colony with one dominant export: rice.

Rice and Wheat as Commodities

Rice as both an export product and the prime staple of Cambodia's Khmer, Vietnamese, and Chinese populations was crucial to determining power dynamics surrounding food in French Cambodia. Rice was also the principal export of a region mostly devoid of heavy industry, an export which needed to be exploited by the French colonial government in order guarantee the colony's profitability. As a commodity, Cambodian rice contributed to funding French occupation in the region while also being sensitive to the vagaries of increasingly volatile global markets.[12] When market volatility threatened rice prices and the metropole faced supply issues relating to wheat at home, the French endeavoured to increase consumption of rice in the metropole, an initiative which met with limited success in part because of the colonial identity attributed to the foodstuff.[13] The conundrum of rice surpluses and bigotry towards colonial foods reached their apex when French efforts to blend rice flour into bread during periods of wheat shortage met stiff opposition at home, a situation studied in depth by Lauren Janes.[14]

348

French Cambodia, as a rice-producing locale dominated by a powerful bread consuming minority, is an ideal case through which to study the emergence of a wheat versus bread binary. Though bread existed as a basic staple in France, a necessity even, within Indochina bread was a source of comfort for French colonists, a food which was not biologically necessary to sustain them but which was deemed integral to preserving their identity. French bread in Cambodia was all the dearer as its production relied on imported wheat flour. This stubborn dependence on food perceived as European was all the more bemusing in the context of a vibrant tropical colony rich in local foods. These local foods were easily affordable to the French agents of empire who occupied positions of privilege within Cambodia's imperial structure. Although French overreliance on bread attracted criticism, this did not impede continued imports of wheat to French Cambodia from as far abroad as Australia, the United States, and Canada.[15] In 1929 Indochina imported over 22 million kilograms of wheat flour, 21.3 million kilograms of which was purchased from British Hong Kong, undermining the profits which the colonizing project sought to attain.[16] Indochina's, and by extension Cambodia's, reliance on foreign flour speaks to the triumph of taste over profit. French inhabitants of the colony attempted to avoid inexpensive Khmer rice in favour of foreign flour produced by their imperial rivals, seemingly with the understanding that wheat was wheat and that any wheat was better than rice.

Wheat, Frenchness, and Colonial Identity

The noteworthy exception to this rule was the French flour imported by the Resident Superior of Cambodia for use by the highest offices of the protectorate. Records show that distinct arrangements were put in place to import 100 kg of French wheat flour for use by the protectorate of Cambodia in the first semester of 1917, despite the scarcity of wheat in the metropole due to the ongoing war.[17] Cambodia's chief civil servant likely sought to make a statement by importing costly French flour, stressing the link between metropole and colony and asserting the resident superior's place at the top of a hierarchy of consumption. While it is unclear how conspicuous his office's consumption of French flour was made to be, the patriotism inherent in this provisioning speaks to the symbolic value of consuming identifiably French bread made from French flour, despite the accessibility of more affordable, and potentially better quality, foreign flour.

Though the resident superior's consumption of French flour demonstrates a potentially fervent sense of national duty, the production of French bread was somewhat more nuanced. French bakers spread throughout the colonies rapidly, and Indochina was no exception. Though some bakeries remained French in name and ownership, the bread consumed by the colonizers does not appear to have remained in French hands for long. For instance, the Pâtisserie Dauphinoise in Dalat in modern day Vietnam sought to evoke France with its name even though its owner, Ban Thaï, was Vietnamese.[18] Though information regarding such examples is relatively scarce, instances such as this one allude to the place that some non-French bakers were able to make for themselves by making use of the colonial reliance on bread to secure survival in a system skewed against them.

349

For French bakers, local peoples provided a source of inexpensive labour. Erica Peters has stressed that upon arrival in Indochina many French bakers took advantage of the positions of power that their nationality granted them to escape the difficult conditions of their trade. Much as a baker in metropolitan France passed off the hardest work to apprentices, the colonizers were quick to pass on the skills of their trade to native peoples who did the brunt of their work.[19] This occurred in part because of a need to provide French-style bread to colonial soldiers and later to other wings of the colonial administration, as evidenced by records from the mixed hospital of Phnom Penh.[20] French bakers were doubtless all too glad to distance themselves from the backbreaking work of the trade, particularly in colonial locales considered by the French to be too hot for habitation, let alone baking.[21] The shifting of this difficult labour and its offloading to the colonial body points toward hierarchies based on class and race in the colonies. The rhetorical commitment to bread in the colony being 'French' and thus acting as a marker of difference seems to have contrasted sharply with the reality of who was actually doing the baking.

The racialization of staple foods in French Cambodia made non-French bakeries targets in an already imbalanced power structure. One archival finding of note chronicled the testing of food for potential adulterants. The 1917 seizure of flour from a Chinese baker in Phnom Penh named Lo Linh is indicative of the suspicion which non-French bakers were subjected. Lo Linh, who had no prior convictions, was suspected of food adulteration alongside three other non-French bakers. The flour and bread seized from these four bakers were all tested chemically for adulterants, with no samples showing evidence of adulteration.[22] Despite the rigorous testing to which these breads were subjected, no records of similar inspections of the few French bakeries in Phnom Penh emerged.

The three European bakeries of Guyonnet, Pétigny, and Roussely which surface most often in Cambodian archival sources not only escaped such scrutiny but also appear as the only bakers that were issued contracts for bread by the colonial government. Calls for tender to supply bread to Phnom Penh's hospital, among other public institutions, were dominated by bids from these European bakeries.[23] In one particularly striking instance Maison Roussely secured government provisioning contracts despite competition from an unnamed bakery which offered bread at a lesser cost. Despite being deemed to be of an 'excessively high' price by the French administration, Maison Roussely's bid won the contract. This inequity was made all the more flagrant by the internal correspondence discussing the tender, which stated directly that the contract was given to Maison Roussely despite the higher price, because the bakery was French while the competitor was not.[24]

Within these French bakeries, the degree to which the bread made was actually mixed by French hands is itself subject to consideration. Considering that 200 kilograms of bread were consumed per capita in 1928, we can reasonably assume that despite the small French population of Cambodia, a substantial quantity of bread was necessary to feed the city's population.[25] This demand sustained multiple European bakeries and generated numerous supply contracts for government institutions such as provisioning contracts dating from 1930 attesting to sales of rice and bread to the mixed hospital of Phnom Penh. Receipts from December of 1930 for the provisioning of the hospital in the previous month mention the purchase of 3900 kilograms of rice at the price of 0$14 per kilogram, bought from a grocer named Song Chhéang Kai, as well as for 721 kilograms of bread purchased from Roussely sold at 0$27 a kilogram, nearly double the cost of rice.[26] The higher cost of the bread provided to the hospital speaks to the willingness of the French government to spend more to be provisioned with their staple food rather than with local rice. In addition to this, the bread provided to the hospital, an average of 24 kilograms a day, testifies to a substantial demand for the French staple, a demand which required many capable bakers to be met. This is particularly noteworthy given that in this period the mechanization of bakeries in industrialized France was only first taking off. In Cambodia, where local labour was inexpensive and plentiful, it seems a natural conclusion that the workforce responsible for baking purportedly French bread in French bakeries was likely composed largely of Indochinese workers.

This is substantiated by police reports that document five employees of the Maison Guyonnet going on strike after being denied payment of their wages. Despite the ethnicity of the workers not being stated, it does not seem to be an overly ambitious leap to assume that these workers were not French. Whereas the manager of the bakery, a M Mignot, is mentioned by name, the anonymity of the workers hints towards a lack of interest in their identity. This insouciance was mirrored by Mignot's lackadaisical approach to paying them wages owed, an attitude unlikely to be directed towards French people in such a small European community. That the document refers to the five workers as members of a larger group goes further in hinting toward the labourer's place in the colonial hierarchy.[27]

Wheat and the Politics of Production in Morocco

Despite the great distance between French Cambodia and Morocco and the radically different crops grown in both locales, the two protectorates demonstrate some remarkable similarities. Much like French Cambodia, the Moroccan protectorate was a monarchy which constituted a thin veneer of independence concealing French rule. As in the Cambodian case, French influence in the protectorate pre-existed official integration into the empire, and the colony's economy was dominated chiefly by agriculture. Similar to Cambodia's relationship to Vietnam, Morocco existed as an agricultural hinterland to the more thoroughly colonized Algeria. Where Cambodia produced rice for export, Morocco produced a variety of cereal crops, of which the most important to the French colonial administration was wheat.

La Crise du Blé and Imagining the Moroccan Breadbasket

During the initial years of occupation, the French saw the golden fields of Moroccan wheat as a potential solution to weaning the metropole off of its increasing dependence on foreign wheat imports. Despite the progressive mechanization of agriculture and developments in milling and farming technology, the first two decades of the twentieth century saw an increase in foreign imports of wheat to France.[28] The foreign wheat imported by the French was often qualified as *demi-dur* (half-hard), defined by a protein level which was higher than that of most French and central European wheats, but lower than those of Morocco.[29] Such wheat varieties, particularly those originating from the United States and Canada, were of excellent quality, suitable for bread baking in addition to being affordable, factors which proved integral to the widespread consumption of foreign wheat throughout France in the beginning of the twentieth century.

Unfortunately for the French government, this reliance on foreign wheat attracted criticism at home. In his 1902 thesis, *la Crise du Blé*, Adrien Moras expounded upon the dangers of import overreliance. Moras described the delicate balancing act that states such as France needed to undergo in an increasingly globalized world, balancing cheap quality imports against independence and food sovereignty.[30] Moras was not alone in discussing the risks of such consumption habits, nor was the French government ignorant of the conundrum in which their dependence on imports placed them. Such fears seem particularly sound when one considers in hindsight the geopolitical tensions ramping up to the First World War and the disastrous effects of the conflict on French agriculture. As such, Morocco's potential to grow wheat suitable for French bread production provided a possible solution to the wheat crisis through the cultivation of good wheat at low prices by benefiting from the fertile soil and inexpensive labour present in the colony. The French control of Morocco, and the colony's proximity to France, made it a theoretically ideal breadbasket.

Soft Wheat, Soft Power

Wheat as a source of power is demonstrated in the initial conflicts of French occupation. Military correspondence from 1916 documents Resident General Lyautey's efforts to subdue Moroccan resistance groups by depriving them of grain.[31] Depriving Moroccans of their basic foodstuffs serves as a key example of hard power at play, a proven control tactic for much of human history. Similarly, French appropriation and settlement of Moroccan farmlands mirrored established patterns of colonization in most settler colonies. In an attempt to limit the length of this paper the cases that I have chosen to dwell on are the softer and more nuanced displays of French power that were exercised through wheat in Morocco.

Aside from armed resistance, the French fantasy of the imperial breadbasket was challenged by the very nature of the wheat which Morocco produced. The goal of creating a Moroccan breadbasket could only be attained by colonizing the very seed and soil of the protectorate. As such, the French wasted no time in turning Morocco's fields over to the production of wheat suitable for baking French bread. Such a transition entailed restructuring the entirety of the protectorate's food system through the use of agricultural schools, the importation of seed wheat, and the creation of local mills and grain elevators.

During French rule, seed wheat was actively imported from abroad and planted in an attempt to shift Moroccan agriculture towards soft wheat production. Though difficult to trace, some records exist of seed being imported from the United States as well as from France intended both for direct planting and for hybridization.[32] Attempts to introduce and hybridize wheats suitable to produce strong bread flours, mimicking those milled from the half-hard and soft wheats of the United States and Canada, were ultimately successful in Morocco. By 1933 this type of wheat occupied more than half of the land seeded by European settlers.[33] Production of softer wheat, which one might imperfectly term as European-style wheat, was disproportionately popular among European settlers. Harder wheat, as the staple for most Moroccans, remained primarily the purview of Moroccan farmers. Though this binary was by no means strict, growing softer wheat positioned French farmers in an optimal position to profit the colonial government's plan to create an export economy in Morocco while leaving the less profitable local market to Moroccan farmers. As French settlers became increasingly entrenched into Moroccan agriculture, the acreage of wheat planted in Morocco increased from 754,905 hectares in 1918 to 1,298,660 hectares in 1933.[34]

This colonial restructuring of Morocco's agriculture bears witness to the success of the protectorate's attempts at imposing an agricultural commodity desirable to the French into Moroccan fields. The spread of wheat production, particularly of softer European-style wheats, could easily be perceived as evidence of successful colonization. Jean Plasse, a French agricultural intern working in Morocco, asserted that the massive growth in wheat production was due to increased European colonization as evidenced by softer wheat occupying more than half of the land seeded by European settlers in the 1932-1933 agricultural year. Plasse described the colonists as being responsible for the planting of softer wheats, having introduced them as a large-scale crop in the region. As such, increasing European-style wheat production was deemed to be a successful way for the French to strengthen their colonial hold and justify their presence in Morocco. Plasse also mentioned that, though geared primarily towards export, the increasing popularity of softer wheat flour among upper classes of Moroccan populations provided internal markets for these new crops. Considering prejudices of the period that tied food to levels of civilization, Plasse's comment can be interpreted as evidence of the achievements of the civilizing mission to 'elevate' the locals to quasi-French status, fulfilling broader colonial goals of Europeanizing subjected populations.[35]

Colonial Infrastructure and the Politics of Production

The work of Plasse and of his fellow interns in agronomy as agents of empire operated hand in hand with the colonial agricultural schools that operated throughout Morocco during colonization. These institutions sought to teach modern European agricultural methods to Moroccan and French farmers alike and appear to have devoted substantial resources to the alleged improvement of Morocco's cereal production.[36] The files dedicated to the French agricultural schools of Morocco and to the works of the agricultural interns stored at the Diplomatic Archives of Nantes testify to the place of agriculture within the colonial project. Over one hundred reports on agriculture in Morocco by interns are catalogued, many of which address wheat production.

One such report on the agricultural cooperative of Beni Sassen documents French wheat breeding trials.[37] Experimental prison farms such as those of Adir, Ali Moumen, and Mazagan express the intensity of the French imperial project as well as the power dynamics displayed by them. The Adir Penitentiary not only produced substantial quantities of wheat but also stored seed and milled it into flour.[38] The softer shaping of Moroccan minds via education in colonial agricultural schools shared common goals with the wheat farming prisons, where labourers were forced to practice European-style agriculture as penance for their crimes against the colonial government.[39] These colonial efforts are two sides of the same coin, demonstrating the various methods of colonization used to force Moroccan agriculture into a form more convenient to the colonizers. The Europeanization of Moroccan wheat agriculture expressed itself not only in the varieties of wheat grown and the appropriation of land by French settlers but also in the adoption of modern Western infrastructure. The construction of French mills, the implementation of Western grain cleaning methods, and the construction of modern grain silos produced concrete markers of colonialism.[40]

By the early 1930s Moroccan wheat production and milling had, in French eyes, largely improved, with some Moroccan flours rivalling those of the finest Canadian and American imports. Flours milled in Morocco from locally grown wheat performed far better than the French wheats which they were tested against in the baking of

353

French-style breads.[41] As of 1934 special dispensations which had been granted to the British consul allowing for the importation of high quality strong flour into Morocco were annulled. The French protectorate justified this action by claiming that Moroccan wheat and milling had reached such a level of quality as to no longer justify the special dispensation that allowed the consulate to import its own flour for baking.[42] Though the overhaul of Moroccan wheat production provided the colonial government with technical success in the early 1930s, the hope that Morocco would become both breadbasket and economic powerhouse was ultimately undermined by the ever worsening markets created by the Great Depression, a glut on the global wheat market, and bumper crops of wheat in metropolitan France.[43]

Conclusion

Wheat in the Modern French Empire provides us with a multi-level understanding of the place of food in shaping power dynamics. It allows insight into the globalization of our food-supply, imploring us to understand how European-style wheat came to be defined and juxtaposed with colonial staples in the far reaches of the empire. The history of bread and the wheat it is made of allows us to witness the process of colonization, while learning about the experience of peoples who were forced to negotiate the fine line between assimilationism and dissent in their everyday choices. The prevalence of *num pang* as a typical food in today's Cambodia and the widespread production of baguettes in Morocco evoke the culinary legacies of French colonialism. These foods point to a legacy of colonialism all the while indicating the ability of colonized populations to make use of painful legacies in order to create new culinary symbols, each with their own inherent meaning. By studying staple carbohydrates such as bread and rice in the context of empire we can develop new understandings of colonialism, provisioning, and food while shedding light on the deep relationship binding food with power.

Notes

1   Louis Cros, *L'Indochine Française pour tous* (Paris : Clichy Seine, Paul Dupont, 1931), p. 376.

2   Adrien Moras, *La Crise du blé* (Paris: A. Rousseau, 1902), Bibliothèque National de France (BNF), MFICHE 8-F-14100, 2.

3   Cros, p. 153.

4   For a more detailed exploration of the place of Canadian wheat, empire, and global trade, see my 'Weaving the Imperial Breadbasket: Nationalism, Empire and the Triumph of Canadian Wheat, 1890-1940', *Journal of the Canadian Historical Association*, 28.1 (2017), 249-75.

5   Steven Kaplan, *Good Bread Is Back* (Durham, NC: Duke University Press, 2006).

6   Rachel Laudan, *Cuisine and Empire: Cooking in World History* (Berkeley: University of California Press, 2013).

7   Erica Peters, *Appetites and Aspirations in Vietnam* (Lanham, MD: AltaMira Press, 2012), p. 155.

8   'Union internationale de la boulangerie et de la boulangerie-pâtisserie', in *Le Boulanger-pâtissier,* July 1938, BNF, JO-63972, 18.

9   Alice Conklin, *A Mission to Civilize* (Stanford: Stanford University Press,1997), p. 256.

10 *Annuaire du Cambodge* 1897, (Phnom Penh), BNF, département Philosophie, histoire, sciences de l'homme, 8-LC32-6.

11 *Annuaire Complet (Européen et Indigène) de Toute l'Indochine, 1933-1934*, n.p. (page located between 737 and 741).

12 *Tableau du Commerce Extérieur de l'Indochine Année 1937-1938*, Fonds de la Résidence Supérieure du Cambodge 1863-1954 RSC 37078, National Archives of Cambodia (NAC); Peter A. Coclanis, 'Distant Thunder', *The American Historical Review*, 98.4 (1993): 1065-70.

13 Lauren Janes, *Colonial Food in Interwar Paris* (London: Bloomsbury Academic, 2016), pp. 2-3.

14 Janes, 193-94.

15 For a more detailed exploration of the provisioning of Indochina with foreign wheat, see my 'Finding France in Flour', in *Routledge Handbook of Food in Asia*, ed. by Cecilia Leong-Salobir (London: Routledge, 2019), pp. 29-38.

16 *Document attached to correspondance between Le Gouverneur Général de l'Indochine Commandeur de la Légion d'Honneur à Monsieur le Résident Supérieur au Cambodge, 5 Juillet 1930*, RSC 2535, NAC, 1930.

17 *Cahiers des Charges*, RSC 37078, NAC, 1916.

18 E.T. Jennings, *Imperial Heights* (Berkeley: University of California Press, 2011), p. 90.

19 Peters, p. 157.

20 *Cahiers des Charges*, FRSC 37078, NAC, 1914.

21 Peters, p. 159.

22 'Répression des Fraudes, procès 3773, 8427, 8428, 8429', FRSC 17855, NAC, 1917.

23 *Acte additionnel prorogeant pour une année, à compter du 1er janvier 1915, le marché du 1er novembre 1913 pour la fourniture de pain nécessaire à l'Hôpital Mixte de Phnôm-Penh du 1er janvier au 31 Décembre 1914, 17 novembre 1914, RSC 37078, NAC; Cahier des Charges Relatif à la fourniture de Pain, de sucre et Chocolat nécessaires aux Élèves du Lycée Sisowath du 1er septembre 1936 au 31 décembre 1937*. RSC 31296, NAC.

24 *Sommaire de l'Affaire Présentée, le 9 Septembre 1935*, RSC 31275, NAC.

25 Cros, p. 376.

26 *Commande 108 faite à Monsieur Song Chhéang Kai à Phnom-Penh pour le compte de l'Hôpital-Mixte* (November 1930), RSC 34420, NAC.

27 *Conflits du Travail*. RSC 28825, February 1938, NAC.

28 *Conflits du Travail*.

29 Pierre Barbade, *Étude et Mesure des qualités mécaniques des pâtes de farine, en vue de leur aptitude à la panification* (Paris: Tripette et Renaud, 1934), BNF, 4-V-12495, 36-37; Robert Geoffroy, *Le Blé, la farine, le pain* (Paris: Dunod, 1939), BNF, 4-S-4546, 43.

30 Moras, p. 2.

31 *Sortie des Grains de la Zone Espagnole, et Ravitaillement des Djebala. Le Colonel Maurial Commandant la Région de Rabat à Monsieur le Résident Général Rabat, le 15 Avril 1916*. Importations – Exportations 1914-1924, Maroc/1MA/100/327, CADN.

32 Louis S. Baritou, *La Coopération Agricole dans la Circonscription des Beni Sassen* (1933), *Mémoires de stage des contrôleurs civils stagiaires 1926-1955 Mémoire No 87 à No 94 Maroc/2mi2344*, CADN, pp. 6, 22.

33 Guillaume Plasse, *L'Office du blé et l'indigène nord-africain* (1940, 26 fol., Mémoire n.92), Maroc/2mi2353, CADN, pp. 60-61.

34 Plasse, pp. 60, 39.

35 Plasse, pp. 59-60, 31, 81-82, 59-60, 32.

36 Baritou, p. 22.

37 Baritou, p. 22.

38 Raymond Mirande, *Un pénitencier au Maroc. L'Exploitation agricole de l'Adir (Annexe d'Azemour) 1928, 58 fol., Mémoire n.134)*, Maroc/2mi2357, CADN, pp. 33-35.

39 Mirande, pp. 2, 22-24, 54, 33, 11, 23-31.

40 Plasse, p. 2; Baritou, p. 21.

41 Plasse, p. 42.

42 *Secrétariat Géneral du Protectorat Note N. 1504 S.G.P. Importation de farines étrangères Rabat, le 29 Juin 1934*, Céréales, farines, bougies, huiles, etc., Maroc/1MA/15/384, CADN, p. 1.

43 Plasse, pp. 83-85.

The Power of Laws and Lies in the Italian Fascist Kitchen

Anne Urbancic

In Italy, as Fascism pointed ever more to inevitable autarky after Mussolini became Prime Minister in 1922, Italian women coped as best they could with the numerous government policies for the Italian larder. Ineluctably, by the early 1940s, Italy was hungry. Numerous cookbooks and magazine columns, full of practical advice that enforced ideology on the dinner plate, came to their aid. The constant barrage of alimentary propaganda diffused everywhere along the peninsula momentarily filled hearts with patriotic fervour and intention to collaborate, but did nothing for the stomach, as Marco Patricelli points out in his study *Il nemico in casa* (*The Enemy in Your Home*).[1] Instead, the political zeitgeist brought privation, strict dependence on autarchic food sources, and rationing. No one, of course, dared mention the ubiquitous presence of the black market, which undermined the shortages even more and led to further ineffective power struggles between legality and illegality. In upbeat, reassuring tones, (mostly) female magazine columnists published articles offering lifestyle as much as they offered recipes of frugality.

Did Italians care about the columnists' advice on how to stand in line with elegance and class while waiting for their allotted food rations? Were Italian housewives flattered by encouragement to keep their kitchens luminous, spotless, happy, even coquettish, all the while maintaining a healthy, hygienic, and odorless environment that would deflect focus from misery and poverty?[2]

Such columns, of course, speak to politics beyond the kitchen. Laws meant to support autarky involved issues such as food ethics. And while we assume the goal of nutritional robustness of Fascist foodways, the determined enforcement of power ignored the lived effects of food scarcity and eliminated any compassion for a people already poor and still in recovery from the devastating shortages in the wake of the First World War, a people who had to find a way to feed themselves in the face of monumental policies that told them that they simply had to do without while pretending they had access to an abundance of food. Mussolini himself claimed in a speech of 18 November 1930 that, after the privation of the Great War, it was 'fortunate that most Italians were not used to eating several times a day'.[3] The politics was one of deliberate deception and obfuscation, a concerted bureaucratic demand for compliance, and a denial of agency, especially women's agency even in the kitchen where they had been relegated by the Fascist regime.

My study considers two cookery books of the time, an influential volume by

Fernanda Momigliano entitled *Vivere bene in tempi difficili: come le donne affrontano le crisi economiche* (*Living Well in Difficult Times: How Women Manage the Economic Crisis*) of 1933, just as autarky was becoming a reality in Italy, and a similar volume by Lunella de Seta, *La cucina del tempo di guerra* (*The Kitchen in Time of War*) of 1942, both reflecting the food laws and realities of Italy at war.

Momigliano's book anticipated what would eventually become ever more stringent government supervision of what Italian families put on their tables. Her opening page alerts her compatriots to the severity of what was to come by repeating four times that theirs was a time of crisis. As the hard times predicted by Momigliano became more evident, other authoritative female voices, self-proclaimed experts who wrote for popular magazines, like Dr. Amal/Petronilla (a pseudonym for Amalia Moretti Foggia who was also a medical doctor), home economist Elisabetta Randi, and others, took up the banner to promote Mussolini's ever more restrictive policies around food through newspapers and magazines intended for their housewife subscribers. Among these was also Lunella de Seta with *La cucina del tempo di guerra*. The politics of their promotion was powerfully cruel: there was increasingly less to bring to the table, but women were pressed to increasingly greater acquiescence to powerful Fascist alimentary regulations.

First, I'd like to contextualize the two works. After his rise to power in 1922, Mussolini and his political regime demanded that Italians comply with new alimentary attitudes and new food ethics as the era of self-sufficiency or autarky began. Carol Helstosky points out that 'the administration of other policies – demographic, economic, imperial – depended on the ability of the regime to control what, and how much, Italians ate'.[4] And while there had been studies of food consumption patterns even before the First World War, from 1929 onward the Consiglio nazionale delle ricerche (National Council of Research) began a concerted effort to study food distribution, requirements, and supplies, with a view to determining how autarky could be supported in the agro-alimentary sector.[5] Most paramount was the policy of *granarizzazione* (the Battle for Grain), the focus on the intensified production of wheat in order to eliminate all foreign imports. Other foodstuffs were also affected, of course.

With an increased reading public, especially among women, new food books and magazines came available, and the Fascist government realized that these were ideal outlets for their foodways propaganda. While titles such as *La cucina italiana: il giornale per le famiglie e per i buongustai* (*Italian Cuisine: Journal for Families and Gourmands*) purported to promote a robust Italian gastronomical climate, their agenda soon included the enforced obligations that women (for these were inevitably intended for women) must strive towards diminished food consumption in their family, with a focus on certain kinds of foods. At the same time, there was a continuous emphasis on Italy's purported abundance with exhibitions such as the Settimana della cucina (The Week of the Kitchen) held in conjunction with the IV Mostra Nazionale dell'Agricoltura (Fourth National Agricultural Exhibition). Schoolchildren from 1934 on wrote compositions and dictations on food themes; in their classrooms they sang a paen to bread.[6]

By the 1930s, self-styled cooking experts, predominantly women, began to use the print media to encourage, cajole, and compel women to fall in line. Suffice it to repeat the observations of Carol Helstosky on the topic: recipes from their pages hardly comprised the stuff of haute cuisine and depended on polenta, puddings, rice molds, offal, and the ubiquitous *minestra* (thick vegetable soup).[7] In 1933, however, it was Fernanda Momigliano, Milanese, Jewish, initially a supporter of Fascism, who anticipated the food future of the country with her small volume entitled *Vivere bene in tempi difficili: come le donne affrontano le crisi economiche*.[8]

Momigliano subscribed, in particular, to the quickly changing role of the urban rather than rural Italian woman. Since, as Luisa Tasca points out, Fascism decreed that women could not make up more than 10% of employees of a company, urban women were largely relegated to the sphere of their homes, a policy promulgated by Maria Diez Gasca at the fourth International Congress of Home Economics (Rome, 1927).[9] This was the birth of the Fascist woman as an Angel of the Hearth.[10]

Momigliano promotes the Fascist ideology for all aspects of domestic life; her book is about food and cooking, but it is also about lifestyle. As will most of the authors after her, she skirts over any profoundly detrimental effects in the main part of her title, as if these could be overcome with a little good will and domestic prudence. Her subtitle reveals a somewhat more insidious agenda: the problems were many, and it was up to the women of Italy to confront and resolve them, at least as far as the home, and specifically the kitchen, were concerned. In many cases, when the family suffers, suggests Momigliano, it is the fault of the woman of the home who should not stop to reflect on negative aspects of Italy's situation, but who should instead do whatever possible to combat them by ensuring that 'a husband, a father, a brother, upon returning from work, will find the house as usual, the table sparkling and shiny, their women smiling' because 'women should never show any sign of crisis in their home'.[11] Her intended reader is primarily a mother with two children, a home in a metropolitan environment, a husband who is an office worker, and a live-in *domestica* or *servetta*. The lifestyle Momigliano advocates for her readers embraces constant frugality, assuring them that even the most important leaders of Italy practised such thrift. Historian Miriam Mafai points out: 'The Fascist kitchen is a frugal one. The King and Queen practised frugality. Mussolini as well (but he out of necessity given that he suffered from a stomach ulcer).'[12] Mafai then indicates precisely the ethical problem evinced by Momigliano's book: a frugal lifestyle for the Italian bourgeoisie 'dominates with an imperative that is both material and moral.'[13] Once the idea of imposed moral behaviour enters the sphere of legally mandated practises in the kitchen, it becomes coercive and ugly.

Momigliano's tone is straightforwardly prescriptive, tending to attitudes of blaming, antagonism, and reproach, as is evident from the very first page of the first chapter, *Il Compito della donna* (*A Woman's Duty*) where she repeats '*C'è la crisi*' (There is a crisis) at the beginning of four separate paragraphs, all on the same opening page. She expertly offers a solution for many aspects of reducing waste in domestic life whether saving on electricity and gas or sewing your own simple outfits. One illustrative example of her severe attitude comes in the section of advice on the annual summer vacation, urging the housewife to forego the idea and instead accept as a source of joy any small pleasures she might invent for her children.[14]

In sections of the volume that focus on food, Momigliano's intransigence and her promotion of government policies on foodways comes to the fore. She offers recipes where of utmost importance were dishes that showed good taste (she does not say 'tasted good'), meaning filling, inexpensive, and easy to prepare. The latter was especially important because it saved time and thus cooking fuel.[15] She proposes quick, economical, and healthy recipes, with thirty *minestre*, seven pasta and seven rice dishes (she recommends pasta over rice, contrary to later Fascist policies), vegetables (predominantly potatoes), and also some meat, in particular beef and veal.[16] There is no attempt to engage the cook with stories or commentary as Pellegrino Artusi had done in his cookbook, a mainstay of the Italian bourgeois household.[17] The recipes are followed by a suggested list of lunch and dinner menus, with amounts to spend monthly on food.[18] Momigliano's recipes are low in sugar so its cost does not factor into the grocery bill; they are low in dairy products and in eggs as well (she does provide a section on eggs later in the book). She does not include much fruit, despite her assertion that fruit should appear at all meals.[19] Beverages are omitted from the weekly expenditures.

It is fascinating to note that at the time of writing, aware of the failure of Mussolini's Battle for Grain, not one meal described in Momigliano's weekly menu includes bread. However, a few recipes call for breadcrumbs, and she counsels that 'bread in broth [...] is an excellent food'. She also reminds housewives that 'bread is [...] one of our most precious foods for which we must have utmost respect; wasting bread [...] is a deplorable habit'. Nonetheless, she then recommends that crumbs be reserved for the birds 'who fill us with happiness through their song and who live their joys and sorrows without demanding anything from humans'.[20]

The food allowance she recommends are for the housewife, her husband, and two children; the maid/cook is not considered.[21] The chapter ends with her assurance that her calculations, monetary and caloric, prove that 'there is no need to stuff oneself; it's sufficient to be watchful of one's diet, without excess, because measured eating is synonymous with health', a nod to the growing Fascist propaganda that Italians should be thin and healthy.[22] She deals with leftovers only briefly, saying they are 'a nightmare for housewives and no one wants to see them reappear at table'; she offers three pages of ways to present them in ways to make them unrecognizable.[23]

With this last piece of advice, Momigliano foresees the difficult years that were to come. Marked changes began after Italy's occupation of Ethiopia in 1936.[24] Fascist food policies began to extol 'the triumph of the kitchen of little or nothing [... where] there wasn't a thing that could not be recycled, masked, pushed as something else. A continuing illusion'.[25]

We come now to a question of ethics: did Momigliano recognize at all the need for human dignity while acting within parameters that demanded a food ethics in compliance

359

with relentless government dictates? She is regressive, rigorously promoting these policies and blaming women for any fragility in adherence. She writes with severe objectivity, but she seems honest in the attempt to help the Italian war effort at least in this one social sector.

While she has left us with a burdensome portrait of food in times of crisis, she never reaches the exaggerated tones of writers like Lunella de Seta, who suggests that food deprivation has a moral and religious hagiography and, in this way, reaches beyond any ethics of human dignity in times of scarcity. What is different about the two? For Momigliano the focus was on a type of alimentary crisis management, but for writers like de Seta, there were almost feverish attempts to impose sham pleasure in eating, and even to take pride in a fake Italian food patrimony.[26]

Lunella de Seta's 1942 book, *La cucina del tempo di guerra* (*The Kitchen in Time of War*), was published by Salani, which had several cookery books on its list during the war.[27] While most scholars dealing with the food and foodways of Fascist Italy quote de Seta, almost nothing is known about her. One source suggests that the name is a pseudonym for a Florentine home economics professor, Elizabetta Randi.[28]

De Seta's book, subtitled *A Practical Manual for Families*, is a call to arms for Italy's women, as her Preface evinces from the outset:

> Today's difficulties show and prove that the war demands also of us women a veiled and humble, but valid and real, personal contribution. Our battle is modest; it's the battle of the stove [...] nothing really in comparison to the true horrors of the war [...]. Let us too fight for Victory [...]. This book wants to be your 'friend', close to the domestic hearth, among the pots and pans.

Appearing two years after the official introduction of food rations, this is a book that fully promotes Fascist policies of repression and creating consensus. Unlike Momigliano, de Seta usually speaks to her readers in the first-person plural to implicate herself in the consensus making as well. From the outset she encourages women to avoid the appearance of poverty, by using appropriate table linens (of dyed cloth so they don't have to be washed as often), dishes with cheerful motifs, and break-resistant glassware produced in Italy, at Empoli. De Seta's tone is light and jovial; however, it deliberately underplays the difficulties of the times: 'We've already told you that your meal will be [...] what it can be in times of war, but – to raise your spirits – set the table carefully, set it beautifully'.[29]

De Seta follows with a series of recipes beginning with broth. But these are not recipes in a traditional sense; instead, they are intermingled with advice on how to attenuate criticism about meals that leave diners hungry. For example, in describing how to make highly diluted soups, she counsels: 'It's up to us to ennoble them, to make these twentieth-century broths with elegance, methodically, with patient trials and through the fruits of experience coupled with continuing research.' De Seta suggests a '*super brodo di guerra*' (Super Broth for Wartime) based on vegetables. Any problem due to lack of resources is quickly dismissed by de Seta's friendly and cheery tone, as if these were minimal. For example: 'What to use on pasta as a sauce? There is very little oil, and just as little butter. So? Stay calm. Stay calm. Forget your classic, or regular pasta sauces.' She advises substituting with diluted tomato sauce or ricotta cheese or a walnut pesto. If olive oil must be used, it should be mixed with flaxseed oil and lots of water. As for meat dishes, she urges women to 'meditate on the solid truth that one can live well on vegetables *alone* whereas meat *alone* would soon have us heading for the cemetery. So then, where is the serious harm of having only little meat?'.[30] By this time Italians were required to follow recommended daily allowances of 120 grams of meat or 200 grams of fish, so she points to canned meat, meat extracts, or meat-based bouillon cubes as meat substitutes.[31]

Later de Seta affirms that 'every family can resolve problems of a healthy and complete diet without becoming a slave to traditional meals'. Suggesting that the housewife might offer what was usually considered an antipasto or hors-d'oeuvre as the main meal after a nutritious soup, she explains that 'in today's required parsimony the names of dishes remain but their purpose is changed, given that foodways have changed'. In other words, simply by calling an antipasto a main dish, the housewife would suggest abundance. Later, de Seta suggests that a dessert made from boiled mashed beans covered in reduced grape must could be called winter strawberries.[32]

The chapter specifically dedicated to vegetables (although in truth vegetables dominate throughout the book) begins with the title 'Long Live...green. "Green" may not be in your pocket, but on your table it's a healthy manna.' De Seta continues with a diatribe against meat, and prompts readers to conserve even the water in which vegetables are boiled to use it in other ways so as to 'enrich our organism with a certain category of vitamins, all necessary for our health'. Later, in her section on eggs, she reminds the housewife that church and state are allied in frugal eating. Earlier, discussing fish dishes for Catholics to consume on Fridays, she reminds the housewife that, though many fish recipes called for frying, we eat to live; we don't live to eat.[33]

De Seta's tone becomes almost menacing in her section on coffee (roasted chicory or barley were favoured since imported coffee was not permitted during the years of autarky). The chapter opens with a warning that 'it is a serious and unpardonable error to try to avoid the very rigorous rules regarding food since in the dark days of wars that are prevalently economic, not to be vigilant and not to reduce your consumption severely can mean that a decisive battle is lost'; however, 'nothing prevents you from enhancing the taste of imitation coffee and increasing its digestive properties with a correction of cognac or grappa etc, for every cup'.[34]

Most importantly, de Seta advises, we must:

> take care in the appearance of food notwithstanding the course, because it means that we can confer something superior to the reality. One eats better! When offered with courtesy and perfect manners even the most miserable lunch can satisy, when presented well. As a matter of fact, this is part of the politics we as women regularly practise: even if we are ugly, when we are well dressed, it's a whole other thing.[35]

She even eschews any advice involving leftovers, letting her readers assume that all the dishes should start 'from scratch' with fresh products. Admitting to using leftovers, it seems, would undo the necessary sleight of hand in the kitchen.

In many ways, de Seta reiterates the work of Momigliano. Both books invite the Italian urban housewife to recognize times of crisis and to be frugal; rationing and autarky were a reality that Italians understood. However, theirs are also pages of hammering home the necessity, even the privilege, of duress in the kitchen. The glimmer of gladness in Momigliano's sharing of breadcrumbs with the birds to gladden our lives with their cheery songs disappears in de Seta's text, where the food chapters end with a menacing message that makes of the demand for frugality a coerced religious experience. She writes on a page dedicated solely to breadcrumbs:

> The Value of crumbs
> The patriotic morale of these hard months of War culminates and must culminate in respect for rigorous frugality in every minimal aspect of life.
> Absolute probity and frugality.
> We must raise ourselves to a mystic frugality, valuing crumbs, leftovers.
> Crumbs must be elevated as symbols.
> They are the remembrance of the words of Christ after the miraculous multiplication of loaves and fishes: Gather all the crumbs so that nothing is lost.'[36]

362

Patriotic morale, mysticism of frugality, and breadcrumbs as symbolic of following Christ's teaching was what the regime demanded from its citizens. Sadly, for Italian women struggling to put food on the table, de Seta's call to fervent spiritual and physical compliance does not include the miracle of the loaves and fishes, only the crumbs.

Her fusion of patriotism, religion and food is unmistakable in its intent to make of women a guilty party should the war not be a triumph. De Seta and Momigliano, and other similar writers of the time, brought the voice of Mussolini directly into Italian kitchens, underscoring that Italian women of the Fascist years could be seen almost as lawbreakers against both body (human and civic) and soul should they not comply with the regime. And although such writers purported to act as a housewife's 'friend', their tone was one of undeniable passive aggression, of deception and prevarication. However, their advice, despite the force of the legal clout of food rationing behind it, was like the super broth for wartime that de Seta promoted: largely insipid and weak.

Notes

1   Marco Patricelli, *Il nemico in casa* (Bari: Laterza, 2014), pp. 58-59. Unless otherwise indicated, all translations in this study are mine.
2   Patricelli, p. 330.
3   Qtd. in Valerio Castronovo, '*Banche e imprese sotto l'ala di stato*', in *Il Sole 24 Ore*, 19 May 2010.
4   Carol Helstosky, *Garlic and Oil: Food and Politics in Italy* (Oxford: Berg, 2004), p. 2.

5 Helstosky, p. 73.

6 Miriam Mafai, *Pane nero. Donne e vita quotidiana nella Seconda guerra mondiale* (Milano: Mondadori, 1987), p. 79. The official words were: 'Love bread/heart of the home/perfume of the table/joy of the hearth/Respect bread/the sweat of your brow/the pride of your work/the poetry of your sacrifice.'

7 Helstosky, p. 8.

8 Fernanda Momigliano, *Vivere bene in tempi difficili: come le donne affrontano le crisi economiche* (Milano: Hoepli, 1933).

9 Rules were somewhat different for rural women and working-class women. See Luisa Tasca, 'The "Average Housewife" in Post-World War II Italy', *Journal of Women's History*, 16.2 (2004), 92-115 (p. 95).

10 Tasca, p. 95. And by contrast, it was also the birth of the much derided 'crisis woman', well-to-do rich woman who was thin, wore make-up and did not have numerous children. For more information see Natasha V. Chang, *The Crisis-Woman: Body Politics and the Modern Woman in Fascist Italy* (Toronto: University of Toronto Press, 2015).

11 Momigliano, pp. 7, 8.

12 Mafai, p. 77; see also Helstosky, p. 99.

13 Mafai, p. 78.

14 Momigliano, pp. 5, 68-75, 90.

15 Momigliano, p. 25.

16 Momigliano, p. 107. However, in 1935 still further restrictions decreed Tuesdays and Wednesdays as non-meat days (Helstosky, p. 6).

17 Pellegrino Artusi's 1891 volume *La scienza in cucina e l'arte di mangiar bene* (Florence: Giunti Marzocco, 1960) was among the first cookbooks in Italy. He complemented his recipes with stories, anecdotes, and friendly advice.

18 Momigliano includes breakfast bread and milk are included in her sample daily calorie intake (p. 115); she calculates the monthly budget at just under 500 lire (pp. 17-24). Later, another such author, Lidia Olinda, recommends a daily food expenditure of 10-13 lire, or between 300 and 390 lire monthly (Helstosky, p. 88). For a full discussion, see Paolo Sorcinelli, *Gli italiani e il cibo* (Bologna: Clueb, 1992), pp. 168-69, and Roberta Pieraccioli, *La Resistenza in cucina* (Monteregio: Ouverture Edizioni, 2014), pp. 18-22.

19 Momigliano, p.110.

20 Momigliano, pp. 102-06.

21 My interviews with several (now elderly) women who served in this capacity confirms that they were given what was left over; often they were so underfed that they resorted to taking stale bread from the larder. They were still in their teens when employed.

22 Momigliano, p. 116. Official posters warned that 'those who eat too much, rob their country'.

23 Momigliano, p. 117.

24 Helstosky, p. 8.

25 Patricelli, pp. 58-59.

26 Helstosky, pp. 9-10.

27 Lunella de Seta, *La cucina del tempo di guerra: manuale pratico per le famiglie* (Firenze: Salani, 1942). More recently the book was republished in facsimile in 2012 by A. Vallardi, although they gave no reason for their decision to bring this particular volume to their reading public. They do not mention the most obvious justification, namely, to commemorate the seventyith anniversary of the original volume. They do maintain that the 346 recipes are valid even today. <http://www.vallardi.it/catalogo/scheda/la-cucina-del-tempo-di-guerra.html> [accessed 8 May 2019].

28 See Diana Garvin, *Feeding Fascism: Tabletop Politics in Italy and Italian East Africa, 1922-1945* (unpublished doctoral dissertation, Cornell University, 2017), p. 159 <doi.org/10.7298/X4HT2M9F>. This brings us to an observation of curiosity: if such is the case, then Randi (under the nom de plume de Seta) actually created a direct marketing competition for her own similar volume, also published in 1942. What purpose this would have is not clear as it is unlikely that Italian women would have

purchased both books.

29 De Seta, pp. 5-6, 9, 16.
30 De Seta, pp. 26, 30, 35, 107.
31 Helstosky, p. 99.
32 De Seta, pp. 147, 149, 310.
33 De Seta, pp. 231, 234, 263, 173.
34 De Seta, p. 321.
35 De Seta, p. 325.
36 De Seta, p. 343.

Subsistence Depression in Alaska: Who Gets Paid?

Nina Vizcarrondo

The foodways of Native Americans have been affected all throughout the United States ever since colonization occurred. Historical accounts of controlling food sources to eradicate the Native population include the mass killing of buffalo in the late 1800s and the inundation of Celilo Falls by the Dalles Dam in the 1950s.[1] That is noting only two of the many instances of this damage that have been actually documented. However, there is one place in particular that has traditionally been harder for colonizing forces to control with regard to food: the isolated last frontier, Alaska.

Alaska is the only state in which subsistence is considered a constitutional right. Subsistence is defined as 'the customary and traditional uses by rural Alaska residents of wild renewable resources for direct personal or family consumption as food, shelter, fuel, clothing, tools, or transportation'.[2] With subsistence being the main source of their food, Alaska Natives are the last of the first hunter gatherers the United States has left. The Alaska National Interest Lands Conservation Act (ANILCA) implies subsistence is constitutional and states its users 'shall be accorded priority over others (commercial and sport fisheries)'. The particular phrasing used in the ANILCA document makes it a tough policy to enforce, as cases have challenged its verbiage, such as *Bobby* v. *Alaska* and *Madison* v. *Alaska*.[3] If subsistence users are granted priority to the resources of Alaska, who exactly does that constitutional right defend when the animal populations start depleting? Alaska Department of Fish and Game studies show that 'rural subsistence users account for 4% of the total fish and wildlife harvest, while 95% goes to commercial interests and 1% goes to sport users'.[4] Although commercial interests do bring money to communities, overharvesting animals that Alaska Natives have historically depended upon for survival for thousands of years is taking a toll on their livelihood throughout the state. Non-diverse government entities, such as the Board of Fish (BOF), are responsible for crucial decisions affecting subsistence harvests of Pacific herring, salmon, and walrus; therefore, they hold the power over food and the responsibility for its injustices in the state of Alaska.

Many Alaska Natives live off of a subsistence-based economy. Subsistence-based economies are composed of hunting, fishing, and a cash component.[5] Many residents of Alaska nowadays, including myself, live somewhat on this subsistence-based economy where gathering or hunting offsets the amount of money spent in the industrialized food system (grocery stores, etc.). This system is then affected by and dependent on a 'complex seasonal round, high participation rates, high production outputs, a domestic mode of production, extensive non-market distribution and exchange networks, traditional systems of land use and occupancy, and mutually supportive subsistence and commercial-wage sectors'.[6] We can see the exchange network at work when, for example, a whale is caught in the North Slope, and it is divided among multiple villages. Each person gets a share.[7] The cash component is based mainly on working for cash wages. Other methods of obtaining cash include selling crafts or receiving the state's Permanent Fund Dividend, the cash reserve (mainly from an oil tax) distributed to all Alaskan residents since the Trans-Atlantic Pipeline was built. With this in mind, the value of fishing and hunting is complicated, because these practices also have cultural value. Traditional foods provide 'spiritual, cultural and traditional values, shelter, medicines, energy, identity and more. The obtaining, processing, storing and consuming of these foods have involved storytelling, dancing, drumming, art, education, language traditions and ceremonies'.[8] These are life factors connected to food that cannot be easily measured in economic terms.

Pacific Herring Roe

The annual spawning of Pacific herring has been an important cultural event for Alaska Natives since time immemorial. Traditional knowledge from Elders recalls the massive herring spawns that occurred throughout the Southeast, compromising the majority of the Tlingit and Haida foodways. The earliest written account of herring roe consumption was when Captain Richard visited Sitka Sound on 2 April 1799: 'The following morning, the natives […] had come thus early to the coast to get a supply of the spawn of a certain fish [herring] which constitutes their principal food in the spring of the year.'[9] As Richard implies, the herring spawned in such vast amounts that their roe filled the shores in thick layers. Traditional knowledge accounts for the once abundant herring roe stacking on the Southeast Alaskan shores.[10] To this day, herring roe continues to be an important food to the Tlingit. The herring spawning in Sitka have now moved away from shore to deeper waters, making gathering difficult. The Tlingit now harvest the eggs by laying hemlock branches tied to buoys in the water for the herring to lay their eggs on. Celebrations such as the blessing of Herring Rock by Kiks.ádi and herring koo.eex (potlatches) honour the arrival of the herring, or 'ya'aw'. Herring are included in many cultural curriculum resources, and the Kik.sadi clan even name their women the herring ladies, noting how vital herring are.[11]

Despite the constitutional subsistence consideration under ANILCA, the predominantly white BOF in Alaska has stopped allowing the Sitka Tribe to provide input on opening the fishery. As previous chair of the subsistence board for Alaska Native Sisterhood camp 4, I have personally been involved and seen how organizations are fighting the state over how they manage the last herring roe fishery in Alaska. The herring roe fishery is one of the most expensive in the world, with Japan willing to pay a high price: herring roe is highly prized as a delicacy in Japan. It is called *kazunoko* or referred to as 'yellow diamonds' by the Japanese, and 60% of the imported herring roe are consumed on New Year's Eve as it signifies 'family prosperity and numerous progenies'.[12] With prices once up to $26 per pound for herring roe, it is no wonder that the Alaska BOF refuses to classify herring as a forage fish. If herring were classified as a forage fish, the BOF would set fishing limitations. Herring are scientifically a forage fish since it makes up the diet of the salmon, whales, and halibut that roam Southeast Alaska waters. Other states, such as Washington, have classified herring as a forage fish, yet Alaska refuses to, presumably because of the money involved.

The traditional knowledge of many Elders shows that the populations of herring are depleting as a result of overfishing. Commercial fishermen are allowed to harvest up to 20% of the population. The westernized formulas to determine how much herring are spawning, resulting in a quota, are failing and do not account for shifting biodynamics. In 2018, commercial fishermen, despite large projections, were able to harvest only a quarter of the quota because of the lack of fish.[13] In 2019, because of a lack of herring of marketable size returning to Sitka to spawn, the fishery was not able to open at all, despite large projections of populations going to return. Now commercial fishermen are concerned as well. The Sitka Tribe of Alaska (STA), Alaska Native Brotherhood, and Alaska Native Sisterhood begged the BOF to lower the harvest quota to only 10% of the herring population, but the board refused to change. Many Tlingit interviewed in the state say they haven't met their 'Amount Necessary for Subsistence' consistently for years. Now the STA is suing the state for overfishing herring and are in a current legal battle to protect this sacred animal that ties them to their history and ancestors.[14]

367

Salmon

When people think of Alaska, they often think of salmon. Many wealthy individuals come to visit Alaska to fish and ship frozen salmon back home, exemplifying a form of neo-colonization. Historical documents show how the exploitation of salmon have impacted Alaskan Native livelihoods. There is a property rights issue when salmon are being overharvested and a certain race then controls access to cash (jobs at canneries) from that resource. This affects two out of the three subsistence-based economy factors earlier mentioned. Throughout the past several years, salmon canneries have depleted salmon populations, forcing Natives to find new locations to fish. Moreover, these canneries refused to hire Alaska Natives.[15] In 1889, Alaska Salmon Co. Fresh Water Bay wrote down an Alaskan Native man named Kah-Chuc-Tee of the Hoo-chee-noo tribe was 'friendly to whites and worthy of doing business with'.[16] Those in power could determine what Native was or was not worthy of trust or even doing business with.

When the United States acquired Alaska from Russia, Alaska Natives were shunned when practicing their culture, and the National Park Service burned off Tlingit salmon smokehouses. At a herring conservation meeting, Sitka Tribe of Alaska were informed of a very difficult debate surrounding National Park Service (NPS) trying to build a salmon smokehouse as reparations to STA. In Sitka, NPS did attempt to make amends by building one salmon smokehouse, but only under one condition – everyone can use it regardless of race. This debate illustrates how colonization goes hand in hand with destroying peoples' food sources.

The size of salmon have considerably decreased. This year will be the sixty-fourth holding of the Sitka Salmon Derby, a fishing competition over who can get the largest salmon. The largest one caught was seventy pounds in 1986, but with each passing year the size of the first-place winner has decreased noticeably.[17] For example, in 2016 it was forty pounds, in 2017 it was thirty-five pounds, in 2018 it was thirty-three pounds, and in 2019 the first place winner is thirty-one pounds. Not only are the salmon getting smaller, but they are also decreasing in numbers. King and pink salmon numbers are the lowest they have been in decades. King salmon numbers are so low that there were state-wide fishery closures. Those who subsist in the Klukwan village kept fishing despite the closure, and wildlife troopers took their nets away.[18] With the pink salmon failing to run in 2016, the commercial fishermen convinced Governor Walker to ask the Department of Commerce for disaster relief. As a result, Congress passed the Magnusen-Stevens Fishery Conservation Act, providing $56.3 million dollars.[19] The government, noting these declines, decided to make monetary reparations to commercial fishermen, whom they thought suffered the most from this downfall – even though, ironically, this downfall has resulted from the inaccuracies of westernized science and its failure to properly predict populations.

Taxpayers had to pay for disaster relief to only one set of the people whose income is dependent on this fish. The fishermen who depend on salmon for subsistence seem to have gotten overlooked, even though their economies rely on its runs just as much. These declines change everything for these people – not only diets, but also traditions such as potlatches to honour those who have 'walked into the forest'. I met an Elder who said that, of all of her loved ones who have walked into the forest, she can only afford to have one potlatch this year because she doesn't have enough salmon.

Indeed, there are a multitude of factors affecting the salmon populations. However, when the equations of entities such as BOF fail to take traditional ecological knowledge into 'data', all are affected. It is an unjust system when only some (majority not Natives) get compensated for it, if constitutionally, under ANILCA, subsistence should take priority over other uses. The issue is much broader than just the compensation – it is about how entire systems and lifestyles are devastated, perhaps beyond repair.

Walrus

Savoonga, Alaska is said to be the 'walrus capital of the world', and its inhabitants call themselves 'the people of the walrus'. Walrus is traditionally used not just for food, but also skin for boats, stomach for drums, and ivory for carving, trading, and more. Whereas not long ago this small community could harvest 300 to 400 walrus in one season, they are now only able to harvest as few as thirty. 'The total loss of our identity is on the line,' stated Mr. Pungowiyi, President of the Native Village of

Savoonga.[20] The people of Savoonga and Gambell Islands, Alaska sought to declare a state of emergency over the lack of the walrus hunt, but the state responded that, 'with no lives in immediate danger, the failed subsistence hunt doesn't qualify under the Alaska Disaster Act'.[21] The state also suggested raising food stamps, which is an unsustainable solution in an isolated place where food prices are already so high. While multiple NGOs have donated food, the government has failed to act. The outcome here is completely different from the situation with pink salmon, presumably because commercial fishermen are not involved with walrus subsistence.

Most accounts attribute the decrease in the walrus population to the thinning of sea ice, but we should also consider the depletion of their primary food source.[22] Walrus primarily feed on pollock, which also happens to be the Filet-O-Fish featured on the McDonald's menu. The McDonald's fishing boat *Alaska Ocean* is said to be one of the largest fishing vessels, with its own processing facility inside. Not only do they catch tons of pollock a day, but they also have millions of bycatch in halibut, which also affects Alaska Native foodways.[23] Powerful organizations like McDonald's reap all the economic benefits whether a fish comes or fails to run, yet they are not held accountable by the state. There is a severe disconnect in food justice here.

Food Justice

The best solution for the state to address this injustice would be to allow Alaskan Natives or Tribes to participate on the Board of Fish and Game, which currently is predominantly white. Failing to draw on the traditional ecological knowledge of the Native Alaskan Tribes in powerful boards such as BOF affects animal populations, and hence affects foodways. It is still data to consider the experiences of peoples who witness first-hand changes occurring faster than westernized scientific ways of knowing can measure. Alternative ways of knowing and traditional knowledge must be taken into consideration when setting harvest levels for those in power, the commercial fishermen. They get paid even if the fish don't show up. The state doesn't have guidelines to compensate those who live off of a subsistence-based lifestyle, yet still have the power to determine it a 'constitutional right'. Having a more diverse board would ideally lead to decisions that are more widely informed by traditional subsistence practices – which would be valuable not only for indigenous people, but also for the land overall: 'After all, our traditional foods are much more than calories or nutrients; they are a lifeline throughout our culture and reflect the health of the entire Arctic ecosystem.[24]

Notes

1   Adrian Jawort, 'Genocide by Other Means', *Indian Country Today*, 24 September 2017 <https://newsmaven.io/indiancountrytoday/archive/genocide-by-other-means-u-s-army-slaughtered-buffa-lo-in-plains-indian-wars-nEWiK2AZik-yWbnFLXOqfw/> [accessed 15 May 2019]; 'Celilo Falls', Columbia River Inter-Tribal Fish Commission <https://www.critfc.org/salmon-culture/tribal-salmon-culture/celilo-falls/> [accessed 15 May 2019].

2   United States Congress, *Alaska National Interest Lands* Conservation Act, p. 590 <https://www.nps.gov/locations/alaska/upload/ANILCA-Electronic-Version.PDF> [accessed 15 May 2019].

3   *Bobby* v. *State of Alaska, Justia US Law* <https://law.justia.com/cases/federal/district-courts/FSupp/718/764/2268787/> [accessed 15 May 2019].

4   Thomas Thornton, 'Alaska Native Subsistence: A Matter of Cultural Survival', *Cultural Survival Quarterly Magazine* (1998) <https://www.culturalsurvival.org/publications/cultural-survival-quarterly/alaska-native-subsistence-matter-cultural-survival> [accessed 15 May 2019].

5   James Fall, 'Why There is a Division of Subsistence at ADF&G', *Alaska Department of Fish and Game* <http://www.adfg.alaska.gov/index.cfm?adfg=wildlifenews.view_article&articles_id=391> [accessed 15 May 2019].

6   Robert Wolfe, 'Subsistence-Based Socioeconomic Systems in Alaska: An Introduction', *Alaska Department of Fish and Game*, 1984 <http://www.adfg.alaska.gov/specialpubs/SP2_SP1984-001.pdf> [accessed 15 May 2019].

7   Daniel Stone, 'Meet the Bowhead Whale Hunters of Northern Alaska', *National Geographic*, December 2018 <https://www.nationalgeographic.com/magazine/2018/12/proof-whale-hunters-northern-alaska/> [accessed 15 May 2019].

8   *Alaskan Inuit Food Security Conceptual Framework* (Anchorage: Inuit Circumpolar Council, 2015), p. 8 <https://iccalaska.org/wp-icc/wp-content/uploads/2016/03/Food-Security-Summary-and-Recommendations-Report.pdf > [accessed 15 May 2019].

9   Robert Schroeder and Matthew Kookesh, 'The Subsistence Harvest of Herring Eggs in Sitka Sound', *Alaska Department of Fish and Game*, 1990 <http://www.adfg.alaska.gov/techpap/tp173.pdf> [accessed 15 May 2019].

10 'Abundance and Use of Herring by Harvey Kitka', *Pacific Herring*, <https://www.pacificherring.org/stories-map> [accessed 15 May 2019].

11 'Pauline Duncan's Tlingit Curriculum Resources', *Alaska Native Knowledge Network* <http://ankn.uaf.edu/curriculum/Tlingit/PaulineDuncan/books/Spawn/spawn.html> [accessed 15 May 2019],

12 George Herrfurth, 'Japan's Herring and Herring Roe Supplies and Trade', *Foreign Fishery Developments*, 48.3 (1986), 60 <https://spo.nmfs.noaa.gov/sites/default/files/pdf-content/MFR/mfr483/Herrfurth.pdf> [accessed 15 May 2019].

13 Emily Kwong, 'Sitka Herring Fishery Closes Early 8,300 Tons Short Of Quota', *Alaska Public Media*, 4 April 2018 <https://www.alaskapublic.org/2018/04/04/sitka-herring-fishery-closes-early-8300-tons-short-of-quota/> [accessed 15 May 2019].

14 Enrique de la Rosa, 'STA Requests State Supreme Court Reversal on Injunction Denial', *KCAW Raven Radio*, 4 March 2019 <https://www.kcaw.org/2019/03/04/sta-requests-state-supreme-court-reversal-on-injunction-denial/> [accessed 15 May 2019].

15 US National Library of Medicine, 'Canneries Deplete Salmon Catch for Alaska Natives', *Native Voices: Native Peoples' Concepts of Health and Wellness* <https://www.nlm.nih.gov/nativevoices/timeline/356.html> [accessed 15 May 2019].

16 US National Library of Medicine, 'Alaska Natives Must Renounce Cultures to Become Citizens', *Native Voices: Native Peoples' Concepts of Health and Wellness* <https://www.nlm.nih.gov/nativevoices/timeline/418.html> [accessed 15 May 2019].

17 '86 Year Old Wins Sitka Salmon Derby With 40 Pound Chinook', *Daily News-Miner*, 7 June 2016 <http://www.newsminer.com/news/alaska_news/year-old-wins-sitka-salmon-derby-with--pound-chinook/article_9c1f9574-2cdf-11e6-8b60-a7d073fa78b7.html> [accessed 15 May 2019].

18 Nathaniel Herz, 'Southeast Alaska's King Salmon are Disappearing, and Fishermen are Grappling with the Consequences', *Anchorage Daily News*, 28 December 2017 <https://www.adn.com/business-economy/2017/12/28/southeast-alaskas-king-salmon-are-disappearing-and-fishermen-are-grappling-with-the-consequences/> [accessed 15 May 2019].

19 Joe Viechnicki, 'Permit Holders, Processing Workers Included in Pink Salmon Disaster Money Draft Plan', *KFSK*, 7 September 2018 <https://www.kfsk.org/2018/09/07/permit-holders-processing-workers-

included-in-pink-salmon-disaster-money-draft-plan/> [accessed 15 May 2019].

20 Lisa Demer, 'For Two Alaska Villages, Walruses Remain Essential As Sea Ice Disappears', *Anchorage Daily News*, 26 May 2017 <https://www.adn.com/features/alaska-news/rural-alaska/2017/05/26/for-two-alaska-villages-walruses-remain-essential-as-sea-ice-disappears-can-it-last/> [accessed 15 May 2019].

21 Suzanna Caldwell, 'Disaster Declared for Subsistence Walrus Hunt on St. Lawrence Island', *Anchorage Daily News* (2013) <https://www.adn.com/rural-alaska/article/disaster-declared-subsistence-walrus-hunt-st-lawrence-island/2013/09/03/> [accessed 15 May 2019].

22 Henry Huntington, 'Effects of Changing Sea Ice on Marine Mammals and Subsistence Hunters in Northern Alaska From Traditional Knowledge Interviews', *Biology Letters* (2016) <http://www.north-slope.org/assets/images/uploads/2016_Huntington_et_al_effect_sea_ice_change_on_mm_and_sub_hunt.pdf> [accessed 15 May 2019].

23 Sienna Hill, 'McDonald's Filet-O-Fish Might Be Causing Some Problems in Alaska', *Business Insider* (2015) <https://www.businessinsider.com/how-mcdonalds-filet-o-fish-impacts-alaskan-communities-2015-7> [accessed 15 May 2019]; Lee Van Der Voo, 'Look Beyond the Label', Slate (2015) <https://slate.com/technology/2015/07/sustainable-mcdonalds-fish-pollock-trawlers-harm-native-alaskan-halibut-fishers.html> [accessed 15 May 2019].

24 Alaskan Inuit Food Security Conceptual Framework', *Inuit Circumpolar Council* (p. 8), <https://iccalaska.org/wp-icc/wp-content/uploads/2016/03/Food-Security-Summary-and-Recommendations-Report.pdf> [accessed 15 May 2019].

Contributors

Vidya Balachander is a food journalist and researcher based in Dubai. Over the last nine years, her work has explored the intersection of food and anthropology, particularly its relationship with politics, society, and culture.

Janet Beizer is Professor of Romance Languages and Literatures at Harvard, specializing in French literature and civilization with a strong penchant for all aspects of Francophone food culture. She is finishing a book called *The Harlequin Eaters: Leftovers and the Patchwork Imagination in Nineteenth-Century Paris*.

An award-winning investigative journalist and the author of seven books on food issues, **Joanna Blythman** was named 2018 Food Writer of the Year by the Guild of Food Writers.

Paul Brummell is a career diplomat, who has served as UK Ambassador to Turkmenistan, Kazakhstan, Kyrgyzstan, and Romania, and High Commissioner to Barbados and the Eastern Caribbean. He is currently head of soft power and external affairs at the Foreign and Commonwealth Office.

Voltaire Cang is an academic researcher based in Tokyo. He researches and writes about Japan's 'intangible' heritage, including food and other cultural practices and traditions.

Janet Clarkson is a general practitioner and lecturer at the School of Medicine at the University of Queensland, Australia. She writes regularly on culinary history and is also the author of *Pie: A Global History*.

Siobhan Dooley is a PhD candidate in the School of English at the University of St Andrews. Her research, which is supported by the Wolfson foundation, focuses on the significance of food and foodways in anglophone writing about South Africa.

Specializing in the Renaissance, **Allison Fisher** earned a PhD in art history from Canada's Queen's University.

Len Fisher is a scientist, author, and broadcaster who won a spoof Ig Nobel prize for using physics to work out the best way to dunk a biscuit. He was a finalist in the recent Global Challenges 'New Shape' competition to find new approaches to resolving global challenges, many of which are related to food.

Scientific Director of the International Union Against Tuberculosis and Lung Disease in Paris, France, now focusing on the COVID-19 pandemic response, **Paula Fujiwara** has interests ranging from the culinary and political history of Japanese Americans to Victorian and Edwardian etiquette books, cookbooks, and household manuals.

L. Sasha Gora is a cultural historian and writer with a focus on food history and contemporary art (often separately but sometimes together). Since 2015, she has been teaching at LMU Munich's Amerika-Institut.

A sociologist, action researcher, and Fair Food tomato enthusiast, **Melissa C. Gouge** conducts engaged research to transform power relations commonly found in traditional scholarship as a Research Affiliate at the Center for Social Science Research at George Mason University in Fairfax, Virginia.

Jennifer Holm is an Assistant Professor of French at the University of Virginia's College at Wise. She studies representations of food and eating in contemporary French literature and film as well as the cultural and political implications of French gastronomy.

Jennifer Hostetter is an Instructor at the University of Central Florida's Rosen College of Hospitality Management. She also runs her own catering and cooking class business. Her writing focuses on the history and culture of food, especially within the context of punishment.

Trained in analytical chemistry and sensory analysis, **Arielle Johnson** worked as the Research and Development Scientist at Noma and is currently the Science Officer on Alton Brown's Food Network show *Good Eats*.

Since 2018, historian **Alex Ketchum** has been the Faculty Lecturer of the Institute for Gender, Sexuality, and Feminist Studies of McGill University. Her research focuses on the role of technology, food, feminism, and environmentalism in twentieth-century social movements in the United States and Canada.

Dorota Koczanowicz is professor of cultural studies at the University of Wroclaw, Poland. She publishes on aesthetics, arts, food, and culture.

Leszek Koczanowicz is professor of Philosophy and Political Science at the SWPS University of Social Sciences and Humanities (Poland). He specializes in the theory of culture, social theory, and cultural aspects of politics. His recent publication is *Anxiety and Lucidity: Reflections on Culture in Times of Unrest*.

Michael Krondl is a food writer, culinary historian, cooking teacher, and artist. His books include *The Taste of Conquest: The Rise and Fall of the Three Great Cities of Spice* and *Sweet Invention: A History of Dessert*.

Christopher Laurent is a cultural anthropologist based in San Francisco, California. His current research focusses on the intersection of Japanese cuisine and ethnic minorities in Japan.

Contributors

Don Lindgren is an antiquarian bookseller specialized in printed and manuscript cookery. His business, Rabelais Inc., acquires, researches, and sells rare books, manuscripts, ephemera, and other materials related to culinary history and culture, and performs appraisal and institutional placement services for collections and archives. In 2019 he published the first part of a multi-volume exploration of the American community cookbook, researched and written with Mark Germer, titled *UnXld: American Cookbooks of Community & Place.*

Lecturer in Medieval History and in Economic and Social History of the Middle Ages at the University of Bari, **Andrea Maraschi** writes about various aspects of food in medieval society.

Jacob Matthews recently graduated from Columbia University with a degree in French and Francophone Studies.

Professor of English at the United States Naval Academy, **Mark McWilliams** has served as Editor of the Oxford Symposium on Food and Cookery since 2011.

Frieda Moran, PhD candidate at the University of Tasmania, is currently researching the cultural history of food safety in Australia.

Simona Moti received her PhD in German Studies from the University of California-Irvine and currently teaches at the Sacramento Waldorf School. Her research focuses on food studies and postcolonial approaches to Central European literature and culture.

Giulia Nicolini is a researcher specialising in food systems at the International Institute for Environment and Development in London.

Féilim Ó Cuireáin is a professional chef who has been working in kitchens across Ireland, the UK, and Europe for the past five years. During this time he has also been involved with projects on food justice and distribution for homeless and isolated communities. His most recent work has been working with refugees and migrants so they can teach cookery classes to the public.

Samantha Presnal is Center for Humanistic Inquiry Fellow and Visiting Lecturer in French at Amherst College. She mines archives, dissects texts, and attempts period recipes to bring to light what people cooked and what it meant in turn-of-the-century France.

Christian Reynolds is Senior Lecturer at the Centre for Food Policy, City University, London. He researches the economic and environmental impacts of food loss and waste, and focuses on the shift towards sustainable diets and cookery.

Charity Robey writes for the *Shelter Island Reporter, Newsday,* and the *New York Times* covering the food, culture, and history of Eastern Long Island. A programming chair for Culinary Historians of New York, she lives in New York City and Shelter Island, New York.

Or Rosenboim is historian of international thought and Director of the Centre for Modern History at City, University of London. Her research explores ideas of world order, empire, and globalism in the twentieth century.

Laura Shapiro is a journalist and culinary historian. Her most recent book is *What She Ate: Six Remarkable Women and the Food That Tells Their Stories.*

Richard Warren Shepro is an international lawyer who also teaches at the University of Chicago. A scholar of French and other food history, he is the author of four previous papers for the Symposium and is a former editor of the *Harvard Law Review.*

Koby Song-Nichols is a PhD student in Chinese diasporic history and food studies at the University of Toronto and University of Toronto Scarborough. With a soft spot for dishes like sweet and sour chicken balls, chili chicken, and chop suey, his current research examines how Chinese Canadian and American communities have shaped, negotiated, and experienced multicultural life in North America through food.

Carolyn Steel is a London-based architect, academic, and writer whose work explores what it means to see the world through the lens of food. She is the author of *Hungry City: How Food Shapes Our Lives* and *Sitopia: How Food Can Save the World.*

David C. Sutton is a literary and archival researcher, Director of Research Projects in the University of Reading Library, and a member of the governing body of the International Council on Archives. His books include *Figs* and *Rich Food, Poor Food.*

Svetlana Tcareva is a PhD candidate in the Slavic Languages and Literatures Department at Yale University. Her research interests include Soviet literature, food studies, horror, and embodiment. She is currently working on her dissertation about gross corporeality and monstrous consumption in Soviet literature and film between 1920 and the 1940s.

After obtaining a Master's in Fine Art in 1998, **Carolyn Tillie** promptly enrolled in cooking school. Combining her education in the arts and gastronomy, she works as an exhibiting artist, curator, and food historian who specializes in researching, creating, and presenting food as an art form.

Nick Tošaj is a professor of history at John Abbott College, a PhD candidate at the University of Toronto, and a lover of carbohydrates. His research focuses primarily on bread, wheat, and staple foods in the modern French empire.

Anne Urbancic, the Mary Rowell Jackman Professor in the Humanities at Victoria College, University of Toronto, specializes in nineteenth- and twentieth-century Italian literature which, to her delight, has led her to the fascinating cookbooks and foodways of Italy in that period.

Nina Vizcarrondo earned her undergraduate degree at New York University in Food Studies. She is a chef and food truck owner in Alaska with a passion for addressing food justice issues.

Alice Mulhearn-Williams is a freelance writer and PhD student in History at NUI Galway. She is researching the sensory history of Ireland's Magdalene laundries.